Court of Federal Claims:

West:	*Esposito v. U.S.*, 70 Fed. Cl. 558 (2006)
CCH:	*Esposito v. U.S.*, 2006-2 USTC ¶ 50,434 (Fed. Cl.)
Thomson Reuters:	*Esposito v. U.S.*, 97 AFTR2d 2006-1733 (Fed. Cl.)

Court of Appeals:

West:	*Home Concrete & Supply, LLC v. U.S.*, 634 F.3d 249 (CA-4, 2011).
CCH:	*Home Concrete & Supply, LLC v. U.S.*, 2011-1 USTC ¶ 50,341 (CA-4).
Thomson Reuters:	*Home Concrete & Supply, LLC v. U.S.*, 107 AFTR 2d 2011-1726 (CA-4).

Supreme Court:

GPO:	*U.S. v. Clintwood Elkhorn Mining Co., Et Al.*, 553 U.S. 1 (2008)
West:	*U.S. v. Clintwood Elkhorn Mining Co., Et Al.*, 128 S. Ct. 1511 (2008)
CCH:	*U.S. v. Clintwood Elkhorn Mining Co., Et Al.*, 2008-1 USTC ¶ 50,281 (USSC)
Thomson Reuters:	*U.S. v. Clintwood Elkhorn Mining Co., Et Al.*, 101 AFTR 2d 2008-1612 (USSC)

Books

Sawyers, R., Raabe, W., Whittenburg, G., and Gill, S., 2014. *Federal Tax Research,* 10th ed. Mason, OH: South-Western.

Journals

Everett, J., Hennig, C., and Raabe, W., Converting a C Corporation Into an LLC, *Journal of Taxation* Vol. 113, No. 2 (August 2010).

Capitalization

Proper nouns and words derived from them are capitalized while common nouns are not. The names of specific persons, places, or things are proper nouns. All other nouns are common nouns. Examples of proper nouns include:

the Congress

Section 172(a)

Regulation § 1.102-1 or the Proposed Regulation (references to regulations in general do not need to be capitalized)

the Fifth Circuit

the Tax Court

a revenue ruling or a private letter ruling

Italics

In handwritten or typed papers underlining represents italics. The titles of books, magazines, newspapers, pamphlets and court cases are shown in italics. Examples of items that are italicized include:

The Wealth of Nations

Journal of Taxation

New York Times

Gregory v. Helvering

Note: Do not italicize the titles of legal documents such as the U.S. Constitution and the U.S. Code.

Federal Tax Research

Federal Tax Research

ELEVENTH EDITION

Roby B. Sawyers, Ph.D., CPA, CMA
North Carolina State University

Steven L. Gill, Ph.D.
San Diego State University

CENGAGE
Learning®

Australia • Brazil • Mexico • Singapore • United Kingdom • United States

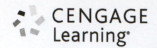
CENGAGE
Learning®

Federal Tax Research, Eleventh Edition
Roby B. Sawyers and Steven L. Gill

Vice President, General Manager, Social Science & Qualitative Business: Erin Joyner

Product Director: Jason Fremder

Senior Product Manager: John Barans

Content Developer: Jonathan Gross

Product Assistant: Aiyana Moore

Manufacturing Planner: Doug Wilke

Art and Cover Direction, Production Management, and Composition: Lumina Datamatics, Inc.

Intellectual Property

   Analyst: Brittani Morgan

   Project Manager: Carly Belcher

Cover Image: Tomasz Zajda/Fotolia LLC

© 2018, 2015 Cengage Learning

ALL RIGHTS RESERVED. No part of this work covered by the copyright herein may be reproduced or distributed in any form or by any means, except as permitted by U.S. copyright law, without the prior written permission of the copyright owner.

For product information and technology assistance, contact us at
Cengage Learning Customer & Sales Support, 1-800-354-9706

For permission to use material from this text or product, submit all requests online at **www.cengage.com/permissions**
Further permissions questions can be emailed to
permissionrequest@cengage.com

Library of Congress Control Number: 2017931304

ISBN: 978-1-337-28298-7

Cengage Learning
20 Channel Center Street
Boston, MA 02210
USA

Cengage Learning is a leading provider of customized learning solutions with employees residing in nearly 40 different countries and sales in more than 125 countries around the world. Find your local representative at **www.cengage.com**

Cengage Learning products are represented in Canada by Nelson Education, Ltd.

To learn more about Cengage Learning Solutions, visit **www.cengage.com**

Purchase any of our products at your local college store or at our preferred online store **www.cengagebrain.com**

Unless otherwise noted, all content is © Cengage Learning

Printed in the United States of America
Print Number: 01   Print Year: 2017

Dedications

This book is dedicated to our academic mentors.

Roby B. Sawyers
David E. Hoffman
Charles W. Christian
J. Hal Reneau
Philip M. J. Reckers
Joseph J. Schultz, Jr.

Steven L. Gill
Susan Porter
Lynne Krapf
Gene Whittenburg

In 2015, we unexpectedly lost out friend and co-author Gene Whittenburg. As one of the original authors of *Federal Tax Research*, Gene helped create this market-leading textbook in an environment where computer-based research was just becoming available. It is simply not possible to quantify the degree of our loss. Gene started his life in a small town in Texas; entered the Navy; served his country in Vietnam; earned bachelors, masters, and Ph.D. degrees; and served as a distinguished faculty member at San Diego State University for almost 40 years. The outpouring of sorrow and gratitude from countless former students and colleagues is a wonderful tribute to Gene's love and devotion to teaching.

Roby B. Sawyers, Ph.D., CPA, CMA, is a professor in the Poole College of Management at North Carolina State University. He earned his undergraduate accounting degree from the University of North Carolina at Chapel Hill, his master's degree from the University of South Florida, and his Ph.D. from Arizona State University. He has taught a variety of undergraduate and graduate tax courses at NC State and has been a visiting professor in the International Management Program at the Catholic University in Lille, France, and the Vienna School of Economics and Business (Wirtschaftsuniversitat Wien). He has also developed and taught continuing education courses for the AICPA, NCACPA, BDO Seidman, McGladrey, Dixon Hughes Goodman, KPMG, and PricewaterhouseCoopers.

In addition to being on the author team of *Federal Tax Research*, Dr. Sawyers writes frequently for leading academic, policy, and professional tax journals.

Steven L. Gill, Ph.D., is an associate professor in the Charles W. Lamden School of Accountancy at San Diego State University. He received a BS in Accounting from the University of Florida, an M.S. in Taxation from Northeastern University (Boston), and a Ph.D. in accounting from the University of Massachusetts. Before entering academia, Professor Gill worked for 12 years in the field of accounting, including roles in public accounting, internal audit, and corporate accounting, and, ultimately, as a vice president of finance.

Professor Gill's research interests include a concentration in taxation including mutual funds and college savings ("529") plans and wider interests in corporate internal control structure and weaknesses, management overconfidence, and earnings quality. Professor Gill has taught at both the undergraduate and graduate levels, and his teaching interests include taxation and financial accounting. In addition to being on the author team of *Federal Tax Research*, Dr. Gill is an author of *Income Tax Fundamentals*.

Brief Contents

Contents

The 11th Edition of *Federal Tax Research* includes the deepest analysis of the online research tools available to assist with tax and accounting research. As a result, we believe that the 11th Edition is indispensable to learning and performing real-world research. New features in the 11th edition include:

- A searchable electronic research case classification matrix. Faculty can search for appropriate cases to assign based on the necessary primary tax authority needed in the case (legislative, administrative, judicial), jurisdiction (federal, state, international), entity type or issue, tax type, the similarity of the research case to the facts in the primary sources, and the expected response (short paragraph, research memo, etc.).

- **Chapter 1**: An updated discussion of Circular 230 and the AICPA Code of Professional Conduct, including the impact of the *Ridgely* and *Loving* cases on the regulation of tax return preparers.

- **Chapter 2**: An updated discussion of research on the CPA exam and the importance of citations in tax research.

- **Chapter 3**: An enhanced discussion of tax treaties and committee reports and how they are used in tax research.

- **Chapter 4**: An expanded discussion of regulations, including the process of proposing and issuing final regulations, and an updated discussion of the authority of regulations post-*Mayo*. The chapter also includes additional discussion of private letter rulings and the cost of requesting rulings, an expanded discussion of the Internal Revenue Bulletin as a source of substantial authority, and a more thorough discussion of the litany of documents issued by the Treasury Department's general counsel, including GCMs, CCAs, and FSAs.

- **Chapter 5**: An updated discussion of burden of proof standards to reflect current law.

- **Chapter 6**: A discussion and demonstration of the new Checkpoint Catalyst tool as well as updated screenshots and guidance related to conducting tax research using Thomson Reuters Checkpoint.

- **Chapter 7**: Updated screenshots and guidance related to conducting tax research using CCH IntelliConnect.

- **Chapter 8**: Updated screenshots and guidance related to conducting tax research using BNA Bloomberg, Lexis Tax Center with Lexis Advance Tax, Westlaw, Lexis-Nexis Academic, and Tax Analysts.

- **Chapter 9**: Enhanced discussion of multistate taxation to better explain state income taxes to novice tax researchers as well as updates to screenshots and use of state and local and international research tools in Checkpoint, IntelliConnect, BNA Bloomberg, Lexis Tax Center, LexisNexis Academic, and Westlaw.

- **Chapter 10**: Updated screenshots and guidance related to the use of the FASB Accounting Standards Codification Research System (CRS).

- **Chapter 11**: Enhanced focus on general writing tips for the tax professional as well as using email and text messages to communicate with clients.

- **Chapter 12**: Updated discussion of the fundamental tenants of tax planning.

- **Chapter 13**: Enhanced discussion of the statute of limitations (moved from Chapter 14 to Chapter 13) as well as taxpayer rights and client confidentiality privilege for nonattorneys.

- **Chapter 14**: New discussion of relief from joint and several liability for innocent spouses.

The book has been prepared as a comprehensive, stand-alone reference tool for the user who wishes to become proficient in federal, multistate, and international tax research as well as financial accounting research. It is written for readers who are familiar with the fundamentals of the tax law, at a level that typically is achieved on the completion of two comprehensive introductory courses in taxation in either the accounting program in a business school or second- or third-year courses in a law school. Nearly every accounting, tax, and tax law student can benefit from the tools and strategies found in this book.

Structure and Pedagogy

Too often, textbooks ignore the detailed, pragmatic approach that students require in developing effective and efficient tax research skills. That is why we have included an unprecedented degree of hands-on tax research analysis throughout the text. This book does not simply discuss tax research procedures or the sources of the tax law, nor does it provide a mere sample of the pertinent tax reference material. Rather, the book reflects our conviction that students learn best by active learning and real-world experience using the most comprehensive and important sources of tax law. We have applied this conviction to the many important features of the 11th Edition, including:

- Dozens of exercises, problems, and research cases in each chapter.

- "Spotlight on Taxation" boxes in every chapter to provide tax news and background information to students.

- Chapters on working with the IRS and on tax practice and administration that provide details on important topics such as preparer penalties, statutes of limitations, and the IRS audit and appeals process.

- Assignments requiring students to construct research memos, client letters, and other elements of a comprehensive client file—vital communication skills they will need in practice.

- Hundreds of reproductions, illustrations, and screen captures from the most important tax reference materials to expose students to the real world of tax research.

- Summary charts, diagrams, and other study aids integrated throughout the text.

Students can access chapter-by-chapter study content at the CengageBrain.com home page and can search by author name, title (*Federal Tax Research*), or ISBN (9781337282987) using the search box at the top of the page. This will bring readers to a link for the 11th Edition of *Federal Tax Research*.

The instructor's portion of the Web site located at www.cengagebrain.com includes the solutions for the end-of-chapter material, a test bank, instructor PowerPoint slides, lecture notes, and the new searchable research case classification matrix to help guide instructors through the course.

Acknowledgments

We are grateful to our supplement authors and reviewers who provided valuable comments and insights, which guided us in the development of the 11th Edition.

Lucia Smeal, Georgia State University

Tad Ransopher, Georgia State University

Tom Purcell, Creighton University

We wish to thank all of the book's student and faculty readers who have provided their detailed feedback and suggestions. Without their responses, our efforts would have been greatly diminished in scope. Any errors, of course, are the sole responsibility of the authors.

We welcome your comments and suggestions for further improvements to this text. Please feel free to use the following addresses to convey these remarks:

Roby B. Sawyers
Department of Accounting, Poole College of Management
NC State University
Raleigh, NC 27695-8113
roby_sawyers@ncsu.edu

Steven L. Gill
Charles W. Lamden School of Accountancy
San Diego State University
San Diego, CA 92182-8221
sgill@mail.sdsu.edu

Roby B. Sawyers
Steven L. Gill

March 2017

PART I

The Tax Research Environment

CHAPTER 1

Introduction to Tax Practice and Ethics

LEARNING OBJECTIVES

- Describe the elements of modern tax practice in the United States.
- Explain and apply the sources of legal and ethical standards that guide those who engage in tax practice.
- Summarize the limitations on tax research by CPAs and other nonattorneys.

CHAPTER OUTLINE

Tax PRACTICE AND TAX RESEARCH have evolved over the last twenty or thirty years into an electronic and often paperless system. For example, in 2016 more than 90 percent of individual taxpayers e-filed their tax returns. In keeping with this continuing transition to an all-electronic tax system, today tax research is almost 100 percent online based. The Uniform CPA Exam recognizes this transition and includes a set of simulation questions that require the candidate to demonstrate accounting and tax research skills by completing short research cases using online searches of authoritative literature, including the Accounting Standards Codification (ASC) and the Internal Revenue Code (IRC). However, before the tax practitioner can complete a tax research project, he or she must understand the tax research process, all its elements, and how each element relates to solving a specific tax problem. The primary purpose of this book is to inform the user on how to effectively obtain tax research results in a timely and efficient manner.

The practice of taxation is the process of applying the tax laws, rules, regulations, and judicial rulings to specific transactions in order to determine the tax consequences to the taxpayer involved. There are many ways to practice tax. Certified public accountants (CPAs), tax attorneys, and enrolled agents often provide compliance and planning services for clients. In addition, tax can be practiced by controllers, chief financial officers (CFOs), tax directors, and other individuals who do tax work as part of their duties within a corporation or other business entity. An understanding of taxation and the tax practice environment is essential to the individual who wants to have a career in the tax area.

Taxation is the process of collecting revenue from citizens to finance government activities. In a modern technological society such as that of the United States, however, taxation comprises an interaction among several disciplines that is far from simple. The tax system is derived from law, accounting, economics, political science, and sociology (Exhibit 1-1). Principles of economics, sociology, and political science provide the environment, while law and accounting precepts are applied in a typical tax practice.

Tax policy questions concerning the effects that a specified tax law change will have on economic growth, the effects of projected inflation on the implementation of the tax law and vice versa, and the effects of the tax law on the United States' balance of payments are addressed by economists. Political scientists, economists, and sociologists examine issues such as who bears the ultimate burden of a tax, how a tax bill becomes

EXHIBIT 1-1:   Elements of Taxation

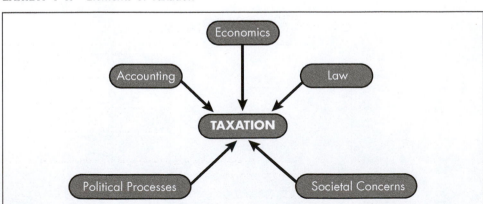

law (including practical effects of the legislative process), the social equity of a tax, and whether a tax is discriminatory. Attorneys interpret taxation statutes and litigate disputes with governmental authorities, and accountants apply the tax laws to current or prospective economic transactions.

1 Elements of Tax Practice

The tax laws of a democratic country such as the United States are created by a political process. In recent years, the result of this political process has been a set of laws that levies taxes on income, sales, estates, gifts, and other items that usually are reflected by the accounting process. Modern tax practice can be separated into three elements: compliance, planning, and litigation, which are all supported by tax research. How these elements of tax practice fit together is illustrated in Exhibit 1-2.

1-1 Tax Compliance

In general, **tax compliance** consists of two separate but related components—tax return preparation and, for certain corporate entities, the preparation of the tax provision on a company's financial statements.

Tax return preparation consists of the gathering of pertinent information, the evaluation and classification of such information, and the filing of necessary tax returns with the appropriate governmental agency. In the United States, this will typically be the Internal Revenue Service (IRS) or the appropriate state agency. Tax compliance also includes other functions necessary to satisfy governmental requirements, such as representation at a client's IRS audit. Non-credentialed tax preparers, enrolled agents (EAs), attorneys, and CPAs all perform tax compliance to some extent. Relatively simple individual, partnership, and corporate tax returns often are completed by non-credentialed tax return preparers. EAs, attorneys, and CPAs usually are involved in the preparation of more complex tax returns; in addition, they provide tax planning services and represent their clients before the IRS at the appeals level.

A corporation's income tax expense as reported on its financial statements is often different from the income tax on its tax return. Financial statements are prepared using generally accepted accounting principles (GAAP) rather than tax law as set out in the IRC, related Treasury regulations, and other administrative pronouncements and court cases. Both tax return preparation and the preparation of the tax provision on financial statements are examined in more detail in later chapters.

EXHIBIT 1-2:   Elements of Tax Practice

1-2 Tax Planning

Tax planning is the process of arranging one's financial affairs to minimize tax liabilities. While this usually means minimizing current tax payments, that is not always the case. Whereas **tax avoidance** is a legitimate objective of modern tax practice, **tax evasion** constitutes the illegal nonpayment of a tax and cannot be condoned. Fraudulent acts of any kind are unrelated to the professional practice of tax planning.

Tax planning can be divided into two major categories: **open transactions** and **closed transactions**. In an open transaction, the tax practitioner maintains some degree of control over the potential tax liability because the transaction is not yet completed; for example, the title to an asset has not yet passed. If desired, some modifications to an incomplete transaction can be made to receive more favorable tax treatment. In a closed transaction, however, all of the pertinent actions have been completed; therefore, tax planning may be limited to the presentation of the facts to the government in the most favorable, legally acceptable manner possible.

SPOTLIGHT ON TAXATION

Is Tax Avoidance Legal?

There is nothing inherently illegal or immoral in the avoidance of taxation (i.e., tax planning) according to the tax system's rules. The eminent judge Learned Hand best expressed this doctrine in the dissenting opinion of *Commissioner v. Newman*, 159 F.2d 848 (CA-2, 1947):

> *Over and over again, courts have said that there is nothing sinister in so arranging one's affairs as to keep taxes as low as possible. Everybody does so, rich or poor, and all do right, for nobody owes any public duty to pay more than the law demands: taxes are enforced extractions, not voluntary contributions.*

1-3 Tax Litigation

A specialized area within the practice of taxation is the concentration on **tax litigation**. Litigation is the process of settling a dispute with another party (in the United States, usually the IRS or a state revenue department) in a court of law. Typically, a tax attorney handles tax litigation that progresses beyond the initial appeal of an IRS or state revenue department audit result. Accountants and other financial advisers can also serve in a support capacity. Later chapters of this book contain additional discussions of the various opportunities and strategies available in tax litigation.

1-4 Tax Research

Tax research is undertaken to answer taxation questions. The tax research process includes the (1) identification of pertinent issues, (2) determination of proper authorities, (3) evaluation of the appropriateness of these authorities, and (4) application of these authorities. Tax research methodology, sources of federal tax law, and tax research tools are examined in Chapters 2 through 8 of this book.

2 Rules and Ethics in Tax Practice

A person who prepares tax returns for monetary or other compensation, or who is licensed to practice in the tax-related professions, is subject to various statutes, rules, and codes of professional conduct. Tax practitioners (as defined by the IRS) are regulated by **Circular 230**, Regulations Governing Practice before the Internal Revenue Service.

The ethical conduct of an attorney is also governed by the laws of the state(s) in which he or she is licensed to practice. Most states have adopted, often with some modification, guidelines that are based on the **American Bar Association (ABA)** Model Rules of Professional Conduct.

Certified public accountants (CPAs) who are members of the **American Institute of Certified Public Accountants (AICPA)** must follow its Code of Professional Conduct and any other rules generated by the state board(s) of accountancy. The AICPA has also produced a series of Statements on Standards for Tax Services (SSTS), which contain advisory guidelines for AICPA members who prepare tax returns. Although CPAs who are not members of the AICPA are not bound by the Code of Professional Conduct and the SSTS, those rules and standards are a useful source of guidance for all members of the profession. In addition, CPAs are regulated by the state(s) in which they are licensed. As a result, there can be additional statutes, regulations, and requirements that must be met by individuals who practice in certain states.

Statutory tax law also specifies certain penalties and other rules of conduct that apply to all tax return preparers. Chapter 14 addresses these rules.

The basic overlapping sources of rules and ethics for tax practitioners are illustrated in Exhibit 1-3.

2-1 Circular 230

Circular 230, which constitutes Part 31 of the Treasury Department Regulations, is designed to provide protection to taxpayers and the IRS by requiring tax practitioners to be technically competent and to adhere to **ethical standards**.[1]

At present, Circular 230 contains the following definition of **practice before the IRS** in Section 10.2 of Subpart A:

> *Practice before the Internal Revenue Service comprehends all matters connected with a presentation to the Internal Revenue Service or any of its officers or employees relating to a taxpayer's rights, privileges, or liabilities under laws or regulations administered by the Internal Revenue Service. Such presentations include, but are not limited to, preparing documents; filing documents; corresponding and communicating with the Internal Revenue Service; rendering written advice with respect to any entity, transaction, plan or arrangement, or other plan or arrangement having a potential for tax avoidance or evasion; and representing a client at conferences, hearings, and meetings.*

2-1a Who May Practice [Circular 230 § 10.3] Under Section 10.3, Subpart A, of Circular 230, the following individuals may practice before the IRS:

1. Attorneys

2. CPAs

3. EAs

4. Enrolled actuaries

5. Enrolled retirement plan agents

6. Registered tax return preparers[2]

---

[1] Circular 230 as revised in June 2014 can be found on the IRS's Website at **www.irs.gov/pub/irs-pdf/pcir230.pdf**.

[2] While the term "registered tax return preparer" is still in Circular 230, as a practical matter it is not being used by the IRS. Preparers who are not CPAs, EAs, or attorneys (called non-credentialed tax return preparers by the IRS) may participate in the voluntary Annual Filing Season Program and receive a certificate from the IRS upon completion of 18 hours of continuing education.

EXHIBIT 1-3:   Sources of Rules and Ethics for Tax Practitioners

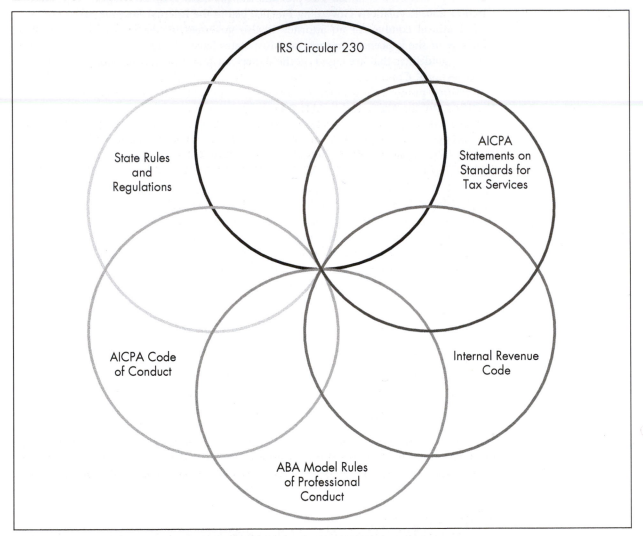

These individuals are collectively referred to as Circular 230 practitioners.

In order to practice before the IRS, an attorney must be a member in good standing of the bar of the highest court in any state, possession, territory, or commonwealth or the District of Columbia. Likewise, CPAs and enrolled actuaries must be qualified to practice in any state, possession, territory, or commonwealth or the District of Columbia. No further substantive examination is required. Applicants for EAs and enrolled retirement plan agents may be granted temporary recognition to practice until the application is approved.

SPOTLIGHT ON TAXATION

CPA Mobility

While CPAs are licensed by their home state, a uniform system allowing CPAs to practice across state lines has been endorsed by the AICPA and the National Association of State Boards of Accountancy (NASBA). A total of 52 states, territories, and

(Continued)

SPOTLIGHT ON TAXATION (CONTINUED)

the District of Columbia have passed mobility laws that essentially allow a CPA with a license from one state to practice outside his or her home state without getting an additional license in the state in which he or she will be serving a client. NASBA and the AICPA sponsor a CPA mobility Website at www.cpamobility.org. After entering your principal place of business where you will be performing services and the type of services you will perform, the site provides a summary of the individual and firm requirements for the target state as well as relevant links.

Individuals who are not attorneys or CPAs can qualify to practice before the IRS by becoming an **enrolled agent (EA)**. An EA is someone who has either passed a special IRS examination or worked for the IRS for five years. The procedures for becoming an EA are detailed in Circular 230, Subpart A, §§ 10.4, 10.5, and 10.6. EAs have the same rights as attorneys and CPAs to represent clients before the IRS. Under Circular 230, an EA must renew his or her enrollment card on a three-year cycle.

The Enrolled Agent Special Enrollment Examination (SEE) is an online exam given throughout the year that consists of three parts covering individual taxation, business taxation and representation, and practices and procedures. For additional information on the SEE, see the Prometric Testing Website: **www.prometric.com/en-us/clients/SEE /Pages/landing.aspx**.

For each enrollment cycle, EAs, like attorneys and CPAs, must meet certain continuing education requirements as defined in Subpart A, § 10.6. For an EA's enrollment card to be renewed, he or she must complete 72 hours (i.e., an average of 24 hours per year) of qualifying continuing education for each three-year enrollment period. In addition, a minimum of 16 hours of continuing education credit must be completed during each year of an enrollment cycle. Subpart A, § 10.6(f) defines what qualifies as continuing education for EAs.

For more information on EAs, see **www.irs.gov/taxpros/agents** and **www.naea.org**.

SPOTLIGHT ON TAXATION

Does the IRS Have Authority to Regulate Tax Preparers?

Two recent court cases have called into question the ability of the IRS to regulate anyone, including CPAs and attorneys who are only providing tax return preparation services. In the *Loving* case, the court said that for purposes of Circular 230, practice must be undertaken by a representative of the taxpayer. A representative must have the authority to bind others, and a tax return preparer filing an amended return does not have that authority. In *Ridgely v. Lew*, the court held that a contingent fee arrangement was allowed in the case of a CPA who filed an amended return for refund for a client before the IRS commenced an audit of the return. The court ruled that under Circular 230, the IRS was limited to regulating practice and that the preparation of an ordinary refund claim did not constitute practice before the IRS. The IRS has not amended Circular 230 language since both of these cases were decided [*Ridgely v. Lew* (114 AFTR 2d 2014-5249, DC Dist Col), and *Loving v. IRS* (111 AFTR 2d 2013-589, DC Dist Col)].

2-1b Limited Practice and Representing Oneself   Enrolled agents, certified public accountants, and attorneys have unlimited representation rights before the IRS. This allows these individuals to represent their clients in matters including audits and payment and collection issues as well as appeals. Practice as enrolled actuaries and enrolled retirement plan agents is limited to specific issues related to the specialty. While Circular 230 provides limited practice rights to registered tax return preparers, effective January 1, 2016, non-credentialed tax return preparers have limited practice rights only if they participate in the IRS **Annual Filing Season Program.**

Limited practice rights allow individuals to represent clients whose returns they prepared and signed, but only before revenue agents, customer service representatives, and similar IRS employees. Non-credentialed tax return preparers who do not participate in the Annual Filing Season Program are allowed to prepare tax returns but have no authority to represent clients before the IRS. Additional information on the status of the new tax return preparer requirements can be found at the IRS Website. The frequently asked questions section on unenrolled preparers and the Annual Filing Season Program are located at **www.irs.gov/tax-professionals/frequently-asked-questions -annual-filing-season-program.**

SPOTLIGHT ON TAXATION

How Many CPAs Are There?

According to NASBA, there were 664,532 active individual CPAs as of April 22, 2016. Over 215,000 of these CPAs have current PTIN numbers. In contrast there are only about 53,000 EAs and 31,000 attorneys with current PTIN numbers. Another 62,000 PTIN holders have received records of completion after participating in the Annual Filing Season Program.

www.irs.gov/tax-professionals/return-preparer-office-federal-tax-return-preparer-statistics www.nasba.org/licensure/howmanycpas/

In Circular 230, the IRS has authorized limited practice rights for certain individuals who are not practitioners. For example, individuals (with proper identification) can represent themselves under § 10.7(a) and participate in IRS rule making as provided for under § 10.7(b). In addition, under § 10.7(c), an individual who is not a practitioner may represent a taxpayer before the IRS in the following situations:

1. An individual may represent a member of his or her immediate family.

2. A regular full-time employee of an individual employer may represent the employer.

3. A general partner or regular full-time employee of a partnership may represent the partnership.

4. A bona fide officer or regular full-time employee of a corporation (including a parent, subsidiary, or other affiliated corporation), an association, or organized group may represent the corporation, association, or organized group.

5. A trustee, receiver, guardian, personal representative, administrator, executor, or regular full-time employee of a trust, receivership, guardianship, or estate may represent the trust, receivership, guardianship, or estate.

6. An officer or regular employee of a governmental unit, agency, or authority may represent the governmental unit, agency, or authority in the course of his or her official duties.

7. An individual may represent any individual or entity before personnel of the IRS who are outside the United States.

Circular 230 requires that such person must not be disbarred or suspended from practice before the IRS or from his or her profession.

2-1c Return Preparation and Application of Rules to Other Individuals [Circular 230 § 10.8]
A compensated individual who prepares or assists with the preparation of all or substantially all of a tax return or claim for refund must have a **preparer tax identification number (PTIN).**[3]

Compensated individuals who prepare less than substantially all of a tax return or claim for refund do not require a PTIN. Nevertheless, they may appear as a witness for the taxpayer before the IRS or furnish information at the request of the IRS or any of its officers or employees [§ 10.8(b)]. A tax return preparer who participates in the Annual Filing Season Program and earns a certificate of completion is subject to the duties and restrictions relating to practice in subpart B, as well as to the sanctions for incompetence and disreputable conduct in subpart C [§ 10.51].

2-1d Duties and Restrictions Relating to Practice before the IRS [Circular 230 Subpart B]
Subpart B of Circular 230 provides a set of rules, duties, and restrictions for those individuals authorized to practice before the IRS:

1. A practitioner must furnish information, on request, to any authorized agent of the IRS, unless the practitioner has reason to believe that the request is of doubtful legality or the information is privileged [§ 10.20(a)].

2. A practitioner who knows of client noncompliance, error, or omission with regard to the tax laws must advise the client of that noncompliance, error, or omission [§ 10.21].

3. A practitioner must exercise **due diligence** in preparing and filing tax returns and other documents relating to IRS matters and in determining the correctness of oral and written representations made to the IRS, the Treasury, and clients. Preparation of tax returns includes normal activities such as determining the questions asked and information requested from clients [§ 10.22]. Due diligence is not defined in Circular 230. However, the U.S. Court of Appeals for the Second Circuit held in *Harary v. Blumenthal*, 555 F.2d 1113 (CA-2, 1977), that due diligence requires that the tax practitioner be honest with his or her client in connection with all IRS-related matters. In determining if a practitioner has exercised due diligence, the IRS uses several factors, including the nature of the error, the explanation of the error, and other standards that apply (e.g., the AICPA SSTS that are discussed later in this chapter). In essence, due diligence means a tax practitioner should use reasonable effort to comply with the tax laws.

   A practitioner will be presumed to have exercised due diligence if the practitioner relies on the work of others and the practitioner used reasonable care in engaging, supervising, training, and evaluating the other person [§ 10.22(b)].

---

[3]IRC § 6109(a)(4) requires tax return preparers to include proper identification of the preparer, his or her employer, or both on any return or claim for refund.

EXAMPLE 1-1

Judy is a CPA who fails to include rental income on a tax return she completed for a client. The omitted rental income was from a new rental property the client purchased this year and therefore had not been reported on prior years' tax returns. The taxpayer did not mention the new rental property to Judy in any communications with her. Under these circumstances, Judy has exercised due diligence in preparing the tax return. However, if Judy also kept the rental income records for the new rental property and still omitted the income from the tax return, then she would not be exercising due diligence.

4. A practitioner must not unreasonably delay matters before the IRS [§ 10.23].

5. A practitioner must not accept assistance from or employ a disbarred or suspended person or a former IRS employee who is disqualified from practice under another rule or U.S. law [§ 10.24].

6. Partners of governmental employees cannot represent anyone for whom the governmental employee-partner has (or has had) official responsibility. For example, a CPA firm with a former IRS agent as a partner cannot represent any taxpayer that was in the past assigned to the IRS agent/partner. Likewise, no former governmental employee shall, subsequent to his or her governmental employment, represent anyone in any matter administered by the IRS if such representation would violate other U.S. laws [§ 10.25].

7. A practitioner may not act as a notary public for his or her clients with respect to any matter administered by the IRS and for which he or she is employed or otherwise involved [§ 10.26].

8. In general, fees for tax work must not be contingent or unconscionable [§ 10.27]. A **contingent fee** is any fee that is based, in whole or in part, on whether or not a position taken on a tax return or other filing avoids challenge by the IRS or is sustained either by the IRS or in litigation. Contingent fees include a fee that is based on a percentage of the refund reported on a return, that is based on a percentage of the taxes saved, or that otherwise depends on the specific result attained. Also, fees are contingent if they include any fee arrangement in which the practitioner will reimburse the client for all or a portion of the client's fee in the event that a position taken on a tax return or other filing is challenged by the IRS or is not sustained, whether pursuant to an indemnity agreement, a guarantee, rescission rights, or any other arrangement with a similar effect. Practitioners may charge contingent fees for services rendered in connection with the IRS's examination of, or challenge to, (1) an original tax return or (2) an amended return or claim for refund or credit for which the amended return or claim for refund or credit was filed within 120 days of the taxpayer receiving a written notice of the examination of, or a written challenge to, the original tax return.[4] The intent of this exception is to discourage the tactical preparation of a refund claim or amended return filed late in the examination process. A practitioner may also charge a contingent fee for services rendered in connection with a claim for credit or refund filed solely in connection with the determination of statutory interest or penalties assessed by the IRS, and for services rendered in connection with any judicial proceeding arising under the Internal Revenue Code.

---

[4]In *Ridgely* (114 AFTR 2d 2014-5249), the District Court for the District of Columbia invalidated the restriction on charging contingent fees in refund actions before an audit is commenced. See Spotlight on Taxation Feature on p. 9.

EXAMPLE 1-2

Oak Corporation has been audited by the IRS for its tax return filed two years ago. The company's controller completed the original return. The IRS is asserting that Oak underpaid its taxes by $100,000. Oak contacted Joe, a CPA, and engaged him to handle the appeals process with the IRS. In this situation, Joe can use a contingent fee arrangement. (For instance, Joe's fee could be 30 percent of any amount by which he could get the IRS to reduce the $100,000 assessment.)

While an **unconscionable fee** is not defined in Circular 230, if a tax practitioner charges a fee that is out of line with some measure of the value of the service provided to a client, then the fee would be unconscionable. For example, a CPA could not charge a fee of $10,000 to an unsophisticated taxpayer (such as an elderly person) for simple tax work that most CPAs would complete for less than $500.

9. In general, a practitioner must, at the request of a client, promptly return any and all of the client's records that are necessary for the client to comply with his or her federal tax obligations. The practitioner may retain copies of the records returned to a client [§ 10.28].

10. No tax practitioner can represent conflicting interests before the IRS unless he or she has the express consent of the directly interested parties [§ 10.29].

11. A practitioner may not use, in any form of public communication or private solicitation, false, fraudulent, coercive, misleading, or deceptive statements or claims [§ 10.30]. Specifically prohibited by the section is the use of the term "certified" by EAs, enrolled retirement plan agents, and non-credentialed preparers in describing their professional designation. If done in a dignified manner, examples of items that a practitioner may communicate to the public include (1) his or her name, address, and telephone number; (2) names of individuals associated with the practitioner; (3) a factual description of services offered; (4) fee information; (5) credit cards accepted; (6) foreign language ability; (7) membership in professional organizations; (8) professional licenses held; and (9) a statement of practice limitations. Copies and recordings of communications must be kept for 36 months.

12. A practitioner may not endorse or otherwise negotiate a taxpayer's refund check [§ 10.31]. This includes directing or accepting payment by any means, electronic or otherwise, into an account owned or controlled by the practitioner by an entity with which the practitioner is associated.

13. Circular 230 may not be construed as authorizing persons not members of the bar to practice law [§ 10.32].

14. Tax advisors should provide clients with the highest quality representation concerning federal tax issues by adhering to best practices in providing advice and in preparing in the preparation of submissions to the IRS [§ 10.33]. Best practices to be observed by all tax advisors include the following:

   A. Communicating clearly with the client regarding the terms of the engagement. For example, the advisor should determine the client's expected purpose for and use of the advice and should have a clear understanding with the client regarding the form and scope of the advice or assistance to be rendered.

   B. Establishing the facts, determining which facts are relevant, evaluating the reasonableness of any assumptions or representations, relating the applicable law (including potentially applicable judicial doctrines) to the relevant facts, and arriving at a conclusion supported by the law and the facts.

C. Advising the client regarding the importance of the conclusions reached, including, for example, whether a taxpayer may avoid accuracy-related penalties under the IRC if a taxpayer acts in reliance on the advice.

D. Acting fairly and with integrity in practice before the IRS.

According to Circular 230, these procedures help to ensure best practices for tax advisors. While best practices are aspirational, note than under § 10.36, tax practitioners with responsibility for overseeing a firm's practice of providing tax advice or of preparing tax returns should take reasonable steps to ensure that the firm's procedures for all members, associates, and employees follow best practices.

15. Section 10.34 of Circular 230 provides practitioners with rules pertaining to preparing and signing tax returns, giving advice to clients, and filing documents, affidavits, and other papers with the IRS. Under § 10.34(a), a practitioner may not sign a tax return that he or she knows (or should reasonably know) contains a position that (1) lacks a reasonable basis, (2) is an unreasonable position under IRC § 6694(a)(2), or (3) is a willful attempt to understate a tax liability or an intentional disregard of rules and regulations as described in IRC § 6694(b)(2). Furthermore, under § 10.34(a), a practitioner should not advise a taxpayer to take a position on a tax return that (1) lacks a reasonable basis, (2) is an unreasonable position under IRC § 6694(a)(2), or (3) is a willful attempt to understate a tax liability or a pattern of intentional disregard of rules and regulations under IRC § 6694(b)(2). Note that a position is considered unreasonable in the standards given here if the tax preparer does not have "substantial authority" for the position, if it is not disclosed on the return. If the position is disclosed, the standard is "reasonable basis." If the position involves a tax shelter or reportable transaction, the preparer must believe it is "more likely than not" that the position will be sustained on its merits.

Section 10.34(b) states that a practitioner should not advise a taxpayer to take a position on a document, affidavit, or other paper submitted to the IRS unless the position is not frivolous. In addition, a client should not be advised to submit to the IRS a document, affidavit, or other paper (1) the purpose of which is to delay or impede the administration of the federal tax laws, (2) that is frivolous, or (3) that contains or omits information in a manner that demonstrates an intentional disregard of rules or regulations.

Under § 10.34(c), a client must be informed of any penalties that are reasonably likely to apply to positions on tax returns or any document, affidavit, or other paper submitted to the IRS. In addition, a client should be informed about steps that can be taken to avoid such penalties.

Normally, under § 10.34(d), a practitioner advising a client or preparing and signing a tax return as a preparer may in good faith rely without verification upon information furnished by the client. However, a practitioner may not ignore the implications of information furnished to, or actually known by, the practitioner, and must make reasonable inquiries if the information as furnished appears to be incorrect, inconsistent with another factual assumption, or incomplete.

SPOTLIGHT ON TAXATION

E-mail Disclaimer

One of the significant changes made in the 2014 revision of Circular 230 was the elimination of the covered opinion rules. As a result, it is no longer necessary for CPAs to use disclaimer language like that given here in e-mails and other written correspondence:

> *I am required by IRS Circular 230 to inform you that, unless otherwise expressly indicated, any federal tax advice contained in this communication, including attachments and enclosures, is not intended or written to be used, and may not be used, for the purpose of (1) avoiding tax-related penalties under the Internal Revenue Code or (2) promoting, marketing, or recommending to another party any tax-related matters addressed herein.*

16. A practitioner must possess the necessary competence to engage in practice before the IRS. Competent practice requires the knowledge, skill, thoroughness, and preparation necessary for the matter for which the practitioner is engaged [§ 10.35].

17. Any practitioner who has (or practitioners who have or share) principal authority and responsibility for overseeing a firm's practice governed by this part, including the provision of advice concerning federal tax matters and preparation of tax returns, claims for refund, or other documents for submission to the IRS, must take reasonable steps to ensure that the firm has adequate procedures in effect for all members, associates, and employees for purposes of complying with this part, as applicable [§ 10.36].

18. In providing written advice concerning federal tax matters (including by means of electronic communication), the practitioner must:

    (i) Base the written advice on reasonable factual and legal assumptions (including assumptions as to future events);

    (ii) Reasonably consider all relevant facts that the practitioner knows or should know;

    (iii) Use reasonable efforts to identify and ascertain the facts relevant to written advice on each federal tax matter;

    (iv) Not rely upon representations, statements, findings, or agreements (including projections, financial forecasts, or appraisals) of the taxpayer or any other person if reliance on them would be unreasonable;

    (v) Relate applicable law and authorities to the facts; and

    (vi) Not, in evaluating a federal tax matter, take into account the possibility that a tax return will not be audited or that a matter will not be raised on audit [§ 10.37(a)(2)].

Reliance on representations, statements, findings, or agreements is unreasonable if the practitioner knows or should know that one or more representations or assumptions on which any representation that is incorrect, incomplete, or inconsistent [§ 10.37(a)(3)].

Government submissions on matters of general tax policy as well as continuing education presentations are not considered written advice for purposes of these rules.

19. A practitioner may only rely on the advice of another practitioner if the advice was reasonable and the reliance is in good faith considering all the facts and circumstances. Reliance is not reasonable when—

    (1) The practitioner knows or should know that the opinion of the other practitioner should not be relied on;

    (2) The practitioner knows or should know that the other practitioner is not competent or lacks the necessary qualifications to provide the advice; or

    (3) The practitioner knows or should know that the other practitioner has a conflict of interest as described in this part.

In evaluating whether a practitioner giving written advice complied with the requirements of this section, the Commissioner will apply a reasonable practitioner standard, considering all facts and circumstances, including, but not limited to, the scope of the engagement and the type and specificity of the advice sought by the client. If the practitioner provides an opinion regarding the promotion, marketing, or recommendation of an entity or plan with a significant purpose of avoidance or evasion of tax, the reasonable practitioner standard will still apply, but emphasis will be given to the additional risk caused by the practitioner's lack of knowledge of the taxpayer's particular circumstances [§ 10.37(c)].

2-2 AICPA Code of Professional Conduct

Members of the AICPA are subject to its Code of Professional Conduct. The Code of Professional Conduct is relevant to all professional services performed by CPAs, including those services provided in the practice of public accounting, private industry, government, or education. The Code of Professional Conduct was designed to provide its members with the following:

1. A comprehensive code of ethical and professional conduct;

2. A guide for all members in answering complex questions; and

3. Assurance to the public concerning the obligations and responsibilities of the accounting profession.

The **AICPA Code of Professional Conduct** was originally adopted in 1988 and has been periodically updated and revised since then. In June 2014, the AICPA issued a new codification of the code, including as a searchable online version available at http://pub.aicpa.org/codeofconduct/Ethics.aspx?_ga=1.59759533.1293052021.1474643050#.

The code begins with a preface which is applicable to all AICPA members, followed by part 1, applicable to members in public practice; part 2, applicable to members in business; and part 3, applicable to all other members including those who are retired or unemployed. Broad conceptual frameworks for members in public practice and members in business are included in parts 1 and 2. The conceptual frameworks recognize that members will often be faced with relationships and circumstances that create threats to the member's compliance with the rules in the code and that the rules and interpretations of those rules do not address all situations. In those situations, the conceptual framework calls for the member to evaluate whether the relationship or circumstance would lead a reasonable person to conclude that there is a threat to the member's acceptable compliance with the rules [1.000.010.01 and 2.000.010.01]. Under the conceptual framework, members must identify threats to compliance, evaluate the significance of the threat, and identify and apply safeguards to eliminate the threat or reduce the threat to an acceptable level.

Depending on the type of member, examples of threats include members not acting with objectivity due to an adverse interest, advocacy threats, familiarity threats due to a long or close relationship with a client, management participation threats, self-interest threats, self-review threats, and undue influence threats [1.000.010.08 and 2.000.010.07].

Safeguards can include those created by the profession, legislation, or regulation; safeguards implemented by the client or firm (for members in public practice); and safeguards implemented by the employing organization (for members in business) [1.000.010.18 and 2.000.010.16]. Examples of safeguards include things like continuing education requirements, external review, effective policies and procedures to address ethical conflict, effective internal control policies, firm leadership, and the "tone at the top." In some cases, the code specifies that no safeguards can eliminate or reduce a threat to an acceptable level [1.000.010.02 and 2.000.010.02].

The preface includes six principles recognizing the profession's responsibilities to the public, to clients, and to colleagues.

2-2a Principles The principles suggest that a CPA should strive for behavior above the minimal level of acceptable conduct required by law and regulations. In addition to expressing the basic tenets of ethical and professional conduct, the principles are intended to provide a framework for the CPA to use in his or her practice. The six principles of professional conduct under the AIPCA Code are the following:

1. Responsibilities—In carrying out their responsibilities as professionals, members should exercise sensitive professional and moral judgments in all their activities [0.300.020.01].

2. The public interest—Members should accept the obligation to act in a way that will serve the public interest, honor the public trust, and demonstrate commitment to professionalism [0.300.030.01].

3. Integrity—To maintain and broaden public confidence, members should perform all professional responsibilities with the highest sense of integrity [0.300.040.01].

4. Objectivity and Independence—A member should maintain objectivity and be free of conflicts of interest in discharging professional responsibilities. A member in public practice should be independent in fact and appearance when providing auditing and other attestation services. The principle of objectivity requires the member to be impartial, intellectually honest, and free of conflicts of interest [0.300.050.01 and 0.300.050.02].

5. Due care—A member should observe the profession's technical and ethical standards, strive continually to improve competence and the quality of services, and discharge professional responsibility to the best of the member's ability. Competence is obtained from a combination of education and experience, beginning with a mastery of the knowledge required to be a CPA and requiring a commitment to learn and improve throughout a member's professional life [0.300.060.01 and 0.300.060.03].

6. Scope and nature of services—A member in public practice should observe the Principles of the *Code of Professional Conduct* in determining the scope and nature of services to be provided.

Each of the principles should be considered in determining whether to provide specific services in individual circumstances and may restrain a member from offering certain services to clients [0.300.070.01 and 0.300.070.03].

2-2b Rules Each part of the Code of Professional Conduct includes rules relevant to members subject to that part. Rules related to (1) independence, (2) contingent fees,

(3) commissions and referral fees, (4) advertising and other forms of solicitation, (5) the handling of confidential client information, and (6) the form of organization and name used are only discussed in part 1, dealing with members in public practice, while more general rules related to (7) integrity and objectivity, (8) general standards, (9) compliance with standards, and (10) accounting principles are discussed in parts 1 and 2. A rule regarding committing acts discreditable to the profession (11) is included in all three parts.

Following the rules, the code includes interpretations of those rules. In the absence of interpretations, members should apply the relevant conceptual framework to the issue or situation in attempting to resolve the question.

Independence Rule [1.200.001].   A member in public practice shall be independent in the performance of professional services. **Independence** is required not only for opinions on financial statements but also for other reports and services for which a body designated by the AICPA has promulgated standards requiring independence. In the absence of interpretations that address a particular relationship or circumstance, a member should evaluate whether the relationship or circumstance would lead a reasonable and informed third party aware of the relevant information to conclude that there is a threat to either the member's or firm's independence that is not at an acceptable level [1.210.010.01]. A member would be in violation of the rule if the member cannot demonstrate that safeguards were applied that eliminated or reduced threats to an acceptable level [1.200.005.02]. Examples of threats include members not acting with objectivity due to an adverse interest, advocacy threats, familiarity threats due to a long or close relationship with a client, management participation threats, self-interest threats, self-review threats, and undue influence threats [1.210.010.10]. In some cases, the code specifies that no safeguards can eliminate or reduce a threat to an acceptable level [1.210.010.11].

Contingent Fee Rule [1.510.001].   A CPA in public practice cannot charge or receive a contingent fee for any professional services from a client for whom the CPA or the CPA's firm performs audits, reviews, certain compilations, or examinations of prospective financial information. For example, a fee schedule of $5,000 for a qualified audit opinion and $35,000 for an unqualified opinion would not be allowed. The rule also prohibits a CPA from charging a contingent fee for preparing an original or amended tax return or a claim for a tax refund.

A **contingent fee** is defined here as a fee established for the performance of any service pursuant to an arrangement in which no fee will be charged unless a specified finding or result is attained, or in which the amount of the fee is otherwise dependent on the finding or result of such service. Solely for purposes of this rule, fees are not regarded as being contingent if fixed by courts or other public authorities or, in tax matters, if determined based on the results of judicial proceedings or the findings of governmental agencies. (This is similar to Circular 230 § 10.27.)

The code provides a number of examples of when a contingent fee is permitted, including representing a client in connection with a revenue agent's examination of their federal or state tax return, filing an amended return claiming a refund based on an uncertain tax issue that is the subject of a case involving a different taxpayer or for which a taxing authority is developing a position, filing an amended return claiming a refund greater than the threshold for review set by the Joint Committee on Taxation or state taxing authority, requesting a refund of overpayments of interest or penalties in circumstances in which the taxing authority has established procedures for the substantive review of such requests, requesting by means of a protest letter or similar document a reduction in a property's assessed value under an established review process for hearing taxpayer arguments, and representing a client in connection with obtaining a private letter ruling or influencing the drafting of a regulation or statute [1.510.010.04]. A contingent fee is never permitted for a return amended because a valid deduction was inadvertently omitted from the original filed return [1.510.010.05].

Commissions and Referral Fees Rule [1.520.001]. A member in public practice cannot charge or receive a commission or referral fee from a client for whom the CPA or the CPA's firm performs audits, reviews, certain compilation work, or examinations of prospective financial information. Thus, under this rule, a CPA who does only tax or other nonaudit work for a client may accept or pay a commission. However, the CPA must disclose the commission to the client or other party in the transaction. In addition, a member who accepts or pays a referral fee for recommending or referring any service of a CPA must disclose that fact.

Advertising and Other Forms of Solicitation [1.600.001]. A CPA in public practice cannot seek clients through false, misleading, or deceptive advertising or other forms of solicitation. In addition, solicitation by the use of coercion, overreaching, or harassing conduct is not allowed. The AICPA has placed no restrictions as to the type, media, or frequency of a CPA's advertisements or on the artwork that is associated with them. Under this rule, an activity would be prohibited if it:

1. Creates false or unjustified expectations of favorable results;

2. Implies the ability to influence any court, tribunal, regulatory agency, or similar body or official;

3. Contains a representation that specific professional services in current or future periods will be performed for a stated fee, estimated fee, or fee range when it was likely, at the time of the representation, that such fees would be substantially increased and the prospective client was not advised of that likelihood; or

4. Contains any other representations that would be likely to cause a reasonable person to misunderstand or be deceived.

For example, a radio spot that states a CPA firm "can beat the IRS every time" would violate the rule.

Confidential Client Information Rule [1.700.001]. While Circular 230 and the AICPA Statements on Standards for Tax Services (see page 22) do not include specific guidance regarding client confidentiality, the AICPA Code of Professional Conduct provides that a member in the practice of public accounting must not disclose confidential client data without the specific consent of the client. Confidential information is defined as any information obtained from the client that is not available to the public [0.400.09]. Relative to disclosure to third parties, Interpretation 1.700.060 notes that the consent should preferably be in writing and should specify the nature of the information that may be disclosed, the type of third party to whom it may be disclosed, and its intended use.

The rule does not apply if:

1. There is a conflict with the Compliance with Standards Rule [1.310.001] or the Accounting Principles Rule [1.320.001];

2. The CPA is served with an enforceable subpoena or summons or must comply with applicable laws and government regulations;

3. There is a review of a CPA's practice under AICPA or state society authorization; or

4. The CPA is responding to an inquiry of an investigative or disciplinary body of a recognized society, or the CPA is initiating a complaint with a disciplinary body. In connection

with this rule, members of the investigative and disciplinary bodies that may be exposed to confidential client information are precluded from disclosing such information.

Interpretations specific to tax engagements deal with situations in which a member withdraws from an engagement due to the discovery of irregularities in a client's tax return [1.700.020.02], and when a member is engaged to prepare a married couple's joint return when that couple is going through a divorce [1.700.030]. In addition, firms sometimes outsource the preparation of tax returns and other services to outside entities. Interpretation 1.700.040 notes that when members use a third-party service provider, threats may exist, and it goes on to require that members enter into contractual agreements with outside service providers to maintain confidentiality and provide reasonable assurance that the outside provider has procedures in place to prevent the unauthorized release of confidential information to others. The interpretation also requires that the member obtain specific consent from the client before disclosing confidential information to the third-party service provider.

SPOTLIGHT ON TAXATION

Confidentiality

A Texas district court held that the identities of taxpayers who hired the accounting firm KPMG to participate in a tax shelter later identified as potentially abusive by the IRS were not protected from disclosure under the IRC § 7525 confidentiality privilege for communications between taxpayers and federally authorized tax practitioners. Disclosing taxpayers' identities to the IRS would only reveal their participation in these shelters, and it would not reveal any confidential communications made regarding these tax shelters. *John Doe 1 & John Doe 2 v. KPMG*, 93 A.F.T.R. 2d 2004-1759 (D.C N. Tex.).

Form of Organization and Name Rule [1.800.001]. CPAs may practice public accounting only in the form of organization permitted by state law or regulation whose characteristics conform to resolutions of the AICPA Council. Under this rule, a CPA cannot practice under a firm name that is misleading. The names of one or more past owners may be included in the firm name of a successor organization. In addition, all partners or members of a firm must be AICPA members if a firm is to designate itself as "Members of the AICPA."

Integrity and Objectivity Rule [1.100.001 and 2.100.001]. The integrity and objectivity rule is included in part 1 and part 2 and accordingly applies to members in public practice and members in business. All professional services by a CPA should be rendered with objectivity and integrity, avoiding any conflict of interest. A CPA should not knowingly misrepresent facts or subordinate his or her judgment to that of others in rendering any professional services. For example, in a tax practice the CPA may be requested to blindly follow the guidelines of a government agency or the demands of an audit client. This rule prohibits such blind obedience. The code specifically recognizes that conflicts of interest may arise in tax contexts including providing tax or personal financial planning services for several members of a family whom the member knows to have opposing interests or when referring a personal financial planning or tax client to an insurance broker or other service provider which refers clients to the member under an exclusive arrangement [1.110.010.04 examples l and m].

General Standards Rule [1.200.001 and 2.300.001].   Both members in public practice and members in business must comply with the following general standards, as well as any interpretations of such standards, of the AICPA Code of Professional Conduct.

1. The CPA must be able to complete all professional services with professional competence.

2. The CPA must exercise due professional care in the performance of all professional services.

3. The CPA shall adequately plan and supervise the performance of all professional services.

4. The CPA must obtain sufficient relevant data to afford a reasonable basis for any conclusion or recommendation in connection with the performance of any professional services.

Competence encompasses not only technical subject matter but also knowledge of the profession's standards and the ability to exercise sound judgment in applying the technical knowledge [1.300.010.01]. At the same time, the code is clear that the member does not assume a responsibility for infallibility of knowledge or judgment [1.300.010.02].

Compliance with Standards Rule [1.310.001 and 2.310.001].   Both members in public practice and members in business, whether providing tax, management consulting, audit, review, compilation, or other professional services, must comply with all standards promulgated by bodies designated by the AICPA Council.

Accounting Principles Rule [1.320.001 and 2.320.001].   Members in business and members in public practice are prohibited from expressing an opinion that financial data of an entity conform to GAAP if those statements or other financial data contain any material departure from the profession's technical standards. Reference to GAAP in this rule means accounting principles as promulgated not only by the Financial Accounting Standards Board (FASB) but also the Federal Accounting Standards Advisory Board (FASAB), the Governmental Accounting Standards Board (GASB), and the International Accounting Standards Board (IASB). In some cases in which a departure is present but the financial statement or other financial data would have been misleading without that departure, a member may be able to comply with this rule by describing the departure, the effect of the departure, and its justification.

Acts Discreditable Rule [1.400.001, 2.400.001, and 3.400.001].   All members including retired members and unemployed members and others subject to the part 3 rules must not commit an act that is discreditable to the profession. Examples include members who violate antidiscrimination laws of the United States, a state, or a municipality, including those related to sexual and other forms of harassment [1.400.010.01, 2.400.010.01, and 3.400.010.01], members who are negligent in the preparation of financial statements or other records [1.400.040, 2.400.040, and 3.400.040], members who solicit or disclose Uniform CPA Exam questions or answers without the AICPA's written permission [1.400.020, 2.400.020, and 3.400.020], and members who fail to comply with applicable federal, state, or local laws regarding the filing of personal tax returns or tax returns of the member's firm or employer or the timely remittance of all payroll and other taxes collected on behalf of others [1.400.030, 2.400.030, and 3.400.030]. Making false, misleading, or deceptive claims about a member's experience or qualifications is also considered a violation of the Acts Discreditable Rule [1.400.090, 2.400.090, and 3.400.090].

2-3 Statements on Standards for Tax Services

To assist CPAs, the AICPA has issued a series of statements as to what constitutes appropriate standards for tax practice. These Statements on Standards for Tax Services (SSTS) delineate a CPA's responsibilities to his or her clients, the public, the government, and the profession. The SSTS is a set of enforceable standards. They are intended to specifically address the problems inherent in the tax practitioner's dual role in serving the client and the public. The statements are intended to supplement, rather than replace, the AICPA Code of Professional Conduct and Circular 230. Furthermore, they are designed to address the development of tax practice as an integral part of a CPA's practice and the changing environment in which tax practitioners must operate, including the rapidly changing tax laws.

2-3a SSTS No. 1: Tax Return Positions   Under SSTS No. 1, a member should determine and comply with the standards, if any, that are imposed by the applicable taxing authority with respect to recommending a tax return position or preparing or signing a tax return. If the applicable taxing authority has no written standards with respect to recommending a tax return position or preparing or signing a tax return, or if its standards are lower than the standards set forth in the SSTS, then the standards in SSTS No. 1 apply. This standard provides that, in providing professional services that involve tax return positions, a member should have a **good-faith belief** that the position, if challenged, has at least a **realistic possibility** of being sustained administratively or judicially solely on its merits. In addition, a member may recommend a tax return position if the member concludes that there is a reasonable basis for the position and advises the taxpayer to appropriately disclose that position. Thus, a member may prepare or sign a tax return that reflects a position if a member has a reasonable basis for the position and that position is appropriately disclosed.

A member may reach a conclusion that a position is warranted based on a well-reasoned construction of the applicable statute, well-reasoned articles or treatises, or pronouncements issued by the applicable taxing authority, regardless of whether such sources would be treated as authority under IRC § 6662 (accuracy-related penalty on underpayments). A position would not fail to meet these standards merely because it is later abandoned for practical or procedural considerations during an administrative hearing or in the litigation process.

In cases in which the member believes that the taxpayer may have some exposure to a penalty, the statement suggests that the member advise the taxpayer of such risk. In cases in which disclosure of a position on the tax return may mitigate the possibility of a taxpayer penalty under the IRC, the member should consider recommending that the taxpayer disclose the position on the return. Additionally, a member should not recommend a tax return position or prepare or sign a tax return reflecting a position that the member knows could exploit the audit selection process of a taxing authority or that serves as a mere arguing position advanced solely to obtain leverage in a potential negotiation with a taxing authority.

Two interpretations of SSTS No. 1 provide additional guidance and examples to aid practitioners in interpreting the standard.[5] Interpretation No. 1-1 notes that the realistic-possibility-of-success standard (satisfied if there is an approximately one-in-three (33 percent) likelihood that the position will be upheld on its merits if challenged) is a lower standard than the substantial-authority standard (interpreted as requiring a 40 percent

---

[5]Full text of the SSTS and interpretations is available at **http://www.aicpa.org/INTERESTAREAS/TAX/RESOURCES/STANDARDSETHICS/STATEMENTSONSTANDARDSFORTAXSERVICES/Pages/default.aspx**.

likelihood) and the more-likely-than-not-standard (requiring a 50 percent likelihood), but it is a higher standard than the reasonable-basis standard (generally interpreted as requiring a 20 percent likelihood of success). Sixteen illustrations provide specific fact situations followed by conclusions as to how SSTS No. 1 should be interpreted.

Interpretation No. 1-2 provides additional guidance with respect to providing services in connection with tax planning, including an additional 19 illustrations intended to show how the standard would apply across the spectrum of tax planning.

2-3b SSTS No. 2: Answers to Questions on Returns   Before signing a return as the preparer, a member should make a reasonable effort to obtain from the taxpayer appropriate answers to all questions on the taxpayer's tax return. If the taxpayer leaves a question on the return unanswered and reasonable grounds exist for not answering the question, the member need not provide an explanation for the omission. The possibility that an answer to a question may prove disadvantageous to the taxpayer, however, does not justify omitting the answer. However, such an omission is acceptable in the following situations:

1. The pertinent data are not readily available and are not significant to the determination of taxable income (or loss) or the tax liability.

2. The taxpayer and member are genuinely uncertain as to the meaning of the question on the return.

3. An answer to a question is voluminous. (However, assurance should be given on the return that the data can be supplied upon examination.) In this regard, a notation on Form 1120 and related schedules that information will be provided on request is not considered acceptable (IRS Brooklyn District Newsletter No. 47, 10/89).

2-3c SSTS No. 3: Certain Procedural Aspects of Preparing Returns   In preparing or signing a return, the member ordinarily may rely without verification on information that the taxpayer or a third party has provided, unless such information appears to be incorrect, incomplete, or inconsistent. A more formal audit-like review of documents or supporting evidence is generally not required for a member to sign the tax return. Where material provided by the taxpayer appears to be incorrect or incomplete, however, the member should obtain additional information from the taxpayer. In situations in which the statutes require that specific conditions be met, the member should determine, by inquiry, whether the conditions have been met. For example, the IRC and IRS regulations impose substantiation requirements for the deduction of certain expenditures. In such a case, the member has an obligation to make appropriate inquiries.

Although members are not required to examine supporting documents, they should encourage the taxpayer to provide such documents when deemed appropriate. For example, in the case of deductions or income from a pass-through entity, such as a partnership, the entity's documents might be useful in preparing the owner's tax returns.

The member should make proper use of the prior year's tax return when feasible to gather information about the taxpayer and to help avoid omissions and errors with respect to income, deductions, and credit computations.

2-3d SSTS No. 4: Use of Estimates   A member may prepare tax returns that involve the use of the taxpayer's estimates if it is impractical to obtain exact data and if the estimated amounts appear reasonable to the member. In all cases, these estimates must be supplied by the taxpayer. However, the member may provide advice in connection with determining an estimate. When the taxpayer's estimates are used, they should be presented in such a manner as to avoid the implication of greater accuracy than exists.

Situations in which the use of estimates may be appropriate include cases in which the keeping of precise records for numerous items of small amounts is difficult to achieve, data are not available at the time of filing the tax return, or certain records are missing.

This statement does not prohibit the use of estimates in making pertinent accounting judgments when such use is not in conflict with the IRC; such judgments are acceptable and expected. For example, the income tax regulations permit the use of a reasonable estimate for accruals if exact amounts are not known.

SPOTLIGHT ON TAXATION

The Cohan Rule

SSTS No. 4 is similar to (and somewhat based on) the estimation rule in the 1930 *Cohan* case [8 A.F.T.R. 10552; 39 F.2d 540; 2 U.S.T.C. ¶ 489]. George M. Cohan was a producer of Broadway shows ("Yankee Doodle Dandy," for example) in the early part of the 20th century. As such, his work involved a substantial amount of travel and entertaining. George did not keep records of these travel and entertaining (T&E) expenses; he just estimated them for tax purposes (more than $55,000 for his 1921 through 1923 fiscal years) and deducted them on his income tax returns. The Board of Tax Appeals (the predecessor to the Tax Court) upheld the IRS's disallowance of all (100 percent) of the estimated T&E deduction because of lack of proper substantiation. However, the Second Circuit Court of Appeals disagreed and said that Cohan obviously incurred such expenses and that a reasonable estimate would be acceptable in calculating taxable income.

This is sometimes referred to as the **Cohan Rule** and is still in effect today. However, Congress has modified the Cohan Rule by changing the IRC for certain transactions. For example, the Cohan Rule may no longer be used to allow the deduction of estimated amounts of certain kinds of business expenses—namely, travel and entertainment expenses (including away-from-home travel expenses) and listed property expenditures (including local travel expenses). The current rules (see IRC § 274) require detailed substantiation of such expenditures.

Although in most cases the use of estimates does not necessitate that the item be specifically disclosed on the taxpayer's return, disclosure should be made when failure to do so would result in misleading the IRS about the accuracy of the return. For example, disclosure may be necessary when the taxpayer's records have been destroyed in a fire or when the taxpayer has not received a Schedule K-1 from a pass-through entity at the time the return is filed. Tax practitioners should inform their taxpayers that the tax law does not allow estimates of certain income and expenditure items, and that more restrictive substantiation requirements apply in cases of certain expenditures, such as travel and entertainment expenses.

2-3e SSTS No. 5: Departure from a Position Previously Concluded in an Administrative Proceeding or Court Decision The recommendation by a member as to the treatment of an item on a tax return should be based on the facts and the law as they are evaluated at the time during which the return is prepared or when it is signed by the member. Unless the taxpayer is bound by the IRS to the treatment of an item in later years, such as by a closing agreement, the disposition of an item in a prior year's audit, or as part of a prior year's court decision, the member is not prevented from recommending a different treatment of a similar item in a later year's return. Thus, a member may sign a return that contains a departure from a treatment required by the IRS in a prior year, provided that the member adheres to the standards in SSTS No. 1.

In most cases, a member's recommendation as to the treatment of an item on a tax return will be consistent with the treatment of a similar item consented to in a prior year's administrative proceeding or as a result of the prior year's court decision. In deciding whether a recommendation contrary to the prior treatment is warranted, the member should consider the following:

1. Neither the IRS nor the taxpayer is bound to act consistently with respect to the treatment of an item in a prior proceeding. However, the IRS tends to act consistently in similar situations.

2. The standards under SSTS No. 1, Tax Return Positions, must be followed. In determining whether such standards can be met, the member must consider the existence of an unfavorable court decision and the taxpayer's consent in an earlier administrative proceeding.

3. In some cases, the taxpayer's consent to the treatment of an item in a prior administrative or judicial proceeding may have been because of a desire to settle the issue or a lack of supporting data, whereas in the current year these factors no longer exist.

4. The tax climate may have changed for a given issue since the prior court decision was reached or the prior administrative hearing concluded.

2-3f SSTS No. 6: Knowledge of Error: Return Preparation and Administrative Proceedings

The member must advise the taxpayer promptly, regardless of whether the member prepared or signed the return in question, when he or she learns of an error in a previously filed tax return, an error in a return that is the subject of an administrative proceeding, or a taxpayer's failure to file a required return. The term "administrative proceeding" does not include a criminal proceeding. Such advice should include a recommendation for appropriate measures the taxpayer should take. However, the member is not obligated to inform the IRS of the situation, nor may he or she do so without the taxpayer's permission, except as provided by law.

The term "error" includes any position, omission, or method of accounting that, at the time the return is filed, fails to meet the standards set out in SSTS No. 1. An error also includes a position taken on a prior year's return that no longer meets these standards because of legislation, judicial decisions, or administrative pronouncements having retroactive effect. However, an error does not include an item that has an insignificant effect on the taxpayer's tax liability. This materiality threshold is not included in Circular 230, Section 10.21.

If the member is requested to prepare the current year's return, and the taxpayer has not taken action to correct an error in a prior year's return, the member should consider whether to proceed with the preparation of the current year's return. If the current year's return is prepared, the member should take reasonable steps to ensure that the error is not repeated.

A member should advise a taxpayer, either orally or in writing, as to the correction of errors in the prior year's return. In a case in which there is a possibility that the taxpayer may be charged with fraud, the taxpayer should be referred to an attorney.

2-3g SSTS No. 7: Form and Content of Advice to Taxpayers

In providing tax advice to taxpayers, the member must use judgment that reflects professional competence and serves the taxpayer's needs. The member must assume that any advice given will be used to determine the manner of reporting items on the taxpayer's tax return; therefore, the member should ensure that the standards under SSTS No. 1 are satisfied. When providing advice that will be relied on by third parties, the member's responsibilities may differ. Neither a standard format nor guidelines have been issued or established that would cover all situations and circumstances involving written or oral advice from a member. When giving such advice to taxpayers, in addition to exercising professional judgment, the member should consider each of the following:

1. The importance of the transaction and amounts involved.

2. The specific or general nature of the taxpayer's inquiry.

3. The time available for development and submission of the advice.

4. The technical complexity involved.

5. The existence of authorities and precedents.

6. The tax sophistication of the taxpayer.

7. The need to seek other professional advice.

8. The type of transaction and whether it is subject to heightened reporting or disclosure requirements.

9. The potential penalty consequences of the tax return position for which the advice is rendered.

10. Whether any potential applicable penalties can be avoided through disclosure.

11. Whether the member intends for the taxpayer to rely upon the advice to avoid potential penalties.

Written communication is recommended in important, unusual, or complicated transactions, while oral advice is acceptable in situations that are more typical. In the communication, the member should advise the taxpayer that the advice reflects his or her professional judgment based on the current situation, and that subsequent developments may affect previous advice, such as stating that the position of authorities is subject to change.

When subsequent developments affect the advice that a member has previously communicated to a taxpayer, the member is under no obligation to initiate further communication of such developments to the taxpayer unless a specific agreement has been reached with the taxpayer or the member is assisting in the application of a procedure or plan relative to such advice.

Exhibit 1-4 summarizes the main topic of each SSTS. The complete text of the SSTS can be found on the AICPA Website at **www.aicpa.org/INTERESTAREAS/TAX /RESOURCES/STANDARDSETHICS/STATEMENTSONSTANDARDSFORTAXSERVICES /Pages/default.aspx.**

EXHIBIT 1-4:   Summary of AICPA Statements on Standards for Tax Services

SSTS	Summary of Contents
No. 1	Specifies the standards for professional services that involve tax positions
No. 2	Explains how a member should handle answering questions on a tax return
No. 3	Describes the procedural aspects of preparing a tax return
No. 4	Defines when a member can use an estimate in preparing a tax return
No. 5	Explains what a member should do about items on a current return when similar items were audited on a prior year's return or were the subject of a judicial hearing
No. 6	States what a member should do upon learning about an error in a prior year's tax return
No. 7	Establishes standards for the giving of tax advice to taxpayers

2-4 Sarbanes-Oxley and Taxation

In 2002, Congress passed the Sarbanes-Oxley Act, which addressed the corporate management abuses that took place during the 1990s and early 2000s. These corporate governance breakdowns culminated in spectacular business failures such as those involving Enron, WorldCom, Global Crossing, Waste Management, Sunbeam, and others, and led to the eventual failure of a Big Five CPA firm, Arthur Andersen. In addition to being a response to corporate governance and accounting transparency failures, the Sarbanes-Oxley Act was a response to the general failure of business ethics, for example, the proliferation of abusive tax shelters and super-aggressive tax-avoidance strategies.

The Sarbanes-Oxley Act made it unlawful for an auditor to provide certain nonaudit services listed in the act. In addition, the act provided that a registered public accounting firm "may engage in any nonaudit service, including tax services, that is not described [in the list of nine specifically prohibited services] for an audit client only if the activity is approved in advance by the audit committee of the issuer" in accordance with the act. The prohibited services are as follows:

1. Bookkeeping or other services related to the accounting records or financial statements of the audit client

2. Financial information systems design and implementation

3. Appraisal or valuation services, fairness opinions, or contribution-in-kind reports

4. Actuarial services

5. Internal audit outsourcing services

6. Management functions or human resources

7. Broker or dealer, investment adviser, or investment banking services

8. Legal services and expert services unrelated to the audit

9. Any other service that the Public Company Accounting Oversight Board (PCAOB) determines, by regulation, is impermissible. For example, PCAOB Rule 3522 states that a registered public accounting firm is not independent of its audit firm if the firm provides to the audit client any nonaudit service related to marketing, planning, or opining in favor of the tax treatment of a transaction that (a) is a confidential transaction; or (b) was initially recommended by the public accounting firm (directly or indirectly) and a significant purpose of which is tax avoidance, unless the proposed tax treatment is at least more likely than not to be allowable under applicable tax laws.

With some exceptions, Rule 3523 prohibits an accounting firm from providing tax services to a person in a financial reporting oversight role at an audit client or to an immediate family member of that person with oversight responsibilities.

Although tax compliance work is not one of the prohibited services, it is subject to the pre-approval process. Guidance related to the pre-approval process is provided by the PCAOB in Rule 3524 and includes requirements that the audit firm describe in writing to the audit committee the scope of the service, the fee structure, and the potential effects of the services on the independence of the firm.

2-5 ABA Model Rules of Professional Conduct

In 1983, the ABA first adopted **Model Rules of Professional Conduct** to serve as guides for attorneys' professional conduct. Revised several times since then, the current rules have been adopted by over 50 states and territories. The Model Rules deal with issues such as confidentiality and conflicts of interest in the client–lawyer relationship, responsibilities to nonclients, and so on. While the Model Rules do not have the force of law, they have been adopted by the appropriate agencies that govern the practice of law in each of the states. In many jurisdictions, the state's supreme court is charged with policing the practice of law; in other states, the legislature bears this responsibility. Attorneys should consult their own jurisdiction's ethical guidelines to determine whether the provisions of the ABA Model Rules, or some modification of these doctrines, have been adopted. The current status of the ABA Model Rules can be found on the ABA Website at **www.abanet.org/cpr/mrpc/mrpc_toc.html**.

3 Nonregulatory Ethical Behavior Models

Since the turn of the 21st century, nonregulatory ethical models have become more relevant and applicable to professions such as accountancy and law. Tax practitioners need to be aware that there is substantially more to ethical behavior than just following the rules of ethics or conduct of professional organizations such as the AICPA or the ABA. The regulatory rules are generally straightforward and usually list a defined set of acts that are prohibited by members of the profession. For example, under SSTS No. 6, a CPA cannot disclose an error in a client's tax return to the IRS without the client's permission. On the other hand, nonregulatory ethics involve making choices that are not always clearly spelled out.

3-1 Ethical Dilemmas and Ethical Reasoning

An ethical dilemma occurs when someone is faced with a situation to which there are no clearly defined answers, such as by regulation or law. In other words, there are multiple "right" answers (or put another way, no obviously wrong answers).

EXAMPLE 1-3

Bill, a CPA, has been requested by his CPA firm employer to join The Macho Men, a private club. Most of the movers and shakers (i.e., clients and potential clients) in town are members of this club. However, the club does not allow female members. If you were Bill, what would you do? How do you think Bill's female co-workers would feel about him joining a club that discriminates against women? There is no "right" answer to these questions because they are ethical dilemmas to which there are several right answers.

As illustrated in this example, making the choice in an ethical dilemma can be complicated. How, then, is a person supposed to deal with a situation such as this? The answer can be assessed using several generally recognized forms of ethical reasoning.

SPOTLIGHT ON TAXATION

Quotation

Ethics is knowing the difference between what you have the right to do and what is the right thing to do.

—Supreme Court Justice Potter Stewart

3-1a Ethical Reasoning There are several approaches to resolving an ethical dilemma. Len Marrella notes that three common lines of reasoning are used to solve an ethical dilemma.[6] These are end-based reasoning, rule-based reasoning, and care-based reasoning. Each of these approaches attempts to provide a framework in which to resolve an ethical dilemma.

3-1b End-Based Ethical Reasoning   End-based ethical reasoning was popular in the 1800s. Its main tenet was that an action was right if it produced at least as much net good as any alternative action could have produced. Hence, an ethical decision was the one that did the most good for the largest number of people. In summary, competing ethical solutions are resolved in terms of the end result.

John Stuart Mill was a proponent of this philosophy. He encouraged individuals to examine the consequences of various alternatives and to rely heavily on facts when making ethical choices.[7] The steps used to apply end-based reasoning can be summarized as follows:

1. Identify the courses of action available.

2. Identify stakeholders who will be affected by the various choices of action and what benefit or harm may come to them as the result of a given choice.

3. Choose the action with the greatest benefits and the least amount of harm.[8]

To a CPA this type of decision-making is similar to cost–benefit analysis. However, applying cost–benefit analysis to an ethical decision is not as easy as applying it to a financial decision. The real problem is that end-based reasoning does not consider justice, fairness, integrity, and similar concepts in arriving at a choice. Ethicists consider this to be one of end-based reasoning's major failings.

3-1c Rule-Based Ethical Reasoning   Rule-based reasoning is based on what is referred to as "Kantian ethics," which were derived from the writing of the German philosopher Immanuel Kant. He held that individual actions should be such that we would accept similar behavior from everyone else. Kant believed rules are made to apply to everyone and there are no exceptions—period. According to Kant, lying and stealing are always unethical, and therefore there is no such thing as a "white lie" to protect someone's feelings or reputation. This thinking today is usually referred to as "zero tolerance" and many times leads to unjust results. For example, what if a six-year-old first grader is expelled from school for bringing a plastic picnic knife to school to eat his lunch, in violation of the no-weapons policy at his school? Is this fair or just?

3-1d Care-Based Ethical Reasoning   Care-based reasoning is found in the moral teachings of almost every culture and religion. In Western culture, it is called the "Golden Rule," which states, "Do unto others as you would have them do unto you." From an ethical reasoning point of view, it advises one to make decisions that would result in the treatment you yourself would like to receive. Care-based reasoning can be described as doing what is fair and just.

3-2 Ethical Professional Behavior

Professional ethical behavior is the result of the interaction of personal morality, social responsibility, business ethics, and other general ethical standards.

---

[6]*In Search of Ethics: Conversations with Men and Women of Character* (DC Press, 2001).

[7]Velasquez, Manuel, et al., "Thinking Ethically: A Framework for Moral Decision Making," *Issues in Ethics*, Vol. 7, No. 1 (Winter 1996).

[8]Ibid.

3-2a Morality

The subject of morality fills tens of thousands of books. Publications as diverse as the Bible and popular novels examine morality in one way or another. When something is judged to be morally right or wrong (or good or bad), the underlying standards on which such judgments are based are called moral standards.

According to some people's moral standards, cheating "just a little" in computing a tax liability is morally acceptable. Most people in the United States believe that everyone cheats a little on their taxes. Cheating significantly may be viewed differently, but where is the dividing line between morally acceptable tax cheating and morally wrong tax evasion? Under the self-assessed tax system in the United States, different moral standards provide different answers—from complete honesty to various degrees of dishonesty. The tax practitioner must be ready to work with clients holding various systems of morality and to accept the consequences of the moral choices made, including the possibility of losing a client, paying fines and penalties to the IRS, or even going to jail.

3-2b Social Responsibility

The tax practitioner must be aware of social responsibility in areas such as environmental protection, equal opportunity, and occupational safety. Since World War II, society has held the business world increasingly responsible for meeting certain noneconomic standards. In 1970, Milton Friedman, the Nobel Prize-winning economist, said that the "social responsibility" of business is merely to increase profits. Nevertheless, the prevailing sentiment today is that businesses and the professions should return something to society to make it better, not just make a profit. For the tax practitioner, this could mean going beyond the minimum legal responsibility to provide equal opportunity in the hiring of employees by making special recruitment efforts, or it could mean volunteering time to help charitable organizations with their tax problems.

3-2c Business Ethics

In recent years, one of the major topics in the business world has been the question of business ethics. Many people believe that ethics has application only in one's personal life, not in the business or professional arena. Like Milton Friedman, they think that the only business of business is to make a profit. This view is popular because people who work in business or professions must concern themselves with producing goods and services to earn a profit, and it is easier to measure profit than it is to make value judgments. People are more comfortable discussing problems in terms of profits than in terms of the ethical impact of the entity and its actions. Few business people and professionals are trained in ethical analysis, and therefore they usually are not familiar with how to evaluate a problem in terms of ethics.

SPOTLIGHT ON TAXATION

Quotation

The income tax has made more liars out of the American people than golf has.
—Will Rodgers

EXAMPLE 1-4

Bruce owns a successful small business. The business is operated as a corporation. During the year, Bruce makes numerous personal long-distance phone calls from the office, uses the company credit card to purchase gas for his family's personal automobiles, sends personal items using the company's FedEx account, and is reimbursed by the company for meals and entertainment expenditures that are primarily personal in nature. These items are deducted by the corporation on its tax return. Would you sign this company's Form 1120 as the tax return preparer? If you also audited this company, what would you do about these transactions?

That business and professional organizations have ethical responsibilities is readily apparent to anyone who reads the popular press. Recent scandals such as the Volkswagen emissions scandal, accounting improprieties at Toshiba, and corruption involving FIFA officials, and the public reaction to those scandals, are prime examples of society holding business to a standard of ethical conduct. Most of the big CPA firms have settled, in or out of court, multimillion dollar lawsuits brought against them for what was, in part, a business ethics failure.

There are many examples of suspect ethics practices in the area of taxation. Following are some classic examples of the aggressive tax planning arrangements that have been promoted over the years by CPAs, lawyers, and others. Each year, the IRS publishes a list of its "dirty dozen" tax scams. In recent years, this list has included offshore tax avoidance, often facilitated by financial organizations, abusive tax shelters, frivolous tax arguments, and return preparer fraud.

SPOTLIGHT ON TAXATION

Shame on You

The taxing authorities of several U.S. states post the names of delinquent taxpayers on their Websites. The stated purpose of the postings is to shame the taxpayers who have not paid their state taxes into paying them. Although this posting clearly is legal, is it ethical? For example, suppose a family has a child with leukemia and has massive medical bills and cannot afford to pay their taxes. Should they be held up to ridicule because they are doing the right thing and taking care of their child, even if it prevents them from paying their taxes?

3-2d Other Ethical Standards The study of nonregulatory ethics could be expanded to cover such other issues as public policy, religious beliefs, and cultural values, issues that are beyond the scope of this text. Most such topics would be addressed in a university course on ethics or business ethics. A tax practitioner can expand his or her understanding of the application of ethics to accounting and business situations by referring to the following books and online resources:

- Leonard J. Brooks, *Business and Professional Ethics for Directors, Executives, and Accountants*, 7th edition (Cengage Learning, 2015).

- *Business Ethics*, the Magazine of Corporate Responsibility, available at **business-ethics.com**.

- Markkula Center for Applied Ethics, **www.scu.edu/ethics/focus-areas/business-ethics/**.

- *Ethical Problems in Federal Tax Practice*, 5th edition (Wolters Kluwer, 2014).

The following are examples of nonregulatory ethics dilemmas that could arise in a business, accounting, or tax setting. As shown in these examples, the application of ethics to tax and business situations is not clear cut. Many times, doing what is "right" may not be possible. The tax practitioner is faced with challenges on how to apply proper business ethics on a daily basis.

EXAMPLE 1-5

Hilary is a CPA who is a sole practitioner. This year, one of her clients, Gold Corporation, opened a new division in Europe. Gold is a longtime client of Hilary's, and she is anxious to keep it. However, Hilary has no experience in international tax and would not be able to give Gold the kind of tax advice needed for the new division. The ethical question is whether Hilary should inform the client of her lack of knowledge in this area and risk losing the client, or whether she should remain silent and "wing it" on the international tax issues. What should Hilary do in this situation?

EXAMPLE 1-6

Patrick is a CPA who is a partner in a successful local CPA practice. The state in which Patrick lives has a 40-hour annual continuing professional education (CPE) requirement. If a CPA does not meet the CPE requirement, the CPA's license will be suspended and he or she will not be able to practice. Patrick is approached by the Flight-by-Night CPE Company about signing up for some of its CPE courses.

The representative tells Patrick that the company will report that Patrick attended the courses so that he gets the CPE credit, even if he does not attend. Because Patrick is overloaded with work, he considers this a "low hassle" way to get his CPA license renewed. Would it be ethical for Patrick to obtain his CPE credit this way?

EXAMPLE 1-7

Devona is an auditor in the Boston office of a large international CPA firm. She is sent on an inventory observation for a new client of the firm's Houston office. The Houston office gives her a 6-hour budget for the job. When she arrives at the client's office, Devona discovers that the Houston office has substantially underestimated the size of inventory to be counted. The client has $20,000,000 in inventory comprising more than 6,000 different items. The client plans to use 20 hours to complete the count. Devona is up for promotion, and she does not want to risk a negative personnel review because she overran the budget on this job. Therefore, she considers spending the budgeted 6 hours on the observation and then signing off in the audit work papers that she completely observed the inventory. Devona thinks this would be acceptable because she perceives there is only a small risk of a material misstatement of the inventory. Would it be ethical for Devona to do this?

EXAMPLE 1-8

Last year, one of Andy's clients, Trout Corporation, had a significant tax problem. Andy needed 35 hours of research time to arrive at an answer to Trout's problem. This year, another of Andy's clients, Bass Corporation, had the same problem. Because of his experience with Trout, Andy could solve Bass's tax problem in 3 hours. The ethical question is whether Andy should bill Bass for 3 hours or 35 hours of professional consulting time. There are two ways to look at this situation. Andy only spent 3 hours on the job, so he should only bill for 3 hours of time. Yet there is "value" in Andy already knowing the approach to take on the Bass matter, so perhaps he should bill for that knowledge and not just for the actual time spent working on the problem. What should Andy do in this situation?

EXAMPLE 1-9

Betty is negotiating a transaction on behalf of one of her clients, John Carp. During the process, Betty becomes aware that the other party to the transaction does not adequately understand the tax consequences of the proposed transaction, which are highly favorable to Carp. In fact, if the transaction were completed as proposed, the other side would suffer significant negative tax consequences. Should Betty inform the other party of the potential negative tax consequences of the proposed transaction?

SPOTLIGHT ON TAXATION

Quotation

When morality comes up against profit, it is seldom that profit loses.
—Shirley Chisholm

3-3 Ethics Training and Education

State boards of accountancy are the organizations with the responsibility to license and regulate the practice of public accountancy in each state. Recently, the state boards as a group have increased the ethics training for initial licensing and license renewals in response to highly publicized ethical lapses. All states have some form of ethics training to become a CPA, and most states have some form of ethics training requirement to maintain a CPA license. These ethics requirements vary from state to state. If one has a question about a state's requirements, it is best to refer to the Internet for the most current information on a specific state. Links to state-specific Websites can be found at the National Association of State Boards of Accountancy Website at **www.nasba.org/stateboards/**.

4 Legal Research by Certified Public Accountants

Over the years, the tax community has addressed the issue of whether the practice of tax law by a CPA or other nonattorney constitutes the **unauthorized practice of law**. The problem stems from the tax law itself, passed in 1913. The provisions of early tax law called for an income tax, but the statute was not specific about the accounting methods to be used in implementing it. In fact, not until 1954 was a formal statutory effort made to address accounting issues in the computation of taxable income. For this reason, many attorneys avoided tax work, allowing CPAs to fill the void.

When a CPA resolves an issue in most nonroutine tax situations, he or she is, to some extent, solving a legal problem. The issue is not whether the CPA is rendering legal service but how much legal service is provided. When does the CPA cross the mythical boundary and begin an unauthorized practice of law? Neither these professions nor the courts have promulgated binding guidelines on this issue. Instead, the federal agencies seem to have taken the lead in attempting to solve this problem.

Lowell Bar Association v. Loeb, 315 Mass. 176, 52 N.E.2d 27 (1943), addressed the issue of the unauthorized practice of law by nonattorneys engaged in tax practice. The Lowell Massachusetts Bar Association sued Birdie Loeb, a commercial tax preparer, for her preparation of simple wage-earner tax returns. On appeal, the court held that the preparation of "simple" tax returns did not constitute the unauthorized practice of

Massachusetts law because tax return preparation could not be identified as strictly within the legal discipline. Tax practice includes interaction among various disciplines, including law, accounting, economics, political science, and others.

Subsequent courts attempted to adopt the *Lowell* "wholly within the field of law" test in other jurisdictions, but they found that defining the boundaries of the legal profession was so difficult and the 1943 opinion was so general and vague that the *Lowell* precedent was of little value in other situations.

Probably the best-known case concerning a tax accountant's unauthorized practice of law is *Bercu*, 299 N.Y. 728, 87 N.E.2d 451 (1949). Bercu was an accountant who consulted with a client concerning whether sales taxes that were accrued, but not yet paid, could be deducted on a tax return. The taxpayer who requested this advice was not one of Bercu's regular clients. Bercu advised the client that the sales tax could be deducted when it was paid. Bercu presented a bill to the client and, when it was not paid, sued the client to collect the fees.

Ultimately, a New York state court of appeals held that it was not proper for Bercu to render services in such a situation. The court indicated that Bercu could have provided this type of service and answered the sales tax question had the service been incidental to the tax return work he regularly performed for his clients.

This "incidental to accounting practice" test became the chief issue in several subsequent cases concerning the unauthorized practice of law. In a Minnesota case, *Gardner v. Conway*, 234 Minn. 468, 48 N.W.2d 788 (1951), a person who was neither an attorney nor a CPA attempted to answer difficult and substantial questions of law. The court held that the practitioner improperly gave advice to the client and rejected the incidental-to-practice test as an approach to providing guidelines for the definition of tax practice.

In a California case, *Agran v. Shapiro*, 127 Cal. App.2d Supp. 807, 273 P.2d 619 (1954), CPA Agran prepared returns, performed research, and represented his clients before the IRS. Agran's preparation of Shapiro's return involved extensive research—including more than 100 court cases, IRC sections, and Treasury Regulations—concerning a question involving the proper treatment of a net operating loss. Upon completion of the work, the CPA presented his bill and, when he was not paid, sued Shapiro to collect. The court held that Agran engaged in the unauthorized practice of law and, therefore, was unable to collect his fees. In its decision, the California Superior Court relied on *Gardner v. Conway* and rejected the incidental-to-practice test that Agran used in his defense. The court did not decide, however, whether the authorization to practice before the IRS preempted the right of the state to regulate tax practice.

In contrast, in *Zelkin v. Caruso Discount Corp.*, the court ruled in favor of the CPA. In this case, Zelkin negotiated with the IRS on behalf of Caruso Corp. in trying to get the IRS to reduce an income tax deficiency. The company refused to pay Zelkin's bill on the grounds that Zelkin was providing illegal services. However, the court found for Zelkin, finding that his research on behalf of the client did not amount to the unauthorized practice of law.[9]

In *Sperry v. Florida*, 373 U.S. 379 (1963), the U.S. Supreme Court held that a federal statute that admitted nonattorneys to practice before federal agencies (in this case, the Patent Office) took precedence over state regulation. In late 1965, Congress enacted Public Law Number 89-332, amending prior law and allowing CPAs to practice before the IRS. Although this law added to the force of the *Sperry* decision as it applied to CPAs, *Sperry* still provides for the preemption of federal regulations and statutes in matters of practice before other federal agencies.

In 1981, the AICPA and the ABA held a conference for attorneys and CPAs to address some of these definitional questions relative to tax practice and the unauthorized

---

[9]186 Cal.App.2d 802, Nov. 28, 1960.

practice of law. The stated purpose of this session was to "promote understanding between the professions in the interests of the client [taxpayers] and the general public." This National Conference of Lawyers and CPAs issued a statement in November 1981, reaffirming that clients (taxpayers) are best served when attorneys and CPAs work together in tax practice. The text of the statement identifies eight areas related to income taxation and three areas related to estate and gift planning in which such professional cooperation should be encouraged. The statement lacks any form of exclusionary language. Indeed, it asserts the following[10]:

> *Frequently, the legal and accounting phases (of tax practice) are so intertwined that they are difficult to distinguish. This is particularly true in the field of income taxation where questions of law and accounting are often inextricably intertwined.*

However, this did not end the argument. In 1997, Arthur Andersen (at the time, one of the largest CPA firms in the country) was charged with the unauthorized practice of law for engaging in estate planning and drafting legal documents such as partnership agreements and stock option agreements. However, the Texas Supreme Court disagreed, finding that the firm's activities did not amount to the practice of law.[11]

Currently, CPAs and other nonattorneys who practice tax law before the IRS are in little danger of entering into the unauthorized practice of law as long as they avoid providing general legal services. This can be accomplished if CPAs and other nonattorneys do not themselves engage in the following kinds of general law activities:

- Expressing a legal opinion on any non-tax matter.
- Drafting wills or trust instruments.
- Drafting contracts.
- Drafting incorporation papers.
- Drafting partnership agreements.

Taxpayers can draft any of these documents themselves without the services of an attorney. If a CPA's client wishes to handle personal legal affairs in this manner, the CPA (exercising caution) can render professional advice without running afoul of the case law concerning the unauthorized practice of law.

As long as CPAs and other nonattorneys stay within the practice of tax, and do not cross over into the practice of general law, the control exercised by Circular 230 and the AICPA Code should ensure that virtually all tax compliance, planning, and research activities that are provided by adequately trained nonattorney CPAs constitute the "authorized practice of tax."

SUMMARY

CPAs, attorneys, EAs, and others who practice before the IRS are faced with various sets of overlapping rules of conduct. Circular 230 applies to anyone who practices before the IRS. The AICPA Code of Professional Conduct applies to members of the AICPA. Members of the legal and public accounting professions are subject to additional codes of ethics and conduct.

---

[10]For a complete discussion of this conference statement, see the *Journal of Accountancy* (August 1982).

[11]Farrell, Elijah D., "Accounting Firms and the Unauthorized Practice of Law: Who Is the BAR Really Trying to Protect?" *Indiana Law Review*, Vol. 33, No. 2 (2000).

Similarly, cultural codes of morality and social responsibility form general boundaries relative to acceptable behavior by a taxpayer or tax professional. When engaged in tax practice, one must always be aware of the appropriate rules of conduct and conduct oneself in accordance with those rules.

KEY WORDS

By the time you complete this chapter, you should be comfortable discussing each of the following terms. If you need additional review of any of these items, return to the appropriate material in the chapter or consult the glossary to this text.

AICPA Code of Professional
   Conduct, p. 16
American Bar Association (ABA),
   p. 7
American Institute of Certified
   Public Accountants (AICPA),
   p. 7
Annual Filing Season Program,
   p. 10
certified public accountant (CPA),
   p. 7

Circular 230, p. 7
closed transactions, p. 6
Cohan Rule, p. 24
contingent fee, p. 12 and p. 18
due diligence, p. 11
good-faith belief, p. 22
enrolled agent (EA), p. 9
ethical standards, p. 7
independence, p. 18
Model Rules of Professional
   Conduct, p. 27

open transactions, p. 6
practice before the IRS, p. 7
realistic possibility, p. 22
tax avoidance, p. 6
tax compliance, p. 5
tax evasion, p. 6
tax litigation, p. 6
tax planning, p. 6
tax research, p. 6
unauthorized practice of law, p. 33
unconscionable fee, p. 13

DISCUSSION QUESTIONS

Note: A copy of Circular 230 is needed to answer many of these discussion questions. Obtain a complete copy of Circular 230 from **www.irs.gov**.

1. In a modern, industrial society, the tax system is derived from several disciplines. Identify the disciplines that play this role in the United States. Explain how each of them affects the U.S. tax system.

2. The elements of tax practice fall into what major categories in addition to tax research?

3. What is tax compliance as practiced in the United States? Give several examples of activities that can be classified as tax compliance.

4. Several groups of individuals do most of the tax compliance work in the United States. Identify these groups and briefly describe the kind of work that each group does. In this regard, be sure to define the term *enrolled agent*.

5. What is tax planning? Explain the difference between tax evasion and tax avoidance and the role of each in professional tax planning.

6. Tax planning falls into two major categories, the "open" transaction and the "closed" transaction. Discuss each type of transaction and describe how each affects tax planning.

7. What is tax litigation? What type of tax practitioner typically handles tax litigation on a taxpayer's behalf?

8. In tax litigation, what is usually the role of a certified public accountant?

9. Define tax research. Briefly describe the tax research process.

10. Who issues Circular 230? Which tax practitioners are regulated by it?

11. CPAs must follow the rules of Circular 230. In addition, CPAs in tax practice are subject to two other sets of ethical rules. Give the name and the issuer of both these sets of rules.

12. In order for them to have limited practice rights, the IRS requires non-credentialed tax return preparers to participate in the IRS Annual Filing Season Program. What does participation require, and why do you think the IRS has made this change?

13. The term "practice before the IRS" includes the representation of clients in the U.S. Tax Court for cases being handled under the "small tax case procedure." True or false? Explain your answer. (IRS adapted)

14. The rules that govern practice before the IRS are found in Circular 230. Discuss what entails practice before the IRS and state which section of Circular 230 contains the definition.

15. There are two ways to become an EA. Briefly explain what they are and give the subpart and section references in Circular 230 where the details of becoming an EA are found.

16. EAs are subject to continuing education (CE) requirements. Briefly describe the CE requirements and give the reference to where the details can be found in Circular 230.

17. Leigh, who is not a Circular 230 practitioner, is employed by Rose, a CPA. One of Rose's clients has been notified that the IRS has selected his 2015 income tax return for audit. Rose had prepared the return and signed it as preparer. Rose has been called out of town on a family emergency and would like for Leigh to represent the client. Leigh cannot represent the client even if she has Rose's written authority to do so and has the client's power of attorney. True or false? Explain your answer. (IRS adapted)

18. Regular full-time employees are allowed to represent certain organizations before the IRS without being a Circular 230 practitioner. Name the organizations that can be represented by full-time employees, and cite where you found that authority in Circular 230.

19. Jane's mother resides in a nursing home and cannot travel. There is a problem with the mother's prior-year tax return, and the IRS needs to discuss the matter with her at the local IRS office. Is it possible for Jane to handle this matter without having to hire professional tax representation? Reference your answer to the appropriate part of Circular 230.

20. A practitioner could be suspended from practice before the IRS if the practitioner employs, accepts assistance from, or shares fees with any person who is under disbarment or suspension from practice before the IRS. True or false? Explain your answer. (IRS adapted)

21. A tax practitioner may not advise a client under Circular 230 to take a position on a document, affidavit, or other paper submitted to the IRS unless the position meets which standard under Circular 230 § 10.34?

22. May Circular 230 practitioners advertise on television? On the Internet? If so, what standards are applied to the advertisements?

23. May a tax practitioner who is a CPA form a CPA partnership with a former IRS agent who is also a CPA? What limits (if any) would be placed on such a partnership?

24. If a tax practitioner finds an error in a prior year's tax return, what action (if any) must he or she take under Circular 230? What subpart and section addresses this situation?

25. Is a tax practitioner required to adhere to the best-practices standard under Circular 230 § 10.33? Explain.

26. What are the four best practices under Circular 230 § 10.33?

27. A practitioner cannot give written advice under Circular 230 § 10.37 in which situations?

28. A compensated individual who prepares or assists with the preparation of all or substantially all of a tax return or claim for refund must have a PTIN. What is a PTIN, and which individual(s) are required to obtain one?

29. Not all individuals who for compensation prepare or assist with the preparation of all or substantially all of a tax return or claim for refund are subject to the duties and restrictions relating to practice in subpart B as well as subject to the sanctions for violation of the regulations in Section 10.51 of Circular 230. Explain.

30. Practicing CPAs generally are subject to the AICPA Code of Professional Conduct. What is its stated purpose?

31. Briefly list and discuss the primary threats to complying with the Independence Rule of the AICPA Code of Professional Conduct.

32. What specific tax-related situations may result in a conflict of interest for members in public practice under the Integrity and Objectivity Rule of the AICPA Code of Professional Conduct?

33. A CPA in public practice must meet certain general standards under § 1.300.001 (the General Standards Rule). Discuss the four general standards of this rule.

34. In each of the following (independent) situations, state which AICPA Code of Professional Conduct rule or principle (if any) is violated by a CPA?
    a. A CPA in public practice opens a tax practice and names the new firm "Jill's Super Tax."
    b. In return for recommending a certain investment to an audit client, a CPA in public practice receives a 5 percent commission from the broker who sells the investments.
    c. The IRS is assessing a taxpayer for an additional $100,000 of tax. A CPA in public practice offers to represent the taxpayer for a fee that is equal to 25 percent of any amount by which he can get the IRS to reduce its assessment.
    d. A CPA in public practice places an advertisement in the local newspaper that states that she is the "Best CPA in the Western World." The advertisement further states that, because of her great skill, the CPA has considerable influence with the IRS and the U.S. Tax Court.
    e. A CPA partnership has eight partners, six of whom are members of the AICPA. On its letterhead, the firm designates itself as "Members of the AICPA."
    f. A CPA who is not in public practice is convicted of helping to run a large illegal drug operation.

35. Under the Confidential Client Information Rule of the AICPA Code of Professional Conduct, a CPA in public practice must not disclose confidential client data without the specific consent of the client. Under what conditions might a disclosure of confidential information without the client's consent be appropriate?

36. What are the SSTS? Who issues them? Discuss their principal objectives.

37. When must a member tax practitioner follow SSTS when preparing or signing a return?

38. What threshold does SSTS No. 1 provide for a tax practitioner regarding tax return positions? Could disclosure of the position influence that threshold?

39. According to SSTS No. 2, a tax return should be signed by a member only after reasonable effort has been made to answer all questions on the return that apply to the taxpayer. What are some of the reasonable grounds under which a member may sign a return as the preparer even though some of the pertinent questions remain unanswered?

40. What guidelines are provided by SSTS No. 3 as to the reliance by a member on information supplied by the taxpayer for use in preparing the taxpayer's return?

41. A member may use estimates in completing a tax return according to SSTS No. 4. When might the use of estimates be considered appropriate?

42. Last year a taxpayer was audited by the IRS and an item of deduction on the tax return was disallowed. On this year's tax return, the taxpayer would like to deduct a similar item. Discuss the circumstances under which a member may allow the taxpayer to take the deduction on the current year's return and still comply with SSTS No. 5. Under what conditions must special disclosure be made by the member?

43. When a member learns of an error in a previously filed tax return or learns of an error during an audit, how is he or she to respond and still be in compliance with SSTS No. 6?

44. What situations are addressed by SSTS No. 7?

45. The Sarbanes-Oxley Act prohibits CPA firms from providing certain services to publicly traded corporate audit clients. Is doing tax compliance work for an audit client one of the prohibited transactions? If such tax work is allowed, who must approve it?

46. Who sets ethical rules for attorneys in the various states?

47. What is an ethical dilemma?

48. The text discusses three types of ethical reasoning. Identify them and give a short description of each.

49. Ethical professional behavior is the interaction of several standards. Identify these standards and briefly describe each.

50. Professor Andy Accrual works for Mega State University. The state has negotiated a set of special airfares with various airlines for state employees to use when traveling on state business. These fares are lower, and they do not have restrictions on changing, cancellation, and so forth. Andy is aware that the airlines never check to see if he is on state business when he books such a fare. He has decided that he would like to go to Hawaii on short notice for a well-earned mini-vacation. When he checks the Internet for airfares, he discovers that the cheapest fare he can find is $700 per person. However, the fare for state employees traveling on business to Hawaii is only $400. Although he is traveling for personal reasons, in your opinion is it ethical to use the special state employee airfare for his vacation? Would this qualify as an ethical dilemma?

51. Donna Deduction is a staff accountant for Dewey, Cheatham, and Howe, LLP. She and other staff raid the office supply cabinet for office supplies to take home to use. In addition to the standard paper, pens, paper clips, and so forth, the staff takes home inkjet cartridges and other high-cost supplies. During the year, Donna takes home supplies worth more than $500. In your opinion, is this ethical behavior? If Donna does a significant amount of work for the firm at home, would your opinion change?

52. How does the term "the unauthorized practice of law" apply to CPAs?

53. List several services or products that a CPA or EA purposely should not make a part of a tax practice in order to minimize exposure to a charge of engaging in the unauthorized practice of law.

EXERCISES

54. Summarize what is discussed in each of the following sections of Circular 230:
    a. Subpart A, § 10.4(c)
    b. Subpart B, § 10.21
    c. Subpart B, § 10.26
    d. Subpart B, § 10.29

55. Summarize what is discussed in each of the following sections of Circular 230:
    a. Subpart C, § 10.51(a)(12)
    b. Subpart A, § 10.6(e)

c. Subpart A, § 10.3(f)

d. Subpart B, § 10.27

56. Summarize what is discussed in each of the following sections of Circular 230:

a. Subpart A, § 10.22(b)

b. Subpart A, § 10.7(c)(1)(vi)

c. Subpart B, § 10.24

d. Subpart B, § 10.34

57. Summarize what is discussed in each of the following sections of Circular 230:

a. Subpart B, § 10.33

b. Subpart B, § 10.35

c. Subpart B, § 10.36

d. Subpart B, § 10.37

58. Which subpart and section of Circular 230 discusses each the following topics?

a. Solicitation

b. Negotiation of a taxpayer's refund checks

c. Who may practice before the IRS

d. Authority to disbar or suspend from practice before the IRS

59. Which subpart and section of Circular 230 discusses each the following topics?

a. Conflicts of interest

b. Disreputable conduct

c. Assistance from disbarred or suspended persons

d. Representing oneself before the IRS

60. Which subpart and section of Circular 230 discusses each of the following topics?

a. Practice of law

b. Information to be furnished

c. Fees

d. Responsibility for correcting errors

61. Which subpart and section of Circular 230 discusses each of the following topics?

a. Best practices

b. The return of client's records

c. Requirements for taking tax return positions

d. Due diligence

62. Summarize what is discussed in each of the following SSTS:

a. SSTS No. 1

b. SSTS No. 4

c. SSTS No. 6

63. What is the precedent-setting value of each of the following cases?

a. *Lowell Bar Association v. Loeb*

b. *Bercu*

c. *Sperry v. Florida*

64. Ms. E is an EA who prepared the tax returns for Mr. A and Mr. B (buyer and seller, respectively). Ms. E may not, under any circumstances, represent A and B before the IRS with regard to this buy and sell transaction. True or false? Explain your answer using Circular 230. (IRS adapted)

65. A full-time employee of a sole proprietorship may represent his or her employer in an examination by the IRS without being a Circular 230 practitioner. True or false? Explain your answer using Circular 230. (IRS adapted)

66. Which of the following is a contingent fee under Circular 230 § 10.27? A fee (1) that is based on a percentage of the refund reported on a return, (2) that is based on a percentage of the taxes saved, or (3) that otherwise depends on the specific result attained.

67. Are CPAs and EAs authorized to practice tax law by Circular 230? Discuss.

68. Which of the following statements may not be used when an EA advertises? Explain your answer. (IRS adapted)
    a. Name, address, and office hours
    b. Names of associates of the firm
    c. Claims of quality of service that cannot be verified
    d. Membership in professional organizations

69. Which of the following statements is unacceptable under the AICPA Code of Professional Conduct for a CPA in public practice? Explain your answer.
    a. Julie Adams, CPA, Fluency in Chinese
    b. Julie Adams, CPA, MBA, Big State University, 2010
    c. Julie Adams, CPA, Free Initial Consultation
    d. Julie Adams, CPA, I Always Win IRS Audits

70. Which of the following situations would most likely result in a violation of the practitioner's ethical standards? Explain your answer.
    a. A CPA (not in public practice) is controller of a bank and grants permission to the bank to use his "CPA" title in the listing of the bank officers in the bank's publications.
    b. A CPA in public practice who is also a member of the bar represents on her letterhead that she is both an attorney and a CPA.
    c. A CPA in public practice, the sole shareholder in a professional accountancy corporation, uses the term "and company" in his firm's title.
    d. A CPA in public practice who writes a newsletter on financial management topics grants permission to the publisher to solicit subscriptions.

71. Which of the following situations would provide an acceptable case for using a taxpayer's estimated figure in the preparation of a federal income tax return? Explain your answer.
    a. The taxpayer has the necessary data available but is busy with a pressing public offering and has not had the time to look through her records for the information.
    b. The data are not available at the time of filing the return, and the estimated amounts appear reasonable to the CPA.
    c. The taxpayer has the data available at the time of filing the return but feels that the data do not fairly represent the results of her business operation and therefore desires to use an "estimate."
    d. The taxpayer, relying on the income tax regulations that allow the use of reasonable estimates under certain circumstances, desires to use an estimate to determine the amount of his deduction for entertainment expenses.

72. According to the AICPA Code of Professional Conduct, CPAs in public practice who are representing a taxpayer in a formal controversy with the government are permitted to receive contingent fees because:

    a. This practice establishes fees that are commensurate with the value of the services rendered.

    b. Attorneys who are in tax practice customarily set contingent fees.

    c. Determinations by tax authorities are a matter of judicial proceedings that do not involve third parties.

    d. The consequences are based on the findings of judicial proceedings or the findings of a government agency. Explain your answer.

73. According to the AICPA Code of Professional Conduct, under what conditions if any can a CPA in public practice disclose confidential client data?

74. A taxpayer's records are destroyed by fire. A CPA prepares the tax return based on estimates and other indirect information she has obtained. Under the SSTS, she should:

    a. Disclose the use of estimates to the IRS.

    b. Not disclose the use of estimates to the IRS.

    c. Charge the taxpayer a double fee.

    d. Not prepare a return based on estimates.

    e. Have an attorney prepare the return. Explain your answer.

75. With regard to the categories of individuals who may practice before the IRS under Circular 230, which of the following statements is correct? Explain your answer. (IRS adapted)

    a. Only Circular 230 practitioners may represent trusts and estates before any officer or employee of the IRS.

    b. An individual who is not a Circular 230 practitioner may appear as the representative of a taxpayer who is a member of his or her immediate family with or without the taxpayer, at an IRS Appeals Office conference.

    c. Under the limited practice provision in Circular 230, only general partners may represent a partnership.

    d. Under the limited practice provision in Circular 230, an individual who is under suspension or disbarment from practice before the IRS may not engage in limited practice before the IRS.

76. If a Circular 230 practitioner knows that a client has not complied with the revenue laws of the United States with respect to a matter administered by the IRS, then the EA, attorney, or CPA is required under Circular 230 to

    a. Do nothing until advised by the client to take corrective action.

    b. Advise the client of the noncompliance.

    c. Immediately notify the IRS.

    d. Advise the client and notify the IRS. Explain your answer. (IRS adapted)

77. Answer each of the following questions:

    a. What is found in Subpart A, § 10.7(a) of Circular 230?

    b. Describe the requirements of § 1.520.001 of the AICPA Code of Conduct.

    c. Which SSTS discusses whether a member may rely without verification on information provided by a taxpayer or a third party?

    d. Under SSTS No. 1, a member must have a good-faith belief that a recommended position has a ___ possibility of being sustained if challenged.

78. Answer each of the following questions:

    a. What is found in Subpart C, § 10.51 of Circular 230?

    b. In Circular 230, where are the rules on knowledge of client omissions found?

    c. Describe the requirements of § 1.400.200 of the AICPA Code of Conduct.

    d. Which SSTS discusses whether a member can recommend that a client depart from a previously concluded tax position?

    e. Under SSTS ___, a member must use judgment that reflects professional competence and serves the taxpayer's needs.

79. The exam to become an EA has three parts. Go to the IRS Website at **www.irs.gov** and determine what is tested on each part of the exam. Describe the content of each part.

80. Go to the IRS Website at **www.irs.gov**. What is the form number of the Application for Enrollment to Practice before the IRS? Print out a copy of the form to hand in.

81. Many states have an ethics education requirement to become a CPA. Determine each of the following state's ethics education requirements to become a CPA:

    a. California

    b. Texas

    c. North Carolina

    d. Your home state

CHAPTER 2

Tax Research Methodology

LEARNING OBJECTIVES

- Demonstrate and elaborate the six steps of the tax research process.
- Discuss the benefits of online tax research and compare and contrast commercial with free tax research services.
- Demonstrate the ability to identify keywords and develop queries in conducting online tax research.
- Explain practical considerations affecting the research process.
- Discuss the role of tax and research on the CPA exam.

CHAPTER OUTLINE

TAX RESEARCH IS THE process undertaken to answer taxation questions relevant to the researcher's needs. The tax research process is a multistep process that includes a model discussed in this chapter. The tax researcher should become efficient at tax research because these professional services can be very expensive for the client, or the time spent on research can take away valuable time that could be used for other activities of the tax practitioner. Unnecessary time spent doing tax research could be used by the tax practitioner to produce additional revenue or to give him or her additional personal time for other activities.

SPOTLIGHT ON TAXATION

The Complexity of Taxation

The complexity of the tax system (and thus tax research) can be shown in a quote by Pam Olson, the former Treasury Assistant Secretary for Tax Policy. When speaking to a group of tax specialists, she quoted an e-mail sent to her by a tax attorney, who said:

It is difficult to predict the future of an economy in which it takes more brains to figure out the tax on our income than it does to earn it.

The tax research process is similar to that of traditional legal research. The researcher must find authority, evaluate the usefulness of that authority, and apply the results of the research to a specific situation. There are two essential tax research skills. The first is the ability to use certain mechanical techniques to identify and locate the tax authorities that relate to solving a problem. The second entails a combination of reasoning and creativity and is more difficult to learn. A tax researcher must begin with native intelligence and imagination and add training and experience properly to apply the information found.

Creativity is necessary to explore the relevant relationships among the circumstances and problems at hand to find a satisfying (and defensible) solution. In many cases, no legal authority will exist that is directly on point for the problem. If such a situation exists, the researcher must combine seemingly unrelated facts, ideas (including those that he or she has derived from previous research work), and legal authority to arrive at a truly novel conclusion. This creative ability of the researcher often spells the difference between success and failure in the research process.

1 The Tax Research Process

As the tax problems of the client become more significant, the related tax research can become time consuming and thus expensive to the client. A moderate tax research problem often takes up to 8 to 10 hours of research time, and the bill for these services is often quite substantial. Because of the costs that are involved, the tax researcher must work as efficiently as possible to obtain the solution to the client's problem. The researcher needs a framework for the research process so that he or she does not waste time and effort in arriving at a solution to the problem.

The tax research process can be broken down into six primary steps (Exhibit 2-1). Tax researchers, especially those without a substantial amount of experience at the task, must approach the resolution of a tax problem in a structured manner so that the analysis of the problem will be thorough and the solution complete.

EXHIBIT 2-1: Steps in the Tax Research Process

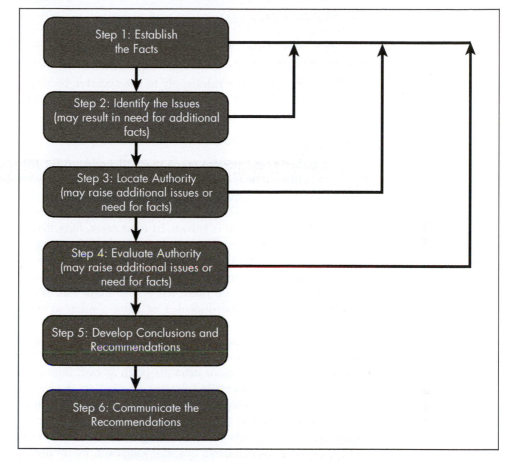

1-1 Step 1: Establish the Facts

All tax research begins with an evaluation of the client's factual situation. To find the solution to a problem, the researcher must understand fully all facts that could affect the related tax outcome. Many beginning tax researchers make the mistake of attempting to research a problem before they completely understand all relevant facts and circumstances.

Moreover, a tax researcher may approach the tax research process so rigidly that he or she ignores new factual questions that arise during the other steps of the research task. The tax researcher may engage in several rounds of fact gathering, including those necessitated by additional tax questions that arise as he or she is searching for or evaluating the pertinent tax authority. These research "feedback loops" are not endless, although they might seem to be. The best tax researcher is one who can balance the need for efficiency against the need for thoroughness.

Significant tax facts that often influence the client's situation include the following:

- The client's tax entity, for example, individual, corporation, or trust.

- The client's family status and stability.

- The client's past, present, and projected marginal tax rates.

- The client's place of legal domicile and citizenship.

- The client's motivation for the transaction.

- The relationships among the client and other parties who are involved in the transaction.

- Whether special tax rules apply to the taxpayer because of the type of business in which the taxpayer is engaged (i.e., he or she is a farmer, fisherman, or long-term contractor).

- Whether the transaction is proposed or completed.

Fact gathering can present many practical problems for the researcher. Often, the client will (wittingly or not) omit information that is vital to a solution. He or she might not believe the information is important or might have personal reasons for not conveying the information to the practitioner. In such cases, the researcher must persist until all the available information is known. In some cases, facts that initially appear to be irrelevant may prove to be important as the research project progresses. The researcher, therefore, should pay attention to and record all details that the client discloses. Efficient tax research cannot be completed until the factual situation is clear; without all the facts at hand, the researcher could make costly false starts that, when additional pertinent facts become known, must be discarded or redone, often at the client's (or, worse, at the researcher's) expense.

In gathering facts relative to a research problem, the researcher also must be aware of the nontax considerations that are pertinent to the client's situation. For example, the client may have economic constraints (such as cash flow problems) that could preclude the implementation of certain solutions. In addition, the client may have personal preferences that will not accommodate the best tax solution to the problem. For instance, assume that the client could reduce his or her own income and estate tax liability by making a series of gifts to his or her grandchildren. However, because the client does not trust the grandchildren's financial judgment, he or she does not want to make any such gifts to them during his or her lifetime. Accordingly, the researcher must look for alternative methods by which to reduce the client's total family tax burden.

1-2 Step 2: Identify the Issues

A combination of education, training, and experience is necessary to enable the researcher to identify successfully all the issues with respect to a tax problem. In some situations, this step can be the most difficult element of a tax research problem.

Issues in a closed-fact tax research problem often arise from a conflict with the IRS. In such a case, one can easily ascertain the issue(s). Research of this nature usually consists of finding support for an action that the client has already taken.

In most research projects, however, the researcher must develop the list of issues. Research issues can be divided into two major categories, namely, fact issues and law issues. **Fact issues** are concerned with information having an objective reality, such as the dates of transactions, the amounts involved in an exchange, reasonableness, intent, and purpose. **Law issues** arise when the facts are well established, but it is not clear which portion of the tax law applies to the issue. The application of the law might not be clear because of an apparent conflict among code sections, because a genuine uncertainty may exist as to the meaning of a term as used in the **Internal Revenue Code** (IRC), or because there are no provisions in the law that deal directly with the transaction at hand.

When undertaking a research project for which the issue may end up being challenged in court, the researcher must be sure to address all the issues in the tax return. The legal concept of **collateral estoppel** bars relitigation on the same facts or the same issues. In other words, if an issue is brought up in a case or should have been brought up in a case, that issue cannot be raised in a different case by a party to the first lawsuit. Therefore, the practitioner must make sure that his or her case is researched fully and that no issues that could be resolved in the client's favor have been overlooked. If such an issue is not addressed in the original case, it may be lost forever.

In many situations, a research project may encompass several tax years. The researcher must be aware of any fact or law changes that occured during each period that might affect the results of the research project. The pertinent facts or law may be subject to changes that will cause the researcher to arrive at different conclusions and recommendations, depending on the tax year involved. Seemingly simple situations can often generate many tax research issues. In the process of identifying tax issues, the researcher might discover that additional facts are necessary to provide sufficient answers for the new questions. The following example illustrates the potential for complexities in merely identifying tax research issues.

EXAMPLE 2-1

The KML Medical Group of Houston would like to hire a new physician who currently works in Atlanta. However, the new physician owns a home in Georgia, and she will sustain a loss on the home if it is sold in the current housing market. KML approached the Happy Care Hospital, the institution at which the group practices, and asked whether it would reimburse the new physician for the loss to facilitate her move to Texas. The hospital agreed to reimburse the physician this year for her $120,000 realized loss.

A tax researcher might address or clarify at least the following issues in making recommendations concerning tax treatment of the reimbursement:

- Why did the hospital reimburse the physician?

- Is there any relationship between the hospital and the KML Medical Group?

- Do any members of the KML Medical Group have an equity or debt interest in the hospital?

- Does the reimbursement constitute gross income to the physician?

- If the reimbursement does constitute gross income to the physician, is it treated as active, passive, or investment income?

- Is the new physician classified as an employee of the hospital?

- Should the hospital report the payment to the physician on a Form 1099 or W-2?

- Should the hospital withhold any income or Federal Insurance Contributions Act (FICA) tax on the reimbursement?

- Can the hospital deduct the reimbursement as a trade or business expense?

- Should the physician consider the reimbursement and/or the loss on the sale of her residence in computing her moving-expense deduction?

- If the reimbursement is considered gross income to the physician, when should the amount be included in the physician's income?

- Is the reimbursement subject to any restrictions, such as the physician's continued employment? For how long?

- Is the reimbursement to the physician considered an additional amount realized on the sale of her residence?

- Can the reimbursement be considered a gift from the hospital to the physician?

Imagine how the question concerning whether the physician's gross income (if any) was ordinary income might lead to further questions concerning her potential employee status, income tax and FICA withholding, and reporting issues.

The process of tax research is iterative in the sense that, once an answer to an issue is found, it often causes a new issue to appear and thus requires the gathering of additional facts. In other words, the tax research process is not strictly linear. This relationship between facts, issues, and answers is illustrated in Exhibit 2-2. The tax research process requires *mechanical skills* and *critical thinking*. Mechanical skills are gained and sharpened through both knowledge and experience. *Knowledge* is usually gained through education in universities and other formal class work. *Experience* is obtained through working in the field and dealing with real tax problems on a recurring basis.

Critical thinking is the hardest skill for the researcher to develop. To some extent, it depends on innate ability, but a person can be taught the elements of logical analysis and can learn to watch for common pitfalls in evaluating information. Being able to analyze and solve a problem is something the tax researcher must master if he or she is to earn a living in this field. Knowledge is useless when it cannot be applied to solve the problem at hand. The following example demonstrates how both mechanical skills and critical thinking are used to solve a tax research problem.

EXHIBIT 2-2:   Interaction among Research Facts, Issues, and Solutions

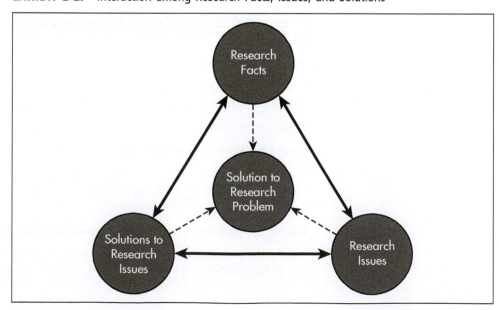

EXAMPLE

This year, Chris Lee, a client of your CPA firm, sold stock in Slippery Bank (a publicly traded company with a limited market) to Kolpin Corporation for $100,000. Chris has records that show the stock was acquired 10 years ago and has a basis of $135,000. He personally owns 30 percent of Kolpin Corporation. At first glance, the tax researcher would conclude that Chris would have a capital loss of $35,000, which would be deductible against his current-year long-term capital gains of $50,000. This situation appears to be straightforward. The problem could become complex, though, if someone at the CPA firm asked questions about the other owners of Kolpin. What if Chris's wife, Judy Lee, owns Kolpin stock? The researcher must back up in the research process and gather more facts to determine how many shares she owns.

Suppose Judy Lee owns 25 percent of the Kolpin stock. Now the tax practitioner (you) is faced with new facts and issues; § 267 of the IRC suggests that the loss might be disallowed. By looking at § 267(b)(2), you would find that losses between an individual and a corporation are disallowed if "more than 50 percent in value of the outstanding stock of which is owned directly or indirectly, by or for such individual." You then need to know what "indirect ownership" is. Looking further in the code, you would find in § 267(c), "An individual shall be considered as owning the stock owned, directly or indirectly, by or for his family." Finally, in § 267(c)(4), you would discover, "The family of an individual shall include only his brother and sisters (whether by whole or half blood), spouse, ancestors, and lineal descendants."

Armed with this new information, it becomes clear that Chris is a related party to Kolpin Corporation within the meaning of § 267. He owns more than 50 percent of the stock, 30 percent directly and 25 percent indirectly through his wife. As a result, the $35,000 capital loss is not allowed to Chris, and he cannot use it to offset his other capital gains.

SPOTLIGHT ON TAXATION

Quotation

There may be liberty and justice for all, but there are tax breaks only for some.

—Martin A. Sullivan

1-3 Step 3: Locate Authority

Once facts have been gathered and the issues defined, the tax researcher must locate legal authority that relates to the issue(s). Authority comes from many sources, including Congress, the courts, and the IRS. Since the inception of the 1913 tax law, several hundred thousand pages of such authority have been produced. To solve a given problem, the researcher must find the appropriate authority in this massive amount of information.

In general, tax authority can be classified as either primary or secondary authority. **Primary authority** is an original pronouncement that comes from statutory, administrative, or judicial sources. **Statutory sources** include the U.S. Constitution, tax treaties, and tax laws passed by Congress. Statutory authority is the basis for all tax provisions. The Constitution grants Congress the power to impose and collect taxes and authorizes the creation of treaties with other countries. The power of Congress to implement and collect taxes is summarized in the IRC, the official title of U.S. tax law. The IRC constitutes the basis for all tax law, and therefore it serves as the basis for arriving at solutions to all tax questions.

The other primary sources of the tax law, administrative and judicial authority, function primarily to interpret and explain the application of the provisions of the IRC and the intent of Congress. **Administrative sources** include the various rulings of the Treasury Department and the IRS, which are issued in the form of regulations, revenue rulings, and other pronouncements. **Judicial sources** consist of the collected rulings of the various courts on federal tax matters. The primary sources of the tax law will be discussed in detail in Chapters 3, 4, and 5. **Secondary authority** consists of interpretations of primary authority and is an unofficial source of tax information. Examples of secondary authority include tax services, journals, textbooks, treatises,[1] and newsletters.

The distinction between primary and secondary sources of authority has become more important since the enactment of IRC § 6662, which imposes a penalty on substantial understatements of tax, except when the taxpayer has "substantial authority" for the position taken on the return. The regulations under § 6662 specify the sources of "substantial authority" to include the provisions of the IRC, temporary and final regulations, court cases, administrative pronouncements, tax treaties, and congressional intent as reflected in committee reports. This list also includes proposed regulations, private letter rulings, technical advice memoranda, actions on decisions, general counsel memoranda, information or press releases, notices, and any other similar documents published by the IRS in the Internal Revenue Bulletin. Treatises and articles in legal periodicals, however, are not considered substantial authority under this statute.

Secondary authority is useful when conflicting primary authority exists, there appears to be no extant primary authority, or the researcher needs an explanation or clarification of the primary authority. During the past 15 years, as the support staffs of government agencies and (especially) federal courts have decreased in number or otherwise become inadequate, more dependence has been placed on the secondary authorities of the tax law, even by the IRS, the Treasury Department, and the court system. The beginning researcher must be careful, though, not to rely too heavily on secondary authority and to always read any pertinent primary authority that is referred to in the secondary sources.

Because of the vast amount of tax authority that is available, the tax researcher would have a tremendous problem in undertaking a tax research problem for a client if it were not for commercial tax services. While the IRC, Treasury regulations, and other administrative pronouncements and many court cases are available through a variety of free searchable online resources (see Exhibit 2-3), these databases are not as comprehensive nor updated as frequently as the commercial databases, generally include nontax resources as well as tax documents, and do not include many of the features of popular commercial databases. On the other hand, a number of publishers have produced

---

[1] A treatise is a lengthy book or article written by an expert that discusses a subject in depth.

EXHIBIT 2-3: Examples of Free Online Tax Resources

Site Name	Internet Address	Description
Internal Revenue Service	**www.irs.gov/**	Includes searchable forms, instructions, publications, and other IRS information.
Congress.gov	**www.congress.gov**	Includes searchable legislative resources including enacted legislation, committee reports, and treaties. The site is generally updated the morning after a session adjourns.
U.S. Tax Court	**www.ustaxcourt.gov/UstcInOp /OpinionSearch.aspx**	Includes T.C. and TC Memo cases from September 25, 1995, and TC Summary cases since January 10, 2001.
Legalbitstream	**www.legalbitstream.com/**	Includes tax cases (since 1990 in most cases), Treasury and IRS materials, and legislative sources in a searchable database. The database is generally updated within one or two weeks after material is made public.
Legal Information Institute (LLI)	**www.law.cornell.edu**	Includes tax and other general law documents including the Constitution, Supreme Court cases, and the U.S. Code (including the IRC) and links to a variety of state and international sources.
NYU GlobaLex	**www.nyulawglobal.org**	Focus is on international and foreign law research including tax.
Google Scholar	**scholar.google.com/**	Includes federal and state court cases including the U.S. Tax Court.
Public Library of Law	**www.plol.org/Pages/Search .aspx**	Includes federal cases from the Supreme Court and Courts of Appeals, state cases back to 1997, and federal and state statutory law and regulations.
Findlaw	**caselaw.findlaw.com/**	Includes links for state and federal laws and a searchable database of summaries of published opinions from selected federal and state courts back to 2000.
Leagle	**www.leagle.com/**	Includes primary case law from all federal courts and all state higher courts. Updated within 24 hours.
Justia	**law.justia.com/**	Includes federal and state case law (but not Tax Court cases), U.S. and state codes, and federal regulations.

coordinated sets of reference materials that organize the tax authority into a usable format, making the IRC and other source documents much more accessible. These commercial tax services are useful in that they often provide simplified explanations with footnote citations as well as examples illustrating the application of the law.

SPOTLIGHT ON TAXATION

Research on irs.gov

The IRS maintains a Website (**www.irs.gov**) on which limited tax research may be conducted. While irs.gov is not a full-service tax research resource, it does contain searchable and downloadable tax information such as tax forms, instructions, publications (e.g., Publication 17), and other IRS information. Irs.gov also has a search engine that allows both basic and advanced searching.

As an example, last year, Doris's daughter and son-in-law moved into her home. This year, Doris has supported both of them for the entire year. Doris would like to know if she can claim a dependency exemption for her son-in-law. Doris could go to irs.gov and click the search button. She could then search terms such as "son-in-law" and "dependent." The IRS search engine will return several IRS publications (e.g., Pub. 17 and 501) that will inform Doris she can claim a deduction for her son-in-law.

Exhibit 2-4 includes examples of the primary commercial tax services. The tax services are discussed in detail in later chapters.

Both CCH and Thomson Reuters provide "citators" as part of their tax services. A citator is an extremely useful reference source that enables the researcher to follow the judicial history of court cases.

EXHIBIT 2-4:   Examples of Commercial Online Tax Resources

Name	Description
Thomson Reuters Checkpoint	Includes research material on federal, state, local, and international taxation. Checkpoint contains analytical material such as the Federal Tax Coordinator 2d and the *United States Tax Reporter.* All public domain information such as the IRC and regulations, U.S. tax treaties, IRS publications and pronouncements, and court cases is available on this system.
Wolters Kluwer CCH IntelliConnect	Includes CCH's tax services (*Tax Research Consultant* and *Federal Income Tax Reporter*) and other federal, state, local, and international legal and tax information. All public domain information such as the IRC and regulations, U.S. tax treaties, IRS publications and pronouncements, and court cases is available on this system.
Tax Analysts Federal Research Library	Includes the IRC, regulations, treasury decisions, IRS taxpayer publications, revenue rulings, revenue procedures, notices and announcements, and more than 100,000 court opinions.
LexisAdvance Tax	Includes federal and state tax research material as well as access to expert analytical materials from CCH, Tax Analysts, and BNA. In addition, LexisAdvance Tax has extensive libraries of newspapers, magazines, journals, and patent records and medical, economic, and accounting databases.
Thompson Reuters Westlaw	Includes all federal, state, local, and international legal sources, including court cases, administrative releases, and statutory information. All government documents (e.g., IRS publications, court cases) are also available on this system. It also offers BNA and some CCH products.
Bloomberg BNA Tax and Accounting	Focuses on providing a practitioner-to-practitioner approach to analysis and commentary through its Tax Management Portfolios, Daily Tax Report, and online content.

EXHIBIT 2-5: Selected Tax Journals

Journal	Publisher	Target Readership
ATA Journal of Legal Tax Research (JLTR)	American Tax Association section of the American Accounting Association	Tax academics and practitioners
Journal of Taxation	Warren, Gorham & Lamont (WG&L), Thomson Reuters	Sophisticated tax practitioners
Practical Tax Strategies	WG&L, Thomson Reuters	Tax practitioners in general practice
The Tax Adviser	American Institute of CPAs	Members of AICPA and
TAXES—The Tax Magazine	Wolters Kluwer Commerce Clearing House	other tax practitioners General tax practitioners

Tax journals are another source of information that can be useful to the tax researcher. By reading tax journals, a tax practitioner can become aware of many current problem areas in taxation and increase awareness of recent developments in the tax law, tax compliance matters, and tax planning techniques and opportunities. The tax researcher typically is interested in publications devoted to scholarly and professional discussions of tax matters. Among these publications, each tax journal usually is written for a specific group of readers. Exhibit 2-5 lists several useful tax journals, their publishers, and the target readership of each.

1-4 Step 4: Evaluate Authority

After the researcher has located authority that deals with the client's problem, he or she must evaluate the usefulness of that authority. Not all tax authority carries the same precedential value. For example, the Tax Court could hold that an item should be excluded from gross income at the same time that an outstanding IRS revenue ruling asserts the item is taxable. The tax researcher must evaluate the two authorities and decide which, if any, of the items of authority are controlling and whether to recommend that his or her client report the disputed item.

In the process of evaluating the authority for the issue(s) under research, new issues not previously considered by the researcher may become known. If this is the case, the researcher may be required to gather additional facts, find additional pertinent authority, and evaluate the new issues. This interaction is illustrated in Exhibit 2-1.

1-5 Step 5: Develop Conclusions and Recommendations

After several iterations of the first four steps of the tax research process, the researcher must arrive at his or her conclusions for the tax issues raised. Often, the research will not have resulted in a clear solution to the client's tax problems, perhaps because of unresolved issues of law or incomplete descriptions of the facts. In addition, the client's personal preferences must also be considered. The "ideal" solution for tax purposes may be entirely impractical because of other factors that are integral to the tax question. In any of these cases, the tax practitioner must use professional judgment in making recommendations based on the conclusions drawn from the tax research process.

When unresolved issues exist, the researcher might inform the client about alternative possible outcomes of each disputed transaction and give the best recommendation for each. If the research involved an open-fact situation (where there is still time to change the actions of the client), the recommendation might detail several alternative courses of future action (e.g., whether to complete the deal or how to document the intended effects of the transaction).

In many cases, the researcher may find it appropriate to present his or her recommendation of the "best" solution from a tax perspective as well as one or more alternative recommendations that may represent much more workable solutions. In all cases, the researcher should discuss with the client the pros and cons of all reasonable recommendations and the risks associated with each course of action.

1-6 Step 6: Communicate the Recommendations

The final step in the research process is to communicate the results and recommendations of the research. The results of the research effort usually are summarized in a memorandum to the client file and in a letter to the client. Both items usually contain a restatement of the pertinent facts as the researcher understands them, any assumptions the researcher made, the issues addressed, full citations to the applicable authority relied upon to support the conclusions, and the practitioner's conclusions and recommendations. An example of the structure of a simple tax research memo is shown in Exhibit 2-6. The memorandum to the file usually contains more detail than does the letter to the client.

1-7 The Citation System

Including correct and full citations to the applicable sources of law referred to in a research memo is a critical component in this step. **Citations** are a type of shorthand system of documentation that help the researcher pinpoint the specific location of the relevant text in the specified authority. For example, in citing an IRC section, the researcher must provide not only the section number but also the subsection, paragraph, subparagraph, and clause if applicable. Citations to court cases help identify the case and the reporter in which the decision was published. The typical citation for a case includes the names of the parties in the case, the volume number and abbreviation of the reporter, a page number showing where the case begins, and the year in which the opinion was issued.

Citations not only document a preparer's research and provide a trail for reviewers to follow but also support that the preparer has met the substantial authority standard. Citations immediately signal to a reader the types of documents and level of authority a researcher is relying upon.

Standard tax citations for statutory, administrative, and judicial sources of law are provided on the inside front cover of this text. More information on citing specific types of administrative and judicial sources of law is provided in Chapters 4 and 5.

The researcher must temper his or her communication of the research results so that it is understandable by the intended reader. For instance, the researcher should use vastly different jargon and citation techniques in preparing an article for the *Journal of Taxation* than in preparing a client memo for a businessperson or layperson who is not sophisticated in tax matters. Additional guidelines and formats for tax research memos, client memoranda, and other means of delivering the results of one's research are provided in Chapter 11. An excellent source to help the tax researcher improve his or her written tax communication is the M.Tx. Writing Website produced by the School of Accountancy at Georgia State University and found at **www2.gsu.edu/~accerl**.

EXHIBIT 2-6: Tax Research Memo Template

Sawyers & Gill, LLP
Certified Public Accountants
1906 Earthquake Street
San Francisco, CA 94102

Relevant Facts and Assumptions:

Specific Issues:

Conclusions:

Support:

Actions to Be Taken:

_____ Discuss with client. Date discussed: _____

_____ Prepare a memo or letter to the client.

_____ Explore other fact situations.

_____ Other action. Describe:

Preparer: _____

Reviewer: _____

2 Conducting Tax Research Using Online Services

The body of knowledge that encompasses the field of taxation grows at a phenomenal pace. During the last several decades, Congress has enacted more than three dozen major tax and revenue bills that have had a significant effect on U.S. taxpayers. Additionally, each year hundreds of new Treasury regulations, court decisions, revenue and private letter rulings, revenue procedures, and technical advice memoranda are issued.

The avalanche of tax-related information is not expected to decrease during the foreseeable future. The abundance of available information as well as the complexity of the tax laws that have been enacted in recent years have made it even more difficult and time consuming to conduct thorough and effective research concerning a tax-related issue.

Whenever a diligent tax professional is providing advice or other services to a client, he or she must be cognizant of the latest legislative changes and judicial decisions. Furthermore, he or she must be able to draw upon, and sort through, the vast body of established tax knowledge and to apply statutes and administrative and judicial rulings to the current tax issue.

Most tax professionals conduct a significant portion of their tax research using online resources available through commercial subscription services or through free tax-related Internet sites.

Online tax research systems are relatively simple to operate. Normally, the user will have no trouble utilizing the system after he or she has devised an effective search command or query. After the documents are retrieved, the user must evaluate them and decide whether further research is required. As in using the tax research methodology itself, online searching requires a combination of technical knowledge, experience, and creativity in approach.

2-1 Benefits of Using Online Tax Services

In tax research, the primary benefit of using an **online tax service** is that such a resource makes it possible for the user to use search terms and queries to search vast amounts of data from legislative, administrative, and judicial sources of tax law. However, that is also one of the primary problems of online research—finding hundreds if not thousands of "hits."

This requires great care (and practice) in developing search terms and often limiting the sources searched. If properly structured, online search queries can result in the research process being conducted with greater speed and thoroughness and can reduce the amount of time spent on that phase of the research task.

Such speed and flexibility are best realized as the researcher moves among pertinent tax documents. This is easily done with the commercial tax services but is often not possible with the free online sources. For instance, the researcher could be reading a court case that refers to IRC § 2032A. By clicking on the link, he or she is taken directly to the text of the code section for direct perusal of the statutory language. Similarly, links can be made to pertinent regulations or to similar court documents in a manner that the researcher may not be able to accomplish with free online services. As available tax documents become more voluminous, the important task of moving among the documents quickly can be accomplished only with an online commercial tax service.

A researcher generally is able to retrieve recent court decisions and administrative rulings from a commercial service almost immediately upon release by the source of the document. In addition, commercial services often include one or more of the daily tax news summaries, such as BNA's *Daily Tax Report* or Tax Analysts' *Tax Notes Today*. In this regard, commercial tax service allows a tax researcher to stay on top of the latest news and developments without incurring additional subscription costs for the stand-alone services.

Factors to consider in choosing among online commercial services include the availability of editorial materials as well as specific resources dealing with special topics—international or multistate taxation, for example. Of course, customer support, training, and pricing are also important considerations.

With several billion searches conducted each day, you might be tempted to do your tax research using the Google search engine or other free online services. While a Google search may do a good job of finding government documents and articles relating to your question, determining whether the material is up to date, reliable, and comprehensive is difficult. Using Google searches as a quick starting point to identify code sections and perhaps reading an article in the popular press about a topic is fine, but it is not the place to conduct sound, supportable tax research.

SPOTLIGHT ON TAXATION

Tax Research Using Google Searches

Suppose your client wants to know whether she can deduct expenses related to landscaping her yard as a home office deduction. A Google search using the natural language question, "Can I deduct expenses for landscaping my yard as a home office deduction?" returns almost 500,000 results. Included is a short article from H&R Block and a question and answer from TurboTax AnswerXchange. However, no support from primary sources of the tax law is provided, and it is impossible to know if the information is current or complete. The search also takes you to the IRS Website and Tax Topic 509—Business Use of a Home. While this page does indeed discuss the basics of deducting business use of a home, it does not include the word *landscape*—hardly a definitive answer for your client!

On the other hand, a search using either a natural language query or terms and connectors using Checkpoint provides a list of resources in relevance order, the ability to link directly to the relevant primary sources of law, documentation of the research steps you took to find an answer, and most importantly, a comprehensive, up-to-date solution.

3 Using a Commercial Online Tax Service to Conduct Tax Research

In the first part of this chapter, we presented a model of the tax research process. In this model, steps 1 and 2 of the tax research model are (1) to establish the facts and (2) to identify the issues related to the research question(s). The third step in the research model is to locate tax authority with which to solve the research question. In most situations, the tax researcher uses an online tax service to find the required authority (or to conclude that there is no authority on the subject). The process of finding tax authority using an online tax research service can be broken down into several steps, as shown in Exhibit 2-7.

3-1 Step 1: State the Issue as a Question

After the tax researcher has established the facts and identified the issues that he or she must resolve, the issues should be stated as a question to be answered. For example, suppose the researcher has a client who is a self-employed attorney. As part of her trade or business, the attorney incurs substantial travel expenses during the year. On a recent business trip in Europe concluding on Friday night, she found that she could save over $600 in airfare by departing on Sunday instead of on Saturday morning. As her hotel room on Saturday night was only an extra $200, she

EXHIBIT 2-7:   Steps in the Online Tax Research Process

Step 1	State the Issue as a Question	The step comes after establishing the facts and identifying the issues.
Step 2	Identify the Keywords	Use words that are on point to get best results.
Step 3	Construct an Online Research Query	Use wildcards and connectors to get the best results.
Step 4	Select a Database and Execute the Search	Use a database that finds what is needed without returning too much information.
Step 5	Interpret and Refine the Search	Results may require the researcher to return to a previous step.

booked the return flight on Sunday. The research question in this situation could be stated as the following:

> *Are the additional travel costs (primarily meals and lodging) of staying over a Saturday night in order to save substantial amounts on airfare deductible?*

3-2 Step 2: Identify the Keywords

Once the research question has been stated, the researcher must next identify the keywords to construct a proper query. In the preceding research question, the keywords could be as follows:

- Meals and lodging

- Travel

- Saturday

- Deductible

- Airfare

The researcher is looking for words that, when entered into a search query, will find tax authority that is "on point." If the correct keywords are not identified, tax researchers might not find the authority needed or could be led down blind alleys.

3-3 Step 3: Construct a Research Query

Commercial services such as Checkpoint and IntelliConnect allow researchers to search using natural language or using terms and connectors. Each has its advantages and disadvantages. Natural language searches are easy for nonexperts in that they allow the researcher to simply state the research question using normal sentence structure. For our research question, we could type the query as, "Can I deduct additional travel costs related to staying over Saturday night to save on airfare?" According to Checkpoint, their natural language search feature (called intuitive search) "takes advantage of historical usage data, giving higher importance to documents that are frequently accessed … as well as our editorial know-how embedded within the content."

On the other hand, a terms and connectors search allows the researcher to specify the exact relationship between words and phrases that describe the tax question, and it often results in a more precise search. For example, a researcher can search for one word

EXHIBIT 2-8: Selected Checkpoint Search Connectors

Connector	Example	Description
And (or a space)	stock and securities stock securities	Finds documents with both the term *stock* and the term *securities* in them.
Or	stock or securities	Finds documents with either the term *stock* or the term *securities* in them.
/n	stock/15 securities	Finds documents in which the term *stock* is within 15 words of the term *securities*.
Not	stock not securities	Finds documents with the term *stock* but not the term *securities*.

within the same sentence as another word. All online tax research systems recognize various types of connectors to construct a research query. Generally, online tax services, such as Thomson Reuters Checkpoint, have 10 to 15 search connectors available, but most tax research searches can be accomplished by using several basic connectors. The syntax of the four most useful connectors in Checkpoint is shown in Exhibit 2-8.

In addition, the tax services allow the use of wildcard (universal) character(s). For example, in Checkpoint, an "*" (asterisk) at the end of a root word finds all variations of that word. Thus, the word *deduct** will find *deduct, deducted, deduction, deductible*, and so on. Other online tax services use similar methods to construct tax research queries.

For our research question, a term and connectors search such as "travel deduct* Saturday" finds all documents including the words *travel* and *deduct* (and its variations), and *Saturday* in the same document.[2]

3-4 Step 4: Select Sources and Execute the Search

Once the query is constructed, the researcher must choose the resources to search. In Checkpoint, the user first identifies the practice area (e.g., federal, state and local, or international) and then whether he or she wants to confine the search to primary source materials such as the IRC, regulations, and cases or also include editorial materials, journals, and other secondary sources of law. The search screen in Checkpoint is shown in Exhibit 2-9.

3-5 Step 5: Interpret and Refine the Search

An online tax search often produces too little or too much information. If there is too little information, the search query must be broadened. For example, other keywords may be used, or proximity connectors may be relaxed. On the other hand, if the query generates too much information, then the search should be tightened. For example, fewer libraries or more unique keywords may be used, or proximity connectors may be used or narrowed.

In our research example, the natural language search of primary materials produced the 100 "best results." Sorting those results by relevance resulted in PLR 9237014 as the most relevant document. Our term and connectors search using "travel deduct* Saturday" resulted in 299 hits, once again with the private letter ruling as the most relevant.

---

[2]In a Checkpoint terms and connectors search, if a space occurs between words, the system assumes it is an "and."

EXHIBIT 2-9:   Checkpoint Query and Database Selection Screen

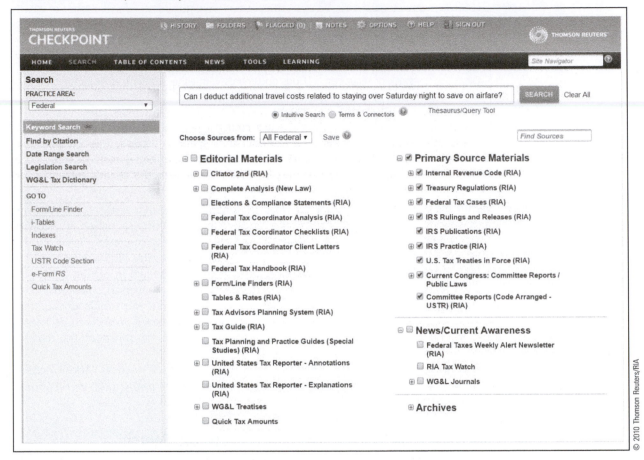

Refining the search by including an additional keyword, *airfare*, substantially narrows the results to only 15 hits. This can be done in the initial search query or by using the "Search Within Results" feature at the top of the Search Results page.

Each online tax service (e.g., LexisNexis, Westlaw, Checkpoint, CCH IntelliConnect) uses its own format for conducting tax searches. However, all services (including those conducted on Google) use the same basic steps in executing such searches. In all online tax services, the researcher must state the issue, select the keywords, construct a query, choose a database, execute a search, and interpret and refine the search.

4 Tax Research Practical Considerations

When a tax researcher undertakes an engagement, there are several practical factors to consider. These factors can influence the research project on several levels. The primary goal of a researcher should be to produce results in the most accurate and efficient manner possible. The following factors should be considered when conducting tax research engagements:

- *Engagement Time Cost.* A tax researcher must be efficient in using his or her time. Research time is very expensive, sometimes amounting to several hundred dollars per hour of cost to the client. The researcher must make sure that the time spent on the project is used efficiently and effectively in order to provide the most value to the client.

- *Potential Tax Liability Involved.* Not every tax research engagement has the same relative value to a client. A tax transaction involving millions of dollars in tax liability is different from one that affects several thousand dollars in tax liability. The researcher has an obligation to a client not to waste the client's money on a low cost/benefit issue. What is the point of incurring $5,000 in research time to save $3,000 in taxes? The new staff researcher should always be aware of the research budget and check with his or her supervisor if the supervisor is concerned about the time spent on a specific research project.

- *Accuracy Threshold.* One of the issues facing a tax researcher is how definitive a research result must be. Is the additional time spent to increase the certainty of a conclusion from 70 percent to 95 percent worth the additional cost? Related to the issue is the amount of tax liability involved along with the client's tolerance for risk.

- *Ethics.* Chapter 1 covered many of the ethical requirements for tax professionals. These requirements should always be kept in mind when undertaking a research project and reaching a conclusion. The final question for the tax researcher should be the following: "Have I met the appropriate ethical standards in reaching my conclusion?"

5 Research and Tax on the CPA Exam

All individuals who wish to obtain a CPA license in one of the 50 states and other jurisdictions (e.g., Puerto Rico) of the United States must pass the CPA examination. The exam is prepared by the American Institute of CPAs and is administered through the National Association of State Boards of Accountancy (NASBA). NASBA information can be found at the following Website: **www.nasba.org/**.

NASBA contracts with testing centers around the United States, which actually give the exam. The CPA exam is an online exam that tests accounting knowledge (e.g., financial accounting, taxation, auditing) and a set of supporting "soft" skills deemed to be important to the practice of public accountancy. CPA exam candidates are required to demonstrate their ability to apply these skills in each section of the Uniform CPA Examination: Auditing and Attestation (AUD), Business Environment and Concepts (BEC), Financial Accounting and Reporting (FAR), and Regulation (REG).

The most recent changes to the exam (effective April 2017) increase the emphasis on higher-order critical thinking and analysis. According to the AICPA, the number of task-based simulations on the exam has increased along with the amount of background material and data provided, requiring candidates to determine what information is relevant to a question. Representative tasks on the exam are intended to combine content knowledge and other skills in the context of work that a newly licensed CPA would be expected to perform. Candidates will receive at least one research question in each section of the exam that requires the candidate to search the applicable authoritative literature and find an appropriate reference.[3]

In the REG section of the exam, broad topics tested include Ethics and Responsibilities in Tax Practice, Federal Tax Procedures, Licensing and Disciplinary Systems, and Legal Duties and Responsibilities. Candidates should be familiar with a number of

---

[3]Next Version CPA Exam Structure, effective April 1, 2017, available at **www.aicpa.org/BecomeACPA /CPAExam/DownloadableDocuments/next-cpa-exam-structure-white-paper.pdf**.

references including the IRC, Circular 230, and other administrative pronouncements regarding federal taxation and the case law on federal taxation.[4]

Representative tasks in these areas include:

1. Recalling the regulations governing practice before the IRS and applying those regulations to a specific scenario.

2. Recalling who is a tax return preparer.

3. Recalling situations in which preparers would be subject to penalties and applying potential penalties given a specific scenario.

4. Explaining the audit and appeals process as it relates to federal tax matters.

5. Explaining the different levels of the judicial process as it relates to federal taxation.

6. Identifying options available to a taxpayer within the audit and appeals process and the judicial process given specific scenarios.

7. Summarizing the requirements for the appropriate disclosure of a federal tax return position.

8. Identifying situations in which disclosure of federal tax return positions is required and identifying whether substantiation is sufficient.

9. Recalling situations that would result in taxpayer penalties and calculating taxpayer penalties relating to federal tax returns.

10. Recalling the appropriate hierarchy of authority for federal tax purposes.

11. Summarizing the rules regarding privileged communications as they relate to tax practice and identifying situations in which communications regarding tax practice are considered privileged.[5]

All these subject areas are discussed in this book. In addition, REG also includes sections on business law, the federal taxation of property transactions (acquisition and disposition of assets, cost recovery, and estate and gift taxation), and the federal taxation of individuals, including concepts such as gross income inclusions and exclusions, reporting of items from pass-through entities, adjustments and deductions for adjusted gross income (AGI), deductions and adjustments from AGI, passive activity losses and loss limitations, filing status and exemptions, and the computation of tax including the alternative minimum tax and tax credits.

REG also includes sections on the federal taxation of entities, including the tax treatment of the formation and liquidation of business entities, differences between book and tax income, C corporations, S corporations, partnerships, limited liability companies, trusts and estates, and tax exempt organizations.

SUMMARY

Tax research is a complex process. The researcher must complete all the steps in the research process to arrive at a solution to or recommendation for the client's tax problem. Moreover, the steps delineated in Exhibit 2-1

---

[4]Coverage and testing of the *AICPA Code of Professional Conduct* is primarily in the AUD section of the exam.

[5]Uniform CPA Examination Regulation (REG) Blueprint, available at **www.aicpa.org/becomeacpa/cpaexam /nextexam/downloadabledocuments/2017-cpa-exam-blueprints.pdf.**

(or iterations of them) must be completed in their proper order to minimize the possibility of errors in evaluating the authority, arriving at conclusions, or making recommendations. If the process is abbreviated, the researcher risks failure to properly serve the client, which could result in the payment of unnecessary taxes by the client or in the payment of damages by the tax practitioner to the client.

KEY WORDS

By the time you complete this chapter, you should be comfortable discussing each of the following terms. If you need additional review of any of these items, return to the appropriate material in the chapter or consult the glossary to this text.

administrative sources, p. 52
citations, p. 56
collateral estoppel, p. 49
fact issues, p. 48

Internal Revenue Code, p. 48
judicial sources, p. 52
law issues, p. 48
online tax service, p. 58

primary authority, p. 51
secondary authority, p. 52
statutory sources, p. 52
tax journals, p. 55

DISCUSSION QUESTIONS

1. What are the purpose(s) of tax research?

2. What are the six basic steps in conducting tax research? Briefly discuss each step in the tax research process.

3. What are the two chief tax research skills, as identified in this text? Explain the importance of each basic skill.

4. The tax researcher must find the facts as the first step in tax research. Give examples of the kind of information that a tax practitioner might want to obtain.

5. What are some of the potential pitfalls in the first step of the tax research process?

6. In each of the following independent situations, indicate whether the item generally would be a **tax (T)** or a **nontax (NT)** consideration in solving a tax research or tax planning problem.

   a. The taxpayer would like to set up a private foundation to reduce her annual income tax liability.

   b. The taxpayer has limited cash flow because of prior investments; therefore, he has limited ability to make "tax-advantaged" investments.

   c. The taxpayer wants to transfer as much of her property to her grandchildren as possible. However, she does not want any of the property to fall into the hands of the grandchildren's mother (her daughter-in-law).

   d. The taxpayer lived through the Great Depression of the 1930s and does not like investments with any risk, such as owning stocks or bonds.

   e. The taxpayer likes to maintain liquid investments, such as money market funds and certificates of deposit in insured banks and savings and loan institutions.

7. In each of the following independent situations, indicate whether the item generally would be a **tax (T)** or a **nontax (NT)** consideration in solving a tax research or tax planning problem.

   a. The taxpayer hates to pay federal taxes. He will take any legal action to avoid paying any federal income, estate, or gift taxes.

   b. The taxpayer does not trust the U.S. banking system and moves all her money to a bank in Switzerland.

   c. The taxpayer is married, and his spouse is financially naive. Since he is in bad health, the taxpayer wants to make sure his wife will be taken care of financially if he were to suddenly die.

    d. The taxpayer wants to purchase rental real estate. He wants to make sure that he will not be subject to a high state tax where he buys.

    e. The taxpayer owns city of San Diego bonds instead of putting his money in a commercial bank.

8. Identify and briefly describe the two major types of tax research issues.

9. What is collateral estoppel? How does it affect tax research and planning?

10. Tax law provisions tend to change over time. Explain how this might affect tax research and planning.

11. In the tax research process, the researcher has an obligation to the client to evaluate authority. Do the precedents in all tax authority carry the same value? Explain.

12. Primary tax authority can be classified as statutory, administrative, or judicial. Briefly describe each.

13. Classify each of the following items as a **primary (P)** or **secondary (S)** tax research authority:
    a. The Internal Revenue Code
    b. A Tax Court case
    c. A textbook on corporate taxation
    d. Treasury regulations
    e. An IRS revenue ruling

14. Classify each of the following items as a **primary (P)** or **secondary (S)** tax research authority:
    a. A U.S. district court case
    b. An IRS revenue procedure
    c. Code § 213
    d. The *Daily Tax Report* newsletter
    e. An article on recent tax rulings on inventory valuation in *Practical Tax Strategies*

15. Classify each of the following items as a **primary (P)** or **secondary (S)** tax research authority:
    a. An article in the *Journal of Taxation*
    b. "Taxes on Parade" (a newsletter)
    c. A U.S. Supreme Court decision on a tax matter
    d. The U.S./Australia Income Tax Treaty
    e. A discussion on earnings and profits in the Checkpoint Tax Coordinator 2d Tax Service

16. What kind of information can be found in a citator?

17. Tax practitioners use the term *tax service* regularly. What is a tax service?

18. What is the target readership of each of the following tax journals?
    a. *TAXES*
    b. *Journal of Taxation*
    c. *Practical Tax Strategies*
    d. *The Tax Adviser*
    e. *The ATA Journal of Legal Tax Research*

19. Specific items of tax authority have different "values" in helping the tax researcher to solve his or her problem. Explain this statement and describe how it applies to the tax research process.

20. Step 5 in the tax research process is concerned with reaching a conclusion or making a recommendation. If one has not found a clear answer to a tax research problem, how is a conclusion or recommendation to be reached?

21. The final step in the research process typically involves a memorandum to the client file and/or a letter to the client communicating the results of the research. List the items that should be found in the body of both of these documents.

22. It has been said that the tax research process is more circular than linear. Do you agree with this statement? Explain your answer.

23. What is deemed to be substantial authority under the IRC § 6662 regulations? Why is this important?

24. Describe an online tax research system. What are the primary advantages of such a system?

25. Give the Web addresses of three *free* online Internet sites where someone could find information on various aspects of taxation.

26. What is the purpose of citing relevant authority in research memos?

27. Briefly describe what is contained in each of the following tax services:
    a. Thomson Reuters CheckPoint
    b. CCH IntelliConnect
    c. LexisAdvance Tax
    d. Westlaw

28. What are the disadvantages of using an online tax service?

29. What are the major steps in developing an effective online tax research query?

30. If you were researching an issue and the computer informed you it had located 1,000 pertinent documents, what would you do to reduce the number of retrieved documents to a more reasonable number?

31. What are the search connectors discussed in the text used by Checkpoint? Describe how each operates.

32. For the following Checkpoint databases, state if they generally contain primary or secondary authority: (1) *Federal Tax Coordinator*, (2) Federal Tax Cases, (3) IRS Rulings and Releases, and (4) WG&L Journals.

33. One of the practical factors that could affect a tax research project is engagement time cost. Discuss how this might influence your completion of a tax engagement.

34. One of the practical factors that could affect a tax research project is potential tax liability involved. Discuss how this might influence your completion of a tax engagement.

35. One of the practical factors that could affect a tax research project is accuracy threshold. Discuss how this might influence your completion of a tax engagement.

36. How might ethics considerations influence a tax research engagement?

37. The Uniform CPA exam has four parts. Briefly summarize the tax and ethics issues covered in the REG section of the exam.

EXERCISES

38. Which of the selected tax journals listed in Exhibit 2-5 can be found online? Which are available through your university's library in either electronic or hard copy?

39. Determine if your campus has any of the following online tax research services available for student use. If a service is available on your campus, describe how you would gain access to that system for research projects in your tax classes.

     a. LexisAdvance Tax

     b. Thomson Reuters Checkpoint

     c. Westlaw

     d. CCH IntelliConnect

40. Go to **irs.gov** and print a copy of the most recent Instructions for Form 3903 of Form 1040.

41. Go to **irs.gov**. Which IRS publication number addresses tax rules that apply to personnel in the armed forces? Print the first page of the IRS publication to hand in.

42. Go to **irs.gov**. What IRS publication number addresses tax rules for pension and annuity income? Print the first page of the IRS publication to hand in.

43. Go to **irs.gov**. Find a copy of Form 1040-PR, the Puerto Rico individual tax return. Print and turn in page 1 of the 1040-PR Form.

44. Go to **irs.gov** and find the most recent IRS Publication 1542, Per Diem Rates. What is the maximum per diem rate for lodging and meals and incidental expenses (M&IE) for each of the following cities?

     a. Miami, Florida

     b. Palm Springs, California

     c. San Antonio, Texas

     d. Springfield, Missouri

     e. White River Junction, Vermont

45. Go to **congress.gov** and search for current legislation dealing with taxation. Provide bill numbers, titles, and the current status for five bills dealing with taxation issues.

46. Jennifer owns 200 acres of land on which she grows flowers to sell to local nurseries. Her adjusted basis in the land is $30,000. She receives condemnation proceeds of $20,000 from the state for 10 acres of her land on which a new freeway will be built. The state also pays her $30,000 for the harmful effects that the increased auto exhaust might have on her flowers. List as many tax research issues as you can to determine the tax consequences of these transactions. Do not attempt to answer any of the questions you raise. Simply identify the research issues.

47. Joey parked his car on the top of a hill when he went to watch the X Games in San Diego. He did not properly set his brakes or curb the wheels when he parked the car. When he returned from the games, he found his car had rolled down the hill, smashed into Nick's house, and injured Nick, who was watching TV in his den. Joey does not have car insurance. List as many tax research issues as you can to determine the tax consequences of this accident. Do not attempt to answer any of the questions you raise. Simply identify the research issues.

48. John and Marsha are married and filed a joint return for the past year. During that year, Marsha was employed as an assistant cashier at a local bank and, as such, was able to embezzle $75,000, none of which was reported on their joint return. Before the defalcation was discovered, Marsha disappeared and has not been seen or heard from since. List as many tax research issues as you can to determine the tax consequences of this crime. Do not attempt to answer any of the questions you raise. Simply identify the research issues.

49. In the current year, Dave receives stock worth $125,000 from his employer. The stock is restricted and cannot be sold by Dave for seven years. Dave estimates the stock will be worth $300,000 after the seven years. List as many tax research issues as you can to determine the tax consequences of this transaction. Do not attempt to answer any of the questions you raise. Simply identify the research issues.

50. On December 1, 2014, Ericka receives $18,000 for three months' rent (December 2014, January 2015, and February 2015) for an office building. List as many tax research issues as you can to determine the tax consequences of this transaction. Do not attempt to answer any of the questions you raise. Simply identify the research issues.

51. Formulate a search query to determine whether your client is required to include in gross income the proceeds from redemption of a tax-exempt bond, purchased in 1998 and called by the school district this year. Redemption proceeds were $190,000, and the 1998 purchase price on the secondary market was $176,000. Give an example of an online search query using only the following Checkpoint connectors: "and," "or," "/n," and "not."

52. Formulate a search query to determine the provisions of the treaty between the United States and Germany relative to graduate fellowship income received by a business student during a summer internship with the German Department of Price Controls. Give an example of an online search query using only the following Checkpoint connectors: "and," "or," "/n," and "not." Give an example of a natural language query for the same issue.

53. Formulate a search query to determine whether your client is required to capitalize fringe benefits and general overhead that is attributable to employees who are building an addition to your client's factory during a "slack time" at work. Give an example of an online search query using only the following Checkpoint connectors: "and," "or," "/n," and "not." Give an example of a natural language query for the same issue.

54. Formulate a search query to determine whether your client can retroactively elect to change its accounting method. Give an example of an online search query using only the following Checkpoint connectors: "and," "or," "/n," and "not." Give an example of a natural language query for the same issue.

55. Formulate a search query to find all the cases in which the word *constructive* occurs within 10 words of the word *dividend*. Give an example of an online search query using only the following Checkpoint connectors: "and," "or," "/n," and "not."

56. Sam Manuel has been employed on a full-time basis as an electrical engineer for the past three years. Prior to obtaining full-time employment, he was self-employed as an inventor of complex electronic components. During this period of self-employment, most of his projects produced little income, although several produced a significant amount of revenue.

    Because of the large expenditures necessary and the failure of the majority of the products to produce a profit, Sam was forced to seek full-time employment. After obtaining full-time employment, he continued to work long hours to perfect several of his inventions. He continued to enjoy relatively little success with most of his products, but certain projects were successfully marketed and generated a profit. For the past two years, Sam's invention activity has generated a net loss.

    a. List as many possible tax research issues as you can to determine whether the losses may be deducted.
    b. After completing your list of tax research issues, list the keywords you might use to construct an online tax research query.

57. Matthew Broadway was a partner in the law firm of Johnson & Smith, a partnership of 20 partners, for the past 10 years. Without the knowledge or consent of the other partners, Matthew worked on a highly complicated acquisition and merger project for six months, at all times using the law firm's resources. Several months later, the firm for which Matthew provided the professional services made out a check for $300,000 to Johnson & Smith. Matthew insisted that the fee should rightly be his, while the firm disputed his claim. Because of the dispute, the fee was held in escrow until the following year when the dispute was settled.

    The dispute was settled with Matthew agreeing to withdraw from the partnership. Included as part of the withdrawal agreement was a clause that specified he would receive $45,000 of the $300,000 fee, with the law firm retaining the remainder. Six months later, Matthew received a total payment of $125,000, which included the $45,000 fee, from Johnson & Smith.

    a. List as many possible tax research issues as you can to determine the tax treatment of the $125,000 payment received by Matthew.

    b. After completing your list of tax research issues, list the keywords you might use to construct an online tax research query.

58. Juanita Sharp purchased a large parcel of property for $120,000. A short time after purchasing the property, Sharp submitted plans for the division of the parcel into six lots and the construction of three single-family residences on three of the lots. The city permits required that the property be divided into six lots and that street improvements and water and sewer access be provided. Sharp spent $22,000 for the street, water, and sewer improvements. As a result of the improvements, the value of each of the three vacant lots increased by $10,000, based on an appraisal completed subsequent to the completion of the improvements. The costs of constructing the three single-family residences totaled $200,000.

    a. List as many possible tax research issues as you can to determine how the original purchase price of $120,000, the $22,000 cost of the improvements, and the $200,000 cost of the construction of the homes should be allocated to the basis of each of the lots for purposes of determining gain or loss on the sale of the lots.

    b. After completing your list of tax research issues, list the keywords you might use to construct an online tax research query.

59. Tom and Donna were divorced three years ago. At the time of their divorce, they owned a residence whose value had significantly increased during the marriage. Tom remained half-owner of the house, but he moved out and allowed Donna to continue living in the house. In the current year, Tom and Donna sold the house for $500,000. Last year, Tom purchased a new house for $390,000.

    a. List as many possible tax research issues as you can to determine tax treatment(s) available to Tom on the sale and purchase of the residence.

    b. After completing your list of tax research issues, list the keywords you might use to construct an online tax research query.

60. Vincent ("Vinny") Vineyard is a very successful physician in Temecula, California. He earns approximately $800,000 per year from his medical practice. His two children have graduated from college, and he and his wife are now "empty-nesters." His son, Vincent Jr., is an officer in the U.S. Navy, and his daughter, Valerie, is an electrical engineer in Texas. Vinny has had an interest in wine and grape growing for many years. Now, with more time to devote to other activities, Vinny recently started a winery with an initial investment of $1,000,000. Since the winery is new, he expects it to be 8 to 10 years before the winery makes a profit. Vinny would like your advice as to any potential tax problems he might have with his new winery investment.

    a. What additional information might you want in this situation?

    b. Where might that information come from?

    c. Are all the given facts pertinent? Which (if any) are irrelevant?

    d. What is the primary research question you would try to answer?

    e. Are there any additional research question(s) you want to address?

61. Ned Naive operated several franchised stores, and at the home office's suggestion, he consolidated its payroll and accounting functions with Andy the Accountant. Andy is not a CPA. Last year, Andy began misappropriating taxpayers' escrowed tax withholdings to himself and failed to remit required amounts for the four quarters. The IRS assessed Ned penalties for failing to make the proper withholding deposits during the year.

    a. What additional information might you want in this situation?

    b. Where might that information come from?

c. Are all the given facts pertinent? Which (if any) are irrelevant?

d. Where might that information come from?

e. What is the primary research question you would try to answer?

f. Are there any additional research question(s) you want to address?

62. Dr. Diego Dissolution is recently divorced and has some questions regarding payments he is making to his ex-wife (Mrs. D.). Diego is 45 years old and has a successful dental practice. Mrs. D. was divorced from her first husband six years ago. Diego is paying $12,000 per month to Mrs. D. He wants to know if the tax payments on the $12,000 per month are deductible.

a. What additional information might you want in this situation?

b. Where might that information come from?

c. Are all the given facts pertinent? Which (if any) are irrelevant?

d. What is the primary research question you would try to answer?

e. Are there any additional research question(s) you want to address?

63. Phred Phortunate won his state lotto two years ago. His lotto ticket was worth $10 million, which was payable in 20 annual installments of $500,000 each. Phred paid $1 for the winning ticket. The lotto in Phred's state does not allow winners to receive their payout in a lump sum. Phred wanted all the money now, so he assigned his future lotto winnings to Unscrupulous Finance Company for a discounted price of $4.5 million. Assignment of lotto winnings is permitted by Phred's state lotto. Phred filed his tax return and reported the assignment of the lotto winnings as a capital gain ($4.5 million, $1 basis) taxable at a 15 percent rate.

a. List as many possible tax research issues as you can to determine whether Phred correctly reported his lotto winnings.

b. After completing your list of tax research issues, list the keywords you might use to construct an online tax research query.

64. The Mucho Oro Indian Tribe operates a casino on its reservation in Arizona. The casino is very profitable, and therefore the tribe has excess money to invest. The tribe is approached by an entrepreneur who wants to build an outlet mall next to the casino. The entrepreneur would like to operate the outlet mall as an S corporation. Both he and the tribe would be shareholders in the new S corporation.

a. List as many possible tax research issues as you can to determine whether this plan of organization would be allowed under the current tax law.

b. After completing your list of tax research issues, list the keywords you might use to construct an online tax research query.

PART II

Primary Sources of Federal Tax Law

CHAPTER 3

Constitutional and Legislative Sources

LEARNING OBJECTIVES

- Describe in detail the nature and structure of the statutory sources of the tax law, including the Constitution, tax treaties, and the Internal Revenue Code.
- Delineate how statutory tax law is created and how tax research resources are generated in this process.
- Demonstrate how to locate the statutory sources of the tax law.
- Discuss how the tax researcher can carefully interpret the Internal Revenue Code.

CHAPTER OUTLINE

WHEN ASKED ABOUT HOW income taxes work, most practitioners respond by mentioning the Internal Revenue Code (IRC) as the backbone of the tax law environment. As mentioned in Chapter 2, tax law stems from three sources: statutory, administrative, and judicial. In the next three chapters, we are going to examine resources a tax researcher might need to consult for each source. These resources will assist the researcher in obtaining the relevant tax law authority necessary to support the correct conclusion and are presented in Exhibit 3-1. Starting in Chapter 6, we will add secondary sources of tax law to the research toolkit, but primary sources such as those covered here are generally required to justify conclusions drawn by a researcher in practice.

1 Sources of Legislative Tax Law

In this chapter, we examine primary sources of tax law that largely stem from **statute** known as legislative or **statutory sources**. Because changes to the IRC are passed by Congress and signed by the executive branch into statutory law through a legislative process, the code is often considered the focal point of legislative tax law. However, other sources such as the U.S. Constitution and international tax treaties are also considered part of legislative tax law. In some instances, tax law can stem from other legislative activity that is not part of the code. Most conclusions from tax research will rely in large part on a legislative source (most likely the code). The sources of federal tax law to be examined here and in the next two chapters are presented in outline form in Exhibit 3-1.

2 History of U.S. Taxation

Although the Massachusetts Bay Colony enacted an income tax law in 1643, the first U.S. income tax was not created until the Civil War. An income tax law was passed at that time to help the Union pay for the cost of fighting the war. This federal income tax law was passed on August 5, 1861. The tax was not generally enforced, but some limited collections were made under the law.

This first federal income tax was levied at the rate of a modest 3 percent on income between $600 and $10,000, and 5 percent on marginal incomes in excess of $10,000. Later, in 1867, the rate was a flat 5 percent of income in excess of $1,000. The Civil War income taxes were allowed to expire in 1872. In 1894, another income tax act was

EXHIBIT 3-1: Framework of Primary Sources of Federal Tax Law

Statutory Sources (Chapter 3)
- U.S. Constitution
- Tax Treaties
- Internal Revenue Code

Administrative Sources (Chapter 4)
- Treasury Regulations
- Revenue Rulings
- Revenue Procedures

- Other Written Determinations
- Miscellaneous IRS Publications

Judicial Sources (Chapter 5)
- Supreme Court
- Courts of Appeals
- U.S. District Courts
- U.S. Court of Federal Claims
- U.S. Tax Court

passed by Congress. By this time, however, the income tax had become an important political issue. The southern and western states generally favored the tax, and the eastern states commonly opposed it. The tax had developed into an important element of the Populist political movement.[1] In *Pollock v. Farmers' Loan & Trust Co.*, 157 U.S. 429 (1895), the Supreme Court held that the income tax was unconstitutional because it was a constitutionally prohibited "direct tax."[2]

The supporters of the income tax decided to amend the Constitution so that there would be no question as to the constitutionality of a federal income tax, applying progressive rates to diverse sources of income. The proposed amendment was sent to the states on July 12, 1909, by the 61st Congress; it was ratified on February 3, 1913. The 16th Amendment to the Constitution states:

> *The Congress shall have the power to lay and collect taxes on incomes, from whatever source derived, without apportionment among the several States, and without regard to any census or enumeration.*

A copy of a 1913 individual tax return (Form 1040) is shown in Exhibit 3-2. It should be noted that individual taxpayers were allowed a $3,000 ($4,000 for married taxpayers) "specific exemption" before they had to start paying income tax at a 1 percent rate. The 1 percent bracket went up to $20,000 of taxable income before a surtax of an additional 1 percent was added. The surtax eventually reached 6 percent at a taxable income of $500,000. Thus, the maximum marginal tax rate in 1913 was 7 percent (1 percent regular tax plus 6 percent surtax).

The 1913 specific exemption is similar to the current standard deduction. If $3,000 in 1913 were price-level adjusted into today's dollars, it would be more than $70,000. Thus, an individual taxpayer would not pay any federal income tax until he or she showed taxable income of more than $70,000 if an equivalent exemption were in place today.

Before the 16th Amendment was ratified, Congress passed a corporate income tax in 1909. This tax also was challenged at the Supreme Court level, in *Flint v. Stone Tracy Co.*, 220 U.S. 107 (1911). The Court held that this tax was constitutional because it was a special form of "excise tax" on the privilege of operating in the corporate form, using income as its base, rather than a (prohibited) direct income tax.

3 Who Pays the Income Tax?

Historically, the 1913 income tax was strictly a tax on wealthy and high-income taxpayers (i.e., a "select tax"). The original post-16th Amendment income tax applied to less than 1 percent of the population (i.e., 1 in every 271 adults). It was not until the end of World War II that the income tax became a broad-based tax that applied to the majority of the population (i.e., a "mass tax"). The percentage of taxpayers subjected to income tax liability has changed over the last few decades, with numbers as high as about 60 percent in 2007 and as low as about 50 percent in 2008 and 2009 after the financial crisis.

3-1 Tax Protesters

Over the years, the income tax has been attacked in the courts on the basis that it is unconstitutional. For instance, some protesters have asserted that because the U.S.

---

[1]For more background on the Populists' ideas, search the Web for the term *populist movement*.

[2]Under the Constitution, direct taxes had to be apportioned among the states on the basis of population, which is not the way income taxes are levied.

EXHIBIT 3-2: 1913 Individual Form 1040

TO BE FILLED IN BY COLLECTOR.	Form 1040.	TO BE FILLED IN BY INTERNAL REVENUE BUREAU.
List. No.	**INCOME TAX.**	File No. ....
.... District of	**THE PENALTY** FOR FAILURE TO HAVE THIS RETURN IN THE HANDS OF THE COLLECTOR OF INTERNAL REVENUE ON OR BEFORE MARCH 1 IS $20 TO $1,000. (SEE INSTRUCTIONS ON PAGE 4.)	Assessment List ....
Date received		Page .... Line ....

UNITED STATES INTERNAL REVENUE.

RETURN OF ANNUAL NET INCOME OF INDIVIDUALS.

(As provided by Act of Congress, approved October 3, 1913.)

RETURN OF NET INCOME RECEIVED OR ACCRUED DURING THE YEAR ENDED DECEMBER 31, 191 ....

(FOR THE YEAR 1913, FROM MARCH 1, TO DECEMBER 31.)

Filed by (or for) .... of ....

(Full name of individual.)   (Street and No.)

in the City, Town, or Post Office of .... State of ....

(Fill in pages 2 and 3 before making entries below.)

1. GROSS INCOME (see page 2, line 12) . . . . $ ....

2. GENERAL DEDUCTIONS (see page 3, line 7) . . . . $ ....

3. NET INCOME . . . . $ ....

Deductions and exemptions allowed in computing income subject to the normal tax of 1 per cent.

4. Dividends and net earnings received or accrued, of corporations, etc., subject to like tax. (See page 2, line 11) . . . $ ....

5. Amount of income on which the normal tax has been deducted
and withheld at the source. (See page 2, line 9, column A) ....

6. Specific exemption of $3,000 or $4,000, as the case may be.
(See Instructions 3 and 19) . . . .

Total deductions and exemptions. (Items 4, 5, and 6) . . . . $ ....

7. TAXABLE INCOME on which the normal tax of 1 per cent is to be calculated. (See Instruction 3) . $ ....

8. When the net income shown above on line 3 exceeds $20,000, the additional tax thereon must be calculated as per schedule below:

					INCOME.	TAX.
1	per cent on amount over $20,000 and not exceeding $50,000 . .	$	$ ....
2	"	"	50,000	"	"	75,000 .	....
3	"	"	75,000	"	"	100,000 .	....
4	"	"	100,000	"	"	250,000 .	....
5	"	"	250,000	"	"	500,000 .	....
6	"	"	500,000	. . . .	....

Total additional or super tax . . . . $ ....

Total normal tax (1 per cent of amount entered on line 7) . . $ ....

Total tax liability . . . . $ ....

SPOTLIGHT ON TAXATION

The question of who pays a tax is not always as straightforward as who makes the payment. Economists use the term *tax burden* to more aptly describe which taxpayer bears the burden of the economic consequences of a tax. For example, although a retail store often makes the payment to the state for state sales taxes, the burden is generally thought to fall on the consumer.

currency is no longer based on the gold standard, the 16th Amendment's basis for measuring income, and therefore the tax itself, is invalid. Others have asserted that the federal income tax law forces the taxpayer to surrender his or her Fifth Amendment rights against self-incrimination. Federal courts, however, have denied virtually all of the protesters' challenges.

Congress has passed several laws to discourage tax protesters. Penalties that can be associated with filing a tax return with a **frivolous position** include penalties for the failure to pay, the failure to file, failure to pay estimated tax, the additional penalties under § 6651(f), accuracy-related penalties under § 6662, fraud penalties under § 6663, and erroneous claim for refund penalties under § 6676. Under § 6702, a $5,000 penalty is imposed for frivolous tax returns. The IRS periodically publishes notices which include a list of tax positions identified as frivolous. For example, a taxpayer claiming to be a citizen of a sovereign state (one of the 50 U.S. states) and thus not subject to U.S. taxation or arguing that he or she is not subject to U.S. income taxes under religious or moral beliefs are both on the list of frivolous positions. In 2016, the IRS released *The Truth about Frivolous Tax Arguments*, a 71-page document detailing the tax law (legislative, administrative, and judicial) that debunks most of the frivolous tax myths (see **www.irs.gov** for more detail).

The Tax Court can impose a penalty, not to exceed $25,000, if the taxpayer brings a frivolous matter before the court. Under §§ 6673 and 6702, a frivolous matter is one in which the intent is to delay the revenue collection process and the proceedings are found to be groundless, or the taxpayer unreasonably failed to pursue available administrative remedies. Sanctions can also be imposed against tax practitioners who participate in the litigation of frivolous tax return positions.

SPOTLIGHT ON TAXATION

Quotation

Like moths to a flame, some people find themselves irresistibly drawn to the tax protester movement's illusory claim that there is no legal requirement to pay federal income tax. And, like moths, these people sometimes get burned.

—Hon. Michael S. Kanne, 7th Circuit, U.S. Court of Appeals,
in *U.S. v. Sloan*, 939 F. 2d 499 (7th Cir. 1991)

4 U.S. Constitution

The U.S. Constitution is the source of all federal laws of the country, including both tax and nontax provisions. In addition to the 16th Amendment, however, the Constitution contains other provisions that bear upon the taxation process. For example, the Constitution provides that Congress may impose import taxes but not export taxes. Moreover, the constitutional rights of due process and of the privacy of the citizen apply in tax, as well as nontax, environments.

The Constitution also requires that taxes imposed by Congress apply uniformly throughout the United States. For instance, it would be unconstitutional for Congress to impose one federal income tax rate in California and another rate in Vermont. Moreover, except as provided by the 16th Amendment, the Constitution still bars per capita and other direct taxes, unless the revenues that are generated from these taxes are apportioned to the population of the states from which they were collected.

The federal courts have upheld the constitutionality of the estate and gift taxes because they are in the form of excise taxes on (the transfer of) property rather than direct taxes on individuals. Thus, one can conclude that, for better or worse, most future judicial challenges to the constitutionality of the elements of the federal tax structure probably will be fruitless.

One can find the original U.S. Constitution at the National Archives Museum in Washington, DC. Transcriptions can be found from many sources, including the National Archives Website (**www.archives.gov**). A convenient online printed version of the U.S. Constitution is also made available by the U.S. Government Publishing Office (**www.gpo.gov**).

An excerpt from the U.S. Constitution can be found in Exhibit 3-3.

EXHIBIT 3-3:   United States Constitution Excerpt (with Original Spelling)

WE THE PEOPLE of the United States, in Order to form a more perfect Union, establish Justice, insure domestic Tranquility, provide for the common defence (sic), promote the general Welfare, and secure the Blessings of Liberty to ourselves and our Posterity, do ordain and establish this Constitution for the United States of America.

Article I
Section. 1. *All legislative Powers herein granted shall be vested in a Congress of the United States, which shall consist of a Senate and House of Representatives.*

Section. 2. *The House of Representatives shall be composed of Members chosen every second Year by the People of the several States, and the Electors in each State shall have the Qualifications requisite for Electors of the most numerous Branch of the State Legislature.*

No Person shall be a Representative who shall not have attained to the Age of twenty-five Years, and been seven Years a Citizen of the United States, and who shall not, when elected, be an Inhabitant of that State in which he shall be chosen.

Representatives and direct Taxes shall be apportioned among the several States, which may be included within this Union, according to their respective Numbers, which shall be determined by adding to the whole Number of free Persons, including those bound to Service for a Term of Years, and excluding Indians not taxed, three fifths of all other Persons. The actual Enumeration shall be made within three Years after the first Meeting of the Congress of the United States, and within every subsequent Term of ten Years, in such Manner, as they shall by Law direct. The Number of Representatives shall not exceed one for every thirty Thousand, but each State shall have at Least one Representative; and until such enumeration shall be made, the State of New Hampshire shall be entitled to chuse (sic) three, Massachusetts eight, Rhode Island and Providence Plantations one, Connecticut five, New York six, New Jersey four, Pennsylvania eight, Delaware one, Maryland six, Virginia ten, North Carolina five, South Carolina five, and Georgia three.

When vacancies happen in the Representation from any State, the Executive Authority thereof shall issue Writs of Election to fill such Vacancies.

The House of Representatives shall chuse (sic) their Speaker and other Officers; and shall have the sole Power of Impeachment.

Section. 3. *The Senate of the United States shall be composed of two Senators from each State, chosen by the Legislature thereof, for six Years; and each Senator shall have one Vote.*

Immediately after they shall be assembled in Consequence of the first Election, they shall be divided as equally as may be into three Classes. The Seats of the Senators of the first Class shall be vacated at the Expiration of the second Year, of the second Class at the Expiration of the fourth Year, and of the third Class at the Expiration of the sixth Year, so that one third may be chosen every second Year; and if Vacancies happen by Resignation, or otherwise, during the Recess of the Legislature of any State, the Executive thereof may make temporary Appointments until the next Meeting of the Legislature, which shall then fill such Vacancies.

No Person shall be a Senator who shall not have attained to the Age of thirty Years, and been nine Years a Citizen of the United States, and who shall not, when elected, be an Inhabitant of that State for which he shall be chosen.

The Vice President of the United States shall be President of the Senate, but shall have no Vote, unless they be equally divided.

5 Tax Treaties

Tax treaties are agreements negotiated between countries concerning the treatment of individuals and entities subject to tax in both countries. The United States has entered into treaties with most of the major Western countries of the world. The overriding purpose of such treaties (also known as tax conventions) is to eliminate the "double taxation" that the taxpayer would face if his or her income were subject to tax in both countries. For example, a U.S. citizen who has generated income from an investment in the United Kingdom usually would be allowed a credit on her U.S. income tax return to the extent of any related UK taxes that she paid.

In the United States, tax treaties are normally negotiated under the Department of Treasury. Once the negotiations are complete, the treaty is submitted by the president to the Senate for ratification by at least a two-thirds majority. After Senate approval, the treaty gains the force of law once the president notifies the treaty partner country in accordance with the treaty terms.

SPOTLIGHT ON TAXATION

Treaties are often negotiated by the U.S. Treasury Department; however, before becoming effective, the Senate must ratify the treaty. According to the U.S. Department of State (**www.state.gov/s/l/treaty/pending/**), the Senate has over 40 treaties pending ratification, some as old as 1949 and some as recent as 2016. Included in the list are new or amended income tax treaties with countries such as Japan, Poland, Spain, Chile, and Hungary. The Senate has not ratified any tax treaties since 2010, when Rand Paul was elected senator and he put a "hold" on ratifications due to concerns with information privacy.

Any tax matter can be covered in a tax treaty with another country. Many times, there are multiple tax treaties with a given country. For example, one treaty will address income tax issues, while another treaty covers estate tax, and a third treaty addresses excise taxes. Although each treaty can be different, many are based on a model tax treaty and are only slightly modified. Thus, the structure and language of U.S. tax treaties can be fairly consistent, but a researcher should never assume that any particular treaty is the same as other treaties without reading the provisions in detail.

Treaties may be terminated in several ways. They may expire because of a specific congressional time limitation, be superseded by a newer treaty, or be terminated by the countries' mutual actions.

Treaties often contain unusual language that a new researcher may not be accustomed to. For example, many treaties are titled as **conventions** and amended by documents known as **protocols**. To assist with the interpretation of tax treaties, often a Treasury Department **technical explanation** is also provided. The technical explanation is a guide to help understand the treaty and generally reflects the policies behind treaty provisions, as well as understandings reached during the negotiations with respect to the application and interpretation of the treaty. In addition, a **Senate executive report** is often prepared by the Senate Foreign Relations Committee, and the Joint Committee on Taxation will also issue reports on treaties at times. Because the Government Publishing Office no longer prints complete copies of treaties, the treaty and related documents can be scattered on different sites on the Internet, such as those of the Treasury Department, the State Department, or the Senate. Fortunately, both Thomson Reuters Checkpoint and CCH IntelliConnect contain treaties and most collateral documents in the treaty sections of the databases. Tax treaties can also be found in the IRS Website at **www.irs.gov/Businesses /International-Businesses/United-States-Income-Tax-Treaties-A-to-Z**.

Tax researchers often find it necessary to examine the provisions of tax treaties.

EXAMPLE 3-1

Chiang Jiang is a U.S. citizen and operates her own business consulting firm specializing in financial services industry consulting. Chiang enters into a consulting arrangement with the National Bank of China. Under the arrangement, Chiang will travel to Shanghai and perform services for the bank for a term of about 90 days. During the visit, Chiang will work in the bank's offices and stay in a hotel. The bank will pay her $45,000 for her professional services. Chiang has no other business in China during any prior year. Chiang knows that U.S. tax law requires her to pay U.S. income taxes on her income earned in China. Chiang is trying to determine if her income earned in China will also be subjected to Chinese income taxes.

Exhibit 3-4 presents excerpts of the U.S.–China tax treaty that can be used to help resolve Chiang's tax issue. Chiang can refer to a number of sections of the U.S.-China Tax Treaty. Article 13, related to independent personal services would appear to speak to Chiang's business activities in China. Chiang is performing consulting services which certainly would appear to fit the professional services classification. Article 13 states that professional services will only be taxed in the "other" state (which for Chiang is China) if present in China for more than 183 days. Chiang's work is expected to last only 90 days and she does not expect to be in China for other work; thus it would appear that Chiang is not taxable in China. Also, per a review of Article 5, especially section 3, of the U.S.-China Tax Treaty, Chiang does not have a fixed base in China as she has no permanent establishment in China and does not expect to exceed 183 days. Lastly, if Chiang's work were somehow associated with her business in lieu of independent services, Article 7 with respect to business profits also appears to require permanent establishment before taxation in China would start.

In addition to the tax treaties, the U.S. government enters into non-tax international agreements that are not formal tax treaties; however, in many respects they function like one. Along with other provisions, these agreements address tax issues involving the parties associated with the agreement. Examples of such international agreements include the North American Free Trade Agreement (NAFTA) and the General Agreement on Tariffs and Trade (GATT). Other agreements might address the exchange of tax, banking, and securities information among countries.

Treaties are an important source of federal law. Most treaties do not address tax issues, but the ones that do have far-reaching effects. When dealing with a research problem that has international implications, the researcher must locate, read, and evaluate any tax treaty that applies to the client's problem. The researcher cannot rely on the more typical sources of tax research information because these references usually address only domestic tax precedents. Tax treaties often address issues such as the following:

- How to treat the business and investment income of the visiting taxpayer.

- When the visitor is subject to the host country's tax laws.

- How to offset the possibility of taxing the same income or assets more than once.

- How to compute the taxable amount in the host country.

- To what extent host-country withholding taxes are applied to the visitor's transactions.

- How taxes levied by a state/province/canton are treated by the taxpayer.

- What tax disclosures must be made by the visitor.

Treaties are surprisingly difficult to cite. Many citation suggestions refer to the United States Treaties and Other International Agreements (UST) or Treaties and Other International Acts Series (TIAS). The UST and the TIAS are no longer printed by the Government Publishing Office (last done in 1984). As a result, citing a tax treaty should generally be done as follows: treaty title, signing date (not effective date), parties, subdivision or article, and source. As an example, the treaty presented in Exhibit 3-4 could be cited as Income Tax Convention, November 21, 1986, United States—The People's Republic of China, Article 5, Thomson Reuters Checkpoint U.S. Tax Treaties in Force.

The Constitution provides that "Laws of the United States which shall be made in pursuance thereof; and all Treaties made, or which shall be made, under the Authority of the United States, shall be the supreme Law of the Land." An IRC provision and a provision under a treaty will sometimes conflict. In such a case, both provisions cannot represent the law; the one adopted later in time generally controls.

EXAMPLE 3-2

Prior to 1980, the United States negotiated treaties with several countries that allowed foreign taxpayers to sell U.S. real estate and not pay tax on gains. Under these treaties, nonresident aliens and foreign corporations could avoid U.S. taxes on real estate if the gains were treated as capital gains and were not effectively connected with the conduct of a U.S. business. Because of this favorable treatment for foreign investors, many U.S. farmers felt foreign investors were bidding up the price of farmland in the United States.

This and other concerns led Congress to pass the Foreign Investment in Real Property Tax Act (FIRPTA) of 1980. Under § 897, FIRPTA makes gains and losses by nonresident aliens and foreign corporations taxable by treating such transactions as effectively connected with a U.S. trade or business. This provision overrides any treaties in effect at that time by making foreign capital gains on real property taxable for transactions after 1984.

This later-in-time rule appears to be a simplistic approach to the complex interaction of the IRC and treaty provisions. The courts have presented interpretive guidelines to be used in resolving interstatutory conflicts. One such guideline is that, where possible, equal effect should be given to both statutes; congressional intent to repeal a statute should not be assumed. A significant judicial history also exists for the interaction of treaties and the IRC. In fact, as with conflicts between statutes, courts usually attempt to reconcile the apparent conflict in a way that gives consideration to both the treaty and IRC provisions.

The equality of the two types of provisions is indicated in § 7852(d) of the IRC, which provides that neither a treaty nor a law shall be given preferential status by reason of its being a treaty or a law. The language of both the IRC and the Constitution make this clear. The only codified exception to this rule is that treaty provisions that were in effect in 1954 and that conflicted with the 1954 code as originally enacted are given precedence over the existing provisions of the 1954 code, but not over later amendments to the code. Section 894 states that due regard shall be given to any treaty obligation of the United States that applies to the taxpayer when applying the provisions of the IRC.

EXHIBIT 3-4:   A Portion of a Tax Treaty

ARTICLE 5

(Permanent Establishment)

1. For the purposes of this Agreement, the term "permanent establishment" means a fixed place of business through which the business of an enterprise is wholly or partly carried on.

2. The term "permanent establishment" includes especially:

   (a)   a place of management;
   (b)   a branch;
   (c)   an office;
   (d)   a factory;
   (e)   a workshop; and
   (f)   a mine, an oil or gas well, a quarry or any other place of extraction of natural resources.

3. The term "permanent establishment" also includes:

   (a)   a building site, a construction, assembly or installation project, or supervisory activities in connection therewith, but only where such site, project or activities continue for a period of more than six months;
   (b)   an installation, drilling rig or ship used for the exploration or exploitation of natural resources, but only if so used for a period of more than three months; and
   (c)   the furnishing of services, including consultancy services, by an enterprise through employees or other personnel engaged by the enterprise for such purpose, but only where such activities continue (for the same or a connected project) within the country for a period or periods aggregating more than six months within any twelve month period.

ARTICLE 7

(Business Profits)

1. The profits of an enterprise of a Contracting State shall be taxable only in that Contracting State unless the enterprise carries on business in the other Contracting State through a permanent establishment situated therein. If the enterprise carries on business as aforesaid, the profits of the enterprise may be taxed in the other Contracting State but only so much of them as is attributable to that permanent establishment.

ARTICLE 13

(Independent Personal Services)

1. Income derived by an individual who is a resident of a Contracting State in respect of professional services or other activities of an independent character shall be taxable only in that Contracting State, unless he has a fixed base regularly available to him in the other Contracting State for the purpose of performing his activities or he is present in that other Contracting State for a period or periods exceeding in the aggregate 183 days in the calendar year concerned. If he has such a fixed base or remains in that other Contracting State for the aforesaid period or periods, the income may be taxed in that other Contracting State, but only so much of it as is attributable to that fixed base or is derived in that other Contracting State during the aforesaid period or periods.

2. The term "professional services" includes, especially, independent scientific, literary, artistic, educational or teaching activities as well as the independent activities of physicians, lawyers, engineers, architects, dentists and accountants.

6 The Legislative Process

To understand how to research tax issues, the tax researcher must have a grasp of the federal legislative process. United States tax law, like automobiles and hot dogs, is created in a multistep process. At each stage in the creation of a tax law, Congress generates additional items of information, each of which may be useful in addressing a client's tax problem.

Most tax legislation begins in the House of Representatives. In the House, tax law changes are considered by the **Ways and Means Committee**. Upon approval by this committee, the bill is sent to the full House of Representatives for its approval. The bill then is sent to the Senate, where it is referred to the **Finance Committee**. After the Finance Committee approves the bill, the proposal is considered by the entire Senate.

If any differences between the House and Senate versions of the tax bill exist (which is almost always the case), the bill is referred to a conference committee, where these differences are resolved. The compromise bill must be approved by both houses of Congress before it is forwarded to the president. If the president signs the bill, the new provisions are incorporated into the IRC.

If the bill is vetoed by the president, however, it is not enacted unless Congress overrides the veto with a sufficient revote. Exhibit 3-5 summarizes the usual steps of the legislative process as it is encountered relative to tax legislation.

EXHIBIT 3-5:   Legislative Process to Amend the Tax Law

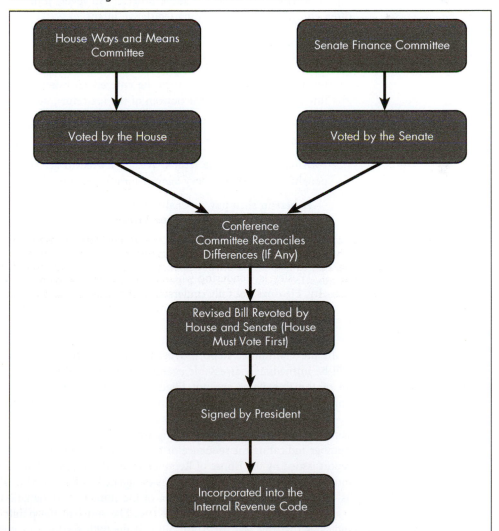

6-1 Committee Reports

As bills pass through the houses of Congress, often the committees that handle the bills will publish reports known generally as **committee reports**. Committee reports explain the elements of the proposed changes to the bill and the reasons for each of the proposals. These committee reports are an important tool for tax researchers. In many situations in which the tax law is unclear or legislation has recently been passed, they can provide insight concerning the meaning of a specific phrase of the statute or the intention of Congress concerning a certain provision of the law. Although not listed in the citation, committee reports are most often issued by the Senate Finance Committee or the House Committee on Ways and Means. If the house and senate versions of the bill are sent to conference, then a **conference committee** report can also be issued. Often the Joint Committee on Taxation, a committee made up of five members of the House and five members of the Senate, will issue reports that explain tax bills but do not constitute legislation. As a result, Joint Committee on Taxation reports on enacted legislation (sometimes known as "Blue Books") carry a lower level of authority than a committee report issued during the legislative process. However, Joint Committee reports are still often considered in determining legislative intent.

EXAMPLE 3-3

Wesley Gripes, a single taxpayer, decided to join the tax protestor movement. On his current year tax return, he entered an asterisk next to each significant line on Form 1040. At the bottom of the tax return, he handwrote the following:

> The entry indicates I am specifically claiming the Constitutional right to remain silent under the 5th amendment.

After mailing in the return, Wesley started to get anxious about the possible penalties the IRS may levy against him under § 6702:

> A person shall pay a penalty of $5,000 if such person files what purports to be a return of a tax imposed by this title but which (a) does not contain information on which the substantial correctness of the self-assessment can be judged....

Wesley is wondering whether his return will subject him to the $5,000 penalty. He does not fully understand what the language of the code section means, so he reviews the Senate Report (S. Rept. 97-530) issued with the law as shown in Exhibit 3-6.

In the Committee Report, Wesley finds that the Senate considers that "the penalty will be immediately assessable against any individual filing a "return" in which many or all of the line items are not filled in except for references to spurious constitutional objections." As a result, it would appear that Wesley is likely to be charged the penalty.

Committee reports generally are referred to by a public law number. The citation contains the session of Congress during which the new legislation was passed, followed by a number indicating the sequence of the report. For example, H. Rept. 107-189 is the 189th report issued by the House of Representatives during the 107th Congress. In a similar fashion, the Tax Reform Act of 1986 was designated as P.L. 99-514. "Public law" is abbreviated as "P.L." in this context. The prefix of the numerical designation (here, 99) refers to the session of Congress that passed the law. The suffix of the public law number (here, 514) indicates that this was the 514th bill that the 99th session of Congress adopted.

EXHIBIT 3-6: Committee Report

Penalty for frivolous returns ('82 Tax Equity and Fiscal Responsibility Act, PL 97-248, September 3, 1982)

Senate Explanation

Present Law.

Under the present law, a taxpayer who files a protest return (such as one refusing to pay tax because the U.S. is no longer on the gold standard) may be subject to a penalty for failure to file a return, or for negligence or fraud. These penalties, however, are measured as a percentage of the underpayment of tax. Thus, if a taxpayer has paid at least the correct amount of tax through estimated tax or wage withholding, there is no penalty for filing a protest return. In addition, even when there is an underpayment, it may take several years of administrative and judicial proceedings before any penalty is imposed.

Explanation of Provision.

The bill provides that an immediately assessable penalty of $500 will be imposed on any individual who files any document which purports to be a return of income tax if (1) the document fails to contain information from which the substantial correctness of the amount of tax shown on the return can be judged or contains information that on its face indicates that the amount of tax shown on the return is substantially incorrect, and (2) such conduct arises from a position taken by the taxpayer on the purported return which is frivolous, or from a desire which appears on the face of the purported return, to delay or impede the administration of the Federal income tax laws. The penalty will be imposed, therefore, only on purported returns that are patently improper and not in cases involving valid disputes with the Secretary. This penalty will not be imposed, of course, in the case of innocent or inadvertent mathematical or clerical errors. *******

For example, the penalty under this provision is immediately assessable against any individual who files, as a purported a document appearing at first glance to be a but which contains altered or incorrect descriptions of line items or other altered provisions. Such purported "returns" are clearly not designed to inform the Secretary of the filer's taxable income and are not in processible form. The penalty will be immediately assessable against any individual filing a "return" in which many or all of the line items are not filled in except for references to spurious constitutional objections. Furthermore, the penalty is available against any individual filing a purported return in which insufficient information to calculate the tax is given or where the information given is clearly inconsistent (as where an individual claims 99 exemptions but lists only a few dependents) or where the return otherwise reveals a frivolous position or a desire to impede the tax laws. Moreover, the penalty could be imposed against any individual filing a "return" showing an incorrect tax due, or a reduced tax due, because of the individual's claim of a clearly unallowable deduction, such as a "gold standard deduction" (i.e., a discount of dollars because the U.S. is not on the gold standard) or a "war tax" deduction under which the taxpayer reduces his taxable income or shows a reduced tax due by that individual's estimate of the amount of his taxes going to the Defense Department budget, etc. In contrast, the penalty will not apply if the taxpayer shows the correct tax due but refuses to pay the tax. In such a case, of course, the Secretary can assess and collect the tax immediately. *******

Because it is unnecessary to determine the taxpayer's true tax liability before imposing the penalty, the penalty is immediately assessable. The deficiency procedures, under which the taxpayer would receive advance notice before assessment, do not apply to this penalty. There is, however, a provision allowing for district court review of the assessment on payment of 15 percent of the amount assessed and the filing of a claim for refund of the amount paid (see sec. 322 of the bill). This district court review is not one with respect to the taxpayer's actual liability for any tax for the taxable year. It is merely a determination of whether the penalty under this provision was properly imposed. The district court's opinion cannot, therefore, have any res judicata or collateral estoppel effect on the issue of the taxpayer's actual tax liability for the taxable year. This penalty is in addition to all other penalties provided by law.

Conference Report

* * * * * *

The conference agreement follows the Senate amendment, except that the exclusion for inadvertent mathematical or clerical errors is deleted as unnecessary.

Senate Explanation

Effective Date.

This penalty will apply to documents filed after the date of enactment.

Congressional sessions last for two years; therefore, the researcher may find it useful to construct a method by which to identify the two-year period in which a tax law was passed. Recent and forthcoming sessions of Congress are identified as follows:

Congressional Sessions	Years
111th	2009–10
112th	2011–12
113th	2013–14
114th	2015–16
115th	2017–18
116th	2019–20
117th	2021–22

6-2 Where to Find Committee Reports

When a new tax law is passed, the pertinent committee reports are released in the IRS's weekly Internal Revenue Bulletin. The texts of the 1954 committee reports relative to the IRC are found not in the Cumulative Bulletin but in the United States Code Congressional and Administrative News. All of the pre-1939 Revenue Act committee reports are reprinted in the 1939 Cumulative Bulletin.

The committee reports and other legislative items can also be found in most subscription online tax services (e.g., Checkpoint) and on various nonsubscription Internet sites, such as the following:

- **http://congress.gov**

- **http://waysandmeans.house.gov**

- **http://finance.senate.gov/**

- **www.jct.gov**

CCH and Thomson Reuters both publish a collection of committee reports (or excerpts thereof) whenever a major new tax law is passed. If a tax researcher wants to find the committee reports that underlie a statutory provision, he or she also can use reference materials that are included in the bodies of most commercial tax services.

Besides the committee reports, the floor debate report may be of value to the tax researcher. The floor debate report includes a summary of what was said from the floor of the House or Senate concerning the proposed bill. It may include some detailed or technical information that is excluded from the committee report(s). The floor debate report is included in the Congressional Record for the day of the debate.

Citations to committee reports will vary depending on source, such as Senate, House, Joint Conference, or Joint Committee on Taxation. For example, a Senate committee report could be cited as S. Rep. 104-281 (to accompany H.R. 3448), P.L. 104-188, Small Business Job Protection Act of 1996. A House report would refer to the House committee, and a Joint Conference report uses *U.S. Congress* and the joint committee's name. Joint Committee on Taxation reports can be cited using the report name, for example, JCX-63-00.

7 Internal Revenue Code

After the 16th Amendment was ratified in 1913, Congress passed a series of self-contained revenue acts, each of which formed the entire income tax law of the United States. For about two decades, Congress passed such a freestanding revenue act every year or two. By the 1930s, however, this series of revenue acts, and the task of rewriting the entire tax statute so often, had become unmanageable. Thus, in 1939, Congress replaced the revenue acts with the Internal Revenue Code of 1939, the first fully organized federal tax law.

Although the concept of a freestanding tax code, as part of the entire United States Code, was a good idea, the organization of the Internal Revenue Code of 1939 left little room to accommodate subsequent changes to the law. Accordingly, the 1939 Code was replaced with a reorganized, more flexible codification in 1954. Because of extensive revisions to the code that were made as part of the Tax Reform Act of 1986, the statute was renamed the Internal Revenue Code of 1986. Thus, although the statute still follows the 1954 numbering system and organization, the official title of the extant U.S. tax law is the *Internal Revenue Code of 1986, as Amended*.

The principal sources of tax laws of the United States since 1913, then, have been identified as follows:

Period	Principal U.S. Tax Law
1913–39	Periodic Revenue Acts
1939–54	Internal Revenue Code of 1939
1954–86	Internal Revenue Code of 1954
1986–Present	Internal Revenue Code of 1986

Many provisions of the 1939 Code were carried over to the Internal Revenue Code of 1954 without substantive change; some of these sections were adopted into the code verbatim, although all sections were renumbered as part of the 1954 reorganization.

SPOTLIGHT ON TAXATION

Growth of the Code

According to the Tax Foundation, an independent tax policy research organization, the 2015 IRC plus the Federal Tax Regulations reached over 10 million words. These two sources of tax law were a mere 1.4 million words in 1955.

The **Internal Revenue Code** is part of the United States Code (USC), which is a codification of all of the federal laws of the United States. The elements of the USC are organized more or less alphabetically by subject and assigned title numbers. Accordingly, the IRC constitutes Title 26 of the USC and is located between Title 25 (Indians) and Title 26 (Intoxicating Liquors). Because tax researchers almost exclusively work with the IRC section of the USC, Title 26 is often omitted from citations. If the researcher is working with other titles of the USC in a document, the complete title number should be used to avoid confusion. In addition, many tax lawyers as a matter of habit will use citations including title number.

7-1 Organization of the Internal Revenue Code

The IRC is organized into an outline form with multiple levels or subdivisions. The primary levels found in the code are as follows:

Subtitles
  Chapters
    Subchapters
      Parts
        Sections
          Subsections

Subtitles of the code are assigned a capital letter to identify them (currently A through K are used). Generally, each subtitle contains all the tax provisions that relate to a well-defined area of the tax law. Exhibit 3-7 identifies the subtitles of the current code.

The tax researcher spends most of his or her time working with Subtitles A, Income Taxes; B, Estate and Gift Taxes; and F, Procedure and Administration. The other subtitles typically are used only from time to time for special research problems.

Each subtitle contains a number of chapters, numbered, although not continuously, from 1 through 100. These chapter numbers do not start over at each subtitle; rather, they are used in ascending order throughout the code. Thus, for example, there is only one Chapter 11 in the IRC, not 11 of them. Each chapter contains the tax provisions that relate to a more narrowly defined area of the tax law than is addressed by the subtitles. Most of the subtitles include several chapters. Exhibit 3-8 examines the numbering system of the chapters of the IRC, concentrating on selected important chapters.

The chapters of the IRC are further divided into subchapters. Typically, a subchapter contains a group of provisions that relate to a fairly specific area of the tax law. Subchapters sometimes are divided into parts, which may be divided into subparts. Letters are used to denote subchapters, and the lettering scheme starts over with each chapter. Thus, there may be a Subchapter A in each chapter.

Many times, tax practitioners use the subchapter designation as a shorthand reference to identify a certain area of taxation. For example, Subchapter C of Chapter 1 of Subtitle A of the IRC includes many of the basic corporate income tax provisions. Thus, when a

EXHIBIT 3-7:   Subtitles of the Internal Revenue Code, as Amended

Subtitle	Tax Law Included
A	Income Taxes
B	Estate and Gift Taxes
C	Employment Taxes
D	Miscellaneous Excise Taxes
E	Alcohol, Tobacco, and Certain Other Excise Taxes
F	Procedure and Administration
G	The Joint Committee on Taxation
H	Financing of Presidential Election Campaigns
I	Trust Fund Code
J	Coal Industry Health Benefits
K	Group Health Plan Requirements

EXHIBIT 3-8: Key Chapters of the Internal Revenue Code

Chapter	Subjects Included
1	Normal Taxes and Surtaxes
2	Self-Employment Tax
6	Consolidated Returns
11	Estate Taxes
12	Gift Taxes
61	Administration/Information
79	Definitions

tax practitioner wants to refer to a corporate tax matter, he or she often simply identifies it as a "Subchapter C" issue. Similarly, "Subchapter K" refers to partnership tax provisions. Exhibit 3-9 shows the various subchapters included in Chapter 1 (Normal Taxes and Surtaxes) of Subtitle A (Income Taxes).

EXHIBIT 3-9: Subtitle A: Table of Contents Excerpt

Subtitle A Income Taxes §§ 1–1564

 Chapter 1 Normal Taxes and Surtaxes §§ 1–1400t

   Subchapter A Determination of Tax Liability §§ 1–59b

   Subchapter B Computation of Taxable Income §§ 61–291

   Subchapter C Corporate Distributions and Adjustments §§ 301–385

   Subchapter D Deferred Compensation, etc. §§ 401–436

   Subchapter E Accounting Periods and Methods of Accounting §§ 441–483

   Subchapter F Exempt Organizations §§ 501–530

   Subchapter G Corporations used to Avoid Income Tax on Shareholders §§ 531–565

   Subchapter H Banking Institutions §§ 581–597

   Subchapter I Natural Resources §§ 611–638

   Subchapter J Estates, Trusts, Beneficiaries, and Decedents §§ 641–692

   Subchapter K Partners and Partnerships §§ 701–777

   Subchapter L Insurance Companies §§ 801–848

   Subchapter M Regulated Investment Companies and Real Estate Investment Trusts §§ 851–860L

   Subchapter N Tax Based on Income from Sources within or without the United States §§ 861–999

   Subchapter O Gain or Loss on Disposition of Property §§ 1001–1111

   Subchapter P Capital Gains and Losses §§ 1201–1298

   Subchapter Q Readjustment of Tax between Years and Special Limitations §§ 1301–1351

   Subchapter R Election to Determine Corporate Tax on Certain International Shipping … §§ 1352–1359

   Subchapter S Tax Treatment of S Corporations and Their Shareholders §§ 1361–1379

Tax researchers must pay careful attention to the subtitle, chapter, and subchapter they are using to support conclusions. For example, a keyword search for *wages* may facilitate the researcher accidentally relying on a code section that addresses wages for employment tax purposes (§ 3121) when the income tax definition under § 61 is the relevant source. Knowing where in the code the section is located is critical to confirming the correct tax law.

Most of the code's subchapters are divided into parts. The parts provide a natural grouping of provisions that address essentially the same issue. Not all subchapters are divided into parts, and occasionally the parts are not numbered consecutively. For instance, the parts of Chapter 1, Subchapter A (Determination of Tax Liability) are as follows:

Part I	Tax on Individuals
Part II	Tax on Corporations
Part III	Changes in Rates during a Taxable Year
Part IV	Credits against Tax
Part V	Repealed
Part VI	Alternative Minimum Tax
Part VII	Repealed [Environmental Tax]
Part VIII	Repealed [Supplemental Medicare Premium]

The most important division of the IRC for the tax researcher is the section, because the code is arranged so that its primary unit is the section number. The sections currently are numbered 1 through 9834, although not all the numbers are used. Each section number is used only once in the code. The researcher can refer to a specific provision of the IRC by its section number and not be concerned about duplication in another part of the law. Indeed, the most common element of the jargon of the tax practitioner community is the code section number, and tax researchers must learn to identify important tax provisions merely by the corresponding section number.

Code sections can be divided into various smaller elements for the convenience of the drafter or user of the section. A section can contain subsections, paragraphs, subparagraphs, and clauses. Sections are denoted by numbers (1, 2, etc.), subsections by lowercase letters (a, b, etc.), paragraphs by numbers, subparagraphs by capital letters (A, B, etc.), and clauses by lowercase roman numerals (i, ii, etc.). In citing a code section, one uses parentheses for each division that occurs after the section number. Occasionally, the code is constructed in a way that includes **flush language**. This is language that does not appear to be associated with any particular subsection, paragraph, or other element of the section.

There are some exceptions to the general formatting of code section citations. For example, Congress has inserted code sections in between other consecutive sections and has had to use a capital letter [e.g., § 25A(b)(1) or § 280F(a)(1)] to accomplish this. The addition of a capital letter results in a different code section. For example, § 25A is a different code section than § 25(a).

Exhibit 3-10 shows the breakdown of code § 121 into its subsections, paragraphs, subparagraphs, clauses, and flush language.

Although there are nearly a thousand code sections, certain ones contain basic principles that affect most tax situations (Exhibit 3-11). The tax researcher should be familiar with this group of code sections for efficient analysis of his or her clients' tax problems.

EXHIBIT 3-10: Interpreting a Code Section Citation

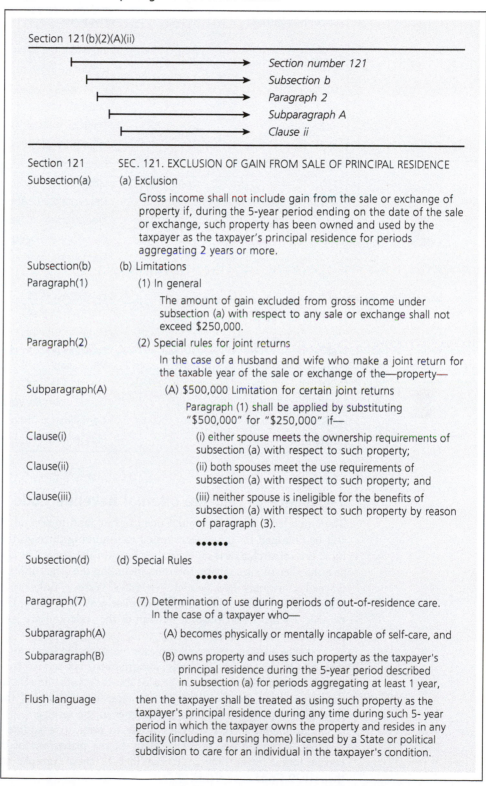

Section 121(b)(2)(A)(ii)

	Section number 121
	Subsection b
	Paragraph 2
	Subparagraph A
	Clause ii

Section 121	SEC. 121. EXCLUSION OF GAIN FROM SALE OF PRINCIPAL RESIDENCE
Subsection(a)	(a) Exclusion
	Gross income shall not include gain from the sale or exchange of property if, during the 5-year period ending on the date of the sale or exchange, such property has been owned and used by the taxpayer as the taxpayer's principal residence for periods aggregating 2 years or more.
Subsection(b)	(b) Limitations
Paragraph(1)	(1) In general
	The amount of gain excluded from gross income under subsection (a) with respect to any sale or exchange shall not exceed $250,000.
Paragraph(2)	(2) Special rules for joint returns
	In the case of a husband and wife who make a joint return for the taxable year of the sale or exchange of the—property—
Subparagraph(A)	(A) $500,000 Limitation for certain joint returns
	Paragraph (1) shall be applied by substituting "$500,000" for "$250,000" if—
Clause(i)	(i) either spouse meets the ownership requirements of subsection (a) with respect to such property;
Clause(ii)	(ii) both spouses meet the use requirements of subsection (a) with respect to such property; and
Clause(iii)	(iii) neither spouse is ineligible for the benefits of subsection (a) with respect to such property by reason of paragraph (3).
	• • • • • •
Subsection(d)	(d) Special Rules
	• • • • • •
Paragraph(7)	(7) Determination of use during periods of out-of-residence care. In the case of a taxpayer who—
Subparagraph(A)	(A) becomes physically or mentally incapable of self-care, and
Subparagraph(B)	(B) owns property and uses such property as the taxpayer's principal residence during the 5-year period described in subsection (a) for periods aggregating at least 1 year,
Flush language	then the taxpayer shall be treated as using such property as the taxpayer's principal residence during any time during such 5- year period in which the taxpayer owns the property and resides in any facility (including a nursing home) licensed by a State or political subdivision to care for an individual in the taxpayer's condition.

EXHIBIT 3-11: Some Important Code Sections

Section Number	Contents
1	Individual Tax Rates
11	Corporate Tax Rates
61	Definition of Gross Income
62	Deductions for Adjusted Gross Income
162	Trade or Business Deductions
163	Interest Deduction
164	Deduction for Taxes
165	Losses
167, 168, 179	Depreciation, Cost Recovery
212	Production-of-Income Expenses
312	Corporate Dividends
351	Forming a Corporation
368	Mergers, Acquisitions, Corporate Break-Ups
469	Passive Activities
501	Tax-Exempt Status
721	Forming a Partnership, LLC
861	Sourcing of International Income and Deductions
904	Foreign Tax Credit
1245	Depreciation Recapture
1504	Consolidated Taxable Income
6662	Penalties for Inaccurate Tax Filings

7-2 Where to Find the Internal Revenue Code

The amended Internal Revenue Code can be found in several places. A print version can still be obtained for those accustomed to thumbing through the large volumes; however, most tax researchers use an electronic form of the code. The code is available for no cost at a number of sites on the Internet, including the Legal Information Institute hosted by Cornell University Law School (the IRS's Website links to this source) and the U.S. House of Representatives at **uscode.house.gov**. Of course, the major tax services also provide a searchable electronic version of the code and are generally kept current as tax law changes are enacted.

The type of tax service will indicate the probable location of the original language of the code in the service. Typically, an annotated tax service (refer to Chapter 2 to review this definition) will include the text of the code with the related section's discussion. On the other hand, a topical tax service typically reproduces the text of the code in an appendix to pertinent chapters or volumes of the service.

Occasionally, a tax researcher needs to refer to a source that originated from the Internal Revenue Code of 1939. Many of the provisions of the 1986 (and 1954) code can be found in the 1939 code. Exhibit 3-12 gives examples of 1986 Code sections and their 1939 Code equivalents.

EXHIBIT 3-12: Examples of 1986 Code Sections Derived from the 1939 Code

1986 Code Section	1939 Code Section
§ 61, Gross Income Defined	§ 22(a)
§ 71, Alimony and Separate Maintenance Payments	§ 22(k)
§ 103, Interest on State and Local Bonds	§ 22(b)(4)
§ 151, Allowance of Deductions for Personal Exemptions	§ 25(b)
§ 162, Trade or Business Expenses	§ 23(a)(1)
§ 172, Net Operating Loss Deduction	§ 122
§ 212, Expenses for Production of Income	§ 23(a)(2)
§ 301, Distributions of Property	§§ 22(e), 115(a), (b), (d), (e)
§ 316, Dividends Defined	§ 115(a), (b)
§ 701, Partners, not Partnership, Subject to Tax	§ 181

Other useful indices to the code itself are provided in commercial tax research services. For example, several useful tables are available from the CCH IntelliConnect Tax Service under its "Current I.R.C. Finding Lists." In Cross-Reference Table I, 1939 code sections are cross-referenced to their 1954 (and 1986) counterparts. In Table II, current code sections are cross-referenced to the 1939 code. Table III cross-references the code sections within the current code.

These three tables can be useful to the tax researcher when he or she needs to find a 1939 code section number, perhaps in interpreting a court case that addresses a pre-1954 code issue, identifying situations in which a code section is referred to elsewhere in the current code, or finding out whether other code sections provide information bearing on the section being reviewed.

One other publication is valuable if the researcher is addressing issues that predate the 1954 code. Seidman's *Legislative History of Federal Income Tax Laws* details the historical evolution of the early tax law. It explains how certain provisions evolved into their current form in the code.

Most tax services also contain information about the history of each code section. Typically, at the end of the text of each code section, or as a related page that can be accessed by linking, the editors include a list of the public laws that have altered or amended the section. This listing generally includes a reference to the section as it existed prior to amendment as well as the effective date of the amendment. The tax researcher must be careful to consider the impact of any such amendments. Exhibit 3-13 illustrates the public law history with respect to a specific code section.

7-3 Interpreting the Internal Revenue Code

One of the greatest problems for a tax researcher is the interpretation of the IRC. Often, code provisions are long, interrelated, and confusing. In researching a client's tax problem, one must read each code section that might apply. Many times, a single phrase or clause in the section may prevent the client from being subject to the provision or may contain other unexpected implications for the client's situation.

A researcher, in his or her initial review, may find the topical index, which is included by most publishers of the code, a useful tool in locating a starting point or the relevant code section. In reading, interpreting, and evaluating a selected code section, the tax

EXHIBIT 3-13: Recent History for Code § 101

In 2006, P.L. 109-280, Sec. 863(a), added subsec. (j) P.L. 109-280, Sec. 863(c)(1), substituted "subsection (f), and subsection (j)" for "and subsection (f)" in para. (a) (1), effective for life insurance contracts issued after 8/17/2006, for a contract issued after 8/17/2006 pursuant to an exchange described in Code Sec. 1035 for a contract issued on or prior to 8/17/2006. For purposes of the preceding sentence, any material increase in the death benefit or other material change shall cause the contract to be treated as a new contract except that, in the case of a master contract (within the meaning of Code Sec. 264(f)(4)(E)), the addition of covered lives shall be treated as a new contract only with respect to such additional covered lives.

In 2003, P.L. 108-121, Sec. 110(b)(1), added para. (i)(4) P.L. 108-121, Sec. 110(b)(2), added "or astronauts" after "victims" in the heading of subsec. (i), effective for amounts paid after 12/31/2002, with respect to deaths occurring after 12/31/2002.

In 2002, P.L. 107-134, Sec. 102(a), added subsec. (i), effective for tax. yrs. end. before, on, or after 9/11/2001. Sec. 102(b)(2) of this Act, provides:

"(2) Waiver of limitations. If refund or credit of any overpayment of tax resulting from the amendments made by this section is prevented at any time before the close of the 1-year period beginning on the date of the enactment of this Act by the operation of any law or rule of law (including res judicata), such refund or credit may nevertheless be made or allowed if claim therefore is filed before the close of such period."

---

researcher must be especially attentive to the language used throughout the section. Many, if not most, code sections contain a general rule, followed by specific conditions that must be satisfied in order to apply the provision and situations under which the taxpayer is not subject to the general rule. In some cases, the exceptions to the general rule are further modified to provide for exceptions to the general exceptions. Moreover, some exceptions to a code section are addressed not within the same section but in another section of the code. Therefore, all relevant provisions must be read carefully.

EXAMPLE 3-4

Paula, a self-employed taxpayer from the United States, is planning on going on a business trip to London to attend a business-related conference. The conference begins on a Monday and ends on Thursday. In order to be in London in time for the start of the conference, Paula's flight will leave on Sunday and arrive the same day. She will spend four nights at the conference hotel (Sunday through Wednesday) and then check out Thursday morning, attend the conference through Thursday afternoon, and then she is taking a train to Windsor outside of London to do some sight-seeing. She will spend Thursday and Friday in Windsor and return home to the United States on Saturday. Paula is wondering what part of her trip is deductible.

Most business expenses are deductible under § 162 of the code:

§ 162(a) There shall be allowed as a deduction all the ordinary and necessary expenses paid or incurred during the taxable year in carrying on any trade or business, including—

(1) a reasonable allowance for salaries or other compensation for personal services actually rendered;

(2) traveling expenses (including amounts expended for meals and lodging other than amounts which are lavish or extravagant under

the circumstances) while away from home in the pursuit of a trade or business; and

Paula sees that business travel expenses away from home are deductible under § 162(a)(2). Her expenses are not extravagant, and her trip is "mostly" related to business. Paula notices that there are no other limitations that apply to her anywhere else within § 162 and thus assumes deductibility.

However, § 274 provides for a number of limitations on expenses.

§ 274(c) Certain foreign travel.

> (1) In general. In the case of any individual who travels outside the United States away from home in pursuit of a trade or business or in pursuit of an activity described in section 212, no deduction shall be allowed under section 162 or section 212 for that portion of the expenses of such travel otherwise allowable under such section which, under regulations prescribed by the Secretary, is not allocable to such trade or business or to such activity.

Armed with the knowledge of § 274(c), Paula now realizes that the portion of her trip associated with personal travel is not deductible. Using the associated Regulations (see Chapter 4), she would need to categorize her expenses as business or nonbusiness related to determine her deductible portion.

However, § 274 also contains an exception to the general rule under § 274(c)(1):

> (2) Exception. Paragraph (1) shall not apply to the expenses of any travel outside the United States away from home if—
>
> (A) such travel does not exceed one week, or
>
> > (B) the portion of the time of travel outside the United States away from home which is not attributable to the pursuit of the taxpayer's trade or business or an activity described in section 212 is less than 25 percent of the total time on such travel.

Now Paula sees that she can take the full deduction for her travel expenses as her entire trip does not exceed one week.

In addition to being aware of the required conditions for application of a section, as well as the exceptions thereto, the researcher must be aware of the definitions of terms used in the section; pertinent definitions may be given within the section or in some other provision of the code. These definitions may be significantly different from the common use of the term.

While many common terms used in the code are defined in IRC § 7701, these definitions may be superseded by material contained within the applicable code section. In addition, the researcher may need to look beyond the code, such as to the regulations or other authority, to determine the conditions that a specific term may encompass. In all cases, the researcher should avoid jumping to premature conclusions until a thorough analysis of all relevant code sections has been completed.

The tax researcher must be careful not to overlook words that connect phrases, such as *and* and *or*. These words have very different logical meanings, and even when the words are "hidden" at the end of the previous clause or subparagraph, they may significantly change the outcome of a research project. The word *and* is conjunctive; the word *or* is disjunctive. If the word *and* lies between two phrases, both of them must be true for the provision to apply to the client's problem. However, if the word *or* lies between two phrases, then only one of them must be true for the provision to apply.

The researcher also must be careful with words that modify percentage or dollar amounts. The phrases "less than 50 percent," "more than 50 percent," and "not less than 50 percent" have very different meanings in determining whether the provisions of a section apply. The researcher also must distinguish between such terms as "30 days" and "one month," because they usually identify different time periods.

Conflicting code sections can also be problematic, as illustrated below.

EXAMPLE 3-5

Paul is a roofing contractor and has a truck he uses 100 percent of the time in his business. The truck cost $35,000 three years ago, and Paul has claimed cost recovery deductions of $24,920 on the truck, which leaves him an adjusted basis of $10,080. Paul sells the truck for $22,080, resulting in a gain of $12,000 on the truck. How is he to treat this gain for tax purposes?

In the IRC, Paul finds that when depreciable property used in a trade or business [§ 1231(b)] is sold, the gain is treated as a long-term capital gain [§ 1231(a)]. Thus, he might report the gain on his tax return as a long-term capital gain. In § 1245(a), however, Paul discovers that gain on depreciable personal property (in this case, the truck) is ordinary income to the extent of depreciation claimed since 1961. Thus, § 1245 would indicate the gain is ordinary, not long-term capital.

How is the problem resolved? In § 1245(d), Paul finds a directive that the recapture provision "shall apply notwithstanding any other provision of this subtitle [of the Code]." As a result, he must report the gain on this tax return as ordinary income, not long-term capital gain.

If Paul had read only § 1231 of the code and not § 1245, he would have arrived at a different conclusion about the gain. In many situations, when code sections conflict, the resolution of the conflict may not be as easy as in this example.

SPOTLIGHT ON TAXATION

Confusion in the Code

Self-employed taxpayers are eligible to deduct a certain amount of their health care insurance premium under § 162(l). In addition, under § 36B (added as part of the Affordable Care Act), certain taxpayers receive a subsidy against their health care premiums through the Premium Tax Credit. Although the code sections seem fairly straightforward, in practice, the amount of the deduction depends on the amount of the tax credit, and the amount of the tax credit depends on the amount of the deduction! This means the logic to calculate both is circular.

When analyzing a provision that recently has been changed by Congress, a researcher must be very careful to cross-reference all uses of terms whose definitions have been affected by the new law. Often, Congress does not use the care necessary to ascertain that all loose ends of new provisions have been tied up. In recent years, almost every major change in the tax law has been followed by a "technical corrections act" to remove errors in implementing and interpreting the new provisions of the law as well as to clarify problems that arise in integrating the new provisions with the existing provisions of the code. Most of these corrections are identified by practitioners whose clients' situations are adversely affected by a given reading of the amended law. Thus, the typical technical corrections act testifies as much to the thoroughness of the practitioners' research as to shoddy drafting of the law by Congress.

Because the provisions of the IRC change frequently, the researcher must be aware of the effective dates of the various changes to the law. A provision may not go into effect immediately upon its adoption by Congress. The date of the act with which the change in law is passed is not always indicative of a provision's effective date. Often, various provisions under the same tax law will become effective on different dates and, in fact, may have effective dates that precede the date of the tax act. Similarly, when a provision of the tax law is deleted from the code, the provision may be left in effect for a designated period of time before it actually expires. Transitional rules may also apply. The effective date for a change in the tax law usually may be found in the explanation of the public laws (or code history) which follows the pertinent code section (see Exhibit 3-13). In some cases, the researcher may need to look to the explanation under another code section for the effective date of a provision. The researcher must be careful to align the client's facts with the effective law at the pertinent dates, or a serious mistake could be made in the research conclusion.

In recent decades, Congress has taken to creating code sections that have annual cost-of-living adjustments. For example, the tax schedules used to compute individual tax liability found in § 1 reflect the tax brackets at the time this section was last amended. As a result, using § 1 to determine current tax liability amounts would result in the incorrect tax. As prescribed in § 1(f)(1), the Treasury Department is required to issue new tables that reflect a cost-of-living adjustment each year; thus the current year tables must be found outside of the code in order to properly calculate the tax.

Congress has also legislated code sections that expire at a set date (often referred to as sunset provisions). Often these are used to prevent revenue erosion over the budget period when the legislation is enacted. For example, § 213(f) provides that the floor for deducting medical expenses for those taxpayers 65 or older is only 7.5% rather than the general floor of 10% for other taxpayers; however, this rule applies only for tax years ending before January 1, 2017, and thus will expire for most individuals in 2016.

Finally, the tax researcher must be aware that not all answers to a tax question will be found in the code. The code may be silent concerning the problem at hand, the application of code language to the fact situation at hand may not be clear, or code sections may appear to be in conflict. Thus, the researcher must look for an answer from other sources, such as tax treaties, administrative rulings (see Chapter 4), judicial decisions (see Chapter 5), or secondary sources of the law. Alternatively, the controlling law may be found in other parts of the USC, such as tariff or bankruptcy laws.

7-4 Citing the Internal Revenue Code

Citing the code, as mentioned previously, generally starts with the IRC section and does not include the complete citation to the USC. Since one of the primary objectives of citing a tax law source is to leave a "trail of breadcrumbs" that a subsequent reader can follow, a tax researcher needs to exercise care when making citations to the code. Some code sections are short, and a simple cite to the section may be meaningful enough to the reader, for example, § 212:

§ 212 Expenses for production of income. In the case of an individual, there shall be allowed as a deduction all the ordinary and necessary expenses paid or incurred during the taxable year—

(1) for the production or collection of income;

(2) for the management, conservation, or maintenance of property held for the production of income; or

(3) in connection with the determination, collection, or refund of any tax.

A citation to § 212 is likely to provide enough detail for the reader to understand the support for the conclusion.

Longer code sections may require a citation that is more focused. For example, § 162 goes from subsection (a) all the way to (q) and would require many printed pages. If the researcher is interested in travel expenses for a reservist in the U.S. armed services, the citation should include detail down to the subsection level of § 162(p) so that the reader can focus directly on the tax law of interest and avoid wasting time reading parts of § 162 that are not relevant. Citations to the code should be at the level of detail (subsection, paragraph, subparagraph, etc.) necessary to provide the easiest trail for a reader to follow.

SUMMARY

The three major sources of statutory tax law are the U.S. Constitution, tax treaties, and the Internal Revenue Code. The tax researcher must thoroughly understand each of these sources and the relationships among them. The Constitution is the basis for all federal laws. The tax treaties are agreements between countries, negotiated by the president and approved by the Senate, that cover taxpayers subject to the tax laws of both countries. The authority of a tax treaty may equal or exceed that of a code section. The greatest volume of tax statutes is found in the Internal Revenue Code, which is Title 26 of the United States Code. The IRC contains the tax laws that Congress has passed, and it is the basic document for most U.S. tax provisions.

KEY WORDS

By the time you complete this chapter, you should be comfortable discussing each of the following terms. If you need additional review of any of these items, return to the appropriate material in the chapter or consult the glossary to this text.

committee report, p. 86
conference committee, p. 86
convention, p. 81
Finance Committee, p. 85
flush language, p. 92

frivolous position, p. 79
Internal Revenue Code, p. 89
protocol, p. 81
Senate executive report, p. 81
statute, p. 76

statutory sources, p. 76
tax treaties, p. 81
technical explanation, p. 81
Ways and Means Committee,
   p. 85

DISCUSSION QUESTIONS

1. Discuss the effect of *Pollock v. Farmers' Loan & Trust Co.* on the development of U.S. income tax laws.

2. The 16th Amendment to the Constitution had a significant effect on the U.S. income tax. What was it?

3. Discuss briefly the events leading to the passage of the 16th Amendment to the U.S. Constitution.

4. What did the U.S. Supreme Court hold in *Flint v. Stone Tracy Co.* in 1911?

5. Tax protesters who file "frivolous" tax returns or bring "frivolous" proceedings before the U.S. Tax Court are subject to certain fines or other penalties. What are the grounds for imposing each penalty? What is the maximum amount of each penalty?

6. Discuss the powers of taxation that are granted to Congress by the U.S. Constitution. Are any limits placed on the powers of Congress to so tax?

7. What is a tax treaty? Explain the purpose of a tax treaty. What matters generally are covered in a tax treaty?

8. When an Internal Revenue Code section and a tax treaty provision appear to conflict, which usually prevails?

9. Describe the ratification process for a tax treaty between the United States and another country.

10. The tax researcher must be able to find descriptions of tax treaties to solve certain tax problems. List different locations where a tax researcher might find a tax treaty.

11. Briefly summarize the usual steps of the legislative process for the development of federal tax legislation.

12. As a bill proceeds through Congress, various committee reports are generated. List the three committee reports that typically are prepared for a new tax law.

13. When are committee reports useful to a tax researcher?

14. What is a public law number? In P.L. 100-203, what do the "100" and the "203" indicate?

15. Where would a tax researcher find pertinent committee reports?

16. In addition to committee reports, which are byproducts to the development of tax legislation, what other report may be of value to the tax researcher analyzing a new provision of the tax law? Why?

17. Discuss the evolution of today's Internal Revenue Code.

18. The Internal Revenue Code is Title 26 of the United States Code. How is the Internal Revenue Code subdivided?

19. How are the subtitles of the Internal Revenue Code identified? What is generally contained in a subtitle?

20. In the citation § 101(a)(2)(B), what does the "a" stand for? What do the "2" and the "B" indicate to a tax researcher?

21. In the citation § 1031(a)(3)(B), what does the "a" stand for? What do the "3" and the "B" indicate to a tax researcher?

22. Are there any exceptions to the general formatting rules for a code section? Give examples.

23. Which subchapter of Chapter 1, Subtitle A contains the code sections relating to:
    a. Corporations?
    b. Mutual funds?
    c. Tax-exempt organizations?

24. Which code section contains the statute for the definition of:
    a. Gross income?
    b. The interest deduction?
    c. Depreciation and cost recovery?

25. Which code section contains the statute for the definition of:
    a. A dependent?

    b. Bad debts?

    c. Alimony payments?

26. The tax researcher must be careful not to overlook connecting words such as *and, or, at least,* and *more than.* Explain why this is important.

27. Not all statutory tax laws are found in the Internal Revenue Code. Is this statement true or false? Discuss briefly.

EXERCISES

28. Locate § 163 of the code and answer the following. Section 163 is part of which:
    a. Title
    b. Subtitle
    c. Chapter
    d. Subchapter

29. Locate § 1245 of the IRC and answer the following. Section 1245 is part of which:
    a. Title
    b. Subtitle
    c. Chapter
    d. Subchapter

30. Locate the committee reports associated with each of the following code sections using a tax service such as Checkpoint. Give the public law (P.L.) number of the most recent committee report and a brief explanation of how the new provision changes the code section for each of the following code sections.
    a. § 25A
    b. § 117
    c. § 163

31. Locate the most recent committee reports associated with each of the following code sections (if any) using a tax service such as Checkpoint. Give the citation to the committee report, the Public Law number, and a brief explanation of how the Public Law is amending the code.
    a. Conference committee report on § 6103
    b. Conference committee report on § 7345
    c. Senate report on § 4980H

32. Log on to **waysandmeans.house.gov**, the Website for the Ways and Means Committee of the U.S. House of Representatives, and answer the following questions:
    a. Who is the chair of the committee?
    b. What is the total number of members on the committee?
    c. How many of the members are from your home state? If none, say so.
    d. The Ways and Means Committee has several subcommittees. Name three of these subcommittees and indicate who chairs each subcommittee.

33. What is found in each of the following subtitles of the Internal Revenue Code?
    a. Subtitle B
    b. Subtitle F

  c. Subtitle A

  d. Subtitle C

34. Each subtitle of the Internal Revenue Code contains several chapters. How are chapters identified? What generally is included in a chapter of the code?

35. Identify the general content of each of the following chapters of the Internal Revenue Code:

  a. Chapter 11

  b. Chapter 61

  c. Chapter 1

  d. Chapter 12

36. Chapters of the Internal Revenue Code are subdivided into subchapters. How are subchapters identified? What is generally contained in a subchapter?

37. What is found in each of the following subchapters of the Internal Revenue Code's income tax provisions (Chapter 1 of Subtitle A)?

  a. Subchapter C

  b. Subchapter J

  c. Subchapter K

  d. Subchapter S

38. Correctly cite the italicized sentence indicated by the dart (▶) in the following passage from the code.

  SECTION 79. GROUP-TERM LIFE INSURANCE PURCHASED FOR EMPLOYEES.

  (a) General rule. There shall be included in the gross income of an employee for the taxable year an amount equal to the cost of group-term life insurance on his life provided for part or all of such year under a policy (or policies) carried directly or indirectly by his employer (or employers); but only to the extent that such cost exceeds the sum of—

  (1) the cost of $50,000 of such insurance, and

  (2) the amount (if any) paid by the employee toward the purchase of such insurance.

  (b) Exceptions. Subsection (a) shall not apply to—

  (1) the cost of group-term life insurance on the life of an individual which is provided under a policy carried directly or indirectly by an employer after such individual has terminated his employment with such employer and is disabled (within the meaning of section 72(m)(7)),

  (2) the cost of any portion of the group-term life insurance on the life of an employee provided during part or all of the taxable year of the employee under which—

  ▶(A) the employer is directly or indirectly the beneficiary, or

  (B) a person described in section 170(c) is the sole beneficiary, for the entire period during such taxable year for which the employee receives such insurance, and

39. Correctly cite the italicized sentence indicated by the dart (▶) in the following passage from the Code:

  SECTION 263A. CAPITALIZATION AND INCLUSION IN INVENTORY COSTS OF CERTAIN EXPENSES

  a. Nondeductibility of certain direct and indirect costs

  1. In general—In the case of any property to which this section applies, any costs described in paragraph (2)—

A. in the case of property which is inventory in the hands of the taxpayer, shall be included in inventory costs, and

B. ▶ *in the case of any other property, shall be capitalized.*

2. Allocable costs

40. What is the general content of each of the following subchapters of Chapter 1, Subtitle A, of the Internal Revenue Code?
    a. Subchapter C
    b. Subchapter K
    c. Subchapter S
    d. Subchapter E

41. What is found in each of the following subchapters of Subtitle A, Chapter 1 of the Internal Revenue Code?
    a. Subchapter B
    b. Subchapter E
    c. Subchapter L
    d. Subchapter F

42. Which subchapter of Subtitle A, Chapter 1 of the Internal Revenue Code contains the provisions related to the following?
    a. Deferred compensation
    b. Partners and partnerships
    c. Corporate distribution and adjustments
    d. Banks

43. Which Internal Revenue Code sections are found in each of these subchapters of Subtitle A, Chapter 1?
    a. Subchapter J
    b. Subchapter A
    c. Subchapter I
    d. Subchapter P

44. Which Internal Revenue Code sections are found in each of these parts of Subtitle A?
    a. Subchapter A, Part IV
    b. Subchapter C, Part II
    c. Subchapter B, Part VIII
    d. Subchapter A, Part I

45. What is covered in Subtitle A, Chapter 2 of the Internal Revenue Code? What Internal Revenue Code sections are included in Chapter 2?

46. What is found in each of the following subchapters of Chapter 1, Subtitle A, of the Internal Revenue Code?
    a. Subchapter D
    b. Subchapter H
    c. Subchapter P
    d. Subchapter L

47. What is the official name of P.L. 114-14? What year was that law enacted? Where did you find your answer?

48. What is the official name of P.L. 112-78? What year was that law enacted? Where did you find your answer?

49. The most important division of the Internal Revenue Code is the section. Sections usually are subdivided into various smaller elements. Name several of these elements and state how they are denoted.

50. Do section numbers repeat themselves or is each one unique?

51. Identify the general contents of each of the following Internal Revenue Code sections:
    a. § 61
    b. § 162
    c. § 1
    d. § 212

52. Identify the general contents of each of the following Internal Revenue Code sections:
    a. § 62
    b. § 163
    c. § 11
    d. § 164

53. Locate § 217 of the IRC. It is found in which
    a. Subtitle of the code
    b. Chapter
    c. Subchapter
    d. Part

54. Locate § 2036 of the IRC. It is found in which
    a. Subtitle of the code
    b. Chapter
    c. Subchapter
    d. Part

55. Use an online tax service (e.g., Checkpoint, LexisNexis, CCH IntelliConnect) to answer the following questions:
    a. What is the general content of Internal Revenue Code § 28?
    b. What is the general content of Internal Revenue Code § 141?
    c. What is the general content of Internal Revenue Code § 166?
    d. Print a copy (maximum of one page) of any one of the above code sections and attach it to your answer.

56. Use an online tax service (e.g., Checkpoint, LexisNexis, CCH IntelliConnect) to answer the following questions:
    a. What is the general content of Internal Revenue Code § 117?
    b. What is the general content of Internal Revenue Code § 165?
    c. What is the general content of Internal Revenue Code § 304?
    d. Print a copy (maximum of one page) of any one of the above code sections and attach it to your answer.

57. Use an online tax service (e.g., Checkpoint, LexisNexis, CCH IntelliConnect) to answer the following questions:
    a. What is the general content of Internal Revenue Code § 25A?
    b. What is the general content of Internal Revenue Code § 67?

    c. What is the general content of Internal Revenue Code § 280G?

    d. Print a copy (maximum of one page) of any one of the above code sections and attach it to your answer.

58. Name several locations where a tax researcher would find the text of the current Internal Revenue Code.

59. If a tax researcher wants to know if there is an equivalent 1939 code section for a specific 1986 code section, how would he or she locate it?

60. One important problem that faces a tax researcher is interpretation of the Internal Revenue Code. Comment on each of the following interpretation problems:

    a. Exceptions to a code section

    b. Words that connect phrases, such as *and* and *or*

    c. Recent changes in the code

    d. Effective dates

    e. Words that modify percentages, dollar amounts, or time

61. Comment on the statement, "All tax questions can be answered using the Internal Revenue Code."

62. Does the United States have an income tax treaty with any of the following countries? If it does, in what year was the treaty signed? State where you found this information.

    a. Japan

    b. United Kingdom

    c. Egypt

    d. Germany

63. Does the United States have an income tax treaty with any of the following countries? If it does, in what year was the treaty signed? State where you found this information.

    a. Australia

    b. Iceland

    c. Jamaica

    d. Sri Lanka

64. Use an online tax service (e.g., Checkpoint, LexisNexis, CCH IntelliConnect) to locate § 117 of the Internal Revenue Code. Answer the following questions:

    a. How many subsections does § 117 include?

    b. How many paragraphs does § 117(b) include?

    c. How many subparagraphs does § 117(d)(2) include?

    d. Print a copy (maximum of one page) of this section and attach it to your answer.

65. Use an online tax service (e.g., Checkpoint, LexisNexis, CCH IntelliConnect) to locate § 385 of the Internal Revenue Code. Answer the following questions:

    a. How many subsections does § 385 include?

    b. How many paragraphs does § 385(b) include?

    c. Print a copy (maximum of one page) of this section and attach it to your answer.

66. Use an online tax service (e.g., Checkpoint, LexisNexis, CCH IntelliConnect) to locate § 280C of the Internal Revenue Code. Answer the following questions:

    a. How many subsections does § 280C include?

    b. How many paragraphs does § 280C(b) include?

    c. How many subparagraphs does § 280C(b)(2) include?

    d. Print a copy (maximum of one page) of this section and attach it to your answer.

67. When was each of the following 1986 code sections originally enacted? State how you obtained this information.

    a. § 843

    b. § 131

    c. § 469

    d. § 263A

68. In which subtitle, chapter, and subchapter of the 1986 code are each of the following sections found?

    a. § 32

    b. § 172

    c. § 2039

    d. § 6013

69. List the first three section numbers and titles of each of the following subchapters of Chapter 1 of the Internal Revenue Code:

    a. Subchapter B

    b. Subchapter E

    c. Subchapter J

    d. Subchapter S

70. Identify the equivalent section of the current code for each of the following sections of the 1939 code. If there is no equivalent section, say so.

    a. § 1

    b. § 113(a)

    c. § 22(a)

    d. § 115(a)

    e. § 181

71. Use an online tax service (e.g., Checkpoint, LexisNexis, CCH IntelliConnect) to locate the following code sections. What other code sections reference each of the sections you found? State which online tax service you used to complete this assignment.

    a. § 72

    b. § 307

    c. § 446

72. Name the article and section of the U.S. Constitution that gives Congress the power to levy a tax.

73. Enumerate the code sections that contain the chief tax law provisions on the following topics:

    a. S corporations

    b. Personal holding company tax

    c. Gift tax

    d. Tax accounting methods

74. Use an online site to determine how many senators are on the Senate Finance Committee. Who is the chair of the Finance Committee? State where you found this information.

75. Use an online site to determine what is contained in each of the following. State where you found this information.

    a. U.S. Const. Art. I, § 9 cl. 3

    b. U.S. Const. Art. I, § 8 cl. 1

    c. U.S. Const. Art. II, § 2 cl. 2

76. Locate and print the first page of a House Ways and Means Committee report using an online site. State where you found this information.

CHAPTER 4

Administrative Regulations and Rulings

LEARNING OBJECTIVES

- Identify the most important administrative sources of the federal tax law.
- Distinguish among the structure, nature, and purpose of regulations, revenue procedures, and IRS rulings.
- Describe how to locate and interpret the precedential value of administrative sources of tax law.
- Explain the elements of common citations for regulations and other IRS pronouncements.
- Describe the contents and publication practices of the Internal Revenue Bulletin and the Cumulative Bulletin.

THE INTERNAL REVENUE SERVICE (IRS), part of the U.S. Treasury Department, is responsible for the administration of the income tax law. The administrative process consists of both interpreting and enforcing the tax laws. The IRS interprets the law by issuing various pronouncements, examples of which include Treasury regulations, revenue rulings, revenue procedures, and letter rulings requested by taxpayers. Enforcement of the tax law by the IRS consists primarily of systematically auditing tax returns and administering an appeals process for taxpayers to arbitrate disagreement with audit results (see Chapters 13 and 14). In addition, the IRS administers a collection process to collect overdue taxes. The Treasury Secretary delegates the ongoing administrative responsibilities for the tax law to the commissioner of the IRS, who is a presidential appointee.

To facilitate the IRS's administration of the tax laws, the Internal Revenue Code (IRC) authorizes the Treasury secretary (or his or her delegate) to prescribe the rules and regulations necessary to administer the code. According to § 7805(a):

> *Except where such authority is expressly given by this title to any person other than an officer or employee of the Treasury Department, the Secretary shall prescribe all needful rules and regulations for the enforcement of this title, including all rules and regulations as may be necessary by reason of any alteration of law in relation to internal revenue.*

This code section gives the IRS general authority to issue binding rules and regulations concerning Title 26 of the United States Code. In practice, most of the IRS's pronouncements are written by IRS staff or by the Office of the Chief Counsel of the IRS, who is an assistant general counsel of the Treasury Department.

The tax researcher must be especially familiar with the five major types of pronouncements that may be forthcoming under this authority: (1) regulations, (2) revenue rulings, (3) revenue procedures, (4) letter rulings, and (5) other IRS notices. Each of these categories is issued for a different purpose and carries a different degree of authority. The remainder of this chapter addresses the nature and location of each of these administrative pronouncements.

1 Regulations

Regulations are issued by the IRS and Treasury Department and constitute official interpretation of the IRC. Regulations are intended to provide guidance on new legislative tax law or perhaps to address issues that have arisen related to existing code. Regulations are not law but rather rules issued by an agency (in this case the Treasury) to provide the IRS's position on the meaning of the law and give directions on how taxpayers might comply. Although not law, regulations retain significant authority and must generally be followed.

Regulations are largely drafted by the Office of the Chief Counsel inside the Treasury. Issues to consider for regulations are identified from various sources such as comments from the commissioner of the IRS, the chief counsel and other Treasury Department staff, taxpayers, practitioners, and outside organizations, as well as other comments on tax law directed at professionals or the taxpaying public. The regulations may also be issued to deal with recent court decisions, common issues dealt with in private letter rulings, and of course, recently enacted legislation.

SPOTLIGHT ON TAXATION

Quotation

The hardest thing in the world to understand is the income tax.

—Albert Einstein

Regulations often begin as an Advance Notice of Proposed Rulemaking (ANPRM), which indicates the Treasury's consideration of an issue for publication of guidance and seeks input from the public about the tax issue. Once the regulations are drafted, a **Notice of Proposed Rulemaking** (NPRM) is issued announcing the proposed regulations. The NPRM includes a preamble explaining the purpose of the regulations, asks for public input, announces a public hearing (if one is to be held), and contains the text of the proposed regulations themselves.

Before and during the hearings process, the NPRMs are referred to as **proposed regulations** and, unlike final regulations, do not have the effect of law. Proposed regulations are useful for understanding the IRS's current position on an issue but generally should not be relied on by a taxpayer unless the IRS provides explicit advice on doing so. For example, in Exhibit 4-1, an excerpt from REG-134016-15, the NPRM on Guidance under Section 355 Concerning Device and Active Trade or Business, which was issued in July 2016, is presented. The proposed regulations appear as part of the Checkpoint tax service (or other tax services).

After the hearings are completed and changes (if any) have been made to the text of the proposed regulations, they are published in the final form of a **Treasury decision (TD)**. **Final regulations** are integrated with previously approved TDs and constitute the full set of IRS regulations. After this integration has occurred, the TD designation is usually dropped, and the pronouncement is simply referred to as a regulation. TDs are

EXHIBIT 4-1: Excerpt from REG-134016-15 and Presentation of Proposed Regulations

Proposed Amendment 1.355-9

§ 1.355-9 Minimum percentage of Five-Year-Active-Business Assets.

(a) Definitions. The following definitions apply for purposes of this section.

(1) Distributing, Controlled. Distributing means the distributing corporation within the meaning of § 1.355-1(b). Controlled means the controlled corporation within the meaning of § 1.355-1(b).

(2) Five-Year-Active Business. Five-Year-Active Business means the active conduct of a trade or business that satisfies the requirements and limitations of § 355(b)(2) and § 1.355-3(b).

(3) Five-Year-Active Business Assets. Five-Year-Active Business Assets of a corporation means its gross assets used in one or more Five-Year-Active-Businesses. Such assets include cash and cash equivalents held as a reasonable amount of working capital for one or more Five-Year-Active

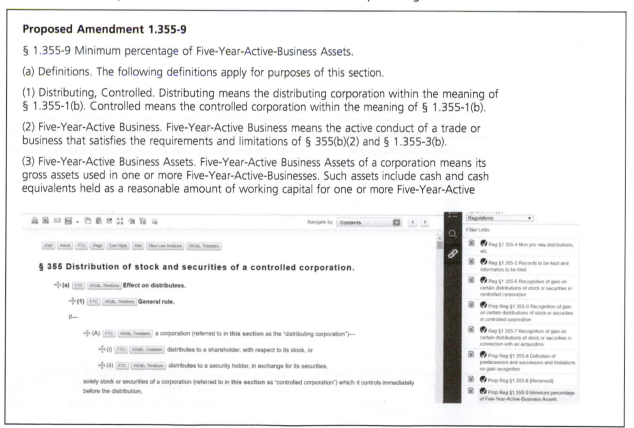

published in the Federal Register and, some time later, in the Internal Revenue Bulletin, discussed later in this chapter.

Although proposed regulations do not carry the same authority as final regulations, temporary regulations have the same authority as final regulations. **Temporary regulations** are not subject to the public hearing procedure that typifies the development of a final regulation, and they are effective immediately upon publication. Although they are effective immediately, the IRS must simultaneously issue the regulations in proposed form; the temporary regulations expire three years after issuance pursuant to the statute. Temporary regulations are issued to provide the taxpayer with immediate guidance concerning a new provision of the law, perhaps concerning filing requirements that must be satisfied immediately or the clarification of definitions and terms. It should be noted that the three-year rule was prospective and that temporary regulations issued prior to November 1988 can still be in effect. For example, parts of the IRC § 469 regulations dealing with material participation by limited partners are still in effect and should be followed by tax practitioners.

Until a temporary regulation is replaced with the final regulation under a code section, the tax researcher should treat the temporary regulation as though it were final. Thus, temporary regulations are fully in effect and must be followed until they are superseded, whereas proposed regulations, having been issued only to solicit comments and to expose the IRS's proposed interpretation of the law, need not be followed as if they were law.

1-1 Authority of Regulations

Observers have identified two distinct categories of regulations, general and specific. General regulations (also called **interpretive regulations**) are issued under the general authority granted to the IRS to interpret the language of the IRC under § 7805(a).

An example of interpretive regulations can be found under IRC § 212, Expenses for the Production of Income. This short code section has many pages of interpretive regulations, providing taxpayers with operational rules for applying this provision to tax situations.

Regulations issued under specific authority are often called **legislative regulations** because they are issued under a specific grant of authority by Congress when the IRC was constructed or revised. Such authority is granted because, in certain (especially technical) areas of the tax law, Congress cannot or does not care to address the detailed or complex issues that are associated with an otherwise defined tax issue. Accordingly, Congress directs the IRS to pronounce regulations on the matter. For example, Congress delegated to the IRS the authority to prescribe regulations necessary to carry out the provisions of IRC § 135, which grants an exclusion for interest on certain U.S. savings bonds used for higher education expenses, including regulations requiring record keeping and information reporting. Under § 136(d)(4), legislative authority is provided:

> *The Secretary may prescribe such regulations as may be necessary or appropriate to carry out this section, including regulations requiring record keeping and information reporting.*

In the course of tax practice, the researcher is occasionally faced with a question concerning the validity of a regulation. If the practitioner disagrees with the scope or language of the regulation, he or she bears the burden of proof of showing that the regulation is improper. This can be difficult. Many regulations simply restate the code or congressional committee reports; they are known as "hard and solid" regulations.

Prior to an important Supreme Court decision in 2011,[1] most professionals considered legislative regulations issued under specific direction to carry higher authority than interpretive regulations issued under general authority. Both types of regulations are now considered equal under the two-part standard developed in the *Chevron* case: (1) if Congressional intent is clear, the regulation will only be invalid if it conflicts with the unambiguous language of the statute; and (2) "if Congress has explicitly left a gap for the agency to fill, there is an express delegation of authority to the agency to elucidate a specific provision of the statute by regulation. Such legislative regulations are given controlling weight unless they are arbitrary, capricious, or manifestly contrary to the statute."[2] Most commentators agree that the overall result of the Supreme Court's reliance on the *Chevron* standard is that greater deference will be paid to Treasury regulations than in the past. Thus, a taxpayer's challenge to a regulation typically must assert an improper exercise of IRS power or an overly broad application of a rule.

In questioning the provisions of a regulation, the tax researcher must be aware of several accuracy-related penalties Congress has enacted in the IRC. For example, a penalty is assessed equal to 20 percent of any underpayment of tax in situations in which the underpayment is found to be because of "negligence" on the part of the taxpayer. Generally, negligence includes any failure to make a reasonable attempt to comply with the code or any evidence of disregard of Treasury rules or regulations. Thus, if a practitioner chooses to ignore an administrative element of the tax law, he or she must possess substantial authority to do so to avoid this penalty or others of its kind. See Chapter 13 for a more detailed examination of these provisions.

1-2 Effective Date of Regulations

In general, a new regulation is effective on the date on which such regulation is filed with the Federal Register.[3] However, there are certain situations in which a regulation can be effective retroactively, including the following:

1. The regulation is filed or issued within 18 months after the date of the enactment of the statutory provision to which the regulation relates.

2. The regulation is designed to prevent abuse by taxpayers.

3. The regulation corrects a procedural defect in the issuance of a prior regulation.

4. The regulation relates to internal Treasury Department policies, practices, or procedures.

5. The regulation may apply retroactively by congressional directive.

6. The Commissioner also has the power to allow taxpayers to elect to apply new regulations retroactively.

In situations in which a regulation applies retroactively, it technically can apply starting with the date of the underlying code section to which it relates. However, the statute of limitations may limit the application of a retroactive regulation in many situations.

---

[1]*Mayo Foundation for Medical Education and Research, et al. v. U.S.*, 131 S.Ct. 704 (January 11, 2011).

[2]*Chevron U.S.A. Inc. v. Natural Resources Defense Council, Inc.*, 467 U.S. 837 (1984).

[3]IRC § 7805(b).

SPOTLIGHT ON TAXATION

Regulations Matter

In 2016, a merger deal valued at about $160 billion between U.S.-based Pfizer and Ireland-based Allergan was scuppered as a result of new tax regulations related to transactions known as corporate inversions. Statements by Allergen CEO Brett Saunders implied the U.S. government was specifically targeting this particular merger: "It really looked like they [U.S. Treasury] did a very fine job of constructing a rule here— a temporary rule—to stop this deal, and obviously it was successful." The Treasury Department took umbrage to the allegations and issued a public release denying specific deal-tampering:

MYTH: Treasury specifically targeted the Pfizer/Allergan merger.

FACT: This claim is baseless. Treasury's most recent guidance is the result of an extensive policy process that began nearly two years ago, long before the Pfizer-Allergan deal was even announced.

Treasury Notes, the Official Blog of the U.S. Treasury Dept., March 6, 2016, **www.treasury.gov/connect/blog/Pages/default.aspx**.

1-3 Citing a Regulation

Tax practitioners use a uniform common system for citing specific regulations. The Treasury assigns to each regulation a unique number, which is broadly based on the code section being interpreted in that regulation. An example of this citation system appears in Exhibit 4-2.

The number to the left of the period in a regulation citation indicates the type of issue that is addressed in the pronouncement. The most commonly encountered types of regulations include the following:

Regulation Type	Topic
1	Income Tax
20	Estate Tax
25	Gift Tax
31	Employment Tax
301	Procedural Matter

Familiarity with this arbitrary numbering system used by the regulations allows tax researchers to immediately identify the general issue that is addressed in a pronouncement. Note that these numbers indicating the type of issue addressed in the regulation do not necessarily correspond to the chapter numbers of the code sections that address the same issues.

The number to the immediate right of the period in the citation of a regulation indicates the code section to which the regulation relates. In Exhibit 4-2, an example of a full citation, one can determine that this is an income tax regulation dealing with § 162 of the IRC. The numbers and letters to the right of the section number denote the regulation number and smaller divisions of the pronouncement. Regulation numbers typically are consecutive, starting with 0 or 1, and follow the general order of the issues that are

EXHIBIT 4-2: Interpreting a Regulation Citation

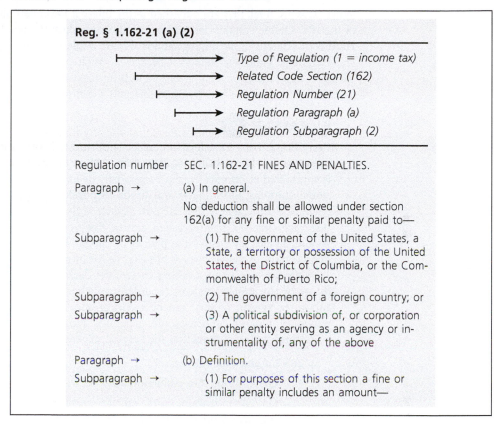

Regulation number	SEC. 1.162-21 FINES AND PENALTIES.
Paragraph →	(a) In general.
	No deduction shall be allowed under section 162(a) for any fine or similar penalty paid to—
Subparagraph →	(1) The government of the United States, a State, a territory or possession of the United States, the District of Columbia, or the Commonwealth of Puerto Rico;
Subparagraph →	(2) The government of a foreign country; or
Subparagraph →	(3) A political subdivision of, or corporation or other entity serving as an agency or instrumentality of, any of the above
Paragraph →	(b) Definition.
Subparagraph →	(1) For purposes of this section a fine or similar penalty includes an amount—

addressed in the corresponding code section. However, the regulation numbers, paragraphs, and so on do not necessarily correspond to the subsection or other division designations of the underlying code section. Because code citations and regulations citations can appear similar, and the content of the regulations can be very similar to that of the code, new researchers should take special care to ensure they are citing the proper source. Failure to include the "Reg." or the regulation type number can leave the reader puzzled as to whether the code or a regulation is being cited.

The numbering system for temporary regulations is similar to the numbering system for the final and proposed regulations; however, usually the reference to, or citation of, a temporary regulation will include a "T" designating the temporary nature of the regulation. Reg. § 1.280H-1T(b)(3) is an example of a citation for a temporary regulation under IRC § 280H.[4]

A regulation can also be cited in a more formal legal format. For instance, the regulation in Exhibit 4-1 could be alternatively cited as: 26 C.F.R. § 1.162-21(a)(2). In this case, the "26" is the number of the Title of the U.S. Code for the IRC, and "C.F.R." is the abbreviation for *Code of Federal Regulations*, the codification of the complete federal agency regulations.

---

[4]Formerly, temporary regulations were designated with an "18" preceding the code section number, e.g. Treasury Temp. Reg. Sec. 18.1862-(b).

1-4 Locating and Using Regulations

When TDs are final, they are published in the Internal Revenue Bulletin, a weekly newsletter of the IRS. Online commercial tax services also reproduce the regulations in their materials. Hard copy editions of the tax regulations also are available from several commercial publishers, including Thomson Reuters Checkpoint, Wolters Kluwer CCH IntelliConnect, and Westlaw. Regulations can be a great tool to better understand the IRC and can often be considered the "first step" when trying to interpret a complex or confusing code section.

EXAMPLE 4-1

Perry Potter runs a small online magic shop and sells magic trick props and supplies through her website, Pigwartz.com. Although almost all of Perry's business is conducted electronically, she occasionally needs to print documents (e.g., occasional shipping documents) and needs to purchase a new printer at a cost of $350. She understands that the new printer is likely to have a useful life of over one year (her old printer lasted almost five years) and wonders whether she should deduct the cost of the printer or capitalize the cost as an asset and then depreciate it. Assume Perry is not eligible for immediate expensing under § 179.

Although not a very exciting choice, the decision to either deduct an expenditure or to capitalize its cost (and deduct its cost through depreciation, amortization, or at time of sale) can be a critical one. Perry knows that ordinary and necessary business expenses are generally deductible under § 162; however, § 263 prohibits the deduction for "capital expenditures":

§ 263 Capital expenditures.

(a) General rule. No deduction shall be allowed for—

(1) Any amount paid out for new buildings or for permanent improvements or betterments made to increase the value of any property or estate.

*****

(2) Any amount expended in restoring property or in making good the exhaustion thereof for which an allowance is or has been made.

§ 263 does not include any specific instructions for regulations to be provided by the Treasury; however, given the broad nature of the guidance reflected in the code, the Treasury issued a series of regulations over the years to assist taxpayers with this mundane but important decision. Like many complex areas of tax law, § 263 regulations include a "-0" regulation [Reg. § 1.263(a)-0], which represents a table of contents for the remaining 16 final or proposed regulations.

Perry finds Reg. § 1.263(a)-1(f), which permits a de minimis safe harbor election to expense certain property.

(f) De minimis safe harbor election.

(1) In general. Except as otherwise provided in paragraph (f)(2) of this section, a taxpayer electing to apply the de minimis safe harbor under this paragraph (f) may not capitalize under § 1.263(a)-2(d)(1) or § 1.263(a)-3(d) any amount paid in the taxable year for the acquisition or production of a unit of tangible property nor treat as a material or supply under § 1.162-3(a) any amount paid in the taxable year for tangible property if the amount specified under this paragraph (f)(1) meets the requirements of paragraph (f)(1)(i) or (f)(1)(ii) of this section.

*****

(ii) Taxpayer without applicable financial statement. A taxpayer electing to apply the de minimis safe harbor may not capitalize under § 1.263(a)-2(d)(1) or § 1.263(a)-3(d) nor treat as a material or supply under § 1.162-3(a) any amount paid in the taxable year for property described in paragraph (f)(1) of this section if—

(A) The taxpayer does not have an applicable financial statement (as defined in paragraph (f)(4) of this section);

(B) The taxpayer has at the beginning of the taxable year accounting procedures treating as an expense for non-tax purposes—

(1) Amounts paid for property costing less than a specified dollar amount; or

(2) Amounts paid for property with an economic useful life (as defined in § 1.162-3(c)(4)) of 12 months or less;

(C) The taxpayer treats the amount paid for the property as an expense on its books and records in accordance with these accounting procedures; and

(D) The amount paid for the property does not exceed $500 per invoice (or per item as substantiated by the invoice) …

In this situation, the regulations provide a substantial additional interpretation of how taxpayers need to implement capitalization treatment of smaller expenditures under § 263. In this way, regulations can be valuable source of guidance for taxpayers. Perry immediately institutes a capitalization policy for her business that expenses all qualifying purchases of property under $500.

2 Revenue Rulings

Revenue rulings are second to regulations as important administrative sources of the federal tax law. A revenue ruling is an official pronouncement of the National Office of the IRS. It deals with the application of the IRC and regulations to a specific factual situation, usually one that has been submitted by a taxpayer. Thus, many revenue rulings indicate how the IRS will treat a given taxpayer transaction. In addition, revenue rulings provide taxpayers with needed information, such as applicable federal interest rates and other items required by taxpayers. These rates are used for complying with required tax law calculations.

Revenue rulings do not carry the force and effect of regulations. Nevertheless, they still provide excellent sources of information for tax researchers. In fact, they are published chiefly for the purpose of guiding taxpayers. Therefore, even for a tax researcher whose client did not submit the original request for the ruling, the result of the ruling is of value if it concerns a transaction similar in nature, structure, or effect to the client's situation. However, as with any administrative source of tax law, reliance should not be placed on a revenue ruling if it has been affected by subsequent legislation, regulations, rulings, or court decisions.

Revenue rulings adhere to a general internal structure, as illustrated in Exhibit 4-3. The typical structure is as follows:

Issue: A statement of the issue in question.

Facts: The facts on which the revenue ruling is based.

Law and analysis: The IRS's application of current law to the issue in the revenue ruling.

Holding: How the IRS will treat the transaction.

EXHIBIT 4-3:   Revenue Ruling Excerpt

Rev. Rul. 2015-11, 2015-21 IRB 975

Issue

Is the capitalized cost of unrecoverable precious metal that is used in various manufacturing processes depreciable under § § 167 and 168 of the Internal Revenue Code?

Facts

Situation 1. A is a contract jeweler who fabricates jewelry to customers' specifications using gold supplied by the customers. A does not maintain an inventory of gold or completed jewelry, but to assist customers A fabricates and maintains gold sample jewelry showing currently available styles. A's samples are not held for sale. Every 3 years A melts down the sample jewelry, recovering 100 percent of the gold content of the jewelry. For A's purposes, the recovered gold is indistinguishable from gold that has not previously been used in sample jewelry and A reuses it in fabricating new sample jewelry. A capitalizes the cost of the gold into the basis of its sample jewelry.

Situation 2. B is a petroleum refiner. As part of its refining process, B uses a catalyst called prills, fabricated from platinum and other chemicals. Based upon engineering studies performed by B, B determines that approximately 10 percent of the platinum initially utilized to fabricate prills is lost over the course of the platinum's reasonably expected useful life in the refining process. The remaining 90 percent of the platinum is recoverable and becomes available to B for other uses. B capitalizes the cost of the platinum.

Situation 3. C manufactures flat glass using the float manufacturing process. This process involves the use of molten tin, which provides the ideal surface to manufacture high-quality, flat glass. During the manufacturing process, the tin declines in purity and volume due to chemical reactions and vaporization. Additional tin is added as needed to maintain the level required for the production of the glass. After approximately 7 years, all of the original tin is lost due to chemical reactions and vaporization. C capitalizes the cost of the initial tin installed in the tin bath.

Law

Section 167(a) provides as a depreciation deduction a reasonable allowance for the exhaustion and wear and tear (including a reasonable allowance for obsolescence) of property used in a taxpayer's trade or business.

Section 1.167(a)-1(a) of the Income Tax Regulations provides that the depreciation allowance is that amount that should be set aside for the taxable year in accordance with a reasonably consistent plan (not necessarily at a uniform rate), so that the aggregate of the amounts set aside, plus the salvage value, will, at the end of the estimated useful life of the depreciable property, equal the cost or other basis of the property.

Section 1.167(a)-1(b) provides that for the purpose of § 167, the estimated useful life of an asset is not necessarily the useful life inherent in the asset but is the period over which the asset may reasonably be expected to be useful to the taxpayer in its trade or business or in the production of his income. This period is determined by reference to the taxpayer's experience with similar property taking into account present conditions and probable future developments.

Section 1.167(a)-2 provides that the depreciation allowance in the case of tangible property applies only to that part of the property which is subject to wear and tear, to decay or decline from natural causes, to exhaustion, and to obsolescence.

Section 1.168(a)-1(a) provides that § 168 determines the depreciation allowance for tangible property that is of a character subject to the allowance for depreciation provided in § 167(a) and that is placed in service generally after December 31, 1986. See § 1.168(a)-1(b). Accordingly, tangible property to which § 1.168(a)-1(a) applies is property that is of a character subject to the allowance for depreciation provided in § 167(a) if the taxpayer shows that the property is subject to exhaustion, wear and tear, or obsolescence, and that the property has a determinable estimated useful life.

Analysis

An asset is depreciable for federal income tax purposes to the extent that the taxpayer can show that the asset is subject to exhaustion, wear and tear, or obsolescence, and that the asset has a determinable estimated useful life. See *O'Shaughnessy v. Commissioner*, 332 F.3d 1125 [91 AFTR 2d 2003-2559] (8th Cir. 2003), aff'g in part, rev'g in part, 2002-1 U.S.T.C. ¶ 50,235, 89 A.F.T.R. 2d 658 (D. Minn. 2001) (allowing depreciation for tin that declined in volume and purity as a result of glass manufacturing process); *Arkla, Inc. v. United States*, 765 F.2d 487 [56 AFTR 2d 85-5446] (5th Cir. 1985), cert. denied, 475 U.S. 1064 (1986) (allowing investment credit and depreciation for unrecoverable cushion gas but not for recoverable cushion gas); Rev. Rul. 97-54, 1997-2 C.B. 23 (adopting the reasoning of *Arkla*, supra). In *O'Shaughnessy*, the Eighth Circuit allowed the taxpayer to depreciate the initial installation of molten tin used in the float manufacturing process of flat glass. The Eighth Circuit concluded that whether an asset is depreciable for federal income tax purposes depends on the taxpayer's showing that the asset is subject to exhaustion and wear and tear. The Eighth Circuit reasoned that the tin's decline in volume and purity as a result of its use in the glass manufacturing process constituted "exhaustion, wear and tear" within the meaning of § 167, and therefore, the taxpayer appropriately depreciated the tin under § 168. In reaching its decision, the court concluded that Rev. Rul. 75-491, 1975-2 C.B. 19 (holding that the initial installation of molten tin used in the float manufacturing process of flat glass is not depreciable), was no longer persuasive insofar as the ruling predated a substantial restructuring of the depreciation rules upon which its holding was based.

O'Shaughnessy, Arkla, Inc., and Rev. Rul. 97-54 require a fact-specific analysis of the extent to which precious metals used in various manufacturing processes are subject to exhaustion, wear and tear, or obsolescence (in other words, the extent to which precious metals are recoverable or unrecoverable) for determining whether such precious metals are depreciable under § § 167 and 168. Accordingly, determining whether and the extent to which an asset is depreciable is based on an examination of the specific facts relating to the asset's use in a taxpayer's trade or business and whether the asset has a determinable estimated useful life. This analysis departs from the analysis previously used in Rev. Rul. 90-65, 1990-2 C.B. 41, as corrected by Announcement 91-15, 1991-5 I.R.B. 49, and Rev. Rul. 75-491.

Rev. Rul. 90-65 and Rev. Rul. 75-491 distinguished the treatment of a precious metal that remains available to the owner but is consumed in production from a material such as "line pack gas" or "cushion gas," which is lost for any other potential use upon its initial installation into a facility (with the facility itself being a depreciable asset). Rev. Rul. 75-491 held that the initial installation of molten tin used in the float manufacturing process of flat glass is not depreciable property. The ruling recognized that, although a portion of the initial tin is consumed in the manufacturing operation, the remaining portion is undiminished in value and once restored to its original level (by adding additional quantities during the year) is property that is "essentially the same that existed at the beginning of the year." Accordingly, the ruling concluded that the initial installation of molten tin was not depreciable and that the cost of tin consumed during the year in the production of the glass was deductible under section 162, subject to being included in inventory as a production cost.

Rev. Rul. 90-65 amplified the holding of Rev. Ruling 75-491 by clarifying that the principles of Rev. Rul. 75-491 apply not only when a recoverable element is used in its natural state, but also when an economically recoverable precious metal is fabricated into items of property used in the taxpayer's trade or business. Specifically, Rev. Rul. 90-65 held that if an economically recoverable precious metal is fabricated into items of property used in the taxpayer's trade or business and the cost of that metal is more than half the cost of the property, the cost of the metal is nondepreciable and is accounted for separately from the item into which it is fabricated.

The analyses in Rev. Rul. 75-491 and Rev. Rul. 90-65 are inconsistent with *Arkla, Inc.* and Rev. Rul. 97-54, which require an analysis of the specific facts surrounding an asset's use in a taxpayer's trade or business when determining whether and the extent to which an asset is depreciable. In addition, Rev. Rul. 75-491 and Rev. Rul. 90-65 have been supplanted by more recent authorities such as *O'Shaughnessy*. Accordingly, this revenue ruling adopts the factual analysis approach as applied by those later authorities. Further, because the factual analysis approach permits depreciation of initial installations of certain precious metals, it is no longer relevant whether the cost of those initial installations is more than half the cost of the overall fabricated property.

In Situation 1, the gold used to manufacture sample jewelry can be recovered and reused by A in A's trade or business in a manner that is indistinguishable from other gold that has never been fabricated, used, and recovered. The utility of the gold does not diminish as a result of its having previously been fabricated into sample jewelry. Accordingly, the gold is not subject to exhaustion, wear and tear, or obsolescence and as a result, is not depreciable.

In Situation 2, approximately 10 percent of the platinum is lost over the course of its expected useful life and is not recoverable for reuse. Accordingly, approximately 10 percent of the platinum will undergo exhaustion, wear and tear, or obsolescence over a determinable useful life. To the extent that the platinum will be lost and is not recoverable for reuse (i.e., approximately 10 percent of the total amount), B may depreciate the capitalized cost of such platinum under § § 167 and 168. To the extent that any of the platinum is recoverable for reuse (i.e., approximately 90 percent of the total amount), B may not depreciate the capitalized cost of such platinum.

In Situation 3, all of the original tin used in the glass manufacturing process is lost due to chemical reactions and evaporation after about 7 years. Thus, all of the original tin will undergo exhaustion, wear and tear, or obsolescence over a determinable useful life. Therefore, C may depreciate the capitalized cost of all the entire original tin under § § 167 and 168.

Holding
The capitalized cost of unrecoverable precious metals that are used in various manufacturing processes is depreciable under § § 167 and 168 of the Code. The capitalized cost of any recoverable precious metal is not depreciable under § § 167 and 168.

Application
Any change in a taxpayer's treatment of the cost of precious metals to conform with this revenue ruling is a change in method of accounting that must be made in accordance with § § 446 and 481, the regulations thereunder, and the applicable administrative procedures. See section 6.01 of Rev. Proc. 2015-14, 2015-5 I.R.B. 450 (or successor guidance). The amount of the § 481(a) adjustment must account for the proper amount of the depreciation allowable that is required to be capitalized under any provision of the Code (e.g., § 263A) as of the beginning of the year of change.

Effect On Other Documents

Rev. Rul. 75-491 is revoked.

Rev. Rul. 90-65 is revoked.

Drafting Information

The principal author of this revenue ruling is Douglas H. Kim of the Office of Associate Chief Counsel (Income Tax and Accounting). For further information regarding this revenue ruling, contact Mr. Kim at (202) 317-7005 (not a toll-free call).

EXAMPLE 4-2

Lisa Hammill owns and operates a business that creates custom-made jewelry pieces for its customers. Because many customers are not familiar with the type of jewelry that can be made, Lisa creates a set of "sample" jewelry items that she presents to show current styles and fashions. These items are not sold to customers. Every three years or so, Lisa melts down the gold and creates new samples. Lisa's initial $10,000 investment in the gold used to make the sample items was recorded as a fixed asset with no useful life and thus remains on her books at that value. Over the last decade or so, as the price of gold per ounce has skyrocketed, she sees the samples as an expensive asset with no cost recovery in the foreseeable future. She is particularly concerned because she has noticed that over time, the amount of gold used for the sample is slowly eroding, attributable to minute portions lost due to scratching, marring, and abrasions while being used as a sample and a very small amount of loss during the melting and reconstruction process. She estimates that of the 20 ounces she originally started with, she loses about one-quarter of an ounce each refabrication (which occurs about every three years). Because she has to replace this small amount every cycle, at current prices, she is starting to notice the cost. Lisa has read the IRC and regulations (there are over 40) related to depreciation and is looking for some clarity.

Exhibit 4-3 contains a revenue ruling that provides guidance to taxpayers on issues similar to those facing Lisa. Three fact situations are presented in the ruling, and although the first fact pattern is about a jeweler, the second fact pattern is actually more closely related to Lisa's use of gold in her store. Like the second situation in the revenue ruling, a portion of the gold is lost as part of the sample process. As a result, Lisa can use Rev. Rul. 2015-11, 2015-21 IRB 975 as part of substantial authority in concluding that she is eligible to take a depreciation deduction for the portion of gold lost in each cycle.

New researchers should be certain to avoid confusing revenue rulings with other forms of rulings, such as private letter rulings (discussed later in this chapter). In addition, as more and more of the code has shifted to requiring annual or quarterly updates for cost-of-living adjustments, interest rates, and mileage rates, revenue rulings (and revenue procedures discussed in the next section) have become an important source of information to interpret how the code is applied in the current year.

2-1 Revenue Ruling Citations

Revenue rulings are published weekly by the IRS in the Internal Revenue Bulletin, which is discussed in more detail later in this chapter. An example of a citation of a revenue ruling is as follows:

Rev. Rul. 2010-5, 2010-4 I.R.B. 312

2010-5 is the Revenue Ruling number (the fifth Revenue Ruling of 2010).

2010-4 is the weekly issue of the Internal Revenue Bulletin (the fourth week of 2010).

I.R.B. is the abbreviation for the Internal Revenue Bulletin.

312 is the page number on which the ruling starts in the Internal Revenue Bulletin. If the page number is not yet available, the date of the revenue ruling is substituted for the page number.

Through 2008, revenue rulings in the I.R.B. were published in twice-yearly bound volumes, named the **Cumulative Bulletin (C.B.)** by the Government Publishing Office (referred to as a permanent citation). An example of such a C.B. citation is as follows:

Rev. Rul. 96-58, 1996-2 C.B. 6

96-58 is the Revenue Ruling number (the 58th Revenue Ruling of 1996).

1996-2 is the volume number of the Cumulative Bulletin (volume 2 of 1996).

C.B. is the abbreviation for the Cumulative Bulletin.

6 is the page number.

Note the two-digit year (96) in this citation. Tax practitioners should be aware of the historical C.B. citation system because many older revenue rulings, which are still in effect, may have research value in future years.

2-2 Locating Revenue Rulings

Generally, the tax researcher must examine every applicable revenue ruling before a tax research project is complete. Revenue rulings can be found in the Internal Revenue Bulletin and by using commercial tax research databases as discussed in Chapter 2. Prior to 1953, revenue rulings were lumped together with other rulings and published by the IRS. For example, 1951 IRS Rulings 13,509 to 13,614 concerned the Tax Court of the United States, income tax, estate and gift taxes, employment taxes, excise tax, miscellaneous rulings, legislation, and committee reports. A tax researcher cannot ignore such rulings simply because they are old; some might still be applicable in certain situations.

SPOTLIGHT ON TAXATION

Decline in the Number of Revenue Rulings Issued

The number of revenue rulings issued by the IRS has dropped considerably in recent years.

Year	Revenue Rulings Issued	Year	Revenue Rulings Issued
1987	142	2011	32
1988	105	2012	33
1989	131	2013	27
1990	112	2014	34
1991	70	2015	26

Of the 26 revenue rulings issued in 2015, 21 were on mundane matters such as interest rates and similar adjustments. In the 1950s, the IRS regularly issued over 600 revenue rulings per year. The reasons given for the decline are varied, but one likely cause is resource constraints on the agency.

3 Revenue Procedures

Revenue procedures deal with the internal practice and procedures of the IRS in the administration of the tax laws. They constitute the IRS's way of releasing information to taxpayers and instructing them on how to comply with certain procedures, such as filing a letter ruling request. Although a revenue procedure may not be as useful as a regulation or a revenue ruling in the direct resolution of a tax research problem, the practitioner still should be familiar with all pertinent procedures.

As mentioned previously, revenue procedures (along with revenue rulings) are one of the primary ways that updates to annual or quarterly information is provided by the IRS to taxpayers. For example, adjustments to income tax brackets for individuals, phase-outs for various deductions, current year credit amounts such as the earned income credit, and a vast wealth of necessary information for any taxpayer or tax preparer are issued through revenue procedures.

EXAMPLE 4-3

Linda and Pat adopted a child in 2016. Adoption is a very expensive process, and thus they are wondering if a tax break might be offered. An examination of the IRC reveals that a tax credit is available under § 23; however, § 23(b)(1) provides for an overall limit of $10,000 and a reduction of the credit for higher income taxpayers starting at $150,000. Linda and Pat are somewhat disheartened as they spent well over $20,000 adopting the child, and their joint income exceeds $200,000. However, Linda and Pat's tax preparer notices § 23(h), which provides for an annual cost-of-living adjustment starting in 2002. The tax adviser reviews the revenue procedures issued in 2015 and notices one related to updating such amounts for the 2016 tax year. An excerpt of the revenue procedure is presented in Exhibit 4-4.

EXHIBIT 4-4:   Excerpt of Rev. Proc. 2015-53, 2015-44 I.R.B. 615

.03 Adoption Credit. For taxable years beginning in 2016, under § 23(a)(3) the credit allowed for an adoption of a child with special needs is $13,460. For taxable years beginning in 2016, under § 23(b)(1) the maximum credit allowed for other adoptions is the amount of qualified adoption expenses up to $13,460. The available adoption credit begins to phase out under § 23(b)(2)(A) for taxpayers with modified adjusted gross income in excess of $201,920 and is completely phased out for taxpayers with modified adjusted gross income of $241,920 or more. (See section 3.19 of this revenue procedure for the adjusted items relating to adoption assistance programs.)

.04 Child Tax Credit. For taxable years beginning in 2016, the value used in § 24(d)(1)(B)(i) to determine the amount of credit under § 24 that may be refundable is $3,000.

.05 Hope Scholarship, American Opportunity, and Lifetime Learning Credits.

(1) For taxable years beginning in 2016, the Hope Scholarship Credit under § 25A(b)(1), as increased under § 25A(i) (the American Opportunity Tax Credit), is an amount equal to 100 percent of qualified tuition and related expenses not in excess of $2,000 plus 25 percent of those expenses in excess of $2,000 but not in excess of $4,000. Accordingly, the maximum Hope Scholarship Credit allowable under § 25(b)(1) for taxable years beginning in 2016 is $2,500.

(2) For taxable years beginning in 2016, a taxpayer's modified adjusted gross income in excess of $80,000 ($160,000 for a joint return) is used to determine the reduction under § 25A(d)(2) in the amount of the Hope Scholarship Credit otherwise allowable under § 25A(a)(1). For taxable years beginning in 2016, a taxpayer's modified adjusted gross income in excess of $55,000 ($111,000 for a joint return) is used to determine the reduction under § 25A(d)(2) in the amount of the Lifetime Learning Credit otherwise allowable under § 25A(a)(2).

As indicated in Rev. Proc. 2015-53, the annual overall adoption credit limitation has increased to $13,460 for 2016, and the income limitation has increased to start at $201,920. Both of these amounts represent substantial increases over the amounts reflected in the original code section.

Revenue procedures are issued in a manner similar to that for revenue rulings. They are published in the weekly Internal Revenue Bulletin. The IRS issues approximately 50 revenue procedures per year. (For example, there were 57 in 2015.)

A revenue procedure is cited using the same system as that for revenue rulings. Thus, a typical current revenue procedure would have the following citation: Rev. Proc. 2010-20, 2010-14 I.R.B. 528.

A revenue procedure is reproduced in Exhibit 4-5. Revenue procedures can be found in the same publications in which revenue rulings are located.

EXHIBIT 4-5: Revenue Procedure Excerpt

Rev. Proc. 2015-42, 2015-36 IRB 310

1. Purpose

This revenue procedure provides the domestic asset/liability percentages and domestic investment yields needed by foreign life insurance companies and foreign property and liability insurance companies to compute their minimum effectively connected net investment income under section 842(b) of the Internal Revenue Code for taxable years beginning after December 31, 2013. Instructions are provided for computing foreign insurance companies' liabilities for the estimated tax and installment payments of estimated tax for taxable years beginning after December 31, 2013. For more specific guidance regarding the computation of the amount of net investment income to be included by a foreign insurance company on its U.S. income tax return, see Notice 89-96, 1989-2 C.B. 417. For the domestic asset/liability percentage and domestic investment yield, as well as instructions for computing foreign insurance companies' liabilities for estimated tax and installment payments of estimated tax for taxable years beginning after December 31, 2012, see Rev. Proc. 2014-53, 2014-19 I.R.B. 573.

2. Changes

DOMESTIC ASSET/LIABILITY PERCENTAGES FOR 2014. The Secretary determines the domestic asset/liability percentage separately for life insurance companies and property and liability insurance companies. For the first taxable year beginning after December 31, 2013, the relevant domestic asset/liability percentages are:

[120.4] percent for foreign life insurance companies, and

[193.3] percent for foreign property and liability insurance companies.

.02. DOMESTIC INVESTMENT YIELDS FOR 2014. The Secretary is required to prescribe separate domestic investment yields for foreign life insurance companies and for foreign property and liability insurance companies. For the first taxable year beginning after December 31, 2013, the relevant domestic investment yields are:

[4.6] percent for foreign life insurance companies, and

[3.9] percent for foreign property and liability insurance companies.

.03. SOURCE OF DATA FOR 2014. The section 842(b) percentages to be used for the 2014 tax year are based on tax return data following the same methodology used for the 2013 year.

3. Application-Estimated Taxes

To compute estimated tax and the installment payments of estimated tax due for taxable years beginning after December 31, 2013, a foreign insurance company must compute its estimated tax payments by adding to its income other than net investment income the greater of (i) its net investment income as determined under section 842(b)(5), that is actually effectively connected with the conduct of a trade or business within the United States for the relevant period, or (ii) the minimum effectively connected net investment income under section 842(b) that would result from using the most recently available domestic asset/liability percentage and domestic investment yield. Thus, for installment payments due after the publication of this revenue procedure, the domestic asset/liability percentages and the domestic investment yields provided in this revenue procedure must be used to compute the minimum effectively connected net investment income. However, if the due date of an installment is less than 20 days after the date this revenue procedure is published in the Internal Revenue Bulletin, the asset/liability percentages and domestic investment yields provided in Rev. Proc. 2014-53 may be used to compute the minimum effectively connected net investment income for such installment. For further guidance in computing estimated tax, see Notice 89-96.

4. Effective Date
This revenue procedure is effective for taxable years beginning after December 31, 2013.

5. Drafting Information
The principal author of this revenue procedure is Sheila Ramaswamy of the Office of Associate Chief Counsel (International). For further information regarding this revenue procedure contact Sheila Ramaswamy at (202) 317-6938 (not a toll free call).

4 Letter Rulings

The term *letter rulings* actually covers a number of different forms of guidance issued by the IRS, including private letter rulings, technical advice memoranda, and determination letters. There are other forms of IRS communications covered later as well.

4-1 Private Letter Rulings

The National Office of the IRS issues **private letter rulings** in response to a taxpayer's request for the IRS's position on a specified tax issue. The IRS has the authority to decline to issue letter rulings under certain conditions, such as when the problem is one of an inherently factual nature. The content, format, and procedures that are used for revenue rulings apply with respect to private letter rulings. The IRS does not publish its reply in the Internal Revenue Bulletin. Rather, it sends its response only to the taxpayer who submitted the request. An excerpt of a private letter ruling is shown in Exhibit 4-6.

EXHIBIT 4-6: Private Letter Ruling

Private Letter Ruling 201616002
This letter responds to the Date1 letter submitted by Taxpayer requesting a ruling that contributions made by Taxpayer pursuant to a political action committee charity match program are deductible under section 162 of the Internal Revenue Code (Code) as ordinary and necessary business expenses. The Date1 letter was supplemented by additional letters dated Dates.

FACTS
Taxpayer, a corporation, is prohibited by the Federal Election Campaign Act (FECA) from contributing to federal election campaigns. 52 U.S.C. § 30118(a); 11 CFR § 114.2(b). Consistent with the FECA, Taxpayer established PAC, which is funded by employees of Taxpayer and its subsidiaries. PAC is a political organization exempt from taxation under section 527 of the Code. PAC's purpose, as stated in its charter, is to "disburse funds to candidates" for public office. The candidates are chosen by PAC's [redacted text].

To incentivize employee contributions of at least Amount1 but not more than Amount2 to PAC, Taxpayer matches each of these contributions with a contribution in the name of the employee to one or more charities selected by the employee. Taxpayer requests a ruling that it may deduct its matching contributions as ordinary and necessary business expenses under section 162 of the Code.

LAW AND APPLICATION
Section 162 of the Code allows a taxpayer to deduct all of the ordinary and necessary expenses paid or incurred during the taxable year in carrying on any trade or business. "Ordinary" has been defined to mean "frequent" or "common" in the

context of the particular business. See *Welch v. Helvering*, 290 U.S. 111, 54 S. Ct. 8, 78 L. Ed. 212, 1933-2 C.B. 112 (1933). "Necessary" has been defined to mean "appropriate and helpful." Id.

Regardless of whether such expenses are "ordinary" and "necessary," deductions for expenses made to political campaigns have long been prohibited. See, for example, § 162(e)(2) (1962) (prohibiting deductions for expenses "for participation in, or intervention in, any political campaign on behalf of any candidate for public office"). Congress expanded this prohibition to disallow a deduction of amounts paid or incurred in connection with a political campaign. See § 162(e)(1)(B), as amended by the Omnibus Budget Reconciliation Act of 1993, P.L. 103-66, § 13222(a).

Under current section 162(e)(1)(B), amounts paid or incurred in connection with participation in, or intervention in, any political campaign on behalf of (or in opposition to) any candidate for public office are not deductible under section 162. Treasury Regulation section 1.162-20(c) further states that, while certain types of expenses with respect to legislative matters may be deductible, other expenditures, including those "for political campaign purposes," are not deductible from gross income. Treas. Reg. § 1.162-20(c).

Courts generally have read the phrase "in connection with" as it appears in the Code broadly. See, for example, *Snow v. Commissioner*, 416 U.S. 500, 94 S. Ct. 1876, 40 L. Ed. 2d 336 (1974) ("In connection with" under section 174); *Conopco v. United States*, 572 F.3d 162 (3rd Cir. 2009) ("In connection with" under section 162(k)(1)); *General Mills v. United States*, 554 F.3d 727 (8th Cir. 2009) ("In connection with" under section 162(k)(1)); but see, *Boise Cascade v. United States*, 329 F.3d 751 (9th Cir. 2003) (stating that the phrase "in connection with" should be read narrowly; requiring one action to be a prerequisite of the other).

Here, the contributions to PAC and Taxpayer's matching contributions are inextricably linked. The contributions to PAC are a prerequisite for Taxpayer's matching contributions. Moreover, Taxpayer's matching contributions are intended to incentivize contributions of Amount1 or more to PAC. Applying section 162(e)(1)(B), the regulations, and case law, we conclude that Taxpayer's matching contributions are "in connection with" a political campaign on behalf of a candidate for public office, and are not deductible under section 162.

This ruling is directed only to Taxpayer. Section 6110(k)(3) of the Code provides that it may not be used or cited as precedent.

This ruling is based upon information submitted by Taxpayer and accompanied by a penalty of perjury statement executed by an appropriate party. This office has not verified any of the material submitted in support of the ruling request, and the material is subject to verification on examination.

In accordance with the Power of Attorney on file with this office, a copy of this letter is being sent to your authorized representatives.

Sincerely,

John P. Moriarty
Acting Associate Chief Counsel
(Income Tax and Accounting)
By: Karin G. Gross
Senior Technical Reviewer, Branch 1
(Income Tax & Accounting)

Requesting a private letter ruling is a fairly involved activity and should not be undertaken lightly. More or less each year for the past few years, the IRS has issued a revenue procedure that details the steps necessary to request a letter ruling (e.g., Rev. Proc. 2016-1, 2016-1, I.R.B. 1). The annual revenue procedure details the types of issues that may be considered in a letter request, who the request should be sent to, the fee required, and of course, a detailed description of what should be included in the request (including a sample letter request). The request letters are not released to the public, only the IRS's response. The 2016 instructions list 18 distinct requirements to be included in a request, including a complete statement of the facts, a statement of supporting and contrary authorities, and an analysis of the material facts. The request should also detail the portions of the letter that the IRS should redact when released. In order to avoid privacy issues, letter rulings often refer to anonymous "Taxpayer A" or "Amount $X." In some cases, if the IRS asserts that the transaction will not receive a treatment favorable to the taxpayer, it will suggest means by which the transaction could be restructured to obtain the favorable treatment.

As shown near the end of Exhibit 4-6, all private letter rulings are issued with a caveat that the ruling applies only to the taxpayer making the request:

> *This ruling is directed only to Taxpayer. Section 6110(k)(3) of the Code provides that it may not be used or cited as precedent.*

This does not mean, however, that letter rulings should be cast aside as useless to the tax researcher. First, private letter rulings are included in the list of authorities constituting "substantial authority" upon which a taxpayer may rely to avoid certain statutory penalties.[5] When the facts of a private letter ruling are similar to the current facts of a taxpayer, from a practical perspective, it seems reasonable to rely on the conclusions in the ruling. A thorough analysis of the authorities cited in the letter ruling generally makes good sense with a keen eye toward identifying possible differences in the fact patterns in the ruling and the facts currently being considered. At a minimum, letter rulings are an important source of information because they indicate how the IRS may treat a similar transaction.

SPOTLIGHT ON TAXATION

Fees for Letter Rulings

From a cost–benefit perspective, a letter ruling for most taxpayers probably does not make financial sense. Some of the fees for letter requests in 2016 are as follows:

Type of Request	Fee
General letter request fee	$28,300
Change in tax year	$4,200
Nonautomatic change in accounting method	$8,600

For taxpayers with gross income of less than $250,000, the general fee drops to $2,200. Thus, tax issues with small financial consequences are generally not an appropriate issue for a letter ruling.

Private letter rulings also constitute an important IRS stimulus for new revenue rulings. When the IRS comes across an unusual transaction that it believes to be of general interest, or when it receives a flurry of letter ruling requests concerning very similar factual situations, a private ruling may be converted into revenue ruling form and published in official administrative sources. The IRS must notify the taxpayer of its intention to disclose the ruling, and the taxpayer has the right to protest such disclosure. Before publication, all aspects of the new ruling, including the statement of facts, are purged of any reference to the taxpayer's name or other identifying information.

---

[5]Reg. § 1.6662-4(d)(3)(iii).

4-2 Technical Advice Memoranda

A **technical advice memorandum (TAM)** is issued by the IRS's Office of the Chief Counsel, typically responding to a request from an IRS official that stems from an audit or a taxpayer request for refund. A TAM and private letter review follow the same general format and thus will appear similar. A TAM, however, generally concerns a completed transaction, whereas a private letter ruling typically is requested by a taxpayer prior to completing a transaction or filing a tax return.

Similar to private letter rulings, a TAM applies strictly to the taxpayer for whose audit it was requested, and it cannot be relied on by other taxpayers. However, once again the information that is contained in the memorandum may be useful to the tax researcher for the insight that it gives concerning the thinking of the IRS relative to a given problem area in taxation.

These memoranda are not included in any official IRS publication, but they are open for public inspection and available from commercial tax research services, as will be discussed in the next section. If the facts or the holding of a technical advice memorandum are thought by the IRS to be of general interest, the memorandum may be converted into revenue ruling format and published by the IRS in the Internal Revenue Bulletin.

4-3 Determination Letters

A **determination letter** is similar in purpose and nature to a private letter ruling, except that it is issued by a local office of the IRS rather than by the national office of the IRS. Because a determination letter is issued by a lower-level IRS official, it usually deals with issues and transactions that are not overtly controversial. For instance, the trustee of a pension plan might request a determination letter to ascertain whether the plan is qualified for the code's tax-favored deferred-compensation treatment.

Determination letters usually relate to completed transactions rather than to the proposed transactions that typically lead to the issuance of a private letter ruling. Determination letters are not included in any official IRS publication, but they are available to the tax researcher from commercial tax research services.

4-4 Precedential Value of Private Letter Rulings, TAMs, and Determination Letters

The precedential value of any of these written determinations is strictly limited.[6] Overall, such pronouncements may not be cited as authority in a tax matter by either the taxpayer or the IRS. However, they can be used as examples of IRS treatment of similar factual patterns when dealing with the IRS. For example, tax practitioners could suggest that a letter ruling be used as guidance in a similar situation during an audit. However, an IRS agent need not follow a letter ruling issued to a different taxpayer.

Taxpayers may rely on private letter rulings, technical advice memoranda, actions on decisions, general counsel memoranda, and other similar documents published by the IRS in the Internal Revenue Bulletin to avoid certain understatement of tax penalties. Nevertheless, use of such pronouncements for this purpose does not expand the general precedential value of these pronouncements with respect to determining a taxpayer's tax liability.

---

[6]IRC § 6110(k)(3).

4-5 Citing Letter Rulings

Because the IRS issues thousands of letter rulings per year, it assigns a nine-digit document number to each written determination for identification purposes. The first four digits indicate the year in which the ruling was issued, the next two numbers denote the week, and the last three digits indicate the number of the ruling for the week. Thus, a lengthy but unique identifier is created for each pronouncement. For example, the number of a letter ruling can be interpreted as follows:

Ltr. Rul. 201323021, where

2013 is the year the ruling is issued.

23 is the week of the year the ruling is issued.

021 indicates that this is the 21st ruling issued that week.

At times, a citation to a private letter ruling may be prefaced with *PLR* (e.g., PLR 201323021) and a technical advice memorandum with *TAM* (e.g., TAM 201544025). Over the years, the names under which these types of documents were issued have changed, so researchers need to be careful when citing.

Before 2000, only a two-digit date was used to signify the year in which the ruling was issued (e.g., 9814026).

98 is the year the ruling is issued.

14 is the week of the year the ruling is issued.

026 indicates that this is the 26th ruling issued that week.

4-6 Locating Written Determinations

If the tax researcher needs access to written determinations to complete a tax research project, they can be found online. The IRS releases sanitized versions of letter rulings (those since 1999) weekly, at **http://apps.irs.gov/app/picklist/list/writtenDeterminations.html.**

In addition, most online commercial tax services have letters ruling available as part of their research data base.

5 Internal Revenue Bulletin

The IRS issues several other types of information that can be of value to the researcher. Most of these are published through the **Internal Revenue Bulletin** (IRB), the instrument used to publish official rulings, procedures, regulations, court decisions, and a wealth of other items of interest to tax professionals. For example, regulations, revenue rulings, and revenue procedures are all released through the IRB. Other important items in the IRB include

- New tax laws issued by Congress

- Committee reports

- Tax treaties

- IRS notices

- IRS announcements

- Notices of proposed rulemaking (including advance notices)

- Actions on decisions

The IRB is available online at **www.irs.gov/irb/** and in a searchable form at **http://apps.irs.gov/app/picklist/list/internalRevenueBulletins.html**. See Exhibit 4-7 for an example of an Internal Revenue Bulletin.

EXHIBIT 4-7: Internal Revenue Bulletin

INTERNAL REVENUE
BULLETIN

IRS

HIGHLIGHTS
OF THIS ISSUE

Bulletin No. 2016–31
August 1, 2016

These synopses are intended only as aids to the reader in identifying the subject matter covered. They may not be relied upon as authoritative interpretations.

INCOME TAX

REG–134016–15, page 205.
Proposed regulations under section 355 of the Internal Revenue Code would clarify the application of the device prohibition and the active business requirement of section 355. The proposed regulations would affect corporations that distribute the stock of controlled corporations, their shareholders, and their security holders.

Rev. Rul. 2016–18, page 194.
Federal rates; adjusted federal rates; adjusted federal long-term rate and the long-term exempt rate. For purposes of sections 382, 642, 1274, 1288, 7872, and other sections of the Code, tables set forth the rates for August 2016.

EMPLOYEE PLANS

Notice 2016–46, page 202.
This notice sets forth updates on the corporate bond monthly yield curve, the corresponding spot segment rates for July 2016 used under § 417(e)(3)(D), the 24-month average segment rates applicable for May 2016, and the 30-year Treasury rates. These rates reflect the application of § 430(h)(2)(C)(iv), which was added by the Moving Ahead for Progress in the 21st Century Act, Public Law 112–141 (MAP-21) and amended by section 2003 of the Highway and Transportation Funding Act of 2014 (HATFA).

ADMINISTRATIVE

Announcement 2016–25, page 205.
This Announcement informs area residents affected by the Southern California Gas Company's natural gas leak at Aliso Canyon that the IRS will not assert that amounts paid either on behalf of or to the residents pursuant to the relocation plan are includible in gross income.

T.D. 9778, page 196.
Final regulations under section 7602 that clarify that persons with whom the IRS contracts for services described in section 6103(n) may be included as persons to receive summoned records and, in the presence and under the guidance of an IRS employee, participate fully in the interview of a summoned witness.

Finding Lists begin on page ii.

The IRB is somewhat like a weekly newsletter in that it is published weekly and contains items that are new or revised during that most recent period. The IRS's Website has each weekly edition going back for many years, but the search function is not particularly useful, thus rendering the Website useful primarily as an archive to download an IRB you identified as relevant through some other source. As a result, most of the major tax services group items published through the IRB as separate items (e.g., regulations, revenue rulings, etc.), which permits a more powerful search using keywords.

6 Acquiescences and Nonacquiescences

When the IRS loses an issue or decision in court, the commissioner may announce an acquiescence or nonacquiescence to the decision. An **acquiescence** indicates that the court decision, although it was adverse to the IRS, will be followed in similar situations. The commissioner determines, at his or her own discretion, the degree of similarity required before the IRS will follow the result that is unfavorable to itself.

A **nonacquiescence** indicates that the IRS disagrees with the adverse decision in the case and will follow the decision only for the specific taxpayer whose case resulted in the adverse ruling. If the IRS wishes to express agreement with only part of the decision that is settled in the taxpayer's favor, the commissioner may nonacquiesce with respect to certain issues. Finally, an acquiescence or nonacquiescence is not issued if the IRS prevails in a court case, because it likely agrees with all pertinent holdings.

Nonacquiescence may indicate to the tax practitioner that the IRS is likely to continue to litigate the issue in future cases that present similar fact patterns. However, the issuance of an acquiescence does not necessarily mean that the IRS agrees with the adverse decision, but only that it will not pursue the matter in a (similar and) subsequent case. Each of these items of information can be useful when the practitioner prepares for, or anticipates, a court challenge to the client's position in a tax matter.

As mentioned, if the IRS has acquiesced to a case, then the taxpayer can rely on that decision as a precedent that will be followed by agents for similar fact patterns. If the IRS has nonacquiesced, however, the taxpayer must evaluate whether to pursue a similar fact pattern in court. Such factors as the cost of litigation plus the probability of winning must be appraised before proceeding with a case similar to one with which the IRS has nonacquiesced.

Occasionally, the IRS changes (with an attendant retroactive effect on taxpayers) its acquiescence or nonacquiescence position by withdrawing the original pronouncement. For example, in *United States v. City Loan & Savings*, 287 F.2d 612 (CA-6, 1961), the court allowed the IRS to withdraw an acquiescence on an issue-by-issue, but not taxpayer-by-taxpayer, basis. This change may occur after only a short time passes or many years later. Such a change in the IRS's position typically is accompanied by a brief explanation of the reason for the change—for example, because of a contrary holding in a subsequent court case or a change in the agency's policy concerning the issue.

IRS acquiescence decisions are driven by related litigation costs, revenue effects, and administrative and policy directives. The IRS issues acquiescences/nonacquiescences as **actions on decision (AODs)**, relative to decisions of the following courts:

- Regular Tax Court

- Memorandum Tax Court

- District Court

- Court of Federal Claims

- Courts of Appeal

IRS actions on decision are currently published in the Internal Revenue Bulletin and before 2009 in semiannual Cumulative Bulletins. They are issued by various branches of the IRS Chief Counsel's office. AODs are public documents, and they generally include the following:

- The issue decided against the government;

- The pertinent facts; and

- A discussion of the reasoning supporting the acquiescence/nonacquiescence decision.[7]

Exhibit 4-8 reproduces an acquiescence from the IRB in which the IRS indicates its position on a case. A citator also can be used to locate and interpret acquiescence and nonacquiescence decisions.

EXHIBIT 4-8:   Action on Decision Excerpt

Action on Decision 2016-01, 2016-16 IRB

Subject: *Cosentino v. Commissioner*, T.C. Memo. 2014-186 [2014 RIA TC Memo ¶2014-186]

Issue: Whether an amount the taxpayers received from an accounting firm, to settle a claim that the taxpayers incurred additional income tax liability because of the firm's advice that they enter into an abusive tax shelter, is excludible from their gross income as a restoration of lost capital.

Discussion: The taxpayers, husband and wife, each had a 50 percent direct interest in a partnership that received rental income from real estate rentals. In 2002, the taxpayers wanted to dispose of a rental property held by the partnership through a like-kind exchange and sought advice from an accounting firm. The accounting firm advised the taxpayers to enter into an abusive tax shelter in an attempt to artificially increase the partnership's basis in the property. In 2003, the partnership disposed of the property in a like-kind exchange with boot. On its 2003 partnership return, the partnership reported a small amount in recognized gain and no deferred gain on the like-kind exchange. Had it not relied on the abusive tax shelter to report an improperly inflated adjusted basis in the relinquished property, the partnership would have reported realized gain of almost $2.4 million, of which almost $2 million would be recognized for 2003. In 2005, upon learning that the transaction was abusive, the taxpayers filed amended returns for 2002 and 2003 to report the correct gain from the like-kind exchange and pay the correct Federal and state income taxes on the recognized gain, as well as interest and penalties. The taxpayers also disclosed their participation in the abusive tax shelter.

In 2006, the taxpayers filed suit against the accounting firm, seeking to recover $640,749.80 in fees, in losses from the transaction, and in income tax deficiencies, interest, and penalties paid to Federal and state tax authorities. In 2007, a settlement was reached in which the accounting firm paid the taxpayers $375,000. The taxpayers did not include any of the settlement proceeds on their 2007 Federal income tax return. In a notice of deficiency, the Service rejected the taxpayer's exclusion of the settlement proceeds.

The Tax Court held that, except for those portions to which the tax benefit rule applies or to which no actual loss on the taxpayers' part was attributable, the settlement proceeds were excludible from gross income because they represented a return of lost capital. The court noted that the taxpayers did not know the transaction advised by the accounting firm was abusive and their intent was to defer gain recognition on the disposition of the rental property through a like-kind exchange. Relying on two cases that the court found similar to this case, and which involved settlement payments in malpractice lawsuits, the court concluded that the taxpayers paid Federal and state income taxes and other expenses they would not have paid had they not relied on the accounting firm's erroneous advice.

The Service disagrees with the Tax Court's holding.

Gross income includes "all income from whatever source derived" unless subtitle A of the Internal Revenue Code provides otherwise. Sec. 61(a).

---

[7]*Taxation with Representation Fund v. IRS*, 485 F. Supp. 263 (DDC, 1990).

"When a claim is resolved by settlement, the relevant question for the tax treatment of a settlement award is: 'In lieu of what were the damages awarded?'" *Milenbach v. Commissioner*, 318 F.3d 924, 932 [91 AFTR 2d 2003-818] (9th Cir. 2003) (quoting *Raytheon Prod. Corp. v. Commissioner*, 144 F.2d 110, 113 [32 AFTR 1155] (1st Cir. 1944)). The payments are includible in gross income if they are to replace lost profits, and are excludible from gross income as a return of capital if they are to compensate for the loss or destruction of capital. See *Milenbach*, 318 F.3d at 933; *Raytheon*, 144 F.2d at 113.

In *Clark v. Commissioner*, 40 B.T.A. 333 (1939), acq. 1957-1 C.B. 4, the Board of Tax Appeals held that the taxpayers, a husband and a wife, could exclude an amount they received from their tax counsel to compensate for additional income tax the taxpayers had to pay because of the tax counsel's error in return preparation. The tax counsel had prepared the taxpayers' joint return. The joint return brought them a less favorable tax outcome than separate returns would have. The Board concluded that the payment was compensation for the taxpayers' "loss which impaired [their] capital," or a return of the lost capital, and was "not income since it was not 'derived from capital, from labor or from both combined.'" *Clark* at 335 (citations omitted).

In Rev. Rul. 57-47, 1957-1 C.B. 23, the Service analyzed the nearly same facts as in *Clark*. The Service held (1) that no taxable income is derived from that portion of the settlement proceeds that does not exceed the amount of tax that the taxpayer was required to pay because of the return preparer's error; and (2) that the remainder of the proceeds that represented interest on the overpaid tax and the fees that the taxpayer paid to the preparer and deducted must be included in gross income.

In *Concord Instruments v. Commissioner*, T.C. Memo. 1994-248 [1994 RIA TC Memo ¶94,248], a taxpayer received $125,000 in settlement of a malpractice claim against an attorney who failed to file a notice of appeal from a Tax Court decision against the taxpayer. The taxpayer was seeking compensation for additional costs incurred (including the deficiency it paid) because of the attorney's failure. Relying heavily on *Clark* and Rev. Rul. 57-47, the Tax Court held that the portion of the $125,000 settlement attributable to the Federal income tax deficiency was excluded from gross income as a restoration of capital.

The Tax Court's reliance on *Clark* and *Concord Instruments* is misplaced. In *Clark*, the taxpayers sustained a loss of capital when they paid the additional tax due to the tax counsel's error. The *Clark* taxpayers could have paid less tax without any change in the facts of their situation if their tax counsel had advised them to file separate returns. The filing of a joint return, not the underlying facts, caused the *Clark* taxpayers' loss by leading them to pay more than the minimum amount of tax they owed based on the transactional facts.

In *Concord Instruments*, the taxpayer's claim against the attorney was that it paid taxes over and above the minimum amount it owed because the attorney failed to file a timely notice of appeal. The court looked to the nature of the taxpayer's claim to characterize the settlement amount the taxpayer received, and found that the amount was to compensate for the loss sustained due to the attorney's negligence that resulted in the taxpayer losing the ability to challenge the merits of the underlying tax liability.

Unlike the taxpayers in *Clark* and *Concord Instruments*, the taxpayers in this case paid the correct amount of Federal income tax based on the transaction they entered into. In this transaction, the taxpayers received taxable boot as part of their consideration upon the disposition of the rental property. When the artificially inflated basis was disregarded, the boot resulted in gain recognition from the exchange and the imposition of tax on that gain. Once this transaction was completed, no choices were available to the taxpayers to reduce this taxable gain. It was the facts of the transaction, and not a failure to make an election or a failure to timely file an appeal, that caused the taxpayers to incur additional tax.

In light of the underlying gain recognition transaction, the amount of tax imposed was not more than what they properly owed on that transaction and, consequently, the taxpayers did not sustain a loss. To the contrary, because the taxpayers received the boot, and because they continued to receive the benefit of both the boot and the basis in the newly acquired real property even after the abusive tax shelter transaction was disregarded, taxpayers financially were in a better (not merely restored) position after the settlement than they were in before entering the transaction.[1]

Accordingly, the settlement amount the taxpayers received is not a restoration of lost capital, but is instead compensation by the accounting firm for a portion of the Federal income tax the taxpayers properly owed, and therefore should be included in the taxpayers' gross income as an accession to wealth.

---

[1] In reaching its holding, the court considered the taxpayers' plan to use a lifetime series of tax-free exchanges, followed by a step up in basis at death, to permanently avoid paying taxes on the gain from these transactions. We disagree with the court's reliance on these facts. The taxpayers' ability to execute that tax planning strategy was purely speculative, and a change in the taxpayers' circumstances, or even a change to the provisions of the Internal Revenue Code, could have altered the strategy at any time.

After the IRS issues such a pronouncement, any reference to the citation for the case includes the abbreviation either "Acq" or "Nonacq" (or, occasionally, "NA") to indicate the subsequent development. However, the AOD itself should not be cited as an IRS precedent.

7 Chief Counsel Memoranda

The office of the IRS's chief counsel generates a wealth of taxpayer guidance through various document types, some of which are no longer issued or have been replaced by a new format.

General counsel memoranda (GCMs) and chief counsel advice (CCA) are prepared by the chief counsel's office and are intended primarily for internal IRS use. CCAs replaced GCMs after 2002. These provide the chief counsel's interpretation of and positions on tax law. Field service advice (FSA) is memoranda that advise IRS attorneys and revenue agents on significant tax issues. These have also been replaced by CCAs.

Litigation guideline memoranda (LGMs) and chief counsel notices (CCNs) are prepared by the national office of the IRS to disseminate policies, procedures, instructions, and other information to litigating attorneys and other employees in the chief counsel's office. LGMs were issued between 1986 and 1999 but are now issued as CCNs.[8] CCNs are a precursor to the Chief Counsel Directives Manual (CCDM), which is part of the Internal Revenue Manual (IRM). The IRM is the operating manual for IRS employees and contains internal guidelines, policies, and procedures to be followed by the IRS. The IRM is available on the IRS Website.

Technical memoranda (TMs) are similar to CCAs and are generally issued to the Treasury Department. TMs have not been issued since 1993.

Chief counsel bulletins are prepared by divisions within the Office of the Chief Counsel and provide updates on recent court decisions and other legal developments.

Generic legal advice (GLA), nondocketed service advice reviews (NSAR), and Service Center advice (SCA) are also issued by the Office of the Chief Counsel and are intended for internal IRS use.

8 Announcements and Notices

The IRS issues **announcements and notices** concerning items of general importance to taxpayers. Announcements are public pronouncements that have immediate or short-term value, such as an approaching deadline for making an election. Notices contain guidance involving substantive interpretations of the code or other provisions of the law that usually have long-term application. IRS notices are sometimes issued in advance of regulations to provide immediate, important guidance to taxpayers and thus are an important source of authority in tax research. A tax practitioner may rely on an IRS announcement or notice as authority for an action but should confirm his or her understanding of the released material using appropriate research techniques. Exhibit 4-9 reproduces a typical notice. Notices and announcements are published in the weekly Internal Revenue Bulletin.

---

[8]The IRS announced in late 2016 that LGMs may now be considered obsolete.

EXHIBIT 4-9: IRS Notice

Notice 2016-12, 2016-12 IRB 312

Purpose
This notice provides the maximum vehicle values for 2016 that taxpayers need to determine the value of personal use of employer-provided vehicles under the special valuation rules provided under section 1.61-21(d) and (e) of the Income Tax Regulations.

Maximum Vehicle Values
The maximum value of employer-provided vehicles first made available to employees for personal use in calendar year 2016 for which the vehicle cents-per-mile valuation rule provided under Regulation section 1.61-21(e) may be applicable is $15,900 for a passenger automobile and $17,700 for a truck or van.

The maximum value of employer-provided vehicles first made available to employees for personal use in calendar year 2016 for which the fleet-average valuation rule provided under Regulation section 1.61-21(d) may be applicable is $21,200 for a passenger automobile and $23,100 for a truck or van.

Effective Date
This notice applies to employer-provided passenger automobiles first made available to employees for personal use in calendar year 2016.

Drafting Information
The principal author of this notice is Kathleen Edmondson of the Office of the Division Counsel/Associate Chief Counsel (Tax Exempt & Government Entities). For further information on this notice contact Ms. Edmondson on (202) 317-6798 (not a toll-free number).

---

9 IRS Publications

The IRS publishes a number of documents designed to assist taxpayers with compliance. Although these should not be relied on by taxpayers (they are not a source of substantial authority), they can be extremely helpful in understanding particular parts of tax law or how to properly execute taxpayer compliance. Two of the largest types are IRS publications and IRS form instructions. **IRS publications** are documents that are arranged by topic and contain a more easy-to-read description of how the tax law works on that topic. IRS Publication 17, Your Federal Income Tax, is a large publication that covers almost all facets of completing the individual income tax return and contains many examples and worksheets to assist taxpayers with individual tax compliance. Some other important topics include the following:

- IRS Publication 946 How to Depreciate Property

- IRS Publication 901 Tax Treaties

- IRS Publication 15 (Circular E) Employer's Tax Guide

A complete list of IRS publications can be found at the IRS Website.

Because IRS publications are not substantial authority, extreme care should be taken when placing any reliance on these documents. IRS publications do not benefit from citations to primary sources of tax law and thus do not replace the work of sound tax research in any way. In addition, IRS publications are not always updated in a timely manner for changes in the tax law and are often thought to be biased in favor of the IRS over the taxpayer.

Almost all IRS forms come with instructions. The IRS forms and instructions are intended to assist taxpayers in complying with reporting requirements under the tax law. Similar to IRS publications, forms and instructions are also not considered substantial authority and caution should be exercised with their use as a source of tax law. However, IRS forms and instructions are not without redeeming value. Often, complex calculations are handled through step-by-step computations on a tax form or in a worksheet in form instructions. These should be used to assist a researcher in understanding the tax law but are in no way a substitute for proper legal sources.

SUMMARY

Administrative pronouncements provide the tax researcher with a significant amount of information from and about the IRS. The primary IRS pronouncements that are of interest to the tax researcher include the regulations, revenue rulings, revenue procedures, and letter rulings. The tax practitioner who performs competent research must be aware of the content and format of each of these items, know how to locate them, appreciate the precedential value of each, and understand how each might affect the client's tax problem. Exhibit 4-10 summarizes the most commonly encountered IRS pronouncements.

EXHIBIT 4-10: Common IRS Pronouncements

Pronouncement	Purpose
Regulation	The official Treasury or IRS interpretation of a portion of the Internal Revenue Code
Revenue Ruling	The IRS's application of the tax law to a specific fact situation and other information for taxpayers (e.g., interest rate adjustments)
Revenue Procedure	A statement of IRS practice or procedure that affects taxpayers or the general public
Notice	IRS release that provides substantive or procedural guidance on an expedited basis
Private Letter Ruling	Statement issued by the National Office of the IRS at a taxpayer's request, applying the tax law to a proposed transaction
Determination Letter	Statement issued by the district director in response to a taxpayer request concerning the application of the tax law to a specific completed transaction
Acquiescence	Acceptance by the IRS of a court decision that held in the taxpayer's favor. Published as an action on decision
Nonacquiescence	Notice that the IRS still disagrees with a court decision that held in the taxpayer's favor. Published as an action on decision
Treasury Decision	A document that explains and contains the text of a final or temporary regulation
Technical Advice Memorandum	A letter ruling issued on a completed transaction, usually during an audit

KEY WORDS

By the time you complete this chapter, you should be comfortable discussing each of the following terms. If you need additional review of any of these items, return to the appropriate material in the chapter or consult the glossary to this text.

acquiescence, p. 130

actions on decision (AOD), p. 130

announcements and notices, p. 133

Cumulative Bulletin (C.B.), p. 121

determination letter, p. 127

final regulations, p. 111

Internal Revenue Bulletin (IRB), p. 128
interpretive regulations, p. 112
IRS publications, p. 134
legislative regulations, p. 112
nonacquiescence, p. 130

Notice of Proposed Rulemaking, p. 111
private letter rulings, p. 124
proposed regulations, p. 111
regulations, p. 110
revenue procedures, p. 122

revenue rulings, p. 117
technical advice memorandum (TAM), p. 127
temporary regulations, p. 112
Treasury decision (TD), p. 111

DISCUSSION QUESTIONS

1. What department and agency of the U.S. government has the responsibility to administer the federal tax laws?

2. Section 7805(a) of the Internal Revenue Code authorizes the IRS to perform what activities?

3. The IRS issues numerous pronouncements. Name and describe four that are the most important in conducting federal tax research.

4. Define the terms *regulation* and *Treasury decision*. Where are TDs published so that interested parties can comment on them?

5. "A tax researcher should not ignore proposed regulations." Comment on this statement.

6. Define and distinguish between general (interpretive) and legislative regulations.

7. What are temporary regulations? What weight do they carry in the tax researcher's analysis?

8. The burden of proof is on the taxpayer to prove that a provision of the regulations is improper. How could this affect one's tax research?

9. In general, what is the effective date of a new regulation?

10. What is a revenue ruling?

11. Describe the structure of a typical revenue ruling.

12. What resources are available to help the tax researcher who wishes to check the status of a revenue ruling?

13. Of what relevance to the tax practitioner is a revenue procedure?

14. Identify three types of letter rulings that are of interest to the tax researcher. Indicate whether each of these rulings is published by the IRS.

15. Which office of the IRS issues private letter rulings? Who may request such a ruling? What kinds of issues are addressed therein?

16. Sometimes a private letter ruling is generalized and included in an official IRS publication. What form does this recast private ruling take?

17. What is a determination letter? Which office of the IRS issues determination letters? What kinds of issues are addressed therein?

18. What is a technical advice memorandum? Who may request it? What kinds of issues are addressed therein? Does the IRS include technical advice memoranda in any official publication?

19. Discuss the precedential value of private letter rulings, determination letters, and technical advice memoranda. What role do these items play in conducting tax research?

20. Which IRS documents are open to public inspection under IRC § 6110?

21. What is the precedential value of an IRS written determination under IRC § 6110?

22. One of the most important IRS publications is the Internal Revenue Bulletin. How often is this document published? Name six items that typically are published in the Internal Revenue Bulletin.

23. Distinguish between a citation with "I.R.B." in it and one with "C.B." in it.

24. Discuss the difference between a revenue ruling and a revenue procedure.

25. In what publication(s) would a tax researcher find the official listing of the IRS acquiescences and nonacquiescences to a Tax Court decision?

26. Can the IRS change its position on acquiescences or nonacquiescences?

27. Must the IRS acquiesce or nonacquiesce to every issue in a court decision?

28. What is the purpose of each of the following?
    a. Technical memorandum (TM)
    b. General counsel memorandum (GCM)
    c. Action on decision (AOD)

29. What is the purpose of each of the following?
    a. Chief counsel notices (CCN)
    b. Service center advice (SCA)
    c. Chief counsel advice (CCA)

30. What is an IRS announcement? When is it used? In your opinion, could a tax practitioner rely on an IRS announcement as authority for a tax return position?

31. What is an IRS notice? When is it used? In your opinion, could a tax practitioner rely on an IRS notice as authority for a tax return position?

32. Why should the tax researcher exercise caution in relying on an IRS publication, such as published instructions to tax forms, in undertaking a research project?

EXERCISES

33. In the citation Reg. § 1.212-3, what do the "1," the "212," and the "3" indicate?

34. Answer the following questions about this citation: Reg. § 20.2039-1(a).
    a. What does the "20" stand for?
    b. What does the "2039" stand for?
    c. What does the "1" stand for?
    d. What does the "(a)" stand for?

35. Answer the following questions about this citation: Reg. § 1.274-6T(a)(2).
    a. What does the "1" stand for?
    b. What does the "274" stand for?
    c. What does the "6T" stand for?
    d. What does the "(a)" stand for?
    e. What does the "(2)" stand for?

36. Answer the following questions about this citation: 26 C.F.R. § 163-10(a)(2).
    a. What does the "26" stand for?
    b. What does the "163" stand for?
    c. What does the "10" stand for?
    d. What does the "(a)" stand for?
    e. What does the "(2)" stand for?

37. Answer the following questions about this citation: 26 C.F.R. §1.61-21(a)(3).
    a. What does the "1" stand for?
    b. What does the "26" stand for?
    c. What does the "61" stand for?
    d. What does the "21" stand for?
    e. What does the "(a)" stand for?
    f. What does the "(3)" stand for?

38. Give the number that is associated with each of the following categories of regulations:
    a. Estate tax regulations
    b. Income tax regulations
    c. Gift tax regulations
    d. Procedural regulations
    e. Employment tax regulations

39. Give the type of regulation associated with each of the following regulation numbers:
    a. 31
    b. 301
    c. 25
    d. 601
    e. 20

40. Explain each of the elements of this citation: Rev. Rul. 2013-5, 2013-9 I.R.B. 525.

41. Explain each of the elements of this citation: Rev. Rul. 96-41, 1996-2 C.B. 8.

42. What is the correct citation for Revenue Ruling 2002-55, which is found on page 529 of the second Cumulative Bulletin volume for 2002?

43. What is the correct citation for Revenue Procedure 94-36, which is found on page 682 of the first Cumulative Bulletin volume for 1994?

44. Construct the permanent C.B. citation for the fifth revenue procedure of 2001, which was published in the second week of the year. It is published on page 164 of the appropriate volume.

45. Explain each of the elements of this citation: Ltr. Rul. 9615032.

46. Explain each of the elements of this citation: Rev. Proc. 2013-14, 2013-3 I.R.B. 283.

47. Explain each of the elements of this citation: Rev. Proc. 2000-41, 2000-2 C.B. 317.

48. Give the title of each of the following:
    a. Publication 17
    b. Publication 225
    c. Publication 334

49. Give the title of each of the following:
    a. Publication 54
    b. Publication 503
    c. Publication 519

50. Locate Revenue Ruling 2016-15. Explain the effect of that ruling on previous Treasury Department pronouncements.

51. Briefly describe the subject of each of the following letter rulings. State the type [private letter ruling (PLR), field service advice (FSA), service center advice (SCA), etc.] of each letter ruling.
    a. 200250019
    b. 200130045
    c. 201449010
    d. 200849015

52. Correctly cite the italicized sentence indicated by the dart (▶) in the following passage from the regulations:

    SEC. 1.162-21 FINES AND PENALTIES.
    a. In general.
       No deduction shall be allowed under section 162(a) for any fine or similar penalty paid to—
       (1) The government of the United States, a State, a territory or possession of the United States, the District of Columbia, or the Commonwealth of Puerto Rico;
       (2) ▶ The *government of a foreign country; or*
       (3) A political subdivision of, or corporation or other entity serving as an agency or instrumentality of, any of the above

53. Correctly cite the italicized sentence indicated by the dart (▶) in the following passage from the regulations.

    SEC. 1.1362-1 ELECTION TO BE AN S CORPORATION.
    a. In general.
       Except as provided in section 1.1362-5, a small business corporation as defined in section 1361 may elect to be an S corporation under section 1362(a). An election may be made only with the consent of all of the shareholders of the corporation at the time of the election. See section 1.1362-6(a) for rules concerning the time and manner of making this election.
    b. ▶ *Years for which election is effective.*
       An election under section 1362(a) is effective for the entire taxable year of the corporation for which it is made and for all succeeding taxable years of the corporation, until the election is terminated.

54. Briefly describe the subject of each of the following letter rulings.
    a. 200940017
    b. 201009014
    c. 201433001
    d. 9544001

55. What is the subject of each of the following revenue rulings?
    a. Rev. Rul. 2015-20
    b. Rev. Rul. 2014-32
    c. Rev. Rul. 77-438
    d. Rev. Rul. 2005-52

56. What is the subject of each of the following revenue procedures?
    a. Rev. Proc. 2015-48
    b. Rev. Proc. 2016-14
    c. Rev. Proc. 2010-51
    d. Rev. Proc. 86-14

57. Read and summarize Announcement 2015-28.

58. Read and summarize Notice 2016-6.

59. Read and summarize Private Letter Ruling 201550029.

60. Read and summarize Technical Advice Memorandum 200449001.

61. What is the subject of each of the following IRS announcements?
    a. Announcement 2016-14
    b. Announcement 2016-4
    c. Announcement 85-181

62. What is the subject of each of the following IRS notices?
    a. Notice 2012-35
    b. Notice 2007-91
    c. Notice 95-50

63. What is the subject of each of the following IRS notices?
    a. Notice 88-115
    b. Notice 96-63
    c. Notice 2016-40

64. What is the subject matter of each of the following technical advice memoranda?
    a. TAM 201445010
    b. TAM 200849015
    c. TAM 7953001

65. What is the subject matter of each of the following technical advice memoranda?
    a. TAM 200703019
    b. TAM 201314043
    c. TAM 9853001

66. Briefly describe the subject matter of each of the following TDs:
    a. T.D. 9762
    b. T.D. 9680
    c. T.D. 9567

67. For each of the following code sections, how many Treasury regulations have been issued? Give the total number of such regulations and the number of the last regulation.
    a. § 102
    b. § 104
    c. § 121
    d. § 338

68. For each of the following code sections, how many Treasury regulations have been issued? Give the total number of such regulations and the number of the last regulation.
    a. § 25A
    b. § 119
    c. § 180
    d. § 305

69. What is the current status of each of the following revenue rulings?
    a. Rev. Rul. 2014-27
    b. Rev. Rul. 90-65
    c. Rev. Rul. 87-34

70. What is the current status of each of the following revenue rulings?
    a. Rev. Rul. 2002-80
    b. Rev. Rul. 2001-31
    c. Rev. Rul. 98-13

71. Locate the pronouncement at 1989-1 C.B. 76.
    a. What is the number assigned to this written determination?
    b. What issue(s) does this written determination address?
    c. What is the holding in this written determination?

72. Locate the pronouncement at 2000-2 C.B. 333.
    a. What is the number assigned to this written determination?
    b. What is the subject matter discussed in this written determination?

73. Locate the pronouncement at 2004-10 I.R.B. 550.
    a. What is the number assigned to this written determination?
    b. What is the subject matter discussed in this written determination?

74. Locate the pronouncement at 2007-17 I.R.B. 990.
    a. What is the number assigned to this written determination?
    b. What is the subject matter discussed in this written determination?

75. Locate the pronouncement at 2006-40 I.R.B. 528.
    a. What is the number assigned to this written determination?
    b. What is the subject matter discussed in this written determination?

76. What is the current status of each of the following IRS pronouncements?
    a. Notice 2010-92
    b. Revenue Ruling 2000-41
    c. Revenue Procedure 89-31
    d. Announcement 99-110

77. What is the current status of each of the following IRS pronouncements?
    a. Notice 2015-79
    b. Revenue Ruling 2004-28
    c. Revenue Procedure 93-15
    d. Announcement 2014-24

78. A member of a tax-exempt business league makes deposits into a strike fund. The contribution reverts to the taxpayer if the fund is terminated. Are these deposits tax deductible?

    Database to search: IRS Technical Advice Memoranda

    Keywords: business, league, strike, fund

79. Can proceeds from a life insurance policy be included in a decedent's gross estate if the policy was purchased by an S corporation for an employee-shareholder?

    Databases to search: IRC and IRS letter rulings

    Keywords: Sec. 2042, life, insurance, estate, inclusion

80. Is a veterinary medical corporation a "personal service corporation" for purposes of the required use of the flat 35 percent tax rate?

    Database to search: revenue rulings

    Keywords: veterinary, personal, service, corporation

81. Are homeowners who claim an itemized deduction for interest paid on adjustable rate mortgages and then receive refunds in a later year required to show the refunds as taxable income?

    Database to search: Announcements

    Keywords: adjustable, rate, mortgage, refund, interest

82. Are points paid by homebuyers on Veterans Affairs (VA) and Federal Housing Administration (FHA) loans deductible in the year the house is purchased?

    Database to search: revenue procedures

    Keywords: loan, origination, fees, VA, FHA

CHAPTER 5

Judicial Interpretations

LEARNING OBJECTIVES

- Describe the structural relationship among the federal courts that hear taxation cases.
- Discuss the constitution of, and procedures concerning, each element of the federal court system hearing tax cases.
- Use proper citation conventions for each of the courts that hear tax cases.
- Recall where Tax Court cases are published for use by tax researchers.
- Describe conditions under which the practitioner might choose each of the trial-level courts for a client's litigation.
- Illustrate working with the format and content of a court case brief.

WHEN A DISPUTE BETWEEN the Internal Revenue Service (IRS) and a taxpayer cannot be settled through the administrative appeals process (Chapter 12), the taxpayer can seek relief via the judicial system. The taxpayer may select one of the three courts in which to initiate litigation. These courts are the Tax Court, U.S. district courts, and the U.S. Court of Federal Claims. If a taxpayer or the IRS disagrees with a lower court decision, an appeal may be made to the appropriate court of appeals and then, finally, to the U.S. Supreme Court. In this chapter, we examine the federal court system as it relates to tax matters, learn to locate various federal tax judicial decisions, and discuss the use of those decisions in solving tax research problems.

1 Federal Court System

If a taxpayer and the IRS cannot reach an agreement concerning a specific tax matter using the administrative review process (i.e., audits and appeals), the dispute may be settled in the federal court system, where either party may initiate legal proceedings. A taxpayer may decide to initiate proceedings as a final attempt to recover an overpayment of tax the IRS refuses to refund or to reverse a deficiency assessment determined by the IRS. Alternatively, the IRS may initiate proceedings to assert its claim to an assessment, enforce the collection of taxes, or impose civil or criminal penalties on the taxpayer.

Judicial decisions are the third primary source of the tax law. The Internal Revenue Code (IRC) is the primary statutory basis for federal tax laws, and the administrative pronouncements of the IRS interpret provisions of the code and explain their application. Frequently, however, additional issues and questions arise regarding the proper interpretation or intended application of the law that are not answered either in the law itself or in the administrative pronouncements. The judicial system is left with the task of resolving these questions. In this process, additional tax law is generated that can carry the full force of the statute itself.

Often, litigation that results in a series of innovative or unexpected judicial decisions regarding tax matters will cause Congress to enact legislation that codifies certain judicial decisions. For example, a 1938 Supreme Court decision (*U.S. v. Hendler*, 303 U.S. 564), where the court held that liabilities transferred in a corporate organization should be treated as "boot," resulted in the 1939 amendment of the IRC to create the exception for liabilities transferred as part of a corporate organization now found within §§ 357, 358, and 368. Sometimes this change to the statutory tax law can occur more slowly, as in the codification of the economic substance doctrine after a long series of court cases (e.g., *ACM Partnership v. Comm.*, 82 AFTR 2d 98-6682; *United Parcel Service of America et al.*, TC Memo 1999-268; and *Winn-Dixie Stores, Inc.*, 113 TC 254 [1999]). After a series of changes such as increases in penalties for tax shelter activity, in 2010 Congress finally conceded and added § 7701(o) providing a definition of economic substance to the code.

Litigation can also result in regulatory action by the IRS, thus creating administrative tax law. For example, *FedEx Corporation v. U.S.*, 291 F. Supp. 2d 699, allowed a taxpayer-friendly immediate business expense deduction for expenditures that the IRS felt were subject to capitalization and depreciation. This provoked the IRS to issue regulations (commonly known as the "tangible property" regulations or the "repair and maintenance regulations") in 2006, again in 2008, and again in 2012, with final regulations issued in 2013. During that time, no substantive changes to the underlying code section were made related to this issue, thus leaving interpretation to the regulations issued by the Treasury.

Most taxpayer disagreements with the IRS are resolved through the administrative process of appeals. Judicial decisions should be given significant weight in arriving at a conclusion or recommendation to a tax problem; however, caution should be exercised when it is apparent from the IRS's prior actions that a given position is almost certain to result in litigation. The costs of litigation, in terms of both money and time, may be prohibitive for many taxpayers.

All litigation between a taxpayer and the government begins in a trial court. If the decision of the trial court is not satisfactory to one of the parties, then the trial court decision may be appealed. The appellate court will review the trial court decision and then either uphold the trial court's decision, modify it in some way, or reverse it. The appellate court can also send a case back to the trial court with explicit instructions for reconsideration.

The federal court system consists of three trial courts and two levels of appellate courts. The three trial courts are the U.S. Tax Court, the U.S. District Court, and the U.S. Court of Federal Claims. The two appellate courts are the U.S. Court of Appeals and the U.S. Supreme Court. Each of the trial courts has different attributes and is designed to serve in a different capacity in the federal judicial system. Exhibit 5-1 diagrams the existing federal court system. An appeal from any of the three trial courts is to the appropriate U.S. Court of Appeals. The taxpayers and the IRS have no direct access to the Supreme Court or any court of appeals.

SPOTLIGHT ON TAXATION

17,000 Pages and Counting

The U.S. Government Printing Office (**www.gpo.gov**) sells a complete set of Title 26 of the U.S. Code of Federal Regulations, which has approximately 13,500 total pages. It also sells the full text of the Internal Revenue Code, which consists of approximately 3,500 pages, bringing the total code and regulations page count to about 17,000. Is it any wonder why there are hundreds of thousands of court cases interpreting the tax law in the United States?

2 Legal Concepts and Terminology

2-1 Burden of Proof

As a general rule, in most litigation the plaintiff (the party initiating the case) has the burden of convincing the court that he or she is correct. Because the taxpayer is the plaintiff (called the petitioner in the Tax Court) in civil tax cases, he or she initially bears the burden of proof. The taxpayer's burden includes two prongs: (1) providing *prima facie* evidence to support a finding contrary to the IRS and (2) proving that the IRS's determination is wrong by a preponderance of the evidence.

However, in a wave of anti-IRS sentiment in 1998, § 7491 was introduced, serving to shift the burden of proof to the IRS if the taxpayer "introduces credible evidence" on any factual issue relevant to the tax liability. The shift to the IRS is conditional on the taxpayer being able to substantiate the item and on the taxpayer having maintained all records and having cooperated with the IRS's reasonable requests for witnesses, information, documents, meetings, and interviews. The shift of burden under § 7491 is not

EXHIBIT 5-1:   Federal Tax System Tax Cases

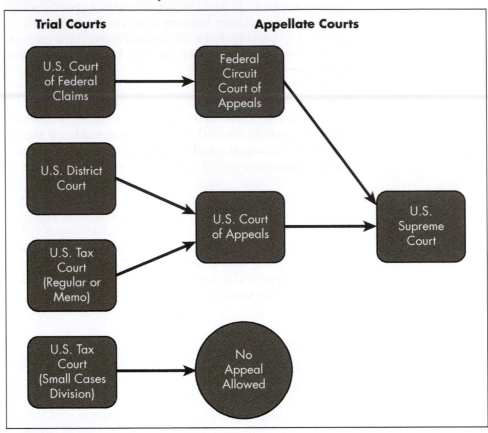

SPOTLIGHT ON TAXATION

Most Litigated Tax Issues

Internal Revenue Code § 7803(c)(2)(B)(ii)(X) requires the National Taxpayer Advocate to identify the 10 tax issues most often litigated in the federal courts, classified by the types of taxpayer affected. The 2015 Annual Report to Congress lists the following 10 issues (**www.taxpayeradvocate.irs.gov**):

1. Summons Enforcement Under IRC §§ 7602, 7604, and 7609
2. Accuracy-Related Penalty Under IRC § 6662(b)(1) and (2)
3. Appeals from Collection Due Process Hearings Under IRC §§ 6320 and 6330
4. Trade or Business Expenses Under IRC § 162 and Related Sections
5. Gross Income Under IRC § 61 and Related Sections
6. Failure to File Penalty Under IRC § 6651(a)(1), Failure to Pay Penalty Under IRC § 6651(A)(2), and Estimated Tax Penalty Under IRC § 6654
7. Civil Actions to Enforce Federal Tax Liens or to Subject Property to Payment of Tax Under IRC § 7403
8. Frivolous Issues Penalty Under IRC § 6673 and Related Appellate-Level Sanctions
9. Relief from Joint and Several Liability Under IRC § 6015
10. Limitations on Assessment Under IRC § 6501

available to corporations, partnerships, or trusts with net worth exceeding $7 million or more than 500 employees. Section 7491 also leaves the burden with the IRS in instances where income has been reconstructed using statistical information, or when the liability is a penalty or addition to tax. There are a small number of other situations in which the burden of proof remains with the IRS, such as the accumulated earnings tax, expatriation, hobby classification when the three-out-of-five rule of § 183(d) is met, and fraud. The burden of proof always remains with the IRS in criminal actions.

When reading a published opinion, the tax researcher should note whether the decision was based in part on the IRS's or the taxpayer's failure to meet a needed evidentiary burden, or whether the IRS or the taxpayer established the position with sufficient proof. The first situation should be considered a weaker precedent than the second. Understanding the "strength" of a court decision is an important part of tax research.

2-2 Common Legal Terminology

Following are some of the common legal terms likely to be encountered by the tax researcher:

- *Ad valorem.* According to value. This term is used in taxation to designate an assessment of taxes based on property value.

- *Appellant.* The party who appeals a decision, usually to a higher court.

- *Bona fide.* In good faith and without fraud or deceit.

- *Certiorari (writ of).* The process by which the U.S. Supreme Court agrees to hear a case, based on the appeal of a lower court decision by one of the parties involved in that decision.

- *Collateral estoppel.* When a fact or issue has been determined by valid judgment, that fact or issue cannot be litigated again by the same parties in future litigation.

- *De facto.* In fact or reality; by virtue of accomplishment or deed.

- *De jure.* In law or lawful; legitimate.

- *De novo.* To hear a trial over again.

- *Defendant.* In civil proceedings, the party that is responding to the complaint; usually the one that is being sued in some matter.

- *Deposition.* An out-of-court statement of a witness under oath, normally taken in question-and-answer form.

- *Dictum (dicta).* A statement or remark in a court opinion that is not necessary to support the decision.

- *En banc.* A decision by the full court instead of a single judge or a selected set of judges. The larger number sits in judgment when the court feels there is a particularly significant issue at stake.

- *Enjoin.* To command or instruct with authority; a judge can enjoin someone to do or not to do some act.

- *Nolo contendere.* A party does not want to fight or continue to maintain a defense; the defendant will not contest a charge made by the government; "no contest."

- *Non obstante veredicto (n.o.v.).* Notwithstanding the verdict; a judgment that reverses the determination of a jury.

- *Parol evidence.* The doctrine that renders any evidence of a prior understanding of the parties to a contract invalid if it contradicts the terms of a written contract.

- *Per curiam.* An opinion "by the court" that expresses its decision in the case but whose author is not identified.

- *Petitioner.* Similar to the plaintiff (always the taxpayer in a Tax Court case).

- *Plaintiff.* The party who initially brings a lawsuit.

- *Prima facie.* At face value; correct on its face unless disproved or rebutted.

- *Pro se.* To represent oneself.

- *Remand.* To send back to a lower court.

- *Res judicata.* The legal concept that bars relitigation on the same set of facts. Because of this concept, taxpayers must make sure that all issues they want (or do not want) to be litigated are included in a case. Once the case is decided, it cannot be reopened.

- *Respondent.* Similar to the defendant and always the IRS in a Tax Court case.

- *Slip opinion.* An individual court decision published separately, shortly after the decision is rendered.

- *Summary judgment.* A court ruling that no factual issues remain to be tried and therefore a cause of action can be decided without trial.

- *Vacate.* A reversal or abandonment of a prior decision of a court.

SPOTLIGHT ON TAXATION

The Tax Court

The Tax Court has two options for taxpayers looking to go to court at a minimum of cost. One is to file as a small tax case (S case), which is held in more cities and is less formal. There is, however, no appeal from an S case. A second option is to file a regular petition to the court and go "pro se," which is to represent yourself. Given the daunting task of self-representation, you can also try and find a low income tax clinic (LITC) nearby. The IRS Website maintains a list and map of LITCs. The Tax Court also provides a video explaining the court process at its Website (**ustaxcourt.gov**).

3 U.S. Tax Court

The U.S. **Tax Court** is a specialized trial court that hears only federal tax cases. For a case to be heard, the taxpayer must petition the court within 90 days after the IRS's mailing of a notice and demand for payment of the disputed amount (a deficiency). The taxpayer need not pay the disputed tax liability before the case is heard.

At this point, it is necessary to understand the difference between an assessment and a deficiency. Some taxes, such as employment taxes, are considered assessed taxes. When a taxpayer files his or her income tax return, the tax is considered to be self-assessed. When a tax has been assessed, the tax must be paid before a refund action may be initiated. There is no Tax Court jurisdiction on these types of assessed taxes. For assessed taxes, the taxpayer would have to bring a refund action in either the Court of Federal Claims or district court. This would mean that any action for employment taxes would have to be brought as a refund action. The taxpayer would need to pay the tax for one employee for one quarter and then sue for the refund. Note, however, that in cases of worker classification, the Tax Court has broader jurisdiction with regard to employment tax issues.

On the other hand, if an income tax return is selected for audit and a deficiency is found, the taxpayer can go to Tax Court without having to first pay the tax. There is no Tax Court review of a filed return unless the return is audited. If a return is not audited, the taxpayer must pay the full amount of tax before suing the government for a refund.

Established by Congress through the IRC and not directly by the U.S. Constitution,[1] the Tax Court's jurisdiction is limited to cases concerning the various Internal Revenue Codes and Revenue Acts that were adopted after February 26, 1926. Before 1943, the Tax Court was known as the **Board of Tax Appeals (BTA)**; it was an administrative board of the Treasury Department rather than a true judicial court. In 1943, the BTA became the U.S. Tax Court, an administrative court, and its status was upgraded in 1969 to that of a full judicial court, with enforcement powers.

Nineteen judges hear Tax Court cases. Each judge is appointed to a 15-year term by the president of the United States, with the advice and confirmation of the Senate. This appointment must be based solely on the grounds of the judge's fitness to perform the duties of the office. A Tax Court judge may be removed from his or her position by the president, after notice and opportunity for public hearing, because of inefficiency, neglect of duty, or malfeasance in office, but for no other reason.

To alleviate the heavy caseload of the appointed Tax Court judges, the chief judge of the court periodically designates additional special trial judges to hear pertinent cases for a temporary period. Limited primarily by the budget granted by Congress, these temporary appointments are useful in decreasing the waiting period for taxpayers who wish to be heard before the court. The decisions of these special judges carry the full authority of the U.S. Tax Court. Senior judges are retired judges who still hear cases from time to time by invitation of the chief judge.

Tax Court judges are tax law specialists, not generalists. Typically, they have acquired many years of judicial or tax litigation experience before being appointed to the Tax Court. Thus, if a taxpayer wants to argue a technical tax issue with the IRS, the Tax Court usually is the best trial-level forum in which to try the case. Tax Court judges are better able to understand such issues than would be a judge in a more general court.

However, the Tax Court may examine an entire tax return for a taxpayer whose case it is hearing while the district court and Court of Federal Claims can address only the specific issue or issues that are involved in the case. If a taxpayer wants only a specific issue (or issues) litigated in a case, then the district court or Court of Federal Claims may be a better forum than the Tax Court.

---

[1] IRC § 7441.

SPOTLIGHT ON TAXATION

Tax Court

When Supreme Court Justice Antonin Scalia passed away in 2016, his replacement nominee was not the only confirmation held up in Senate. Two Tax Court judges were also placed on hold by the Senate despite both being approved by the Senate Finance Committee 26-0 earlier in 2016.

The U.S. Tax Court is a national court, based in Washington, D.C. Its jurisdiction is not limited to a specific geographical region, as is the case with some other federal courts. Taxpayers need not travel to Washington, D.C. to have a case tried before the Tax Court because some of its judges travel throughout the country and are available to hear taxpayer cases in every major city of the United States several times every year. See Exhibit 5-2 for a map showing cities where the Tax Court occasionally holds trials.

When a case is heard before the Tax Court, it usually is presented before only one of the 19 Tax Court judges. Taxpayers cannot request jury trials before this court. After the judge hears the case, he or she prepares a decision that is reviewed by the chief judge of the court. In most instances, the trial judge's opinion stands, but the chief judge can designate the opinion for review by the other members of the Tax Court. Upon their agreement with the decision, the opinion is released. If the case involves an unusually important or novel issue, the entire Tax Court might hear the case. This rare occurrence is identified as a reviewed decision.

EXHIBIT 5-2: Tax Court Trial Locations (2016)

United States Tax Court Places of Trial

▲ Denotes cities in which only small tax case trials are heard.

United States Tax Court Places of Trial

When a court reaches a tax decision, it typically will not compute the tax due from or refund owed to the taxpayer. The computation of this amount is left to be determined by the IRS and the taxpayer. The court will compute the tax only if the government and the taxpayer cannot agree. When the Tax Court reaches a decision without calculating the tax, the decision is said to be entered under **Rule 155**. See *Julie A. Toth*, 128 T.C. 1 (2007), for an example of how the Tax Court enters a decision under Rule 155. For Tax Court decisions prior to 1974, this practice was referred to as Rule 50.

Accounting professionals, including CPAs, enrolled agents, and even those not holding one of these credentials, may represent taxpayers before the Tax Court if they pass a special admission exam authorized under § 7452 of the IRC. The exam is a rigorous, four-hour essay test given only in even-numbered years and is administered only in Washington, D.C. The exam consists of four parts: (1) the Tax Court rules of practice and procedure (25 percent), (2) substantive federal tax law (40 percent), (3) the federal rules of evidence (25 percent), and (4) legal ethics (10 percent), including the American Bar Association's Model Rules of Professional Conduct.[2] Applicants must achieve a grade of at least 70 percent in each area of the Tax Court exam to pass. Successful candidates are admitted to practice before the Tax Court and can fully represent their clients before the court in the same manner that attorneys are allowed to practice before the court.

3-1 Regular and Memorandum Decisions

The Tax Court issues two kinds of decisions: regular and memorandum. A **regular decision** (recently 30–35 cases per year) generally involves a new or an unusual point of law, as determined by the chief judge of the court. If the chief judge believes that the decision concerns only the application of existing law or an interpretation of facts, then the decision is issued as a **memorandum decision** (250–350 cases per year).

Over the years, however, this classification scheme has not always been strictly followed by the court. Many of its memorandum decisions address significant points of law or other issues important to the tax researcher. Accordingly, the researcher should not ignore memorandum decisions. If issues or points of law pertinent to the problem at hand are addressed, both regular and memorandum decisions of the Tax Court should be considered by the taxpayer.

3-2 The *Golsen* Rule

Because the Tax Court is a national court, it hears cases that may be appealed to courts of appeals (discussed later in this chapter) in different geographical regions, or circuits. Because these courts of appeals occasionally disagree on tax issues, the Tax Court is faced with a dilemma. For example, one court of appeals may have held that a specific item is deductible in computing taxable income, while another has held against such a deduction. Which precedent should the Tax Court follow?

Under *Golsen*,[3] the Tax Court will follow the court of appeals that has direct jurisdiction over the taxpayer in question. If the court of appeals that has jurisdiction over the taxpayer has not ruled on the matter, then the Tax Court will decide the case on the basis of its own interpretation of the disputed provision.

This ***Golsen* rule** means the Tax Court may reach opposite decisions, based on identical facts, for taxpayers differentiated solely by the geographical area in which they live.

---

[2]www.ustaxcourt.gov/forms/Admission_Nonattorney_Form.pdf.

[3]54 T.C. 742 (1970).

The tax researcher must be aware of the *Golsen* rule in analyzing cases that may be affected by it.

3-3 Small Tax Cases

Small tax cases (called S cases) may be handled under simpler, less formal **small tax case procedures,** similar to those in a small claims court. In a deficiency case, if the amount of a disputed deficiency, including penalties (but not interest), does not exceed $50,000, then a taxpayer may choose to have the case heard as a small tax case. In a collection action, the total unpaid tax (including interest and penalties) for all years cannot exceed $50,000. Generally, the Tax Court will agree with the taxpayer's election to follow the small tax case procedures as long as the case qualifies.

The hearing is conducted as informally as possible, and the taxpayer may represent himself or herself, that is, act *pro se.* Of course, the taxpayer may be represented by an attorney or nonattorney admitted to Tax Court practice if he or she so desires. Neither elaborate written briefs nor formal oral arguments are required for S cases. Issues brought before this forum generally are fact based; for example, does the taxpayer have the necessary documentation to claim the earned income tax credit?

At any time before a decision is final, the Tax Court may interrupt a small tax case hearing and transfer the case to the regular Tax Court for trial. This might occur, for example, when important facts or issues of law, more suitably heard in the more formal Tax Court context, become apparent only after the proceedings have begun.

Small tax case decisions, called **summary opinions,** are not officially published by the government. Nevertheless, they are available for review by tax researchers and taxpayers through commercial publishers. Small tax case decisions cannot be used as precedent when dealing with the IRS; however, they do provide insight into how the Tax Court has treated similar tax situations.

While the relaxed procedures and rules of evidence and the ability to represent oneself in an S case may be appealing to a taxpayer, there is no right of appeal from a decision in an S case. The decision of the small tax case judge is final and may not be appealed by the taxpayer or the government.

3-4 Locating and Citing Tax Court Decisions

Tax Court regular decisions are published by the Government Printing Office (GPO) in a set of bound reporters called the Tax Court of the United States Reports. These volumes are cited as "T.C." The Board of Tax Appeals had its own reporter, called the United States Board of Tax Appeals, cited as "BTA."

Because many months may elapse between the release of a Tax Court decision and its publication in a bound reporter, such decisions receive both a temporary and a permanent citation. The **temporary citation** is structured as follows:

Francis T. Foster, et ux. v. Commissioner, 138 T.C. ___ (2012), No. 4, where

138 is the volume number.

T.C. is the abbreviation for the Tax Court Reporter.

___ indicates the page number, which is to be determined later.

No. 4 is the number of the case.

(2012) is the year of the decision.

The temporary citation includes no page number for the case because the opinion has not yet been published. All proper citations either italicize or underline the name of the court case; major elements of the citation are separated by commas. The **permanent citation** for the same case is reported as follows:

Francis T. Foster, et ux. v. Commissioner, 138 T.C. 51 (2012)

138 is the volume number.

T.C. is the abbreviation for the Tax Court Reporter.

51 is the page number.

(2012) is the year of the decision.

The same citation procedure is used with respect to Board of Tax Appeals cases, substituting "BTA" for the "T.C." identification.

Most court case citations include the names of both parties involved. However, this convention is ignored for most Tax Court citations because all such cases involve the taxpayer bringing suit against the government to avoid payment of disputed tax liabilities. Thus, a traditional citation for the above case would be *Jones, III, Carl H. v. Comm.* (or, more precisely, *Carl H. Jones, III, v. Commissioner*). Nonetheless, common practice allows the tax researcher to omit the reference to the defendant in the action (i.e., the government or the IRS Commissioner) because such reference could be inferred from the notation for the court in which the lawsuit is heard.

Once the GPO publishes the decision in the permanent bound edition of the regular Tax Court cases, the temporary citation becomes obsolete. Indeed, this procedure for disclosing the citation for a case (i.e., Name–Volume Number–Reporter–Page Number–Year) is common among all American courts. When regular Tax Court opinions are published in the online services such as Thomson Reuters Checkpoint or CCH IntelliConnect, the periods and spaces are dropped from the citation (e.g., Francis T. Foster, et ux., 128 TC 51).

Memorandum decisions are not published by the GPO. They are included in reporters that are published by CCH and by Thomson Reuters. The CCH reporter is cited as "T.C.M.," and the Thomson Reuters reporter is cited as "TC Memo."

Using the same citation conventions, the general and permanent citations, respectively, for a Tax Court memorandum decision would appear as follows:

General

Chi Wai, T.C. Memo 2006-179, where

T.C. Memo is a reference to a Tax Court memorandum decision.

2006 is the year of the decision.

179 is the decision number.

Permanent Thomson Reuters

Chi Wai, TC Memo 2006-179, where

TC Memo is the Thomson Reuters Tax Court Memorandum reporter.

2006-179 is the paragraph number.

Permanent CCH

Chi Wai, 92 T.C.M. 181 (2006), where

92 is the volume number.

T.C.M. is the CCH Tax Court Memorandum reporter.

181 is the page number.

(2006) is the year of the decision.

One can observe from the citations that the opinion was issued in 2006 because all Tax Court Memorandum Decisions for that year are cited using paragraph numbers that begin with 2006. Again, the citation omits the reference to the government, typically "v. Comm.," as this is common among all Tax Court cases. As with regular Tax Court decisions, the temporary citation becomes obsolete when the permanent bound edition of the memorandum reporter is published.

Besides the traditional hard copy published sources for Tax Court decisions, these decisions also are available through online tax services such as Thomson Reuters Checkpoint, CCH IntelliConnect, and LexisNexis.

4 District Courts

The U.S. **district courts** are a trial-level federal court that hears tax cases. Unlike the Tax Court, however, the district courts hear cases involving legal issues based on the entire U.S. Code and are not limited to just the Internal Revenue Code. District court judges typically are generalists rather than specialists in federal tax laws. The same district court judge might render opinions concerning matters of tax law, civil rights, bank robbery, interstate commerce, kidnapping, fraud, and so on.

The district courts are further distinguished from the Tax Court in that a taxpayer who disagrees with the IRS may take his or her case to the appropriate district court only after paying the disputed tax liability; thus, in the typical district court taxation case, the taxpayer sues the government for a refund of the disputed tax liability.

There are 94 different district courts throughout the United States, and at least one in each state and the District of Columbia. Typically, the taxpayer will request a hearing before the district court that has jurisdiction over the location in which he or she lives or conducts business.

Similar to most Tax Court cases, district court cases are heard before one judge. In the appropriate district court, the taxpayer can request a jury trial concerning a tax case (or certain other federal matters). This opportunity may be useful if the taxpayer wants to argue an "emotional" issue rather than a technical one, or if the taxpayer or his or her associates are particularly credible witnesses (and thus have a good chance of winning a jury trial). Limited to decisions concerning questions of fact, juries occasionally can be persuaded in a tax case to hold for the taxpayer when a judge might not be so inclined.

Because the district courts are general in nature and do not specialize in tax matters, over time their decisions can vary significantly among the districts. Some of their decisions have important precedential value and can be relied on by the tax researcher; however, many of these decisions are poorly structured or poorly conceived from a technical standpoint and represent candidates for overturn on appeal. Note also that district court decisions are not binding outside of the jurisdiction of that particular district court. The tax researcher must examine these decisions carefully to assess their probable use as a precedent before using them to help solve a client's tax problem.

4-1 Locating and Citing District Court Decisions

District court tax decisions are published in three different reporters. West Publishing includes such cases in its *Federal Supplement Series*; citations for these cases include the "F. Supp." (cases before 1998), the "F. Supp. 2d." (1998–2013), or the "F. Supp. 3d." (cases since 2014) abbreviation. The series contains all decisions of the district courts designated for publication, including those for the numerous nontax cases. Most university and law school libraries subscribe to the *Federal Supplement Series*.

However, it is a waste of money for the tax researcher to subscribe to this series to obtain just the tax decisions that are rendered in the district courts. Instead, the tax researcher can use special tax case reporters that include only tax decisions selected from all of the decisions of the federal courts except the Tax Court. (As we discussed earlier, the Tax Court's regular and memorandum decisions are published in specialized reporters, so they do not present a budgeting problem of this sort.)

Thomson Reuters's specialized tax reporter is titled *American Federal Tax Reports*, abbreviated in citations as **AFTR**. The first series of the reporter includes cases concerning pre-1954 code litigation, the second series includes cases that address issues relative to the 1954 code, and the third series includes cases under the 1986 code.

CCH's specialized federal tax case reporter is known as *United States Tax Cases*, which is abbreviated as **USTC** in traditional citations. Do not confuse this abbreviation with that for the U.S. Tax Court, which we have identified as "T.C." Occasionally, the West citation (F. Supp.) is referred to as the primary citation for a case, and the CCH and Thomson Reuters reporters are used for secondary citations since they only contain tax decisions. The AFTR2d and USTC reporters each publish 1,000 to 1,500 tax cases in a typical year from courts other than the U.S. Tax Court.

Besides the traditional published primary and secondary court reporters, online court reporters are also available. The online reporters have their own citations, and they usually cross-reference one or more of the standard printed reporters (West, Thomson Reuters, and CCH). An illustration of various citations for a district court case follows.

4-2 Court Reporters

West:	*Bohall, Patrick L. v. U.S.,* 602 F. Supp. 2d 187 (DCt. D.C. 2009)
Thomson Reuters:	*Bohall, Patrick L. v. U.S.,* 103 AFTR2d 2009-1338 (DCt. D.C.)
CCH:	*Bohall, Patrick L. v. U.S.,* 2009-1 USTC ¶ 50,307 (DCt. D.C.)

Each of these citations indicates both the specific district court that heard the case and the year in which the opinion was issued. Given publication time lags, however, this may not match the year in which the reporter volume was published. Unless necessitated by such a delay, a proper citation need not include in the parentheses the year in which the opinion was issued, in all but a West citation.

Notice that more than one volume of the USTC reporter was published by CCH in 2009, as indicated by the volume number, and that this reporter uses paragraph numbers to organize the opinions. Other elements of the citations are familiar. A complete citation for this case, using traditional form, would appear as follows:

Bohall, Patrick L. v. U.S., 602 F. Supp. 2d 187; 103 AFTR2d 2009-1338; 2009-1 USTC ¶50,307 (DCt. D.C.).

5 Court of Federal Claims

The U.S. **Court of Federal Claims** is the newest of the trial-level courts. Created on October 1, 1982, by the Federal Courts Improvement Act (P.L. 97-164), the U.S. Court of Claims and the U.S. Court of Customs and Patent Appeals were reorganized into two new courts. The trial division of the U.S. Court of Claims became the new U.S. Claims Court, and the remaining appellate divisions of both courts became the new Court of Appeals for the Federal Circuit, discussed later. The forum was renamed the U.S. Court of Federal Claims in 1992.

Sixteen judges sit on the Court of Federal Claims. Its jurisdiction lies in hearing cases concerning all monetary claims against the federal government, only one type of which is in the form of tax refunds. Thus, the taxpayer must pay the disputed tax and sue the government for a refund in order for the case to be heard in the Court of Federal Claims. Similarly, like the district court but unlike the Tax Court, the Court of Federal Claims is composed of judges who, with only a few exceptions, are not specialists in technical tax law. The Court of Federal Claims does not allow jury trials.

The U.S. Court of Federal Claims is a national court located in Washington, D.C. However, because the Court of Federal Claims judges regularly travel to the major cities of the country and hear cases in these various locations, in a manner similar to that of the Tax Court, one need not go to Washington, D.C. to present a case before the Court of Federal Claims.

Moreover, because the Court of Federal Claims is a national court that must follow the decisions only of the Federal Circuit of the Court of Appeals, it is not bound by the geographical circuit courts of appeals that have ruled on similar cases nor by the court of appeals for the circuit in which the taxpayer works or resides. This may be important to a taxpayer whose circuit has held adversely to his or her position on the disputed issue: if the case were presented to the appropriate district court, or to the Tax Court (recall the *Golsen* rule), the precedent of the adverse ruling would be adopted by those trial courts, but the Court of Federal Claims is not so bound. Thus, if federal circuit precedent is more favorable to the taxpayer than the taxpayer's own circuit court, the taxpayer should consider initiating a case in the Court of Federal Claims.

5-1 Locating and Citing Court of Federal Claims Decisions

Before October 1982, all U.S. Court of Claims decisions concerning both tax and nontax issues were published in *West's Federal Reporter*, second series. (This reporter is now in its third series.) Citations to the reporter use the abbreviations "F.2d" or "F.3d," as applicable. Current decisions of the U.S. Court of Federal Claims can be found in West's primary reporter, *U.S. Court of Federal Claims*, which can be cited by using the abbreviation "Fed. Cl." In addition, tax decisions of the old U.S. Court of Claims and the new U.S. Court of Federal Claims are available through several secondary published and online reporters. U.S. Court of Federal Claims decisions are published in CCH's USTC, Thomson Reuters's AFTR2d, and other places in printed form and online.

Examine the following proper primary and secondary citations for decisions of the U.S. Court of Federal Claims. All elements of these citations are familiar to us. As is most often the situation, when a decision is issued and published in the same year, one need not be redundant in identifying the given year in the body of the citation because the reader can infer the year from other aspects of the listing. A complete citation of the case would include references to all of the publications, in the form indicated previously.

5-2 Court Reporters

West:	*Liu v. U.S.*, 93 Fed. Cl. 184 (2010)
CCH:	*Liu v. U.S.*, 2010-1 USTC ¶ 50,456 (Fed. Cl., 2010)
Thomson Reuters:	*Liu v. U.S.*, 105 AFTR 2d 2010-2883 (Fed. Cl., 2010)

As a general tax court, the U.S. Court of Federal Claims has generated decisions that cannot easily be anticipated. Practitioners usually should pursue a case in the U.S. Court of Federal Claims when the applicable U.S. District Court and U.S. Tax Court decisions are adverse to the taxpayer or when a nontechnical matter lies at the heart of the taxpayer's case.

6 Courts of Appeals

The first level of federal appellate courts is the U.S. **courts of appeals**. Like the district court and Court of Federal Claims, the courts of appeals consider issues in both tax and nontax litigation, although the courts of appeals generally will hear only cases that involve a question of law. Seldom will a circuit court of appeals challenge the trial court's findings as to the facts.

Congress has created 13 courts of appeals: 11 are geographical in that they are responsible for cases that originate in designated states; one is assigned to Washington, D.C.; and one is known as the Court of Appeals for the Federal Circuit. This last court hears tax and other cases that originate only in the Court of Federal Claims. The other courts of appeals consider tax and nontax issues brought from the Tax Court or a district court for an assigned geographical region.

The 11 geographical courts of appeals are organized into geographical circuits, each of which is assigned a number. Practitioners commonly refer to the circuit courts by this number. For example, the court of appeals designated to hear cases that originate in Seattle typically is referred to as the Ninth Circuit Court of Appeals. Exhibit 5-3 shows the jurisdiction of each of the 11 geographic courts of appeals and district court jurisdictions. Approximately 20 judges have been appointed to each of the circuit courts. Typically, a three-judge panel hears a court of appeals case. Jury trials are not available in these courts.

EXHIBIT 5-3: Courts of Appeals and District Court Jurisdictions of the United States

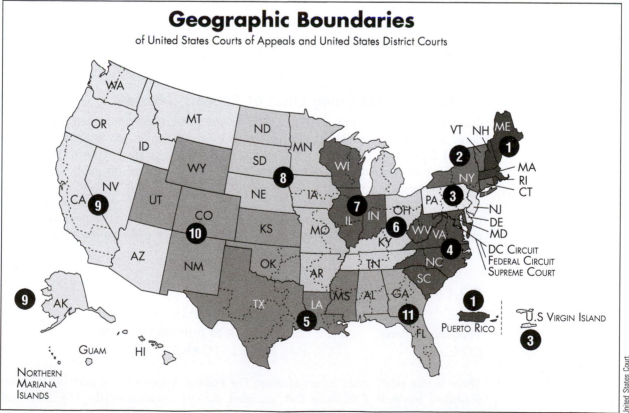

A court of appeals decision carries precedential weight because each circuit is independent of the others and must follow only the decisions of the U.S. Supreme Court. Because the Supreme Court hears only about a dozen tax cases annually, the court of appeals, in most situations, represents the final authority in federal tax matters. Thus, a researcher generally must follow the holding of a tax decision issued by the court of appeals for the circuit in which the client works or resides if the controlling facts or issues of law are sufficiently similar.

Decisions by the circuit court in which the taxpayer works or resides should be given primary consideration, even if the researcher has found that another circuit court has held in the taxpayer's favor in a similar case. For example, if a taxpayer lives in San Antonio, and the Fifth Circuit has held that an item similar to the taxpayer's does not qualify as a deduction, then the deduction most likely should not be claimed, even if the Seventh or Eighth Circuit has held that the deduction is available. Under the *Golsen* rule, the unfavorable Fifth Circuit decision will apply to the taxpayer at the trial-court level, even though the U.S. Tax Court will be forced in this example to render opinions that are inconsistent among taxpayers.

If, however, in the same example, the Fifth Circuit had not yet ruled on the issue, and the favorable Seventh Circuit ruling is available, then the researcher may be more comfortable in following the decision of the "outside" circuit. Prior decisions of courts of appeals are of great importance in the construction of subsequent decisions by another circuit, and the researcher rightly can place precedential value on the holdings of other circuits in anticipating the proper position for a client.

Therefore, in general, the courts of appeals decisions most important to a given taxpayer are those issued by the circuit in which he or she works or resides. In addition, however, these observations can be made: Second, Ninth, and D.C. Circuit decisions are especially important because of their numerous innovative, unusual, and controversial judicial interpretations of the tax laws, and because their jurisdictions include the two most populous states in the nation and the nation's capital.

6-1 Locating and Citing Court of Appeals Decisions

Court of appeals decisions are reported in several general and specialized tax publications. All court of appeals decisions designated for publication are included in West's *Federal Reporter* (F.2d or F.3d). However, not all decisions are published. In general, only those decisions deemed of precedential value are designated for publication by the court of appeals.

Published tax cases from the courts of appeals can be found in the *United States Tax Cases* (USTC) and in the *American Federal Tax Reports* (AFTR). The familiar citation conventions are used in the following examples of primary and secondary citations for a court of appeals decision.

6-2 Court Reporters

West: *U.S. v. Hills,* 618 F.3d 619 (CA7, 2010)
Thomson Reuters: *U.S. v. Hills,* 106 AFTR 2d 2010-5909 (CA7, 2010)
CCH: *U.S. v. Hills,* 2010-2 USTC ¶50,570 (CA7, 2010)

There is one other court report of note. The Federal Appendix is a case law reporter published by West Publishing that publishes judicial opinions of the U.S. courts of appeals that have been not been selected for publication. Such "unpublished" cases are ostensibly without value as precedent. However, the Supreme Court made a change to the Federal Rules of Appellate Procedure in 2006 to say that federal circuit courts are not allowed to prohibit the citation of unpublished opinions issued on or after January 1, 2007. Westlaw abbreviates citations to the Federal Appendix as Fed. Appx. An example of a Fed Appx. citation is as follows:

Kohn v. Comm. 377 Fed. Appx. 578 (CA8, 2010)

7 Supreme Court

The U.S. **Supreme Court** is an appellate court and the highest court in the nation. Article III of the Constitution created the Supreme Court and extended to it judicial power "to all cases of law and equity, arising under this Constitution, the laws of the United States, and treaties ..." Thus, concerning all areas of federal law, the Supreme Court is the final level of appeal and the sovereign legal authority.

The Supreme Court meets and hears cases only in Washington, D.C. If a taxpayer wants to have his or her case heard by the Supreme Court, the taxpayer and counsel must travel to the nation's capital to present the arguments. The Supreme Court is a nine-justice panel; all nine justices hear every case that the Court agrees to consider. The Court does not conduct jury trials.

A U.S. citizen has no automatic right to have his or her case heard by the Supreme Court. Permission to present the case must be requested by petitioning the court to grant a **writ of certiorari**. If the Court decides to hear the case, then "certiorari is granted;" if the Court refuses, then "certiorari is denied." Four justices must agree to grant the petition. One must treat a Supreme Court decision as having the full force of the law; although Congress might repeal the challenged statute or the federal administration might refuse to fund or enforce the underlying law and related activities, neither the citizen nor the government can appeal a Supreme Court decision.

As we have discussed, however, certiorari is granted in very few tax cases. Only about a dozen appeals relating to tax issues—state, local, and federal; income, property, sales, estate, and gift; individual, corporate, and fiduciary—are heard by the Supreme Court in a typical year. In most cases, those petitions granted involve an issue at conflict among the federal circuits or a tax issue of major importance. For instance, the court might hear a client's case concerning the inclusion in gross income of life insurance proceeds if many similar cases had been brought before the various federal courts and huge tax liabilities were under dispute, or if two or more of the circuits had issued inconsistent holdings on the matter.

In denying the petition for certiorari, the Supreme Court is not "upholding," or in any way confirming, a lower court decision. Rather, the court is simply declining to rule on that case at that time. Denying certiorari may mean that the court does not consider the case to be important enough to consider during its limited sessions. However, the court gives no indication of why it declines to hear a case. The lower court's decision does stand, but one cannot infer that the decision necessarily is correct or that it should be followed in the future by other taxpayers whose situations are similar. These matters of unsettled law must be analyzed using the tax researcher's professional judgment.

7-1 Locating and Citing Supreme Court Decisions

At least four different general and specialized reporters publish all the tax-related Supreme Court decisions. CCH includes such cases in the *United States Tax Cases* (USTC), and

SPOTLIGHT ON TAXATION

The Supreme Court's Love Affair with Tax Law

If [a United States Supreme Court Justice is] in the doghouse with the Chief [Justice], he gets the crud. He gets the tax cases …

—Harry Blackmun, Supreme Court Justice

Thomson Reuters publishes them in the *American Federal Tax Reports* (AFTR, AFTR2d, or AFTR3d). The GPO publishes the *United States Supreme Court Reports*, which contains all tax and nontax decisions of the Court. In common citation convention, references to this service are abbreviated as "U.S." In addition, West Publishing includes all Supreme Court decisions in the *Supreme Court Reporter* (S.Ct.).

In the following examples of proper citations, one can infer from the GPO and West citations that the case was heard by the Supreme Court, and any further reference to that forum (e.g., as U.S. Supreme Court (USSC) would be redundant). In addition, if a case involves an issue of pre-1954 *Code* tax law, the first series of the AFTR service would be cited.

7-2 Court Reporters

GPO:	*U.S. v. Home Concrete & Supply, LLC et al.*, 566 U.S. _____ (2012)
West:	*U.S. v. Home Concrete & Supply, LLC et al.*, 132 S.Ct. 1836 (2012)
Thomson Reuters:	*U.S. v. Home Concrete & Supply, LLC et al.*, 109 AFTR 2d 2012-1692 (USSC, 2012)
CCH:	*U.S. v. Home Concrete & Supply, LLC et al.*, 2012-1 USTC ¶ 50315 (USSC, 2012)

EXAMPLE 5-1

Ann Tenna is an assistant director of finance and revenue for the Media Division of the U.S. Federal Communications Commission (FCC). Part of her role is the collection of regulatory fees of over $380 million per year from the cable and satellite television industry. For her services as an employee of the FCC, Ann is paid a generous salary plus a good benefits package as an employee of the federal government. Each year, Ann spends quite a bit of time travelling from station to station leading a team of auditors to determine whether or not the fee amounts paid to the FCC by a station are accurate. Because Ann's audit team are strong performers, from time to time, she treats them to a dinner at the end of the audit wrap-up. These dinners tend to be just a bit on the expensive side and thus are not covered under the FCC's travel reimbursement policy. As a result, Ann covers the cost of the meals out-of-pocket. Her costs in the most recent year were just over $4,600.

Ann is aware that, typically, unreimbursed business expenses of an employee are subject to the 2 percent floor under § 67. Given her income, this ends up being a substantial limitation on her ability to deduct these costs as business expenses. Recently, however, Ann discovered § 62, which defines adjusted gross income as gross income less trade or business deductions. Unfortunately, Ann notes that under § 62(a)(1),

> the deductions allowed by this chapter (other than by part VII of this sub-chapter) which are attributable to a trade or business carried on by the taxpayer, if such trade or business does not consist of the performance of services by the taxpayer as an employee.

Since Ann is an employee, she feels trapped again by the 2 percent floor limitation and starts to give up when she notices § 62(a)(2)(C), which permits deductions for certain expenses of officials:

> The deductions allowed by section 162 which consist of expenses paid or incurred with respect to services performed by an official as an employee of a State or a political subdivision thereof in a position compensated in whole or in part on a fee basis.

Ann feels this is excellent news because she recognizes that her agency, and especially her division, is paid for by the fees of the television and cable operators in the United States. She feels that her position is almost certainly paid for out of the fees paid by the FCC licensees and, as such, the deductions are not limited to the 2 percent floor. Ann reviews the regulations pertaining to § 62 and finds no further interpretation of § 62(a)(2)(C) and thus feels she is on comfortable grounds with her deduction.

Ann's CPA, Anita Dufresne, is less certain. Her sense is that the permission to deduct costs as an "above-the-line" expense not subject to the 2 percent floor is directed at employees that also perform services to the public and are paid directly by the fees. Anita's research reveals the Tax Court case presented in Exhibit 5-4.

EXHIBIT 5-4: Tax Court Decision

Official Tax Court Syllabus

Ps claimed above-the-line deductions under IRC sec. 62 on their 2008, 2009, and 2010 tax returns for expenses related to H's position as a public official. R examined Ps' 2008, 2009, and 2010 returns and determined that while H was entitled to certain deductions for expenses, he could deduct them only as unreimbursed employee business expenses, which would not reduce Ps' tax [pg. 24] liability. R also determined that Ps were liable for accuracy-related penalties under IRC sec. 6662(a).

Held: Under IRC sec. 62(a)(2)(C), a "fee based" public official is an official who receives fees directly from members of the public in compensation for services provided. H, a state-court judge, is a public official but did not personally retain any of the money paid as fees to him. Therefore, he is not a public official compensated on a fee basis, and can deduct his unreimbursed employee business expenses only below the line.

Held, further, Ps are not liable for 20 percent accuracy-related penalties under IRC sec. 6662(a).

Counsel

Stephen Edward Silver and Derek W. Kaczmarek, for petitioners.

Alicia E. Elliott, for respondent.

HOLMES, *Judge*

Michael Jones is an Arizona judge who claimed deductions on his 2008, 2009, and 2010 tax returns for unreimbursed business expenses related to his official position. The Commissioner argues that these expenses should reduce only his taxable income, and not his adjusted gross income, which means that the deductions would be less valuable. This is the general rule for those who are employees, but Judge Jones argues that he falls within an exception to this rule for employees in positions "compensated in whole or in part on a fee basis."

The section of the Code on which he relies—section 62(a)(2)(C)—is one which neither we nor any other court has ever analyzed and one we've mentioned only once (and that was in a nonprecedential opinion).[1]

FINDINGS OF FACT

I. *Judge Jones*

In Arizona the governor appoints judges on the advice of a nominating committee. After their appointment, judges face retention elections every four years. As part of this process, judges undergo performance reviews every two years. These reviews consist of a series of surveys from litigants, jurors, attorneys, and even some citizens at large. The results are then passed to a special commission of attorneys and judges who review the survey responses and make their findings available to the public. The voters use information and feedback gleaned from the surveys to make informed decisions about which judges to keep on the bench.

Judge Jones was appointed to the Maricopa County Superior Court in 1995. He remained in that position during the tax years at issue; and even though he retired in January 2012, the county's chief judge still recalls him to active duty to hear cases a couple days each month. He is highly regarded. Not only did he never lose a retention election, but he has remained throughout his career one of the highest scored judges in the largest county in Arizona.[2]

II. *Judge Jones's Expenses*

The superior court is the general jurisdiction court for each county in Arizona. The Maricopa County Superior Court handles civil cases over $1,000, family law, juvenile matters, and felonies; and is also Arizona's statewide tax court. Ariz. Const. art. VI, sec. 14.

Maricopa County Superior Court is funded in part by the collection of fees.[3] See Ariz. Rev. Stat. Ann. sec. 12.284 (West 2003 & Supp. 2015). Individuals must pay the superior court clerk fees for various case filings, petitions, writs, the filing of any documents, and the issuance of any licenses or certificates. Id. The county does not, however, receive fees paid for wedding ceremonies—judges are allowed to collect those directly (although Judge Jones himself did not charge for weddings during the years at issue).

Maricopa County Superior Court judges are paid a regular salary-funded equally by the county's general fund and by the [pg. 25] State.[4] They receive regular paychecks and a Form W-2 at the end of every year. Items like federal income tax and state income tax are withheld from each paycheck. Judges are also eligible for benefits provided by the state or the county—whichever they choose. Judge Jones, like many other judges on the court, was a member of the Elected Officials' Retirement Plan—he and other participating judges were informed yearly how much fee revenue was paid over to fund the retirement plan. He began receiving payments from the plan, however, only after his retirement in 2012.

When Judge Jones began judging, his court's budget allowed him to make reasonable expenditures for supplies and even the occasional special request. But steep spending cuts led to very tight budgets in Maricopa County during the years at issue. To save jobs, the county slashed discretionary funds. Reimbursements for court travel, for example, were limited to one annual, mandatory judicial conference. And though judges could still get mileage for travel in their official capacity, there was no longer a budget for office supplies or other equipment. Despite these cuts, the county still lost 425 staff positions.

The cutbacks were so severe that Judge Jones took it upon himself to make up for some of the gap. For example, because he held so many pretrial conferences in his chambers, he spent money decorating his office so that it would appear more professional. When he needed a new computer monitor in his courtroom, he bought one himself. And in lieu of bonuses, he personally bought gift cards for high performing members of his chambers staff to "encourage them" and to "make them work harder."

Judge Jones was also in demand as a seminar speaker. He was invited especially often to presentations on Maricopa County's innovative Mental Health Court, which he has played an important role in creating.

---

[1] See *Davis v. Commissioner*, T.C. Summ. Op. 2010-89. (All section references are to the Internal Revenue Code in effect for the years at issue. All Rule references are to the Tax Court Rules of Practice and Procedure.)

[2] He did have one blemish on his record—he admitted that he never volunteered for tax cases because he "never had an interest."

[3] Arizona law (as in effect in 2008, 2009, and 2010) also sent some of the fees collected to the Elected Officials' Retirement Plan and to the county's general fund. See Ariz. Rev. Stat. Ann. sec. 12.284.03 (West 2003 & Supp. 2015).

[4] Halfway through 2010 Maricopa County became responsible for 100 percent of Maricopa County judges' salaries—meaning that for that tax year, Arizona paid only about one-quarter of Judge Jones's salary. See Ariz. Rev. Stat. Ann. sec. 12-128 (West 2003).

This court was the venue for competency cases, and many professionals in the State, both legal and nonlegal, became interested in it. Though his attendance at these seminars was encouraged to the extent that he would disseminate and bring back new ideas and techniques, the court could not reimburse him. So Judge Jones paid his own way to attend—bringing back new skills that eventually led to the creation of two other "problem solving courts." More basic expenditures included water (because the court turned off the water fountains), snacks for employees, and batteries to keep the court's clocks working.

III. *Judge Jones's Returns*

Judge Jones consulted with a tax professional before filing his returns for the 2008 and 2009 tax years. His CPA came on the recommendation of several other court employees, and Judge Jones—a meticulous recordkeeper—turned over several boxes of documents to him each year. He and the CPA would then sit down and go through his receipts to determine what was deductible. Judge Jones credibly testified that his CPA had researched the issue and advised him that these unreimbursed expenses should be deductible above the line. For lack of a more obvious place to put it, the CPA reported it on line 21 of Form 1040. And for 2008 and 2009, Judge Jones ultimately claimed deductions for his expenses on his returns in two places: in a negative amount on line 21 on Form 1040 ("Other income—As per IRC 7701(A)(26)")—making his deductions above the line—and (possibly as an alternative position) on line 21 ("Unreimbursed employee expenses") of Schedule A.

Judge Jones prepared his 2010 return the same way with a different accountant—his first CPA had died. This new accountant, also a CPA, agreed with the old one that a judge's unreimbursed expenses should be allowed as an above-the-line deduction. The only difference in his advice was where to claim that deduction. So for 2010 Judge Jones claimed his deduction on line 24 of Form 1040 ("Certain business expenses of reservists, performing artists, and fee-basis government officials") per the [pg. 26] advice of his CPA. Judge Jones currently maintains that all of his deductions belong "above the line" on line 24 of his Form 1040.

The Commissioner initially disallowed Judge Jones's deductions in full. Later, the parties agreed that several deductions would be allowed. Though the Commissioner still contends that many of the expenses aren't deductible, the primary issue for decision is whether Judge Jones is considered an official compensated on a "fee basis."[5] We tried the case in Arizona, where Judge Jones has resided ever since he filed his petition.

OPINION

I. *Background: Section 162 and Section 62*

Section 162 allows deductions for trade and business expenses. Section 62(a)(1) allows deductions for those expenses to be made from gross income in computing AGI except for those expenses incurred by a taxpayer *as an employee*. A taxpayer who is an employee may instead deduct his unreimbursed employee business expenses in computing his taxable income only to the extent that they exceed 2 percent of his adjusted gross income (AGI). Secs. 162(a), 67(a); *Orvis v. Commissioner*, 788 F.2d 1406, 1408 [57 AFTR 2d 86-1356] (9th Cir. 1986), aff'g T.C. Memo. 1984-533 [¶84,533 PH Memo TC].

Section 62(a)(2), though, carves out five narrow exceptions to this general rule. The one that this case is about is in section 62(a)(2)(C) and is an exception for unreimbursed business expenses "paid or incurred with respect to services performed by an official as an employee of a State or political subdivision thereof in a position compensated in whole or in part on a fee basis." The parties agree that at least some of Judge Jones's expenses are allowed by section 162, that he is an employee of Arizona, and that he incurred these expenses with respect to his services. The sole issue for us to decide is whether Judge Jones is "in a position compensated in whole or in part on a fee basis." To figure that out, we need to decide what it means to be compensated on a fee basis and then whether any of Judge Jones's compensation comes from fees. If we decide against Judge Jones's position, the Commissioner wants to add penalties to any underpayments.

II. *Defining "Fee Basis"*

The Commissioner wants us to interpret "compensated on a fee basis" to mean something like "paid by a member of the public for a service rendered by a judge who receives the fee." Judge Jones argues that "in a position compensated in whole or in part on a fee basis" means something like "a position *funded* in whole or in part by fees paid by members of the public for services rendered by judges." Neither the Code nor the regulations define what "fee basis" means, and the case law is similarly stubborn in its silence.

We begin with the text of the statute. We afford a statute its plain and ordinary meaning. *Crane v. Commissioner*, 331 U.S. 1, 6 [35 AFTR 776] (1947); *Yari v. Commissioner*, 143 T.C. 157, 164 (2014); *Dobra v. Commissioner*, 111 T.C. 339, 345

---

[5] Judge Jones produced all his records at trial. We bifurcated the case, with this opinion coming first, because the parties agree that the remaining disputes about particular expenses would affect Judge Jones's deficiency only were we to rule in his favor on the question we address here.

(1998). We avoid interpretations that "would produce absurd or unreasonable results." *Yari v. Commissioner*, 143 T.C. at 164 (quoting *Union Carbide Corp. v. Commissioner*, 110 T.C. 375, 384 (1998)). And we interpret statutes "in their context and with a view to their place in the overall statutory scheme." *FDA v. Brown & Williamson Tobacco Corp.*, 529 U.S. 120, 133 (2000) (quoting *Davis v. Mich. Dep't of Treasury*, 489 U.S. 803, 809 [63 AFTR 2d 89-1174] (1989)).

We begin with the dictionary. "Compensation" has two common meanings. The first is an award or recompense for an injury, as when we say someone injured by a tortfeasor or whose property is taken by the government is entitled to "compensation." See Black's Law Dictionary 301 (8th ed. 2004); see also Webster's Third New International Dictionary 463 (2002). The second is something of value—usually money, though it's common enough for economists and businessmen to speak of "nonwage compensation," exchanged for the provision of services. See, for example, Gillian Lester, "A Defense of Paid Family [pg. 27] Leave," 28 Harv. J. L. & Gender 1 (2005); John A. Litwinski, "Human Capital Economics and Income," 21 Va. Tax Rev. 183 (2001); see also Black's Law Dictionary 301; Webster's Third New International Dictionary 463.

Exchange in the sense of a balancing of accounts is the key here, as when Thoreau spoke metaphorically: "If we will be quiet and ready enough, we shall find compensation in every disappointment." I To Myself: An Annotated Selection from the Journal of Henry D. Thoreau 10 (Jeffrey S. Cramer ed., Yale Univ. 2007). Or Emerson:

> human labor, through all its forms, *** is one immense illustration of the perfect compensation of the universe. The absolute balance of Give and Take, the doctrine that every thing has its price, — and if that price is not paid, not that thing but something else is obtained, and that it is impossible to get any thing without its price, — is not less sublime in the columns of a ledger than in the budgets of states, in the laws of light and darkness, in all the action and reaction of nature. *** Ralph Waldo Emerson, Compensation, in The Selected Works of Ralph Waldo Emerson (Graphic Arts Books ed., 2011).

These ordinary uses of "compensation" to mean "something of value given in exchange for" are echoed elsewhere in the law. Section 1402(c) defines the term "trade or business" for the purposes of self-employment income. It says:

> Trade or Business. — The term "trade or business," when used with reference to self-employment income or net earnings from self-employment, shall have the same meaning as when used in section 162 (relating to trade or business expenses), except that such term shall not include —
>
> > (1) the performance of the functions of a public office, other than the functions of a public office of a State or a political subdivision thereof with respect to fees received in any period in which the functions are performed in a position *compensated solely on a fee basis*** [Emphasis added.]

There's nothing useful in the section 1402 regulations on this question, but the Commissioner does have some subregulatory guidance. Revenue Ruling 74-608, 1974-2 C.B. 275, construes compensation by fees the same way the Commissioner wants us to in this case. It says that a public official is compensated by "fees" if he receives them directly from members of the public, but not if he is paid from a government fund. Id. If the "public official receives his remuneration or salary from a government fund and no portion of the monies collected by him belongs to or can be retained by him as compensation, the remuneration is not 'fees' under section 1402(c)(1)."[6] Id., 1974-2 C.B. at 276. Note that, although section 1402(c) refers to officials compensated *solely* on a fee basis and section 62 refers to officials compensated in *whole or in part* on a fee basis, the difference has no effect on the meaning of the more general phrase "compensated solely on a fee basis."

Moreover, section 3401(a) also distinguishes between "fees" and wages paid to public officials. Section 31.3401(a)-2(b)(1) of the regulations under that section distinguishes between those public officials compensated by fees and those who receive salaries from the government:

> (b) *Fees paid a public official.* (1) Authorized fees paid to public officials such as notaries public, clerks of courts, sheriffs, etc., for services rendered in the performance of their official duties are excepted from wages and hence are not subject to withholding. However, salaries paid such officials by the Government, or by a Government agency or instrumentality, are subject to withholding.

Other federal laws give us even more hints—for example, the Social Security [pg. 28] Administration adopted a definition (identical to the one that the Commissioner used in his revenue ruling) for applying section 218 of the Social Security Act:[7]

---

[6]We aren't bound by revenue rulings, but we pay attention to them based on "their persuasiveness and the consistency of the Commissioner's position over time." *Webber v. Commissioner*, 144 T.C. __, __ (slip op. at 48) (2015) (noting what administrative lawyers call Skidmore deference); see *Skidmore v. Swift & Co.*, 323 U.S. 134, 140 (1944). (And we let taxpayers rely on them even more, because we treat revenue rulings "as concessions by the Commissioner where those rulings are relevant to our disposition of the case," so that taxpayers may rely on favorable ones. *Rauenhorst v. Commissioner*, 119 T.C. 157, 171 (2002).)

[7]Section 218 of the Social Security Act allows the Social Security Administration to enter into an agreement with any state to provide Social Security benefits to its employees. 42 U.S.C. sec. 418(a)(1) (2006). If a state asks, these agreements exclude those who are compensated on a fee basis. Id. subsec. (c)(3).

When a public official receives remuneration for services in the form of a "fee" directly from members of the public with whom he or she does business, that is considered to be a "fee." Otherwise, if payment is made to a public official from government funds, and no portion of the monies collected by him or her belongs to or can be retained by him or her as compensation, that remuneration is not considered to be a "fee." Social Security Administration, Title II: State & Local Coverage-Commissioner's Ruling on Definition of A "Fee" for Social Security Coverage Purposes Under Section 218 of the Social Security Act. SSR 92-4P (Mar. 20, 1992), available at www.socialsecurity.gov/OP_Home/rulings/oas.

The Fair Labor Standards Act (FLSA) generally requires employers to pay employees overtime when they work more than 40 hours in a week. 29 U.S.C. sec. 207(a)(1) (2006). But the FLSA regulations exclude some professional employees compensated on a fee basis from that requirement. 29 C.F.R. sec. 541.300(a) (2009). These regulations also provide that [a]n employee will be considered to be paid on a "fee basis" within the meaning of these regulations if the employee is paid an agreed sum for a single job regardless of the time required for its completion. These payments resemble piecework payments with the important distinction that generally a "fee" is paid for the kind of job that is unique rather than for a series of jobs repeated an indefinite number of times and for which payment on an identical basis is made over and over again. Payments based on the number of hours or days worked and not on the accomplishment of a given single task are not considered payments on a fee basis. Id. sec. 541.605(a).

We also have to conclude that the Commissioner's position is the more reasonable one. An enormous number of government agencies, courts, departments, and boards receive fee income. See, for example, Tax Court Rules of Practice and Procedure App. II (U.S. Tax Court filing fee). If Judge Jones's construction of section 62(a)(2)(C) were correct, all the positions in all these government bodies would be "position[s] compensated in whole or in part on a fee basis." This would create a caste of employees—those employed as government "officials"—who would be exempt from the rule Congress chose to enact that limits the deductibility of unreimbursed employee expenses. Maybe Congress could do that, but it didn't do so plainly. Business expenses are also usually thought deductible because they are an ordinary and necessary requirement for producing income. But Judge Jones's reading of section 62 would uncouple the deductibility of an expense from the income it produces—once a *position* was funded in part by fees, any employee holding that position would be entitled to unlimited deduction of his unreimbursed business expenses regardless of whether those expenses had anything to do with those fees.

We think all this makes the Commissioner's reading the better one. It's consistent with the ordinary public meaning of the term, consistent with his own construction of a similar clause in section 1402, and consistent with other federal statutes' and regulations' definitions of compensation on a fee basis.

We therefore hold that for Judge Jones to take his deductions above the line he must show that he received fees directly from the public in exchange for services that he rendered. We find that he can't do this. He doesn't retain fees collected by his court as compensation for his services. His salary is paid from the county's general fund—that salary may be funded in part by fees, but these fees aren't paid in exchange for services that Judge Jones renders himself and Judge Jones isn't paid them directly. [pg. 29]

III. *Judge Jones's Compensation*

Judge Jones also argues that even if the phrase "fee basis" means that his compensation must come directly from the public he serves, he is still a fee basis official for two reasons: first, because the court automatically remits a portion of the fees paid by the public not just to its general fund but directly to the judges' retirement plan, and second because judges in Maricopa County are allowed to collect fees for performing wedding ceremonies.

While it's true that a portion of the fees that the superior court collects is automatically remitted to the Elected Officials' Retirement Plan, in which Judge Jones and other superior court judges participate, those fees aren't paid directly to him by the public, and aren't distributed to him until several years later. In fact, during the tax years at issue, Judge Jones didn't receive any compensation from his retirement plan as he hadn't yet retired. We therefore also hold that Judge Jones wasn't compensated on a fee basis via his retirement plan.

The argument about fees from weddings is a bit different. It's true that superior court judges in Maricopa County are entitled to receive fees directly from the public for performing wedding ceremonies. Collecting fees is discretionary, however, and Judge Jones admitted during trial that he waived fees for weddings he performed during the tax years at issue. If we read section 62 as telling us to look at Judge Jones's individual circumstances and ask if his individual position was compensated even "in part on a fee basis," we would have to answer "no."

But he makes a subtler argument that section 62(a)(2)(C) tells us not to focus on the particulars of his situation but to step back and look at whether his type of position—i.e., superior court judge—is one "compensated in whole or in part on a fee basis." Just because he himself wasn't compensated on a fee basis doesn't mean that he wasn't in a *position* that was "compensated in whole or in part on a fee basis." If any superior court judge was taking a fee for even a single wedding, wouldn't that make the position of superior court judge one compensated at least in part on a fee basis?

This isn't a bad question. But let's take another look at section 62(a)(2)(C). It allows as a deduction from gross income in computing AGI [t]he deductions allowed by section 162 which consist of expenses paid or incurred with respect to services performed by an official as an employee of a State or a political subdivision thereof in a position compensated in whole or in part on a fee basis.

And now consider this hypothetical: A Maricopa County Superior Court judge gets a call to perform a wedding in the far reaches of Arizona. The fee is $200, but he has to pay $120 for a motel, another $20 for gas and $10 for tolls. These are expenses that he incurs to produce fee income that goes directly to him. Should he report $200 in extra income and practically speaking (because of the 2 percent limit) get no useful deduction for the $150 in expenses that he incurred to make the $200 in fee income? Maybe the right way to read section 62(a)(2)(C) is that it allows a segregation of expenses for public officials compensated in part on a fee basis—allowing them to deduct above the line those expenses incurred to produce fee income, but treating them like all other employees when it comes to any other employee business expenses.

This might be a reasonable reading. It might even be the most reasonable reading of that section. But it's not one we have to make today in light of Judge Jones's honest admission that he married people for free during the years at issue here. We think that the possibility that one of his colleagues was more mercenary than he at weddings can't convert his own position into one "compensated in whole or in part on a fee basis" any more than the collection of even one filing fee by the clerk of his court would.

Section 62(a)(2)(C) tells us to look at the particular situation of individual taxpayers. Is he "*an* official?" Is he "*an* employee of a State *** in *a* position [pg. 30] compensated in whole or in part on a fee basis?" Singular terms in the Code can include their plural form unless "the context indicates otherwise." See *Commissioner v. Driscoll*, 669 F.3d 1309, 1311 [109 AFTR 2d 2012-832] (11th Cir. 2012) (quoting *United States v. Hayes*, 555 U.S. 415, 422 n.5 (2009)), rev'g and remanding 135 T.C. 557 (2010). But, as in Driscoll, we think "a" and "an" are function words used before *singular* nouns and indicate a singular meaning here. See id. at 1312.

No portion of Judge Jones's compensation for his role as a public officer was provided on a fee basis. Rather, he was an employee of the State of Arizona and paid a salary for his work. Thus, his expenses are deductible as unreimbursed employee expenses under section 162 and should be reported as miscellaneous itemized deductions subject to a 2 percent floor. We hold for the Commissioner on this issue.

IV. *Accuracy-Related Penalties*

The only other issue for decision in this case is whether Judge Jones is liable for accuracy-related penalties for the 2008, 2009, and 2010 tax years under section 6662. Under section 6662(b)(2), a penalty is appropriate when an underpayment of tax is attributable to "[a]ny substantial understatement of income tax." An understatement of tax is "substantial" if it exceeds the greater of $5,000 or "10 percent of the tax required to be shown on the return." Sec. 6662(d)(1)(A). The Commissioner satisfies his burden of production because Judge Jones's understatement of tax exceeds $5,000 (and 10 percent of the tax required to be shown on the return for each tax year at issue). See sec. 6662(b)(2).[8]

Judge Jones can avoid the penalties by showing evidence that his mistake was reasonable and in good faith. See sec. 6664(c)(1); sec. 1.6664-4(a), Income Tax Regs. In making our decision, we examine all the relevant facts and circumstances, including his efforts to determine his proper tax liability and whether he relied in good faith on professional advice. See sec. 1.6664-4(a), Income Tax Regs.

Reliance on a preparer excuses a taxpayer from an accuracy-related penalty only if his reliance was reasonable. Neonatology Assocs., P.A. v. Commissioner, 115 T.C. 43, 99 (2000), aff'd, 299 F.3d 221 [90 AFTR 2d 2002-5442] (3d Cir. 2002). Reliance is reasonable if:

- the adviser was a competent professional with sufficient expertise to justify reliance;
- he provided necessary and accurate information to the adviser; and
- he actually relied on the adviser's judgment in good faith. Id.

We find Judge Jones's testimony as to his CPAs' expertise credible. Though neither CPA testified[9] as to his education, Judge Jones testified that each had several years of experience and came highly recommended by other members of the

---

[8]Section 6662 penalties are also appropriate where an underpayment of tax is attributable to a taxpayer's "[n]egligence or disregard of rules or regulations," and the Commissioner asserts both arguments. Sec. 6662(b)(1).

[9]We note that one of the two CPAs Judge Jones relied on to prepare his return had died before trial.

court. We are satisfied that Judge Jones provided all of the relevant paperwork to his CPAs—he even discussed each individual deduction with them.

We find that Judge Jones reasonably relied on professional advice. Even without a CPA to back him up, we have no doubt about Judge Jones's good faith in taking the position that he did. We also find that the position he took was quite reasonable in the absence of any case law or regulation. This is one of those Code sections that has some ambiguity in it and that no court has ever looked at before in any depth.

Though in the end we agree with the Commissioner, we see no justification for penalties. We find for Judge Jones on this issue.

Decision will be entered under Rule 155.

After reviewing the case, Anita confirms her initial thoughts. Ann is not compensated by the public on a fee basis. Ann's compensation comes entirely from her salary paid by the FCC, and she is not eligible for the benefit of an above-the-line deduction that would escape the 2 percent floor limitation.

8 Case Briefs and Headnotes

Most court reporters contain a brief case summary at the beginning of a case called a **headnote**. Headnotes, which are usually inserted by the court reporter editors, are useful in helping the researcher quickly determine if a particular case is of interest. A court case may contain several issues; therefore, there may be several headnotes for any one case. In addition to using headnotes, tax researchers have found that the construction of a concise case brief is of great value to them, both when they return to a client's research problem or planning environment after a period of time passes and in using the given case in constructing a research analysis for another client. However, the reader should be careful to distinguish this concise research tool from the case briefs required as part of the procedure of most court hearings. The latter is a lengthy written argument of a party's position in the case that includes a detailed analysis of all authority on which the litigant relies.

A proper tax research **case brief** presents in summary fashion, ideally not exceeding one page, the facts, issue(s), holding, and analysis of the chosen court case. From such a brief, the researcher can discover in a very short period whether the full text of the case is of further use in the present analysis. If the briefed case does warrant further examination, the researcher can locate it (or any other cases that are cited in the brief itself) very quickly.

Study carefully the format of the case brief in Exhibit 5-5. Notice that the indicated tax research issues correspond with each of the analyses and holdings of the court, as indicated by the numbers of the brief's outline format. Finally, notice that citations to other cases, or to administrative proclamations, are complete and somewhat detailed, helping to facilitate further research.

EXHIBIT 5-5: Court Case Brief Illustrated

CITATION	*U.S. v. Stephen W. Bentson,* 947 F.2d 1353; 92-1 USTC ¶50,048; 68 AFTR2d 5773 (CA-9, 1991).
ISSUE(S)	(1) Does the IRS's failure to comply with the Paperwork Reduction Act (PRA) preclude a taxpayer from being penalized for failing to file a tax return and cause charges against him to be dismissed?
	(2) Could the IRS penalties be avoided because the Form 1040 had not been published in the Federal Register?

	(3) Could the IRS penalties be avoided because of a lack of proof that Bentson had failed to file returns?
FACTS	For the tax year 1982, Bentson filed a "protest tax return." He refused to supply information other than his name, address, Social Security number, and signature. The rest of his Form 1040 was filled with asterisks, and he attached a statement asserting that to supply other information violated his Fifth Amendment constitutional right. No tax returns could be located for 1983 and 1984. Bentson was charged by the IRS with three counts of willful failure to file tax returns. A district court bench trial was held. After the close of the government's case, Bentson moved for dismissal, relying on *U.S. v. Kimball*, 896 F.2d 1218, vacated, 925 F.2d 356 (CA-9, 1991).
HOLDING	The district court granted Bentson's motion as to the first count only. He was found guilty on two counts and sentenced to eight months' incarceration followed by three years of probation, and a $2,000 fine. The Ninth Circuit affirmed the lower court's decision.
ANALYSIS	(1) Bentson argued the IRS failed to comply with the Paperwork Reduction Act and relied on the original *U.S. v. Kimball*. This decision was reversed in 1991 (see 925 F.2d 356). The Ninth Circuit held that the public protection provision of the Paperwork Reduction Act is not a defense to prosecution.
	(2) Bentson argued that Form 1040 and the instructions constitute a "rule" for purposes of the Administrative Procedures Act (APA) and therefore must be published in the Federal Register to be valid. The Ninth Circuit ruled this argument had no merit.
	(3) Bentson argued the IRS had not proved he did not file tax returns for 1983 and 1984. This argument was rejected because Bentson had already made a binding judicial admission to the contrary.

SUMMARY

The tax practitioner must possess a working knowledge of the federal court system to address tax research problems. The researcher must understand the role of the courts in generating federal tax law, the relationship of the courts to one another, the Constitution, and the jurisdiction of each court, where to locate an appropriate decision, and how to interpret that decision.

Exhibit 5-6 offers a summary of some of the attributes of the trial-level courts discussed in this chapter. Because of differences among courts, the tax adviser might want to choose one trial-level court instead of the others to accommodate a client's special needs or circumstances.

Exhibit 5-7 summarizes the decisions available in each of the tax case reporter services discussed in this

EXHIBIT 5-6:   Selected Attributes of Trial-Level Courts

Item	Tax Court	District Court	Court of Federal Claims
Jurisdiction	Tax cases only	Legal issues based on entire U.S. Code	Monetary claims against U.S. government
Judges	Tax law specialists	Tax law generalists	Tax law generalists
Domain	National court, but judges travel	Limited geographical area	National court, but judges travel
Jury trial available?	No	Yes, if question of fact	No
Number of judges	One, reviewed by the chief judge; en banc hearing for certain issues	One	One to five hearing case
Small cases procedure	Yes	Not available	Not available
Payment of tax	Trial, then payment	Payment, then trial	Payment, then trial
Precedents court must follow	Supreme Court; pertinent circuit court; Tax Court	Supreme Court; pertinent circuit court; own district court	Supreme Court; federal circuit court of appeals; Court of Federal Claims

EXHIBIT 5-7: Court Decision Reporter Summary

Publisher, Common	I. BY REPORTER	
	Reporter, Common	**Decisions Included**
Primary Reporters		
T.C. (B.T.A.)	GPO	Regular Tax Court (BTA) decisions
T.C.M.	CCH	Tax Court Memorandum decisions
T.C. Mem. Dec.	Thomson Reuters	Tax Court Memorandum decisions
F. Supp.	West	District court decisions
Fed. Cl.	West	Court of Federal Claims decisions
F.3d (F.2d)	West	"Published" decisions of U.S. Court of Appeals and pre-1982 Court of Claims decisions
Fed. Appx.	West	All unpublished decisions of U.S. Court of Appeals since 2001
U.S.	GPO	All Supreme Court decisions
S.Ct.	West	All Supreme Court decisions
Secondary Reporters		
USTC	CCH	Selected tax cases from all federal courts except the Tax Court
AFTR series	Thomson Reuters	Selected tax cases from all federal courts except the Tax Court

Court	II. BY COURT		
	Publisher	**Citation**	**Reporter**
Supreme Court			
All cases	West	S.Ct.	*Supreme Court Reporter*
	GPO	U.S.	*U.S. Supreme Court Reports*
Tax only	CCH	USTC	*U.S. Tax Cases*
	Thomson Reuters	AFTR series	*American Federal Tax Reports*
Courts of Appeals			
All published cases	West	F.3d (F.2d)	*Federal Reporter, 3d (2d) series*
All unpublished cases (since 2001)	West	Fed. Appx.	*Federal Appendix*
Tax only	CCH	USTC	
	Thomson Reuters	AFTR series	
Tax Court			
Regular	GPO	T.C.	*United States Tax Court Reports*
Memo	CCH	T.C.M.	*Tax Court Memorandum Decisions*
	Thomson Reuters	T.C. Memo	*Tax Court Memorandum Decisions*
District Court			
All cases	West	F.Supp	*Federal Supplement Series*
Tax only	CCH	USTC	
	Thomson Reuters	AFTR series	
Court of Federal Claims			
All cases post-1982	West	Fed. Cl.	*U.S. Court of Federal Claims*
Tax only	CCH	USTC	
	Thomson Reuters	AFTR series	

EXHIBIT 5-8:   Citation Conventions and Observations

- The common form of a citation is as follows: case name–volume–number–reporter–page number–court–year.
- The AFTR second series began with 1954 IRC cases.
- The B.T.A. became the U.S. Tax Court in 1943.
- The U.S. Court of Claims became the U.S. Claims Court in 1982 and the U.S. Court of Federal Claims in 1992.
- Unless the case was published in a year different from that in which it was heard, the USTC volume number (and many AFTR page numbers) includes a reference to the year, so the year need not be repeated in the citation.
- The S.Ct. and U.S. citations imply that the case was heard in the U.S. Supreme Court, so the court abbreviation need not be repeated in the citation.
- The government need not be mentioned in a typical Tax Court citation.
- Although they are not published in a printed court reporter, U.S. Tax Court small case summary opinions are available after 2000 through online tax services (e.g., Thomson Reuters and CCH).

chapter. With the variety of tax publications available, choices must be made so that the practitioner's tax research budget can be used effectively, without sacrifice of his or her ability to solve the client's problems.

Finally, a number of observations concerning citation conventions can be made. Review the citation examples given in this chapter to verify the list shown in Exhibit 5-8 and to add your own observations to it.

KEY WORDS

By the time you complete this chapter, you should be comfortable discussing each of the following terms. If you need additional review of any of these items, return to the appropriate material in the chapter or consult the glossary to this text.

AFTR (American Federal Tax Reports), p. 155
Board of Tax Appeals, p. 149
case brief, p. 167
Court of Federal Claims, p. 155
courts of appeals, p. 157
district courts, p. 154

Golsen rule, p. 151
headnote, p. 167
memorandum decision, p. 151
permanent citation, p. 153
regular decision, p. 151
Rule 155, p. 151
Small tax case procedures, p. 152

Supreme Court, p. 159
summary opinion, p. 152
Tax Court, p. 148
temporary citation, p. 152
USTC (United States Tax Cases), p. 155
writ of certiorari, p. 159

DISCUSSION QUESTIONS

1. Who can initiate a court case that deals with a tax matter—the taxpayer or the IRS?

2. Explain the general organization of the federal court system for cases concerning federal tax issues.

3. May a taxpayer take his or her tax case directly to the U.S. Supreme Court?

4. Who has the burden of proof in most cases involving the tax law? Why?

5. The U.S. Tax Court hears only certain types of cases. Identify those cases.

6. The U.S. Tax Court has undergone an evolution since it was founded. What happened to its structure in 1926, 1943, and 1969, respectively?

7. How many judges sit on the U.S. Tax Court? What is the length of time of the appointment of each judge?

8. The U.S. Tax Court is a national court that meets in Washington, D.C. Does this mean that the taxpayer and his or her attorney must travel to Washington to have a case heard?

9. May a taxpayer have a jury trial in the U.S. Tax Court?

10. What does the term *en banc* mean?

11. Distinguish among a regular, memorandum, and summary decision of the Tax Court.

12. The U.S. Tax Court is a national court that hears cases of taxpayers who may appeal to various geographical courts of appeals. How does the Tax Court reconcile the opposite holdings of two or more of these courts of appeals for taxpayers who work or reside in different parts of the country?

13. What is the small tax case procedure of the U.S. Tax Court? What is the maximum amount of the deficiency that can be the subject of a small tax case hearing? Comment on the trial procedures in small tax cases.

14. Where are regular Tax Court decisions published? Illustrate the elements of both a temporary and a permanent regular Tax Court citation. Explain what each part of the citation means.

15. Tax Court memorandum decisions are not published by the federal government. However, commercial reporters include these decisions. Illustrate the elements of both a temporary and a permanent citation for a Tax Court memorandum decision, using both the CCH and Thomson Reuters reporters. Explain what each part of the citation means.

16. What is the jurisdiction of a U.S. District Court?

17. Can Tax Court summary opinions be cited as precedent? Discuss.

18. Must the taxpayer pay the disputed tax deficiency to the government before his or her case will be heard in a district court? In the U.S. Court of Federal Claims? In the U.S. Tax Court?

19. Which of the trial courts is most appropriate for a taxpayer who wishes to limit the judicial review of the relevant year's tax return to the specific issue(s) involved in the case?

20. Which of the trial courts would best serve a taxpayer litigating an issue of a technical tax nature? Why?

21. Is a federal district court a national court? How many judges hear a case brought before a federal district court?

22. Name the three court case reporters that publish tax and nontax district court decisions. Illustrate the elements of a citation that might be found in each reporter. Explain what each part of the citation means.

23. Differentiate between a primary and a secondary case citation.

24. What types of cases are heard by the U.S. Court of Federal Claims?

25. How many judges are appointed to the U.S. Court of Federal Claims?

26. Is the U.S. Court of Federal Claims a national court? Must a taxpayer go to Washington, D.C. to present a case to this court?

27. Name the three court case reporters that publish U.S. Court of Federal Claims decisions. Illustrate the elements of a citation that might be found in each reporter. Explain what each part of the citation means.

28. Are the U.S. courts of appeals national courts? What type of cases do they hear?

29. Identify the circuit court that would hear the case of a taxpayer who lives or works in each of the following areas:

    a. Texas
    b. New York
    c. California
    d. Colorado
    e. A case that is appealed from the U.S. Court of Federal Claims

30. Identify the circuit court that would hear the case of a taxpayer who lives or works in each of the following areas:

    a. Idaho
    b. Indiana
    c. South Carolina
    d. Puerto Rico
    e. Guam

31. Identify the circuit court that would hear the case of a taxpayer who lives or works in each of the following areas:

    a. Arizona
    b. Alabama
    c. Alaska
    d. Arkansas
    e. Washington, D.C.

32. Identify the circuit court that would hear the case of a taxpayer who lives or works in each of the following areas:

    a. Nebraska
    b. Nevada
    c. New Hampshire
    d. New Mexico
    e. New Jersey

33. Each court of appeals has approximately 20 judges. How many of these judges hear a typical case?

34. Name the three court case reporters that publish court of appeals decisions. Illustrate the elements of a citation that might be found in each reporter. Explain what each part of the citation means.

35. Can a taxpayer have a jury trial before a court of appeals?

36. What is the highest court in the United States? What is its jurisdiction? Where does it hear cases?

37. How does one petition the Supreme Court to hear one's tax case?

38. How many justices are appointed to the Supreme Court? How many hear each case?

39. Why does the Supreme Court hear so few tax cases?

40. Differentiate between the Supreme Court's overturning of a lower court's decision and its denial of a writ of certiorari.

41. Name the four court case reporters that publish Supreme Court decisions. Illustrate the elements of a citation that might be found in each reporter. Explain what each part of the citation means.

42. Is it possible for a taxpayer to have a jury trial before any of the trial courts? Before a court of appeals? Before the U.S. Supreme Court?

43. Discuss the precedential value of a court of appeals decision. Which court of appeals decisions are most important to a specific taxpayer?

44. In the (fictitious) citation *Gomez v. U.S.,* 104 T. C. 123 (2009), what does the "104" stand for? The "T.C."? The "123"?

45. Which court would have issued the (fictitious) *O'Dell v. U.S.,* 98 T.C.M. 86 (2009) decision? What does each element in the citation mean?

46. In the citation *Simons-Eastern v. U.S.,* 354 F. Supp. 1003 (D.Ct., Ga, 1972), the "F. Supp." tells the tax researcher that the decision is from which court?

47. By using only the citation, state which court issued each of the following decisions. If you cannot determine which court by looking at the citation only, say so.
    a. *Davis v. U.S.,* 43 Fed. Cl. 92 (1999)
    b. *D.C. Crummey v. U.S.,* 68-2 USTC ¶ 12,541
    c. *U.S. v. Goode,* 86 AFTR2d 2000-7273
    d. *James v. U.S.,* 81 S.Ct. 1052 (1961)

48. What is a case headnote? How might it be useful to the tax researcher?

49. By using only the citation, state which court issued each of the following decisions. If you cannot determine which court by looking at the citation only, say so.
    a. *Douglas, Christopher,* T.C. Memo 1994-519
    b. *Takaba, Brian* G., 119 T.C. 285
    c. *Botts, Roy* R., T.C. Summary Opinion 2001-182
    d. American Airlines, Inc., 40 Fed.Cl. 712

EXERCISES

50. Locate the court case *Central Labor's Pension Fund v. Heinz,* 541 U.S. 739 (2004). Using only the headnotes, answer the following questions:
    a. What issue(s) did the court address?
    b. What was the ruling of the court?

51. Locate the court case *Ellis v. Jarvis et al.,* 117 AFTR 2d 2016-1932. Using only the headnotes, answer the following questions:
    a. What issue(s) did the court address?
    b. What was the ruling of the court?

52. Locate the court case *Vichich,* 146 T.C. No. 12 (2016). Using only the headnotes, answer the following questions:
    a. What issue(s) did the court address?
    b. What was the ruling of the court?

53. Locate the court case *David H. Hoffman, et ux.,* T.C. Memo 2016-69. Using only the headnotes, answer the following questions:
    a. What issue(s) did the court address?
    b. What was the ruling of the court?

54. Locate the court case *Million Hussein*, T.C. Summary 2015-59 and answer the following questions:
    a. What issue(s) did the court address?
    b. What was the ruling of the court?

55. Locate the court case *Clayton v. Comm.*, 2015-1 USTC ¶ 50, 110, 114 AFTR 2d 2014-6818. Using only the headnotes, answer the following questions:
    a. What issue(s) did the court address?
    b. What was the ruling of the court?

56. Locate the court case *Byrne v. U.S.*, 127 Fed. Cl. 284 (2016). Using only the headnotes, answer the following questions:
    a. What issue(s) did the court address?
    b. What was the ruling of the court?

57. Find the court decision located at 145 T.C. 145.
    a. Which court heard the case?
    b. Who was the judge(s)?
    c. In what year was the case decided?
    d. What was the issue(s) involved?

58. Find the court decision located at 144 T.C. 279.
    a. Which court heard the case?
    b. Who was the judge(s)?
    c. In what year was the case decided?
    d. What was the issue(s) involved?

59. Find the court decision located at 142 T.C. 297.
    a. Which court heard the case?
    b. Who was the judge(s)?
    c. In what year was the case decided?
    d. What was the issue(s) involved?

60. Find the court decision located at T.C. Memo 2013-144.
    a. Which court heard the case?
    b. Who was the judge(s)?
    c. In what year was the case decided?
    d. What was the issue(s) involved?

61. Find the court decision located at T.C. Memo. 2015-189.
    a. Which court heard the case?
    b. Who was the judge(s)?
    c. In what year was the case decided?
    d. What was the issue(s) involved?

62. Find the court decision located at T.C. Memo. 1992-204.
    a. Which court heard the case?
    b. Who was the judge(s)?
    c. Which tax year(s) is in question and in what year was the case decided?
    d. Which code section(s) was at issue?

e. What was the issue(s) involved?

f. Which party prevailed in the decision?

63. Find the court decision located at T.C. Summary Opinion 2013-21.

a. Which court heard the case?

b. Who was the judge(s)?

c. Which tax year(s) is in question and in what year was the case decided?

d. Which code section(s) was at issue?

e. What was the issue(s) involved?

f. Which party prevailed in the decision?

64. Find the court decision located at T.C. Summary Opinion 2015-65.

a. Which court heard the case?

b. Who was the judge(s)?

c. Which tax year(s) is in question and in what year was the case decided?

d. Which code section(s) was at issue?

e. What was the issue(s) involved?

f. Which party prevailed in the decision?

65. Find the court decision located at 108 AFTR 2d 2011-5569.

a. Which court heard the case?

b. Who was the judge(s)?

c. Which tax year(s) is in question and in what year was the case decided?

d. Which code section(s) was at issue?

e. What was the issue(s) involved?

f. Which party prevailed in the decision?

66. Find the court decision located at 2014-2 USTC ¶50,516.

a. Which court heard the case?

b. Who was the judge(s)?

c. Which tax year(s) is in question and in what year was the case decided?

d. Which code section(s) was at issue?

e. What was the issue(s) involved?

f. Which party prevailed in the decision?

67. Find the court decision located at 67 AFTR2d 91-718.

a. Which court heard the case?

b. Who was the judge(s)?

c. Which tax year(s) is in question and in what year was the case decided?

d. Which code section(s) was at issue?

e. What was the issue(s) involved?

f. Which party prevailed in the decision?

68. Find the court decision located at 101 AFTR2d 2008-1612.

a. Which court heard the case?

b. Who was the judge(s)?

c. Which tax year(s) is in question and in what year was the case decided?

    d. Which code section(s) was at issue?

    e. What was the issue(s) involved?

    f. Which party prevailed in the decision?

69. If your last name begins with the letters A–L, read and brief the following cases:

    a. *Sorensen*, T.C. Memo. 1994-175

    b. *Keller*, 84-1 USTC ¶9194.

    If your last name begins with the letters M–Z, read and brief the following cases:

    c. *Washington*, 77 T.C. 601

    d. *Tellier*, 17 AFTR2d 633

70. Read and brief the following cases:

    a. *Rownd*, T.C. Memo. 1994-465

    b. *Arnes*, 93-1 USTC ¶50,016.

71. Read and brief the following cases:

    a. *Willie Nelson Music Co.*, 85 T.C. 914

    b. *Green v. U.S.*, 117 AFTR 2d 2016-700.

72. Read and brief the following cases:

    a. *Gregory v. Helvering*, 55 S.Ct. 266 (1935)

    b. *Hunt*, T.C. Memo. 1965-172

73. Read and brief the following cases:

    a. *Fulcher, Douglas* R., T.C. Summary Opinion 2003-157

    b. *The Boeing Company and Consolidated Subs.*, 91 AFTR2d 2003-1088 (123 S.Ct. 1099)

74. Read and brief the following cases:

    a. *Thornton v. Commissioner*, 2003-2 USTC ¶50,695

    b. *Stamoulis v. Commissioner*, T.C. Summary Opinion 2007-38

75. Use a tax service to give two parallel citations for *U.S. v. D'ambrosia*, a Seventh Circuit Court of Appeals case decided in 2002. Using only the headnote(s), determine the issue(s) in this case.

76. Use a tax service to give three parallel citations for *Baral v. U.S.*, a Supreme Court case decided in 2000. Using only the headnote(s), determine the issue(s) in this case.

77. Use a tax service to give three parallel citations for *Falstone, Inc. v. Commissioner*, a Ninth Circuit Court of Appeals case decided in 2003. Using only the headnote(s), determine the issue(s) in this case.

PART III

Research Tools

CHAPTER 6

Thomson Reuters Checkpoint

LEARNING OBJECTIVES

- Complete the research process using an illustrative example and the Checkpoint tax service.
- Describe the major research databases of Checkpoint.
- Use keyword, content, index, and citation searches to identify relevant materials in Checkpoint.
- Use the RIA Checkpoint Citator to confirm the current status of sources of tax law.
- Identify key sources of current tax news and information available in Checkpoint.

CHAPTER OUTLINE

1 Using Tax Services for Research

WHEN A CLIENT CONTACTS A TAX ADVISER with a tax situation, the adviser has a professional responsibility to provide the best tax advice possible and also to ensure that the advice meets the professional standards under the taxing authority's rules. In addition, tax advisers are not likely to meet with much commercial success if they do not provide well-researched and constructed solutions to their client's tax problems. Further, tax practitioners are being more closely scrutinized by the IRS and the Securities and Exchange Commission (SEC) as a result of increases in regulation. This heightened oversight increases the importance of conducting quality tax research that is carefully documented. Many sources of tax law can be found on the Internet for free. For example, the IRS offers links to free access to the Internal Revenue Code, Treasury regulations, and anything published in the Internal Revenue Bulletin on its website (**http://www.irs.gov/Tax-Professionals/Tax-Code,-Regulations-and-Official-Guidance#guidance**). The U.S. Tax Court offers its opinions since the mid-1990s online (**https://www.ustaxcourt.gov/**). With a number of primary tax sources available via the Internet for free, one might wonder why tax practitioners are willing to bear the substantial costs associated with subscribing to commercial tax and legal services. By organizing the copious assortment of primary and secondary tax law sources, these services facilitate more efficient, effective, and comprehensive searches for solutions to tax questions than a typical Internet search would produce. In addition to organizing the sources of tax law into a single database system, **commercial tax services** also provide editorial explanations and expert analysis of primary tax law. Because the tax law can be quite complex, the plain-English commentary alone can be worth the cost of the services. Thus, the value of a commercial service is to act as an index for and explanation of primary and secondary tax law source materials. Most tax practitioners avail themselves of the benefit of a tax service, as there are services priced to fit the needs (and pocketbooks) of even the smallest tax office.

While one of the main features that practitioners appreciate in a commercial service is the editorial explanation, only reckless (or inadequately trained) tax practitioners confine their analysis to this commentary. The tax services should efficiently direct the researcher to the germane primary sources of the controlling law. It is the ethical and professional duty of tax researchers to evaluate the primary sources themselves and ascertain whether any developments have occurred recently that may change or alter the results of the initial research.

This chapter concretely applies the basic steps for developing effective and efficient tax research based on the process introduced in Chapter 2 and by utilizing the Checkpoint commercial tax service to find a solution to an actual tax question. The features of Checkpoint, both tax and legal, are explored on this journey.

The commercial providers of tax services offer a plethora of tax products (databases) that can be bundled in a variety of ways. This chapter's description of the tax databases within Checkpoint might not be what is available by subscription to the reader. Each tax professional, firm, and library should perform a cost–benefit analysis and purchase only those resources that it finds useful and can afford. In addition, the tax services are constantly updating their products to maintain their competitive edge. Therefore, the current appearance of the tax services and products offered may differ from those presented in this text. Nevertheless, the basic methodology described in this text should apply to whatever tax databases and products are available to the reader, regardless of their visual presentation.

2 Thomson Reuters Checkpoint

Checkpoint is a commercial tax and accounting research service offered by Thomson Reuters. Checkpoint offers integrated source materials and analysis for tax, accounting, auditing, and corporate finance. The service has been designed to assist researchers in finding answers quickly through customizable search options, integrated links, and time-saving tools. Nontax materials from sources such as the Financial Accounting Standards Board (FASB) and Securities and Exchange Commission (SEC) are available in the same software platform, allowing all users to find information in a similar fashion whether the researcher is a tax or financial accounting expert. Access to the entire Checkpoint library is available from just one screen. The results can then be narrowed using the filter options provided. Documents found as a result of searches can be flagged or saved as favorites for future review.

3 Illustrative Research Example

As with learning to drive an automobile, the procedural knowledge necessary to become an effective researcher can only be acquired through hands-on practice. The remainder of this chapter is designed to guide you through a basic use of Checkpoint and is not a substitute for you actually performing the research. Using the service as you follow the text presentation of the research steps is a highly effective method of learning this material.

Lorna Kolbear, a resident of South Carolina, knew that her son, Steven, was something special at an early age. By the age of 7, Steven showed an extensive talent for political satire and frequently held talk shows with his friends or his six brothers in their modest one-bedroom apartment. Lorna was a single mother and immediately started the work of grooming Steven for a career in television and film. She frequently sacrificed her own needs for those of Steven, especially when it came to Steven's budding career as an actor. Lorna transported Steven to a variety of auditions and tryouts and paid for drama classes and acting instruction as she could afford it. When Steven was in high school, his on-stage and on-camera talents were becoming well known. Articles on his latest comedic ventures were frequently published in the local newspapers. This publicity caught the eye of Quarterlodeon VP for Development, Dorothy Player. Dorothy's primary job was to sign new young talent for the Quarterlodeon Network's lineup of television programming.

Dorothy began to follow Steven's career closely and, as a measure of goodwill, even hired a couple of Steven's older brothers into the production crews at Quarterlodeon Studios; however, she stayed away from contacting Steven directly because of her understanding that Lorna felt strongly that Steven should finish high school. Dorothy met frequently with Lorna, recognizing early on that Lorna was matriarch of the Kolbear household and made all the family decisions.

Two days after Steven graduated from high school, Dorothy approached Lorna at the Kolbears' South Carolina apartment to begin negotiations with her. Lorna, as it turns out, knew nothing about television or film and even less about studio contracts but forged ahead with the negotiations anyway. A deal was finally reached, later that year but before Steven's 18th birthday. The deal included, among other things, a $150,000 signing bonus for Steven, of which $50,000 would be paid to Lorna. Lorna felt that "he would never have been the actor he is and been able to sign this lucrative contract without my tireless efforts." These amounts were to be paid as soon as the contract was executed and did not *require Steven to perform any services whatsoever after that time. Under the terms of the contract, Steven would be prohibited from signing with another studio or network for a period of five years.*

As was standard with all contracts with minor (under age 18) actors, the network insisted that Lorna sign the parental consent. Note that under South Carolina law, Lorna is entitled to all the earnings of her minor children (unless separately emancipated by South Carolina law). Steven was not emancipated.

3-1 Approaching the Research Problem

Regardless of the research method used, the starting point in approaching any tax research problem is to formulate the various tax questions to be answered and identify the issues associated with the questions. The tax question for the Kolbear case appears to be the following: What is the appropriate tax treatment of Steven's signing bonus? This first formulation of the tax question should not be considered its final version. As the research progresses, other issues are likely to be identified, causing some refinement of the tax research questions and necessitating the development of new ones. Recall the iterative nature of tax research as discussed in Chapter 2 and presented in Exhibits 2-1 and 2-2.

Research questions are gradually refined to their final states as all the associated issues are identified. However, this refinement does not guarantee that controlling authority will be found to provide a definite answer to the tax research question. The final conclusion may be that one solution appears more supportable than another. There may be a conflict between the likely interpretation of the facts and circumstances by the IRS and the taxpayer. Considering the probable stance the courts would take may be relevant when weighing the solution to the research question. In most tax research engagements, professional judgment is required because the controlling law is imprecise and can be interpreted differently by the taxpayer, the IRS, and the courts. It is this professional judgment that taxpayers are seeking when they hire CPAs for tax assistance.

Based on the initial question formulated, the main issues in the Kolbear case appear to be the timing of the taxability of the signing bonus, the attribution of the income to either Steven or his mother, Lorna, and the possible deduction of the payment by Steven to his mother for her services in negotiating the contract.

3-2 Accessing Tax Information

Researching the tax law is more of an art than a science, and researching tax issues effectively and efficiently requires a broad knowledge of tax law, a reasonable level of experience with the tax research tools, and persistence (a small dose of luck never hurts, either). One of the most important steps in the tax research process is to consider the question, "Where do I start?" Since most students have little to no tax research experience and a wealth of tax law to pore over, this task can be daunting. The key to effective tax research is finding the pertinent material necessary to formulate an informed conclusion about the optimum treatment of the transaction.

Most tax services, including Checkpoint, offer four primary ways to search for information: (1) keyword search, (2) contents search, (3) index search, and (4) citation search. Keyword searches are very similar to the typical web search performed on an Internet browser using Google, Bing, or some other common search engine. Contents searches are similar to examining the table of contents for a book and trying to locate the chapter relevant to the search. Using an index search is no different than simply flipping to the index at the end of a book and looking up the key word or words that might direct you to the proper page. Citation searches require that the researcher already have a good idea of the IRC section, regulation, ruling, or other known source of tax law that might apply. Before performing a search, the researcher must have a thorough understanding of what information is being searched.

4 Databases

Checkpoint, like most tax services, organizes information by database. Traditionally, databases are classified into two general types: annotated and topical. **Annotated tax services** are organized by Internal Revenue Code section number. They may also be called compilations because they compile an editor's explanation and evaluation with the Code section as well as its recent committee reports and regulations, and they provide **annotations** (i.e., brief summaries) of related court cases and administrative rulings. **Topical tax services**, on the other hand, divide the tax law into transactions and related subject matter with underlying tax principles as an organizing format. Thus, the material follows logical threads that connect noncontiguous code sections. Since the electronic services are developed from published services, they are generally organized as topical and annotated databases; however, this structure may not be apparent.

One of the greatest benefits of any Internet service is the currency of the information provided. Most services update text on a daily or continuous basis. Still, daily updating does not necessarily mean that what happened yesterday will be accessible today; processing time still is required. However, daily updating does mean that as soon as the information is processed it can be entered into the system.

Accessing Checkpoint requires a subscription, including a login and password. The method by which you access Checkpoint can vary depending on the subscription a school or company has obtained. The Checkpoint HOME screen presented in Exhibit 6-1 provides the entry point to starting tax research.

A particular user's HOME screen may differ depending on the default or personalized setup provided by the school or company. More often than not; however, the starting point will be the Checkpoint SEARCH screen presented in Exhibit 6-2.

EXHIBIT 6-1: Checkpoint Home Screen

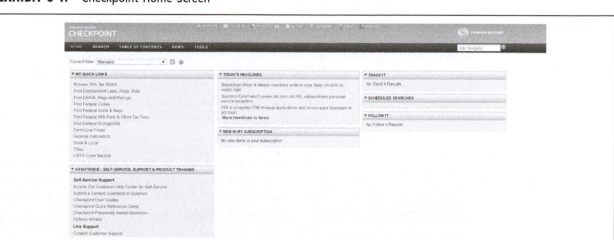

EXHIBIT 6-2: Checkpoint Search Screen

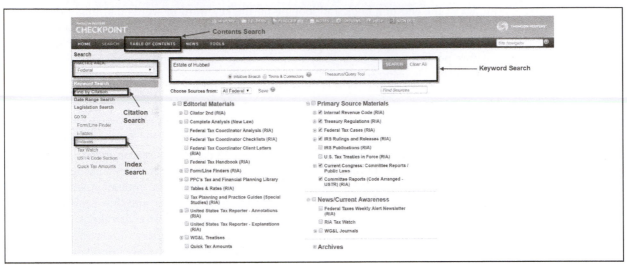

The SEARCH screen is organized to facilitate quick access to the research methods most frequently used by the practitioners. As presented in Exhibit 6-2, the focus of Checkpoint is on keyword searches; the KEYWORD SEARCH Box is located at the top center of the search screen. A contents search can be launched by clicking on the TABLE OF CONTENTS button at the top of the screen, and Index searches are started either through the INDEX button in the left sidebar (the left-hand portion of the screen) under GO TO or through the TABLE OF CONTENTS. Citation searches are also accessed through the left sidebar.

In Checkpoint, the database areas are known as practice areas. PRACTICE AREAS are available to select using the drop-down arrow as presented in the left sidebar of Exhibit 6-2. Practice areas are organized at the highest level to help users identify specific areas of tax or accounting that may apply to the situation. Among the choices are Federal; State & Local; Estate Planning; Pension & Benefits; International; Payroll; Accounting, Audit and Corporate Finance; and All Practice Areas. The practice areas available vary based on the subscription purchased. The information presented in the search screen will change based on the practice area selected. For most subscriptions, the federal practice area includes EDITORIAL MATERIALS (secondary sources), PRIMARY SOURCE MATERIALS, LEGISLATION, and NEWS/CURRENT AWARENESS, as shown clockwise from top left in Exhibit 6-2. Recall that primary authority is what professional standards dictate that tax advisers must understand to achieve substantial authority under IRC § 6662 and IRC § 6694. Primary sources are the statutory, administrative, and judicial sources discussed in previous chapters and presented as shown under that heading in Exhibit 6-2.

Checkpoint offers access to a variety of primary source materials under the FEDERAL TAX practice area. As shown in Exhibit 6-3, all these can be found under the PRIMARY SOURCE MATERIALS heading. The detail of each source can be displayed by clicking the [+] next to any heading as shown in Exhibit 6-3. A more complete listing of primary source materials in Checkpoint is presented in Exhibit 6-4.

EXHIBIT 6-3: Checkpoint Primary Source Materials Screen

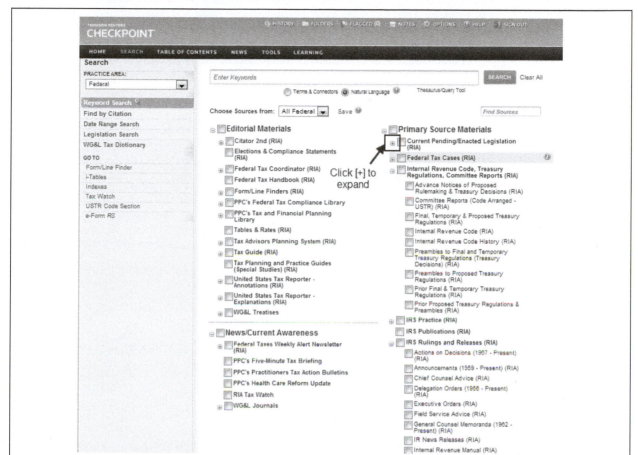

EXHIBIT 6-4: Checkpoint Primary Source Materials

Code, Regulations, Committee Reports	The complete Internal Revenue Code plus the full text of all final, temporary, and proposed regulations and committee reports. It is continuously updated to reflect new developments and is thoroughly indexed for instant access. Code & Regulations is organized by code section to help streamline your research.
Current Pending/ Enacted Legislation	Enacted and pending legislation of the current Congress. Committee reports and tables of amended code sections, also of the current Congress.
Federal Tax Cases	Contains the full text of tax cases heard in the regular federal court system. • American Federal Tax Reports (1860–previous year)—The AFTR series contains decisions of federal tax cases that were not heard in Tax Court. AFTR includes: All U.S. Supreme Court cases that deal with federal taxes • All U.S. Court of Appeals cases that deal with federal taxes • All significant U.S. District Court and Claims Court cases that deal with federal taxes • American Federal Tax Reports (Current Year)—the full text of tax cases gives you the complete history of all tax cases. Each case is preceded by headnotes that identify the issues and summarize the court's finding and rationale.

- Tax Court & Board of Tax Appeals Memorandum Decisions (1928–previous year)—the full text of all reported and memo decisions that address new issues and require revision to an existing law or a new law.

- Tax Court & Board of Tax Appeals Reported Decisions (1924–previous year)—the full text of all Tax Court and Board of Tax Appeals decisions that address new issues and require revision to an existing law or a new law.

- Tax Court & Federal Procedural Rules—the full text of all Tax Court Rules and Federal Rules of Appellate Procedure.

- Tax Court Memorandum Decisions (Current Year)—the full text of all reported and memo decisions, featuring official pagination as it appears in the GPO U.S. Tax Court Reports.

- Tax Court Reported Decisions (Current Year)—the full text of all Tax Court decisions that address new issues and require revision to an existing law or a new law.

- Tax Court Summary Opinions

IRS Practice

Provides all strategies and solutions needed when representing a client before the IRS. A reference addressing the rapidly changing and increasingly complex area of tax procedure. This authority presents the procedural changes, IRS restructuring, and ongoing revisions to the Internal Revenue Manual.

Topics include:

Ethics Materials

How to Use the Internal Revenue Manual

Internal Revenue Manual Index

ISP Materials

Internal Revenue Manual

MSSP Training Guide

Market Segment Understandings Guidelines

IRS Publications

The full text of all IRS publications, organized by publication number.

IRS Rulings and Releases

Actions on Decisions (1967–Present)—Prepared when the IRS loses an issue/issues in a court case.

Announcements (1959–Present)

Chief Counsel Advice—Generated by the Chief Counsel's Office, by request from the IRS, usually to assist in the preparation of a revenue ruling or private letter ruling.

Delegation Orders (1956–Present)—Generated by the Treasury Department.

Executive Orders—Generated by the chief executive (president or state governor).

Field Service Advice—IRS Field Service Advice (FSA) Memorandums are released by the IRS Office of Chief Counsel to provide consistent legal advice to IRS Field Service and related IRS functions with respect to their tax administration responsibilities.

General Counsel Memoranda (1962–Present)—Generated by the Chief Counsel's Office, by request from the IRS, usually to assist in the preparation of a revenue ruling or private letter ruling.

IRS News Releases—Released by the IRS's Public Affairs Office whenever important information must be released to the public.

IRS Business Operating Divisions—Reports and documents released by the IRS Business Operating Divisions (Advance Pricing Program and Large and Mid-Size Business).

Notices (1980–Present)—Provide substantive or procedural tax law guidance.

	Other FOIA (Freedom of Information Act) Documents—Other IRS documents available through the FOIA.
	Other IRS Documents—Miscellaneous IRS documents.
	Private Letter Rulings & Technical Advice Memoranda (1954–Present)
	Revenue Procedures (1955–Present)
	Revenue Rulings (1954–Present)
	Service Center Advice—IRS Service Center Advice (SCA) Memorandums are released by the IRS Office of Chief Counsel to provide consistent legal advice to IRS service centers and related IRS functions with respect to their tax administration responsibilities.
U.S. Tax Treaties in Force	The U.S. Bilateral Tax Treaties Database features expert in-depth analysis and full official text of every treaty, protocol, and agreement between the United States and foreign countries relating to income, estate and gift tax, shipping and transportation, exchange of information, and Social Security totalization.
	Treasury technical explanations, Senate committee reports, reports of the Secretary of State, and other related documents are also included. Look to this database for the latest cases and rulings along with the status and content of new treaties and protocols. All are accompanied by annotated summaries and additional direct links to article-by-article analysis.

SPOTLIGHT ON TAXATION

Thomson Reuters

Checkpoint is currently owned and operated by Thomson Reuters. Reuters originates with the Reuters Agency, founded by Paul Julius Reuter in 1851 in London. Reuter's established itself as a leading news agency and was the first to report Abraham Lincoln's assassination. Roy Thomson was also a news man and started his business through the purchase of a newspaper in Ontario, Canada, in 1934. His business took off with the granting of the rights to operate a television station in Scotland. In 2015, Thomson Reuters had revenues of more than $12 billion. It currently sells a variety of products such as Westlaw (discussed in Chapter 8), the ONESOURCE portfolio of corporate tax compliance software, and the Web of Science citation index and has more than 200 bureaus associated with its continuing Reuters News Service. At one time, Thomson Higher Education owned the textbook you are currently reading! Amazingly, the Thomson family still owns more than one-half of the company.

While considered secondary authority, editorial content can be extremely helpful in providing assistance to the tax adviser to find and understand the relevant primary authority. A typical Checkpoint subscription will contain three main editorial sources of interest, especially to new researchers: (1) Federal Tax Handbook, (2) Federal Tax Coordinator (FTC), and (3) United States Tax Reporter (USTR). These tax sources can be found under the EDITORIAL MATERIALS heading in the main window (see Exhibit 6-2). A complete list is presented in Exhibit 6-5, with these three highlighted. The databases available will vary by subscription; thus, not all of those listed below may be available.

EXHIBIT 6-5:   Checkpoint Editorial Source Materials

Source	Description
Checkpoint Catalyst	Digital portfolios topically organized that provide a synopsis of a particular tax area through editorial commentary. Contains additional functionality such as embedded workflow tools.
Citator 2d	The Citator 2d notes specific relationships between cases (i.e., if a case has overruled another case). It also tracks a case issue individually allowing the practitioner to follow the key issues of the case. Citator is completely integrated, to allow you to cite check all cases quickly and to see all the activity for a given case in one place.
Election & Compliance Statements	Practice aids, including statements and forms required to be filed with the IRS to elect tax treatment or comply with rules.
Federal Tax Coordinator	Analyzes in integrated subject matter arrangement the IRC and all important federal tax legislation, regulations, cases, and rulings.
Federal Tax Handbook	An accurate and easy-to-use reference for day-to-day tax questions on the most current tax years.
Form/Line Finders	Practice aids with line-by-line summaries for individual, corporate, partnership, estate, gift, trust, and exempt organization returns.
PPC's Federal Tax Compliance Library	PPC Deskbooks: Individual titles focused on how to prepare IRS tax returns.
PPC's Tax and Financial Planning Library	PPC Guides: Individual titles that provide planning guidance.
Tables & Rates	Federal rate and tax tables, withholding, CONUS, OCONUS, AFR, COLAs, savings bond redemption, leased auto, excise, etc.
Tax Advisors Planning System	Individual titles, written by expert practitioners, that provide general tax guidance and planning aids, including customizable sample documents.
Tax Guide	Covers tax law in a summary fashion, organized by topic.
Topic Indexes	Indexes that divide the Tax Guide Analysis and the Tax Guide Tables, Rates & Calendars into functional components and list each item alphabetically.
Tax Planning & Practice Guides (Special Studies)	New law highlights and planning materials on topics of current interest organized by year.
United States Tax Reporter	A comprehensive and up-to-date source of federal tax law, regulations, committee reports, cases, rulings, explanations, and federal forms. Annotations, organized by both code section and legal issues, cite RIA's *American Federal Tax Reports*, and other widely known case reporters.
WG&L Treatises	Discussion, analysis, and strategies by renowned experts covering specific tax topics.

Both the Federal Tax Handbook and the Federal Tax Coordinator are organized by topic. As discussed earlier and presented in Exhibit 6-6, a topical organization simply means that tax law and transactions are organized by related subject matter.

The **Federal Tax Coordinator (FTC)** is generally considered the most comprehensive of the three editorial sources. This is Checkpoint's flagship editorial content, in which tax experts are being constantly drawn upon to evaluate and explain tax law in a more understandable but still comprehensive fashion. Each section and subsection of the IRC and regulations are broken down, explained in a detailed fashion, and organized by topic.

The **United States Tax Reporter (USTR)** is an annotated tax service, which is organized by Internal Revenue Code section number and presented in Exhibit 6-7. This database has RIA-provided explanations and annotations, which are court cases that have tax law related to the selected code section. Cases and rulings that are very recent are first reported in the Advance Annotations database.

EXHIBIT 6-6: Federal Tax Coordinator Topical Organization

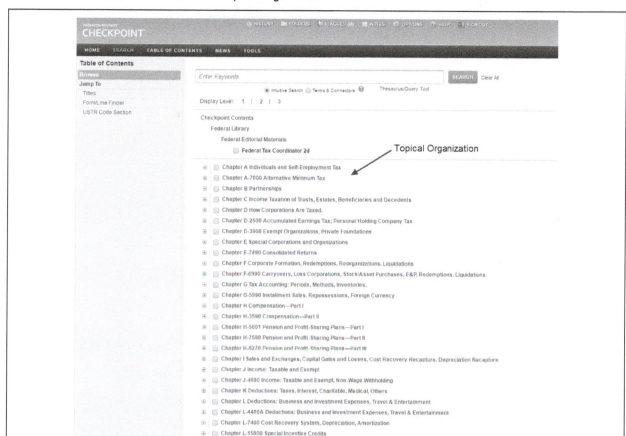

The **Federal Tax Handbook** is a quick way to find general information about a topic of interest. Organized by topic, the Federal Tax Handbook provides less detailed explanations of tax law. It does not provide the same exhaustive analysis as the other two Checkpoint editorial services but might be the fastest service to review because of its relative brevity.

SPOTLIGHT ON TAXATION

Tax Service History

The *United States Tax Reporter*, the annotated tax service offered by Checkpoint, did not start out with this name. Prentice Hall published this tax service from 1924 to 1990 as *PH Federal Taxes.* In November 1989, Maxwell MacMillan bought the service and merely replaced Prentice Hall's name as the publisher. In September 1991, Thomson acquired Maxwell MacMillan. *PH Federal Taxes* became part of the Thomson Reuters offerings in 1992, when its name was changed to the *United States Tax Reporter.*

EXHIBIT 6-7: United States Tax Reporter (USTR) Code Arranged Annotations and Explanations

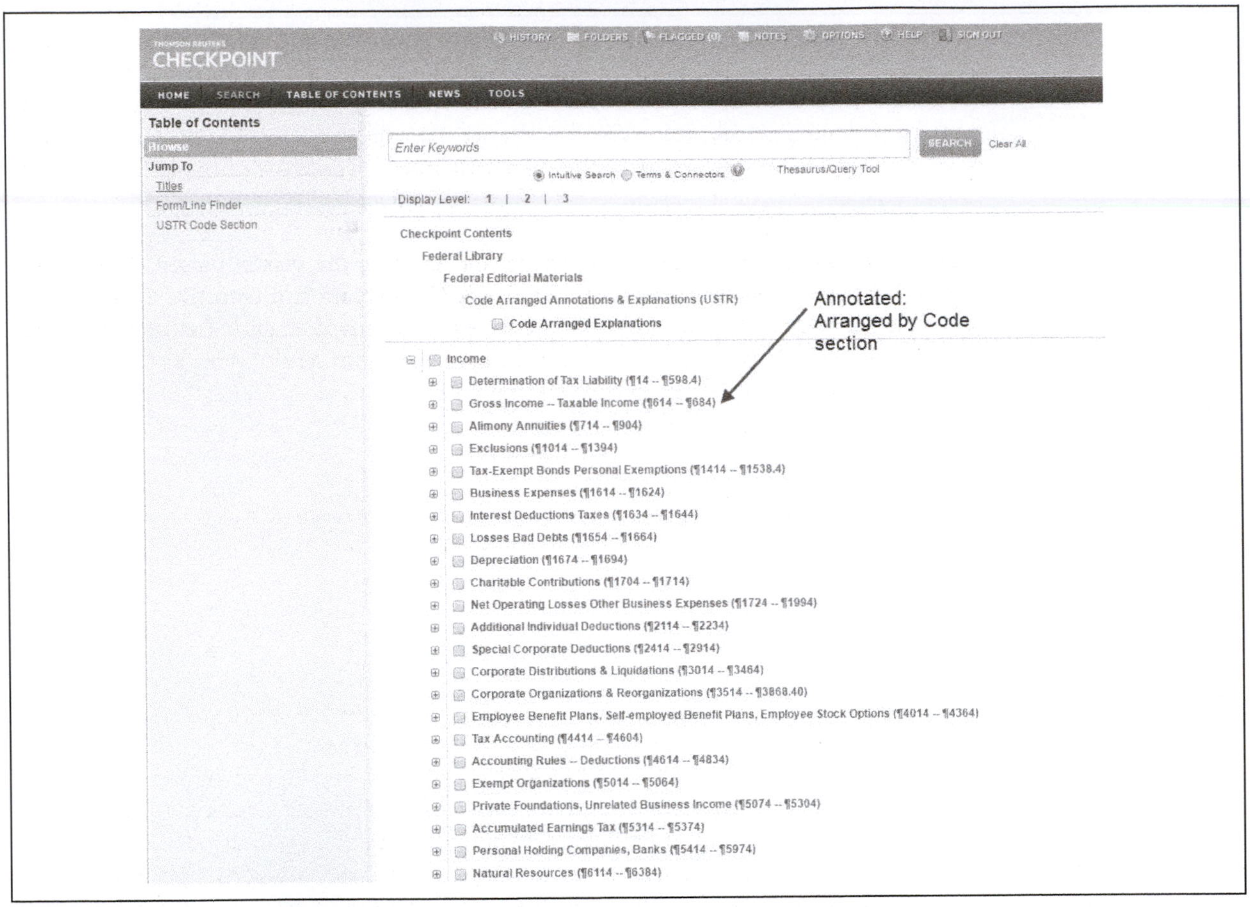

5 Finding Relevant Tax Information

With so many varied sources and types of tax law available, one of the primary challenges to tax research is actually finding the materials and content necessary to respond to a tax issue. Different issues call for different levels of research and varied degrees of certainty, but ultimately, tax advisers must be confident in their response so that their clients can continue to count on them as a reliable source of professional tax advice. Once the source or sources of tax law have been identified, the researcher turns to finding the source documents that will support a conclusion. In Checkpoint, there are four primary search methods: (1) keyword, (2) contents, (3) index, and (4) citation. Each of these may have an advantage over any other based on the researcher's experience or degree of comfort with a particular area of tax law. Most researchers will use all four at one time or another during their careers, and overreliance on any one type of search may do an injustice to the researcher's work in a situation in which a nonfavored approach is the most efficient.

5-1 Keyword Search

As mentioned previously, performing a **keyword search** in Checkpoint is very similar to performing a search on the Internet using a search engine, with one very important difference: selection of the database(s) to search. Although Checkpoint permits users to search their entire subscription, the number of nonrelevant hits is likely to increase with each additional source included, making it more difficult to identify the relevant tax law.

Instead, researchers should select only the database(s) of interest. Returning to the illustrative research example, the search can be limited to only the Federal Tax practice area by selecting that practice area in the left hand window. By clicking the box beside the main headings in the main window, for example EDITORIAL MATERIALS, all databases within that heading are selected. Click the same box and all selections will be cleared from that heading. To clear all database selections, click CLEAR ALL by the search button in the top next to the KEYWORD SEARCH bar. To start the search for the illustrative example, the researcher might select the editorial materials, the primary materials, or both.

Keyword searches are initiated by entering words or phrases into the keyword search box at the top center of the search screen and clicking the SEARCH button. Checkpoint offers two types of keyword searches: **Terms & Connectors** and **Intuitive Search**. With an intuitive search, the tax question is entered in standard English (natural language) words, phrases, or sentences. Checkpoint recognizes if a sentence, terms and connectors, or a citation has been entered and attempts to provide the most relevant results. With an intuitive search, Checkpoint takes advantage of historical usage data, giving higher importance to documents that are frequently accessed, as well as embedded editorial knowledge. This type of search is useful when the researcher is unsure as to which keywords would be the most effective. If keywords can be identified by the researcher, the terms and connectors search is more appropriate.

For the illustrative example, a keyword search can be performed by selecting three sources: the FEDERAL TAX COORDINATOR, the FEDERAL TAX HANDBOOK, and the UNITED STATES TAX REPORTER Explanations. Be sure to select INTUITIVE SEARCH under the search box. Next enter the phrase *what is the tax treatment of a child's income* and click the SEARCH button at the top of the main window (see Exhibit 6-8). If the TERMS & CONNECTORS search method is selected, Checkpoint provides a warning message informing the researcher that certain terms are unacceptable. However, an intuitive search will accept nuisance words such as "what" or "is." Checkpoint allows keyword searches as key terms, exact phrases, or using Boolean connectors, proximity connectors, or wildcards. For example, searching "what is the tax treatment of a child's income" and using the quotation marks will provide the results of a search for that exact phrase (a search that returns no results since that *exact phrase* must appear in the database but does not).

EXHIBIT 6-8: Keyword Search Selection of Content to Search

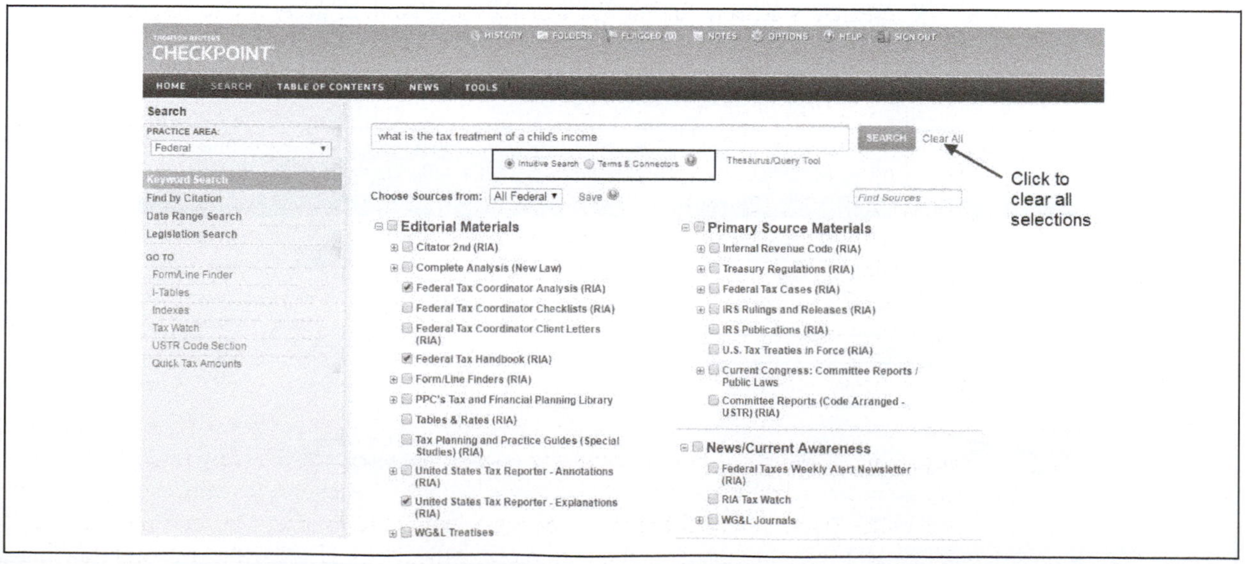

When a keyword search is performed in Checkpoint, the source selections shown in the main page are replaced by a SEARCH RESULTS page. This page shows which sources have materials relevant to the search and the number of documents found within each source. If the earlier described search using the intuitive search alternative is performed, the results show hits in all three of the sources we selected as presented in Exhibit 6-9. The SEARCH RESULTS screen can be modified to present the results in three different ways: (1) as a source list (as shown in Exhibit 6-9), (2) as all documents, and (3) as the table of contents. The view can be selected by clicking the terms located under the Search Results heading. As previously mentioned, the SOURCE LIST view shows the title of the source and the number of hits. The ALL DOCUMENTS view shows the database location and title of each document found, sorted either by relevance or by source. The TABLE OF CONTENTS view offers the opportunity to drill down into the sources, looking only at the contents that contain a hit for the search.

Using the SOURCE LIST to view the results described above and presented in Exhibit 6-9, there are more than 70 hits just in the Federal Tax Coordinator. Checkpoint provides a star next to the [+] to indicate which sources contain the most relevant results. Rolling the cursor over those stars provides a count of how many of the 10 most relevant hits are contained within that source. To examine the three most relevant hits only, expand the view of any source by clicking [+] next to the source name. To examine details of the all hits in a source, the researcher clicks on either the title of the source (e.g., ANALYSIS/FEDERAL TAX COORDINATOR) or the number of hits (e.g., 70). If the search results are too broad, the researcher has the option to refine the original search by entering a new or previous keyword(s) and using the SEARCH WITHIN RESULTS button located under the original keyword search.

The document-by-document results of the example search are presented in Exhibit 6-10. These results can be organized in two different ways: (1) by relevance (the typical default) or (2) by table of contents. Sorting by relevance uses Checkpoint's ranking system to put the most relevant documents at the top of the list. The relevance score is indicated by the stars to the left of each document. Sorting by Table of Contents presents the results in the order in which they appear in that source. In the results presented in Exhibit 6-10, the keywords are highlighted by Checkpoint in the excerpt of each document. These excerpts are controlled by the SHOW WORDS AROUND HITS option located on the upper right of the Search Results screen. Clicking the box either eliminates the excerpts, leaving only the titles of each source document, or (as currently shown) presents a selection of the source with the words that are around the keys words in the search. By clicking either the DOCUMENT icon or the document title, the source document itself is presented in the main window.

EXHIBIT 6-9:   Illustrative Example Keyword Search Results Page

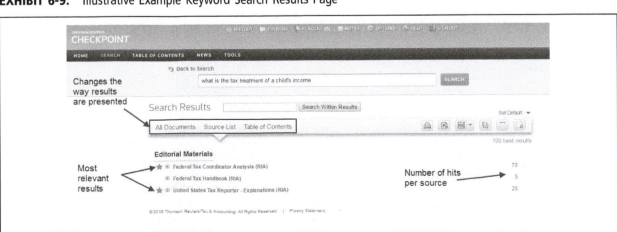

EXHIBIT 6-10: Illustrative Example Results List by Relevance

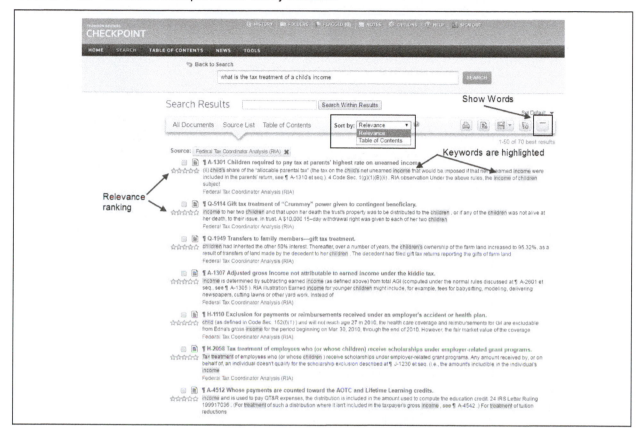

A quick glance at the results from all three sources shows that the solution to the illustrative example is not yet apparent. The keyword search could be improved in a number of ways. Recall the search string, "what is the tax treatment of a child's income." Although an intuitive search can handle these terms, words such as "tax" and "what" are not likely to provide an improvement in the search results. Another problem is the number of unrelated documents in the results of searching the editorial sources.

As an alternative, all primary sources can be selected and searched using a terms and connectors search with keywords "treatment," "child," and "income" (do not use quotation marks in the actual search). This search results in more than 9,000 total hits—a daunting number to be sure. However, by selecting the results in the Internal Revenue Code, the most relevant hit is § 73 Services of Child (see Exhibit 6-11).

When a source document such as § 73 is opened from the results of a search, the typical default is for navigation by keyword (see Exhibit 6-11). The NAVIGATE BY setting is used to change the way a researcher can page through the source documents. NAVIGATE BY KEYWORD advances the document either to the next or previous keyword hit in the document (if shown off screen) or to the next (or previous) document in the results list (if the entire document can be seen in the main window). NAVIGATE BY DOCUMENT allows the researcher to skip to the next or previous document in the results list. NAVIGATE BY CONTENTS allows the researcher to advance forward or back in the source that contains the document. For example, if a researcher is looking at IRC 73 and is navigating by contents, the previous document is § 72 and the next document is § 74, because those are the previous and following document in that source (the IRC).

EXHIBIT 6-11:   Illustrative Example Results Source Document

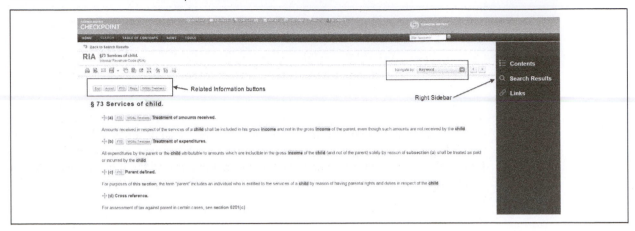

When the source document is opened in the main window, the right sidebar has a number of useful options that can be used by clicking any of the three choices. The choice of SEARCH RESULTS provides the results (sorted by whatever the selection had been on the previous results screen, i.e., by relevance or by contents). By clicking CONTENTS, the exact location within the database of the document or "breadcrumb" is shown. This can be particularly helpful for new researchers, who might not be as familiar with the source materials and must verify whether they are looking at an editorial or a primary source. LINKS provides a very efficient way to find related materials (and can serve as a substitute to the related information buttons discussed later). When LINKS is selected, a drop-down menu appears, which the researcher can use to select the type of link desired. For a source document from the Internal Revenue Code (such as § 73), explanations and annotations from the USTR, explanations from the FTC, regulations, and treatise information are all available under the drop-down menu. Different source documents provide different LINKS options. The choice of a LINKS option produces a list of related documents from that source in the right sidebar. The results of all three right-sidebar options for § 73 are presented in Exhibit 6-12. These same options for identifying related information are also available as buttons at the top of the main window (see Exhibit 6-11).

EXHIBIT 6-12:   Illustrative Example of Options in Right Sidebar

Although it may not yet be obvious to the new researcher, IRC § 73 is likely to be the primary source of tax law on the issue in the illustrative example. Section 73(a) states that "amounts received in respect of the services of a child shall be included in his gross income and not in the gross income of the parent, even though such amounts are not received by the child." Interpretation of the code, whether attempted by a new or experienced researcher, can be a tricky endeavor. However, as described above, Checkpoint offers a number of simple links to other explanatory materials. Researchers who identify a code section that seems to be on topic may want to first link to the related regulations because these form the administrative law that provides well-vetted (though not often well-understood) explanations of the code. Clicking the REGS button (or using the links in the right sidebar) reveals that IRC § 73 has only one regulation, Reg. § 1.73-1. The link to the regulation (or for that matter, any of the other related information link sources if selected instead) appears in the right window. If the researcher wishes to return to the three right-sidebar options, the small x in the upper right corner will close the related documents list, or any of the three icons can be clicked to bring up these options (see Exhibit 6-13).

Clicking on the regulation on the right sidebar opens a new tab in the browser with the Reg. § 1.73-1 document (see Exhibit 6-14), which states as follows:

Compensation for personal services of a child shall, regardless of the provisions of State law relating to who is entitled to the earnings of the child, and regardless of whether the income is in fact received by the child, be deemed to be the gross income of the child and not the gross income of the parent of the child. Such compensation, therefore, shall be included in the gross income of the child and shall be

EXHIBIT 6-13: Illustrative Example Related Information Buttons

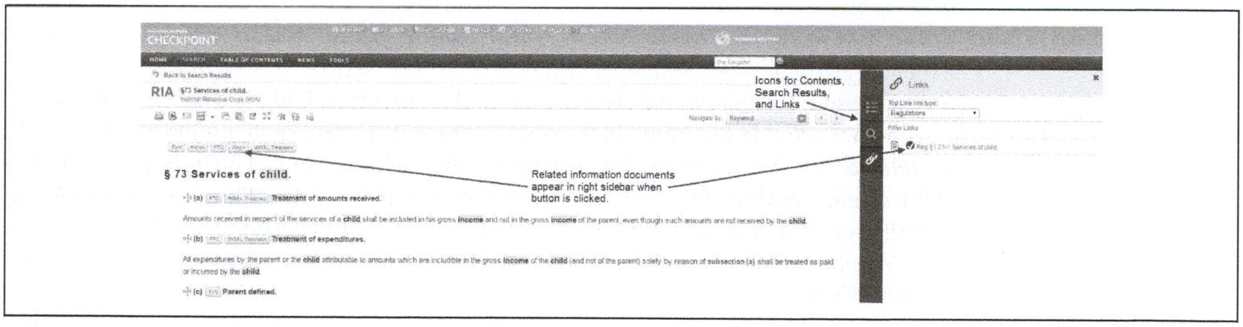

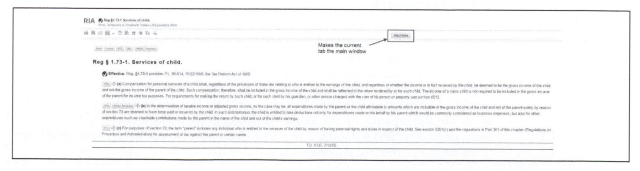

EXHIBIT 6-14: Illustrative Example Document Tab

reflected in the return rendered by or for such child. The income of a minor child is not required to be included in the gross income of the parent for income tax purposes.

As it relates to the illustrative example, between the code and the regulations thereunder, it is starting to appear that the payments to Lorna (the parent) are going to be treated as taxable payments to Steven (the child) under § 73.

Note that the new window with the regulation document does not have the right sidebar and also lacks a number of the options that are available on the main window. In this way Checkpoint preserves the search and its results in the main window but allows the researcher to review sources documents for relevance. If the document is useful, it can be printed, saved as a file, or exported from the document window. If the document is not relevant, the tab can simply be closed to return to the existing search in the main window. If the researcher finds that the new document is pertinent to the search and wants the related information links made available, the MAXIMIZE button in the upper right corner (see Exhibit 6-14) will replace the existing main window with this document and all the related information links become available.

Returning to the illustrative example, the annotations provide a link to ¶735.01(15) of the USTR, which provides a brief explanation related to a court case in which a portion of a signing bonus for a baseball contract was paid to a mother but found to be income of her son (*Richard A. Allen*, 50 T.C. 466, and affirmed by the 3rd Circuit Court of Appeals). In this case, the higher court (the appellate court) did not provide any information other than affirming the Tax Court's decision. As a result, the research value for the illustrative example's issue is to be found in the lower court's decision. A review of the case appears to support the earlier hypothesis that all $200,000 of the income (both Steven's share and his mother's share) will be reportable by Steven.

Before moving on to an alternative search method, consider our original keyword search, "what is the tax treatment of a child's income." Are there improvements that could be made to this search string that might offer the same or more direct results? For example, the search contains the word "tax." When searching a database of tax law, this term is not likely to add considerable differentiation to the search. New researchers may want to experiment with alternative searches using the **Boolean connectors** and **proximity connectors** presented in Exhibit 6-15. For example, results found in the previous example search would suggest that terms such as "child," "parent," "income," "compensation," and "services" would all be suitable keywords. Various proximity connectors such as /n, /s, or /p are likely to find materials relevant to the illustrative example.

5-2 Index Search

New researchers may find it difficult to use the **index search** and the contents search (discussed later) because of their relative lack of experience with the language and structure of the existing tax law. That said, at times the index search can be an efficient way to find the relevant tax law quickly with little guess work. The advantage of an index search is that, because individuals create indexes, the *tax meanings of the words* are considered as well as the context in which the words are found. The researcher has the ability to use the expertise of the indexer in locating the primary documents of interest. Some researchers find it beneficial to start with an index search to help identify effective terms for their general keyword searches.

EXHIBIT 6-15: Checkpoint Boolean and Proximity Connectors

To locate documents:	Using Search Method:	Use:	Example:
containing all of my exact keywords	Terms & Connectors	space, &, AND	funding deficiency funding & deficiency funding AND deficiency
containing all of my keywords, including variations	Intuitive Search	&	funding & deficiency
containing my exact phrase	Terms & Connectors	" "	"funding deficiency"
containing my phrase within 3 words of one another	Intuitive Search	" "	"funding deficiency"
containing any of my exact keywords	Terms & Connectors	OR, |	funding OR deficiency funding | deficiency
containing any of my keywords, including variations	Intuitive Search	OR, |	funding OR deficiency funding | deficiency
contains one exact keyword but excludes another entirely	Terms & Connectors	^	funding ^ deficiency
contains one keyword (including variations), but excludes another entirely	Intuitive Search	^	funding ^ deficiency

To locate documents:	Use:	Example:
containing variations of my keywords	* (asterisk)	deprecia*
disabling automatic retrieval of plurals and equivalencies	# (pound sign)	#damage (retrieves only damage, not damages)
containing single-character variations	? (question mark)	s?????holder (retrieves stockholder, shareholder)
containing compound words	- (hyphen)	e-mail (retrieves e-mail, e mail, email)

To locate documents:	Use:	Example:
containing terms that occur at least # times	atleast#()	atleast5(customer)

To search for a word or phrase:	Use:	Example:
within n words of another (in any order)	/# (where # equals number)	"disclosure exception" /7 negligence
within n words of another (in exact order)	pre/# (where # equals number)	"disclosure exception" pre/7 negligence
within the same sentence (20 words) as another (in any order)	/s	"disclosure exception" /s negligence
within the same sentence (20 words) as another (in exact order)	pre/s	"disclosure exception" pre/s negligence
within one paragraph (50 words) as another (in any order)	/p	"disclosure exception" /p negligence
within one paragraph (50 words) as another (in exact order)	pre/p	"disclosure exception" pre/p negligence

Checkpoint contains a number of useful indexes to search. As one might expect, each of the typical editorial sources—the FTC, the USTR, and the Federal Tax Handbook—has its own topical index that can be searched individually; if all indexes are selected, all may be searched at once. In addition, Checkpoint provides an index for three of the primary sources as well: the current Internal Revenue Code, the Final and Temporary Regulations, and the Proposed Regulations.

New researchers are likely to begin with the secondary sources, which in Checkpoint includes the FTC, the USTR, and the Federal Tax Handbook. As an example, an index search of the FTC can be started from the SEARCH window by clicking on INDEXES under GO TO in the left sidebar. Each of the available indexes in a subscription will be presented in the main window. Using the [+] to expand the tree will reveal the topical index for the FTC (see Exhibit 6-16). The FTC index can be expanded several times revealing sections of the index based on main headings within that letter. The selection boxes next to any letter can be used to select only words starting with certain letters to perform a keyword search at any time. Note that the index for that letter can also be promoted to the main window by clicking the letter itself (this will eliminate the tree structure for the remaining letters. showing only the selected letter) as shown in Exhibit 6-17.

Clicking each index title opens that portion of the index in the document window as presented in Exhibit 6-18. Note that items denoted with two dots are the main headings and those with three dots are subheadings under that main heading. Once the index is opened in the main window, the table of contents for that part of the index can also be presented in the right sidebar (see Exhibit 6-18). This allows the researcher to conveniently scan parts of the index located adjacent to one another. The breadcrumb located above the right sidebar is also clickable, allowing the researcher to return to a higher level within the index in order to continue searching other parts of the index.

EXHIBIT 6-16:   Checkpoint Editorial Materials Index Search

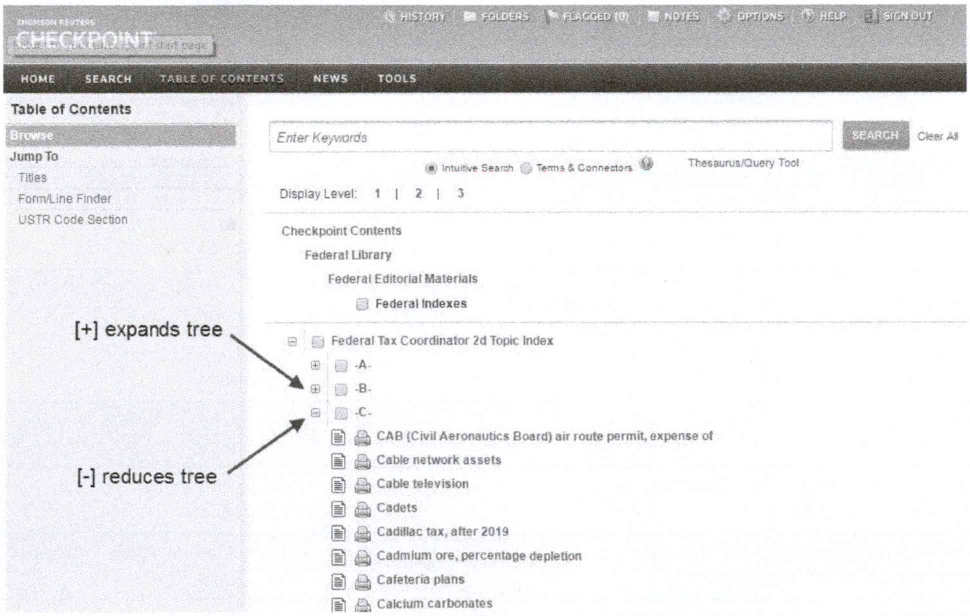

EXHIBIT 6-17: Checkpoint Index Promotion Example

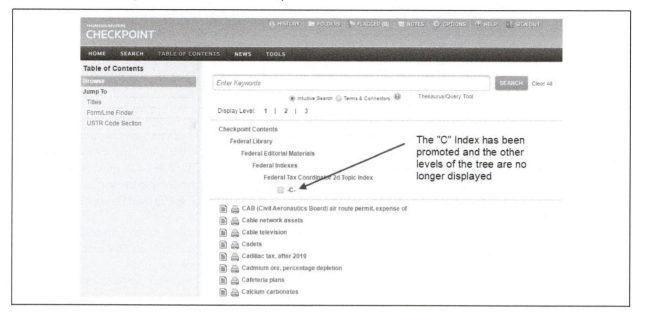

EXHIBIT 6-18: Checkpoint Index Search Results

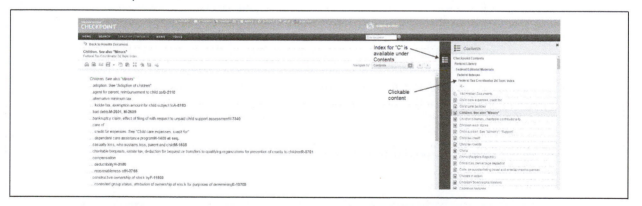

While a researcher might choose to look in the FTC index under the letter C for "children," unfortunately there are hundreds of entries to examine. This is where experience can assist the researcher. Knowing specifically that the topic of interest is related to the tax treatment of the compensation of a child, a researcher might select Children and under that index scroll down the page and find Compensation, which provides a link to ¶H-3180, which is the introduction to the portion of Chapter H of the FTC on compensation, specifically, compensation of minors. This provides a brief overview of the topic, stating that "amounts received for the services of a minor child are included in the child's gross income and not in the gross income of the child's parents." Although this alone may suffice to provide the researcher the necessary support, in order to examine the rest of the chapter on the compensation of minors, the MAXIMIZE button can be clicked to bring the document to the main window. Checkpoint can also present the contents of the chapter in the right sidebar (see

EXHIBIT 6-19:   Checkpoint Maximize Document

Exhibit 6-19). The subsequent paragraph (¶H-3181) presents a more complete explanation of IRC § 73 and provides the footnote links to the primary sources, including § 73, the regulations to § 73, and the *Allen* case.

Another way to find information in the index is to use a keyword search within the index itself. Instead of entering the index and clicking the letter, another option would be to click the box next to the letter and perform a keyword search on just that letter (or a selection of letters) within the index. Referring back to the illustrative example, if the FTC Index for C is selected and a search for "child compensation" is run, the results will show each of the topical areas within the index that contains those terms. Clicking on any of the topical areas listed will open that portion of the index, and each of the keyword terms will be highlighted for easy identification. By opening any of the indexes, the NAVIGATE BY drop-down will open in the top right corner to advance to the next keyword in the items in the results list.

Checkpoint has a THESAURUS/QUERY tool to help researchers improve keyword searches and thus more efficiently find the relevant source documents. As shown in Exhibit 6-20, the THESAURUS/QUERY tool is opened by clicking on the right-hand side under the KEYWORD SEARCH box. The box that opens on the main window has four primary functions: (1) RESTRICTIONS, (2) TOOLS, (3) THESAURUS, and (4) SPELLING.

EXHIBIT 6-20:   Checkpoint Thesaurus/Query Tool

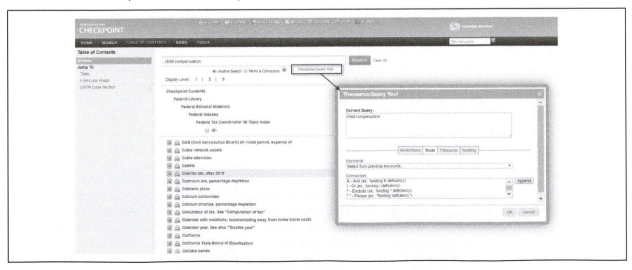

The RESTRICTIONS option is available only when using an intuitive search. The researcher can use the RESTRICTIONS link to refine the search by requiring or excluding words from the search phrase. Each of the terms in the link can be specifically either included or excluded from the search. The TOOLS option provides a history of recently used keywords since the user started that Checkpoint session (or previous sessions if the subscription allows it). In this way, previous versions of the keyword search can be reviewed. In addition, the list of connectors and a brief example can be clicked on to introduce more complexity and, it is hoped, better search results. The THESAURUS option provides a list of synonyms and related terms that can be included in the search. For example, "child" has 25 related terms, including terms such as *student*, *successor*, and *under-age*. Researchers can use these terms when the previously selected term is not the one most likely used in the tax nomenclature. An option to include all alternative terms is also available, but note that the maximum number of characters in a keyword search is 500. In Checkpoint, a keyword search will not attempt to find all synonyms of the keyword entered. For example, a search for "progeny compensation" will not find the same results as one for "child compensation," although they are listed as synonyms in the thesaurus. The SPELLING option allows the researcher to determine if a spelling error is partially to blame for a lack of results. For example, if compensation is misspelled as "compensashun," the spelling tool will identify the word as unrecognized and provide recommended alternatives.

5-3 Contents Search

A **contents search** can be appropriate if the researcher has a reasonably good idea of the area of tax law, either topically or by code section, where the solution to the issue might be found. The contents search can also be an important method for limiting the number of documents retrieved and better guaranteeing their pertinence. Like an index search, a contents search can be used in conjunction with a keyword search once the most relevant portion of the database is found. The contents search method treats electronic tax services as if they were printed published services. Accordingly, researchers can drill down through the table of contents of a service just as they would thumb through the pages if they had books in front of them.

SPOTLIGHT ON TAXATION

Public Laws and Private Laws

Most statutes passed in the United States are given a public law number by the Office of the Federal Register. These laws are published as slip laws (as a separate pamphlet) and then in the United States Statutes at Large (often abbreviated as stat.) and then finally, the Federal Register. However, there are also private laws. A private law is intended to apply to a specific individual, entity, or group, as opposed to a public law which is intended to apply to everyone. For example, in 2006, Pvt. L. 109-1, known as the Betty Dick Residence Protection Act, required the Secretary of the Interior to consent to an individual continuing to live on property that otherwise would have reverted back to National Park Service after 25 years. Private laws used to be quite common in the United States; however, over time, most government agencies were granted enough power to deal with unique exceptions without requiring congressional action.

EXHIBIT 6-21:   Checkpoint Contents Search Topical Service

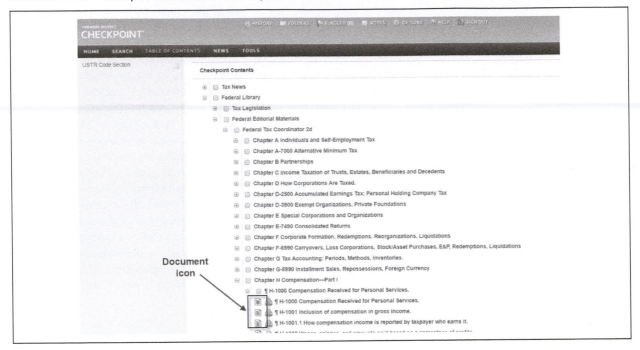

In Checkpoint, a contents search is performed by selecting the TABLE OF CONTENTS tab above the keyword search box (see Exhibit 6-2). The table of contents for each library within the Checkpoint subscription appears in the main window. By repeatedly clicking the [+] SIGN by the content of choice, the researcher can drill down into the level most likely to cover the tax source of interest. As presented in Exhibit 6-21, by clicking [+] sign for the FTC, the contents of that book are revealed. With each subsequent click, the limbs of the tree are opened until ultimately the document level is reached (no [+] sign, only the document icon will be shown). For the illustrative example, a combined contents and keyword search might represent a practical solution. If Chapter H Compensation Parts I and II of the FTC are selected to search and the keywords "child income parent" are used, the related paragraphs previously discussed (H-3181) are located efficiently.

Using the contents search for a code-organized (annotated) source such as the IRC itself or the USTR follows a very similar process to a search of a topically organized source, as presented previously. Obviously, in this case, the contents are organized by code section, which means that some degree of knowledge of the structure of the Internal Revenue Code is extremely helpful in finding the most relevant materials. As described in Chapter 3, the code structure is not without meaning, and thus the structure can be utilized with some success by even the newest of researchers. For the illustrative example, drilling down into the USTR allows the researcher to identify the Alimony Annuities section (IRC §§ 71–86) fairly quickly. The USTR uses the related code section as the first digit(s) of the paragraph number. For example, as shown in Exhibit 6-22, annotations and explanations related to IRC § 73 are numbered ¶734.XX and ¶735.XX. The explanation provided by the USTR in ¶735.01(15) gets to the heart of the illustrative example and provides links to the specific content and eventually back to the important primary sources.

EXHIBIT 6-22: Checkpoint Contents Search Annotated Service

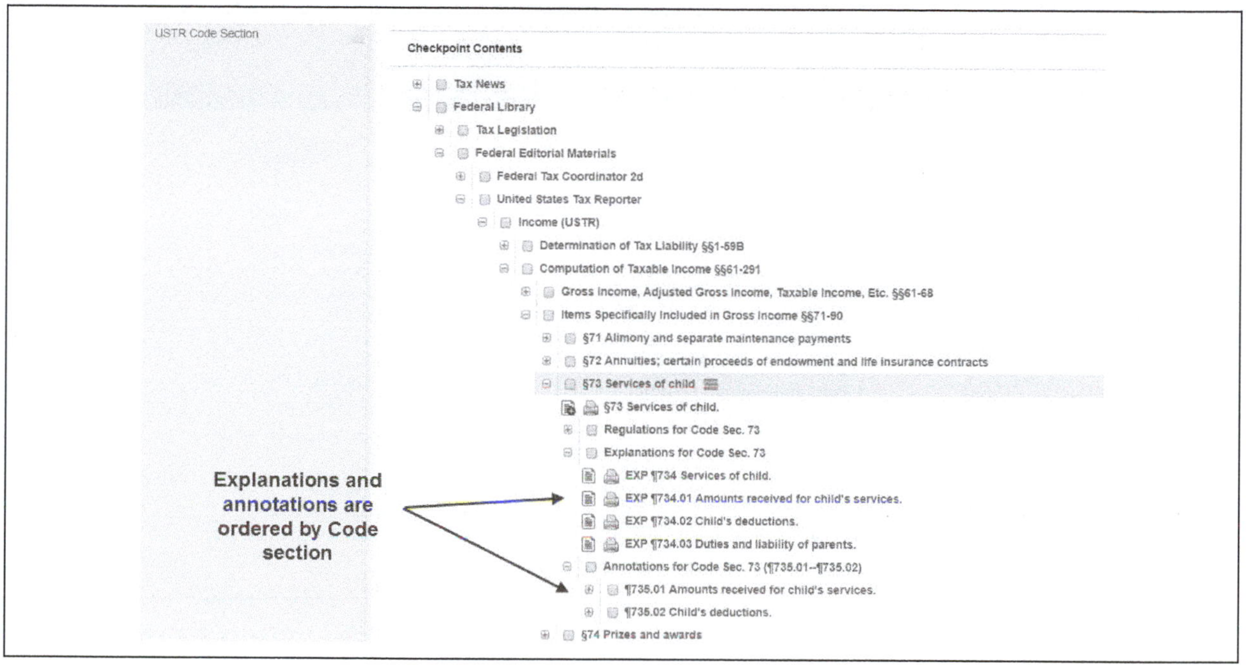

5-4 Citation Search

The final way to search through most tax services is the **citation search** (not to be confused with using a citator, discussed later in this chapter). Checkpoint offers the ability to find documents by citation in virtually all its databases. The key to a citation search is that you must know the code section, regulation, ruling, paragraph, or other source document by its citation form. To perform a citation search in Checkpoint, simply click on FIND BY CITATION in the left sidebar (see Exhibit 6-2) or hold the cursor over the search tab at the top of the main window as shown in Exhibit 6-23.

Checkpoint provides a template that can be completed for each type of possible source as indicated in the left sidebar. For example, to enter a code or regulation citation, CODE AND REGS must be selected in the left sidebar. Cases, revenue rulings, revenue procedures, and many other sources can be searched by citation by selecting the proper template in the left sidebar as shown in Exhibit 6-24.

If, in the illustrative example, the researcher was already aware that IRC § 73 might apply to the situation, using the Citation search to find the code section as the starting point for identifying related documents might be the most efficient choice. Once the code section is located, continued research is simplified by use of the RELATED INFORMATION buttons located above the code section title (similar to those shown in Exhibit 6-11). These buttons will lead the researcher to committee reports, regulations, explanations, annotations, and other related documents in the tax service. However, relying exclusively on code section searches may be more time consuming than Contents or Keyword searches when several code sections are relevant to the research issue.

Primary sources other than the Internal Revenue Code can be found though a citation search. Recall that in the previous research on the illustrative example, a Tax Court ruling, *Allen v. Commissioner*, 50 T.C. 466 (1968), was located and provided additional details on the tax treatment of this particular issue. If the citation for that court case is

EXHIBIT 6-23: Checkpoint Search by Citation

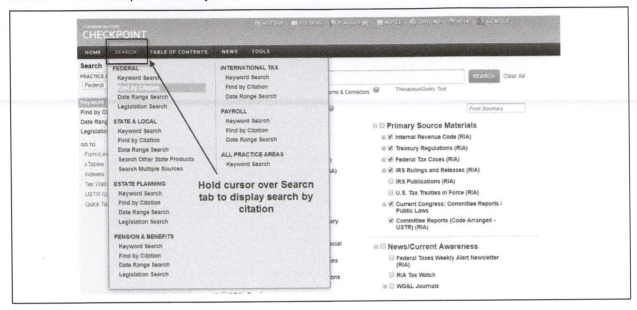

EXHIBIT 6-24: Example of Checkpoint Citation Template

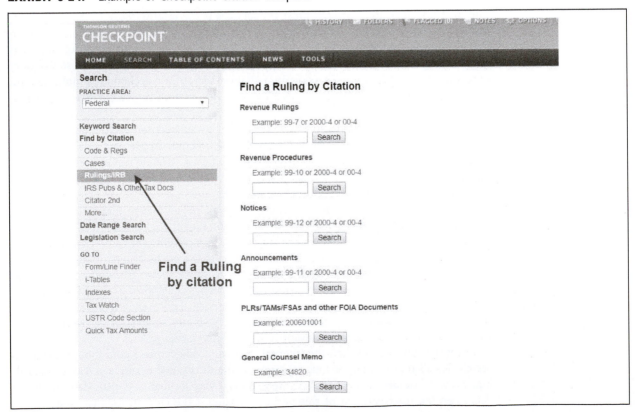

known, then the case can be found quickly by entering the citation into the citation search. The search window allows various citation forms to be used, depending on the case reporter source of the ruling. Checkpoint's database of court cases is limited to cases that cover tax issues and thus reflects Checkpoint's best efforts to identify court rulings that have a tax impact.

SPOTLIGHT ON TAXATION

Citation Forms

There are seemingly endless ways to identify extracts of statutory, administrative, and judicial law by using a citation—a way of providing reference to an authoritative source. By using citations, the tax researcher establishes the credibility of his or her conclusion by identifying the primary sources of tax law but also leaves a trail of bread crumbs for any future reviewers to follow. Unfortunately, citation forms—the way these bread crumbs are structured and formatted—are as varied as the code is long. This book provides its own citation form (see inside front cover). Other popular forms of citation can come from the *Bluebook* (prepared by distinguished law schools in the United States), the *Chicago Manual of Style*, the *MLA (Modern Language Association) Style Manual*, and the APA (American Psychological Association) style, among others. To confuse matters further, many state court systems (e.g., New York and California) as well as the U.S. Supreme Court use their own individual citation styles.

6 Citators

Besides confronting the tremendous volume of tax law, tax practitioners face the added dilemma that the tax law is in a constant state of change. The IRC is changed frequently by passage of federal legislation. Regulations are proposed, finalized, and withdrawn. Administrative rulings are issued, modified, superseded, and revoked or made obsolete by changes in the tax law. A case decided at one level may be appealed, with the higher court overruling the lower court's decision. A court may see a flaw in the reasoning it or another (equal or lower) court used in deciding an earlier case, or a court may use a different line of reasoning to reach a distinct decision in an area previously reviewed by other courts. When a court takes any action that relies on, rejects, or affects the holding of another case, the acting court refers to the affected case in its opinion. All this results in a tangle of inter-references among a vast number of cases. This daily change in the tax law makes it very difficult for a tax practitioner to know what law is current and what has been superseded or overruled.

Recall from the research process explained in Chapter 2 that an evaluation of the relevant primary authority must occur before conclusions can be developed. The evaluation of tax authority includes not only determining whether the authority is still valid but also making judgments regarding the precedential value of the primary sources. Common law relies heavily on the **precedential value** of cases, which can be defined as the legal authority established by the case. The legal authority of prior cases is considered when judges are issuing opinions in subsequent cases that contain similar facts or legal issues. Tax law also relies on the precedential value of tax cases and administrative rulings for guidance. The tax law attempts to maintain consistency in the treatment of similar issues so taxpayers can anticipate the acceptable application of the law to their own situations. Each appellate opinion sets a precedent that applies to later cases.

It is important for the researcher to consider a case in context, to trace its judicially derived decision, and to monitor the reaction of subsequent court cases. This is even more important when the opinion is innovative.

Since practitioners must rely on tax law that is constantly evolving, they must determine if subsequent events have affected the legal standing of the sources upon which they rely. Thus, they need a tool to help them ascertain which legal sources provide strong precedents and which have little or no value. The tax professional could follow the reference threads from case to case or ruling to ruling, but this would be extremely tedious and would only identify earlier cases and rulings and not later sources that may have altered or overruled the case or ruling of interest. This latter information is critical for determining the validity of the document of interest. This section provides the most common methodology for ensuring that the tax laws, cases, and administrative documents supporting a client's tax position are up to date.

A **citator** is a tool through which a tax researcher can learn the history of a legal source and evaluate the strength of its holdings. Citators follow the threads in subsequent sources and typically summarize, in shorthand form, where the threads lead and what they mean. Before a researcher relies on the opinion in a case or analysis in a ruling (or even commits the time to read the document), it is important to ascertain its legal standing. Thus, when a case or ruling relevant to a client's tax situation is found, it is imperative that a citator be examined to determine how later legal sources have considered the document of interest. Because the legal profession has long recognized the need for this specialized information, citators were developed in the late 1800s, many decades before online searches were possible.

To avoid confusion, it is important to learn the specific terminology that describes references between cases. When one case refers to another case, it cites the case. The case making reference to the other case is called the **citing case**. The case that is referenced is the **cited case**. The citing case will contain the name of the cited case and where the cited case can be found. The reference is called its **citation**. Although based on the same principle, a citator is not the same as the *citation search* described previously in this chapter.

A citator is a service that indexes cited cases, gives their full citations, and lists the citing cases and where each citing case can be found. A significant older case, one that establishes an important legal principle, may have been cited by hundreds of other cases. Thus, its entry in a citator would be extremely long and complex. A very recent case, or one examining a narrow aspect of the law, would have few cites, if any.

A citator will not provide all types of information about a case or a ruling. For instance, it does not guide the researcher to documents related to a case or ruling that do not specifically cite it. Also, citators may not always indicate when a case or ruling is no longer valid because of changes in the code, unless the code itself specifically identifies the case or a subsequent document makes a specific reference to the code overriding the case. This is because citators are created by searching primary sources for cites to the case or ruling. A researcher could perform the same search by using the case name or its official cite in a keyword search of databases containing all primary sources. Without access to a tax service, you might try a simple Google or Bing search on the case name. However, sifting through the results would be an arduous task and very inefficient.

Given the vast number of court cases and rulings issued annually, the citator is a vital tool in the research process. If the primary sources have *not* been checked through a citator, the research process is not complete. Not all citators are the same. For example, they may organize the lists of citing cases in distinctive schemes. Shepard's citator (discussed in Chapter 8) comes with color-coded symbols that allow the researcher to quickly identify the type of impact that a later court case made have had on the existing case under review. Depending on the researcher's purpose, one citator may be more appropriate than another. For example, a citator may list only citations that have a major impact on the logic or holding of the cited case. Another may list all citations. A researcher who is initially checking to make sure a case has not been overruled would prefer the former. The citations may be annotated to indicate the type of impact the citing case has on the cited case (e.g., modified, overruled, or followed). A trial court case may be appealed, and each appellate court that hears the case creates additional citations. Because each of these decisions may be cited in other documents, a citator can organize cases by jurisdictional level.

Checkpoint's **RIA Citator** can be found in two ways. The first and probably least direct way is by using the TABLE OF CONTENTS tab located above the main window. From here, the case name or ruling number (among other sources) can be found by drilling down into the document. The most recent cases and rulings can be found in the **Advance Citator**. However, generally a citator is used once the source document has already been located and the next step is to verify that document's current status. In the illustrative example, *Allen v. Commissioner*, 50 T.C. 466 (1968) was found to be a case of interest. If that case document is brought up in the main window as found in the previous searches, one of the relevant information links presented at the top of the window is CITATOR. By clicking the CITATOR button, the links in the citator to that or related cases appears in the right sidebar as shown in Exhibit 6-25 (notice that the original case stays in the main window). The citator can also be accessed through the LINKS option in the right sidebar.

Now the researcher can simply click on the case name of the current case (*Richard A. Allen*, 50 T.C. 466) and the citations related to that case are opened in a new window as shown in Exhibit 6-26.

The RIA Citator provides the judicial history of the *Allen* case, noting that the case was later affirmed by the higher court. In addition, the citator provides all the cases that have cited the *Allen* case and a brief explanation of what the citation pertains to. For example, **Cited Favorably** indicates that the court cited *Allen* and used the holding in *Allen* to support the current case. **Cited without Comment** generally means that the *Allen* case was cited but may not have been an important determining factor in the subsequent case. Other citator explanations can include reversing a previous decision or distinguishing a subsequent holding from the previous case somehow. Researchers must pay

EXHIBIT 6-25: Example of Checkpoint Citator Button

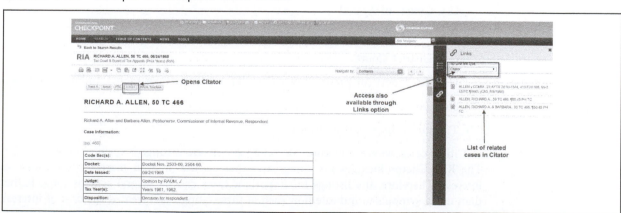

EXHIBIT 6-26: Checkpoint's RIA Citator

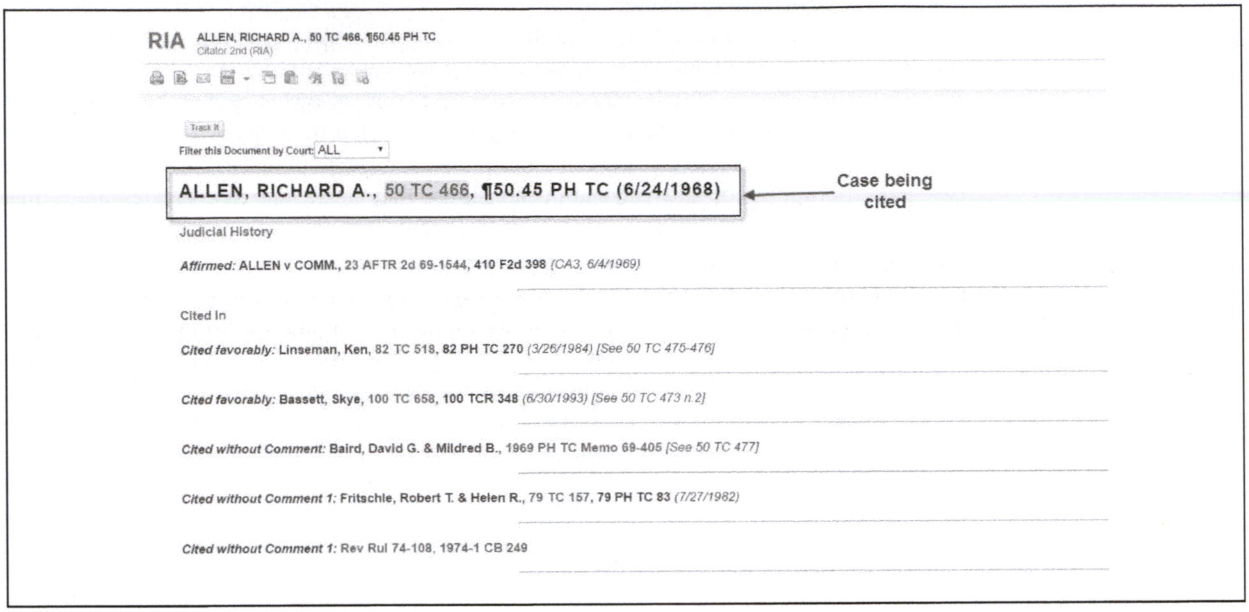
RIA ALLEN, RICHARD A., 50 TC 466, ¶50.45 PH TC
Citator 2nd (RIA)

Track It

Filter this Document by Court: ALL

ALLEN, RICHARD A., 50 TC 466, ¶50.45 PH TC (6/24/1968)

Judicial History

Affirmed: ALLEN v COMM., 23 AFTR 2d 69-1544, 410 F2d 398 *(CA3, 6/4/1969)*

Cited In

Cited favorably: Linseman, Ken, 82 TC 518, 82 PH TC 270 *(3/26/1984) [See 50 TC 475-476]*

Cited favorably: Bassett, Skye, 100 TC 658, 100 TCR 348 *(6/30/1993) [See 50 TC 473 n.2]*

Cited without Comment: Baird, David G. & Mildred B., 1969 PH TC Memo 69-405 *[See 50 TC 477]*

Cited without Comment 1: Fritschle, Robert T. & Helen R., 79 TC 157, 79 PH TC 83 *(7/27/1982)*

Cited without Comment 1: Rev Rul 74-108, 1974-1 CB 249

careful attention to cases that reverse or distinguish the case being cited because of the possibility that the case may have been overturned or the court has changed the interpretation of parts of the tax law, thus necessitating additional research.

RIA Citator first lists the citations for cases that are in complete agreement with the cited case. Next, citing cases are listed that discuss the holdings or reasoning of the cited case but do not refer to a specific paragraph or headnote. Finally, cases are listed in order of the headnote issue they address. The headnote number references allow the researcher to restrict a search to only those citing cases with issues that are relevant to the client's factual situation. The RIA Citator bases its headnote designations on the AFTR series, as that reporter also is a Checkpoint product.

Within any of the citing groupings—complete agreement, no specific headnote, Headnote 1, Headnote 2, and so on—citing cases and rulings are listed in the following order:

- U.S. Supreme Court
- U.S. Courts of Appeal
- U.S. Court of Federal Claims (or predecessor court)
- U.S. District Court
- U.S. Tax Court (or predecessor court—BTA, regular then memorandum decisions)
- State courts
- Treasury rulings and decisions

Citing cases within any court or ruling group are arranged in chronological order. The RIA Citator includes tax citing cases that discuss or even merely cite the case of interest. Therefore, the listings for important cases can be several screens long. Rather than using symbols to indicate how each of these citing cases treated the case of interest, the RIA Citator uses short, easy-to-understand, descriptive phrases.

Upon identifying administrative rulings (e.g., revenue rulings, revenue procedures, notices, general counsel memoranda) that appear to support a client's tax position, it is crucial for a researcher to determine if they are still in effect and represent the current view of the IRS. Rulings are continually clarified, modified, superseded, or revoked. What is good law at one point (e.g., Rev. Rul. 2008-19 issued March 27, 2008) may not be so a few months later (modified by Rev. Rul. 2009-3 on January 29, 2009).

The steps in checking the validity of rulings are the same as with a court case. The RIA Citator furnishes templates for most IRS administrative rulings. The search results for rulings provide a hyperlink to the actual ruling and then its judicial history. In this case, the judicial history shows the effect the ruling of interest had on other administrative pronouncements, and the effect subsequent administrative pronouncements had on the ruling of interest. If there are any citing court cases, these are listed after citing rulings and before lesser pronouncements (such as notices). It is always important to check pertinent pronouncements through a citator.

Citators are not foolproof guarantees that a court case remains on point. For example, a court ruling may have an adverse holding for the IRS. As a result, Congress may enact new legislation that changes the tax law based on the court's ruling. If a similar case has not been tried in which the court describes the change in tax law, there may be no subsequent citing cases, and the researcher might believe that the court's ruling would stand under current tax law, which may not be the case. The RIA Citator, like most other citators, does not provide information to warn the researcher that the underlying tax law may have changed and the holding is stale. It remains the researcher's duty to examine the date of the case and consider any subsequent changes to the code or other tax law that may affect the way the courts would examine the same situation today.

7 Other Tax Law Sources

Although the vast majority of tax law, including almost all primary tax law sources, can be found in the tax services such as Checkpoint, tax professionals also need to consider new developments, recently issued treatises and journal articles, and other tools that may be available to assist with staying on top of their tax practice and serving their clients. Three additional sources of helpful tax information can be found in Checkpoint: Checkpoint Catalyst, tax treatises, tax periodicals, and other research tools. The availability of these items depends on your school's or employer's subscription.

7-1 Checkpoint Catalyst

Checkpoint Catalyst is the newest research tool introduced by Thomson Reuters in 2014. Intended to make research more intuitive, Catalyst was developed with assistance from tax professionals to facilitate the practice of tax law and was designed for the digital online world rather than being a converted printed format. The look and feel is not dissimilar to the BNA Bloomberg portfolios discussed in Chapter 8.

Catalyst is a series of portfolios arranged by topic (see Exhibit 6-27). There are currently Catalysts for a number of main tax areas such as corporations, partnerships, S corporations, tax accounting, and others. More Catalysts are being developed to add to the library over time. Like other sources, the Catalysts can be searched using keywords, contents, and citations (indexes are not yet available for this database).

As shown in Exhibit 6-28, each topic contains a number of subtopics that describe finite portions of the tax issues related to that topic. Topics are updated every four to six weeks to keep the topics current.

EXHIBIT 6-27:   Title Checkpoint Catalyst Library

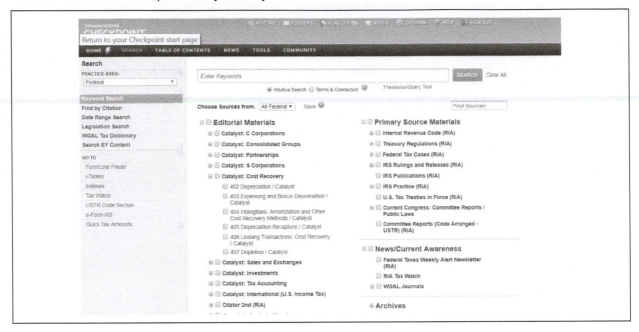

EXHIBIT 6-28:   Title Checkpoint Catalyst Subtopics

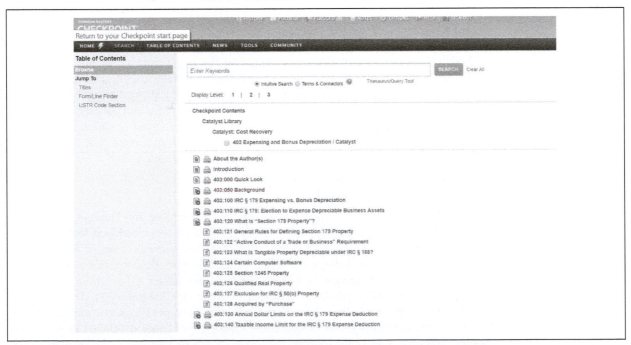

Exhibit 6-29 shows the details included in the Catalyst product. Each subtopic comes with a synopsis to assist the researcher in whether more research in that area is necessary. The editorial commentary is linked to primary sources through footnotes that use a "popup" format rather than taking the researcher to the end of the document. Like other

EXHIBIT 6-29: Title Checkpoint Catalyst Document and Footnotes

EXHIBIT 6-30: Title Checkpoint Catalyst Right Sidebar

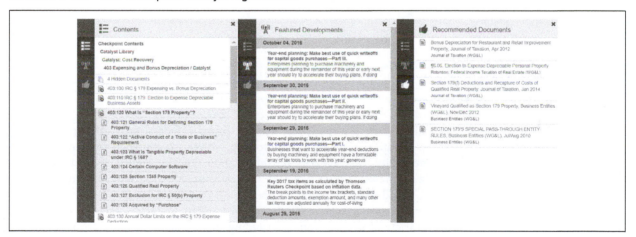

parts of the Checkpoint service, the right sidebar provides options for the researcher to use to assist in solving issues.

As shown in Exhibit 6-29, three options are available: (1) Contents, (2) Featured Developments, and (3) Recommended Documents. All three options are presented side by side in Exhibit 6-30.

Contents provides the location of the document inside the database, just as with the other Checkpoint databases. Featured Developments are the news items and updates released since the last update of the subtopic and provide quick reference to proposed or enacted changes to that subtopic area of tax law. Recommended Documents are a selection of articles and coverage provided in the tax treatises and periodicals included in the Checkpoint subscription.

7-2 Tax Treatises

Tax treatises are editorial analyses that provide in-depth coverage of a particular tax area. Written by prominent experts in the specific field, a treatise offers numerous

EXHIBIT 6-31:   Checkpoint Treatises and Periodicals

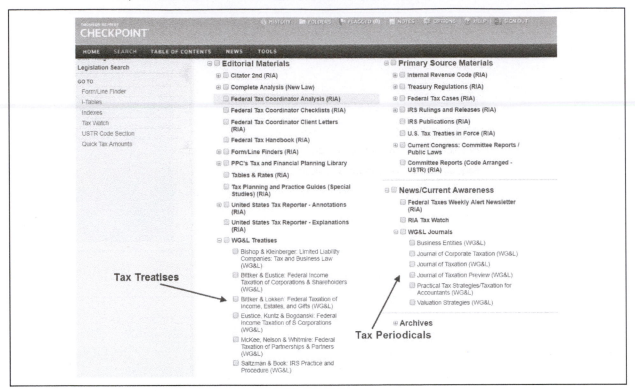

examples and insights on a single tax area, for example, federal taxation of partners and partnerships. Treatises provide a compromise between comprehensive coverage of a topic and the ability to locate relevant information quickly. Topics covered tend to be those that tax professionals are likely encounter in practice. Coverage is more comprehensive than would likely be found in a periodical or journal article.

Checkpoint offers the Warren Gorham and Lamont (WG&L) series of tax treatises related to a variety of taxation topics, including subject matter such as corporate, international, and partnership taxation. Checkpoint also offers treatises on less common topics such as tax fraud and evasion, civil tax controversies, and the alternative minimum tax. The treatises are a rich source of information on these topics and can be found under WG&L TREATISES on the search screen as presented in Exhibit 6-31.

Each treatise contains multiple chapters of information organized by topic. A partial list of WG&L treatises is presented in Exhibit 6-32. The number of treatises available may vary depending on the Checkpoint subscription. Similar to the other explanatory materials in Checkpoint, within the treatise the explanations are accompanied by footnote links to the primary source materials. Typically, a treatise is searched by entering the table of contents in the browser window; however, treatises can be included in the selection of possible databases when performing a keyword search.

7-3 Tax Periodicals

Tax periodicals contain articles and news briefs that are designed to keep readers up to date in specific or general areas of the tax law. These articles might contain an in-depth review of a recently decided court case, a broad analysis of the factors relevant to a

EXHIBIT 6-32:   Checkpoint Partial List of WG&L Treatises

WG&L Federal Treatises
The Alternative Minimum Tax
The Consolidated Tax Return
Electronic Commerce: Taxation and Planning
Federal Income Taxation of Banks & Financial Institutions
Federal Income Taxation of Corporations & Shareholders
Federal Income Taxation of Corporations & Shareholders: Forms
Federal Income Taxation of Individuals
Federal Income Taxation of Intellectual Properties & Intangible Assets
Federal Income Taxation of Passive Activities
Federal Income Taxation of Real Estate
Federal Income Taxation of S Corporations
Federal Tax Accounting
Federal Tax Collections, Liens, & Levies
Federal Taxation of Financial Instruments & Transactions
Federal Taxation of Income, Estates & Gifts
Federal Taxation of Partnerships & Partners
IRS Practice & Procedure
IRS Procedural Forms & Analysis
Limited Liability Companies: Tax & Business Law
Litigation of Federal Civil Tax Controversies
Partnership Taxation
Principles of Financial Derivatives: U.S. and International Taxation
Real Estate Forms: Tax Analysis & Checklists
Structuring and Drafting Partnership Agreements
Subchapter S Taxation
Taxation of Regulated Investment Companies & Their Shareholders
Tax Fraud & Evasion: Offenses, Trials, Civil Penalties [Vol. 1]
Tax Fraud & Evasion: Money Laundering, Asset Forfeiture, Sentencing [Vol. 2]
Tax Planning for Transfers of Business Interests
Taxation of Exempt Organizations
WG&L Tax Dictionary

practitioner's decision on whether to make a certain tax accounting election, or a call for reform of a statute by a neutral (or biased) observer. Tax articles can suggest new viewpoints on tax issues, give guidance for solving complex problems, or just explain a new law in a readable form.

Checkpoint provides access to WG&L's flagship journals on tax news and analysis, such as the *Journal of Taxation*, *Practical Tax Strategies*, and *Valuation Strategies* as shown in Exhibit 6-31. These periodicals contain critical analyses by tax experts including academics, professionals, and other tax practitioners. Articles can cover a variety of tax topics and vary from a brief overview of a potential tax bill to an in-depth analysis of a detailed area of tax law to a thought piece on how tax reforms might alter the business landscape. As with all Checkpoint databases, all the current news and journal information can be searched using the keyword search by selecting those sources.

7-4 Utilizing Treatises and Periodicals in Tax Research

With the right treatise or article that is on point with a tax issue, the practitioner is able to, in effect, use the author as a research associate by capitalizing on the author's expert judgments and references, thereby saving hours of research time. Keep in mind, however, that tax treatises and periodicals are secondary sources of the tax law and therefore should not be cited as a controlling authority, especially when primary sources supporting the position are available. Fortunately, in the online environment, researchers can use the treatise or article references to find the pertinent primary tax sources simply by clicking on the appropriate link. In addition, articles are written based on the existing tax law and are not updated to reflect any changes in the tax law since publication. With those caveats aside, researchers who ignore the tax treatises and periodicals might be accused, at best, of reinventing the wheel and, at worst, of professional malpractice.

Traditionally, citing treatises and articles in professional tax research is limited to two situations: (1) the researcher is referring to the author's analysis and conclusions as stated in an article or (2) the researcher cannot find any controlling primary sources of law and a secondary source addresses the issues. Tax articles are now being cited more frequently in case opinions. When lacking both relevant primary law sources and adequate judicial staff, the authors of these case opinions may draw on tax articles to support the views of the court. In any event, it is imperative that researchers understand the practical implications of using secondary law sources.

7-5 Other Research Tools

Checkpoint also provides access to and interpretation of current events and changes in tax law. Most of these sources of tax information can be found in the NEWS tab located above the main window (see Exhibit 6-33). In addition to daily tax events that are posted on the CHECK-POINT NEWS and the HOME tabs, a variety of tax news can also be found under each practice area. News and new tax developments are provided each day for federal and state tax issues under the FEDERAL TAX UPDATES and STATE & LOCAL TAX UPDATES. These sources, along with the numerous updates contained in the NEWSLETTER LIBRARY, ensure that Checkpoint provides all information necessary for a tax professional to monitor and examine the latest federal tax law changes from a variety of sources, such as new legislation, Treasury rulings and other guidance, the White House, and of course recently decided court cases.

Lastly, Checkpoint also has developed a variety of tools (see Exhibit 6-1) that can be accessed from the Checkpoint HOME SCREEN. Charts that provide quick access to tax rates, deduction limits, depreciation tables, and other frequently used tax information are available at a single click. Online calculators to assist with loan amortization and life expectancy computations are just a few examples of the bevy of tools made available to subscribers. Although specific tools are not available in all subscriptions and are not always useful for tax research, researchers should be aware of their existence in order to

EXHIBIT 6-33:   Checkpoint News Tab

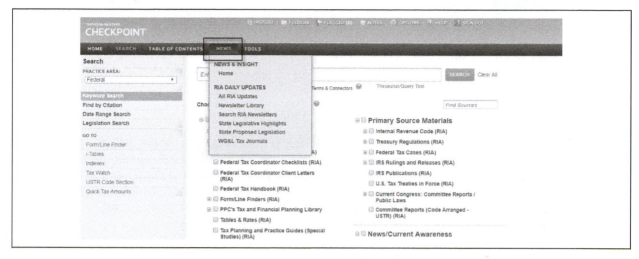

find information quickly and in a manner that can be customized to a particular client. The tools, forms, and other practice aids, although beyond the scope of this text, provide a wealth of efficiency-making improvements for those in tax practice.

SPOTLIGHT ON TAXATION

Frivolous Taxes

Each year, the IRS receives a large number of tax returns filed by taxpayers who, relying on false, frivolous, or phony arguments, claim zero tax liability. Each year, the IRS issues a list of the Dirty Dozen: scams being used that frequently end with bad results for the taxpayer. Common tax-avoidance schemes such as asserting that "the payment of federal income tax is voluntary," "taxes are not legal because the 16th Amendment was never ratified," or "taxpayers are entitled to a refund of all Social Security taxes paid over a lifetime" have become common enough that the IRS has issued a 60-plus page document explaining why these schemes have not been supported in the courts. *The Truth about Frivolous Tax Arguments* is available on the IRS Website.

SUMMARY

Many commercial services are available for performing tax research, and no one service is the best for all practitioners. While the services provide different features, all are most efficient when the organization of the service facilitates research of the issues in a client's tax situation. Thus, each tax service has its place in tax research, and practitioners must determine which products they are most comfortable with and which fit their firms' normal research requirements.

Changes in technology and the tax services are continual. The same changes occur in the practitioner's business. Consequently, the practitioner's comfort level with products and technology and the research needs will change over time. Practitioners should evaluate their tax resource choices often, and at the least once a year, when it is time to renew services.

The tax researcher should employ commercial services as gateways to the primary sources and not as a substitute for primary source research. Tax services can make the research process more efficient and productive, but their use should not replace a thorough review of primary sources and the researcher's professional judgment.

KEY WORDS

By the time you complete this chapter, you should be comfortable discussing each of the following terms. If you need additional review of any of these items, return to the appropriate material in the chapter or consult the glossary to this text.

Advance Citator, p. 207
annotated tax service, p. 183
annotations, p. 183
Boolean connectors, p. 196
Checkpoint, p. 181
Checkpoint Catalyst, p. 209
citation, p. 206
citator, p. 206
cited case, p. 206
cited favorably, p. 207

cited without comment, p. 207
citing case, p. 206
commercial tax service, p. 180
contents search, p. 201
Federal Tax Coordinator (FTC), p. 188
Federal Tax Handbook, p. 189
index search, p. 196
intuitive search, p. 191
keyword search, p. 190

precedential value, p. 205
proximity connector, p. 196
RIA Citator, p. 207
tax periodicals, p. 212
tax treatises, p. 211
terms & connectors, p. 191
topical tax services, p. 183
United States Tax Reporter (USTR), p. 188

DISCUSSION QUESTIONS

1. What is the function of a commercial tax service?

2. Why would a practitioner need a tax service when most primary tax sources are available for free on the Internet?

3. Describe the four common search methods used in RIA Checkpoint.

4. Compare and contrast the general organization of an annotated tax database with that of a topical tax database.

5. Checkpoint makes extensive use of the left sidebar. Describe at least three different types of information or options that may be presented in the left sidebar.

6. Name at least two practice areas in Checkpoint and describe the contents briefly.

7. Select three different primary sources, one from each area of tax law (legislative, administrative, and judicial), and provide a specific example of a source that is available in Checkpoint.

8. Compare and contrast primary and editorial materials and explain the ways in which each can be important to a tax researcher.

9. List the three significant editorial services provided by Checkpoint and discuss the differences between them.

10. Why should a researcher avoid searching all the practice areas of Checkpoint in a single keyword search?

11. Why are the footnote links in Checkpoint's editorial services so important to tax researchers?

12. Explain how the RELATED INFORMATION buttons provide researchers with an efficient researching capability.

13. Explain the difference between a terms and connectors search and an intuitive search.

14. Describe the Boolean connectors, proximity connectors, and wildcard characters available in Checkpoint.

15. What is an advantage to using an index search to find documents of interest?

16. How can a researcher narrow down a search through the index for only specific relevant terms and avoid scrolling through the entire alphabet?

17. Describe how your search results would differ if you use the asterisk wildcard versus place the search term in quotation marks, for example, *dependent*, *"dependent"*, *depend**. List a few synonyms of dependent from the Checkpoint thesaurus.

18. Why should a Contents search typically be left to a more experienced researcher?

19. Explain how a citation search differs from using a citator.

20. Why does the researcher need to determine the precedential value of a case?

21. Why is it difficult to know whether a document retrieved four months ago is still valid law? Which tool in Checkpoint might help a researcher confirm the current status of a case or ruling?

22. Describe the function of a citator in the tax research process.

23. Distinguish between the following terms: *cited case, citing case, citation,* and *cites*.

24. Citators do not provide all the information related to a case. What kind of information do citators not provide?

25. In what way is finding an article on point with a practitioner's tax issue similar to hiring someone to do the research?

26. Why are tax journals and newsletters generally not cited as authority in professional tax research? When would it be appropriate to cite tax journals or newsletters as authority?

EXERCISES

27. Use the Checkpoint Federal Practice Area to answer the following questions:
    a. What are the thesaurus alternatives for "like-kind"?
    b. On the search screen, expand the FTC by clicking on the + before the title. What subheadings are listed?
    c. Expand the IRS Rulings and Releases (RIA). From what year are revenue rulings available?
    d. There are three access points for current legislation. What are these three points?

28. Use the Checkpoint Federal Practice Area, Go To in the left sidebar to answer the following questions:
    a. What is the title of the lead article for the most recent RIA Tax Watch?
    b. When selecting USTR Code Section, what are the choices given for the first and the second selections that must be made (blue circles 1 and 2)?
    c. Which templates are available in the Form/Line Finder?
    d. Which tables are available in the "i-Tables" tool?

29. Use Checkpoint to answer the following questions:
    a. Select the Estate Planning Practice Area. Which templates are available for Code & Regs? Now select the Payroll Practice Area. Indicate any differences in the templates available for IRC & Regs.
    b. Select the Federal Practice Area. Under Find by Citation, select More … In what year was the oldest general counsel memorandum available in Checkpoint issued?
    c. Select the Federal Practice Area and expand the heading under IRS Rulings and Releases. Place the cursor over General Counsel Memoranda and click on the Contents icon that appears on the right. What is the exact date of the oldest general counsel memorandum issued available in Checkpoint?

    d. Select the Federal Practice Area. What type of documents may have the Date Range Search applied to them? What are the oldest available dates for these documents?

    e. Select the Federal Practice Area. Under Find by Citation, select More … then Revenue Ruling. List the Revenue Rulings discussing § 1250. (Hint: Use Retrieve Rulings By Code Section at Issue.)

30. Use the Tool Tab in Checkpoint to answer the following questions:

    a. What is the 1040 Tax Tool under Tax designed to do?

    b. George and Martha are twins, both about to become tax accountants and broke. However, with their new tax jobs starting soon, Martha decides to start saving $200 per month and intends to keep saving $200 per month for 30 years. George, on the other hand, desperately wants a new sports car and thus decides he is going to wait 5 years before starting his $200 per month savings plan. George figures $200 per month for 5 years is only a difference of $12,000, and what difference will delaying his savings really make? Assuming a 6 percent rate of return, using the Savings tools in Checkpoint, what is the difference in the future value of Martha's and George's savings plans?

    c. Under Tools/Mortgage/15 Year vs. 30 Year, what is the difference in total interest paid if Old Mother Hubbard is going to take out a $400,000 mortgage and has a 25 percent marginal tax rate when the 30-year rate is 4 percent and the 15-year rate is 3.25 percent? What will the increased monthly payment be for the 15-year mortgage?

    d. With the Tax tool found on the Tool Tab, determine the marginal tax rate for a single taxpayer earning $60,000 who has one dependent child and takes the standard deduction. List the average rate also.

31. Use the Checkpoint Federal Practice Area to answer the following questions:

    a. What is the title of IRC § 178?

    b. What regulations were issued on this code section? What are their titles?

    c. What code section is added to Reg. § 1.178-1(a) by the proposed regulation?

    d. Which FTC paragraphs furnish an analysis of § 178(a)? What explanation paragraphs are linked to all of § 178?

    e. Which Tax Court case is related to § 178 and amortization of grazing rights?

32. Use the Checkpoint Federal Practice Area Indexes to answer the following questions:

    a. Which federal primary source materials have indexes?

    b. In the FTC Topic Index, determine which paragraph(s) discuss the manufacturer's excise tax on racing car tires (Hint: Look under R for racing).

    c. Using the paragraphs found in the previous part, determine which revenue ruling holds that the tire excise tax depends on the type of tire and not the use of the tire when sold.

    d. In the Current Code Topic Index, determine which code section provides the amount of excise taxes on vaccines.

    e. When was the effective date of the change from different rates on vaccines to a uniform rate?

    f. Find the House committee report related to the change to a uniform rate. According to the report, why was the vaccine excise tax originally established?

33. Use Checkpoint to answer the following questions regarding the ability to expense advanced mine safety equipment.

    a. Using "expense mine safety equipment" as keywords (not in quotation marks), search FTC and determine which paragraph provides an introduction to this issue.

    b. Use Navigate by Contents from the previous paragraph and determine which paragraph provides a definition of advanced mine safety equipment for purposes of expensing?

    c. Use the same keywords in part a, but search USTR—Explanations. What paragraph discusses expensing advanced mine safety equipment?

  d. What primary source is cited by both the FTR and the USTR as the source of the solution?

  e. Use the same keywords and search the Federal Tax Handbook. At what level of detail does the Federal Tax Handbook describe the election to expense advanced mine safety equipment?

34. Use Checkpoint to answer the following questions:

  a. Using Form/Line Finder, locate directions for line 35 on Form 1040 for 2015. What is the paragraph number and topic?

  b. For the last few years, certain real property was eligible for expensing under § 179. Using the keywords *qualified real property 179* find the paragraph of the USTR Explanations that explains the type of qualified property that can be expensed.

  c. Using the Go To: USTR Code Section under Table of Contents, select the Income button under "Choose USTR Tax Type" and the Current button under "Choose Current or Repealed" and enter Code Section 179. Which sources related to § 179 are displayed?

  d. Under Find by Citation, Select More…, then American Federal Tax Reports (Prior Years). In the Retrieve Case by Name, Tax Years, etc., enter 2014 in Year Issued box, S.Ct. in Court example, and Kennedy in Judge Name. Provide the citations for the case(s) that are retrieved.

35. Use Checkpoint to answer the following questions:

  a. What Practice Areas are available in Checkpoint?

  b. What materials are offered in the Archive Materials (Search screen bottom right) for 2014?

  c. When would a practitioner want to use the Archive Materials?

  d. Locate repealed § 341 using USTR Code Section. What area of the tax law did this section cover and when was the repeal effective?

36. Use Checkpoint to answer the following questions:

  a. List three Credit Card tools offered on the Tools Tab that would be personally beneficial to your financial planning.

  b. Where can you find online support and training in Checkpoint?

  c. What is the definition of a mixing bowl transaction (use the WG&L Tax Dictionary)?

37. Use the RIA Citator to evaluate 59 A.F.T.R. 2d 87-392.

  a. What is the name of the case and what are its parallel citations?

  b. In which circuit court was this case heard?

  c. What are the two main issues in the case?

  d. For the professional fees discussed in the case, which two categories were considered? What did the court decide with respect to each?

  e. Have any other cases cited *McCarthy*? Does it modify any previous cases?

  f. Use the FTC related information button and discuss whether this holding would be true for a transaction today.

38. Find the *Santa Clara Valley Housing Group* case decided in 2010.

  a. What is its citation?

  b. Using the citator, determine how many related cases are listed. Of those, which are actually related directly to the issue in the 2010 case?

39. Find the *Parker v. Comm.* decision from 1997.

  a. What is the citation for this case?

  b. How many times has this case been cited by the First Circuit Court of Appeals?

  c. Are there any cases that are distinguished from *Parker*?

40. Using the Federal Practice area, select the Citator 2nd and search for the keywords "2009-47."
    a. Why are so many documents retrieved for this citation?
    b. Use Find by Citation and locate Rev. Proc. 2009-47. What is its title?
    c. Identify by citation the effect this revenue procedure had on earlier pronouncements.
    d. Identify by citation the effect later pronouncements had on this revenue procedure.
    e. Is the revenue procedure that superseded 2009-47 still applicable to the current year?

41. Use the RIA Checkpoint Citator 2nd to evaluate the 2002 *Gwendolyn A. Ewing* Tax Court case.
    a. What is its citation and what tax issues does the case address?
    b. What is the case's direct judicial history?
    c. Where is the case annotated in the United States Tax Reporter?
    d. The *Robert Haag* case cites the 2002 *Ewing* case at 94 A.F.T.R. 2d 2004-6667. What is the *Haag* case's treatment of the *Ewing* case?

42. Find the Supreme Court case involving *Corn Products Refining Company* (not the one in which rehearing was denied).
    a. What is the citation for the case?
    b. How many Supreme Court cases cite the *Corn Products* case?
    c. Find the related Supreme Court case involving *Arkansas Best*. What is the secondary source cited by the court in the opinion?
    d. Use the citator to examine cases that have cited *Arkansas Best*. Does the case appear to have been reversed or overturned?
    e. Using the related information links to the FTC, what is the current application of *Arkansas Best* and *Corn Products*?

43. Use RIA Checkpoint Citator 2nd to evaluate *Deluxe Check Printers, Inc.*, 15 Cl. Ct. 175.
    a. Which tax years were in question in the case? How was the case treated upon appeal? What is the citation of the court of appeals case?
    b. Which doctrine is the basis for part B of the Court of Federal Claims decision? Where is this doctrine discussed in the FTC?
    c. Which cases and rulings distinguish themselves from the *Deluxe Check Printers* Court of Federal Claims case?
    d. How many cases were cited by the *Deluxe Check Printers* decision? (Hint: Check Citing, NOT cited). Does this number of cases seem logical?

44. Use the RIA Checkpoint Citator 2nd to evaluate Revenue Ruling 2001-60.
    a. What is the ruling's complete citation?
    b. What was the effect of Rev. Rul. 2001-60 on Rev. Proc. 99-49 and Rev. Rul. 55-290?
    c. Which IRS revenue procedures favorably cite Rev. Rul. 2001-60?
    d. What issue does Rev. Rul. 2001-60 address?

CCH IntelliConnect

- Complete the research process using an illustrative example and the CCH IntelliConnect tax service.
- Describe the major research databases of CCH IntelliConnect.
- Use keyword, content, index, and citation searches to identify relevant materials in CCH IntelliConnect.
- Use the CCH Citator to confirm the current status of sources of tax law.
- Identify key sources of current tax news and information available in CCH IntelliConnect.

1 Using Tax Services for Research

WHEN A CLIENT CONTACTS A TAX ADVISER with a tax situation, the adviser has a professional responsibility to provide the best tax advice possible and also to ensure that the advice meets the professional standards under the taxing authority's rules. In addition, tax advisers are not likely to meet with much commercial success if they do not provide well-researched and constructed solutions to their clients' tax problems. Further, tax practitioners are being more closely scrutinized by the IRS and the Securities and Exchange Commission (SEC) as a result of increases in regulation. This heightened oversight increases the importance of conducting quality tax research that is carefully documented. Many sources of tax law can be found on the Internet for free. For example, the IRS offers links to free access to the Internal Revenue Code, Treasury Regulations, and anything published in the Internal Revenue Bulletin on its Website (**www.irs.gov/Tax-Professionals/Tax-Code,-Regulations-and-Official -Guidance#guidance**). The U.S. Tax Court offers its opinions online since the mid-1990s (**www.ustaxcourt.gov/**). With a number of primary tax sources available via the Internet for free, one might wonder why tax practitioners are willing to bear the substantial costs associated with subscribing to commercial tax and legal services. By organizing the copious assortment of primary and secondary tax law sources, these services facilitate more efficient, effective, and comprehensive searches for solutions to tax questions than a typical Internet search would produce. In addition to organizing the sources of tax law into a single database system, **commercial tax services** also provide editorial explanations and expert analysis of primary tax law. As the tax law can be quite complex, the plain-English commentary alone can be worth the cost of the services. Thus, the value of a commercial service is to act as an index for and explanation of primary and secondary tax law source materials. Most tax practitioners avail themselves of the benefit of a tax service, as there are services priced to fit the needs (and pocketbooks) of even the smallest tax office.

While one of the main features that practitioners appreciate in a commercial service is the editorial explanation, only reckless (or inadequately trained) tax practitioners confine their analysis to this commentary. The tax services should efficiently direct the researcher to the germane primary sources of the controlling law. It is the ethical and professional duty of tax researchers to evaluate the primary sources themselves and ascertain whether any developments have occurred recently that may change or alter the results of the initial research.

This chapter concretely applies the basic steps for developing effective and efficient tax research based on the process introduced in Chapter 2 and by utilizing the CCH IntelliConnect commercial tax service to find a solution to an actual tax question. The features of CCH IntelliConnect, both tax and legal, are explored on this journey.

The commercial providers of tax services offer a plethora of tax products (databases) that can be bundled in a variety of ways. This chapter's description of the tax databases within IntelliConnect might not be what is available by subscription to the reader. Each tax professional, firm, or library should perform a cost–benefit analysis and purchase only those resources that it finds useful and can afford. In addition, the tax services are constantly updating their products to maintain their competitive edges. Therefore, the current appearance of the tax services and products offered may differ from those presented in this text. Nevertheless, the basic methodology described in this text should apply to whichever tax databases and products are available to the reader regardless of their visual presentation.

2 CCH IntelliConnect

Commerce Clearing House (CCH) IntelliConnect is a comprehensive commercial tax service offered by Wolters Kluwer. Wolters Kluwer is a Netherlands-based firm with a variety of information services in the health, risk, tax, accounting, and legal fields.

IntelliConnect is designed to be intuitive so that researchers can start searching effectively with little training. Access to the entire CCH library is available from just one screen. The results can then be narrowed using the filter options provided. A useful feature allows opening multiple searches (up to eight) with the ability to toggle back and forth between them. In addition, for researchers performing searches on and off all day, IntelliConnect may be launched in the morning and left open all day.

3 Illustrative Research Example

As with learning to drive an automobile, the procedural knowledge necessary to become an effective researcher can only be acquired through hands-on practice. The remainder of this chapter is designed to guide you through a basic use of IntelliConnect and is not a substitute for you actually performing the research. Using the service as you follow the text presentation of the research steps is a highly effective method of learning this material.

Lorna Kolbear, a resident of South Carolina, knew that her son, Steven, was something special at an early age. By the age of 7, Steven showed an extensive talent for political satire and frequently held talk shows with his friends or his six brothers in their modest one-bedroom apartment. Lorna was a single mother and immediately started the work of grooming Steven for a career in television and film. She frequently sacrificed her own needs for those of Steven, especially when it came to Steven's budding career as an actor. Lorna transported Steven to a variety of auditions and tryouts and paid for drama classes and acting instruction as she could afford it. When Steven was in high school, his on-stage and on-camera talents were becoming well known. Articles on his latest comedic ventures were frequently published in the local newspapers. This publicity caught the eye of Quarterlodeon VP for Development Dorothy Player. Dorothy's primary job was to sign new young talent for the Quarterlodeon Network's lineup of television programming.

Dorothy began to follow Steven's career closely and, as a measure of goodwill, even hired a couple of Steven's older brothers into the production crews at Quarterlodeon Studios; however, she stayed away from contacting Steven directly because of her understanding that Lorna felt strongly that Steven should finish high school. Dorothy met frequently with Lorna, recognizing early on that Lorna was matriarch of the Kolbear household and made all the family decisions.

Two days after Steven graduated from high school, Dorothy approached Lorna at the Kolbears' South Carolina apartment to begin negotiations with her. Lorna, as it turns out, knew nothing about television or film and even less about studio contracts but forged ahead with the negotiations anyway. A deal was finally reached later that year but before Steven's 18th birthday. The deal included, among other things, a $150,000 signing bonus for Steven, of which $50,000 would be paid to Lorna. Lorna felt that "he would never have been the actor he is and been able to sign this lucrative contract without my tireless efforts." These amounts were to be paid as soon as the contract was executed and did not require Steven to perform any services whatsoever after that time. Under the terms of the contract, Steven would be prohibited from signing with another studio or network for a period of five years.

As was standard with all contracts with minor (under age 18) actors, the network insisted that Lorna sign the parental consent. Note that under South Carolina law, Lorna is entitled to all the earnings of her minor children (unless separately emancipated by South Carolina law). Steven was not emancipated.

3-1 Approaching the Research Problem

Regardless of the research method used, the starting point in approaching any tax research problem is to formulate the various tax questions to be answered and identify the issues associated with the questions. The tax question for the Kolbear case appears to be the following: What is the appropriate tax treatment of Steven's signing bonus? This first formulation of the tax question should not be considered its final version. As the research progresses, other issues are likely to be identified, causing some refinement of the tax research questions and necessitating the development of new ones. Recall the iterative nature of tax research as discussed in Chapter 2 and presented in Exhibits 2-1 and 2-2.

Research questions are gradually refined to their final states, as all the associated issues are identified. However, this refinement does not guarantee that controlling authority will be found to provide a definite answer to the tax research question. The final conclusion may be that one solution appears more supportable than another. There may be a conflict between the likely interpretation of the facts and circumstances by the IRS and the taxpayer. Considering the probable stance the courts would take may be relevant when weighing the solution to the research question. In most tax research engagements, professional judgment is required because the controlling law is imprecise and can be interpreted differently by the taxpayer, the IRS, and the courts. It is this professional judgment that taxpayers are seeking when they hire CPAs for tax assistance.

Based on the initial question formulated, the main issues in the Kolbear case appear to be the timing of the taxability of the signing bonus; the attribution of the income to either Steven or his mother, Lorna; and the possible deduction of the payment by Steven to his mother for her services in negotiating the contract.

3-2 Accessing Tax Information

Researching the tax law is more of an art than a science, and reaching tax issues effectively and efficiently requires a broad knowledge of tax law, a reasonable level of experience with the tax research tools, and persistence (a small dose of luck never hurts, either). One of the most important steps in the tax research process is to consider the question, "Where do I start?" Since most students have little to no tax research experience and a wealth of tax law to pore over, this task can be daunting. The key to effective tax research is finding the pertinent material necessary to formulate an informed conclusion about the optimum treatment of the transaction.

Most tax services, including IntelliConnect, offer four primary ways to search for information: (1) keyword search, (2) contents search, (3) index search, and (4) citation search.

Keyword searches are very similar to the typical web search performed on an Internet browser using Google, Bing, or some other common search engine.

Contents searches are similar to examining the table of contents for a book and trying to locate the chapter relevant to the search. Using an index search is no different than simply flipping to the index at the end of a book and looking up the key word or words that might direct you to the proper page. Citation searches require that the researcher already have a good idea of the code section, regulation, ruling, or other known source of tax law that might apply. Before performing a search, the researcher must have a thorough understanding of what information is being searched.

4 Databases

IntelliConnect, like most tax services, organizes information by database. Traditionally, databases are classified into two general types: annotated and topical. **Annotated tax services** are organized by Internal Revenue Code section number. They may also be called compilations because they compile an editor's explanation and evaluation with the code section as well as its recent committee reports and regulations, and they provide **annotations** (i.e., brief summaries) of related court cases and administrative rulings. **Topical tax services**, on the other hand, divide the tax law into transactions and related subject matter, with underlying tax principles as an organizing format. Thus, the material follows logical threads that connect noncontiguous code sections. Since the electronic services are developed from published services, they are generally organized as topical and annotated databases; however, this structure may not be apparent.

One of the greatest benefits of any Internet service is the currency of the information provided. Most services update text on a daily or continuous basis. Still, daily updating does not necessarily mean that what happened yesterday will be accessible today; processing time still is required. However, daily updating does mean that as soon as the information is processed, it can be entered into the system.

Accessing IntelliConnect requires a subscription, including a login and password. The method by which you access IntelliConnect can vary depending on the subscription a school or company has obtained. The IntelliConnect home screen presented in Exhibit 7-1 provides the entry point to starting tax research.

A particular user's home screen may differ depending on the default or personalized setup provided by the school or company. Typically, the IntelliConnect screen is made up of no fewer than three separate areas. The portion at the top is known as the NAVIGATION BAR, where you can enter search strings, select content to search, access your history and saved searches (if enabled in your subscription), and log out of the system (which is recommended in order to free up a user license). The second important portion of the screen is the left panel, known as the BROWSE menu or BROWSE window. The BROWSE window contains all the content in the IntelliConnect subscription and can be presented, based on the researcher's choice, in TREE view or in LIBRARY view in the upper right of the BROWSE window. TREE view displays the content in the form of a tree, with branches displayed with each click of the [+] buttons. LIBRARY view presents the titles to each source in a typical by-title manner. In addition, the typical IntelliConnect subscription allows researchers to set up MY FAVORITES to identify the most commonly used databases more quickly. The next important area of the screen is the DOCUMENT LIST window (sometimes known as the RESULTS window). Once a search is performed, the results of that search appear in the

EXHIBIT 7-1: CCH IntelliConnect Home Screen

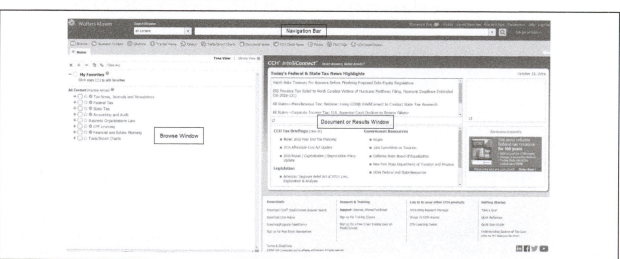

DOCUMENT LIST, to be selected to view or not. Finally, when a document is selected for viewing, a fourth window, known as the DOCUMENT window or simply the DOCUMENT, appears.

In IntelliConnect, the database areas are known as practice areas. Practice areas are presented in the BROWSE window and are organized at the highest level to help users identify specific areas of tax or accounting that may apply to that situation. The contents of each practice area can be displayed by clicking on the + sign and can be hidden by clicking the − sign. For example, within the Federal Tax practice area, IntelliConnect provides databases that include editorial content and primary source content. Recall that primary authority is what professional standards dictate that tax advisers must understand to achieve substantial authority under IRC § 6662 and IRC § 6694. Primary sources are the statutory, administrative, and judicial sources discussed in previous chapters and presented as shown in the BROWSE window in Exhibit 7-2.

EXHIBIT 7-2:   Primary Sources and Expanding and Contracting Lists

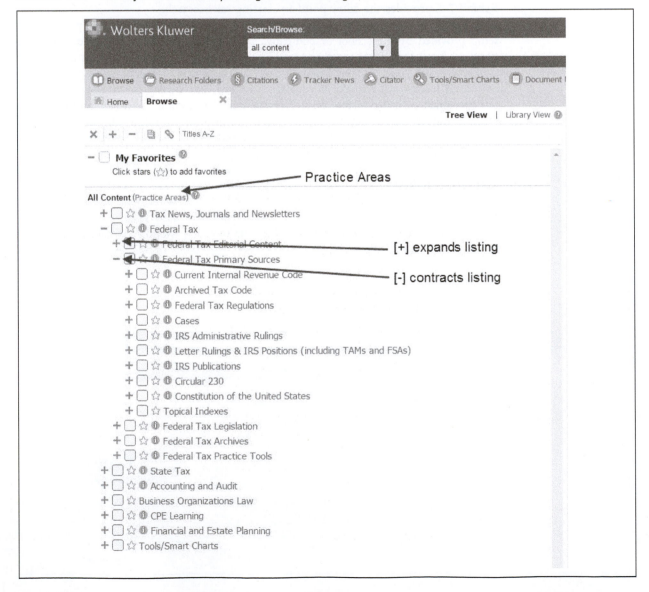

IntelliConnect offers access to a bevy of primary source materials. As shown in Exhibit 7-2, these can be found under the FEDERAL TAX PRIMARY SOURCES heading in the BROWSE window in the left panel. The up-to-date version of the Internal Revenue Code for research on current year tax issues and a history of the code for tax issues from previous years are both available. Final, temporary, and proposed regulations are all contained within the FEDERAL TAX REGULATIONS heading. The CASES heading contains court cases related to federal taxes at the trial, appellate, and Supreme Court levels, including the different types of Tax Court cases (e.g., regular versus memorandum). A more complete listing of primary sources in IntelliConnect is presented in Exhibit 7-3.

EXHIBIT 7-3:   CCH IntelliConnect Primary Source Materials

Current Internal Revenue Code	• Up-to-date version of the Internal Revenue Code
	• Code history dating back to 1986 code
	• Various other statutes covering tax issues
	• Finding lists (cross-reference to older versions of the code)
	• Public laws since 1971 that updated the code
Archived Tax Code	• Code from 1939 and 1954 with some committee reports from that time
Federal Tax Regulations	• Final, temporary, and proposed Treasury Regulations
	• Circular 230
Cases	• Tax Court decisions (regular, memorandum, and small case)
	• Board of Tax Appeals cases (predecessor to the Tax Court)
	• Rules of Procedure for Tax Court, Supreme Court, and other federal courts
IRS Administrative Rulings	• Treasury Decisions
	• Notices of proposed rulemaking (form by which regulations are proposed)
	• Revenue procedures
	• Revenue rulings
	• IRS notices, announcements, and press releases
	• Treasury Department news releases
	• IRS acquiescence/nonacquiescence announcements
	• IRS fact sheets (information and statistics about the federal tax system and the IRS)
	• Executive Orders issued by the president
	• Other IRS documents
Letter Rulings and IRS Positions	• IRS letter rulings and TAMs (technical advice memoranda)
	• Chief counsel advice, field service advice, and IRS service center advice, miscellaneous IRS memoranda (IRS internal communications)
	• Litigation guideline memoranda (communications between IRS and its attorneys)
	• IRS information letters
	• General counsel memoranda
	• Actions on decisions

	• Technical memoranda (not the same as TAMs, these record transmission of TDs for documentation in the Federal Register)
	• IRS audit positions (information used by IRS revenue agents to resolve audit issue and procedures)
IRS Publications	• Current IRS publications
Circular 230	• Circular 230
Constitution of the United States	• The U.S. Constitution
Topical Indexes	• Topical indexes for the code, final and temporary regulations, and proposed regulations

SPOTLIGHT ON TAXATION

Field Service Advice Memoranda

Field service advice (FSA) memoranda are available to the tax community, thanks to Tax Analysts. In 1993, Tax Analysts filed a request under the Freedom of Information Act to have FSA memoranda become subject to public disclosure. The IRS declined this request because these documents contained "return information" or were protected by the attorney–client privilege and therefore were not available for public disclosure. Tax Analysts took the question to court, and in 1996, a district court ordered the IRS to release the FSAs to the general public.

The court indicated that FSAs are similar to general counsel memoranda (GCMs), also considered public information. They contain legal analysis and conclusions of the law and are not "return information" under any reasonable interpretation of IRC § 6103. Further, just because an IRS attorney declares FSAs to be "return information" does not make them so. FSAs are merely memoranda routinely used by the IRS as guidance in conducting audits and therefore are applied by the IRS in its dealings with the public.

While considered secondary authority, editorial content can be extremely helpful to the tax adviser in finding and understanding the relevant primary authority. A typical IntelliConnect subscription will contain three editorial sources of interest, especially to new researchers: (1) U.S. Master Tax Guide, (2) Tax Research Consultant, and (3) Standard Federal Tax Reporter. A complete list of secondary sources is presented in Exhibit 7-4, with these three highlighted. The databases available vary by subscription; thus, not all those listed in the following discussion may be available. These tax sources can be found under the FEDERAL TAX EDITORIAL CONTENT heading in the BROWSE window. Both the Master Tax Guide and the Tax Research Consultant are organized by topic. As discussed earlier and presented in Exhibit 7-5, a topical organization simply means that tax law and transactions are organized by related subject matter. The **Tax Research Consultant** is generally considered the most comprehensive of the three editorial sources. This is the flagship editorial content of IntelliConnect, in which tax experts are being constantly drawn upon to evaluate and explain tax law in a more understandable but still comprehensive fashion. Each section and subsection of the IRC and regulations are broken down and explained in a detailed fashion.

EXHIBIT 7-4: IntelliConnect Editorial Source Materials

Accounting for Uncertain Tax Positions	Support materials, tools, and practice aids necessary to structure and complete compliance under FASB Codification Topic 740, Income Taxes.
Business Entity Planning	Guidance regarding what type of business entity will work to the greatest advantage of the investors and guidance about how to set up the organization. Also includes the *Partnership Tax Watch Newsletter*, the *S Corporations Guide Report Letter*, and the *LLC Advisor Newsletter*, plus the *Business Entity Planning Smart Charts*, decision trees, and checklists.
Health Care Reform	Includes the Affordable Care Act: Law, Regulatory Explanation, and Analysis, tax briefings about health reform and the net investment income tax, and a suite of interactive research aids. It also includes the Health Reform Analysis Locator, which provides coverage of topics related to health reform.
Interactive Research Aids	Interactive web applications that cover a broad range of tax topics on individuals, entities, business, employers, sales, accounting, international, and procedure.
Quick Answers	Access to key information such as tax rates, charts, and checklists.
Specialty Tax Areas	Publications and products related to specific specialty areas within federal taxation, including *U.S. Master Estate and Gift Tax Guide*, *Excise Tax Analysis*, *Executive Compensation Expert Library*, *Real Estate Tax Commentaries*, *Tax Practice and Procedure Commentaries*, *Business Strategies*, *U.S. Master Depreciation Guide*, *Tax Practice Guides*, *Social Security Benefits Explained*, and *Employee Benefits Analysis*.
Standard Federal Tax Reporter	A code-arranged reporter covering the federal income tax. The full text of an Internal Revenue Code section, with brief legislative history notes, followed by the relevant committee reports, final, temporary, and proposed regulations, editorially prepared explanations, and annotations.
Tax Research Consultant	A practical focus on income, estate and gift, payroll, and excise tax laws organized and divided into 36 topics.
U.S. Master Tax Guide	Explanations of federal income taxes for individuals, partnerships, corporations, estates, and trusts as well as new rules established by key court decisions and the IRS. The guide also includes a tax calendar, taxpayer-specific return flowcharts, lists of average itemized deductions, selected depreciation tables, tax rate tables, and checklists of income, deduction, and medical expense items.

The **Standard Federal Tax Reporter** is an annotated tax service, which is organized by Internal Revenue Code section number and presented in Exhibit 7-6. This database contains the code section, the legislative history (committee reports), related Treasury Regulations, CCH-provided explanations, and annotations, which are court cases that have tax law related to the selected code section. In many ways, the Standard Federal Tax Reporter has the relevant primary and secondary tax law in one place.

The **U.S. Master Tax Guide** is a quick way to find general information about a topic of interest. Organized by topic, the Master Tax Guide provides less detailed explanations of tax law. It does not provide the same exhaustive analysis as the other two CCH editorial services but might be the fastest service to review because of its relative brevity. It is not unusual for tax professionals to maintain a paper copy of the U.S. Master Tax Guide as a quick nonelectronic reference.

EXHIBIT 7-5:   Tax Research Consultant Topical Organization

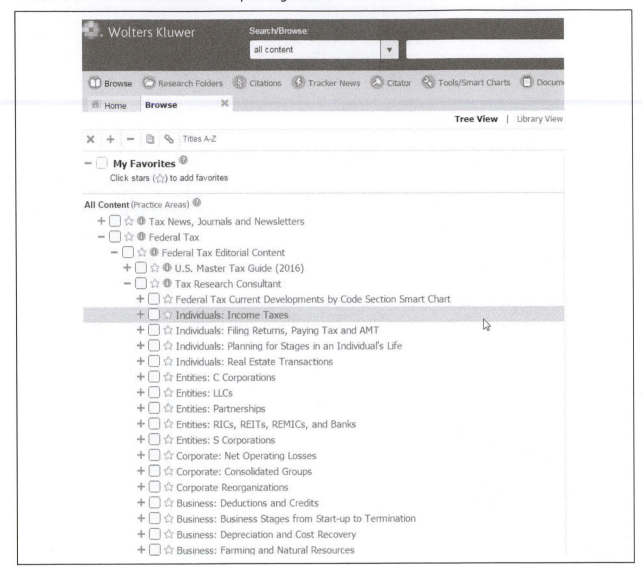

SPOTLIGHT ON TAXATION

CCH History

CCH first published the Standard Federal Tax Reporter in 1913 as a 400-page document. Not coincidentally, this was the first year of the modern income tax in the United States. The 2013 edition of the same Standard Federal Tax Reporter is a remarkable 25-volume, 73,954-page behemoth. Thankfully, with the advent of online and mobile access tax services such as CCH's IntelliConnect, trees around the world can feel safer.

EXHIBIT 7-6: Standard Federal Tax Reporter Annotated Organization

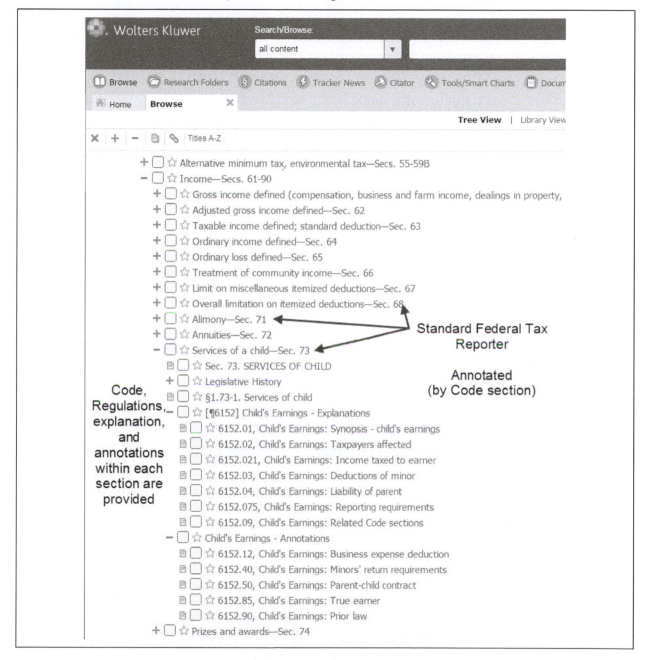

5 Finding Relevant Tax Information

With so many sources and types of tax law available, one of the primary challenges of tax research is actually finding the materials and content necessary to respond to the tax issue. Different issues call for different levels of research and varied degrees of certainty, but ultimately, tax advisers must be confident in their responses so that their clients can continue to count on them as reliable sources of professional tax advice. Once the source or sources of tax law have been identified, the researcher turns to finding the source documents that will support a conclusion. In IntelliConnect, there are four primary search methods: (1) keyword, (2) contents, (3) index, and (4) citation. Each of these may have an advantage over any other based on the researcher's experience or degree of comfort with a particular area of tax law. Most researchers will use all four at one time or another during their careers, and overreliance on any one type of search may do an injustice to the researcher's work in a situation in which a nonfavored approach is the most efficient.

5-1 Keyword Search

As mentioned previously, performing a **keyword search** in IntelliConnect is very similar to performing a search on the Internet using a search engine with one very important difference: selection of the database(s) to search. Although IntelliConnect permits users to search their entire subscription, the number of nonrelevant hits is likely to increase with each additional source, making it more difficult to identify the relevant tax law. Instead, researchers should select only the database(s) of interest. Returning to the illustrative research example, the search can be limited to only the Federal Tax practice area by clicking the box next to the practice area name in the BROWSE window. By clicking the + symbol beside the practice area, the databases within that area are revealed. To start the search for the illustrative example, the researcher might select the editorial content, the primary content, or both.

As presented in Exhibit 7-7, if both are selected, the SEARCH/BROWSE drop-down menu in the NAVIGATION bar automatically chooses selected content.

When the keyword search is performed by entering the phrase "what is the tax treatment of a child's income" and clicking the GO button in the NAVIGATION bar, IntelliConnect opens up a new tab, and the results appear in the DOCUMENT LIST AND RESULTS window

EXHIBIT 7-7:   Keyword Search Selection of Content to Search

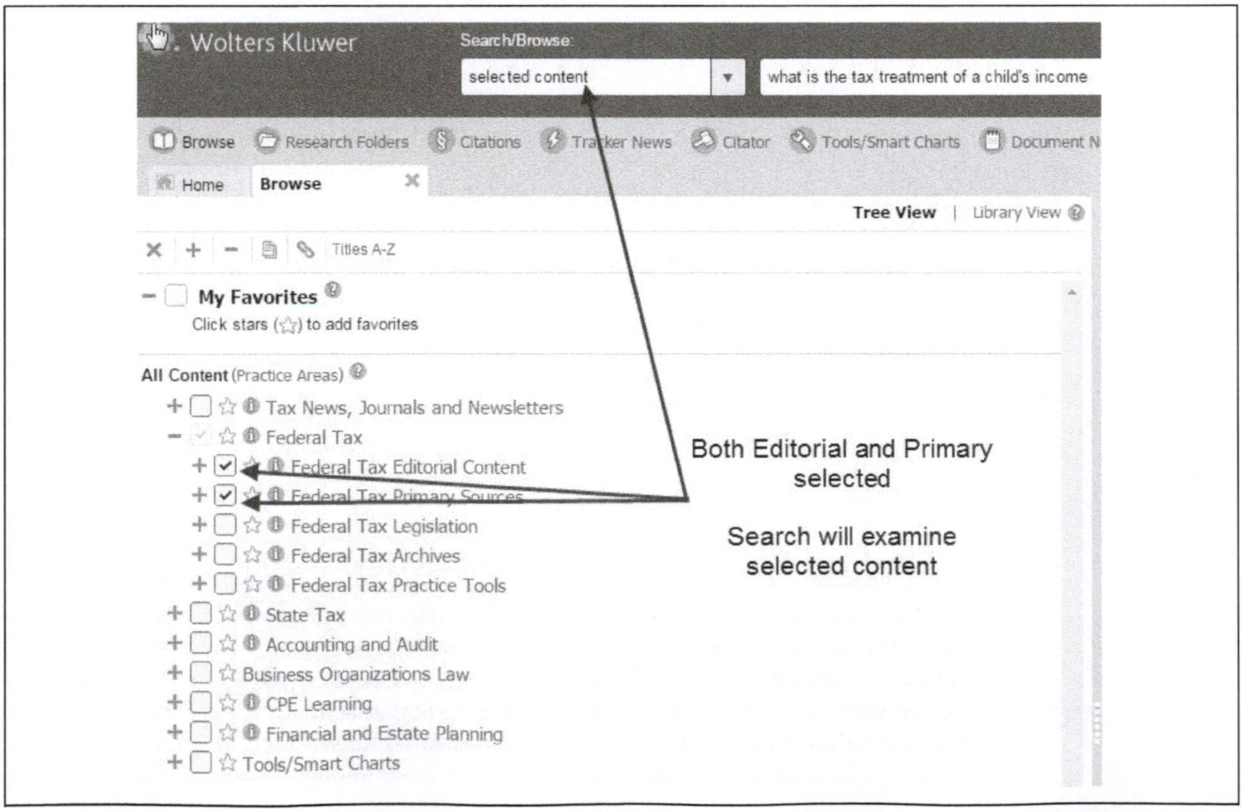

EXHIBIT 7-8: Illustrative Example Keyword Search Document List

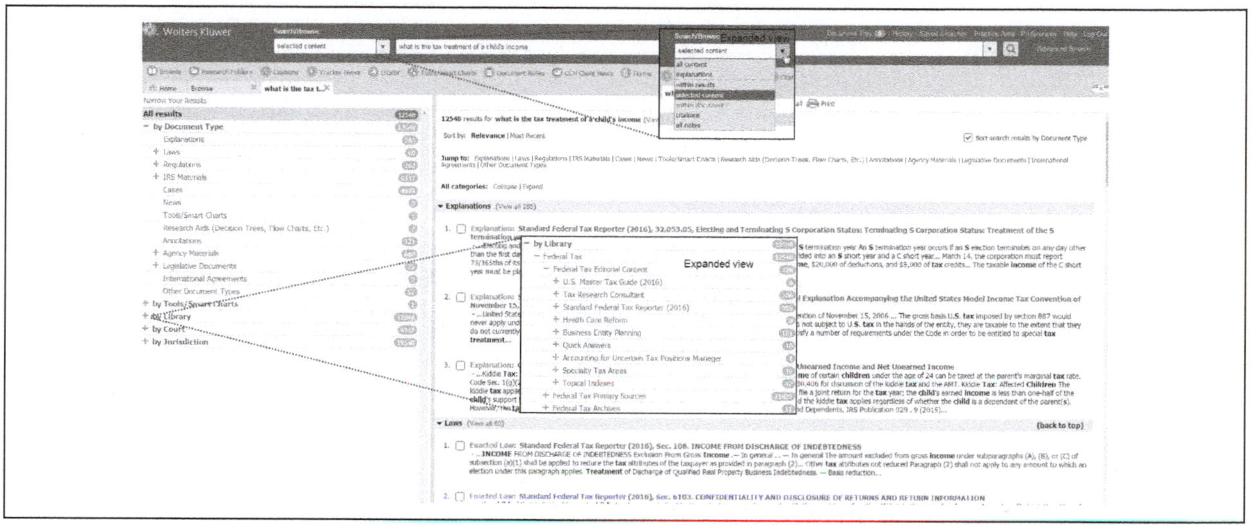

(new left pane) as shown in Exhibit 7-8. The DOCUMENT LIST AND RESULTS and the SEARCH/ BROWSE drop-down both provide a means to refine the search even further. As shown in Exhibit 7-7, the SEARCH/BROWSE drop-down can be used to search within the results or to narrow the search to only certain selected sources (e.g., explanations). Another way to refine the sources in the results is to expand the BY LIBRARY by clicking the [+]. This provides a more detailed list of results in the DOCUMENT LIST in the left pane. If any of the listed libraries is selected, the left pane will adapt to that source, and the RESULTS window will display only those search results (see Exhibit 7-8). Previous keyword search history can be revealed by clicking the drop-down for the KEYWORD SEARCH box. Similar to typical search engines, IntelliConnect ignores nuisance words such as *of* and *a*. IntelliConnect allows keyword searches as key terms, exact phrases, or using Boolean connectors, proximity connectors, or wildcards. For example, searching "what is the tax treatment of a child's income" and using the quotation marks will provide the results of a search for that exact phrase (a search that returns no results since that *exact phrase* must appear in the database but does not).

Depending on the default setup of the IntelliConnect subscription, the results can be displayed by document type or across all sources in the selection, by relevance or date. The typical setup is for the top three documents (by relevance) to be presented. However, all the results for any or all databases can be displayed by clicking VIEW ALL at the top of each different source. In the RESULTS window on the left (which has replaced the BROWSE window on this tab), the document types are listed along with choices to display the results by LIBRARY, COURT, or JURISDICTION. New researchers may find it most helpful to review the explanatory sources first to get a feel for the language and terms of the tax issue being researched. The results of the illustrative search reveal a section of the Tax Research Consultant titled Income Taxation of Children in ¶18,150 and specifically, ¶18,154.05 (as shown in Exhibit 7-9). By simply clicking on the result, the document is opened in the DOCUMENT WINDOW as shown in Exhibit 7-10. With the document open, the results are shifted to the top of the window, while the actual selected document is shown in the lower half. The document displayed can be navigated using the IN RESULTS arrows to find **keywords**. The documents adjacent to the results document can be reviewed by using the READ PREVIOUS or READ NEXT DOCUMENT buttons near the top of the document window. Not much meaningful

EXHIBIT 7-9:   Illustrative Example Selected Document List

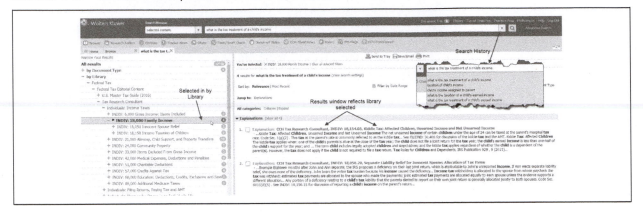

EXHIBIT 7-10:   Illustrative Example Document View

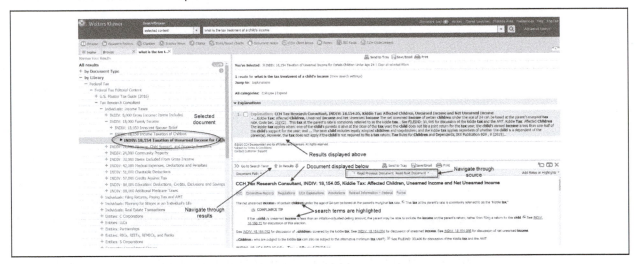

information can be drawn from ¶18,154.05 with respect to the illustrative example; however, the researcher can probably sense they are in the right area. By using the READ PREVIOUS buttons, the research can backtrack through the Tax Research Consultant to find the start of the section (¶18,150), which is a general discussion of the topic that reveals the following:

> *Several rules govern the taxation of children. First, a child with earned income in excess of the filing threshold is a separate taxpayer who must file an individual return, and is generally taxed as a single taxpayer.*

This passage explains that a child's income is reported on the child's tax return even if received by the parent (see Exhibit 7-11). The DOCUMENT WINDOW can be expanded by using the icons in the upper right corner to present a larger window.

This explanation reveals that a child's income is reported in the child's tax return even if received by the parent. Recall that the source document is the Tax Research Consultant, which is a secondary source; however, primary sources must be used to support conclusions. Conveniently, the explanations are laden with footnotes that link back to the primary source materials as presented in Exhibit 7-11. Simply click on the footnote, and the source for the explanation is presented. Click on the source document, and that primary source is opened in the document window as shown in Exhibit 7-12.

EXHIBIT 7-11:   Illustrative Example Footnote Link to Primary Sources

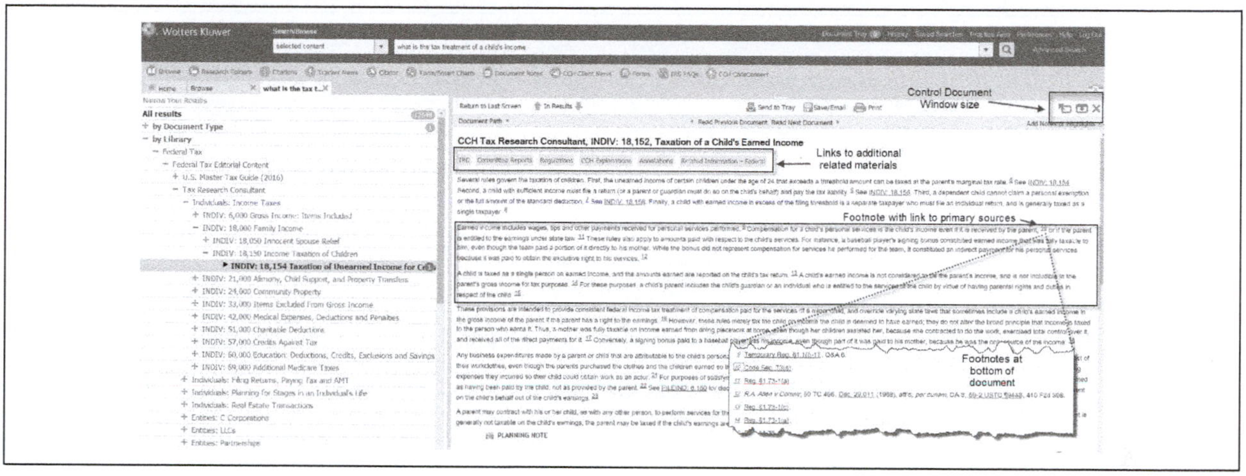

Note also that at the top of both the explanations (Exhibit 7-11) and the code section (Exhibit 7-12) documents, IntelliConnect provides links to jump to a variety of related sources. For example, in Exhibit 7-11, buttons to jump to the Internal Revenue Code, related committee reports, regulations, and other sources are provided. The links are available in the primary source documents (in this case the Internal Revenue Code) as shown in Exhibit 7-12. In this way, researchers can toggle back and forth between secondary sources if they need additional interpretation of the tax law and the primary sources in order to document the substantial authority necessary to achieve a reliable conclusion. Researchers who are not familiar with the organization of the databases can determine exactly where they are in the database by clicking the DOCUMENT PATH tab in the top of the document window (see Exhibit 7-12). Whether a primary or a secondary source, the document path will present the precise location in the table of contents where the document resides.

Returning to our illustrative example and Exhibit 7-12, the search has revealed IRC § 73(a), which states the following:

> *Amounts received in respect of the services of a child shall be included in his gross income and not in the gross income of the parent, even though amounts are not received by the child.*

In order to better understand the language of the code section, the researcher should also examine the Treasury Regulations that interpret that code section. By clicking the

EXHIBIT 7-12:   Illustrative Example of Primary Source—Internal Revenue Code

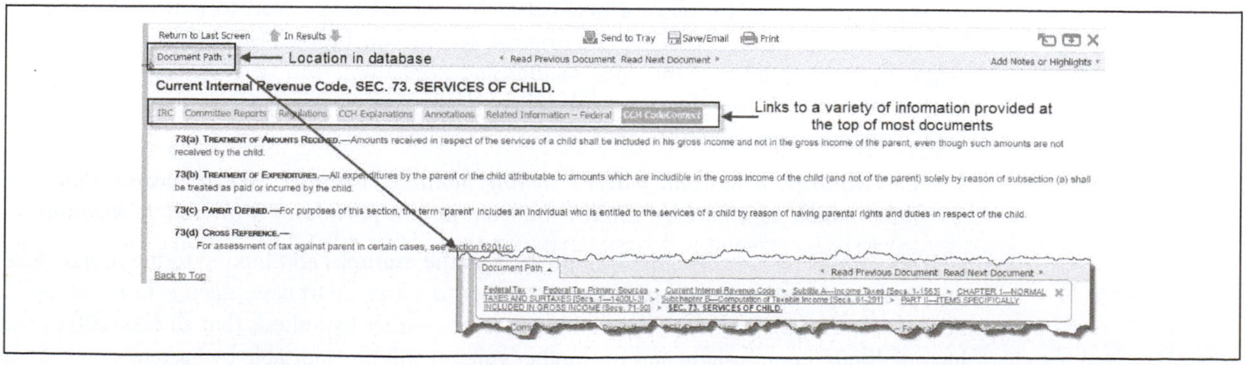

EXHIBIT 7-13:   Illustrative Example Related Document Link to Regulations

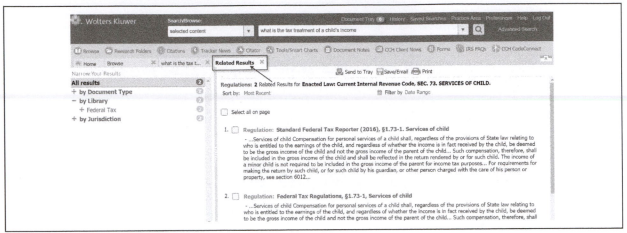

REGULATIONS button at the top of the code section in the DOCUMENT window, the regulations on IRC § 73 are presented in the DOCUMENT LIST AND RESULTS window on yet another new tab (see Exhibit 7-13). The REGULATIONS button and the other links to additional materials are called collectively the RELATED DOCUMENTS links.

Recall that the regulations are a primary source of administrative tax law. In the illustrative example, results show that there is only one regulation for IRC § 73, Reg. § 1.73-1 (available in both the Federal Tax Regulations database and the Standard Federal Tax Reporter), which states the following in subsection (a):

> *Compensation for personal services of a child shall, regardless of the provisions of State law relating to who is entitled to the earnings of the child, and regardless of whether the income is in fact received by the child, be deemed to be the gross income of the child and not the gross income of the parent of the child. Such compensation, therefore, shall be included in the gross income of the child and shall be reflected in the return rendered by or for such child.*

Thus far, the results in the illustrative example indicate that a child is to report the income from his or her services irrespective of who is paid. At this point, a researcher should start to feel fairly comfortable that the correct solution to the tax issue is being formulated. However, it is important that researchers examine other sources of tax law to seek out evidence that supports or contradicts the conclusion they have hypothesized thus far.

As the illustrative example points out, IntelliConnect tracks a researcher's work over time by creating history tabs at the top of the page (see Exhibit 7-13) that capture the search at different points. By clicking on a tab, a researcher can be brought back to a previous search in order to follow a new research trail that might lead to new sources of tax law. In the illustrative example, the original search can be recalled and the explanation originally used to identify the code section and regulations can be reviewed again. Upon further review, one sees that the explanation in the Tax Research Consultant (see Exhibit 7-11) contains the following:

> *For instance, a baseball player's signing bonus constituted earned income that was fully taxable to him, even though the team paid a portion of it directly to his mother.*

This sounds remarkably similar to the facts of the example, and linking to the source document through the footnote brings the researcher to a Tax Court case, *Allen v. Commissioner*, 50 T.C. 466 (1968). The case appears to support the earlier hypothesis that all $200,000 of the income (both Steven's share and his mother's share) will be reportable by Steven.

EXHIBIT 7-14:   CCH IntelliConnect Boolean and Proximity Connectors

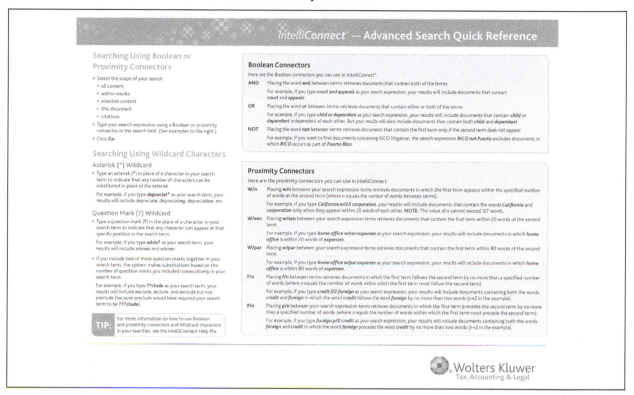

Before moving on to an alternative search method, consider our original keyword search, "what is the tax treatment of a child's income." Are there improvements that could be made to this search string that might offer the same or more direct results? For example, the search contains the word *tax*. When searching a database of tax law, this term is not likely to add considerable differentiation to the search. New researchers may want to experiment with alternative searches using the **Boolean connectors** and **proximity connectors** presented in Exhibit 7-14. For example, results found in the previous example search suggest terms such as *child, parent, income,* and *services* that would all be suitable keywords. Various proximity connectors such as *W/n, W/sen,* or *W/par* are likely to find materials relevant to the illustrative example.

A relatively new feature of IntelliConnect is the Quick Answer box that can appear when a common search is performed. For example, a search for mileage rate will result in a number of results and a Quick Answer box that lists the business standard mileage rates for the recent years. IntelliConnect continues to add additional Quick Answers in an effort to speed up the time to perform common searches.

5-2 Index Search

New researchers may find it difficult to use the **index search** and contents search (discussed later) because of their relative lack of experience with the language and structure of the existing tax law. That said, at times the index search can be an efficient way to find the relevant tax law quickly with little guesswork. The advantage of an index search is that, because individuals create indexes, the *tax meanings of the words* are considered as well as the context in which the words are found. The researcher has the ability to use the expertise of the indexer in locating the primary documents of interest.

EXHIBIT 7-15:   CCH IntelliConnect Editorial Materials Index Search

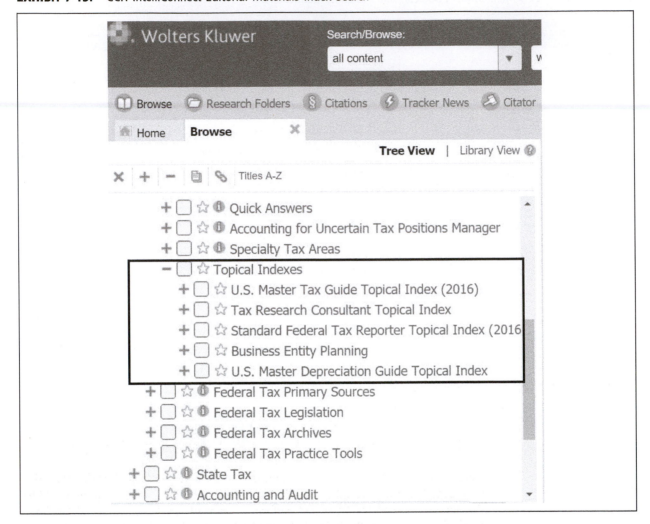

Some researchers find it beneficial to start with an index search to help identify effective terms for their general keyword searches.

IntelliConnect contains a number of useful indexes to search. As one might expect, each of the typical editorial sources—the U.S. Master Tax Guide, the Tax Research Consultant, and the Standard Federal Tax Reporter—has its own topical index that can be searched individually, or if all indexes are selected, all may be searched at once. In addition, IntelliConnect provides an index for three of the primary sources as well: the current Internal Revenue Code, the final and temporary regulations, and the proposed regulations.

New researchers are likely to begin with the editorial sources. As an example, an index search of the Tax Research Consultant can be started by expanding the Federal Tax Editorial Content in the browse window. The last item under that subheading will be topical indexes. Using the + to expand, the tree will reveal the topical index for the three major editorial services, as shown in Exhibit 7-15.

Expanding the tax research consultant Topical Index reveals the alphabet with a selection box and a document icon next to each letter. The selection boxes can be used to select only words starting with certain letters to perform a keyword search at any time. The document icon to the left of each letter opens that portion of the index in

EXHIBIT 7-16:   CCH IntelliConnect Index Search Results

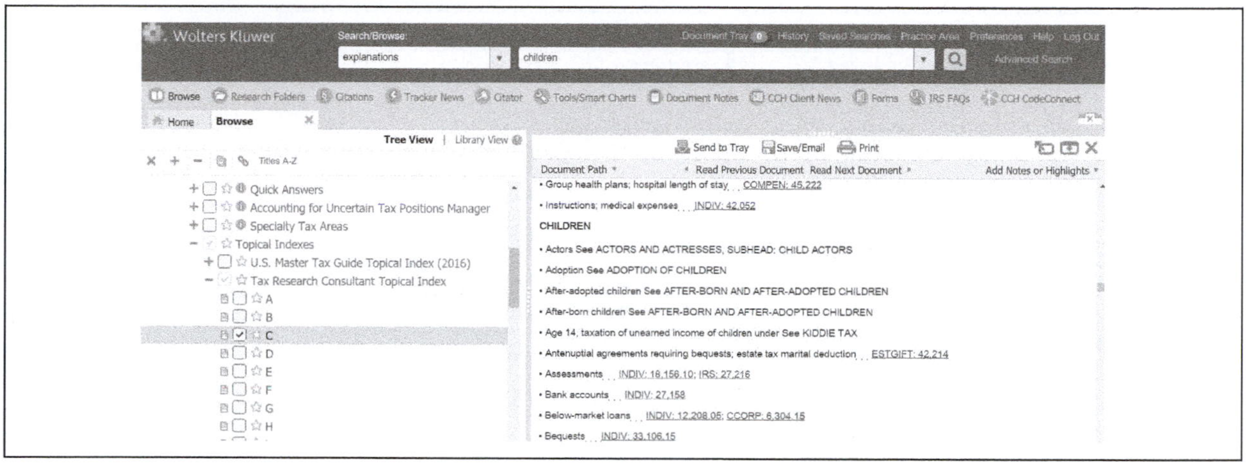

the DOCUMENT Window as presented in Exhibit 7-16. Note that items denoted with a single dot are the main headings, and those with two dots are subheadings under that main heading. In rare instances, subheadings at the level of three dots or more are used.

While a researcher might choose to look under the letter *C* for *children*, unfortunately there are hundreds of entries to examine. This is where experience can assist the researcher. Knowing specifically that the topic of interest is related to the tax treatment of the income of a child, a researcher might scroll down and find Tax Treatment under the Children heading, which provides a link to INDIV 18,150, which is ¶18,150 of the Tax Research Consultant chapter on individuals. This paragraph discusses primarily the unearned income of children under age 24 but provides links to other paragraphs in the Federal Tax Consultant, including ¶18,152, which was the source located in the keyword search example presented previously in this chapter (see Exhibit 7-10).

Another way to find information in the index is to use a keyword search within the index itself. Instead of entering the index and clicking the DOCUMENT icon, another option would be to click the box next to the letter and perform a keyword search on just that letter (or a selection of letters) within the index. Referring back to the illustrative example, if the Index for C is selected and a search for "child earned income" is run, the document window shows the entire C index. In the top left corner of the document window, the GO TO SEARCH TERM arrows allow the researcher to advance throughout the document to the first and each subsequent keyword search term. The key terms will be highlighted (see Exhibit 7-17).

There are several ways to reduce the number of hits in a search. Since the key words earned and income can be used more appropriately as the phrase "earned income," the keyword search can be rerun using either "earned income" in quotation marks or using the proximity connector "income f/1 earned" in the keyword search. A fairly small number of clicks through the GO TO SEARCH TERM window will eventually reveal the same ¶18,152 of the Federal Tax Consultant that has been previously mentioned.

IntelliConnect has a well-designed thesaurus that searches for more than just the root terms used in your keywords. By clicking VIEW SEARCH SETTINGS (near the top of Exhibit 7-17), the additional terms used in the search are revealed as *children*, *kid*, and *minor*. The automatic use of the thesaurus can be turned off by selecting advanced search in the top right corner of the search bar and clicking off the check mark next to APPLY THESAURUS. Note that putting "child" in quotation marks will not turn off the thesaurus for that keyword.

EXHIBIT 7-17: CCH IntelliConnect Keyword Search within and Index Search

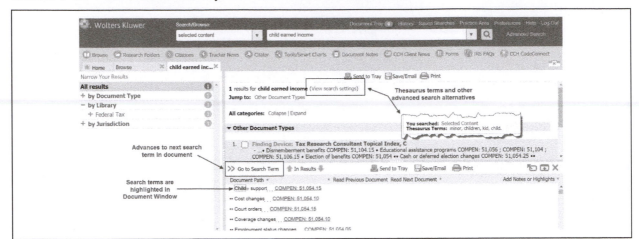

5-3 Contents Search

A **contents search** can be appropriate if the researcher has a reasonably good idea of the area of tax law, either topically or by code section, where the solution to the issue might be found. The contents search can be an important method for limiting the number of documents retrieved and better guaranteeing their pertinence. Like an index search, a contents search can be used in conjunction with a keyword search once the most relevant portion of the database is found. The contents search method treats electronic tax services as if they were printed, published services. Accordingly, researchers can drill down through the table of contents of a service just as they would thumb through the pages if they had books in front of them.

In IntelliConnect, a contents search is largely performed through the BROWSE window by consistently clicking the + signs by the practice area and content of choice. As shown in Exhibit 7-18, by clicking the + sign for the Tax Research Consultant in the Federal Tax practice area, the contents of that "book" are revealed. With each subsequent click, the limbs of the tree are ultimately opened until the document level is reached (no + sign, only the document icon will be shown). As it relates to the illustrative example, at this point it would be difficult to replicate the steps of an inexperienced researcher based on what has been performed previously in the chapter. Given the previous searches, finding the Individual chapter of the Tax Research Consultant and locating ¶18,152 is a fairly simple process.

Using the contents search for an IRC organized (annotated) source such as the code itself or the Standard Federal Tax Reporter follows a very similar process to the search of

EXHIBIT 7-18: CCH IntelliConnect Contents Search Topical Service

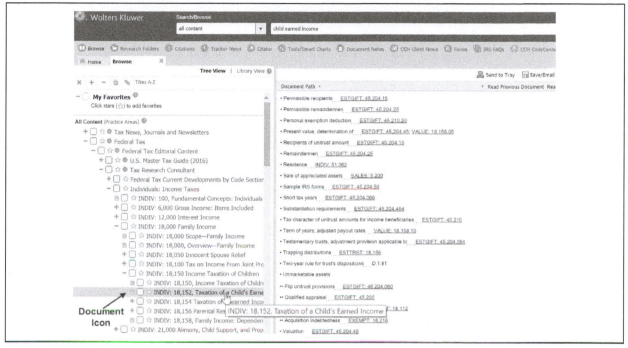

EXHIBIT 7-19: CCH IntelliConnect Contents Search Annotated Service

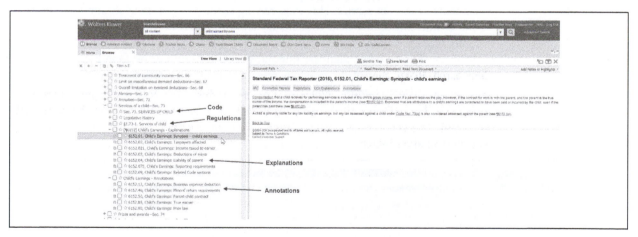

a topically organized source, as presented previously. In this case, the contents are organized by code section, which means that some degree of knowledge of the structure of the IRC is extremely helpful in finding the most relevant materials. As described in Chapter 3, the code structure is not without meaning, and thus the structure can be utilized with some success by even the newest of researchers. For the illustrative example, drilling down into the Standard Federal Tax Reporter allows the researcher to identify the income section (IRC §§ 61–90) fairly quickly (see Exhibit 7-19). The explanation provided by the Reporter in the overview gets to the heart of the illustrative example and provides links to the specific content and eventually back to the important primary sources. In addition, as previously described, the Standard Federal Tax Reporter presents not just explanations but also the code section itself, legislative history, the related Treasury Regulations, and annotations, which are the related court cases on the topic presented in the code section. In this way, primary sources are available in the BROWSE window with no additional searching required.

5-4 Citation Search

The final way to search through most tax services is the **citation search** (not to be confused with using a citator, discussed later in this chapter). IntelliConnect offers the ability to find citations in virtually all its databases. The key to a citation search is that you must know the code section, regulation, ruling, paragraph, or other source document by its citation form. To perform a citation search in IntelliConnect, simply click on CITATIONS above the BROWSE window (see Exhibit 7-20). IntelliConnect provides a template that can be completed for each type of possible source. In addition, the sources can be limited by selecting the appropriate source from the BROWSE window in the left pane. For example, if Federal Tax Primary Sources is already selected in the BROWSE window, then the related sources will be displayed in the citation search template as shown in Exhibit 7-20. If only Cases or Regulations or some other source is selected, then only those documents are presented in the citation search template.

If in the illustrative example, the researcher was already aware that § 73 might apply to the situation, using a Citation Search to find the code section as the starting point for identifying related documents may be the most efficient choice. Once the code section is located, continued research is simplified by use of the buttons located above the code section title (similar to those shown in Exhibit 7-12). These buttons will lead the researcher to committee reports, regulations, explanations, annotations, and other related documents in the tax service. However, relying exclusively on code section searches may be more time consuming than contents or keyword searches when there are several code sections relevant to the research issue.

Primary sources other than the Internal Revenue Code can be found through a citation search. Recall that in the previous research on the illustrative example, a Tax Court case ruling, *Allen v. Commissioner*, 50 T.C. 466 (1968), was located and provided additional details on the tax treatment of this particular issue. If the citation for that court

EXHIBIT 7-20:   CCH IntelliConnect Citation Search

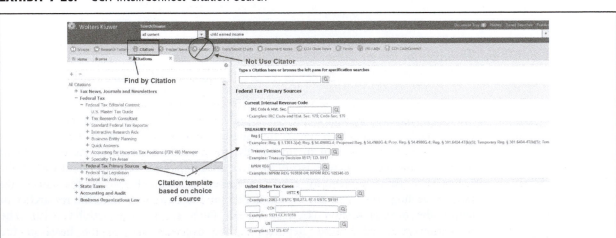

case is known, then the case can be found quickly by entering the citation into the citation search. The search window allows various citation forms to be used depending on the case reporter source of the ruling. IntelliConnect's database of court cases is limited to cases that cover tax issues and thus reflects CCH's best efforts to identify court rulings that have a tax impact.

SPOTLIGHT ON TAXATION

Citation Forms

There are seemingly endless ways to identify extracts of statutory, administrative, and judicial law by using a citation—a way of providing reference to an authoritative source. By using citations, the tax researcher establishes the credibility of his or her conclusion by identifying the primary sources of tax law but also leaves a trail of bread crumbs for any future reviewers to follow. Unfortunately, citation forms—the way these bread crumbs are structured and formatted—are as varied as the IRC is long. This book provides its own citation form (see inside front cover). Other popular forms of citation can come from the *Bluebook* (prepared by distinguished law schools in the United States), the *Chicago Manual of Style*, the *MLA* (Modern Language Association) *Style Manual*, and APA (American Psychological Association) style, among others. To confuse matters further, many state court systems (e.g., New York and California) as well as the U.S. Supreme Court use their own individual citation styles as well.

6 Citators

Besides confronting the tremendous volume of tax law, tax practitioners face the added dilemma that the tax law is in a constant state of change. The IRC is changed frequently by passage of federal legislation. Regulations are proposed, finalized, and withdrawn. Administrative rulings are issued, modified, superseded, and revoked or made obsolete by changes in the tax law. A case decided at one level may be appealed, with the higher court overruling the lower court's decision. A court may see a flaw in the reasoning it or another (equal or lower) court used in deciding an earlier case, or a court may use a different line of reasoning to reach a distinct decision in an area previously reviewed by other courts. When a court takes any action that relies on, rejects, or affects the holding of another case, the acting court refers to the affected case in its opinion. All this results in a tangle of inter-references among a vast number of cases. This daily change in the tax law makes it very difficult for a tax practitioner to know what law is current and what has been superseded or overruled.

Recall from the research process explained in Chapter 2 that an evaluation of the relevant primary authority must occur before conclusions can be developed. The evaluation of tax authority includes not only determining whether the authority is still valid but also making judgments regarding the precedential value of the primary sources. Common law relies heavily on the **precedential value** of cases, which can be defined as the legal authority established by the case. The legal authority of prior cases is considered when judges are issuing opinions in subsequent cases that contain similar facts or legal issues. Tax law also relies on the precedential value of tax cases and administrative rulings for guidance. The tax law attempts to maintain consistency in the treatment of similar issues, so taxpayers can anticipate the acceptable application of the law to their own situations. Each appellate opinion sets a precedent that applies to later cases.

It is important for the researcher to consider a case in context, to trace its judicially derived decision, and to monitor the reaction of subsequent court cases. This is even more important when the opinion is innovative.

Since practitioners must rely on tax law that is constantly evolving, they must determine if subsequent events have affected the legal standing of the sources upon which they rely. Thus, they need a tool to help them ascertain which legal sources provide strong precedents and which have little or no value. The tax professional could follow the reference threads from case to case or ruling to ruling, but this would be extremely tedious and would only identify earlier cases and rulings and not later sources that may have altered or overruled the case or ruling of interest. This latter information is critical for determining the validity of the document of interest. This chapter provides the most common methodology for ensuring that the tax laws, cases, and administrative documents supporting a client's tax position are up to date.

A **citator** is a tool through which a tax researcher can learn the history of a legal source and evaluate the strength of its holdings. Citators follow the threads in subsequent sources and summarize, in shorthand form, where the threads lead and what they mean. Before a researcher relies on the opinion in a case or analysis in a ruling (or even commits the time to read the document), it is important to ascertain its legal standing. Thus, when a case or ruling relevant to a client's tax situation is found, it is imperative that a citator be examined to determine how later legal sources have considered the document of interest. Because the legal profession has long recognized the need for this specialized information, citators were developed in the late 1800s, 100 years before online searches were possible.

To avoid confusion, it is important to learn the specific terminology that describes references between cases. When one case refers to another case, it cites the case. The case making reference to the other case is called the **citing case**. The case that is referenced is the **cited case**. The citing case will contain the name of the cited case and where the cited case can be found. The reference is called its **citation.** Although based on the same principle, a citator is not the same as the *citation search* described previously in this chapter.

A citator is a service that indexes cited cases, gives their full citations, and lists the citing cases and where each citing case can be found. A significant older case, one that establishes an important legal principle, may have been cited by hundreds of other cases. Thus, its entry in a citator would be extremely long and complex. A very recent case, or one examining a narrow aspect of the law, would have few cites, if any.

A citator will not provide all types of information about a case or a ruling. For instance, it does not guide the researcher to documents related to a case or ruling that do not specifically cite it. Also, citators may not always indicate when a case or ruling is no longer valid because of changes in the code, unless the code itself specifically identifies the case or a subsequent document makes a specific reference to the code overriding the case. This is because citators are created by searching primary sources for cites to the case or ruling. A researcher could perform the same search by using the case name or its official cite in a keyword search of databases containing all primary sources. Without access to a tax service, you might try a simple Google or Bing search on the case name. However, sifting through the results would be an arduous task and very inefficient.

Given the vast number of court cases and rulings issued annually, the citator is a vital tool in the research process. If the primary sources have *not* been checked through a citator, the research process is not complete. Not all citators are the same. For example, they may organize the lists of citing cases in distinctive schemes. Shepard's citator (discussed in Chapter 8) comes with color-coded symbols that allow the researcher to quickly identify the type of impact that a later court case may have had on the existing case under review. Depending on the researcher's purpose, one citator may be more appropriate than another. For example, a citator may list only citations that have a major impact on the logic or holding of the cited case. Another may list all citations. A researcher who is initially checking to make sure that a case has not been overruled would prefer the former. The citations may be annotated to indicate the type of impact the citing case has on the cited case (e.g., modified, overruled, or followed). A trial court case may be appealed, and each appellate court that hears the case creates additional citations. Because each of these decisions may be cited in other documents, a citator can organize cases by jurisdictional level.

The **CCH Citator** can be found in two ways. The first and most direct way is by using the CITATOR link located above the BROWSE window as shown in Exhibit 7-21.

From this screen, the case name or citation can be entered. In the illustrative example, *Allen v. Commissioner*, 50 T.C. 466 (1968), was found to be a case of interest. However, if the name *Allen v. Commissioner* is entered into the case name box, no documents are found. Recall from Chapter 5 and the citation forms listed on the inside front cover of the text that "v. Commissioner" is generally omitted from the standard citation format for a Tax Court case. However, a researcher can still find the *Allen* case in a number of ways. Because *Allen* is such a common name, entering "Allen" into the case name box will locate too many cases to scroll through. An alternative is to enter a more complete version of the case name, which is Richard Allen. Another alternative is to enter 50 T.C. 466 into the complete citation box. Finally, the CITATOR TEMPLATE shown in the CITATOR window contains all the common citation forms used in IntelliConnect and can be used as well.

The CCH Citator does not list A.F.T.R. (RIA citation format) citations and does not support A.F.T.R. citations with a template, nor will it recognize them as complete citations. Not accepting A.F.T.R. citations can cause problems when a journal article, published by

EXHIBIT 7-21:   CCH Citator

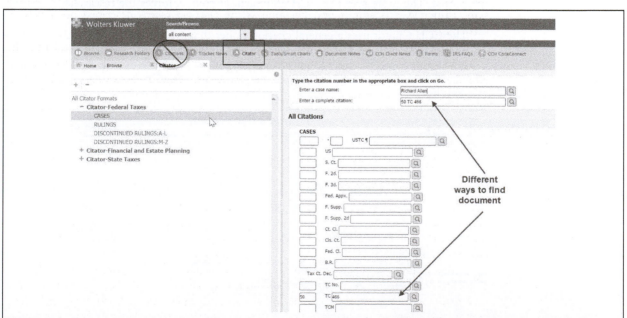

WG&L, for example, contains an A.F.T.R. 2d cite for a case with a common taxpayer name but the practitioner has access only to the CCH Citator and CCH court reporters.

The second way to use the citator on a case in IntelliConnect is directly from the case itself. For example, if during the course of researching the illustrative example, the researcher finds *Allen v. Commissioner*, simply clicking the CITATOR button above the BROWSE window opens up the citator for the case displayed in the document window. The results of running the citator on *Allen* are presented in Exhibit 7-22. CCH's citator acts as an annotation reference as well as a citator, by listing paragraph references where the case is examined in the Standard Federal Tax Reporter. This feature reduces the search time required to locate supplemental information regarding a case or ruling of interest. The tax service discussions help the researcher evaluate the case or ruling in the context of relevant code sections, regulations, and administrative sources of tax law.

Black bullets (Exhibit 7-22) in the results designate the cases in the direct history of the case of interest. For the *Allen* case, the Tax Court case was appealed to, and the ruling was ultimately affirmed by the Third Circuit Court of Appeals. Generally, the highest level court to address the case is listed first, and the trial-level court is listed last and generally in reverse chronology within each level of the court system. Next, other cases citing the *Allen* case are listed. Consequently, the court path chosen by the parties may not be as quickly identifiable as with other citators.

The CCH Citator lists the citing cases for each decision of the case. The decisions of the court of original jurisdiction, appeals court, and Supreme Court are all in one listing. However, only those citing cases that the CCH editors believe will serve as useful guides in evaluating the cited case's effectiveness as precedent are listed. Thus, the tax researcher is directed to those cases that may be most likely to develop, explain, criticize, or otherwise evaluate a cited case. This is in contrast to other citators (such as Shepard's, discussed in Chapter 8), which provide all cases mentioning the cited case and have separate listings for each court-level decision. Although the latter practice provides a level of thoroughness that may be useful, the CCH editorial screening procedure guards against the possibility of being overwhelmed by the sheer volume of citing cases presented. The more selective CCH approach, of course, forces the researcher to rely on an editor's evaluation concerning the usefulness of the citing cases.

The CCH Citator uses a general citation rather than a specific location citation, which means that the citation for the citing case is the first page of the citing case and not the

EXHIBIT 7-22: CCH Citator Results

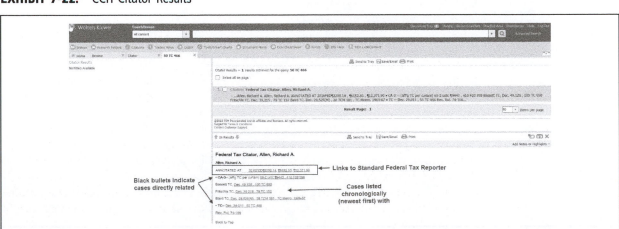

point where the case of interest is discussed by the citing case. If the citing case is long, the researcher can waste valuable time identifying where the citing case discusses the case of interest. The easiest way to find the exact citation is to use the Find function within your browser (Ctrl-F) and type in the case name (or some other unique identifier).

The CCH Citator provides the citation to its court reporter, the U.S. Tax Cases (U.S.T.C.), and no more than two other parallel citations. Most other citator services list most, if not all, parallel citations. CCH also does not have a Table of Authorities or similar function.

Finally, the CCH Citator does not provide evaluations of the citing cases (Exhibit 7-22) nor references to headnotes. While the CCH U.S.T.C. provides headnote information and back references to its tax service, it does not number or label this analysis. The omission of these evaluation sources is a significant drawback of the CCH Citator. However, recall that CCH experts have already combed through the citing cases to select the most relevant ones. With cases having numerous issues and lists of citing cases, knowing how each citing case interpreted the different tax issues can substantially reduce the number of cases the researcher reads. The only information that can be gleaned from glancing at the *Allen* citator entry is that Allen was affirmed by the appellate court and has a fairly small number of cases citing it. One cannot even tell if the decision is still valid, which is critical when relying on the *Allen* case.

7 Other Tax Law Sources

Although the vast majority of tax law, including almost all primary tax law sources, can be found in the tax services such as CCH IntelliConnect, tax professionals also need to consider new developments, recently issued treatises and journal articles, and other tools that may be available to assist with staying on top of their tax practice and serving their clients. Three additional sources of helpful tax information can be found in IntelliConnect: tax treatises, tax periodicals, and CLIENTS' TOOLS. The availability of these items depends on your school's or employer's subscription.

7-1 Tax Treatises

Tax treatises are editorial analyses that provide in-depth coverage of a particular tax area. Written by prominent experts in the specific field, a treatise offers numerous examples and expert insights on a single tax area, for example, federal taxation of partners and partnerships. Treatises provide a compromise between comprehensive coverage of a topic and the ability to locate relevant information quickly. Topics covered tend to be those that tax professionals are likely to encounter in practice. Coverage is more comprehensive than would likely be found in a periodical or journal article.

IntelliConnect offers tax treatises related to corporate, partnership, S corporation, and limited liability company taxation. Treatises are a rich source of information on these topics and can be found under TAX TREATISES in the BROWSE window. Each treatise contains multiple chapters of information organized by topic. Similar to the other explanatory materials in IntelliConnect, within the treatise the explanations are accompanied by links to the primary source materials. In addition, by clicking the RELATED INFORMATION button that appears at the top of each page, all the typical IntelliConnect databases that cover that specific topic are revealed in the document window for further research. Typically, a treatise is searched by entering the TABLE OF CONTENTS in the BROWSE window; however, treatises can be included in the selection of possible databases when performing a keyword search.

7-2 Tax Periodicals

Tax periodicals contain articles and news briefs that are designed to keep readers up to date in specific or general areas of the tax law. These articles might contain an in-depth review of a recently decided court case, a broad analysis of the factors relevant to a practitioner's decision on whether to make a certain tax accounting election, or a call for reform of a statute by a neutral (or biased) observer. Tax articles can suggest new viewpoints on tax issues, give guidance for solving complex problems, or just explain a new law in a readable form.

IntelliConnect provides access to CCH's flagship journal on tax news and analysis, *TAXES—The Tax Magazine*. This monthly magazine contains critical analyses by tax experts including academics, professionals, and other tax practitioners. Articles cover a variety of tax topics and vary from a brief overview of a potential tax bill to an in-depth analysis of a detailed area of tax law to a thought piece on how tax reforms might alter the business landscape. As with all other databases in IntelliConnect, all the current news and journal information can be searched using the keyword search by selecting those sources.

CCH publishes a newsletter for tax professionals titled the **CCH Federal Tax Weekly**. This brief weekly publication is prepared by CCH staff, including tax lawyers and accountants, who receive additional input from tax professionals. The newsletter covers IRS tax guidance, tax litigation, congressional developments, and practitioner reactions to tax planning news and trends. The Current folder contains the current year's newsletters while the Archive includes previous years. **CCH Tax Briefings** and PwC Insights (a publication by PricewaterhouseCoopers) are also available in this practice area. These are short newsletter-style documents that cover any major tax legislation recently passed or important court cases recently decided. If Congress passes a new tax bill or a major court ruling on taxes is made, a tax researcher can find a quick explanation of the development's effects, prepared by experts who have been following the tax or case throughout its evolution.

7-3 Utilizing Tax Treatises and Periodicals in Tax Research

With the right treatise or article that is on point with a tax issue, the practitioner is able to, in effect, use the author as a research associate by capitalizing on the author's expert judgments and references, thereby saving hours of research time. Keep in mind, however, that tax treatises and periodicals are secondary sources of the tax law and therefore should not be cited as a controlling authority, especially when primary sources supporting the position are available. Fortunately, in the online environment, researchers can use the treatise or article references to find the pertinent primary tax sources simply by clicking on the appropriate link. In addition, articles are written based on the existing tax law and are not updated to reflect any changes in the tax law since publication. With those caveats aside, researchers who ignore the tax treatises and periodicals might be accused, at best, of reinventing the wheel and, at worst, of professional malpractice.

Traditionally, citing treatises and articles in professional tax research is limited to two situations: (1) the researcher is referring to the author's analysis and conclusions as stated in an article, or (2) the researcher cannot find any controlling primary sources of law and a secondary source addresses the issues. Tax articles are now being cited more frequently in case opinions. When lacking both relevant primary law sources and adequate judicial staff, the authors of these case opinions may draw on tax articles to support the views of the court. In any event, it is imperative that researchers understand the practical implications of using secondary law sources.

7-4 Other Research Tools

CCH also provides access to and interpretation of current events and changes in tax law. All these sources of tax information can be found in the TAX NEWS, JOURNALS AND NEWS-LETTERS area of content in the BROWSE window (see Exhibit 7-23). In addition to daily tax events that are posted on the IntelliConnect homepage, a variety of tax news can also be found under the practice areas. News and new tax developments are provided each day for federal and state tax issues under TODAY'S FEDERAL AND STATE TAX NEWS HIGH-LIGHTS. In addition, under FEDERAL TAXES (see Exhibit 7-23), IntelliConnect provides all the information necessary for a tax professional to monitor and examine the latest federal tax law changes from a variety of sources, such as new legislation, Treasury rulings and other guidance, the White House, and of course recently decided court cases. This source also includes press releases and other federal-tax-related information released by government agencies and Congress.

Although not available on many school-provided subscriptions, IntelliConnect also allows users to establish CCH CLIENT NEWS to have specific updates or new information e-mailed directly. For example, if a researcher were interested in getting the latest information on federal legislation on applying state sales taxes on Internet purchases, a channel could be set up using key words and specific news sources within IntelliConnect to provide the latest congressional action cases or other information with respect to this topic.

Another source for the latest tax news is the ADVANCE RELEASE documents available under the Tax News Journals and Newsletters practice area. This library of information includes the full text of source documents released within the last 90 days by the IRS or the courts. New Treasury Regulations that are made available for comment can be found here. The CCH LEGISLATION NEWSWIRE follows bills introduced or passed through either or both houses of Congress. Clicking on the link provides access to CCH's public Website and the blog-type webpage that covers tax legislation and other tax headlines on an ongoing basis.

EXHIBIT 7-23:   IntelliConnect News and Journals

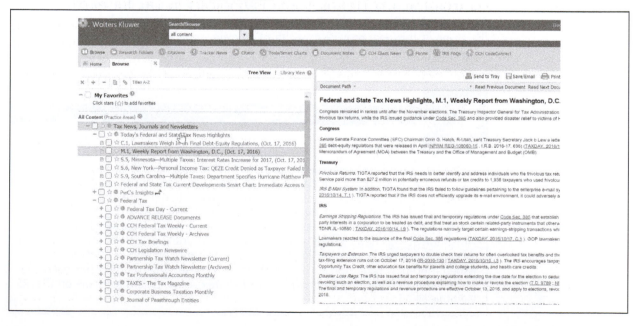

EXHIBIT 7-24: IntelliConnect Tools and Smart Charts

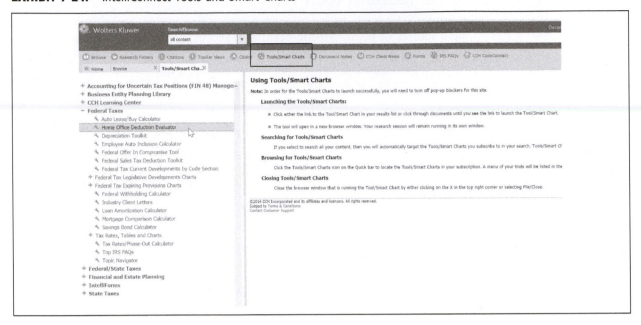

Finally, CCH also has developed a variety of tools that can be accessed from the TOOLS/SMART CHARTS tab above the BROWSE window (see Exhibit 7-24). Charts that provide quick access to tax rates, deduction limits, depreciation tables, and other frequently used tax information are available at a single click. Online calculators to assist with loan amortization and life expectancy computations are just a few examples of the bevy of tools made available to subscribers. Although specific tools are not available in all subscriptions and not always useful for tax research, researchers should be aware of their existence in order to find information quickly and in a manner that can be customized to a particular client. The bevy of tools, forms, and other practice aids, although beyond the scope of this text, provide a wealth of efficiency-making improvements for those in tax practice.

SPOTLIGHT ON TAXATION

Frivolous Taxes

Each year, the IRS receives a large number of tax returns filed by taxpayers who, relying on false, frivolous, or phony arguments, claim zero tax liability. Each year, the IRS issues a list of the Dirty Dozen: scams being used that frequently end with bad results for the taxpayer. Common tax-avoidance schemes asserting that "the payment of federal income tax is voluntary," "taxes are not legal because the 16th Amendment was never ratified," or "taxpayers are entitled to a refund of all Social Security taxes paid over a lifetime" have become common enough that the IRS has issued a 60-plus page document explaining why these schemes have not been supported in the courts. *The Truth about Frivolous Tax Arguments* is available on the IRS Website.

SUMMARY

Many commercial services are available for performing tax research, and no one service is the best for all practitioners. While the services provide different features, all are most efficient when the organization of the service facilitates research of the issues in a client's tax situation. Thus, each tax service has its place in tax research, and practitioners must determine which products they are most comfortable with and which fit their firms' normal research requirements.

Changes in technology and the tax services are continual. The same changes occur in the practitioner's business. Consequently, the practitioner's comfort level with products and technology and the research needs will change over time. Practitioners should evaluate their tax resource choices often, and at the least once a year, when it is time to renew services.

The tax researcher should employ commercial services as gateways to the primary sources and not as a substitute for primary source research. Tax services can make the research process more efficient and productive, but their use should not replace a thorough review of primary sources and the researcher's professional judgment.

KEY WORDS

By the time you complete this chapter, you should be comfortable discussing each of the following terms. If you need additional review of any of these items, return to the appropriate material in the chapter or consult the glossary to this text.

annotated tax service, p. 224
annotations, p. 224
Boolean connectors, p. 237
CCH Citator, p. 245
CCH Federal Tax Weekly, p. 248
CCH IntelliConnect, p. 222
CCH Tax Briefings, p. 248
citation, p. 244

citation search, p. 242
citator, p. 244
cited case, p. 244
citing case, p. 244
commercial tax service, p. 222
contents search, p. 240
index search, p. 237
keyword search, p. 232
precedential value, p. 243

proximity connectors, p. 237
Standard Federal Tax Reporter, p. 229
tax periodicals, p. 248
Tax Research Consultant, p. 228
tax treatises, p. 247
topical tax services, p. 225
U.S. Master Tax Guide, p. 229

DISCUSSION QUESTIONS

1. What is the function of a commercial tax service?

2. Why would a practitioner need a tax service when most primary tax sources are available for free on the Internet?

3. Describe the four common search methods used in CCH IntelliConnect.

4. Compare and contrast the general organization of an annotated tax database with that of a topical tax database.

5. IntelliConnect contains four important windows that are used to search and present tax information to the researcher. Name the four windows and provide a brief description of each.

6. Name at least two practice areas in IntelliConnect and describe the contents briefly.

7. Select three different primary sources, one from each area of tax law (legislative, administrative, and judicial), and provide a specific example of a source that is available in IntelliConnect.

8. Compare and contrast primary and editorial materials and explain the ways in which each can be important to a tax researcher.

9. List the three significant editorial services provided by IntelliConnect and discuss the differences between them.

10. Why should a researcher avoid searching all the practice areas of IntelliConnect in a single keyword search?

11. Why are the footnote links in IntelliConnect's editorial services so important to tax researchers?

12. Explain how the RELATED DOCUMENTS links provide researchers with an efficient researching capability.

13. What do the HISTORY tabs in IntelliConnect provide to the researcher?

14. Describe the Boolean connectors, proximity connectors, and wildcard characters available in IntelliConnect.

15. What is an advantage to using an index search to find documents of interest?

16. How can a researcher narrow a search through the index for only specific relevant terms and avoid scrolling through the entire alphabet?

17. Describe how your search results would differ if you use the asterisk wildcard versus placing the search term in quotation marks and/or turning off the thesaurus: for example, *dependent*, *"dependent,"* and *depend**, with or without the thesaurus applied.

18. Why should a contents search typically be left to a more experienced researcher?

19. Explain how a citation search differs from using a citator.

20. Why does the researcher need to determine the precedential value of a case?

21. Why is it difficult to know whether a document retrieved four months ago is still valid law?

22. Describe the function of a citator in the tax research process.

23. Distinguish between the following terms: *cited case*, *citing case*, *citation*, and *cites*.

24. Citators do not provide all information related to a case. What kind of information do citators not provide?

25. In what way is finding an article on point with a practitioner's tax issue similar to hiring someone to do the research?

26. Why are tax journals and newsletters generally not cited as authority in professional tax research? When would it be appropriate to cite tax journals or newsletters as authority?

EXERCISES

27. Using CCH IntelliConnect Tax Research Consultant:
    a. What is the heading for paragraph INDIV 100?
    b. What is the heading for paragraph CCORP 100 (under Entities)?
    c. What is the last paragraph number in EXCISE?
    d. What is the first item listed in the index to the Tax Research Consultant under the letter H?

28. Using CCH IntelliConnect Tax Research Consultant:
    a. Using the + symbols in the BROWSE window, how many subheadings for Individuals exist in the contents?
    b. What paragraph covers the basis allocation for charitable deductions for bargain sales to charity?
    c. In the Tax Research Consultant, select the following headings to perform a keyword search for the term *auto*: ¶39,000 Personal Deductions and ¶51,000 Charitable Deductions (perform your search without quotation marks). How many documents are in the results window?

    d. In the Tax Research Consultant, select the following headings to perform a keyword search for the term *auto*[*]: ¶39,000 Personal Deductions and ¶51,000 Charitable Deductions (perform your search without quotation marks). How many documents are in the results window?

    e. Explain why the searches in parts c and d above bring up different numbers of results.

29. Using a contents search in IntelliConnect's Standard Federal Tax Reporter:

    a. What is the title of I.R.C. § 265?

    b. How many regulations exist related to § 265?

    c. What is the paragraph number of the explanations covering "wholly exempt" income?

    d. Using a contents search, locate the § 265 related annotations and provide the name of the case that discussed legal fees and expenses for a wrongful death claim against a father serving as administrator of his son's estate.

30. You are trying to find the current standard deduction amount for an individual.

    a. Using a contents search, locate Chapter 1 (Individuals), Computation of Tax Liability, in the U.S. Master Tax Guide for the most current year. What is the standard deduction for a single filer for the most current year?

    b. Browse the contents of the Standard Federal Tax Reporter and select Deductions—Secs. 161–249. How many results do you get when you perform a keyword search for that selected content in the Standard Federal Tax Reporter for the keywords "standard deduction" (without quotation marks)?

    c. Reperform the search in part b, except now use the keywords "standard deduction" (using quotation marks)—how many results?

    d. How many of the results from the search performed in part c are from the Internal Revenue Code?

    e. Use the history tabs and click on the browse tab (your U.S. Master Tax Guide document [paragraph 126] should still be in the window). What is the primary source link for the most recent standard deduction amounts?

31. Use the current Internal Revenue Code in the IntelliConnect Federal Tax database to answer the following questions:

    a. Which code sections result from a search for "tackle box" in the current code?

    b. Examine the resulting code sections. What is the rate of tax imposed on the sale of a tackle box?

    c. In the code section that provides the rate of tax on tackle boxes, use the RELEVANT DOCUMENT link to CCH Explanations. Based on the resulting explanations, what is the maximum excise tax amount on fishing rods or poles (if any)?

    d. Change the selection in the Search/Browse drop-down menu next to the NAVIGATION BAR to Within Document, and keyword search for "quiver." Does an article designed solely for transporting arrows when not in use meet the definition of a taxable quiver?

    e. Follow the footnote link to the primary source on quivers. Which regulation covers this topic?

32. Use the CCH IntelliConnect Federal Tax database to answer the following questions:

    a. What are the major Federal Tax database categories provided?

    b. Select 2007 in the Federal Tax Archives. What is the highest amount of taxable income a single tax-payer can earn before paying a 35 percent marginal tax rate in 2006? (Hint: Use the Master Tax Guide—2007.) When would it be useful to know what the IRC was in a prior year?

    c. Find the Action on Decisions listed in Letter Rulings & IRS Positions and perform a keyword search for "Milligan." Did the IRS acquiesce to the *Milligan* decision?

    d. Look at Bills Worth Watching in the Federal Tax Legislation database. Which bills does CCH think are worth watching?

33. Use the CCH IntelliConnect Browse to locate topical indexes for answering the following questions:
    a. What are the major headings for the letter "Y" in the current Internal Revenue Code topical index?
    b. What are the first and last countries listed under the letter "I" in the Tax Research Consultant topical index?
    c. Find the topical index for the Protecting Americans from Tax Hikes Act of 2015 (under Federal Tax Legislation). What is the treatment of death benefits paid to the surviving spouse of a public safety officer killed in the line of duty?
    d. Explain the function of the Topic Navigator that is located in the TOOLS/SMART CHARTS, Federal Taxes (if your subscription has this).

34. Use the CCH IntelliConnect Browse function and select the Federal Tax Editorial Content heading to answer the following questions:
    a. Using Quick Answers Tax Rates, Tables and Credits, determine the personal exemption amounts for the previous three years.
    b. In the Interactive Research Aids for Tax Research Consultant, for Individuals, who is the author of the decision tree for qualified moving expenses?
    c. Using the Master Tax Guide, determine whether the Adoption Credit is a refundable or nonrefundable credit. In which paragraph number is the discussion of this credit located?
    d. What is the most recent Joint Committee on Taxation *Bluebook* available in the Federal Tax Legislation heading?

35. Use the CCH IntelliConnect Practice Tools database to answer the following questions:
    a. Using the Election and Compliance Toolkit, determine what election might need to be made to elect to expense the cost of property under IRC § 179 (not mine equipment or in a controlled group) and when the election is due.
    b. Using the Depreciation Toolkit, determine the depreciation in year 5 for $45,000 of Dairy Cattle, 150 percent DB method for Farm Property with a half-year convention.
    c. Using the Federal/State Taxes, Tax Calendar, prepare a calendar for the current year for all taxes for the state within which your college is located. Print one month that shows payment due dates.
    d. Explain whether the Practice Tools offered in the Main Menu (where BROWSE, CITATIONS, and so forth are located) are the same as in the Practice Tools, listed in the expanding BROWSE option.

36. Use CITATIONS in the main menu to perform a citation search for the following exercises:
    a. Find paragraph BUSEXP 24,118.30 in the Federal Tax Consultant. What issue does this discuss? (Hint: Federal Tax Consultant (FTC) citations must have both the comma in the paragraph and the trailing 0 after the decimal.)
    b. Find IRC § 221 in the Standard Federal Tax Reporter. What does this code section deal with?
    c. From § 221 in the Standard Federal Tax Reporter, use the Document Path and select Interest on Education Loans—Sec 221. In the BROWSE window, expand the tree for § 221. Which Standard Federal Tax Reporter paragraph covers this issue?
    d. Return to the CITATIONS tab and select current Internal Revenue Code from the Federal Tax Primary Sources heading. Use the citation template to find § 221. Using Document Path, confirm whether the Standard Federal Tax Reporter is available from the Document path links.
    e. Use the RELATED DOCUMENTS button for ANNOTATIONS at the top of § 221. Which paragraph of the Standard Federal Tax Reporter is shown?

37. Use the CCH IntelliConnect Tax Research Consultant to perform a keyword search on the topic of making an election to defer the determination of whether an activity is not engaged in for profit (hobby) until after the fourth year. Use the following terms: "hobby election defer."
    a. How many results were found? How many are shown?

b. Open the document STAGES: ¶9,062.10. Check the document path. Based on the document path, which topic is covered by this broad section of the Tax Research Consultant?

c. Read the document and find the link that discusses filing Form 5213. Which paragraph is linked to?

d. Expand the results in the results window to reveal all results. What is the paragraph of the two results found in the BUSEXP chapters?

e. Start a new search of the Tax Research Consultant but this time use the following keywords: "profit motive election defer." What is the first result listed? Which search terms resulted in a more direct search? Why?

38. Using CCH IntelliConnect, perform a keyword search on the topic of making an election to defer the determination of whether an activity is not engaged in for profit (hobby) until after the fourth year. Use the following terms: "hobby election defer."

a. Use the Standard Federal Tax Reporter and the Tax Research Consultant and perform the search separately in each; then use the Standard Federal Tax Reporter and the Tax Research Consultant together in the same search. Which approach provided the best search results for finding the applicable tax law?

b. Use the results of the previous search, links, and related documents buttons to identify the code section applicable to this issue.

c. How does the code section answer the question regarding how to make the election?

d. Using the RELATED DOCUMENTS button for Regulations, what does Reg. § 1.183-3 say about making the election?

e. Which regulation discusses the election, and what is the status of the regulation? When was it issued?

39. Use the IntelliConnect Citations to answer the following questions:

a. What does IRS Notice 2016-55 discuss? On what date was it issued?

b. Who is the author of "New Temporary Regulations Restrain Inversions" in *TAXES—The Tax Magazine*, Vol. 94, No. 10?

c. What is the title of IRS Publication 946?

d. What is the title of P.L. No. 114-239?

40. Use the CCH IntelliConnect Federal Tax to answer the following questions:

a. Find the Code Sections Added Amended or Repealed under Federal Tax Legislation. What public laws (numbers) amended the code in the current year?

b. Is a former IRS employee eligible to become an enrolled agent without taking an exam? How many years does the former IRS employee have to apply for treatment as an enrolled agent? (Hint: See Circular 230.)

c. Where can you find guidance on how to write an offer in compromise?

d. Use the Checklist for Deductions in the U.S. Master Tax Guide to determine whether conventions on cruise ships are deductible. Once found, use Related Information and Related Documents to find the code section that covers the deduction for conventions on cruise ships. What is the section? Use as specific a citation form as possible.

41. Use the CCH IntelliConnect Citator to answer the following questions regarding Notice 2010-10:

a. Where is the notice located in the Internal Revenue Bulletin?

b. Where is the notice annotated?

c. What other notice has Notice 2010-10 been cited in?

42. Use the CCH IntelliConnect Citator to evaluate the 1956 *William George* Tax Court case.

a. What is the citation for the case?

b. What is the title of the paragraph where *George* is annotated?

    c. What Code section is related to the *George* case?

    d. A revenue ruling cites the George case. What is the citation and title? How does the revenue ruling evaluate the *George* case?

43. Use CCH IntelliConnect Citator to answer the following questions:

    a. Find the discontinued Miscellaneous MS 347; 1950-1 C.B. 281 ruling. (Hint: Use Cumulative Bulletin citation to find it.) What is its current standing and why?

    b. Find court decision 93 T.C. 67. Give the name of the case and all its parallel citations.

    c. Find Treasury Decision 9568. Give the date it was filed with the Federal Register, code sections to which it applies, and the dates of any corrections.

44. Use the CCH IntelliConnect Citator to evaluate the 290th revenue ruling issued in 1955.

    a. What is its complete Cumulative Bulletin citation? Is this revenue ruling still valid?

    b. What tax issue does the revenue ruling address?

    c. List the citations of any cases that cite Revenue Ruling 1955-290.

    d. In what paragraph of the CCH service was this ruling initially discussed?

45. Use the CCH IntelliConnect Citator to answer the following questions regarding the 19th revenue procedure of 2002:

    a. What does this procedure address? Which code sections are involved?

    b. What is its current status?

    c. What types of pronouncements have cited this procedure? What is the most current citing of the procedure?

46. Use the CCH IntelliConnect Citator to evaluate the 2006 *Gwendolyn A. Ewing* case.

    a. What is the case's citation, and what tax issues does the case address?

    b. What is the case's direct judicial history?

    c. Where is the case annotated in the Standard Federal Income Tax Reporter?

    d. The *Haag* case (2005-1 U.S.T.C. ¶50,131) cites *Ewing*. What is the *Haag* treatment of the *Ewing* case?

CHAPTER 8

Other Tax Services and Tax Periodicals

LEARNING OBJECTIVES

- Utilize the major features of other tax and legal commercial services for research.
- Use keyword, citation, and content searches to identify relevant materials in other commercial services.
- Research tax topics in the numerous tax periodicals and journals available outside of the tax services.

CHAPTER OUTLINE

IN ADDITION TO THE TWO MAIN SERVICES covered in Chapters 6 and 7,[1] a number of other tax services are available for use by tax professionals. These services can be as comprehensive as Thomson Reuters Checkpoint and Wolters Kluwer IntelliConnect but tend to be less widely adopted by colleges and universities. The lower subscription adoption rate, however, should not be seen as a signal of lower quality or less valuable information. Each of the services covered in this chapter contains much, if not all, of the information provided in the two major players in the tax services industry. In some instances, even more information or a unique form or structure that many tax professionals find advantageous can be found. Excepting issues of cost, at least one of these other services would be a beneficial addition to any tax service portfolio.

Another valuable source of tax information is the wealth of tax periodicals and journals. Tax periodicals contain a variety of articles and news briefs that are designed to keep readers up to date in specific or general areas of the tax law. These articles might contain an in-depth review of a recently decided court case, a broad analysis of the factors relevant to a practitioner's decision on whether to make a certain tax accounting election, or a call for reform of a statute by a neutral (or biased) observer. Tax articles can suggest new viewpoints on tax issues, give guidance for solving complex problems, or just explain a new law in a readable form. All of these resources are very useful to tax practitioners.

1 BNA Bloomberg

BNA Bloomberg Tax & Accounting Center (BNA) offers numerous products covering all areas of tax and accounting. Many are available on mobile devices though the Quick Tax Reference app. However, BNA is best known in the tax community as the publisher of the **BNA Tax Management Portfolios.** The portfolios are unique because they are written for professionals, by professionals. Practitioners are the preferred authors because they are more sensitive to the information requirements of other practitioners. For this reason, the BNA portfolios are a favorite research tool of individuals practicing tax. Most commercial tax and legal services (e.g., Checkpoint, IntelliConnect, LexisNexis, and Westlaw) offer the portfolios on their web platforms as add-on subscriptions.

SPOTLIGHT ON TAXATION

BNA

In 1926, David Lawrence started the *United States Daily* as the country's "first truly national newspaper." In 1929, Lawrence established Bureau of National Affairs (BNA) as a division of the United States News Publishing Company for the purpose of reporting, interpreting, and explaining the workings of the federal government and its impact on national economics. After the passage of the 1954 Internal Revenue Code, Leonard L. Silverstein, an attorney and a former IRS chief counsel, partnered with BNA to create the Tax Management Portfolios. He realized that there was a need for specialized tax information written by leading tax practitioners. Today, BNA is owned by Bloomberg, provides 350 news services, and is the largest independent publisher of business and government analysis for professionals.

---

[1]This chapter assumes that either Chapter 6 or 7 has already been covered and that a basic understanding of how a tax service operates has been achieved.

EXHIBIT 8-1: BNA Source Materials

Expert Analysis	BNA's Portfolios along with Fast Answers (a set of FAQs by tax area) and State Tax Navigators
News and Commentary	Extensive information and a variety of sources such as the Daily Tax Report, Financial Planning Journal, Green Incentives Monitor, International Tax Monitor, and many more
Laws & Regulations and Agency Documents	Internal Revenue Code, Treasury Regulations, and a variety of other primary sources of federal and state tax law
Cases	Federal and state tax cases from trial and appellate level courts
Practice Tools	Forms, form guides, charts, and tables for a variety of federal and state taxes
Tax Prep Guides	How-to guides to assist practitioners in preparing common tax forms and schedules
Indexes and Finding Aids	Topical indexes of portfolios and various other sources within the BNA service
Events and Training	Access to BNA training
States	Access to a cross-section of state tax-related sources such as the portfolios, state legislation and regulations, and court cases

BNA is best known for its portfolio series; however, BNA also offers access to a wealth of other tax law and information. Access varies by subscription level, but in addition to the portfolios, BNA offers a number of additional sources as presented in Exhibit 8-1. EXPERT ANALYSIS is the area containing the vast majority of the portfolios (discussed in greater detail in subsequent sections) that represent the hallmark of the BNA service. NEWS AND COMMENTARY has a wealth of information and a variety of sources such as the *Daily Tax Report, Financial Planning Journal, Green Incentives Monitor, International Tax Monitor*, and many more. The primary sources of tax law such as the Internal Revenue Code and regulations are contained within the LAWS & REGULATIONS and AGENCY DOCUMENTS areas. The CASES area contains relevant tax cases. Like the other two major players, BNA also offers a wealth of tools and practice aids for professionals to use for assistance in servicing clients. The STATES practice area is an organization of materials from other sources but structured by state. Thus, if a researcher is looking for all the materials available for a particular state, this link provides the most efficient route.

1-1 BNA Portfolios

The more than 500 BNA portfolios are classified into five series: Federal, Estate, International, State, and Accounting. The size of the portfolio library varies as topics are added, deleted, or combined. As shown in Exhibit 8-2, BNA's online offering is structured similarly to those of other tax services. A list of practice areas is provided in tabs across the top, with the detail of each tab presented in the main window. Access to each area is based on the specific subscription. The portfolios can be accessed directly by clicking on the headings under EXPERT ANALYSIS. Portfolios are grouped by area of common topic into COLLECTIONS (e.g., there are multiple portfolios on income tax accounting that will be displayed if one clicks on that heading).

1-2 Searching the BNA Collections

BNA offers four different ways to do a keyword search in the tax databases: Quick Search, Advanced Search, Go To, and Guided Search. Each of these search techniques is located at or near the QUICK SEARCH box located in the upper right corner of the main

EXHIBIT 8-2:   BNA Main Window

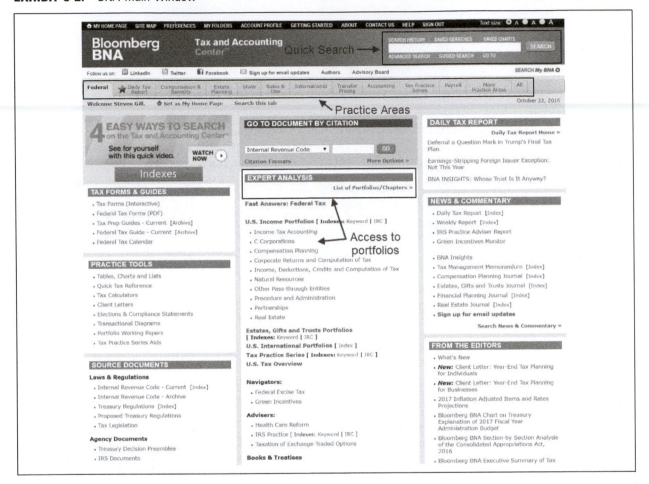

screen. As with other keyword search functions, to perform a quick search, enter the terms in the SEARCH box and click SEARCH. The entire BNA subscription is searched unless a collection has been previously selected. If a portfolio or collection has been selected by browsing to that portfolio or collection, the choice to search just that collection or all items is made available under the QUICK SEARCH box. Boolean and proximity connectors are available to use as presented in the BNA Help Table shown in Exhibit 8-3.

The search function in BNA ignores certain terms because of their frequency of usage in language. BNA refers to these as "stop words." If stop words are included with other terms in a search, they are ignored. If the only terms in a search are stop words, the search will result in an error. Stop words are listed in Exhibit 8-4.

The advanced search provides additional flexibility and depth for the search and can be accessed by clicking ADVANCED SEARCH under the quick search box as presented in Exhibit 8-2. Once the advanced search page is open, the researcher must (1) select the collection(s) to search, (2) enter the terms to search for, (3) select the fields to search (if desired), and (4) limit the search to documents within certain dates (if desired). The Boolean connectors or search operators presented in Exhibit 8-3 are available to click within the ADVANCED SEARCH to enter the connector into the keyword search. As presented in Exhibit 8-5, the researcher selects a collection to search by clicking the box(es)

EXHIBIT 8-3: BNA Search Connectors

Operator	Description of Function	Example
And	Find x **and** y in same document. A blank space between terms also indicates the **and** operator.	Find petroleum **and** election **and** eligibility.
	Note: the ampersand character "&" is not a search operator; it is searched as a character.	Search results list files containing *petroleum*, *election*, and *eligibility*.
Or	Find either x **or** y in the same file. The symbol | **(vertical line)** also indicates the use of the **or** operator.	Find petroleum **or** oil. Search results list files containing either term or both terms.
Not	Find x but **not** y in the same file.	Find petroleum **not** oil.
		Search results list files containing the term *petroleum* but not the term *oil*.
		Note: When using **not** with the **date** search operator, be sure to place parenthesis around the **not** statement. Thus, ("exxon valdez" not gulf) date(year to date) is a valid search, while "exxon valdez" not gulf and date(year to date) is not.
""	Find an exact phrase, ordered as listed within the quotation marks.	Find "stipulated election agreement"
		Search results list files containing the words together and in order: **stipulated election agreement**
near/n	Find x within **n** words of y, in any order; n = a number.	Election **near/2** stipulated
		Search results list files containing *election* within two words of *stipulated*.
/s	Find x and y within the same sentence in any order.	Election**/s** stipulated
		Search results list files containing *election* and *stipulated* within the same sentence in any order.
/p	Find x and y within the same paragraph in any order.	Election**/p** agreement
		Search results list files containing *election* and *agreement* in the same paragraph.
?	Wildcard that replaces one character at a time. Use more? to replace more characters, if needed.	Peter??n search results list files containing *peterson* and *petersen*.
	Wildcard that replaces zero or more characters in a word or number.	Elect*
		Search results list files containing *electric*, *electric's*, *electrical*, *electronic*, *elective*, *elects*, *elected*, *election*.
*	**note:** This wildcard must follow a root of at least three characters.	**note:** el*, 3* yield no search results.

adjacent to the desired publications. The arrows next to each heading allow the area to be expanded to show available content within each heading. A single collection or multiple collections can be selected to search simultaneously. Search terms are entered into the appropriate box and can be searched; however, BNA also offers an alternative to search specific fields within the documents. The FIELDS selection allows for the option to search only the selected field. The fields are populated in the drop-down menu based on the collections selected previously. Searching SHARED FIELDS will present all the fields that are shared within the databases selected, whereas showing the FIELDS FROM ALL SELECTED COLLECTIONS will present all the fields in each collection (whether they are shared across collections or not). The advanced search option also permits a DATE-RANGE LIMITATION on the

EXHIBIT 8-4: BNA Stop Words

about, above, along, also, although, am, an, and, any, are, aren't

be, because, been, but, by

cannot, could, couldn't

did, didn't, do, does, doesn't

either, etc, even, ever

for, from, further

get, gets, got

had, hardly, has, hasn't, have, having, he, hence, her, hereby, herein, hereof, hereon, hereto, herewith, him, his, how, however

is, if, into, it, its

more, most, mr

nor, now, not

of, onto, other, our

really

said, she, should, shouldn't, since, so, some, such

than, that, the, their, them, then, there, thereby, therefore, therefrom, therein, thereof, thereon, thereto, therewith, these, they, this, those, through, thus

under, until, unto, upon

very

was, wasn't, we, were, what, when, where, whereas, whereby, wherein, whether, which, while, who, whom, whose, why, with, without, would, wouldn't

you, your

search. In a similar way, an additional search capability can be found on the main page. Within many of the content areas is a SEARCH function (see Exhibit 8-2) that performs much like a preselected advanced search wherein only the collections within that heading are searched.

BNA also offers a GUIDED SEARCH. This search technique is similar to browsing and then searching within the browsed documents where the documents have been organized according to type or content area. As shown in Exhibit 8-6, BNA groups related portfolios and other sources for easy selection for searching. Across the top of the guided search page are practice areas that offer differing sets of sources for the guided search. In addition, using the SEARCH INDIVIDUAL PORTFOLIOS AND CHAPTERS option allows the researcher to identify specific portfolios to search, as shown in Exhibit 8-7.

The final search option located around the quick search box is the GO TO search. As presented in Exhibit 8-8, GO TO functions very much like the "find by citation" process in Checkpoint or IntelliConnect.

1-3 Browsing the BNA Collections

Since each portfolio covers by design a specific set of topics, browsing through the portfolios by content can be an efficient way to find the topic of interest. Browsing simply requires the researcher to select the practice area of interest (top of Exhibit 8-2) and then click on the collection of choice and continue to drill down to the source document level, as shown in Exhibit 8-9. BNA offers a SPLIT SCREEN feature that allows the portfolio table of contents to be presented in the left window and the documents in the right. This allows the researcher to quickly scan the portfolio for the relevant content.

EXHIBIT 8-5: BNA Advanced Search

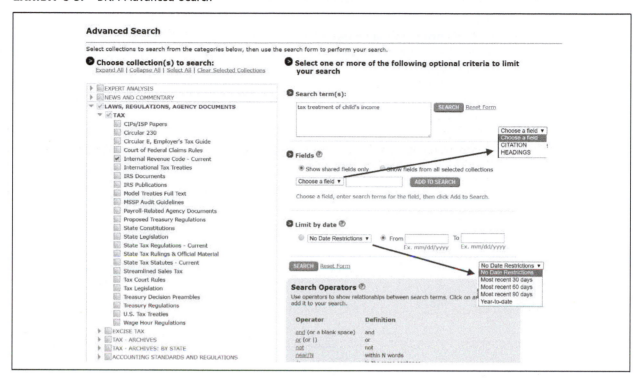

EXHIBIT 8-6: BNA Guided Search

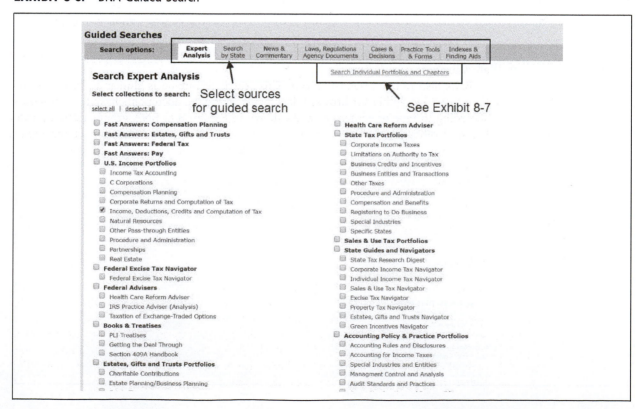

EXHIBIT 8-7: BNA Guided Search of Individual Portfolios and Chapters

Search Individual Portfolios and Chapters ⑦

Note: You may search a maximum of five portfolios and chapters.

Select portfolios and chapters to search:
(You can double-click the options to move them.)

- 508: The Economic Substance Doctrine
- 509: Principles of Capitalization
- 510: Section 199: Deduction Relating to Income Att...
- 512: Tax Incentives for Production and Conservatio...
- 514: Tax Incentives to Hire, Retain, or Compensate...
- 515: Divorce and Separation
- 517: Educational Expenses and Credits
- 518: Exclusion of Scholarships and Other Receipts ...
- 519: Travel and Transportation Expenses — De...
- 520: Entertainment, Meals, Gifts and Lodging...
- 521: Charitable Contributions: Income Tax Aspects
- 522: Tax Aspects of Settlements and Judgments
- 523: Deductibility of Legal and Other Professional...
- 524: Deductibility of Illegal Payments, Fines, and...
- 525: State, Local, and Federal Taxes

[Add →]
[← Remove]
[Clear All]

Your Current Selections:
(You can double-click the options to move them.)

U.S. INCOME PORTFOLIOS
    513: Family and Household Transactions

Choose field(s) to search:

Case Citations ⑦
[   ]

Source Citations ⑦
[   ] [USC ▼] [   ]

[Tax Code   ▼] [   ]
Word(s)
[   ] [SEARCH] Reset Form

Need help? View our search tips or try the Advanced Search.

EXHIBIT 8-8: BNA Go To Search

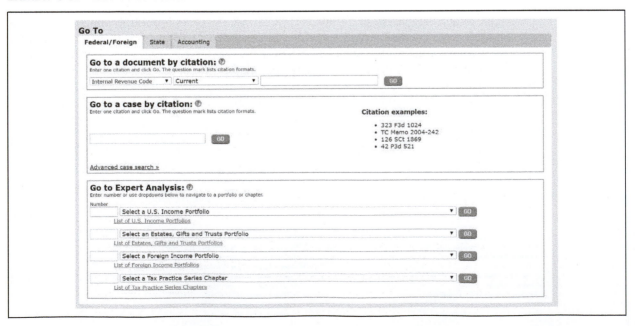

Go To

Federal/Foreign   State   Accounting

Go to a document by citation: ⑦
Enter one citation and click Go. The question mark lists citation formats.

[Internal Revenue Code ▼] [Current ▼] [   ] [GO]

Go to a case by citation: ⑦
Enter one citation and click Go. The question mark lists citation formats.

[   ] [GO]

Citation examples:
- 323 F3d 1024
- TC Memo 2004-242
- 126 SCt 1869
- 42 P3d 521

Advanced case search »

Go to Expert Analysis: ⑦
Enter number or use dropdowns below to navigate to a portfolio or chapter.

Number
[   ] [Select a U.S. Income Portfolio   ▼] [GO]
    List of U.S. Income Portfolios

[   ] [Select an Estates, Gifts and Trusts Portfolio ▼] [GO]
    List of Estates, Gifts and Trusts Portfolios

[   ] [Select a Foreign Income Portfolio   ▼] [GO]
    List of Foreign Income Portfolios

[   ] [Select a Tax Practice Series Chapter   ▼] [GO]
    List of Tax Practice Series Chapters

EXHIBIT 8-9: BNA Browse Portfolios

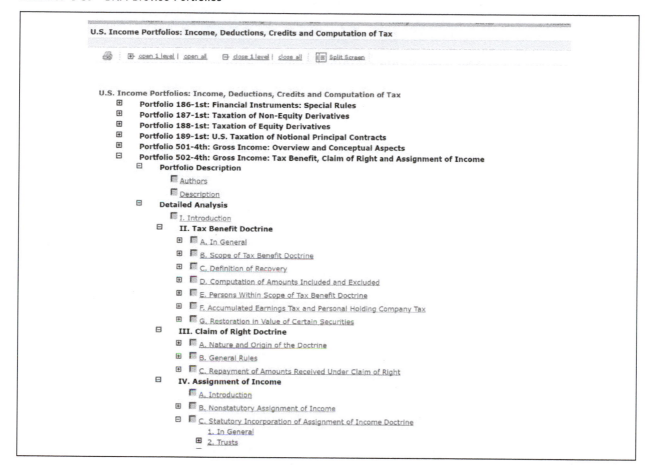

While the number of portfolios appears vast, the series is not truly comprehensive. As with any topical service, it would be impossible to cover every issue that a practitioner may encounter in the course of business. However, practitioners who identify a portfolio on point with an issue generally have completed their search. It is likely that the portfolio will address the issue in a comprehensive manner.

Each BNA portfolio begins with a description that provides a brief overview of the topic and the order in which the materials are presented. The table of contents (TOC) follows this description. The remainder of the portfolio contains four sections: (1) Portfolio Description, (2) Detailed Analysis, (3) Working Papers, and (4) Bibliography. The portfolio sections are updated in response to important tax developments, and when necessary, the complete portfolio is rewritten.

As with other topical services, the IRC, regulations, rulings, and court opinions are integrated into the analysis with citation footnotes, or the relevant portions are included in the text, as shown in Exhibit 8-10. In addition to analysis, the authors identify potential pitfalls, probable IRS positions, effective tax planning techniques, and alternative means of structuring transactions in a tax-favored manner.

The Working Papers section of the portfolios is perhaps the service's most unique and useful feature. This material includes practitioner checklists, reproduced IRS forms (interactive for online version and occasionally filled in for an illustrative fact situation),

EXHIBIT 8-10:   BNA Portfolio Example

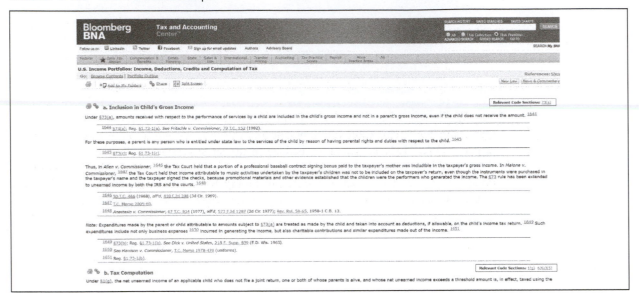

computation worksheets, sample draft agreements and contract clauses, sample board or shareholder resolutions and employment contracts, reproductions of pertinent primary sources, and other practical materials that can assist the professional in implementing tax planning techniques and procedures.

The Bibliography section of a portfolio has a comprehensive listing of the primary (Official) and secondary (Unofficial) sources of the tax law utilized by the author(s) in preparing the portfolio. Finally, this section of the portfolio often includes a listing of journal articles and treatises that are relevant to the portfolio topic.

SPOTLIGHT ON TAXATION

George Boole

All the tax services discussed in this textbook refer to Boolean connectors. These are named after famous mathematician George Boole. From an early age, George was destined to leave his mark on the world. He started school before he reached the age of two. By age 14, he could speak and understand Latin and Greek, and he mastered French, German, and Italian a short time later. George's most well-known contribution is Boolean algebra. In the world of taxes, it might work like this:

x is the set of all property that is real property.
y is the set of all property that is personal use property.
x + y is the set of property that is real OR personal use.
xy is the set of property that is real AND personal use.
z is the set of all property that is in the United States. z(x + y) = zx + zy because the set of U.S. property that is either real or personal use is the same as the set of property that is U.S. and real or U.S. and personal use.

In 1937 this logic was found to be useful in describing electric switching circuits. Binary numbers (0 and 1) combined with Boolean algebra paved the way for the electronic circuits used in modern computers.

2 Westlaw

Thomson Reuters, the same company that offers Checkpoint, also offers tax research capabilities through its **Westlaw** service. The Westlaw service is legally oriented because it was designed by attorneys, for attorneys. Because of this orientation toward the legal profession, Westlaw is less represented than Checkpoint and IntelliConnect in accounting firms; however, virtually all law schools train their students using the Westlaw system. A few years ago, Westlaw introduced the WestlawNext legal research service; however, in 2016 Westlaw returned to their eponymous named product, Westlaw, once again. The latest generation search engine and research simplification features introduced as part of WestlawNext remain embedded in the latest version of Westlaw.

A complete Westlaw subscription contains more than 2.2 billion documents organized into more than 20,000 databases, including BNA Tax Management Portfolios, all of the Checkpoint products, some CCH products, law reviews, legal texts, various tax news services, and the WG&L treatises, manuals, journals, and newsletters. Also included in Westlaw are the popular South-Western Federal Taxation textbook series and a topical tax service called Mertens Law of Federal Income Taxation. Like BNA, Westlaw is accessible via the Internet and through wireless mobile devices.

Many schools and universities subscribe to the **Westlaw Campus Research** product. Campus Research has a more limited range of data than the full Westlaw subscription. The basic searching strategies discussed in this section, however, are similar in all versions of Westlaw. Campus Research includes a much larger range of court cases than only the tax-related cases included in Checkpoint or IntelliConnect. Similarly, Campus Research includes the U.S. Code, regulations, and administrative decisions for a broad array of laws, not just the tax titles (see Exhibit 8-11). A partial list of sources available within Campus Research is provided in Exhibit 8-12. A researcher can examine the complete list of sources available by clicking the Tools tab and then selecting My Content.

2-1 Searching Westlaw

The WELCOME TO WESTLAW CAMPUS RESEARCH screen shown in Exhibit 8-11 is designed to have the same look and feel as a typical browser search. The KEYWORD SEARCH box is located at the top of the window and treats the terms as a natural-language search. As mentioned previously, the WestSearch search engine is designed to tailor search results to the most relevant items based on the expertise of experienced law researchers. Boolean

EXHIBIT 8-11: Westlaw Welcome Screen

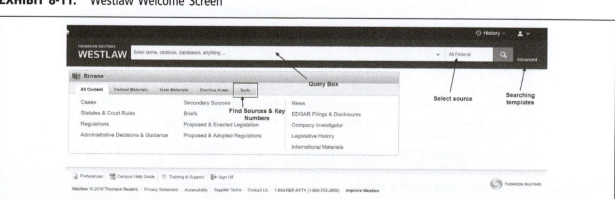

EXHIBIT 8-12:   Westlaw Campus Research Sources

Cases	Court cases from federal, state, and U.S. possession courts available to browse by jurisdiction or by topic
Statutes and Court Rules	Federal, state, and U.S. possession statutes and court procedure rules available to browse by jurisdiction or by topic
Regulations	Federal, state, and U.S. possession regulations available to browse by jurisdiction or by topic
Administrative Decisions and Guidance	Federal government agency administrative decisions, including Equal Employment Opportunity Commission, National Labor Relations Board, and Sarbanes Oxley decisions
Secondary Sources	Includes American Law Review, American Jurisprudence 2d, and a variety of law reviews and journals. Sources may also be browsed by topic
Briefs	Court briefs, petitions, and joint appendices from the U.S. Supreme Court
Proposed and Enacted Legislation	U.S. Public Laws
Proposed and Enacted Regulations	Items published in the Federal Register

terms and connectors may also be used to further hone the search. Exhibit 8-13 presents the Boolean terms and connectors used by Westlaw.

Boolean terms and connectors may also be used by clicking ADVANCED, located to the right of the search button (see Exhibit 8-11). The ADVANCED SEARCH template provides descriptions of the connectors and terms in a way that largely eliminates the need to remember the symbols. The search can also be tailored to certain sources in a number of different ways. The ALL FEDERAL drop-down box located to the right of the keyword search box (see Exhibit 8-11) can be clicked to limit search sources to only the ones selected.

Once a search is performed, the results are presented in the main window as shown in Exhibit 8-14. The terms used in the search are highlighted for quick identification. The

EXHIBIT 8-13:   Westlaw Boolean Terms and Connectors

!	Search for words with multiple endings	Depend! will search for depend, depended, dependant, dependent, dependable, etc.
*	Search for words with variable characters	*ffect will search for affect and effect
#	Search for exact match	#dependent will search for dependent but not dependents
/p	Both terms within the paragraph	Minor /p child
+p	First term must precede the second term within the same paragraph	Organization +p costs
/s	Both terms within the same sentence	Like-kind/s exchange
+s	First term precedes second term in same sentence	Real +s property
/n	Terms must appear within n terms of each other where n is a number	Immediate w/4 expense
+n	The first term precedes the second term by no more than n terms	Barack w/2 Obama
% (BUT NOT)	Excludes documents with the term	Amortization % patent

EXHIBIT 8-14: Westlaw Search Results Screen

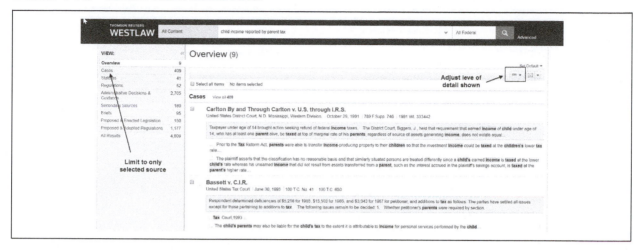

search results can be organized in a number of different ways using options built into West-law. For example, the level of detail can be adjusted to show more of the document or just the title using the box on the upper right side of the results window. Typically, the default setting is to show an overview of the search results; however, the results can be narrowed to only the specific sources required by choosing the selected heading under VIEW on the left side of the results window. Once a specific area is selected, a number of additional filters will be presented to help refine the search even further (see Exhibit 8-15). From these

EXHIBIT 8-15: Westlaw Refine Search Screen

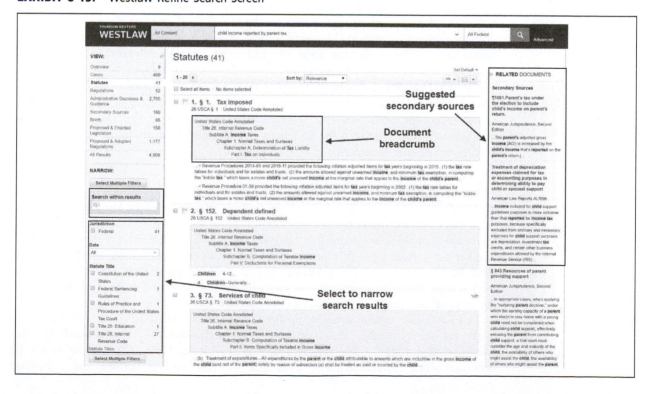

EXHIBIT 8-16:   Westlaw Document

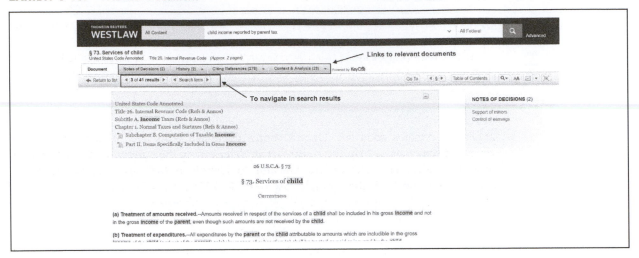

items the researcher can search for key terms within the results or narrow to a certain source or sources. Westlaw will also suggest some secondary sources on the right that have been selected to explain the relevant search terms.

Once a specific document is selected, Westlaw displays that document in the main window along with some important information and additional research assistance (see Exhibit 8-16). The bread crumb for the document is shown above the document, providing information, especially useful to novice researchers, about the location of the document within the database. In addition to the document itself, several related sources are provided at the bottom of the document (not shown), such as links to other sources within Westlaw. Several navigation tools at the top of the document allow the researcher to move forward or back in the search results, by search term, or within the documents source. Above the navigation tools are additional links to relevant documents and sources, presented in the tabs across the top of the results window.

Campus Research also permits browsing the sources using the tabs on the main window (Exhibit 8-11) to examine many of the more common sources of research grouped by jurisdiction or topic. Note that browsing often results in only the most current items and generally will require some additional searching to find anything other than the most recent source documents.

2-2 KeySearch and KeyCite

KeySearch uses the West Key Numbering System, which organizes key issues found in court cases into hundreds of numbered topics. These topics are further subdivided, with the result that there are more than 100,000 unique key numbers! To identify the key number for a legal topic of interest, select the TOOLS tab (see Exhibit 8-11) and select WEST KEY NUMBER SYSTEM. The particular key number can be selected for searching only cases within that area of content. For example, the key number for Taxation is 371, and the Internal Revenue Code is found at Key Number 220.

The KeySearch option, available on the KEY NUMBER screen (not shown), formulates a query for the researcher based on underlying terms for the topic selected by the researcher and adds the key numbers associated with the topic. This type of search is beneficial when the researcher is unfamiliar with the area of tax law and is having difficulty pinpointing keywords to use as search terms. The researcher can determine what type of cases to search or decide to search treatises or journals and law reviews. Only one of these categories, however, may be searched at a time. The researcher may add other search terms to ensure the results will be relevant.

As discussed previously, Westlaw is structured for legal research. It was designed by attorneys, for attorneys. Since court cases are essential sources in most areas of law, taxation included, the citation applications are the centerpiece of the Westlaw service. Thus, Westlaw's citators are also very effective for validating statutes, regulations, and administrative rulings.

KeyCite, Westlaw's citation research service, helps determine whether a case, law, or regulation remains good law. Once a source document is located, Westlaw provides a variety of materials to help the researcher in determining the current status of that case or source document. The easiest indicator to identify is the KEYCITE STATUS FLAG. As shown in Exhibit 8-17, the example case (30 T.C. 757) has a yellow KeyCite status flag. The KeyCite status flags are red or yellow. A red flag indicates the case is no longer good law for at least one of the points of law made. A yellow flag means the case has some negative history but has not been overturned or reversed. The meanings are largely the same for flags associated with statutes. The tabs across the top of the document provide relevant citations and information that help the researcher understand why a yellow or red flag was chosen. For example, the NEGATIVE TREATMENT tab will provide a list and links to the cases, rulings, or other documents containing conclusions contrary to the one in the case in question. The HISTORY tab provides a history of the case or ruling and can be shown as a list or a graphic. KeyCite and Shepard's Citator (part of LexisNexis, discussed later in this chapter) have an unparalleled position among citators because of their rigor at identifying relevant materials affecting cases and laws. The CITING REFERENCES tab provides a list of the relevant cites to the case in question. The depth-of-treatment symbols help the researcher determine the current status of the case in question. Further, the Westlaw quotation mark symbol identifies which cases the case at hand quotes. The evaluation symbols are also provided for the cited cases.

EXHIBIT 8-17:   Westlaw KeyCite Status Flag

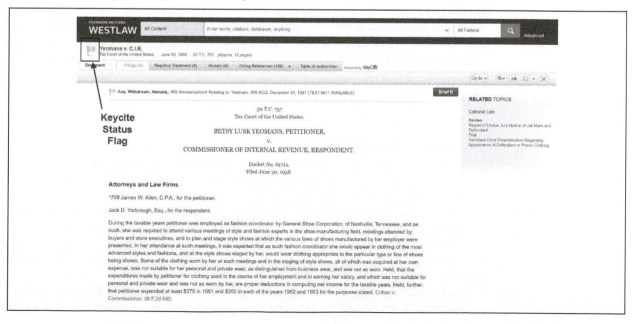

Although often left to the lawyers, Westlaw provides an excellent research tool through the power of the citator and the depth of the information available. Even a researcher with expertise in Checkpoint or IntelliConnect should consider an additional search in a Westlaw system before finalizing the answer to a research question. The Key-Cite system may highlight information that had been overlooked by the researcher, especially in situations in which the case or law has been cited repeatedly, thus making the distinguishing cases harder to identify.

SPOTLIGHT ON TAXATION

Sources Used by U.S. Corporate Tax Professionals

The Tax Executive Institute's (TEI) 2011–2012 Corporate Tax Department Survey of more than 500 chief tax officers found that the most commonly used tax research source was governmental websites, which 73 percent of respondents used. Other sources commonly used by respondents were Thomson Reuters Checkpoint (68%), various accounting firm websites (65%), Google (59%), BNA portfolios (51%), CCH IntelliConnect (49%), BNA *Daily Tax Report* (34%), *Tax Notes Today* (26%), and law firm websites (25%). Less frequently used were Lexis (9%) and Westlaw (3%).
Source: TEI 2011–2012 Corporate Tax Department Survey

3 LexisNexis

The amount of information available on the LexisNexis system is staggering. With billions of searchable documents from more than 45,000 legal, business, and news sources, LexisNexis is possibly the world's largest full-text information resource. Perhaps the only tax services not available on LexisNexis are its competitors Checkpoint and Westlaw. LexisNexis can be accessed through mobile devices as well as conventional personal computers.

LexisNexis contains data and information that go well beyond the realm of tax law. In fact, LexisNexis is so large that the sheer volume of information can be overwhelming to a new researcher. Like so many of the other tax services, LexisNexis has a variety of subscription levels that offer different databases and news sources depending on the product selected. This textbook concentrates on two of those alternatives: (1) Lexis Advance Tax and (2) LexisNexis Academic.

3-1 Lexis Advance Tax

Realizing how important tax research has become, LexisNexis developed a service exclusively for tax practitioners called **Lexis Advance Tax** (Lexis Tax). This service is designed to streamline tax research by having an interface separate from LexisNexis (although still part of the Lexis Advance product) and giving the practitioner the ability to conduct a single search across the full content of this service. Lexis Tax is a second-generation tax research service and a distinct improvement over the previous Lexis Tax Center interface. Searching or browsing sources is considerably easier and is quite similar to the other tax services.

The tax materials currently available in Lexis Tax are extensive and include primary sources (Internal Revenue Code, regulations, cases, IRS pronouncements, and public records) and the analytical materials of Tax Analysts, Bender, and many others. Tax Center also contains two LexisNexis-specific tax services under the LexisNexis Tax Advisor name—Federal Code Reporter and Federal Topical. These editorial tax services are similar to the annotated and topical services available in Checkpoint and IntelliConnect. Different packages are available depending on the specific needs of the tax professional's practice. Consequently, the package described in this chapter may vary from the service available to the reader. The SOURCES tab on the Lexis Tax home page provides the details of all the sources available in a subscription.

Tax Center's opening research option (Exhibit 8-18) presents the practitioner with a wide variety of databases organized by areas called pods. Like other tax research services, Lexis Tax uses a combination of browse and search functions to permit the researcher to keyword search in a large number of sources or to better define the sources so as to perform a more focused search. The broad KEYWORD SEARCH is available from the home page and can be used to search all sources within the practice area in Lexis Tax (the Federal practice area is shown in Exhibit 8-18 with the other practice areas shown in the inset). Boolean connectors are available in the Lexis Tax system and are presented in Exhibit 8-19.

One of the unique offerings in the Lexis Tax keyword search is the option to use segments to direct the search toward specific items. This search can be performed directly from the broad search on the home page. All documents within Lexis Tax have a common structure composed of natural parts knows as segments. Different types of documents can be constructed of different segments. A search can be restricted to a certain segment by using the segment name followed by the keywords in parentheses. For example, the U.S. Cases database contains the segment *writtenby* to allow the researcher to find cases with certain judges as the author. A search for *writtenby(o'conner)* will result in all documents with the *writtenby* segment and O'conner as the author. The number of segments is about 50 and is increasing. A complete list of segments can be found in the HELP function within Lexis Tax. Once a researcher becomes familiar with some of the

EXHIBIT 8-18: Lexis Tax Home Page

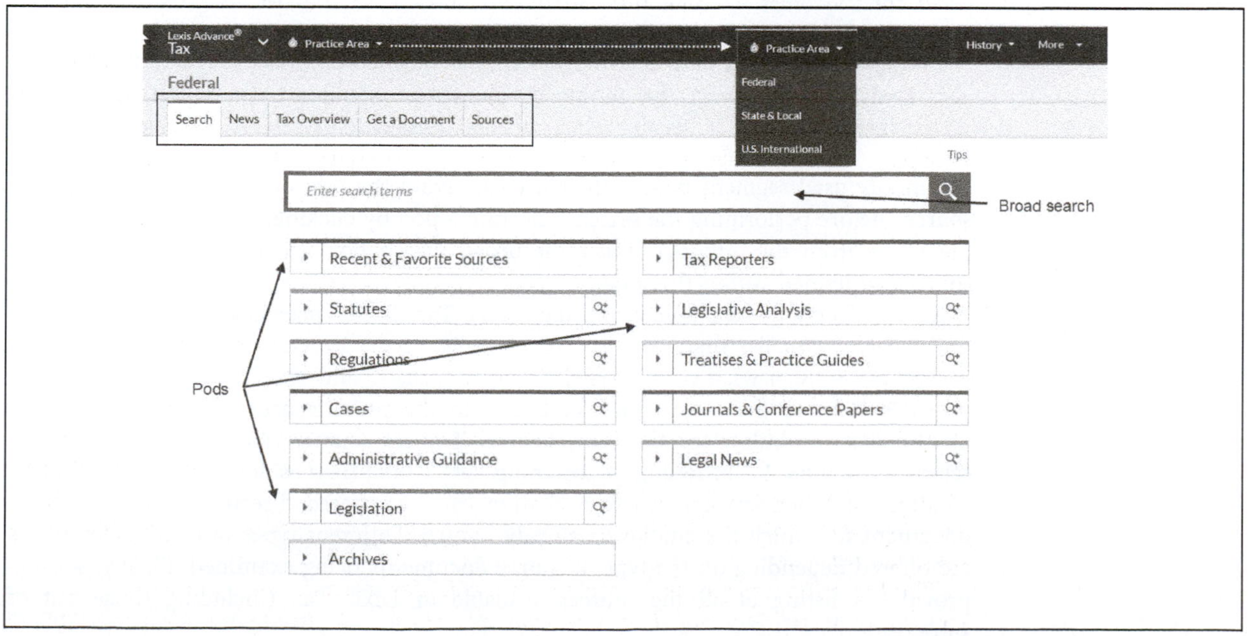

EXHIBIT 8-19:   Lexis Tax Connectors

Connector	Use	Example
and (includes &)	Find words that may appear anywhere in the document	budget and deficit
near/n	Find words within n words of each other in the document	fiduciary near/10 breach
atleastn	Find documents that contain at least n instances of a word	atleast10(recapture)
or (same as using a space between words)	Find contains that can contain either or both words	ship or vessel or boat
and not (same as andnot, but not, butnot)	Find documents that exclude the words	capital and not gains
w/n (same as /n)	First word appears within n words of the second word	vicious w/3 dog (vicious /3 dog)
w/p (same as /p)	Find words within the same paragraph	retirement w/p benefit (retirement /p benefit)
w/s (same as /s or w/sent)	Find words within the same sentence	earnings w/s taxation (earnings /s taxation or earnings w/sent taxation)
w/seg	Find words inside a segment of a document (e.g., headline, body, etc.)	unreported w/seg income
onear/n (same as pre/n)	Find documents where the first word precedes the second by not more than n words	overtime onear/3 compensation
pre/s (same as +s)	First word precedes second word by about 25 words	overtime pre/s compensation
pre/p (same as +p)	First word precedes second word by about 75 words	overtime pre/p compensation
! (same as *)	Find root word plus all words made by adding letters	employ!
?	Find variations of a word using any letter in replacement of ?	wom?n

commonly used segment names, their use can avoid the task of having to select certain sources before performing the search. Selecting a pod by clicking the magnifying glass by the name from the offerings under the broad search box will limit the search to the sources contained within that pod.

Other functions available from the Lexis Tax home page are the options listed under each particular practice area. For example, in the Federal practice area presented in Exhibit 8-18, NEWS, TAX OVERVIEW, GET A DOCUMENT, and SOURCES are available. NEWS provides links to the most recent additions to the practice area. TAX OVERVIEW opens up the search window for the Lexis Federal Topical source, where a tax area can be selecting by topic for browsing or searching. GET A DOCUMENT is consistent with "find by citation" in other services, where a citation can be entered directly to find a specific document for which the citation is already known. Different types of citation templates are offered depending on the type of source documents being examined. Finally, SOURCES provides a listing of all the sources available in Lexis Tax (including those out of subscription).

EXHIBIT 8-20: Lexis Tax Related Documents

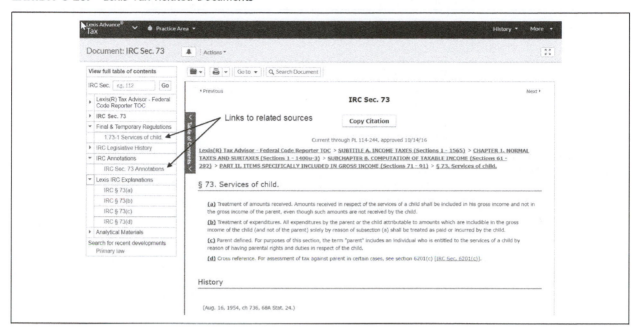

Once a document is found, the Lexis Tax system provides common links to other related documents in the left window. As shown in Exhibit 8-20, the small arrows to the left of each related source can be clicked to reveal the details of what documents are linked directly. As shown in Exhibit 8-21, the Lexis Tax Advisor provides explanatory materials that are linked to primary sources materials contained elsewhere in the Lexis Tax product. Like other services, a bread crumb is listed so the researcher can identify the document and the source at any time.

The results of a broad keyword search are displayed in Exhibit 8-22. The results include a large number of documents (since no restrictions on sources were used) and are almost certain to require refinement. The results are presented with keywords highlighted and can be displayed with detail or by name only using the view icons in the upper right. There are two ways to refine the broad keyword search from the RESULTS page. As presented in Exhibit 8-23, the source of the documents can be limited to one of the selections in the upper left window. Once a source is selected, further refinements are also made available in the lower left window to specify a narrower choice within that source. The results of selecting the Internal Revenue Code are shown in Exhibit 8-24. The refinement choices are shown in the left window so the researcher is aware of the limitations placed on the search. Each document has associated explanatory descriptions such as a summary bread crumb and indication as to whether the document was recently viewed.

3-2 LexisNexis Academic

LexisNexis offers to academic institutions and public libraries a customized version of its services, **LexisNexis Academic.** While the complete LexisNexis flagship service provides full-text documents from more than 6,000 publications, most library subscriptions do not carry all the offerings. Thus, the databases available to the reader may differ from that demonstrated in this section.

EXHIBIT 8-21: Lexis Tax Document

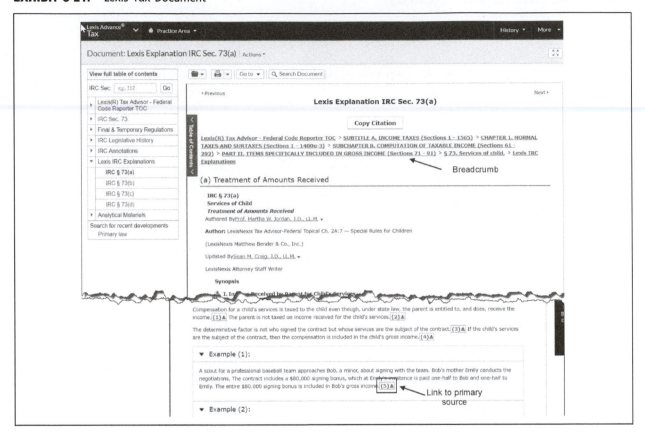

EXHIBIT 8-22: Lexis Tax Broad Search Results

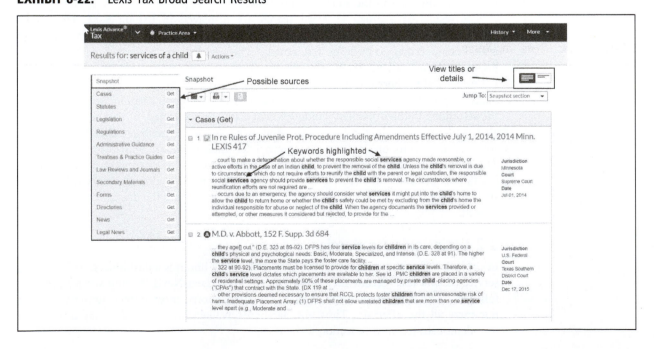

EXHIBIT 8-23: Lexis Tax Search Refinement

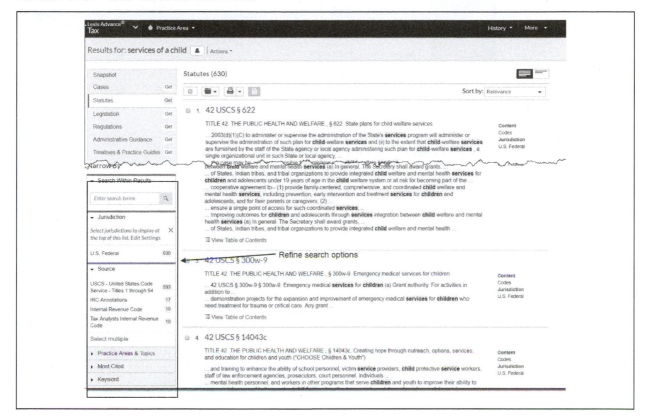

EXHIBIT 8-24: Lexis Tax Result

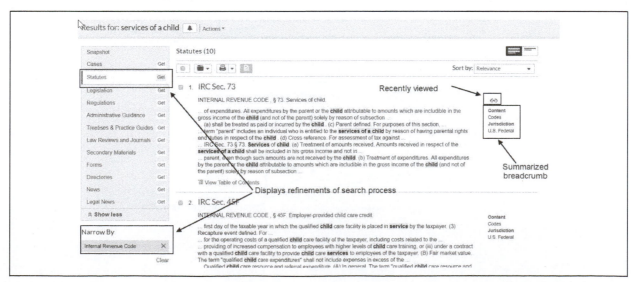

SPOTLIGHT ON TAXATION

Taxes and Literature

The Internal Revenue Code is not known for its literary excellence but rather its length. Court opinions can also be dry reading. However, in T.C. Summary Opinion 2004-94, Judge Holmes took a slightly different approach. The case involved a taxpayer who was both a professor and a playwright. The taxpayer attempted somewhat aggressive deduction strategies, and, in what has to be one of the more interesting opinions, the judge writes:

> Dramatists used to finish with some rhymes,
> Mostly iambs with a pinch of dactyly,
> But in these more prosaic times
> Works usually end more matter-of-factily.

The court rejected most of the taxpayer's deductions.

LexisNexis has a basic keyword search bar that is available on the home page upon entry into the system (see Exhibit 8-25). This will search newspapers, federal and state cases, company profiles, and law reviews. This search functions much like the keyword searches in other research services. There are also three drop-down choices near the bottom of the home page that permit a quick search of news sources, federal and state cases, and company information, all with preset citation-style fields to assist the researcher find a specific document. To find a case quickly or to search common news sources, the home page search functions are efficient, but most tax researchers are looking for information beyond the sources included in those searches. There are two basic methods for finding

EXHIBIT 8-25:   LexisNexis Home Page

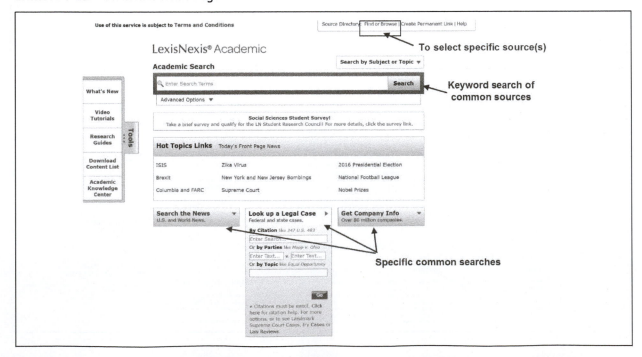

sources: (1) FIND and (2) BROWSE. The FIND function is used when a specific source is desired; whereas the BROWSE function permits the researcher to review a bevy of sources within the service and make a selection or selections of the sources to be searched. The buttons are located at the top of the home page as shown in Exhibit 8-25.

Using FIND requires a two-step process: (1) Use a keyword search to find the sources to examine and (2) once the sources are selected, use a keyword search to search for the desired document(s). To begin step 1, click the FIND function to present a new search screen that is used to find sources but not documents (see Exhibit 8-26). Because the LexisNexis libraries are so exhaustive, the researcher can narrow the source search down to selected types of publications, topics, industries, or types of law using each of the four boxes displayed on the FIND SOURCES page. Keywords are entered into the KEY-WORD SEARCH box, and by clicking the FIND SOURCES button, the results of the source search replace the main page (Exhibit 8-27). Now the specific source(s) can be selected by clicking the box to the left of the title, and the researcher can proceed with a keyword search

EXHIBIT 8-26: LexisNexis Find Sources

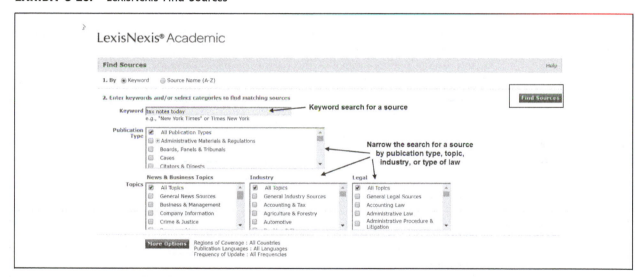

EXHIBIT 8-27: LexisNexis Find Sources Results

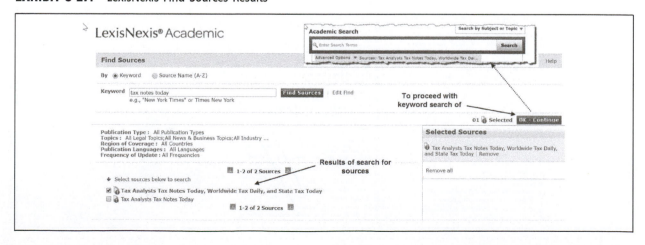

of the source using the OK CONTINUE button as shown in Exhibit 8-27. The resulting page (shown as the inset in Exhibit 8-27) looks a great deal like the home page, except now the selected source is listed.

If the specific source(s) is not known, or multiple sources from a variety of different types of publication are desired, the BROWSE function is likely to be more efficient. Located toward the top of the home page (Exhibit 8-25), the BROWSE function allows the researcher to narrow down the sources through a series of selections. As Exhibit 8-28 indicates, the BROWSE SOURCES option has three numbered steps to follow. In Step 1, select the type of source. This displays a list of law areas (not shown). Frequently, TAXATION LAW is selected by tax researchers. In Step 2, filter the sources by country, region, publication type, and source type (multiple, single, or all sources). In Step 3, the researcher selects which categories of legal sources (databases) to view. Each selected source appears in the right frame with the ability to remove any or all of them. Clicking the OK CONTINUE button located above the selected sources accesses the search screen for performing keyword searches.

The results of a LexisNexis Academic search are presented in Exhibit 8-29. LexisNexis Academic offers several ways to tailor the results to the specific search or researcher. The results may be listed by relevance, chronological date, or publication date. The results summary in the left window of Exhibit 8-29 also may be personalized to list by category or publication name. If the documents retrieved are not on point, the researcher may use the EDIT SEARCH option located at the top of the page to return to the original keyword entry box; if too many documents are returned, the SEARCH WITHIN RESULTS option on the right side at the top of the results window allows the researcher to add keywords to

EXHIBIT 8-28:   LexisNexis Browse Sources

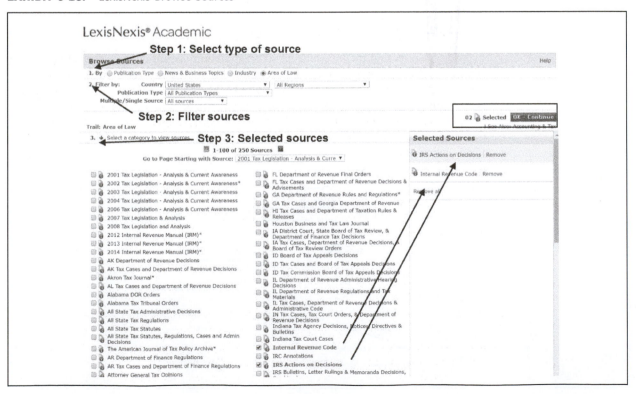

EXHIBIT 8-29: LexisNexis Academic Search Results

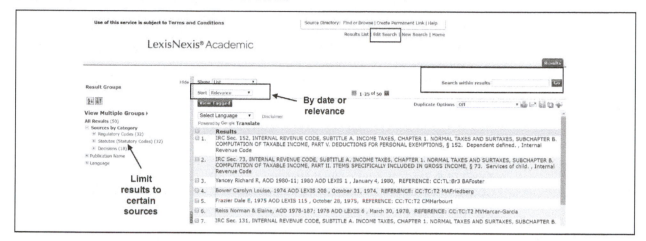

narrow the results. Selecting one of the document titles displays the document. Lexis-Nexis Academic has a KWIC (key words in context) view, which highlights the terms entered as keywords. If the SEARCH WITHIN RESULTS option has been applied, only the words used for narrowing the search will be highlighted. The documents retrieved are full text and may be downloaded, e-mailed, or printed from the browser.

The improvements made by LexisNexis to Academic have dramatically increased the usefulness of this service for performing tax research. LexisNexis has plans to introduce a new look in 2017 (after this book has gone to print), which promises to be even more user-friendly.

3-3 LexisNexis and Shepard's Citators

Shepard's was the first major publisher to understand the commercial value of citators. It became the leading publisher of citators, and thus its name has become synonymous with the act of citing. In fact, the process of evaluating the validity of a case and locating additional authority is often called **Shepardizing** a case. Many attorneys view Shepard's as *the* citator service and all other services as mere imitations. This may have been true in the past, but the current competitors have just as much to offer as the original.

The **Shepard's Citators (Shepard's)** are currently available in many formats and by many delivery means, including mobile devices. In this section, use of Shepard's via LexisNexis Academic is presented.

To get the Shepard's citation for a case you have found, click on the symbol at the top left corner of the case (as shown in Exhibit 8-30) or use the NEXT STEPS drop-down menu in the upper right corner to Shepardize. The symbol (known as the Shepard's Signal Marker) in the upper left indicates the general results that the Shepard's citator will yield. A legend of the signal markers is presented in Exhibit 8-31.

The results of the Shepard's summary contain extensive information stemming from the analysis performed on the citing cases and other sources. This information can be structured in a number of different ways, which is particularly important if a case has been cited repeatedly. As shown in Exhibit 8-32, the citing cases may be restricted to only those with positive or negative analysis. The RESTRICT BY function opens a new search window so that certain terms, jurisdictions, or types of analysis can be selected.

EXHIBIT 8-30:   LexisNexis Shepardizing a Case

EXHIBIT 8-31:   Shepard's Signal Markers

Red Octagon	Warning	Negative treatment such as overruled, superseded, revoked, obsolete, or rescinded
Orange Q	Questioned	Validity of the finding questioned by citing references
Yellow Triangle	Caution	Possible negative treatment such as limited, criticized, clarified, modified, or corrected
+ in green diamond	Positive	Holding is affirmed, followed, or approved
A in blue circle	Analysis	The citing references have some analysis considered neither positive nor negative, such as appeal denied or writ denied
I in blue circle	Citation information	The citing references applied no analysis and simply cite the case

The ability to organize citing cases provides the researcher with more information about a cited case more quickly than can be done with either Checkpoint or CCH's citators. The unrestricted Shepard's summary shown in Exhibit 8-32 provides a snapshot of what an analysis of all citing cases has produced. The citing cases are listed in order of court and then by date. In addition, any additional sources, such as treatises or law reviews, also are listed at the bottom (not shown).

The prior direct history and subsequent appellate history developed by Shepard's are also provided to give the complete procedural posture for the case of interest. Many researchers prefer to start their analysis of a case with the most recent citing cases and work backward to earlier cases. Using this method, they can quickly identify the current status of the cited case. For example, a steady stream of recent favorable references probably indicates that the holding of the original case is still valid and strong, whereas a list of recent negative comments or a scarcity of references may indicate a weak or out-of-date decision. The citator portion of a research project is complete when the researcher is satisfied that the status of the case is sufficiently confirmed.

At this point, the researcher should examine some of the citing cases, especially if the cases found initially support the client's position but the facts are somewhat different. The citing cases may provide support with more similar facts. Descriptions such as "cited by," "followed by," and "criticized by" all denote different treatment by the courts and should be examined as necessary.

Shepard's TABLE OF AUTHORITIES (TOA) is a type of citator service, but it has a different purpose than regular citators. Rather than furnishing a history of a case and a list of

EXHIBIT 8-32: LexisNexis Shepard's Citation Results

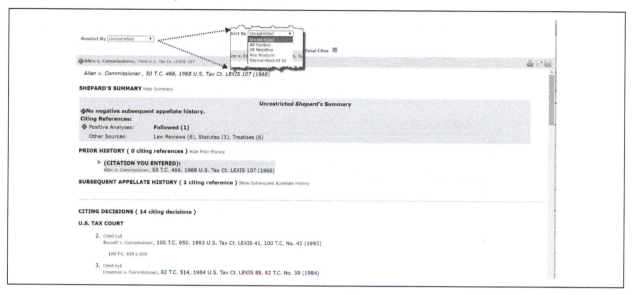

citing cases, as shown in Exhibit 8-33, the TOA lists the cases the case of interest referred to and to what extent it relied on those cases. This saves the researcher from having to enter each of these cases in the regular citator and consequently is a tremendous time-saving tool. If a researcher is using a more robust version of LexisNexis, such as Lexis Advance, the TOA is easily accessed from any case document.

The TOA lists the cited cases by jurisdiction (e.g., U.S. Supreme Court, federal court of appeals, district court). For each case, the TOA furnishes the same information that

EXHIBIT 8-33: LexisNexis Shepard's Table of Authorities

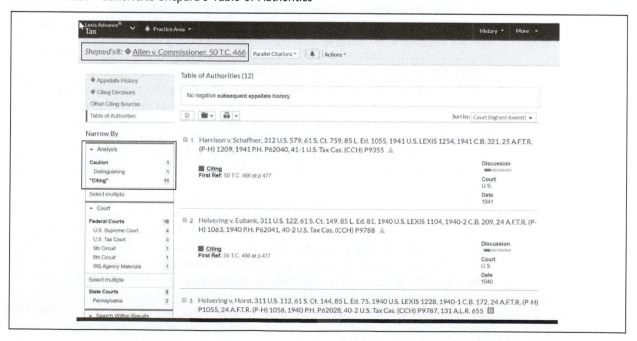

the researcher would obtain if each case was separately checked through the regular Shepard's citator. Thus, the TOA lists the full case name and the decision's citation (with parallel citations). It also provides an assessment of how the case of interest evaluated the cited cases and the page in the case of interest on which the cited case is discussed. The cited cases themselves are evaluated based on their history and are assigned a Shepard's at-a-glance signal (e.g., stop sign, triangle) indicating their current status.

4 Tax Analysts

Tax Analysts is best known in the tax community for its outstanding news publications *Tax Notes* and *Tax Notes Today*. However, Tax Analysts has recently increased the power and reach of their online Tax Notes research service. The Tax Analysts web platform now contains over 4.2 million documents, and Tax Analysts continues to produce a variety of comprehensive state, federal, and international news, analysis, and commentary publications for tax professionals on a daily, weekly, monthly, and quarterly basis.

4-1 Databases

The Tax Analysts web platform now has extensive primary and editorial sources available to subscribers. Among the primary source materials are the Internal Revenue Code, regulations, revenue rulings, revenue procedures, IRS announcements and notices, letter rulings, and a large number of relevant court cases. Tax Analysts also includes access to over 10,000 worldwide tax treaties (including tax treaties to which the United States is not a party). Interestingly, Tax Analysts also provides a directory of tax-exempt organizations and a directory of tax professionals working in industry and government. In addition to *Tax Notes* and *Tax Notes Today*, Tax Analysts provides a multitude of other editorial sources of tax information such as *State Tax Notes*, *Tax Notes International*, *Exempt Organization Tax Review*, *Insurance Tax Review*, and a large number of in-depth articles written by experts on a wide variety of topics.

The Tax Analysts home page is the starting point for accessing all the information in the Tax Analysts web platform. As shown in Exhibit 8-34, Tax Analysts offers a number of ways to search and browse the databases in the service. Near the top of the page are four different browsing options: (1) TAX TOPICS, (2) KEY DOCUMENTS, (3) CONTRIBUTORS, and (4) JURISDICTIONS. Each of these organizes the underlying documents differently. For example, as shown in Exhibit 8-35, the TAX TOPICS organizes tax information by topic. Similarly (but not shown), KEY DOCUMENTS organizes the material by type of source (e.g., IRS revenue rulings or court opinions); CONTRIBUTORS is organized by author, and JURISIDICTIONS by the country of origin. As shown in Exhibit 8-35, a keyword search can be performed to help identify the topic, document, contributor, or jurisdiction of interest.

If a particular source is wanted, the PUBLICATIONS tab in the upper right side of Exhibit 8-34 can be presented by dragging the cursor over the tab and revealing each of the sources in the subscription. Once a source is selected, an appropriate search box will appear tailored specifically for that source. As an example, in Exhibit 8-36, the *Tax Notes* publication has been selected and can be searched using keywords or browsed by date. Once the search has been entered, the RESULTS page is presented (see Exhibit 8-37) with the results on the right and the advanced search options on the left. Advanced search options include searching by date, document type, jurisdiction, subject area, IRC section, author, and court. Results can be sorted by date or relevance as well.

EXHIBIT 8-34:   Tax Analysts Home Page

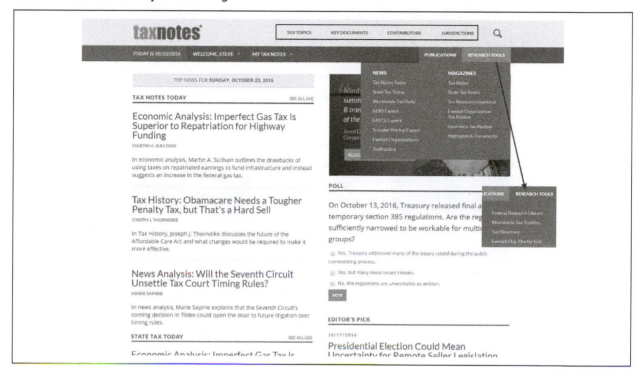

EXHIBIT 8-35:   Tax Analysts Tax Topics Search

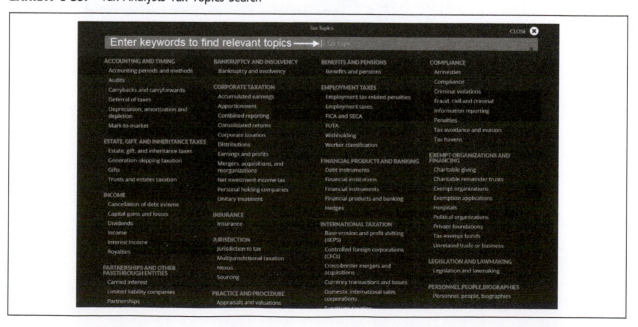

EXHIBIT 8-36: Tax Analysts Tax Notes Search

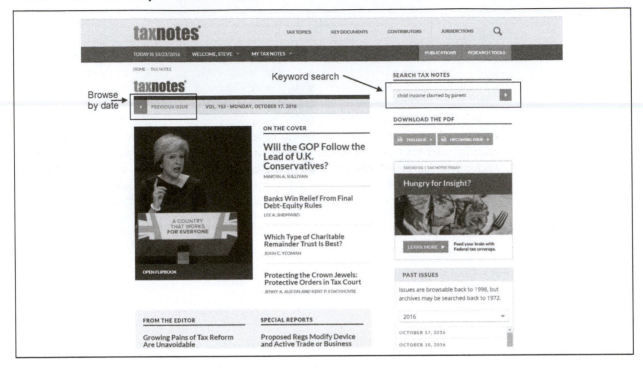

EXHIBIT 8-37: Tax Analysts Results Page

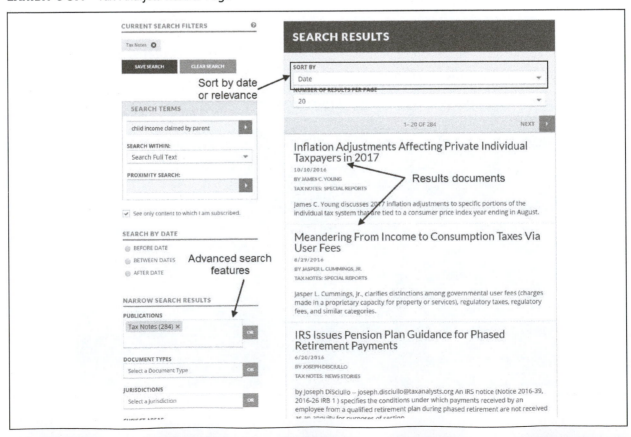

The RESEARCH TOOLS tab (shown in the inset in Exhibit 8-34) provides access to the complete Federal Research Library (FRL), tax treaties, the directory of tax managers, and the exempt organization list. The FRL has the broadest set of underlying databases and sources and can also be searched. As shown in Exhibit 8-38, the FRL is the repository for the vast majority of primary sources of tax law in the Tax Analysts web platform. Using the left side of the page, the entire FRL can be searched, or each of the underlying sources can be searched as needed. The right side of the page presents some of the most significant recent documents to be added to the FRL.

When a broad search is wanted, the magnifying glass (see Exhibit 8-39) can be used to open up a keyword search of the entire service. The Boolean search connectors common in other tax services are also available in Tax Analysts with explanation available by clicking under the search box. The ADVANCED SEARCH capabilities are also available to refine the search as needed by clicking just to the right of the keyword search box. A number of fields are available to refine the search by date, IRC section, author name, and a number of other fields (not shown).

As mentioned previously, the flagship products of the Tax Analysts family are the *Tax Notes* series. The daily Tax Analysts news services, available only online, offer up-to-the-minute coverage of federal, state, and international tax news. The weekly print series includes *Tax Notes*, *State Tax Notes*, and *Tax Notes International*. *Tax Notes Today* (TNT) is updated continually throughout the day, not just once a day, so

EXHIBIT 8-38: Tax Analysts Federal Research Library

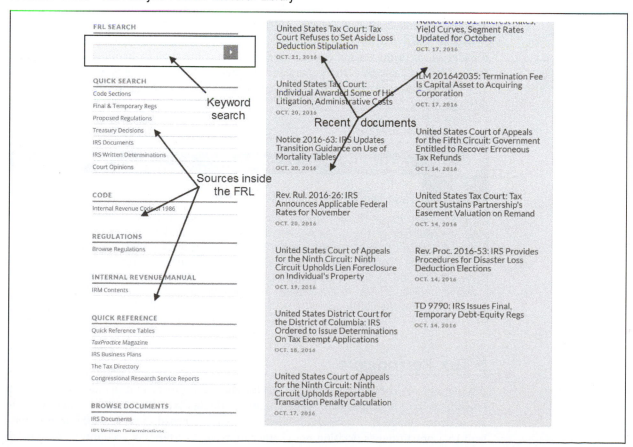

EXHIBIT 8-39:   Tax Analysts Broad Search

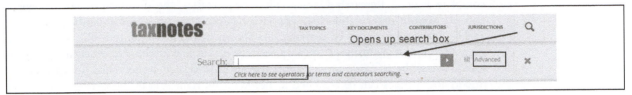

practitioners can be as up to date as they desire. The amount of information included in these newsletters is staggering. TNT, for instance, includes the following:

- Commentary and analysis by experts

- Internal Revenue Bulletins, IRS correspondence, and other administrative rulings; final, temporary, and proposed regulations, and public comments on proposed regulations

- Congressional actions, legislation, and correspondence, including tax committee reports

- Court cases

The content of the weekly *Tax Notes* publication is similar to that of TNT and the Weekly Report, published by BNA (discussed later in this chapter). However, *Tax Notes* includes in-depth analysis of court decisions, regulatory pronouncements, and policy-oriented research submitted by tax professionals and academics. Special sections provide news and practice tips specifically for accounting and tax practitioners. The addition of a broader set of primary sources combined with the continuing in-depth analysis provided by Tax Analysts expert authors increases the chances that researchers will start using the Tax Analysts web platform for more than a reliable source of up-to-date news releases through *Daily Tax Notes*.

SPOTLIGHT ON TAXATION

Field Service Advice Memorandums

Field service advice (FSA) memorandums are available to the tax community thanks to Tax Analysts. In 1993, Tax Analysts filed a request under the Freedom of Information Act to have FSA memorandums become subject to public disclosure. The IRS declined this request, because these documents contained return information or were protected by the attorney–client privilege and therefore were not available for public disclosure. Tax Analysts took the question to court, and in 1996, a district court ordered the IRS to release the FSAs to the general public.

5 Tax Periodicals

Tax periodicals contain a variety of articles and news briefs that are designed to keep readers up to date in specific or general areas of the tax law. These articles might contain an in-depth review of a recently decided court case, a broad analysis of the factors relevant to a practitioner's decision on whether to make a certain tax accounting election, or a call for reform of a statute by a neutral (or biased) observer. Tax articles can suggest new viewpoints on tax issues, give guidance for solving complex problems, or explain a new law in a readable form. All these resources are very useful to tax practitioners.

With an article that is on point as to a tax issue, the practitioner is able to, in effect, use the author of the article as a research associate by capitalizing on the author's expert judgments and references, thereby saving hours of research time. Keep in mind, however, that tax periodicals are secondary sources of the tax law and therefore should not be cited as controlling authority, especially when primary sources supporting the position are available. The article's references can lead to the pertinent primary tax sources. With that caveat aside, researchers who ignore the tax periodicals might be accused, at best, of reinventing the wheel, and at worst, of professional malpractice.

Traditionally, citing articles in professional tax research is limited to two situations: (1) the researcher is referring to the author's analysis and conclusions as stated in an article or (2) the researcher cannot find any controlling primary sources of law, and a secondary source addresses the issues. Tax articles are now being cited more frequently in case opinions. When lacking both relevant primary law sources and adequate judicial staff, the authors of these case opinions may draw on tax articles to support the views of the court. In any event, it is imperative that researchers understand the practical implications of using secondary law sources. Tax periodicals can be categorized according to the depth of the coverage of their articles and the audience for which they are written. From the most extensive coverage to the least, they are as follows:

- Annual proceedings
- Scholarly reviews
- Professional journals
- Newsletters

Although each publication has unique attributes, several general characteristics of each category will be identified. This discussion provides an initial introduction to the broad market of secondary-source tax commentary.

5-1 Annual Proceedings

Every year, several annual conferences for tax practitioners and academics take place. Usually sponsored by a professional organization, law school, or an educational agency, these conferences generally last from two to five days. The agenda at these conferences may include lectures, paper presentations with or without discussions, panel discussions, seminars, demonstrations, and luncheon addresses. Often, the conference speakers allow the sponsoring agency to publish their presentations in proceedings from the meeting.

These annual proceedings are distributed to conference participants and later to the general public in the form of a collection of articles. Most of these papers exhibit considerable depth of coverage and practical insight. They can be a valuable resource for the tax researcher. A few of the established academic tax conferences and the years they started are the following:

- National Tax Association, 1907
- New York University Institute on Federal Taxation, 1942
- William and Mary Tax Conference, 1954
- University of North Carolina Tax Symposium, 1997

- University of Chicago's Annual Federal Tax Conference, 1947

- University of Southern California's Tax Institute, 1948

- Tulane Tax Institute, 1952

5-2 Scholarly Reviews

All major law schools and a few business schools produce publications referred to as law reviews or academic journals. These publications are edited either by faculty members or by students under the guidance of the school's faculty. Most law reviews also use an outside advisory board comprised of practicing attorneys and law professors at other universities to aid in selecting and reviewing articles. The articles appearing in these scholarly reviews are usually written by tax practitioners, academics, students, or noted commentators.

Some law schools produce journals that are limited to a specific area of law, such as constitutional or labor law. Most of the general law reviews feature one to three tax articles per year; however, some law reviews are dedicated exclusively to tax matters. The following are several law reviews that concentrate on taxation issues:

- *Akron Tax Journal*, University of Akron School of Law

- *Ohio Tax Review*, Capital University Law & Graduate Center

- *Florida Tax Review*, University of Florida College of Law

- *Tax Law Review*, New York University School of Law

- *The Tax Lawyer* and *The State and Local Tax Lawyer*, Georgetown University and the American Bar Association (ABA)

- *Virginia Tax Review*, University of Virginia School of Law

Besides law schools, academic organizations such as the National Tax Association (NTA) and the American Taxation Association (ATA) publish scholarly journals and proceedings from their annual conferences.

5-3 Professional Journals

Tax journals are published for the purpose of keeping tax practitioners abreast of current changes and trends in the tax law. This category, commonly referred to as professional or practitioner journals, includes publications from professional organizations as well as commercial companies. Examples of the former are the AICPA's *The Tax Adviser* and journals published by state accountant or attorney professional organizations.

Because the commercial publications are numerous, the tax coverage in these journals can accommodate the needs of both general tax practitioners and those who specialize in a specific area of tax law. For example, journals such as WG&L's *Journal of Taxation* and *Practical Tax Strategies* and CCH's *Taxes—The Tax Magazine* cover a variety of tax areas, whereas journals such as BNA Tax Management's *The Compensation Planning Journal* and WG&L's *Journal of Taxation of Investments* cover only specific topics. Further, the articles appearing in these journals also vary greatly in their coverage, from very complex articles with an exceedingly narrow focus to extremely practical articles designed for immediate implementation. Major changes in the tax law or important court decisions spawn numerous articles in the various periodicals on the same or similar topics.

To accommodate the tax practitioner's need for timely information, most of the multitopic tax journals are published monthly, whereas the more specialized tax journals tend to be issued on a quarterly basis. Practitioners with subscriptions to Internet services may obtain their journals through their online services. For example, a subscriber to Checkpoint may add subscriptions to the WG&L journals. To ensure the quality of their articles, journals seek commentaries prepared by appropriate tax experts. In each case, an editorial review board assesses the timeliness, accuracy, and readability of each article before it is accepted for publication.

5-4 Newsletters

The major tax services include a tax newsletter as part of the service. The Internet services tend to have daily newsletters, whereas the published services send the newsletters weekly. These newsletters help the subscriber keep abreast of important tax law developments. They are designed to give the practitioner both a capsulated summary of tax law modifications and references to paragraphs within the tax service materials that contain more detailed analysis. Some of these newsletters also publish information concerning tax seminars and professional meetings, short reviews of (or citations for) selected current tax articles, and editorial highlights concerning recent tax developments. Popular newsletters include those published by Tax Analysts, BNA, CCH, and Thomson Reuters.

5-5 BNA Publications

One of the most important tax newsletters available to practitioners is the Bloomberg **BNA Daily Tax Report (DTR)**. DTR is available online; through wireless devices, including iPhones; and in hard copy. Subscribers may also receive notification of breaking tax news as soon as it occurs with DTR real-time e-mail alerts. Showing both breadth in coverage and a quality of analysis similar to the Tax Analysts TNT, DTR offers up-to-date information concerning statutory, administrative, and judicial tax law developments that affect state, federal, and international taxation. In addition, the newsletter contains interviews with governmental officials, articles reviewing current events, and the full text of key documents discussed in the newsletter. Some of these documents are not available from other tax services. Monthly and quarterly indexes are provided.

DTR offers the equivalent of 30 to 50 pages of single-spaced printed copy every weekday. Because this is clearly too much data to digest every day, DTR is organized to facilitate the subscriber to access only the material of greatest interest. While the content section lists only the title of each note by category, the highlights provide brief paragraphs describing the notes. With hyperlinks, the subscriber can access the actual governmental document on which the story is based, through TaxCore (included with the subscription to DTR). TaxCore contains a wide variety of full-text primary tax materials that is updated daily. It provides a categorization of sources to facilitate retrieving the document of interest. The source categories include Congressional, Treasury, Court, IRS, State and Local, White House, and International. TaxCore may also be obtained separately from DTR.

Receiving such extensive tax news on a daily basis is costly. However, DTR (as well as many newsletters produced by other publishers) is available online to subscribers of Westlaw, LexisNexis, and various other services. Thus, by subscribing to one of the major tax database systems, the practitioner has access to DTR at a small or zero incremental cost.

Similar to Tax Analysts, BNA publishes a weekly newsletter as well as a daily one. The BNA *Weekly Report* coverage is similar to that of DTR but is more in depth. In addition, it contains articles on news and emerging tax topics. The comprehensive index makes it easy to locate items of interest. In addition to other weekly, biweekly, and monthly newsletters, BNA publishes journals in the areas of financial planning, real estate, compensation planning, international, and estates, gifts, and trusts. It also has a research service, Tax Practice Library, that includes a topical service providing analysis, examples, and practice tools such as client letters, line-by-line form guidance, checklists, and interactive tax forms.

5-6 Locating Relevant Tax Articles

Numerous online search indexes and databases such as Google Scholar, JSTOR, Business Source Premier, Thomson Reuters Web of Science, and ABI/Inform facilitate locating tax, business, and law review articles pertinent to the practitioner's research. These search programs index thousands of periodicals. Most indexes focus on a keyword search strategy and allow the researcher to determine the connectors (e.g., *and, versus, or*) among the words or phrases. Since these indexes are not exclusively for tax research, they will not be reviewed.

Additional resources for locating tax articles are the major tax services. Each service offers access to a variety of journals and law reviews in searchable databases, but no service imparts access to the majority of the tax periodicals. The CCH Federal Tax Articles (FTA) and WG&L's Index to Federal Tax Articles (IFTA) are the two indexes specifically designed for locating tax articles. Unfortunately, both indexes are offered only in print and are not available online. This is frustrating for subscribers to online services such as IntelliConnect, Checkpoint, and Westlaw, because these indexes would be most useful in an electronic format. The FTA index has many outstanding features that make it one of the best tax indexes available. It is known for the concise abstracts it furnishes for each article cited in the index. Reading these abstracts helps the practitioner reduce false starts that commonly occur when trying to find pertinent articles based solely on their titles. These abstracts are organized around an Internal Revenue Code framework.

This organization system also helps the researcher find articles addressing the code section he or she is investigating. CCH updates this index monthly, so the citations are timely. Because the FTA current volume (since 2004) is a loose-leaf service, the updates provide new pages that either replace existing pages or are added to the contents of the volume. Besides listing the filing instructions for the new pages, the Report Letter presents the highlights of the most interesting new developments, seminars, and tax conferences.

Approximately 250 journals, law reviews, papers, and proceedings are included in the index. The topics covered in the FTA include federal income, excise, estate, gift, and employment taxation. The main division of the index, called Articles by Code Section, gives the full citation for each article and its abstract. This cumulative index gives code section numbers with a brief description of the section as its headings. Articles can also be located by using the topic and author indexes. Each of these indexes refers the researcher to the Articles by Code Section division through a system of paragraph numbers.

5-7 Citing Articles in Tax Periodicals

The citation for a printed tax journal article should take the following standard format:

> *Sanders, Debra, Susan Gill, and Jill Zuber. 2009. Deductibility of bankruptcy costs and the origin of the claim. The Tax Advisor 40 (8): at 528.*

Notice the proper placement of capital letters, periods, commas, and italics in the citation. The denotation "at 528" indicates that the researcher is referencing or quoting from a specific page of the article. If the entire article were being referenced, the citation would merely contain the beginning page number of the article. For the citation above, this would be "… 40 (8): 526."

Unfortunately, the proper citation for articles found on the Internet is not as well established as for printed materials. A problem that complicates matters is deciding how to characterize the Internet material being cited. For example, is the material a journal article, a newsletter, a report, or a blog? Who is the author? When was the resource generated? Once all this information is determined (which might not be easy to do), a generally safe citation format to follow is that of a printed document with additions or deletions as necessary. The following would be an acceptable format for a journal article found on the Internet:

Sullivan, Paul. 2013. When Converting a Roth I.R.A. back to a Traditional One Makes Sense. New York Times (October 4, 2013). Retrieved October 4, 2013 from **http://www.nytimes.com/2013/10/05/your-money/when-converting-a-roth-ira-back-to-a-traditional-onemakes-sense.html?ref=incometax&_r=0**

Website addresses are generally case and punctuation sensitive. Therefore, one should ignore normal grammar rules when providing uniform resource locators (URLs) and place no punctuation (such as a period or a comma) at the end of a URL. It is important to indicate the date on which the document was retrieved because documents and URLs may change or be removed.

SUMMARY

Many commercial services can be used to perform tax research, and no one service is the best for all practitioners. Although the services provide different features, all are most efficient when the organization of the service facilitates research of the issues in a client's tax situation. Thus, each tax service has its place in tax research, and practitioners must determine which products they are most comfortable with and which fit their firms' normal research requirements.

Changes in technology and the tax services are constant. The same changes occur in the practitioner's business. Consequently, the practitioner's comfort level with products and technology and the research needs will evolve. Practitioners should evaluate their tax resource choices often, at least once a year when it is time to renew their services.

The tax researcher should employ commercial services as gateways to the primary sources and not as a substitute for primary-source research. Tax services can make the research process more efficient and productive, but they should not replace a thorough review of primary sources and the researcher's professional judgment.

KEY WORDS

By the time you complete this chapter, you should be comfortable discussing each of the following terms. If you need additional review of any of these items, return to the appropriate material in the chapter or consult the glossary to this text.

BNA Bloomberg Tax & Accounting Center, p. 258

BNA Daily Tax Report, p. 291

BNA Tax Management Portfolios, p. 258

Lexis Advance Tax, p. 272

LexisNexis Academic, p. 275

DISCUSSION QUESTIONS

1. How can finding a BNA portfolio on point with a practitioner's tax issue be like hiring someone to do the research?

2. How is each BNA portfolio arranged?

3. Describe the Working Papers section of a BNA tax management portfolio.

4. Who designed Westlaw? What is its target market?

5. The opening screen in Westlaw is designed to look and feel like what other kind of search?

6. How is a space between keywords interpreted by Checkpoint, CCH IntelliConnect, Westlaw, and LexisNexis?

7. What are KeySearch and the West Key Number System?

8. What are the major analytical materials offered through Lexis Advance Tax?

9. Using an example, describe the steps a researcher might take after using a broad keyword search to narrow the search down.

10. What is Lexis's Get a Document feature similar to in the other tax services?

11. What is LexisNexis Academic?

12. How are tax materials accessed on LexisNexis Academic?

13. Why might some researchers find the citators in Westlaw or Shepards' superior to those found in Checkpoint or IntelliConnect?

EXERCISES

14. Use the BNA Tax and Accounting Center to answer the following questions:
    a. Which U.S. Income Portfolios cover gross-income related topics?
    b. Find the *Green Incentives Monitor*. How many days in the month of September 2016 did the *Green Incentives Monitor* publish an article under the News heading?
    c. Find the table of contents for the Employment Tax Withholding Requirements in the Tax Practice Series on Compensation Planning. What is the paragraph on statutory employees? Once found, open the document and then click Chapter Outline at the top of the page. What is the paragraph that covers income tax withholding on fishing crews?
    d. Perform a search of the source documents to locate an IRS publication covering moving expenses.

15. Use the BNA Tax and Accounting Center to answer the following questions:
    a. Use the Guided Search function and select Fast Answers: Federal Tax. What revenue procedure covers the safe harbor for deducting home-office expenses in lieu of actual expenses?
    b. Perform a keyword search for all collections using keywords 2012-62. How many documents are found? In which collection is the actual IRS Notice 2012-62?

    c. Use the Go To function to find IRS Notice 2012-62. What is the website to determine if your area is in a drought?

    d. Using Advance Search/Laws, Regulations, Agency Documents/Tax/IRS Documents, search for notice 2012-62. Which other IRS notice other than the listed notice is found? Is the listed notice related?

16. Use the BNA U.S. Income portfolios to answer the following questions:

    a. Use the keyword index for the U.S. Income portfolios and find New York Liberty Zone. What is the portfolio number (and section) that discusses the definition of New York Liberty Zone property?

    b. In the portfolio identified in a, what is demonstrated in Worksheet 5?

    c. What is the portfolio number (and section) that discusses in general the timing of deductions under the all-events test for an accrual-based taxpayer?

    d. In the portfolio identified in c, who is the author of the portfolio?

17. Use the BNA Tax and Accounting Center to answer the following questions:

    a. What options are available in the Advanced Search?

    b. What actions do the following search operators (connectors) perform: spaces between words, question mark (?), and asterisk (*)?

    c. Using a Guided Search, what options are available besides a keyword search?

    d. How does the Go To option function?

18. Use the BNA Tax and Accounting Center to answer the following questions:

    a. Use a Go To search to find 30 T.C. 757. What is the issue in this case?

    b. Using a Guided Search, determine which Expert Analyses cite 30 T.C. 757.

    c. Using an Advanced Search, select Cases and Decisions, choose the Attorney field, and enter the name Gill. Limit the dates to the year 2012. In what Tax Court case(s) was Gill the lawyer?

    d. Using Advanced Search and using the Search Indexes & Finding Aids, enter *qualified production activity income* as the search term. What is cross-referenced in the results of this search from the U.S. Portfolios index?

19. Use the BNA Tax Management portfolios to answer the following questions:

    a. What is the portfolio number (and section) that discusses the issue of a stuffing allocation to a redeeming hedge-fund partner?

    b. Which Sales and Use Portfolio discusses the true object test for sales and use taxes on information services?

    c. Which portfolio contains a worksheet demonstrating the attribution rules between family members for IRC § 267? What is the worksheet number?

20. Use Westlaw Campus Research to answer the following questions:

    a. Find Reg. § 1.61-11. What is the subject matter of this regulation?

    b. Which American Law Reports—Tax covers the theft of grain as a casualty or theft loss under IRC § 165?

    c. Find 169 A.L.R. Fed. 1. What issue does this source discuss?

    d. Which court case that appears in 169 A.L.R. Fed. 1 examines the timing of worthless bad debt because of a check returned unpaid?

    e. Which items in Westlaw cite the court case found in d above?

21. Use Westlaw Campus Research to answer the following questions:

    a. What is the Westlaw Key Number for Gross Income under Taxation?

    b. Find *Stewart v. U.S.*, 106 F.2d 405. Which court presided over this case?

   c. According to Westlaw's KeyCite flag, what is the status of this case?

   d. Which court reversed the decision cited in b?

22. Use Westlaw Campus Research to answer the following questions:

   a. What is the New Mexico regulation that defines "base income?"

   b. Find the *Armstrong v. Commonwealth of the Northern Mariana Islands* Supreme Court action that occurred in June 2010. Was certiorari granted?

   c. How many law reviews are available as secondary tax sources?

   d. Who wrote the article "Tax Compliance as a Wicked System" in the *Florida Tax Review*?

23. Use Westlaw Campus Research to answer the following questions:

   a. Using Find Case by Party Name, locate the 2008 Supreme Court case, *Boulware*. Provide the Federal, Westlaw, RIA, and CCH citations for the case.

   b. Under Practice Areas, what secondary resources are available for Securities?

   c. Select one of the resources located in b and determine its contents.

   d. Find IRC § 67. Using the Context and Analysis tab, what is the reference to the Encyclopedia that covers the deduction of impairment-related work expenses? Based on this analysis, are these expenses subject to the 2 percent floor?

24. Use Westlaw Campus Research to answer the following questions:

   a. Find the House proceeding during which the bill to add flu vaccines to the list of taxable vaccines was discussed on the House floor and was passed by the House. What is the date of this proceeding and who introduced the discussion?

   b. Indicate your search strategy for a. Include your search terms, databases chosen, and search iterations.

   c. Which statutes were affected by the new public law related to including flu vaccines on the taxable list?

   d. Which key number is suggested for this code section?

25. Use Westlaw Campus Research to answer the following questions:

   a. What is subchapter B of title 26, subtitle A, chapter 1 of the Code of Federal Regulations?

   b. What IRC section covers the inclusion of the rental value of parsonages?

   c. What is the key number for medical deductions?

   d. In the *Jack L. Hargrove* case, why was certiorari granted by the Supreme Court in 2010?

26. Use Lexis Advance Tax to answer the following questions. (Hint: Click on the "i" for information.)

   a. What is the frequency and update schedule for the IRS Chief Counsel Advice?

   b. Since when have California Attorney General opinions been included in Lexis Advance Tax?

   c. Who publishes the LexisNexis Tax Advisor—Federal Topical?

   d. Select LexisNexis Tax Advisor—Federal Topical database. Perform a natural-language search to determine the tax treatment of stock redeemed from a deceased shareholder. Perform the same search using terms and connectors. List your natural-language search and the number of documents it retrieved. Provide the same information for the terms and connectors search. Explain why one was a more effective search.

27. Use Lexis Advance Tax to answer the following questions. (Hint: Use More Sources.)

   a. What is the update schedule for the IRS Chief Counsel Advice?

   b. Which law reviews are offered as separate databases?

   c. Use the Lexis Tax Advisor—Federal Code Reporter to find IRC § 74. What is the title of the Analytical Materials?

   d. What is the title of the first article in Tax Analysts *Tax Notes Today*?

28. Use Lexis Advance Tax to answer the following questions:
    a. Select the Tax Overview tab. What are the three segments that can be searched in the search word *drop-down*?
    b. Select the News Tab. What sources are listed?
    c. Select the Sources tab. What document is the last one listed under the letter E?

29. Using Lexis Advance Tax, answer the following questions:
    a. Use the Tax Overview tab and determine what the title of Chapter 1G:2 of Volume 1G is.
    b. Use the Treatises and Practice Guides pod and search for exempt organizations on the Internet. How many hits are there in Treatises and Practice Guides results?
    c. Select the Treatises and Practice Guides pod and search the Internet in the heading segment of document[s] and exempt within one word of organization? How many hits are there in the results?
    d. Reperform the search in part c, except search the title segment. How many "hits" did you get?

30. Use the LexisNexis option to answer the following questions:
    a. Perform a search for the source revenue procedure. Does a source that contains the IRS revenue procedures result?
    b. Use the BROWSE option to find a source, and restrict the search to the Taxation Area of Law and select United States as the country. Which of the sources that start with IRS have the revenue procedures (Hint: Click on the *i*)?
    c. Search the Internal Revenue Code for *income services child*. Search the results for *parent* and then select the first document. Click the right arrow near the top [1 of XX]. What keyword is highlighted in each document as you scroll through document by document?
    d. Continuing from part c, use the Next Steps drop-down menu and select Back to Original Results and Go. What keywords are highlighted in each document as you scroll through document by document?

31. Use LexisNexis Academic to answer the following questions:
    a. From the home page, select Search by Subject or Topic, select the Tax Law database, and perform a terms and connectors search using the following terms: *taxing*, *barter*, and *baby-sitting* with "and" connectors. How many law review documents are in the results?
    b. From the results in a, what is the sales tax treatment of baby-sitting services when provided by a health club?
    c. From the results in b, find the article from the *Catholic University Law Review*. Do a search within results for the word tomatoes. What is the result?

32. Use LexisNexis Academic to answer the following questions:
    a. Using the judge's last name Sotomayor, determine the treatments of the petitions for writ of certiorari decided on October 7, 2013. Also provide the full name of each case and from which court of appeals the writ originated.
    b. When using terms and connectors searches, what do the following connectors mean? W/10; PRE/ 20; NOT W/seg; and ATLEAST5. (Hint: Click on Tips for using search connectors.)

33. Use LexisNexis Tax Law to answer the following questions:
    a. What types of sources are provided in the Tax Law library? (Hint: After selecting Tax Law, use Advanced Search to reveal the sources.)
    b. Furnish the title of the most recent *UCLA Law Review* article that discusses the zombie apocalypse.
    c. One of the sources in Tax Law is *The Tax Adviser*. What is the coverage period for this journal, and how often is this journal published? (Hint: Use the *i* button.)
    d. What is the title and citation for the *Tax Notes Today* article that discusses tax issues related to marijuana dispensaries?

34. Use LexisNexis Academic Browse Sources by Area of Law, Taxation Law to answer the following questions:
    a. How many United States sources (U.S. All Regions) are available for the Treatises & Analytical Materials library?
    b. Locate the most recent article in the Legal News publication database Tax Analysts Tax Publications (Country United States, All Regions) discussing Cambodia.
    c. Using Browse Sources, select the Cases for Publication Type for the United States, West region. Which states' cases are included in the West region?
    d. Select the Administrative Materials for Publication Type for the United States, and Region California. What sources are offered in the browse option?

35. Use Tax Analysts *Tax Notes* to answer the following:
    a. Perform an advanced search and find the article on Donald Trump's tax loss possibly relating to an S corporation. Who was the author of that article?
    b. In the article found in a, which cited court case dealt with the use of forgiveness of debt to create an S corporation basis to permit a large loss?
    c. What did Johnson conclude about a Gitlitz driven loss?

Multijurisdictional Taxes

LEARNING OBJECTIVES

- Apply the tax research process to state and local taxes.
- Describe the general constraints of a state taxation system.
- Identify the major features of state tax services.
- Compare and contrast the search methodologies that are available for each of the state tax services.
- Describe the basic framework for international taxation.
- Describe and contrast the major features of international tax services.
- Develop search methodologies applicable to each of the international services.
- Identify which tax services are most appropriate for different international research objectives.

CHAPTER OUTLINE

TAX RESEARCH EXTENDS BEYOND the confines of simple federal tax research. The state and local tax environment is becoming increasingly complex and challenging to navigate as a result of the states' expansion of their taxing systems and collection efforts. Additionally, more and more U.S. companies are finding themselves operating in the global economy in a more significant way. The realm of multijurisdictional taxation is no longer limited to large multinational corporations. Even a small Internet-based business can find itself with a large global footprint. Tax professionals need to find a way to extend their expertise into the same jurisdictions as their clients. In addition to understanding how the states deal with transactions that cross state borders, practitioners will need to increase their understanding of both how the United States deals with taxing foreign transactions and how foreign countries will tax U.S. companies. Fortunately, the tax services have recognized the expansion of the tax professionals' purview and continue to offer new and expanded offerings into the world of multijurisdictional tax. The first half of this chapter deals with researching state tax issues while the second half deals with researching international tax issues.

1 State and Local Tax

State and local tax planning and compliance has become big business for accounting and tax law firms. In today's market, practitioners who service their clients successfully recommend tax solutions that are not only consistent with clients' overall financial goals but also help clients minimize their state and local tax burdens. Consequently, the tax professional must stay current in this area of tax law even though this specialized area can represent an additional burden on the practitioner's time.

There are numerous reasons for emphasizing state and local tax planning. For many businesses this is an untapped planning opportunity regarding which practitioners can offer expertise, which is especially important as many of the most productive federal tax planning opportunities for businesses have been limited by tax law changes. While the amount of any single tax paid to an individual state by a business may be relatively small, in aggregate, according to the Council on State Taxation, business taxpayers paid an estimated $688 billion in state and local taxes in fiscal year 2014. Coordinated state tax planning can substantially reduce state taxes, especially for taxpayers that operate in a variety of state and local taxing jurisdictions and have some flexibility as to where their property and labor force are located.

All states possess the authority to tax. Generally, local governments must be specifically authorized to impose taxes by state statutory or constitutional provisions. These authorizing provisions, in turn, regulate the rates and operation of local government taxes. Courts in some states, however, have ruled that the power to impose taxes can be implied from broad home-rule provisions. These rules grant partial autonomy to local governmental authorities under general state constitutional provisions.

The **Supremacy Clause** in the U.S. Constitution governs potential conflicts between federal and state law. This clause does not confer absolute superiority to federal laws over state laws, but instead dictates when a conflict between federal and state law must be resolved in the federal government's favor. Federal laws are "supreme" only if made "in pursuance of the Constitution."[1] Thus, for example, federal laws cannot override powers reserved to the states under the Constitution, such as a state's police powers. The modern view of the Supremacy Clause holds that federal law can preempt state law when Congress by express provision so provides or when Congress legislates in such a way as to indicate that it intends for the federal law to "occupy the field." Another important application of the Supremacy Clause concerns the taxation by the states of federal-government

---

[1]*Marbury v. Madison*, 5 U.S. 137 (1803).

operations. If states were permitted to tax the federal government, the federal government's constitutional functions would be impeded. Thus, the Supremacy Clause in the Constitution immunizes the federal government from taxation by the states.

2 Importance of State and Local Taxes

State and local taxes are playing an ever-increasing role in the tax planning of businesses and individuals alike. Often, greater revenues are needed to meet the demands of constituents, so states often must raise the tax burdens of residents. Businesses take the level of state and local taxation into consideration when deciding where to locate new plants or headquarters. This analysis includes not only business taxes but also the individual taxes of the personnel relocating to the new location. Exhibit 9-1 provides the top and bottom 10 states based on per capita state and local tax-burden rank, and also the percentage of personal income represented by that amount. The differences are striking. Alaska has gone from the number-one rank in 2012 to the last rank in 2015 as taxes from oil and gas have dropped significantly.

Many state constitutions constrain the types of taxes that may be imposed within the state and/or set upper limits on tax rates. Therefore, states may be forced to resort to alternative methods for generating revenues, such as trying to expand the scope of nexus,

EXHIBIT 9-1: Ten Top and Bottom State and Local Tax Collections per Capita 2015

Rank	State	Tax Collection $ per Capita	Largest Source of Tax Revenues
1	North Dakota	7,583	Severance[a]
2	Vermont	4,861	Property
3	Hawaii	4,530	Sales
4	Connecticut	4,520	Personal Income
5	Minnesota	4,452	Personal Income
6	Wyoming	4,020	Sales
7	Massachusetts	3,976	Personal Income
8	New York	3,952	Personal Income
9	California	3,862	Personal Income
10	Delaware	3,715	Corporate License
41	Alabama	2,008	Sales
42	Texas	2,005	Sales
43	South Carolina	1,967	Sales
44	Missouri	1,965	Personal Income
45	South Dakota	1,950	Sales
46	Georgia	1,931	Personal Income
47	Tennessee	1,924	Sales
48	New Hampshire	1,870	Sales
49	Florida	1,836	Sales
50	Alaska	1,170	Sales

[a]Severance taxes are imposed on the removal (severance) of natural resources.

Source: U.S. Census Bureau data. 2015 State Tax Collections and Populations Estimates July 1, 2015.

increase compliance, and impose substantial penalties. As failure to comply with state and local tax laws becomes more costly, businesses and individuals are requesting additional research from their tax professionals to help manage this significant tax burden.

SPOTLIGHT ON TAXATION

State Business Tax Climate 2017

With the myriad differences between states relating to sources of income, types of taxes, and tax rates, it can be challenging to determine with any precision exactly what the tax burden will be in a particular state. The Tax Foundation, a nonpartisan educational foundation, prepares a tax-climate ranking for states, presented here:

2017 State Business Tax Climate Index

Note: A rank of 1 is best, 50 is worst. Rankings do not average to the total. States without a tax rank equally as 1. DC's score and rank do not affect other states. The report shows tax systems as of July 1, 2016 (the beginning of Fiscal Year 2017).
Source: Tax Foundation.

■ 10 Best Business Tax Climates

■ 10 Worst Business Tax Climates

TAX FOUNDATION   @TaxFoundation

Source: Tax Foundation (**www.taxfoundation.org/**).

Exhibit 9-2 illustrates the increase in the state taxes over time. In 1970, the tax collected by states was $48 billion, whereas by 2015 the amount rose to over $900 billion. Thus, state and local taxes have increased on average by just under 7 percent per year.

3 Legal Perspective

Federal and state constitutional provisions play an integral role in state tax planning. The constitutional validity of state tax laws is still challenged in the courts today, whereas the constitutionality of federal taxes is rarely questioned anymore. State and local tax

EXHIBIT 9-2: State Tax Collections

Year	Collections ($B)
1970	48.0
1980	136.9
1990	307.1
2000	551.9
2010	703.4
2015	916.5

Source: U.S. Bureau of the Census.

challenges address not only whether the taxes fall within the purview of the state constitution but also whether the laws are federally constitutional. The federal clauses most frequently providing the basis for state taxation disputes are the Supremacy Clause, related to the hierarchy of tax law, and the Commerce and Due Process Clauses, related to the states' power to tax out-of-state individuals and entities.

SPOTLIGHT ON TAXATION

Tax Freedom Day

Every year the Tax Foundation determines "Tax Freedom Day," the hypothetical day when taxpayers have earned enough money to pay all their taxes and now can "work for themselves." In 2016, the National Tax Freedom Day was April 24. The latest measured tax freedom day was May 1, 2000. Since that time, the date has fluctuated between April 8 and April 27. Depending on the state in which you live, your Tax Freedom Day may be earlier or later than the national average. In 2016, the earliest dates were for Mississippi and Tennessee in early April. The latest dates were for Connecticut (May 21), New Jersey (May 12), and New York (May 11).

TAX FREEDOM DAY AND TAX BURDEN, 1940–2013

Year	Tax Freedom Day	Individual Income Taxes as Share of GDP
1940	March 7	0.9%
1950	March 31	5.6%
1960	April 12	7.6%
1970	April 19	8.6%
1980	April 21	8.7%
1990	April 21	7.9%
2000	May 1	9.9%
2010	April 11	6.1%
2016	April 24	8.7% (estimated)

For details, go to **www.taxfoundation.org/taxfreedomday**.

3-1 Taxing Out-of-State Taxpayers

Without constitutional limits, states might choose to impose taxes on any individual or entity with any connection whatsoever to that state. From a state revenue perspective, such an approach might lead to higher tax revenues, but from the taxpayer's perspective, requirements to file tax returns in every state, even when the taxpayer's connection to that state is minimal, would place an administrative compliance burden that, pragmatically, most taxpayers would be unwilling to subject themselves to. In recognition of not only administrative burdens but also constitutional notions of federalism and the protection of individuals, the states' power to tax out-of-state individuals and entities has been restricted by the federal government under three constitutional clauses and one public law. Federal restrictions apply not only to the income taxation of out-of-state taxpayers but also to the ability of states to force out-of-state businesses to collect and remit sales and use taxes on their sales to in-state residents.

3-2 Due Process Clause

Section 1 of the 14th Amendment to the Constitution (the **Due Process Clause**) states that "… No state shall make or enforce any law which shall … deprive any person of life, liberty, or property, without due process of law." Due process is directed toward the fairness of governmental activities and is concerned with whether the tax in practical terms has a rational relationship to the opportunities, benefits, or protections offered or provided by the state. This "fairness" test is satisfied when an out-of-state entity "purposefully avails itself of the benefits of an economic market in the foreign State."[2] The U.S. Supreme Court has applied the Due Process Clause to limit the territorial scope of a state's taxing authority in interstate commerce cases. States have lost cases in two key situations, as follows:

- States seek to tax out-of-state businesses whose connections or nexus with the state are not sufficient to satisfy the Due Process Clause.

- The tax imposed does not fairly reflect the taxpayer's activities in the state.

To be successful in applying a tax, states must prove that the business has a minimum connection to the state and that the taxing base for the interstate enterprise includes only amounts fairly apportioned to its activities within the state.[3] The Due Process Clause does not guarantee that the benefits received by an interstate enterprise will have any direct relationship to the amount of taxes paid to that state. To be fairly related to the services provided by a state, the tax need only be assessed in proportion to the business's activities within the state. As articulated in *Commonwealth Edison Co. v. Montana*, 453 U.S. 609 (1981), "(A) tax … is a means of distributing the burden of the cost of government. The only benefit to which the taxpayer is constitutionally entitled is derived from his enjoyment of the privileges of living in an organized society, established and safeguarded by the devotion of taxes to public purposes."

The Due Process Clause does not require a physical presence by the out-of-state entity for a state to have taxing jurisdiction. Thus, an economic presence rising above a de minimis level is sufficient to tax under the Due Process Clause. However, this same level of contact might not be sufficient to create the substantial nexus within the state as required by the Commerce Clause.

---

[2]*Quill Corp v. North Dakota*, 504 U.S. 298 (1992).

[3]*Miller Brothers Co. v. Maryland*, 347 U.S. 340 (1954).

3-3 Commerce Clause

Article 1, Section 8, Clause 3 (the **Commerce Clause**) of the U.S. Constitution states that "the Congress shall have power … to regulate commerce with foreign nations, and among the several states. …" The goal of the Commerce Clause is to create a national economy unencumbered by discriminatory, arbitrary jurisdictional standards of the states. Although phrased as a grant of power to Congress, it has long been interpreted as a constraint on the states' ability to tax interstate trade.

The Commerce Clause has a long history of Supreme Court actions. The interpretation of the clause as it now stands is based on the case *Complete Auto Transit Inc. v. Brady,* 430 U.S. 274 (1977). The case involved a tax being imposed on companies for the privilege of conducting interstate transportation businesses. Corporations involved in intrastate and interstate commerce were all subject to the tax. In unanimously deciding that the tax was valid, the Supreme Court established the four criteria now regarded as controlling as to whether a state may tax interstate commerce without the tax becoming an unreasonable burden:

(1) A tax may be imposed if the activity includes a substantial connection (**nexus**) with the taxing state,

(2) the tax burden is fairly apportioned,

(3) the tax does not discriminate against interstate commerce, and

(4) the tax fairly relates to the services provided by the state.

Thus, businesses involved in interstate commerce should be subject to a tax burden related to their fair share of the state's costs of providing benefits to the taxpayer.

In *Quill Corp. v. North Dakota,* 504 U.S. 298 (1992), the U.S. Supreme Court ruled that the Commerce Clause mandated that a taxpayer must have some *physical presence* in a state to be subject to collection responsibility for the state's use tax. Although *Quill* deals with use tax and not income tax, the Court's discussion of the Due Process and Commerce Clauses sheds some light on their application to income taxes. The *Quill* decision was based on the fact that the burden on an interstate business is so great that it poses a barrier to interstate commerce. It has been suggested that the protection from sales taxation offered by *Quill* may not last forever. As it gets easier to comply with the sales and use tax obligation, the argument used in *Quill* regarding the burden on interstate commerce becomes less relevant.

Many of the court cases related to the states' power to define nexus relate to sales tax rather than income taxes. Caution should be used when talking about nexus in general terms because the activities that create sales tax nexus and income tax nexus are likely to be similar but not identical. In general, income tax nexus can be created when a taxpayer receives income from sources within a state, owns or leases property in a state, or has employees who perform significant activities within a state. On the other hand, for sales and use tax nexus, *Quill* requires a physical presence, essentially a brick and mortar structure such as a store, an office, or a distribution center.

While *Quill* may eventually be overturned, the issue of whether states can require out-of-state businesses to collect sales and use taxes for online sales within a state has been taken up by Congress and may be resolved through legislation. Although no legislation has thus far been passed, bills have been introduced in Congress for several years to require remote sellers to collect state sales tax on Internet sales, and the concept has been gaining congressional support. Titled the "Marketplace Fairness Act" or "Main Street Fairness Act," the proposals are designed to address the states' loss of tax revenues from online sales as well as the competitive disadvantage of brick and mortar companies that must collect state and local sales taxes on their retail sales. Under its Commerce power, Congress could give the states the power to make out-of-state businesses collect sales taxes when selling their online products.

3-4 Equal Protection Clause

Although not relied upon as often as the other constitutional clauses to challenge state taxation, the **Equal Protection Clause** of the 14th Amendment prevents states from implementing discriminatory tax classifications. Contained in Article 14, § 1, the clause provides that no state shall "deny to any person within its jurisdiction the equal protection of the laws." The type of cases in which the U.S. Supreme Court has struck down state tax statutes on equal protection grounds generally involve state laws that discriminate against nonresidents or out-of-state businesses. Recent cases have involved state tax amnesty programs[4] and state taxation of certain professions, such as professional athletes.[5] However, unless the classification is "suspect," such as based on race, the courts will defer to state law as long as there is "… a rational relationship between the disparity of treatment and some legitimate governmental purpose."[6]

3-5 Public Law 86-272

In 1959, Congress addressed the issue of what kind of employee activities within states could create nexus. **Public Law 86-272** (15 U.S.C. §§ 381–384) prevents the income taxation of an out-of-state business if a company's only business within the state is the solicitation of orders for sales of tangible personal property. Note that many states take the position that this protection does not extend to franchise taxes, commercial activities taxes, or gross receipts taxes, which may not be considered income taxes.

The Supreme Court has clarified that the definition of "solicitation of orders" goes beyond merely making requests for sales—it includes the entire process associated with requesting orders by out-of-state businesses. Activities that are ancillary to obtaining orders are considered part of the solicitation. Further, activities that are beyond solicitation of orders, but are trivial, are considered de minimis and do not violate the solicitation of orders protection. Having an office located in a state, even if solely for the solicitation of orders, is not de minimis and can subject a business to state taxation.[7]

SPOTLIGHT ON TAXATION

Quill's Legal Precedent at Risk

For years the physical presence standard established under *Quill* has withstood the test of time; however, recent challenges appear to put the continuance of *Quill* under doubt. In a Supreme Court case [*DMA v. Brohl*, 135 S.Ct. 1124 (2015)], in a concurring opinion Justice Kennedy wrote, "Given these changes in technology and consumer sophistication, it is unwise to delay any longer a reconsideration of the Court's holding in *Quill*. A case questionable even when decided, *Quill* now harms States to a degree far greater than could have been anticipated earlier."

Those wishing to challenge *Quill* need no additional invitation. A number of cases are currently pending at lower level courts.

---

[4]*Armour v. Indianapolis*, 566 U.S. _____ , 132 S.Ct. 2073 (2012).

[5]*Hillenmeyer v. City of Cleveland*, Ohio S.Ct., Dkt. No. 2014-0235, 04/30/2015, petition for cert. denied, U.S. S.Ct., Dkt. No. 15-435, 11/09/2015.

[6]*Armour v. Indianapolis*, 566 U.S. _____ , 132 S.Ct. 2073 (2012).

[7]*Wisconsin Department of Revenue v. William Wrigley, Jr., Co.*, 505 U.S. 214 (1992).

4 State Tax Structure

Many states have modeled their income tax structures on the federal tax system. All of the states have adopted constitutions and typically use three branches of government: legislative, executive, and judicial. Tax statutes are enacted by the state legislatures. These statutes are signed by the state governor, just as federal tax laws are signed by the president. Regulatory agencies similar to the IRS issue pronouncements on tax matters and administer the tax law. Finally, state courts hear cases regarding tax matters.

4-1 Constitution

While each state's taxing system is unique, they are all constrained by the U.S. Constitution and federal laws. As discussed in the prior section, many clauses of the U.S. Constitution are applied to state taxation, yet only two clauses explicitly restrict states' taxation: the Import/Export Clause and the very specific Duty of Tonnage Clause. Both of these prohibit states from charging taxes on imports or exports without the consent of Congress. As import/export taxes have become less important at the federal level, so have these clauses.

Although the federal laws may appear to dominate state tax issues, it is actually each state's own constitution that is considered the fundamental taxing law because a constitution places the most relevant restrictions on the state's authority to assess taxes. Generally, state constitutions limit the rates and types of taxes that can be imposed, and they require that tax laws show uniformity, provide equal protection, and have a public purpose. Because elected legislative bodies enact taxes, there is an eminent presumption of validity for a state's taxing laws. It is the ultimate role of the courts to ensure that state legislatures act within the restraints of federal and state constitutions.

Requiring that tax revenues be generated only for a public purpose is a lofty sounding limitation on a state's ability to tax. However, the definition of "public purpose" is rarely included in constitutions, so the courts have rendered (sometimes vague and broad) interpretations in their decisions for specific taxes. Since the legislature represents a state's citizens, federal and state courts generally accept the legislative interpretation of the concept.

4-2 Legislative

State legislatures are responsible for enacting laws regarding state revenue sources and consequently pass bills amending and augmenting their state's tax code. While federal revenue bills constitutionally must start in the House of Representatives, this is not a requirement in all state legislatures. In fact, the jurisdictions of the legislative houses vary from state to state, and there tends to be a significant overlap in their functions. Nebraska avoids this duplication by having only one legislative body. Once the tax bills are passed by the legislatures and signed by the governor, they are incorporated into the state's statutory structure.

State tax codes can provide research challenges for tax practitioners. Each state organizes its tax code based on different criteria and has a different numbering system for its tax law. This means that even the practitioner who knows that corporate income tax laws are found in the 300 sections of the Internal Revenue Code (IRC) must conduct a new search for the state corporate income tax laws, if they even exist!

EXHIBIT 9-3:   States without Certain Types of Taxes

Type of Tax	States with No Such Tax
Corporate Income	Nevada, South Dakota, Washington, Wyoming
Personal Income	Alaska, Florida, Nevada, South Dakota, Texas, Washington, Wyoming
Sales	Alaska, Delaware, Montana, New Hampshire, Oregon

States place varying reliance on the IRC. Some states piggyback most of their individual and business income tax provisions on to the IRC, whereas other states have adopted substantial differences. A current trend in state income tax law is to selectively enact changes made by Congress, especially when the federal changes reduce the state's tax base in a manner the state can ill afford. For instance, some states have refused to adopt the IRC § 199 domestic-production-activities deduction simply because they cannot afford the resulting loss of revenue. Some states adopt federal income tax law as of a certain time and thus do not adopt the most recent changes that may have been enacted by the U.S. Congress. Therefore, the practitioner must be diligent in finding possible differences in state and federal income tax law when providing tax planning or advice to clients.

Income tax is not the only tax that states utilize, and income taxes may not be the most important revenue generator for the state. In fact, several states do not assess any income taxes. Rather, states rely on a multitude of other taxes, including sales/use, real and personal property, excise on products, severance on natural resources, gaming/gambling, estate/inheritance, and gift taxes. Many states are enacting taxes that are assessed on assets or transactions of service industries, communication and computer operations, and financial enterprises. The mix of taxes varies greatly from state to state. Exhibit 9-3 lists some of the more common omissions of major taxes imposed by each state.

4-3 Administrative

Once tax statutes are enacted, they must be interpreted and enforced. These duties fall to administrative agencies created by either statutory or constitutional provisions. In most states, the Department of Revenue (Department of Taxation, State Tax Commission, etc.) is the main administrative agency for this purpose. Other smaller agencies administer the more specialized taxes, such as employment, tobacco, or fuel taxes. California is an exception in that it has two revenue agencies, the Franchise Tax Board (income and franchise taxes) and the State Board of Equalization (most other taxes).

It has been said that whoever has authority to interpret the law is really the lawmaker, and it is the state revenue agencies that play this role for the state tax laws. These agencies publish regulations, rulings, and various other authoritative pronouncements as aids in interpreting and applying the law to a specific situation. As in the federal system, it is the courts' duty to ensure that the administrative agencies do not overstep their authority.

Most state revenue agencies issue rulings for specific taxpayers, similar in nature to private letter rulings (PLRs) issued by the IRS. As with PLRs, the letters are for the exclusive use of the taxpayer requesting the guidance and usually cannot be relied upon by other taxpayers as authority. These private rulings, however, may provide taxpayers with hints as to the revenue agency's position on a particular issue and, therefore, are useful to the practitioner.

Federal regulations and rulings may be pertinent to state tax issues. For states that piggyback income, estate, or other taxes onto federal statutes, guidance in interpreting the law will come from the federal pronouncements. As previously stated, the degree to which states follow federal income tax or other tax law varies greatly.

4-4 Judicial

State judicial systems are, for the most part, patterned on the federal system. Most states use three levels of courts: supreme courts, appeals (appellate) courts, and trial courts. However, some states have only one appeals-level court, whereas others have four levels by adding a county or district trial court with limited jurisdiction. The functions of the levels of state courts are similar to the federal functions. The trial courts establish the facts and apply the law to these facts. The appeals courts review the trial courts' application of the law to the set of facts. They generally rely on the trial courts' finding of the facts. The state's supreme court usually holds powers corresponding to the U.S. Supreme Court; it is the final interpretation of an extant law of the state, but its precedents apply only to the state in which it is located. For those states that use only two levels of courts, the functions of the appeals and supreme courts are conjoined.

While most states do use a three-tier judicial system, the courts' names might not clearly indicate the courts' relative levels. A superior court is likely to be a trial court or can be an appellate court, but it probably is not the highest court of the state. Most of the intermediate courts have the words *appeals* or *appellate* in their names. However, the highest court of a state can also be called the court of appeals. In New York, for example, the supreme court is the trial court, and the highest court is called the court of appeals. The most diversity among states is with the trial courts. There are county, municipal, circuit, district, and superior trial courts, just to name a few. Each state has organized its trial courts to meet the needs of its residents and judicial system.

Whereas the federal judicial system includes a court specifically for tax cases, the Tax Court, most states do not have an equivalent. Rather, there may be administrative (quasi-judicial) tribunals authorized to expedite settlements of tax disputes. The decisions of these tribunals generally are available to the public, but they tend to have little precedential value. The findings generally apply only to the taxpayer bringing the dispute. As with other such documents, they can shed light on the state's position on a particular issue.

Tax services like IntelliConnect and Checkpoint do not offer separate state tax reporters (e.g., AFTR) but they both cull important state tax cases to provide to subscribers.

5 Multistate Taxation

Companies conducting business in more than one state are generally going to be subject to multistate taxation for each state in which they have nexus. Given the complexity of business organizations, it can be quite difficult to determine what share of business income a state is entitled to tax. In more than 40 of the states that impose a corporate income tax, the starting point in determining state taxable income is federal taxable income as reflected on the corporate income tax return (Form 1120) or taxable income before the dividends-received deduction. As mentioned earlier, however, each state is free to define taxable income in a manner consistent with that state's system of taxes. As a result, federal taxable income is often adjusted by whatever differences exist between federal tax rules and that particular state's tax rules. Common modifications include the following:

- Adding back interest on state and municipal obligations if not exempt for state purposes (net of expenses).

- Subtracting interest on U.S. obligations, which is taxable for federal purposes but not state purposes (net of expenses).

- Adding back state income taxes deducted in computing federal taxable income.

- Subtracting refunds of state income taxes.

- Subtracting federal income tax paid. (A limited deduction is allowed in a few states.)

- Adding back federal depreciation, amortization, and depletion in excess of that allowed by the state or subtracting state depreciation, amortization, and depletion in excess of the federal amount.

- Adjustments of gain or loss on asset dispositions because of depreciation differences.

- Adjustments for differences between federal and state net operating losses.

The total income of a business as recalculated under a particular state's rules is often referred to as the state tax base. This does not represent the state taxable income of a business as each state is generally not entitled to the entire scope of multistate income generated by that business. Rather, the income of a multistate company must be divided among the states in which it conducts business. Most states use a system of **allocation** and **apportionment** to divide the income. Under this method, certain types of **nonbusiness income** are traced (allocated) directly to their geographic source or other connection with a state and attributed solely to that state. The definition of nonbusiness income tends to be fairly narrow and is typically limited to interest, dividends, rents, and royalties. For example, interest is most often allocated directly to the state in which the commercial domicile of the business is located. The commercial domicile is the location of central management and not necessarily the state of incorporation.

Income other than nonbusiness income is considered **business income** and is apportioned among the states in which the company is doing business (has nexus). With apportionment, there is no attempt to trace items of income to the state in which the income was generated. Rather, a formula is used to arrive at an approximation of a business's income that should be attributed to a particular state. Formula apportionment divides a multistate company's tax base among the states in which it does business by applying a fraction representing the ratio of in-state factors to total factors. Historically, the most common apportionment formula has been a three-factor equally weighted formula that considers the ratio of in-state property, payroll, and sales to overall property, payroll, and sales. However, today most states use formulas that weight sales more heavily than the other factors. The general formula for the calculation of state taxable income is as follows:

	Federal taxable income
+/−	State adjustments
=	State tax base
−	Allocable income
=	Apportionable income
×	Apportionment factor
=	Apportioned income
+	Allocated income
=	State taxable income
×	State tax rate
=	State tax liability

In most states, nonbusiness income is allocated to a jurisdiction while business income is apportioned. However, it is not always easy to determine if income is business or nonbusiness. In order to create a greater uniformity and consistency in the measurement and determination of business and nonbusiness income, the **Uniform Division of Income for Tax Purposes Act (UDITPA)** was drafted by the National Conference of Commissioners on Uniform State Laws in 1957.

Under UDITPA, business income is defined as income that arises from transactions and activities in the regular course of the taxpayer's business. It includes income from tangible and intangible property if the acquisition, management, and disposition of the property constitute integral parts of the taxpayer's regular trade or business operations.

Interest, dividend, and patent and royalty income can be either business or nonbusiness income. For example, interest derived from notes received from the sale of regular merchandise would be business income. Interest received by banks on loans made to customers is business income, as is interest earned on money held for escrow purchases.

Interest earned from investing excess cash holdings is treated as nonbusiness income. Dividends received from stock held for investment to meet a specific business objective such as bonding or obtaining a source of supply is classified as business income.

In 1967, the **Multistate Tax Commission (MTC)** was created through an organization of state governments called the Multistate Tax Compact. The MTC believes that greater uniformity in multistate taxation will ensure that interstate commerce is more fairly taxed, lessen compliance costs for taxpayers and revenue agencies, and reduce the potential for congressional intervention in state fiscal authority. The MTC closely follows state developments in the rules related to allocation and apportionment of taxable income and communicates that information back to member states.

The MTC has strongly encouraged states to adopt the uniform tax law and abide by its regulations. It has been only moderately successful in this endeavor, however, as only 15 states plus the District of Columbia have become compact members and enacted the multistate tax compact into their state laws, while 7 states are sovereign members that support the general purposes of the MTC. Another 26 states are associate members that participate in commission meetings, programs, and projects. Two states, Nevada and Virginia, are not members.

SPOTLIGHT ON TAXATION

Quotation

The way taxes are, you might as well marry for love.

—Joe E. Lewis

6 Illustrative Research Example

A sample research project will be used to demonstrate effective state tax research methods. It is important that you attempt this research project using the various tax services available to you. The procedural knowledge necessary to perform state tax research effectively can be acquired only through hands-on practice. The remainder of this chapter is designed to guide you through the basic tax services—it is not a substitute for actually performing the research yourself.

Research Project: *Vincent Lopez is expanding his Virginia-based accounting practice by entering into some large engagements in Maryland and West Virginia. It is very likely*

Vincent will need to open a new office to handle the new client business. Vincent would like to know the sales tax implications for this business. Specifically, on which services must Vincent charge sales tax, and are there any tax incentives available to Vincent's firm?

This type of project is very common in state research. Expansion of a business into a new geographic area requires a large number of considerations, including many tax-related issues. It is always important to remember that tax is only one of the many possible consequences of a business decision or transaction, and that tax researchers' attention must be given to the relative importance of taxes with regards to all other factors.

7 Checkpoint State and Local Tax (SALT) Service

Thomson Reuters Checkpoint State and Local Tax (SALT) service is a comprehensive analysis of state and local taxes for all 50 states and the District of Columbia (D.C.). The service is designed to let the researcher designate the states, types of taxes, and documents to be searched. Any or all of the states' taxes and documents may be searched simultaneously. Essentially all taxes imposed by states and most enacted by localities are covered in this service.

As with the federal Checkpoint materials, editorial explanations and annotations are an integral part of this service. The explanations are particularly useful when investigating a state's taxes with which you are unfamiliar, such as the Ohio commercial activity tax (CAT) or the business and occupation (gross revenue) tax of Washington State. The explanations contain links to all the supporting materials, making retrieval a seamless process. The annotations for court and agency decisions also are linked to their primary sources.

The core tax information available in the SALT practice area can be found in the State and Local Tax Reporters. There is a reporter for each state, and each reporter contains rates, explanations, annotations, statutes, regulations, tax cases, rulings, and other official state tax material. Depending on the subscription, the corporate tax reporter or the sales and use tax reporters may also be available. These are subsets of the main reporters.

The Checkpoint feature CompareIt enables the researcher to compare the tax treatment of an item in one state to its treatment in another state or the federal treatment. This makes it easy to compare the tax treatment of an item in multiple states, and it eliminates the need to return to the list of documents when performing multiple state searches, as would be necessary with the illustrative research example. CompareIt is available only for explanatory materials and not for state statutes or regulations.

As with the federal databases, the SALT databases can be entered using the three search methods: keyword search, citation, and contents. The multistate search option is different, though. As a variant of a keyword search, it is demonstrated under the KEYWORD SEARCH heading.

The search screen for Checkpoint (Exhibit 6-2, Chapter 6) allows the researcher to choose a practice area. Upon selecting STATE & LOCAL, Checkpoint offers a list of the states as shown in Exhibit 9-4. All the states or any number of separate states may be designated for the search. At this juncture, one cannot enter keywords.

Checkpoint requires that a type of tax and document be specified before a keyword search may occur. Exhibit 9-5 displays the choices for taxes and documents. The offerings appearing on this screen are customized to the state(s) selected in the previous screen. Accordingly, this full list of taxes would not be offered for every state. Again, any or all of the taxes and document databases may be marked for the search.

EXHIBIT 9-4: Checkpoint State and Local Practice Area

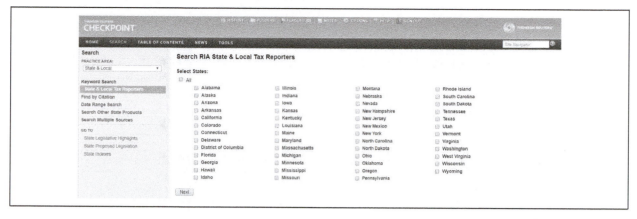

EXHIBIT 9-5: Checkpoint Select State Tax and Document Type

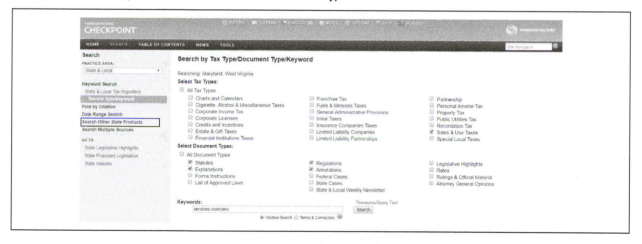

With respect to the illustrative example, Maryland and West Virginia were selected in the list of states, Sales and Use Tax was checked for the Tax Type, and several document types were marked in the document-type section (Exhibit 9-5).

The search results link to explanations, regulations, and rulings pertaining to the sales taxes on accounting services in Maryland (Exhibit 9-6). By reading these documents, the illustrative example can be analyzed. In addition, by clicking the COMPAREIT button at the top of the page, the other states appear in the right window, allowing the researcher to quickly link to the explanation of the same issue in one of the other state reporters.

Rather than going through the process of designating taxes and documents, the SEARCH OTHER STATE PRODUCTS option is also available, as shown in Exhibit 9-5. This accesses secondary sources, such as RIA newsletters and journals, state legislation and regulations, federal cases on state topics, and other state tax materials depending on the subscription (not shown). These databases may be searched using keywords or citations, depending on the nature of the database.

EXHIBIT 9-6:   Checkpoint State Document Screen and CompareIt

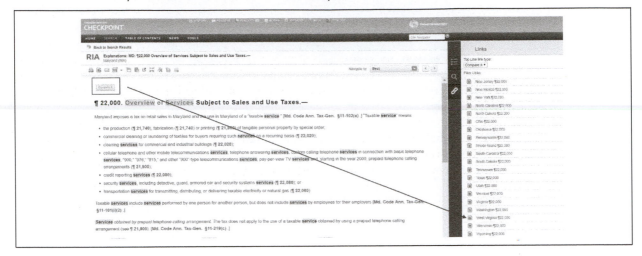

As can be seen in Exhibit 9-7, one of the search choices offered is SEARCH MULTIPLE SOURCES. A comparison of Exhibit 9-5 and Exhibit 9-7 reveals that the document categories are not similar for these two keyword search functions. In fact, SEARCH MULTIPLE SOURCES is designed for entering keywords, selecting document sources, and searching. This closely resembles the Federal Practice Area keyword search format (Exhibit 6-2, Chapter 6), and the same thesaurus and query tool functions are available.

Similar to the Catalyst product described in Chapter 6, Checkpoint also provides Catalyst explanations for certain state tax issues. As presented in the inset in Exhibit 9-7, Catalyst is organized by topic and then, within each topic, by state. The documents provided in Catalyst are designed to be easy to understand and permit researchers to find answers to common questions much more efficiently.

The *All State Tax Guide* is a concise state-by-state analysis of all major taxes, with citations to state materials (see access on Exhibit 9-7). The *Guide* covers interstate law,

EXHIBIT 9-7:   Checkpoint State Multistate Sources

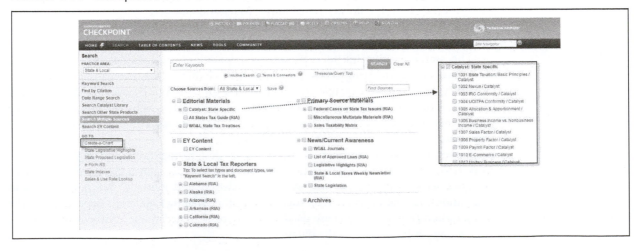

income allocation and apportionment, uniform acts, and the MTC. It offers numerous tables, charts, and checklists for a variety of tax data as well as calendars for important reporting dates and monthly listings of recently approved state and local tax laws. The list of official state contacts makes it easy to find an address or phone number for taxing authorities.

The latest news on state tax developments, including the *State & Local Taxes Weekly* newsletter, is available on the Search Multiple Sources screen shown in Exhibit 9-7. This newsletter offers practice-oriented analysis from national experts and breaking news, organized by state, making it easy to identify what is of interest to the practitioner. Also included in SEARCH MULTIPLE SOURCES is the *Journal of Multistate Taxation and Incentives*. The full-length articles in this journal generally report on multistate tax issues with an emphasis on practical planning opportunities, whereas the short technical comments focus on emerging tax issues for particular states.

The CREATE-A-CHART feature facilitates the building of multistate charts that can cut across a variety of taxes and/or states. These convenient summary charts can be exported to a word-processing or spreadsheet document. The product supports linking information on the charts to controlling authority and/or Checkpoint's explanation paragraphs. These links are maintained when the chart is exported. The practitioner can access CREATE-A-CHART through SEARCH MULTIPLE SOURCES as shown in Exhibit 9-7 and designate the type of tax (e.g., income), a chart type (e.g., tax rates, starting point for computing taxable income), and which states to include in the comparison. More than 100 chart types are offered in CREATE-A-CHART.

Along with primary sources, editorial materials, current newsletters, and journals, as shown in Exhibit 9-7, SEARCH MULTIPLE SOURCES also offers the Miscellaneous Multistate Materials database. This database consists of materials from the Multistate Tax Compact, the Multistate Tax Commission, and the Federation of Tax Administrators. It also contains numerous multistate agreements and acts, formulas for apportionment and allocation of income, and federal laws on state taxation.

Because the SEARCH MULTIPLE SOURCES option lacks a tax-type indicator, the type of state tax being investigated must be included as a keyword to narrow the results to the particular tax of interest. For the illustrative research example, from the SEARCH MULTIPLE SOURCES search screen, Maryland's and West Virginia's state tax reporters can be selected (not shown). The keyword search would need to include "sales taxes" in order to produce results similar to those using Search States in Exhibit 9-5.

Unlike the Federal practice area, the SALT materials do not allow state citation searches directly on the opening screen. Rather, only federal cases on state tax issues may be searched without selecting a state. Recall that the FEDERAL CASES ON STATE TAXES database is located within the SEARCH OTHER STATE PRODUCTS tab. The Federal Cases database may be searched by name of the plaintiff or the defendant, citation, or keyword. Since customized templates for the different court reporters are not furnished, the researcher must know the proper format for the citation.

State statutes, regulations, rulings, and cases may be located by citation, but a state must be chosen before these options appear. The citation templates are customized based on the state selected (Exhibit 9-8), and only one state's citations may be searched at a time. If more than one state is chosen in SEARCH STATES, then the FIND BY CITATION option is not offered.

SEARCH STATES also supports a keyword search for courts and other rulings using date restrictions. These searches also require a state to be selected before the options are accessible because the listings of courts and ruling types are also customized by state. While these are technically keyword search options, the taxpayer's name may be entered as the keyword, thus functioning similar to a citation search. The ability to restrict the search by date is particularly useful when updating a previously searched tax issue.

EXHIBIT 9-8:   Checkpoint State Find by Citation

The Checkpoint SALT service supports TABLE OF CONTENTS (TOC) and INDEX searches. These methods allow the researcher to treat the tax service as if it were in a printed book. Thus, as in a book, the TOC and index can be browsed for the topic of interest. In many cases, this methodology for searching is more efficient than the keyword search. By narrowing the search by focusing on the contents of databases, fewer extraneous documents are retrieved when a keyword search is performed. The limitation with this type of search is that only those databases containing TOCs or indexes are searchable.

The Checkpoint TOC option is available from all screens. Therefore, the researcher does not need to be in the State and Local practice area to begin a TOC search. The methodology that is effective in a federal TOC search also would be appropriate for the SALT search. Besides the editorial materials, Catalyst, and newsletters, each state has a listing in the TOC.

One of the most useful subheadings listed for each state is the Index. By drilling down through the Index, the same documents previously identified for the illustrative example can be found. Starting with Maryland and drilling down into Sales—Use and then Introduction in the Index, the researcher will find the document in Exhibit 9-6. If the listing under the contents is long, using the "CTRL-F" command to bring up the "FIND" box, and entering a relevant term will display the entries desired. These drill-down techniques are efficient in locating pertinent documents; however, the drawback is that each subheading must be examined separately. Access to each state's index is also furnished when it is the only state selected for the SEARCH STATES option.

8 CCH IntelliConnect State

Like Checkpoint, Commerce Clearing House's IntelliConnect (CCH) includes a complete state tax service. This research tool allows for keyword searches across as many databases as the researcher would wish to select. For state tax research, IntelliConnect has a STATE TAX LIBRARY that can be browsed in order to select the specific sources required (shown in Exhibit 9-9).

The backbone of the IntelliConnect state tax service is the STATE TAX REPORTERS. This service combines detailed explanations, primary source materials, and practical compliance guidance. All major taxes imposed by states and localities are covered by the service. Although the explanations are organized by tax type, with links to related primary sources,

EXHIBIT 9-9: IntelliConnect State Tax Browse Window

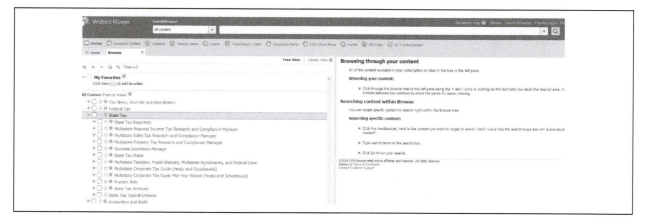

EXHIBIT 9-10: IntelliConnect State Tax Reporters

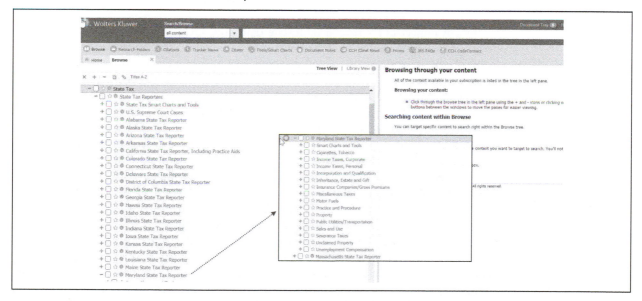

state material is retrieved by selecting the state(s) of interest. Previous versions of the state tax reporters are maintained in the archives to enable research of tax issues for prior years.

Checkpoint requires the researcher to identify the type of documents to be searched, but as a default, IntelliConnect assumes all materials are of interest. The list of document types searched can be reduced by selecting the state tax area in the BROWSE feature, as shown in Exhibit 9-10. The STATE TAX REPORTERS may also be searched using keywords or the TOC.

Searching the STATE TAX REPORTERS for a solution to the illustrative example begins by selecting STATE TAX from the choices presented in Exhibit 9-9 and drilling down into the STATE TAX REPORTERS, and further refining the selection to sales and use taxes and then, if desired, to the specific source of materials on that topic, such as state explanations.

Exhibit 9-11 presents one of the explanations on services for sales and use tax in the Maryland state tax reporter. The results are in the document window, all primary sources are linked via footnote, and related information buttons are across the top of the window.

EXHIBIT 9-11: IntelliConnect State Tax Documents

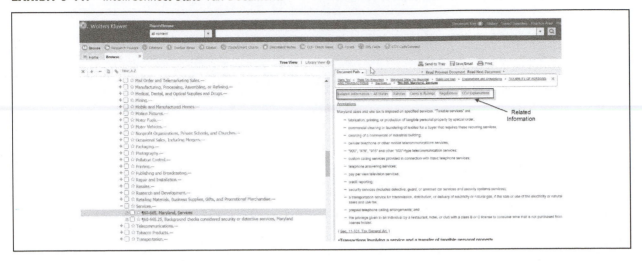

IntelliConnect offers several multistate databases, including business, personal, property, and sales tax guides. Each is designed to be an all-in-one guide emphasizing multistate planning yet delivering state-by-state details for every topic. Cost-effective planning ideas are presented, and the "at-a-glance" charts are effective in finding quick answers to each state's treatment of key taxes.

Included with the specialized multistate databases is the *State Tax Guide*. This is similar to the *Master Tax Guide,* as it is intended for finding quick answers to everyday questions on taxes levied in every state. Thus, its treatment of tax issues is very concise—state tax statutes and pronouncements are summarized rather than reproduced. Each state has a page listing its major taxes, tax base and rates, and due dates. There also are charts for most taxes that provide each state's imposition and rates. This publication can be an extremely efficient tool when all that is needed is a short answer to a simple question or a comparison among a few states on a particular tax.

The CCH State Tax NexusExpert (not shown) provides guidance that helps researchers determine whether common business activities are likely to create nexus for corporate income tax or sales and use purposes. The Business Incentives Manager provides explanations for state-level business tax incentives by industry and category to assist in exploring possible tax incentives.

The latest in state legislative actions is found in the PRACTICE AIDS section of the STATE TAX tab, as shown in Exhibit 9-12. This Week's Legislative Activity, Regulatory Activity, Current Year's Final and Pending Legislation, and Prior Year's Enacted Legislation are located in the practice aids. In addition, Tax Law by State contains primary tax law for each state. The constitution for each state, its revised (consolidated) statutes, city and/or county ordinances, and uncodified (unconsolidated) statutes are obtainable through Tax Law by State.

The last feature in the state tax library is the state topical indexes to the multistate tax guides. Each state also has its own index, but these are accessed through the state tax reporter TOC for the state. The major advantage of using an index is that the definition of the term is considered, not just its occurrence in the document.

State citation searches are conducted in the same manner as a federal citation search. Using CITATIONS from the quick bar and drilling down into the particular state for searching presents templates that are appropriate for state citation searches, as can be seen in Exhibit 9-13.

EXHIBIT 9-12: IntelliConnect Multistate Practice Aids

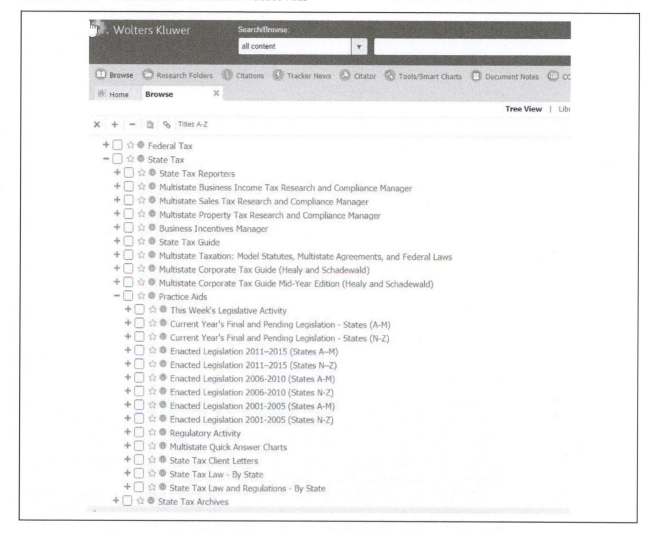

9 Bloomberg BNA

BNA is known for the quality of its federal tax portfolios, and it has added an ever-expanding set of state tax portfolios to the library of offerings. The BNA product makes finding state tax information easier than ever. The core materials in the expert analysis section are the state tax portfolios, the sales and use tax portfolios, and the state tax navigators. The portfolios are designed to address a multistate understanding of the state tax issues associated with business taxes, nexus, incentives, and procedure and administration. A small number of states have their own reporters (such as California [five portfolios], New York, Illinois, and others). The sales and use tax portfolios are structured similarly, with the bulk of the content geared toward a multistate overview and small number of portfolios for certain states. The state tax navigators, on the other hand, are structured by type of tax such as corporate, individual, sales and use, and others, as shown in Exhibit 9-14. The navigators can be used for drilling down into in the browse window until the area of interest is located, as shown in Exhibit 9-15.

EXHIBIT 9-13: IntelliConnect State Find by Citation

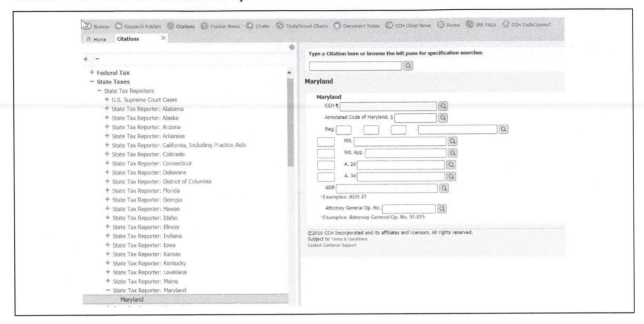

EXHIBIT 9-14: BNA State Tax Page

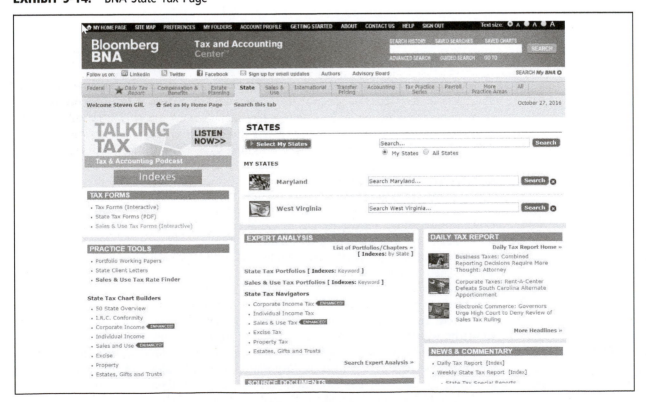

EXHIBIT 9-15: BNA State Tax Navigators

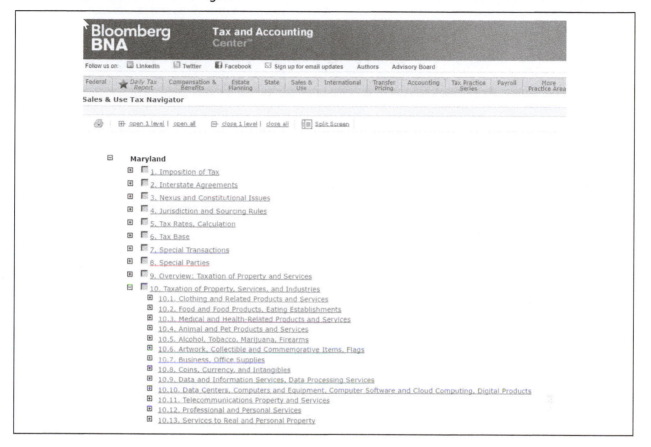

Another way of finding state tax information is to use a state-specific keyword search directly from the State Tax screen in BNA. As shown in Exhibit 9-14, using the SELECT MY STATES button near the top of the main window allows the researcher to select only the states of interest for a set of keyword searches. For the illustrative example, Maryland and West Virginia have been selected, as shown in Exhibit 9-14. Now the keyword search will be restricted to information that pertains to those two states. The search will cross over a number of different state tax sources, including the state tax navigators and any related state statutes, regulations, rulings, and cases. The results of such a search are shown in Exhibit 9-16.

10 Lexis Advance Tax

Lexis Advance Tax provides state-by-state access to all the state-level tax laws and regulations and a host of analysis and other editorial materials as well. Exhibit 9-17 shows the multistate pods available in Lexis Advance Tax.

A wide range of state tax news is also provided with Lexis Advance Tax state information, including the Tax Analysts State Tax Notes and State Tax Notes Today, as shown in Exhibit 9-18.

11 LexisNexis Academic

As with federal tax research using LexisNexis Academic (discussed in Chapter 8), state tax sources can be found through the BROWSE or FIND features. By using BROWSE and

EXHIBIT 9-16: BNA My State Search

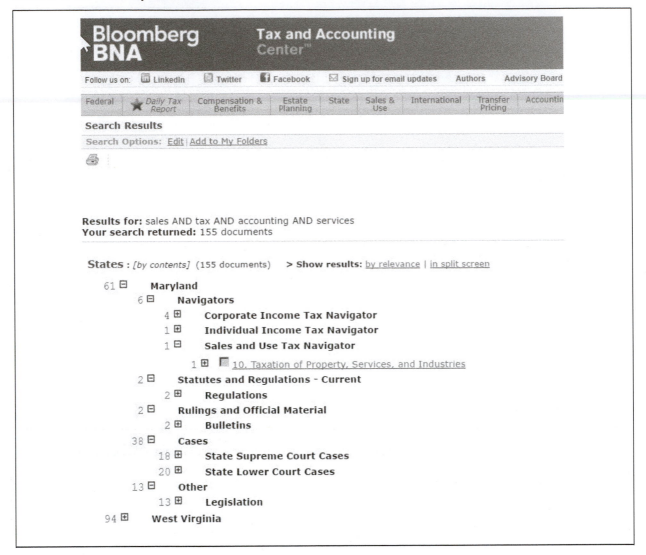

selecting taxation law as the area of law, the opportunity to select an individual state will be available under the Region drop-down menu as shown in Exhibit 9-19. The sources available for that state can be selected to search consistently with the same treatment as discussed in Chapter 8.

Exhibit 9-20 illustrates that using Search by Subject or Topic from the search home page and selecting Tax Law will permit the selection of certain tax law sources in the Advanced Options. Common state tax sources include All State Statutes, Regulations, and Cases & Admin Decisions, which provides a single source for all state-level tax law. The sources included under Combined Federal & State Tax Journals are presented in the inset in Exhibit 9-20. A keyword search of these sources can be performed directly from the main search page.

EXHIBIT 9-17: Lexis Advance Tax State Sources

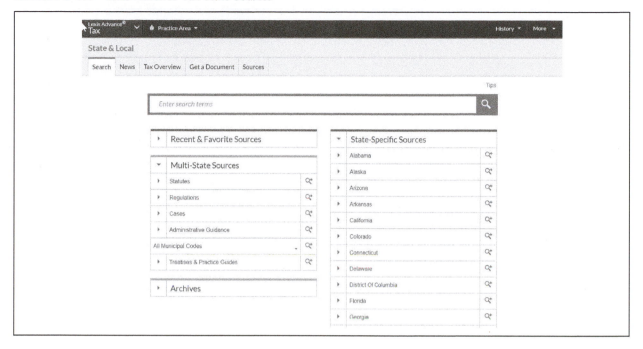

EXHIBIT 9-18: Lexis Advance Tax State Tax News

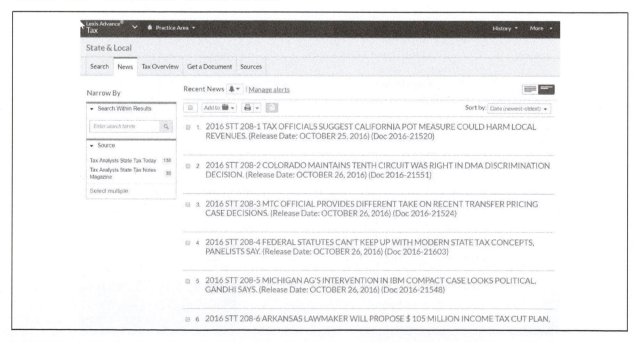

EXHIBIT 9-19: Lexis Nexis Academic Browse State Sources

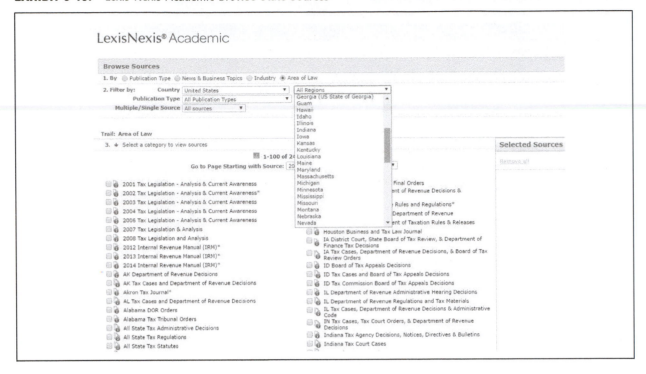

EXHIBIT 9-20: Lexis Nexis Academic Search Tax Law—States

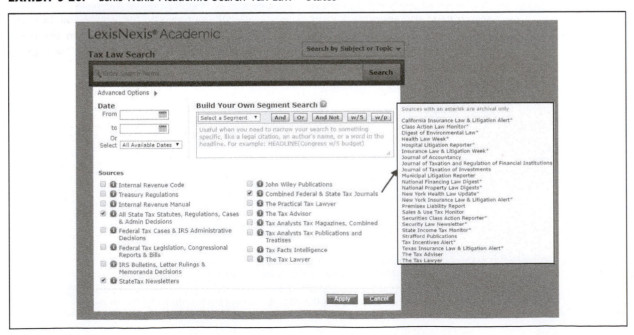

EXHIBIT 9-21: Lexis Nexis Academic State Statutes and Regulations Search

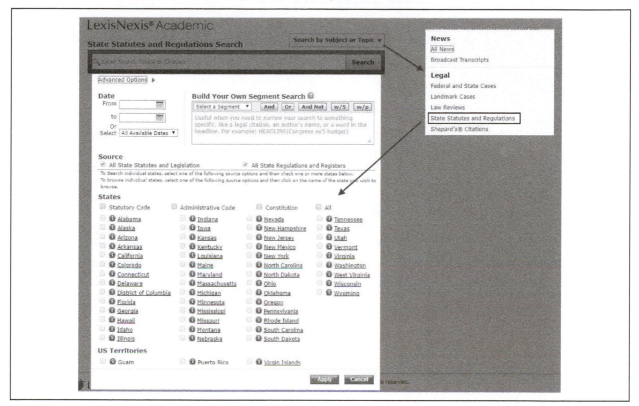

Finally, as presented in Exhibit 9-21, using Search by Subject or Topic from the main search page and selecting State Statutes and Regulations selects that source and also creates a more detailed search opportunity under the Advanced Options from the main search page. A specific state or states can be selected along with restricting the sources to only statutory or administrative codes.

SPOTLIGHT ON TAXATION

State Tax Incentives

All 50 states and the District of Columbia offer some form of tax incentives for business that are considering expanding or relocating to the state or jurisdiction. Incentives offered include exemptions or abatements of business, income, property, and sales and use taxes, and they can apply to business activities that create jobs, provide for capital investment, increase research and development expenditures, or are related to certain industries. One such industry to garner significant attention is the film-production industry. Hollywood's influence is felt in more places than California. Not all analysts believe that the film-production tax breaks are making a substantial difference to state economies. It might be that the economic benefits states expect to gain from the movie industry are creating a made-for-Hollywood story!

12 Westlaw State Services

Westlaw Campus Research contains an extensive library of databases for state tax research. Exhibit 9-22 shows how to reach these sources through the STATE MATERIALS tab. By selecting the state, the lists of sources for that state appear in the main window, as shown in Exhibit 9-23. These sources can be keyword searched as with other Westlaw data.

13 Other Resources

Warren, Gorham & Lamont (WG&L) publishes the *State Taxation* treatise by Jerome R. Hellerstein and Walter Hellerstein. This two-volume treatise, currently in its third edition, is possibly the most comprehensive single work on state and local taxation. The

EXHIBIT 9-22:   Westlaw Campus Research State Materials Tab

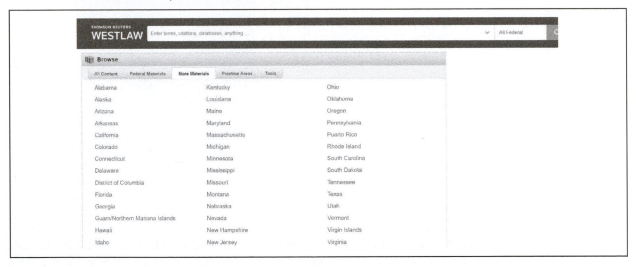

EXHIBIT 9-23:   Westlaw Campus Research State Sources

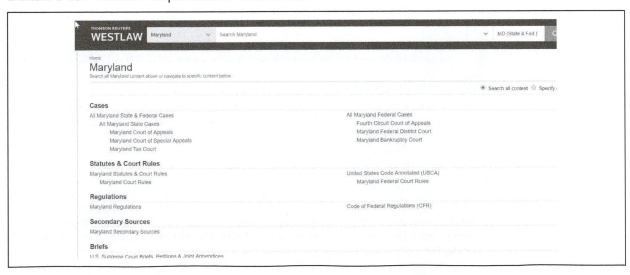

authors have undertaken the ambitious task of assembling a comprehensive review of all state and many local tax laws, plus the court decisions interpreting those laws. Because few published works address state taxation in such a thorough manner, *State Taxation* has been cited by many state courts and even the U.S. Supreme Court as the authority on state taxation. Westlaw and RIA offer this treatise as part of their SALT services, and it is also available in print.

The *Multistate Corporate Tax Guide* published by CCH is another useful treatise. The *Guide* focuses on key corporate tax issues in sales and use taxation and income-based taxes for all states and some localities such as New York City and D.C. The treatise provides quick access, via numerous charts, to each state's position statements on tax issues. Much of the analysis is based on data collected through questionnaires completed by the top state officials who interpret and apply the state laws. To ensure timeliness and relevancy of the information, the treatise is updated mid-year with a supplement.

14 Periodicals and Internet Sites

State tax journals and newsletters contain a variety of articles and news briefs that are designed to keep readers current with regard to developments in general areas of state and local taxation and tax issues specific to a given state. These articles may contain, for example, an in-depth review of a recently decided court case, a broad analysis of state tax factors that should be considered in tax planning, or a call for reform of a statute by a neutral (or biased) observer. The articles can suggest new approaches to tax problems, give guidance for solving complex problems, or just explain a new law in a readable form.

Two important state taxation journals are the *Journal of Multistate Taxation and Incentives* (WG&L), which releases 10 issues per year, and *Journal of State Taxation* (CCH), published bimonthly. Both of these journals focus on practical solutions to state and local taxation issues as well as creative planning strategies for multistate business operations and individuals with multistate tax liabilities. These journals keep the subscriber informed on critical areas of state and local taxation nationwide and provide expert assessments of important cases and their potential impacts.

Generally there are reviews of current state legislative issues to keep the reader up to date on state proposed, pending, or enacted legislation. Articles may cover legal, accounting, and business aspects of multistate entities. Both journals also focus on incentives offered by states to encourage business growth and expansion.

Tax Analysts publishes two influential state tax periodicals, *State Tax Notes* and *State Tax Today*. Like the Tax Analysts flagship, *Tax Notes*, *State Tax Notes* is an authoritative source for news and commentary on state and local taxation. This weekly publication provides the latest news from all 50 states and D.C., plus in-depth analysis from leading experts in state taxation. Summaries of all judicial, administrative, and legislative developments are also included in *State Tax Notes*.

The purpose of *State Tax Today* is to furnish the most current state tax news on a daily basis. It covers every state, D.C., and U.S. territories. There are links to full-text state documents and U.S. Supreme Court, state supreme court, and appellate court decisions. In addition to news briefs, *State Tax Today* has in-depth analytical articles, commentaries, and special reports.

Many of the other tax publishers provide state newsletters. For example, the *Tax Management Weekly State Tax Report* is the BNA analog to the Tax Analysts *State Tax Notes*. It gives a state-by-state analysis of state codes and regulations, state administrative and judicial court decisions, and state administrative pronouncements, as does *State Tax Notes*. Other state newsletters and reports published by BNA include the following:

- *State Tax Legislation Monitor*
- *State Insights & Commentary*
- *State Tax Regulation Monitor*
- *Weekly State Tax Report*
- *Multistate Tax Report*
- E-mail Highlights (notification of the week's state tax highlights)

The CCH newsletter is called *State Tax Day,* and RIA's is *State & Local Taxes Weekly.* Both are offered through the publishers' Internet tax services.

The Tax and Accounting Sites Directory Website (**www.taxsites.com**) contains links to numerous tax resources on the Internet. The state and local listing has links to each state's taxing agency, legal information, organizations, and government sites. In addition, links to general locators, sales/use tax, news topics, organizations, tax rates and data, state tax guides, and e-commerce taxes are included in the state and local screen.

15 International Taxation

The U.S. Department of State recognizes 195 countries in the world today, and each can have its own tax rules and regulations. Consequently, global businesses must maneuver through a tangled web of tax laws that are likely to be unfamiliar to most tax professionals. Intricate (sometimes tax-motivated) intercompany transactions and transfer pricing further compound the complexity and create an international tax environment that can be an unmanageable labyrinth for many companies.

Fortunately, international tax specialists can help with the perplexing compliance obligations and foster the alignment of a company's tax strategies with its business needs. The ultimate tax planning goal of most tax directors of large, multinational companies, however, is quite simple—to reduce the company's overall global effective tax rate. Navigating the road that leads to this goal is the challenge. This chapter provides a brief overview of international taxation, especially from a U.S. perspective, and explains some of the more popular international tax research resources available.

Global business transactions create distinctive tax concerns for both the native country and the temporary resident or transaction country. The native country is where the taxpayer is a citizen or legal resident or where an entity is incorporated or organized. The transaction country is where the income is earned or the transaction completed. International tax provisions generally are concerned with two potential tax situations: the native country's taxation of its citizens' foreign-source income (outbound) and the transaction country's taxation of foreign taxpayers earning income within its borders (inbound).

From an economic perspective, the objective of the international tax rules of each country should be to ensure that the taxing systems interact efficiently and to prevent, to the extent possible, the double taxation of income while encouraging investment within the country's boundaries. At the same time, each country wants to promote global commerce but not erode its domestic tax base for generating revenues. Such tax objectives can be in conflict, and these conflicts are the cause of the complexity and often situation-specific rules found in international tax laws.

15-1 International Tax Models

There are two alternative conceptual models on which countries could base their international tax schemes: worldwide and territorial. Under a **worldwide model**, a country imposes taxes on residents based on their worldwide income, regardless of its source. This would include income earned in other countries and even income earned by foreign subsidiaries, whether or not the profits are distributed (repatriated) to the parent company. All expenses associated with the earning of foreign income are deductible currently. Because the foreign-earned income also may be taxed by the transaction country, the native country would allow a foreign tax credit for taxes paid to other countries. In practice, no country uses a pure worldwide model of taxation.

Under a **territorial model**, a country taxes only income that is earned within its own borders. A business would not be taxed on income earned outside the native country or income of its foreign subsidiaries, even when the income is repatriated to the parent company. Because the foreign income is not taxed within the native country, there is no need for a foreign tax credit. Foreign income is taxed only once, and that is by the foreign country. Accordingly, deductions associated with the foreign income are disallowed. Most territorial models have anti-abuse provisions for certain types of portable income.

The United States uses a blended model that taxes the worldwide income of U.S. citizens and domestic corporations and the income of foreign entities that is connected with U.S. business. However, U.S. taxes do not apply to the foreign income of U.S.-owned corporations incorporated abroad until that income is brought back to the United States. As a result, a U.S. firm can indefinitely defer U.S. tax on its foreign income until, with some exceptions, such time as the foreign corporation repatriates its earnings to its U.S. parent.[8] By allowing tax deferral on foreign-subsidiary income, the blended model employed in the United States encourages domestic corporations to retain earnings in foreign countries and postpone repatriation as long as possible. Given that most countries enjoy a corporate marginal tax rate lower than that of the United States, this provides a substantial tax planning opportunity but also causes numerous opportunities for U.S. tax base erosion.

Another important feature of the U.S. tax system is a **foreign tax credit**. Even though the United States taxes worldwide income of domestic entities, it also allows a limited credit for foreign taxes paid. This treatment reduces double taxation that would otherwise apply to income earned overseas and taxed in the foreign jurisdiction. The credit is limited to the amount of U.S. taxes that would be due on the income; thus the United States collects its share of taxes where the U.S. tax rate is greater than that of the foreign country. If foreign taxes exceed the U.S. tax, the excess foreign taxes cannot be credited.

U.S. tax law uses a territorial approach for taxing non-U.S.-citizen taxpayers. For instance, the income of a Ugandan citizen is subject to U.S. federal income tax but only if that income is earned within the United States. The Ugandan person's income attributable to sources outside the United States is not taxable within the United States. Thus, the current U.S. international taxing system applies both the worldwide model (for citizens and resident aliens) and the territorial model (for nonresident aliens) concurrently.

---

[8]Certain types of portable income and income with little or no economic connection with the foreign country (called Subpart F income) earned by controlled foreign corporations trigger immediate U.S. tax as a constructive dividend.

SPOTLIGHT ON TAXATION

Hold the Mayo on Mine, Please

U.S. companies often fret over the relatively high marginal tax rate paid on corporate taxable income in the United States (35 percent). As the economy has seen some shifting from heavy capital manufacturing into technology products for which the true value lies not in the costs of the parts and labor to assemble the product but rather the innovative research and development that went into designing the product, more and more profits can be tied to the intellectual property (IP) associated with the product rather than to its materials. Unlike large and expensive factories, IP is rather easy to move around the world —simply transfer the patents to a tax haven where the associated profits will be taxed at a lower rate (or perhaps not at all). One unique plan for implementing this type of profits offshoring is known as the Dutch sandwich. In a Dutch sandwich, a U.S. company establishes an Irish subsidiary that is controlled from a tax haven like Grand Cayman, and thus profits are funneled into Grand Cayman. Profits from the sale of the product in the United States are offset by the royalties paid to the Irish/GrandCayman subsidiary. In order to capture even more of the profits from non-U.S. customers, another Irish subsidiary is established (this one controlled from Ireland), and sales profits from non-U.S. customers are funneled to Ireland, which has a low 12.5% corporate tax rate. However, to eliminate some of the already low-tax profits, a Netherlands subsidiary can be sandwiched between the two Irish subsidiaries and voila: a Dutch sandwich! Hungry yet?

15-2 Transfer Pricing

As businesses expand beyond their home country's borders, the legal and supply-chain structures can become extremely complex. For example, a company may develop a technology and secure its rights in one country, manufacture the product in a number of other countries, and distribute the product around the world from several distribution centers. Many firms will, for both tax and legal purposes, establish separate subsidiaries in each country. Although for financial statement purposes only the consolidated income will be reported, for each taxing jurisdiction the taxable income earned will depend on the costs that the subsidiaries charge each other at each step of the business process.

Transfer pricing is often used to refer to the price-setting process between related parties. For example, assume a U.S. bicycle manufacturer wishes to sell its products in the Netherlands and establishes a branch in the Netherlands. Under the U.S. tax system, all the income earned (including the branch under the worldwide part of the U.S. system) will be taxable in the United States. However, only the profits earned in the Netherlands will be taxable in that country. If we assume that the product costs $1,000 to produce, $100 to distribute, and is typically sold for $1,200, what should the transfer price to the Netherlands branch be?

One choice might be to set the transfer price at $1,000. Then the Netherlands will tax $200 of profit. On the other hand, perhaps the Netherlands branch does not bear any real risk for the sale of that bicycle and the profits should merely represent the cost to the Netherlands to distribute the bicycle. Thus the transfer price would be $1,100. Extending that idea just a bit further, perhaps the Netherlands branch is merely another cost center of the entire business and does not warrant any profit margin at all. In this case, the transfer price equals $1,200.

Each of the alternatives has significant ramifications to the taxing jurisdictions as well as the taxpayers. If tax rates differ between the countries, taxpayers have incentives to manipulate transfer prices in order to report low taxable income in the high-tax country and high taxable income in the low-tax country.

Most countries require a transfer-pricing scheme that adheres to an arm's-length principle, which means that prices should be the same as they would have been had the parties to the transaction not been related to each other. In practice, an arm's-length price may be difficult to establish. As a result, companies with international intercompany transactions may enter into advance pricing agreements (APAs) with the IRS. APAs establish a safe-harbor transfer-pricing method for the taxpayer.

SPOTLIGHT ON TAXATION

Transfer Pricing's Cost to the Fisc

Manipulating transfer prices costs the United States and other countries significant tax revenue. In the largest tax dispute in its history, in 2006 the IRS settled a multi-year transfer-pricing suit with pharmaceutical company Glaxo SmithKline Holdings for $3.4 billion. In 2008, the company lost a similar suit with the Canada Revenue Agency, resulting in additional taxes of $51.5 million. In this suit, the Canadian company purchased ranitidine (the active ingredient in Zantac) from an affiliated company in Switzerland. The price paid by the Canadian company exceeded C$1,500 per kilogram (Canadian dollars) at a time when other Canadian drug manufacturers purchased ranitidine at a price of C$200 to C$300 per kilogram.[9]

15-3 Sourcing of Income and Deductions

The geographical source of income has a direct bearing on its tax treatment. U.S. citizens are taxed on their worldwide income, but income earned in other countries may receive tax relief through a number of IRC provisions. Foreign taxpayers (also known as nonresident aliens), on the other hand, generally are subject to federal taxes only on U.S. source income. Consequently, the sourcing rules often are the starting point in researching international tax issues.

The source of income is dependent on performance location and/or property location. Income from interest and dividends generally is sourced by the residency of the payer. Thus, dividends from a domestic corporation and interest from a state bond are sourced within the United States. To attract foreign investment, however, the United States allows a tax exemption on interest paid from a U.S. bank to a nonresident. For income from property, such as rents, royalties, or gains from property sales, it is the location of the property that is relevant.

Sales of inventory often are sourced by the location of the transaction, not by the origin of the inventory. Thus, inventory purchased in a foreign country but sold within the United States produces domestic sourced income. Income for personal services usually is sourced according to where the services are performed, not the residency of the compensating entity or the citizenship of the personal service provider. Finally, sourcing rules apply to deductions as well as to income.

Since the U.S. tax is based on taxable income, deductions and losses must be apportioned between domestic and foreign-source gross income. The U.S. rules for allocation and apportionment are very broad and attempt to match gross income with the deductions incurred to create that income. Deductions for expenses and losses directly related to a transaction or

---

[9]"Transfer Pricing Costs U.S. at Least $28 Billion," Martin A. Sullivan, *Tax Notes International*, March 29, 2010; "Lessons from the Great White North and Down Under—Thoughts on Recent Transfer Pricing Decisions," Louis Tassé, *Tax Notes International*, June 22, 2009.

activity are called *definitely related* deductions and are relatively simple to allocate. For example, cost of goods sold is allocated to the sales income to which it relates.

Expenses that either are not attributable to any specific income source or are associated with more than one source are known as *not definitely related* deductions and must be apportioned. Typically, these expenses are grouped by class of gross income and then apportioned between foreign and U.S. sourced income. There are also a number of special apportionment rules for items such as interest expense, research and experimentation costs, and losses on sales of real property. All the rules and regulations that govern allocation and apportionment are complex and beyond the scope of this text.

SPOTLIGHT ON TAXATION

Organisation for Economic Cooperation and Development

The Organisation for Economic Cooperation and Development (OECD) is an association of countries that believe in democratic governments and market economies. The goals of the OECD are to assist developing countries, support sustainable economic growth, boost employment, raise living standards, maintain financial stability, and generally contribute to world trade. Through its monitoring of world economies, the OECD has become known as one of the most reliable and prolific publishers of economic and social data and statistics. The OECD plays a prominent role in fostering good governance and helps to obtain multilateral economic agreements for individual countries that want to participate in the global economy. It is a forum where peer pressure can act as a powerful incentive. The OECD has released 15 action steps directed at helping countries reduce base erosion and profit shifting (BEPS). The full effect of the BEPS actions (such as country-by-country reporting) is already starting to be felt around the world.

15-4 Tax Treaties

Although the calculation of worldwide tax liability is affected by foreign tax laws, international taxation in the United States is governed by the IRC and by tax treaties. **Tax treaties**, negotiated by the Treasury Department and signed by the president, are bilateral agreements regarding the treatment of residents (not necessarily citizens) of the foreign country and the United States.

Generally, treaties are negotiated to prevent double taxation by providing reduced tax rates and reduced withholding rates or by exempting certain types of income from taxation. The incomes that receive reduced rates and exemptions vary among countries. Most income tax treaties contain what is known as a saving clause that prevents U.S. residents from using treaty provisions to avoid taxes on U.S. source income. The United States has tax treaties with more than 60 countries, as enumerated in Exhibit 9-24.

The IRC and tax treaties may provide conflicting treatment of some types of foreign-sourced income. Unlike most countries, the United States does not consider treaty provisions to take precedence over the code. Rather, to the extent possible, the code and treaties should be applied in harmony with each other. If this is not possible, then the most recently issued provision generally prevails. Some U.S. states do not honor the provisions of tax treaties, and U.S.-adopted tax treaties usually do not address state and local tax issues.

EXHIBIT 9-24: U.S. Income Tax Treaty Countries

Armenia	Iceland	Philippines
Australia	India	Poland
Austria	Indonesia	Portugal
Azerbaijan	Ireland	Romania
Bangladesh	Israel	Russia
Barbados	Italy	Slovak Republic
Belarus	Jamaica	Slovenia
Belgium	Japan	South Africa
Bulgaria	Kazakhstan	Spain
Canada	Korea	Sri Lanka
China	Kyrgyzstan	Sweden
Cyprus	Latvia	Switzerland
Czech Republic	Lithuania	Tajikistan
Denmark	Luxembourg	Thailand
Egypt	Malta	Trinidad
Estonia	Mexico	Tunisia
Finland	Moldova	Turkey
France	Morocco	Turkmenistan
Georgia	Netherlands	Ukraine
Germany	New Zealand	United Kingdom
Greece	Norway	Uzbekistan
Hungary	Pakistan	Venezuela

Source: **www.treasury.gov/resource-center/tax-policy/treaties/Pages/treaties.aspx**, accessed on December 4, 2016.

SPOTLIGHT ON TAXATION

Tax Treaties

A tax treaty requires Senate confirmation once negotiations by the Treasury are complete. However, since 2010, no tax treaties have been signed. Senate confirmation of tax treaties has been blocked through the sole efforts of Rand Paul, senator from Kentucky, on the grounds of privacy of U.S. taxpayer information. As a result, the following tax treaties are pending ratification:

Hungary (submitted to Senate November 2010)

Luxembourg (November 2010)

Switzerland (January 2011)

Chile (May 2012)

Spain (amendments, May 2014)

Poland (May 2014)

Japan (amendments, April 2015)

Vietnam (pending)

If there is no U.S. treaty covering income from a particular country, all taxable income from the country is included in the tax base of U.S. citizens and residents. This income also is likely to be taxed by the foreign country. To mitigate double taxation of this income, the foreign-income exclusion, the foreign-tax credit, and other more specific provisions were legislated.

The remainder of this chapter reviews a sample of the commercial international tax service providers. As discussed in Chapters 6, 7 and 8, these providers offer a plethora of tax products that can be bundled in a variety of ways. Thus, the tax services described in this chapter may not describe the set of resources available to the reader. Furthermore, the tax services update their products continually to maintain their competitive edge, and this is especially true in the international arena. Therefore, the current appearance of the tax services may differ from those presented in this text. However, the research concepts still are applicable.

16 Researching International Tax

Most international tax research can be broken down into two primary areas for a tax professional: (1) researching the U.S. tax treatment of a transaction with some connection to the United States based on U.S. tax law, or (2) researching how a foreign country might tax a transaction based on the foreign country's local tax law. Of course, some situations call for both types of research plus everything in between. The vast majority of tax service materials made available to U.S. tax professionals are focused on item (1) above—the taxation of a transaction by the United States. Due to the cost and special language skills often required, interpretation of detailed non-U.S. law is left to local experts from that country, and therefore much of what is generally available to examine in the United States is an overview of the foreign country's tax laws.

17 Checkpoint

Thomson Reuters offers a variety of international products that may be bundled with Checkpoint (see Chapter 6 for discussion) to meet the particular needs of a practitioner's international research. In the INTERNATIONAL PRACTICE AREA, editorial materials can be distilled down to four sources as shown in Exhibit 9-25: (1) INTERNATIONAL TAX SYSTEMS AND TAX PLANNING TECHNIQUES offered by Sweet and Maxwell, (2) RIA INTERNATIONAL PORTFOLIOS, (3) TAX TREATY EXPLANATIONS provided by WG&L, and (4) the WG&L TREATISES ON INTERNATIONAL TAXATION. Other international materials include the international newsletters and journals provided by Checkpoint, the U.S. tax treaties available as a primary source of U.S. tax law, and information available under the OTHER INTERNATIONAL PRODUCTS area in the left-hand window. Like other Checkpoint databases, these can be keyword searched or browsed through the table of contents to find the relevant information.

The INTERNATIONAL TAX SYSTEMS AND TAX PLANNING TECHNIQUES offered through Checkpoint and authored by Sweet and Maxwell cover international tax planning techniques for multinational companies and include a large number of country-specific titles. A sample of the titles available is presented in Exhibit 9-25.

The RIA INTERNATIONAL PORTFOLIOS are a selection of relevant tax planning portfolios written by experts that cover some of the primary tax topics of interest to international businesses. These portfolios, updated monthly, focus on specific issues relevant to taxpayers with international business. Each portfolio includes commentary, advice supported by detailed explanations, integrated planning ideas, and the current rules with citations to the controlling authorities. In addition, practice aids similar in nature to

EXHIBIT 9-25: Checkpoint International Practice Area

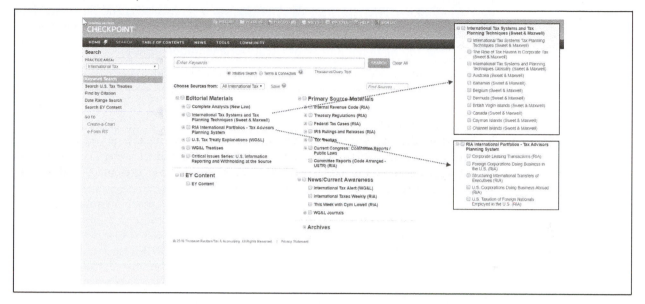

EXHIBIT 9-26: Checkpoint International Tax Treaties

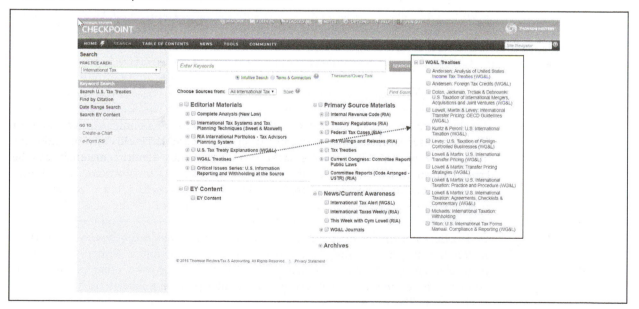

those offered by BNA's Tax Management Portfolios are furnished. The list of RIA portfolios is shorter than BNA's offerings, but the quality is outstanding. These are presented in Exhibit 9-25 as an inset. A multitude of other Checkpoint products may be available based on the particular subscription. Some of these are discussed later in this chapter.

Checkpoint also offers a wide selection of treatises that focus on international tax law. As shown in Exhibit 9-26, Checkpoint can contain treatises on tax treaties, foreign tax credits, transfer pricing, and withholding. Available treatises will depend on the subscription.

SPOTLIGHT ON TAXATION

International Bureau of Fiscal Documentation (IBFD)

The International Bureau of Fiscal Documentation (IBFD) is a not-for-profit organization organized in 1938 to provide authoritative expertise to tax practitioners around the globe with regard to cross-border taxation. The IBFD relies on independent tax research as well as its research specialists to contribute international tax information and education materials to its customers. Originally the IBFD was simply a tax document repository, but now it focuses on research products, which it distributes to both the private and public sectors.

Because it is an independent agency, the IBFD strives to produce objective and unbiased products, including software, tax courses, personalized client research (for private and governmental use), daily newsletters, journals, and numerous books on international tax issues. Besides its publications, the IBFD has a library that is regarded as the world's leading resource for international and comparative taxation. Free online access to this library is available at **www.ibfd.org**.

Another useful service accessible through Checkpoint is the RIA INTERNATIONAL TAX LIBRARY (ITL). Unlike other RIA tax products, ITL is a comprehensive set of analytical treatises and texts. A U.S. bilateral tax treaty database is included for accessing primary sources. Thus, the ITL lacks a central RIA editorial service such as the Federal Tax Coordinator. Newsletters and journals are included to keep the practitioner up to date on global taxation.

Checkpoint offers the unique RIA INTERNATIONAL CREATE-A-CHART function that facilitates the creation of tax-comparison charts with links to controlling authority, detailed explanations, and analysis by WG&L treatises. These links are maintained when the chart is exported to a word-processing file. The Create-a-Chart feature develops personalized charts of pertinent information for countries selected by the practitioner. CREATE-A-CHART currently offers more than 75 chart types on topics such as alimony, air and ship transport, capital gains, dividends, charitable contributions, and pensions.

18 CCH IntelliConnect

CCH offers numerous international tax products that provide timely and authoritative materials with practical analysis and understandable explanations written by experts in this field. To provide these products, CCH has teamed up with other publishers and authors. For example, CCH offers the BNA international publications and the CCH Global Daily Tax News.

All of CCH's international tax services may be accessed through the IntelliConnect platform, thus simplifying the search process for those practitioners already familiar with this service. Browsing the INTERNATIONAL TAX area furnishes access to the TAX TREATIES, U.S. INTERNATIONAL TAX COMPLIANCE AND PLANNING, and vast array of WORLDWIDE BUSINESS TAX GUIDES (see Exhibit 9-27). The Tax Treaties library provides complete and up-to-date coverage of more than 7,100 international tax agreements and protocols for more than 200 countries.

Also available are a series of WORLDWIDE BUSINESS TAX GUIDES (see Exhibit 9-28). The Worldwide Business Tax Guides provide, in a practical, easy-to-read format, a practical,

EXHIBIT 9-27: CCH IntelliConnect International

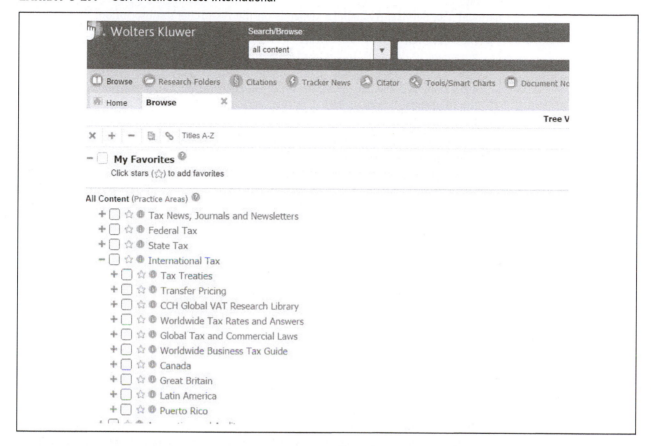

EXHIBIT 9-28: CCH IntelliConnect Worldwide Business Guides

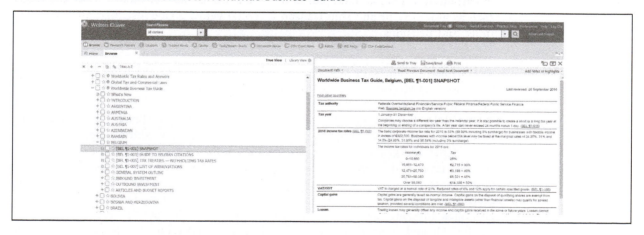

integrated look at almost 50 countries' key tax issues that arise when planning the development and growth of a corporation's foreign business. Issues such as minimizing risk, reducing costs, and increasing productivity are covered by the in-depth commentary on all forms of doing business in a country.

Following is a list of some of the most useful resources offered within the CCH International Tax Service. Availability depends on the researcher's subscription.

- *International Tax Treaty Expert Library.* Thousands of treaties (with amended language in context) and related documents, such as diplomatic notes and protocols, are available, and all are in English. The treaties cover income, estate, and gift taxes, sea and air transport, and information-exchange agreements. Some of the analytical works included in the service are *Klaus Vogel on Double Taxation Conventions; International Taxation, U.S. Taxation of Foreign Persons & Foreign Income; The Compatibility of Anti-Abuse Provisions in Tax Treaties with EC Law; The Impact of Community Law on Tax Treaties—Issues and Solutions*; and *The 1996 United States Model Income Tax Convention, Analysis, Commentary and Comparison.*

- *Transfer Pricing.* There are four publications on transfer pricing: (1) *Tax Treatise: Transfer Pricing Rules Compliance and Controversy*, (2) *International Transfer Pricing*, (3) *U.S. Transfer Pricing Guide*, and (4) *Developing a Transfer Pricing Policy.* All four are written by subject-matter experts.

- *U.S. International Tax Compliance and Planning.* This library contains four outside-authored explanations of U.S. international tax rules: (1) International Taxation: U.S. Taxation of Foreign Persons and Foreign Income, (2) International Taxation: Corporate and Individual, (3) Practical Guide to U.S. Taxation of International Transactions, and (4) International Tax Commentaries.

- *Worldwide Tax Rates and Answers.* This area provides corporate tax rates by country, including national and local tax rates, as well as current forms and instructions for countries around the world.

- *International Tax Planning Library.* This library consists of three comprehensive publications and a practical newsletter exploring tax planning issues from around the world. The three publications cover international tax planning for corporations, expatriates, and migrants, plus offshore financial centers for more than 40 countries.

19 Bloomberg BNA

As with its U.S. and state coverage, BNA has also developed a rich set of international portfolios that are part of the BNA Tax and Accounting Center's International offerings (see Exhibit 9-29).

The BNA International Tax Library includes almost 100 BNA Tax Management Portfolios written by leading experts in international taxation and business. The topics covered run the gamut from the foreign tax credit, to international aspects of Social Security taxes and foreign estates, to nontax issues such as the regulation of foreign investments and currency exchange controls. There are more than 15 portfolios dedicated to transfer pricing in the accompanying Transfer Pricing Library; more than 40 portfolios covering the taxation of business operations in specific countries (Country Portfolios); and more than 40 portfolios covering taxation of U.S. persons' foreign income, taxation of foreign persons' U.S. income, and provisions applicable to U.S. and foreign income (see Exhibit 9-30). The Country Portfolios address not only income taxation but also indirect taxes, such as the value-added tax (VAT) and other special taxes unique to the various countries.

As with the BNA U.S. Income Library, each BNA Tax Management Portfolio contains excerpts from primary sources, such as the IRC, regulations, and IRS pronouncements.

EXHIBIT 9-29: BNA Tax and Accounting Center International

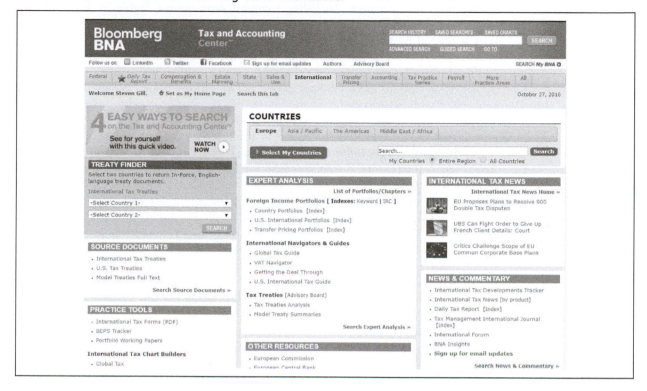

EXHIBIT 9-30: BNA International Portfolios

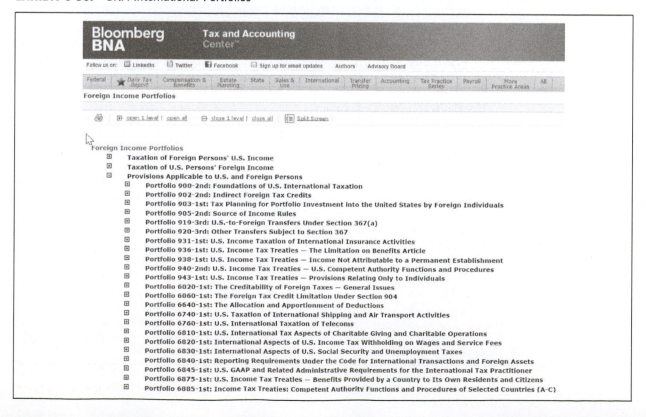

For tax treaties, the portfolios furnish not only the text but all relevant materials for interpreting the agreements, including technical explanations, legislative histories, and judicial interpretations. Practical advice for complying with the local business and tax laws is offered by notable practitioners in the Detailed Analysis section. The Working Papers section contains interactive and IRS forms, sample elections, official documents, and legal forms (some filled in as examples). These portfolios are updated regularly.

The BNA International tab was developed to communicate accurate and detailed analysis of worldwide taxation as well as regular international news updates. Thus, in addition to the Country Portfolios, the typical BNA international tax library offers a variety of news and analysis libraries, shown in Exhibit 9-29, to the international tax practitioner. Included are the *International Journal* and *International Tax Monitor* that follow major tax developments in key jurisdictions; *Tax Planning International Review* and *International Journal*, both providing monthly analysis on international tax developments and treaty changes; and *Tax Planning International* for both Europe and Asia-Pacific. Transfer-pricing updates appear in the accompanying Transfer Pricing Library, featuring the *Transfer Pricing Report* and *Transfer Pricing International Journal*.

Including the portfolios, these sources represent the core of BNA's international tax reference data. The GLOBAL TAX GUIDE provides country-specific information on tax rates for corporate, personal, withholding, and other taxes (see Exhibit 9-31). These rates are summarized in the Worldwide Tax Table, which presents key rate information for many countries in a single source and can be found under Expert Analysis on the main international tab (see Exhibit 9-29).

EXHIBIT 9-31:   BNA Global Tax Guide

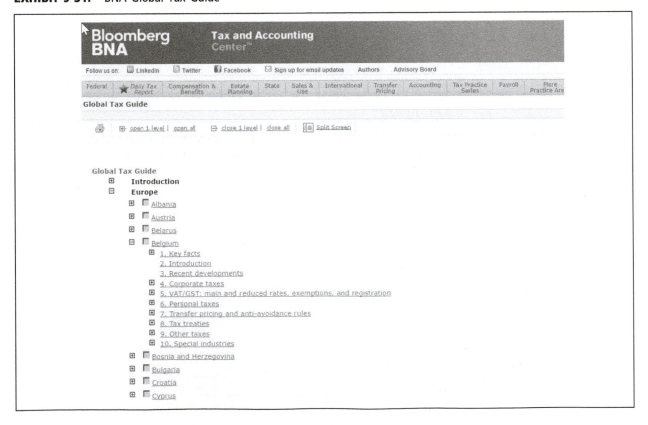

19-1 Tax Treaties

Tax treaty information, including the official treaty language and analysis of the treaty, is available under the TAX TREATIES heading on the international tab (see Exhibit 9-29). U.S. treaties can be accessed quickly on the U.S. treaties heading, and other countries' treaties may be examined using the select-a-country drop-down menu.

20 Westlaw

Westlaw offers two portals to international taxation materials: through a separate service, Westlaw International; and through the standard Westlaw subscription. These services are not widely available to schools other than law schools, so they are only briefly discussed here.

The Westlaw INTERNATIONAL tab provides access to documents on a variety of international topics, one of which is tax law (located in Topical under the Westlaw International Subscriptions heading). The databases generally cover U.S. taxation and its treaties, with analysis supplied by the Law of Federal Income Taxation (Mertens) tax service.

Specific country headings, such as for Australia and Canada, have tax as one of the practice areas and thus provide access to the country's tax laws. However, the countries available may be limited by the user's subscription. Finally, while International Practice Areas might seem to be a logical avenue for finding tax databases, taxation is not listed under this heading.

Westlaw also offers the IRS INTERNATIONAL tab. This tab contains many of the same databases available under the INTERNATIONAL tab but is focused on international tax and has a number of primary and editorial materials, both for the United States and for other countries. BNA, WGL, and other popular treatises and analyses are available.

A more fruitful means of entry into Westlaw's international taxation resources is through the tax library (TAX tab). This portal furnishes access to the RIA and BNA international materials (primary and editorial) that were discussed previously in this chapter as well as international journals, WG&L treatises, and texts.

21 LexisNexis

LexisNexis has built impressive international tax libraries by amassing documents and services developed by other publishers. The Lexis Advance Tax and Academic services contain the international publications by BNA, CCH, Wiley, and Tax Analysts as well as publications written by recognized experts in the international field.

The INTERNATIONAL practice area in Lexis Advance Tax displays source pods in numerous categories. One of the primary international sources is the Rhoades and Langer International Taxation and Tax Treaties series as presented in Exhibit 9-32.

Lexis Advance Tax also offers the business primers, "DOING BUSINESS IN ..." for a variety of countries (see Exhibit 9-33). These portfolios provide an overview of the country's business environment, including its taxing structure. Clicking on the title will either access the document or display the document's TOC, as Exhibit 9-33 shows for the Doing Business in France portfolio.

22 Tax Analysts

The Tax Analysts *Worldwide Tax Treaties* includes several features to enhance the ability to compare, side by side, income tax treaties. Easy-to-read tables compare the tax rates on various types of income and withholding rates among more than 170 taxing

EXHIBIT 9-32:   Lexis Advance Tax International

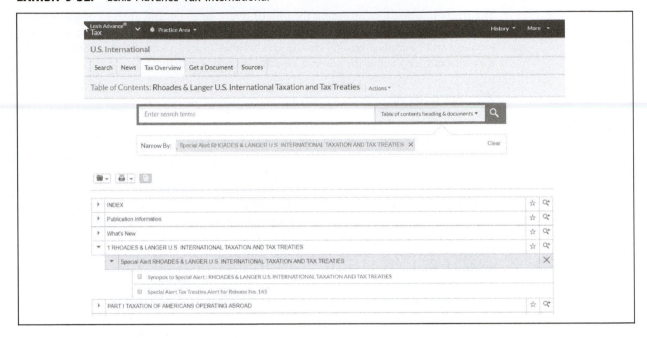

EXHIBIT 9-33:   Lexis Tax Center Doing Business in Guides

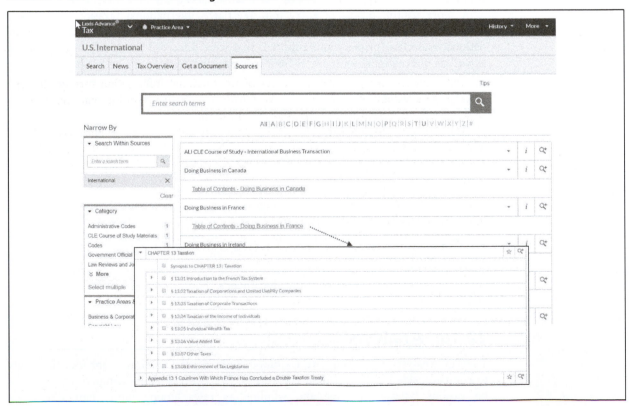

EXHIBIT 9-34:   Tax Analysts Tax Treaties

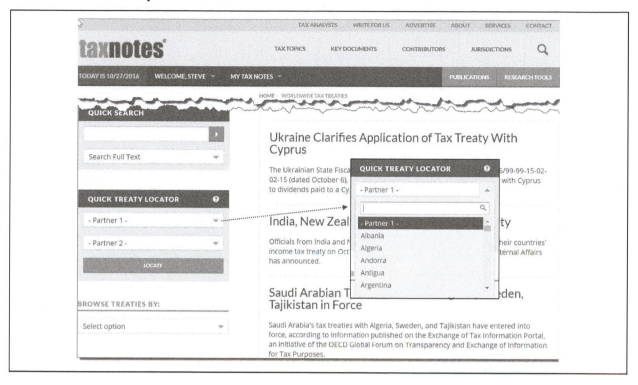

jurisdictions worldwide. The original, in-force, pending, terminated, and unperfected treaties can be viewed separately. Access to treaties using the Quick Treaty Locator is shown in Exhibit 9-34.

Tax Analysts also provides a rich set of international information through its daily updates to a variety of publications. *Worldwide Tax Daily* offers international news on a daily basis organized by country and organization.

Tax Analysts also publishes *Tax Notes International*, a weekly publication that provides tax news, commentary, and in-depth analysis of legislative, judicial, and administrative tax developments from more than 180 countries. Full-text tax documents also are available with *Tax Notes International*.

23 LexisNexis Academic

The international content of LexisNexis Academic relies heavily on Tax Analysts for most of its sources, as Exhibit 9-35 demonstrates. Access to the international documents is easiest through the Sources Tab.

24 Internet Sites

The Tax and Accounting Sites Directory Website (**www.taxsites.com**) contains links to numerous tax web pages, one of which is designated for international tax topics. This is an excellent starting point for Internet international tax searches. Links to tax sites for more than 80 countries are given as well as references to international tax associations and IRS resources. A long list of other sources also is provided.

EXHIBIT 9-35:   LexisNexis Academic International

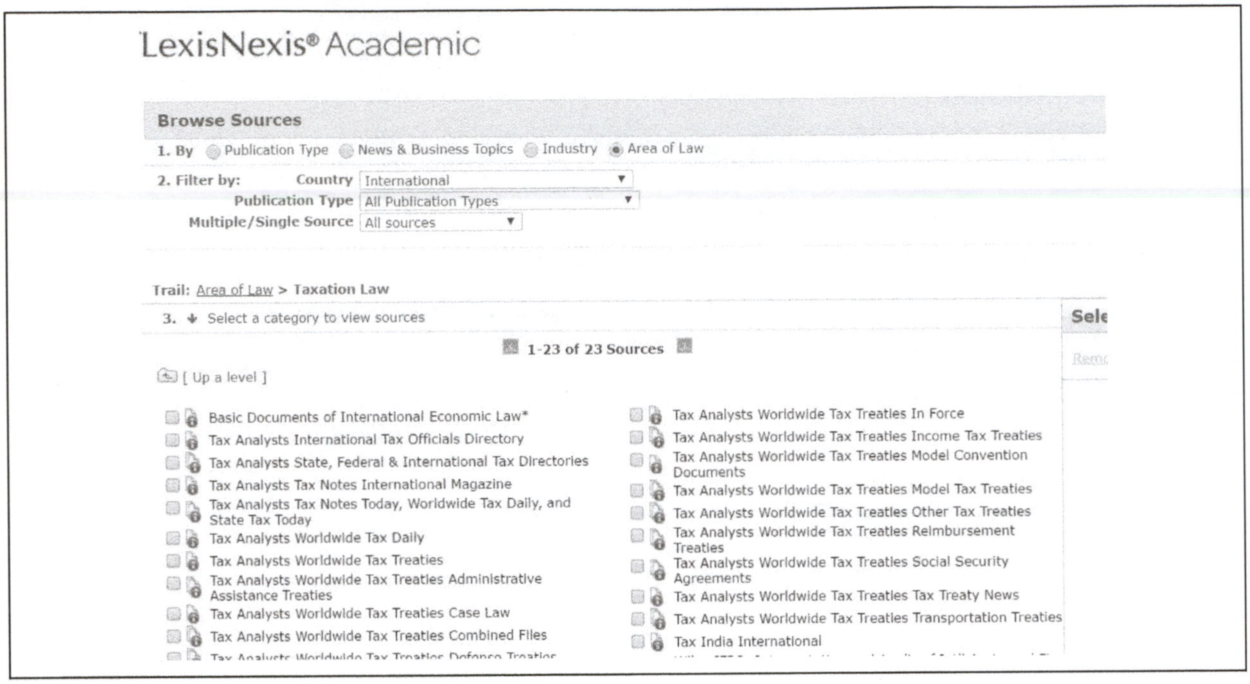

SUMMARY

The world is shrinking as more companies enter the global economy. Only the smallest businesses operate in a single country, much less a single U.S. state. No longer do only large, multinational companies maintain international offices. Now, many middle-market and owner-managed firms are expanding into the international markets of Europe and the Pacific Rim. Thus, it is no longer a luxury to employ staff who are knowledgeable about international taxation. With so much of a business's tax bill being composed of nonfederal taxes, planning for state and local taxation has also become more important to taxpayers and therefore to tax researchers.

The demand for tax advice in the non-U.S. federal area is rapidly growing, and the major players in the research service industry (CCH, LexisNexis, Thomson Reuters, Westlaw, and BNA) continue to expand their international offerings. As the importance of multijurisdictional taxation continues to explode, the tax services will develop more targeted products to serve the needs of the tax practitioners. Consequently, jurisdictional research tools will likely be among the fastest changing component of the major tax services.

KEY WORDS

By the time you complete this chapter, you should be comfortable discussing each of the following terms. If you need additional review of any of these items, return to the appropriate material in the chapter or consult the glossary to this text.

Commerce Clause, p. 305
Due Process Clause, p. 304
foreign tax credit, p. 329

Equal Protection Clause, p. 306
Multistate Tax Commission
   (MTC), p. 311

nexus, p. 305
Public Law 86-272, p. 306
Supremacy Clause, p. 300

tax treaties, p. 332
territorial model, p. 329
transfer pricing, p. 330

Uniform Division of Income for
  Tax Purposes Act (UDITPA),
  p. 311

worldwide model, p. 329

DISCUSSION QUESTIONS

1. Why are taxpayers emphasizing multijurisdictional tax planning?

2. Why is state and local tax planning becoming more important?

3. Describe the different constitutionality challenges with regard to federal and state taxes.

4. Discuss the supremacy provision in the U.S. Constitution.

5. What are the two constitutional limitations and one public law that serve to limit the ability to tax out-of-state taxpayers?

6. Explain what "due process" means with respect to taxing out-of-state businesses.

7. What are the four criteria for imposition of state taxation set forth in *Complete Auto Transit, Inc.*?

8. What protection from taxation does *Quill* afford an out-of-state taxpayer?

9. Describe how a mail-order business uses P.L. 86-272 to avoid taxation by states.

10. Explain how the passage of a state tax bill is similar to the passage of a federal law.

11. When would federal rulings be pertinent to state tax issues?

12. List some of the more common modifications to federal income to arrive at state income.

13. Describe the differences between allocation and apportionment.

14. What are the purposes of the MTC?

15. What is included in the Checkpoint state legislation database?

16. What is the function of the CompareIt feature in Checkpoint?

17. Compare the Multiple Sources search with the State and Local Taxes initial search option in Checkpoint.

18. Discuss the citation search capabilities in the Checkpoint State & Local Tax practice area.

19. How are specific states' tax laws selected using CCH IntelliConnect?

20. Describe some of the multistate sources available in IntelliConnect.

21. Describe the parts of a typical BNA state portfolio.

22. Explain whether one can search the same libraries with the LexisNexis Academic Search engine and its Sources engine.

23. What citator service is used in LexisNexis Academic?

24. Describe the easiest way to find state tax law data in Westlaw Campus Research.

25. Name two state taxation journals and indicate who publishes each.

26. What are the major models for developing international taxing systems?

27. What is the worldwide model of international taxation? Explain whether a corporation with only domestic income or a company with foreign income would pay more taxes under this model.

28. What is the territorial model of international taxation? Under this model, what rate of tax does a native corporation pay on its foreign income?

29. Describe whether the United States uses a worldwide or territorial model.

30. What are the general rules for sourcing income?

31. What are the general rules for assigning expenses to certain sources of income?

32. How does transfer pricing complicate international tax matters for large multinational companies?

33. Describe the standard for transfer pricing in most countries.

34. Describe the functions of the OECD.

35. If a provision of the Internal Revenue Code and a tax treaty are in conflict, which rule prevails?

36. Describe the two primary areas of international tax research.

37. Describe the four editorial materials offered in Checkpoint's International Tax practice area.

38. What is the content of the Worldwide Tax Guides maintained in IntelliConnect?

39. What kinds of information are provided in the Working Papers section of the International BNA Tax Management Portfolios?

40. What are the three main areas in the BNA International Tax Library?

41. What organization provides the international treaty analyses for Lexis Advance Tax?

EXERCISES

State Exercises

42. Locate the Website for the MTC.
    a. Define the three levels of membership in the MTC.
    b. Provide a brief summary of one of the latest articles in the Multistate Tax Commission Review. (Hint: Publications are found in Resources.)
    c. What is the Nexus Program? When was it founded?
    d. How does a taxpayer initiate joint audits?
    e. The MTC provides a link to the Federation of Tax Administrators (FTA). What is the title and date of the most recent FTA meeting?

43. Use the Checkpoint State & Local practice area to locate the *Bacchus Imports Ltd. v. Herbert H. Dias* case using the Federal Cases in the State Taxes option.
    a. What is the citation for the case, and what court heard this case?
    b. Which clauses of the U.S. Constitution did *Bacchus* allege were violated?
    c. Must the names of the plaintiff and defendant in the case be entered to find the case? Explain your response.
    d. Read this case. Perform a keyword search to locate the case without using the plaintiff or defendant names. If necessary, use the Search Within Results feature. What keywords did you use for the general search and (if necessary) for your follow-up search?

44. Use the Checkpoint State & Local practice area to answer the following questions:
    a. Select the state in which the university you are attending is located and go to the next screen.
    b. What corporate items are provided in the tax-type list? Is there a tax on intangibles, mortgages, or stock transfers?
    c. Select Florida (or Washington if your university is in Florida) as the state of interest and go to the next screen. What tax types are different between the two states?
    d. Select the state in which the university you are attending is located. What is the rate of tax per pack of cigarettes? Compare your state's rate to that of Washington State. In what order are the tax types listed? In what order are the document types listed?

45. Use the Checkpoint State & Local practice area to answer the following questions:
    a. For the state of your choice, compare the listing of documents available under the option Select Document Types in the Search States (SALT) with the list for the same state in the TOC.
    b. Using the index in the TOC for the state reporter for Illinois, what are the listings for the letter "H" under the "stamp" heading?
    c. In the Hawaii TOC, what is the fee for filing articles of incorporation for an LLC?
    d. In the Miscellaneous Multistate Materials TOC, what are the U.S. statute titles listed for federal laws on state taxation?

46. Use the CCH IntelliConnect State Tax to answer the following questions regarding the state in which the university you are attending is located:
    a. What is the title of the most recent article in *State Tax Day* related to this state?
    b. What is the most recent court case in the news for this state?
    c. In the explanations of the state tax reporters, perform a keyword search using the term "escheat." What does this term mean, and to what does it apply? In which paragraph did you find the answer?
    d. Using the topical index for *Multistate Property Tax Guide*, perform a keyword search for "damaged property." In which paragraph are the rules for damaged property covered?

47. Use the CCH IntelliConnect State Tax to answer the following questions:
    a. Does Hawaii allow estates a personal exemption? If yes, what is the amount, and which state statute allows such amount?
    b. Using the Browse window, drill down into any state with a corporate income tax and find the explanation for the sales factor under allocation and apportionment. Then use the Related Information All States button to show the results for all states. Now clear that search, select all the state tax reporters, and do a keyword search for "sales-factor apportionment." Explain why one search method might be preferable to the other.
    c. Use the thesaurus (under advanced search) and find the synonyms for the term "devise."

48. Use the CCH IntelliConnect State Tax to answer the following questions:
    a. Did Alaska ever have a personal income tax? If yes, in what year did Alaska repeal the tax?
    b. Use the Multistate Quick Answer Charts to determine the diesel fuel tax for the state in which your university is located. Which state has the highest diesel fuel rate?
    c. What, if any, tax legislation was enacted by the state in which your university is located this week? How about since the beginning of the year?
    d. Determine which states have Jai Alai taxes.

49. Use Lexis Advance Tax to answer the following questions:
    a. Use the Florida Practice Insights to determine whether having a third party sell your out-of-state corporation's gift cards in its Florida stores is likely to create nexus.

b. What section of the Florida code covers the issue in the previous question?

c. Are there any cases related to this issue (Hint: Use the Case Notes at the bottom of the Florida Statute document)?

50. Use Lexis Advance Tax to answer the following questions:

a. Which chapter of *Bender's State Taxation: Principles and Practice* covers sales and use tax nexus?

b. Using the information found in part a, what are the names of the cases that cover the basis of the economic-nexus argument?

c. Which well-known retailer and which U.S. state were at the center of the *Geoffrey* case?

51. Using the LexisNexis Academic Sources option to do the following:

a. Find the law review article from 2014 that results from a search for "dutch sandwich," using quotes for this search. What are the title, author, and publication?

b. What sources are available for the state of Delaware in the Taxation area of law?

c. What are the title and author of the most recent article in the *Florida Tax Review* with these three separate keyword terms: *property*, *tax*, and *abatement*? Did you use a natural-language or terms and connector search?

52. Use LexisNexis Academic Search option Legal to answer the following questions:

a. Locate the following court case: T. C. Memo 1986-512. What is its citation, what court heard it, and when was it decided?

b. Apply the Shepard's Citator to the above case. How many citing decisions are there for this case? How many headnotes?

c. Should the finding in this case be relied upon?

53. Use LexisNexis Academic to answer the following questions:

a. Select Sources, By Area of Law—Taxation, Filter by—West. Which states does LexisNexis Academic consider western states?

b. What treatises and analytical materials are provided for the western states?

c. In what year was the current Missouri constitution adopted?

54. Use the service of your choice (RIA, CCH, LexisNexis, or Westlaw) to answer the following questions:

a. Locate *Complete Auto Transit Inc. v. Brady*. What type of tax was being examined in the case? Provide two parallel citations for the case and the name of the justice delivering the opinion.

b. Locate *Quill Corp. v. North Dakota*. What was the disposition of the case by the Supreme Court? Provide two parallel citations for the case and the name of the justice delivering the opinion. Name any justices who filed dissenting opinions.

c. Locate *Wisconsin Department of Revenue v. Wrigley*. What tax years are reviewed by the case? Provide two parallel citations for the case. Who were the attorneys for the respondent and the petitioner? Were there any dissenting opinions?

d. Locate *Commonwealth Edison Co. v. Montana*. What is the type of tax that was being questioned in the case? Provide two parallel citations for the case. What two federal clauses were addressed in the case?

55. Use the Westlaw Campus Research State Materials practice area to answer the following questions:

a. What document types are available under the State Materials tab for the state of Maine?

b. Select All Maine State Cases from part a above and search for tax and bowling. Find *State v. Haines*. What is the date of this ruling, and what was the opinion of bowling at the time?

c. From the previous case, use the Citing references tab and find *Barnes v. Hathorn*. What was the date of the ruling, and what was the nonbowling nuisance in *Barnes*?

56. Use Westlaw Campus Research to answer the following questions regarding the *Jensen* 178 Cal. App. 4th 426 case:
    a. In what year was the case decided and by what court?
    b. Examine the headnote. What three holdings did the court determine?
    c. What does the history tab say about the ruling?
    d. Which two judges concurred with Judge Boren's ruling?

57. Use the BNA Tax and Accounting Center States tab to answer the following questions:
    a. Is there a portfolio for each state? Which state has the most portfolios?
    b. Generally, what are the portfolio series numbers for the portfolios that address state business entities and transaction issues?
    c. What are the title and number of the portfolio that addresses the federal constitutional limitations on state taxation?
    d. Which portfolio discussed the Illinois sales and use tax on professional and personal services?

58. Use the BNA Tax and Accounting Center States tab for the following questions:
    a. What is the title of State Portfolio 1550? How many worksheets are included in this portfolio?
    b. Which portfolio explains the state tax effects of the QSSS election for S corporations?
    c. How many basic forms of drop-shipment transactions are there? In which portfolio did you find your answer?

59. Locate state tax newsletters to answer the following questions:
    a. What is the title of the most recent article in Tax Analysts' *State Tax Today* that discusses royalty trusts?
    b. What is the most recent article in BNA's *Tax Management Weekly State Tax Reporter* that discusses the streamlining of sales taxes?
    c. What is the title of the most recent article in CCH's *State Tax Day* on gasoline taxes?
    d. What is the title of the most recent article in CCH's *State Tax Review* that discusses sales tax obligations of advertising agencies?
    e. What is the subject of one of the most recent articles in RIA's *State & Local Taxes Weekly* newsletter?

60. Find an article in the *Journal of Multistate Taxation and Incentives* on each of the following topics. Provide the authors, article title, and date published.
    a. The ad valorem property taxes on a baseball stadium.
    b. The most recent economic incentives provided to the film industry.
    c. Credits and exemptions used by Mississippi to promote the development of broadband technology.
    d. The most recent article on the dividends-received deduction.

61. Use the *Journal of State Taxation* to answer the following questions:
    a. What is the title of the most recent article on Web-related activities and potential nexus problems?
    b. What are the volume and number of the most current issue? What is the lead article?
    c. Who is the current editor of the journal? Is anyone on the advisory board from the university you attend? If yes, list the name(s).
    d. Who is the author of the article titled "A Deal's a Deal: Why State Cannot Unilaterally Amend the Multistate Tax Compact"? What are the year, volume, and issue number in which the article appears?

62. Use Internet sites to answer the following questions:
    a. Provide the links to three News & Topics sites provided by Tax Sites for states (**www.taxsites.com**).
    b. Visit three national associations that are concerned with state tax issues. Provide the Websites' URLs.

c. Visit the Website of your state's agency responsible for taxation (the Department of Revenue, for many states). Provide the URL for this agency. For California, provide both agencies' URLs.

d. Select an adjacent state and give a summary of one of its taxes. (You could use Alaska and Hawaii as a pair.)

International Exercises

63. Use the BNA Tax and Accounting Center International tab to answer the following questions:

a. Which countries are included in Tax Planning International Asia-Pacific?

b. Using the Tax Treaties Comparison Tool, prepare a comparison chart of the U.S.–Austria Treaty and the U.S.–Canada Treaty. How do the definitions of permanent establishment differ?

c. Does Switzerland have a tax treaty with China? Does Switzerland have a treaty with Ghana?

d. In which language does BNA have the Switzerland–Ghana treaty?

64. Use the BNA Tax and Accounting Center International tab to answer the following questions:

a. What is the proper citation for the most recent article in the European Tax Service on the United Kingdom's VAT?

b. Who are the authors of the Tax Management International Forum for the Netherlands?

c. Use the Quick Search option to determine how many articles Bert Mesdom has written.

65. Use the BNA Tax and Accounting Center International tab to answer the following questions:

a. What collections are available under the Foreign Income Portfolios heading when using a Guided Search?

b. What is the lead report in the most recent *International Tax Monitor*?

c. What countries are included in Middle East/Africa in the Global Tax Guide collection?

66. Use the BNA Tax and Accounting Center International tab to answer the following questions:

a. What is the name of a limited liability company in Colombia?

b. What section of the French tax code provides the general rules for transfer pricing?

c. Use the Advanced Search option to locate a 2012 article discussing China continuing to offer VAT refunds for the animation industry. Provide the source of the article.

67. Use Lexis Advance Tax to answer the following questions:

a. According to Tax Havens of the World, who granted an exemption on taxes to the Cayman Islands and why?

b. Who is the author of *International Estate Planning*?

c. What is the title of Chapter 8 of the *Foreign Tax & Trade Briefs for Iraq*?

68. Use the International Practice area of Lexis Advance Tax to answer the following questions:

a. How many treatises and practice guides are found for a search of William H. Byrnes?

b. Which countries does Bhutan have tax treaties with?

c. How many treaty documents cover the Bhutanese tax treaties?

d. In which article of the 2006 U.S. Model Income Tax Treaty is permanent establishment discussed?

69. Use Tax Analysts or LexisNexis Academic to answer the following questions:

a. What tax treatment does the Argentina–France treaties indicate for earnings of nonresident students? What is the effective date of the agreement?

b. What is the title and date of the most recent article regarding Iceland in the Tax Analysts' *Worldwide Tax Daily*?

c. What is the title and date of the most recent article on the European VAT in the Tax Analysts' *Tax Notes International*?

70. Use RIA materials to answer the following questions:
    a. What international sources are included in the International News/Current Awareness source heading?
    b. Which paragraph of the *RIA Tax Treaty Editorial Explanations* discusses the taxation of visiting students under the U.S.–Estonia treaty?
    c. What are the title and date of the most recent article in *The Journal of International Taxation* that discusses BEPS? What is BEPS?

71. Use RIA materials to answer the following questions:
    a. What are the countries listed as tax havens in the International Tax Systems and Planning Techniques database?
    b. What International Create-a-Charts are available for the taxation of students and trainees?
    c. Who are the authors of the treatise titled *U.S. Taxation of International Mergers, Acquisitions & Joint Ventures*?

72. Use CCH IntelliConnect to answer the following questions:
    a. What is the most recent article on UK VAT exemptions in the *Global Daily Tax News*? What does it discuss?
    b. Which article of the Estonia treaty discusses the U.S. taxation of students, apprentices, and trainees from Estonia?
    c. Use the *Worldwide Tax Guide for Bahrain*. What is the web address for the Bahrain Tax Authority?

73. Use CCH IntelliConnect to answer the following questions:
    a. How is a resident of Bermuda defined in its treaty with the United States?
    b. What legislation exists in Azerbaijan to deal with intercompany transfer pricing?
    c. What is the title of article 20 in the 2014 OECD Model Tax Convention on Income and Capital?

CHAPTER 10

Financial Accounting Research

LEARNING OBJECTIVES

- Describe the basics of deferred taxes and accounting for income taxes.
- Explain the source and structure of international accounting standards.
- Identify and use the features of the FASB Accounting Standards Codification Research System.
- Identify which tax services offer accounting research and what information is available.

CHAPTER OUTLINE

FOR BUSINESSES REQUIRED to prepare financial statements in accordance with U.S. **Generally Accepted Accounting Principles (GAAP)** or International Accounting Standards (IAS), the computation of income tax expense requires expertise in accounting for income taxes. Increasingly, tax professionals are finding that an understanding of financial accounting for income taxes is a required competency.

The likelihood of a tax professional being asked to prepare, review, or audit the income tax provision reflected in the balance sheet, income statement, and footnotes of financial statements has grown substantially since the passage of the Sarbanes-Oxley Act. Simply put, it is no longer sufficient to understand tax planning and compliance without also gaining a much deeper understanding of accounting for income taxes under the financial accounting guidance framework applicable to businesses both in the United States and abroad.

In order to effectively work with income tax provisions, a tax professional must be able to understand not only the accounting guidance for income taxes but also the financial accounting guidance related to other complex business transactions. It is important that the differences between financial statements and tax returns be identified and reflected properly in the income tax provision.

Consequently, tax professionals must understand how to research the tax law and also financial accounting rules related to businesses. This chapter provides an overview of the topical area most likely to be important to tax researchers, accounting for income taxes, as well as a detailed description of the content, structure, and use of the FASB Accounting Standards Codification Research System (CRS).

1 Accounting for Income Taxes

Intuitively you might assume that a company would account for income taxes on an as-paid basis, reflecting the amount of income tax liability actually owed to all jurisdictions for the particular period of time. However, many items of income and expense are not treated the same for financial statement or book purposes as they are for tax purposes, and such an income tax number would not meaningfully reflect the income taxes associated with the pretax income presented on the financial statements.

A corporation's financial statements are prepared in accordance with GAAP and follow the matching principle in which the expenses related to earning income are reported in the same period as the income, without regard to when the expenses are actually paid. The purpose and objective of the financial statements are very different from the objective of the corporation's income tax return.

Under both U.S. GAAP and IAS, the amount of tax expense reflected in the financial statements is made up of both current and deferred components. While the current tax expense theoretically represents the taxes actually payable to (refund receivable from) the government, the deferred tax expense (or benefit) represents the future tax cost (or savings) connected with income reported in the current-period financial statements.

Differences between the book basis and the tax basis of items affecting income tax are recorded as deferred tax assets (representing future deductions) or deferred tax liabilities (representing future includable income). Consequently, tax professionals must be able to identify not only the tax treatment of transactions but also the financial statement treatment for the item.

SPOTLIGHT ON TAXATION

Taxes Subject to the Deferred Tax Model

The deferred tax model of taxes applies to all federal, state, foreign, and local taxes based on income. However, other taxes, such as payroll, property, sales, value-added, net capital, and taxes based on capital expenditures, are not included. Generally, nonincome taxes are recognized in the period those costs are incurred for financial statement purposes.

2 GAAP and the Financial Accounting Standards Board (FASB)

In the United States, GAAP comes under the purview of the **Financial Accounting Standards Board (FASB)**. As stated by the FASB:

> *Since 1973, the FASB has been the designated organization in the private sector for establishing standards of financial accounting. Those standards govern the preparation of financial statements. They are officially recognized as authoritative by the SEC (Financial Reporting Release No. 1, Section 101, and reaffirmed in its April 2003 Policy Statement) and the AICPA (Rule 203, Rules of Professional Conduct, as amended May 1973 and May 1979).*

Prior to the 1970s, accounting standards were promulgated by groups formed under the umbrella of the American Institute of Certified Public Accountants (AICPA). Seeking additional independence, primary responsibility was shifted to the FASB in 1973; however, accounting guidance continued to be issued by various groups within the AICPA.

For example, the AICPA continued to issue statements of position (SOPs) and industry accounting and auditing guides. Although subordinate to statements issued by FASB, these types of guidance continued to have effect until 2009, when the bevy of different sources and statements were brought together into the **FASB Accounting Standards Codification (ASC)**. The ASC is now the primary accounting guidance for most businesses.

The U.S. **Securities and Exchange Commission (SEC)** was granted authority for the oversight of the U.S. capital markets in 1934. It is the SEC's responsibility to:

- Interpret federal securities laws;

- Issue new rules and amend existing rules;

- Oversee the inspection of securities firms, brokers, investment advisers, and ratings agencies;

- Oversee private regulatory organizations in the securities, accounting, and auditing fields; and

- Coordinate U.S. securities regulation with federal, state, and foreign authorities (**www.sec.gov/about/whatwedo.shtml#create**).

Thus, for public companies, the SEC retains standard-setting authority. In most instances, the SEC continues to rely on the private standard setters. However, the SEC has issued a number of forms of guidance, such as Regulation S-X, staff accounting bulletins, and others that have also been codified by the SEC. Some portion of the SEC guidance is generally available in the ASC as supplemental material.

3 International Standards

In order to deal with the proliferation of country- or jurisdiction-specific accounting principles, the **International Accounting Standards Board (IASB)** was formed. By creating a set of high-quality, understandable, enforceable, and globally accepted **international financial reporting standards (IFRS)**, the IASB attempts to deliver its mission:

- Bring transparency by enhancing the international comparability and quality of financial information, enabling investors and other market participants to make informed economic decisions;

- Strengthen accounting ability by reducing the information gap between the providers of capital and the people to whom they have entrusted their money;

- Contribute to economic efficiency by helping investors to identify opportunities and risks across the world, thus improving capital allocation (**www.ifrs.org/About-us /Pages/IFRS-Foundation-and-IASB.aspx**).

To assess the progress toward global adoption of IFRS, the IASB has gathered information on the profiles of 147 countries—including the G20 (the 20 countries with the largest global economies)—to determine the level of IFRS adoption. Of the 147 countries, 122 require the use of IFRS for all or most publicly accountable companies. In many countries where IFRS has not been adopted as the primary standard, the use of IFRS is permitted.

The current position of the Securities and Exchange Commission is that the United States does not support the adoption of the IFRS as the standards of record; however, the FASB continues to work cooperatively with the IASB when issuing standards. Current international guidance for accounting for income taxes (IAS 12) is similar in many ways to guidance provided in the ASC (ASC 740). Both use a deferred tax framework for reporting income tax expense. Given the existing importance of international accounting standards and the potential for more widespread adoption, tax professionals should continue to monitor changes in international standards related to accounting for income taxes and other relevant transactions.

4 The FASB Codification

Today, the codification is the single source of authoritative U.S. GAAP for private companies. All previous U.S. GAAP standards issued by the standard setters described previously have been superseded. Thus, all other accounting literature not included in the codification is considered nonauthoritative.

For companies registered with the SEC (public companies), the SEC's laws and regulations as well as federal securities laws continue to apply. Certain guidance is not within the scope of the codification, such as international accounting standards issued by the IASB, guidance for non-GAAP financial statements such as cash basis or other comprehensive basis of accounting, governmental accounting standards, and audit guidance.

SPOTLIGHT ON TAXATION

The House of Generally Accepted Accounting Principles (GAAP)

Prior to the codification, the list of standards and guidance was extensive. Thankfully, the codification has reduced this to a single source. Precodification literature issued by various standard setters includes:

1. Financial Accounting Standards Board (FASB)
   a. Statements (FAS)
   b. Interpretations (FIN)
   c. Technical Bulletins (FTB)
   d. Staff Positions (FSP)
   e. Staff Implementation Guides (Q&A)
   f. Statement No. 138 Examples

2. Emerging Issues Task Force (EITF)
   a. Abstracts
   b. Topic D

3. Derivative Implementation Group (DIG) Issues
4. Accounting Principles Board (APB) Opinions
5. Accounting Research Bulletins (ARB)
6. Accounting Interpretations (AIN)
7. American Institute of Certified Public Accountants (AICPA)
   a. Statements of Position (SOP)
   b. Audit and Accounting Guides (AAG)—only incremental accounting guidance
   c. Practice Bulletins (PB), including the Notices to Practitioners elevated to practice Bulletin status by Practice Bulletin 1
   d. Technical Inquiry Service (TIS)—only for Software Revenue Recognition

The five-year codification project had the following three primary goals:

1. Simplify user access by codifying all authoritative U.S. GAAP in one spot.

2. Ensure that the codified content accurately represents authoritative U.S. GAAP.

3. Create a codification research system that is up to date for the released results of standard-setting activity.

The main advantage of the codification is the move away from a standards-based model of organization to one based on topical area. For example, guidance for accounting for income taxes, although found primarily in SFAS109, previously could also be found in a number of other statements, interpretations, and Emerging Issue Task Force findings. Under the codification, guidance for income taxes is found in ASC 740.

5 FASB Accounting Standards Codification Research System (CRS)

As part of the codification, the FASB also developed the **FASB Accounting Standards Codification Research System (CRS)**. The goal was to create a research system that should reduce the amount of time and effort required to solve an accounting research issue and ensure that researchers are examining the most current guidance available.

Codification users are able to identify all related content in one location much more easily than by researching the previous standards. The FASB suggests the following steps when conducting research:

1. Browse the topical structure and related tables of contents. Because all related content is organized topically, users should be able to identify most content by topical browsing.

2. Use the text-search feature only for very specific items (e.g., guidance about inducements). Text search is based on specific language. Deviations from a selected search expression will lead to certain relevant content being excluded from search results. The CRS incorporates certain tools to help overcome the issue, but searching will always be constrained.

The FASB provides online access to the codification. Two levels of service are available: a no-cost basic version that allows the user to browse the codification, print documents, and cross-reference to legacy standards; and a fee-based professional version that provides the same functionality as the basic version, as well as search capabilities and some other functionality to assist researchers with their efforts. The FASB has made the professional version available to most colleges and universities at a reduced rate.

5-1 Structure

As described previously, the codification is organized by topical areas. Each area is broken down into topics, and each topic is further expanded by subtopic, then into sections, and finally into subsections (see example in Exhibit 10-1).

Each area represents a broad category of related guidance, such as "Assets." Topics represent a collection of related guidance for a specific area. Subtopics are subsets of

EXHIBIT 10-1:   Codification Structure

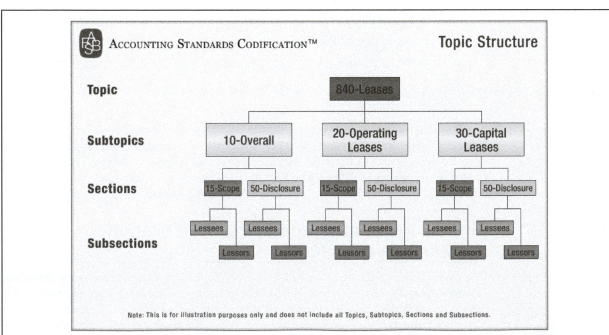

the topics and represent a distinct type or scope of the topic. Sections represent a reflection of the nature of the subtopic, such as measurement, disclosure, and recognition. Subsections are the lowest level of the structure and provide even more granular segregation of material when necessary. For example, under the Expenses area is the Income Taxes topic, and within Income Taxes are a number of subtopics, such as Overall, Intraperiod Tax Allocation, and so on.

Other topics may intersect with the selected topic. These intersection topics tend to relate to a broad transaction category or an industry (e.g., Interim Reporting or Entertainment—Casinos, as in Exhibit 10-2). Within the subtopics are sections (Status, Overview and Background, and Objectives; see Exhibit 10-3) that are expandable into subsections when available.

To assist with the citation of codification topics, the FASB created a numerical system to identify specific parts of the codification. Topics are given a three-digit number between 105 and 999 (see Exhibit 10-4).

EXHIBIT 10-2:   Codification Topics and Subtopics

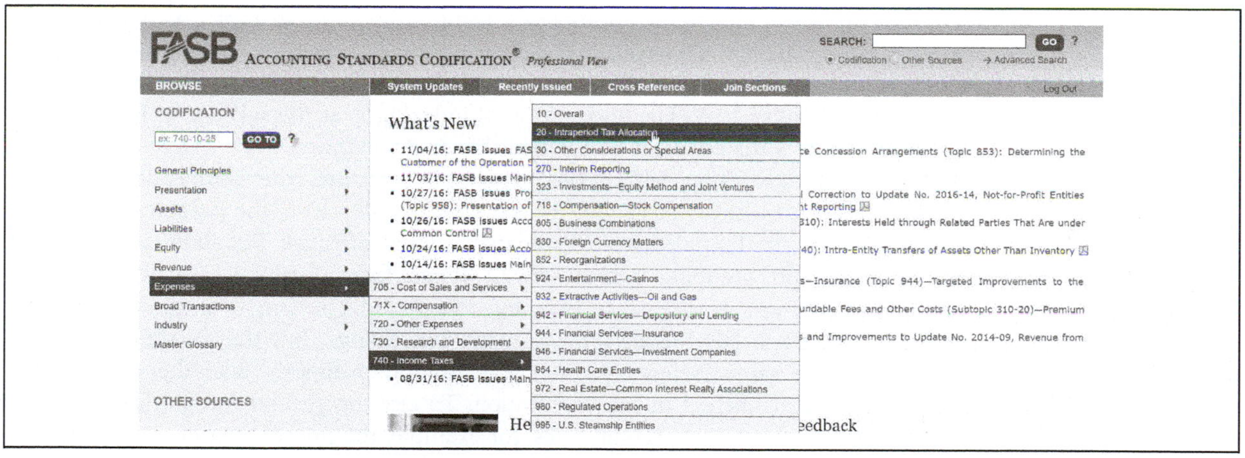

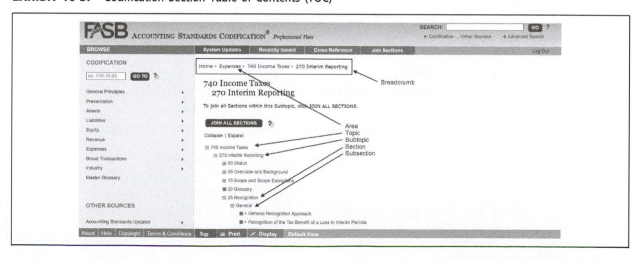

EXHIBIT 10-3:   Codification Section Table of Contents (TOC)

EXHIBIT 10-4:   Topic Numbering System

Topic Number	Description
105–199	General Principles—Broad conceptual matters
205–299	Presentation—Presentation matters only
305–799	Financial Statement Accounts—Organized in financial statement order, e.g., Asset, Liabilities Equity
805–899	Broad transactions—Cut across multiple financial statement accounts and are transaction-oriented
905–999	Industry—Accounting issues unique to an industry such as Airlines, Software, etc.

Intersection topics cut across topics and have a three-digit index as well. For example, topic 270 is Interim Reporting and may be present across any topic within the codification when such material exists. Most subtopics receive a two-digit number between 0 and 99. Sections are also assigned a two-digit number. With the exception of subtopic 10 (Overall), in which the section numbering varies from topic to topic, section numbers assigned are consistent throughout the codification. For example, Status is Section 00 across all subtopics in the codification. A complete listing of the section framework is presented in Exhibit 10-5. The lowest level of indexing is at the subsection level. Within each subsection is the actual guidance available as a paragraph.

When hierarchy exists within the paragraph structure, the codification uses the ">" symbol to present the structure. As shown in Exhibit 10-6, the paragraph grouping on >>Items Always Excluded from Estimated Annual Effective Tax Rate is subordinate to the paragraph grouping >Exclusion of Items from Estimated Annual Effective Tax Rate. Paragraph numbers are expected to be held constant over time. Therefore, should a paragraph be amended, the content will change, but the paragraph number will remain the same. Referencing the ASC should ordinarily take the form of the numerical system inherent in the codification. To cite the general recognition approach to the interim reporting of income taxes, for example, the proper citation would be ASC 740-270-25-1.

EXHIBIT 10-5:   Table of Section Numbers

Section	Description	Section	Description
00	Status	40	Derecognition
05	Overview & Background	45	Other Presentation Matters
10	Objectives	50	Disclosure
15	Scope & Scope Exceptions	55	Implementation Guidance and Illustrations
20	Glossary	60	Relationships
25	Recognition	65	Transition and Open Effective Date Information
30	Initial Measurement	70	Grandfathered Guidance
35	Subsequent Measurement	75	XBRL Elements

EXHIBIT 10-6: Codification Paragraph Hierarchy

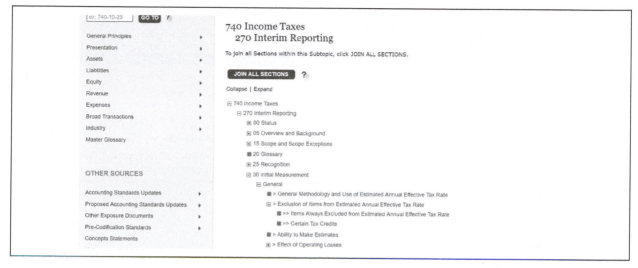

In addition to providing the complete and current guidance for U.S. GAAP, the codification also includes a substantial amount of material issued by the SEC applicable to public companies. The structure of SEC information is very similar to that of the rest of the codification, except for the following:

1. It does not contain the entire population of SEC rules, regulations, interpretive releases, and staff guidance.

2. Each section is preceded with an "S" to indicate that the material originates from SEC guidance.

3. Because the SEC releases do not always lend themselves to the codification framework, the related SEC documentation is provided as issued in Section 99. SEC material does not appear as a section in the BROWSE menus of the Areas and Topics (see Exhibit 10-3); however, SEC MATERIALS are presented on the landing page (see Exhibit 10-7).

5-2 Browsing

Most research using the codification is expected to be performed using the BROWSE function. The codification can be browsed by selecting the specific topic and subtopic desired (see Exhibit 10-7). The page displayed in Exhibit 10-7 is known as a "landing page." All the two-digit subtopics and three-digit intersection topics are displayed on the general topic landing page in an expandable table of contents (TOC) format. By clicking EXPAND under the TOC, all the paragraphs in that topic will be displayed as part of the TOC. Alternatively, any particular subtopic can be expanded by clicking the "+" in front of the title. Note that clicking a broad area or industry topic presented in the TOC on the landing page will bring you to the intersection subtopic within that intersection topic. For example, from the Topic 740 TOC, clicking Topic 718 COMPENSATION—STOCK COMPENSATION brings you to the landing page for Topic 718, with a TOC showing the intersection between Topic 718 and Topic 740 (see Exhibit 10-8). In this way, the codification avoids having the same guidance in two places, once under Topic 740 and then again under Topic 718. Instead, the intersection can be found from either topic.

EXHIBIT 10-7: Codification Section Landing Page

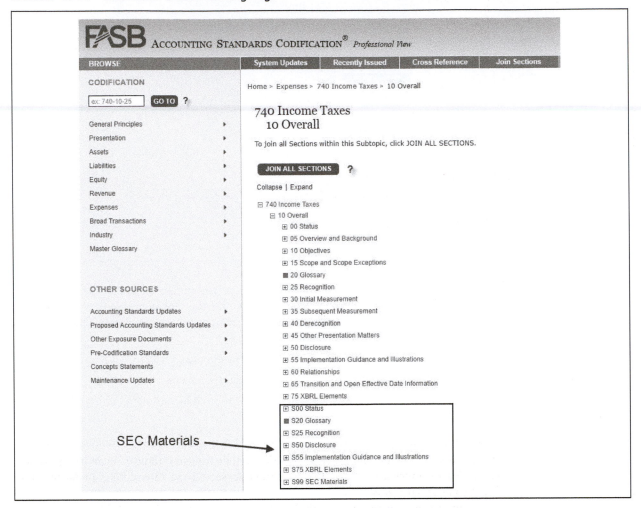

EXHIBIT 10-8: Codification Intersection

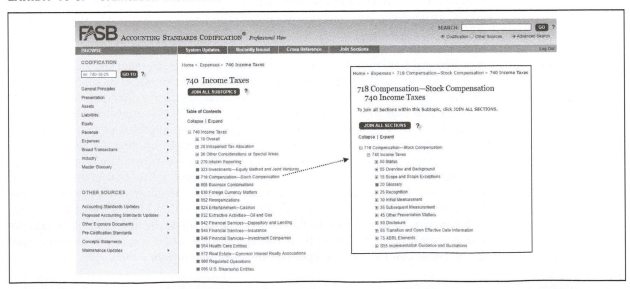

EXHIBIT 10-9: Codification Industry Section

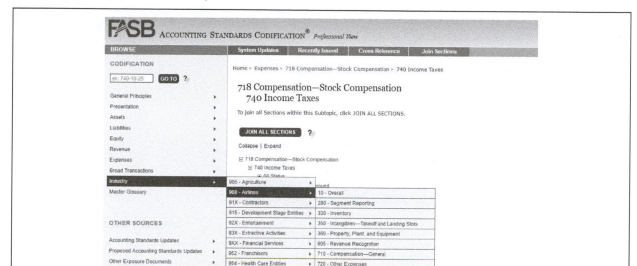

Browsing the industry topics works in a slightly different fashion. By selecting an industry topic from the main menu, the landing page offers a listing of the broad areas and topics that intersect that topic (see Exhibit 10-9). Clicking one of the section titles brings you to the landing page for that topic. Alternatively, the sections can be "joined" using the JOIN ALL SECTIONS button, which then creates a TOC for an industry topic. This allows for continued browsing of that industry topic similar to the other categories of topics and allows the researcher to see all the intersecting guidance for a client's particular industry.

Using the main menu to directly browse to a subtopic is also available (as shown in Exhibit 10-2). By browsing to that level, the subtopic landing page displays the same type of TOC as the topic landing page, but the detail of each section is also displayed (see Exhibit 10-7). Note that a breadcrumb describes the location, where the codification is displayed at all times at the top of the TOC. By clicking JOIN ALL SECTIONS, a single document containing all the sections displayed in the TOC is created to allow for a comprehensive review of all the guidance on that subtopic. Note that a complete document that includes all content included in the TOC is not created.

Selecting a section from the subtopic menu creates the section page (see Exhibit 10-10). The section page is the primary source of research in most instances. The section page comes with a similar TOC and three tabs: (1) DOCUMENT, (2) ARCHIVE, and (3) WHAT LINKS HERE. DOCUMENT is the default tab and displays the actual content (subsections and paragraphs selected). The ARCHIVE tab provides a history of the guidance related to that section, and the WHAT LINKS HERE provides a listing of all other sections within the codification that contain a link back to the current section.

The bottom of the webpage in the codification has a number of helpful tools as well. As shown in the inset in Exhibit 10-10, buttons for TOP, SECTION LINKS, PRINT, DISPLAY, and EMAIL are available and can be activated by rolling the cursor over each. SECTION LINKS

EXHIBIT 10-10:   Codification Section Page

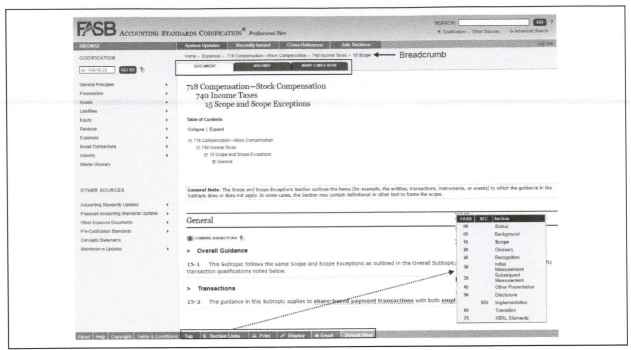

allows for linking easily to the other sections within that subtopic. The section listing contains all the U.S. GAAP guidance and SEC materials by section number and provides the title to each section. The bolded section provides the name of the current section. This is also available in the breadcrumb at the top of the page.

The PRINT function provides a printer-friendly version of the document, with or without legacy sources or the TOC. The suggested method to copy and paste materials from the codification is to use the printer-friendly form of the document prior to the copy and paste procedure. An e-mail of the document can also be sent from this menu. From the section page, all sections can be combined using the COMBINE SUBSECTIONS at the top of the first paragraph, which will create a document that contains all the subsections within the current subtopic. For example, if the current document is 740-10-15 or Income Taxes (740) Overall (10) Scope and Scope Exceptions (15), using COMBINE SUBSECTIONS will create a document with all subsections of subtopic 740-10. Any pending guidance that may have been adopted but is not yet effective is also displayed as part of the subsection information. If the exact location of a paragraph is desired, rolling over the paragraph number provides a detailed trail of location within the codification (see Exhibit 10-11).

Each subtopic includes a glossary section (20) that contains definitions of key words used in that subtopic. The first occurrence of a glossary term in a subsection is also highlighted and linked to that term. If the link is connected to the glossary, then all the locations where that term is used can be displayed by clicking the glossary term itself. The master glossary for all terms can also be found on the main menu.

5-3 Search

The codification also possesses a search function similar to those found in the tax services discussed in prior chapters. Search results include an excerpt from the paragraph

EXHIBIT 10-11: Codification Rollover Breadcrumb

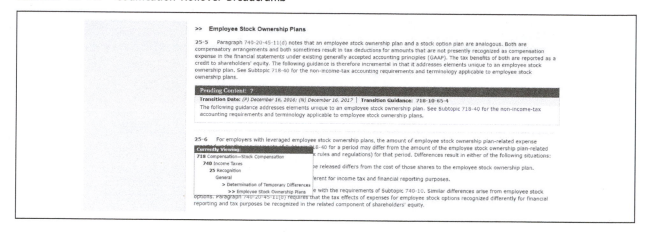

and the numerical location within the codification for each result (see Exhibit 10-12). Narrowing the search results (see the NARROW button on the right of the screen) to provide a more precise result can be achieved in several ways. The RELATED TERM feature presents an opportunity to restrict the search to instances where the original search term and the related words both appear (similar to using the "and" function in the original search).

The search engine identifies commonly used terms and offers them in the related-terms list. The number of results in each area is also presented and allows the original search to be restricted to only the areas desired. Unlike related words, the GO button must be clicked after selecting the area to which the search has been restricted. Once a search has been narrowed by area, the search engine then allows additional narrowing, first by topic (see inset in Exhibit 10-12) and then by subtopic. For a more specific

EXHIBIT 10-12: Codification Search Result

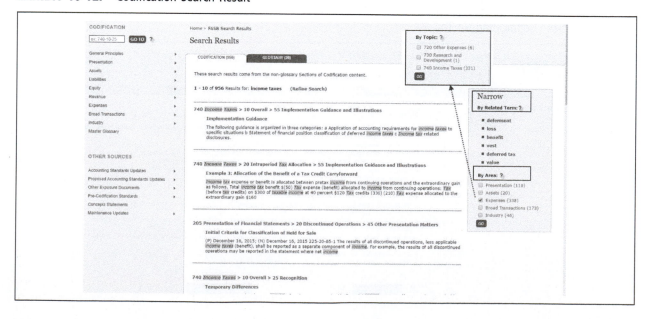

EXHIBIT 10-13: Codification Advanced Search

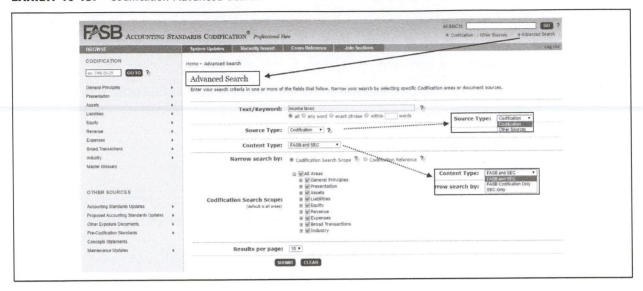

search, the ADVANCED SEARCH feature allows for the narrowing of search results from the original search point (see Exhibit 10-13).

5-4 Go To

The GO TO function works in a similar fashion to a search by citation in a typical tax service. For situations in which the exact location is known, the codification reference can be typed directly into the GO TO box, and the document will be presented immediately. Conveniently, as you type the codification citation into the box, the system will provide a listing of all available content within that topic, subtopic, or section (see Exhibit 10-14).

EXHIBIT 10-14: Codification Go To

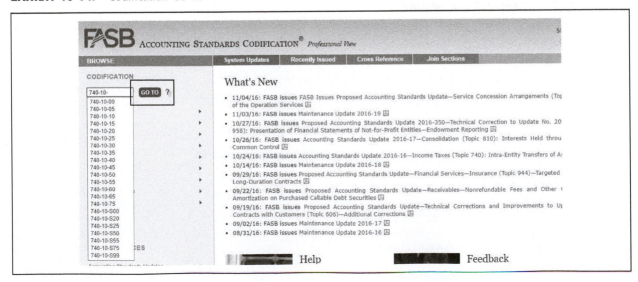

5-5 Join Sections

JOIN SECTIONS allows for joining all related sections of a topic into a single document so that the guidance across all sections within a topic can be reviewed at one time. For example, if a review of all the disclosure requirements for Topic 740 Income Taxes is desired, the JOIN SECTIONS feature allows for the selection of Topic 740 and Section 50 (Disclosure) and first prepares a list of all the sections of disclosure available with that topic (see Exhibit 10-15). The desired sections can be selected and then joined into a single document. Drop-down menus are available when selecting a topic and section. The joined results will include a TOC similar to those presented when browsing.

5-6 Cross Reference

For researchers who are more comfortable with the legacy standards, the codification system provides a CROSS REFERENCE system to allow researchers to locate guidance in the codification using the old guidance or find the old guidance using the new codification reference (see Exhibit 10-16). Any of the original standards are available for the cross-reference report (e.g., FAS, FIN, EITF).

Drop-down menus are available to assist in identifying the proper coding of the old standards. Legacy standard and paragraph numbers are mapped into the codification at the paragraph level and vice versa. The codification paragraph listed in the report is a link to the document itself. Searches for legacy standards using the current codification will provide a report to the original statement and paragraph, but they do not link back to the original document itself. As previously mentioned, cross-references to original guidance can also be found by using the PRINTER FRIENDLY WITH SOURCES function in the PRINT functions.

Certain precodification legacy standards can be located within the codification from the home page (Exhibit 10-3) in the bottom left corner under OTHER SOURCES.

EXHIBIT 10-15: Codification Join Sections

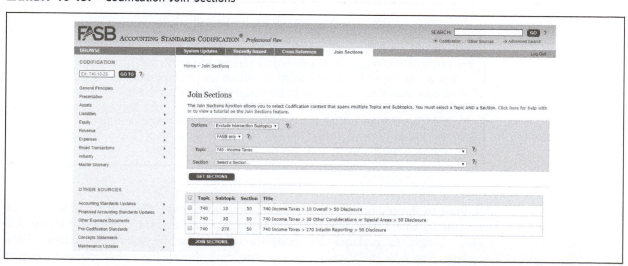

EXHIBIT 10-16:   Codification Cross-Reference

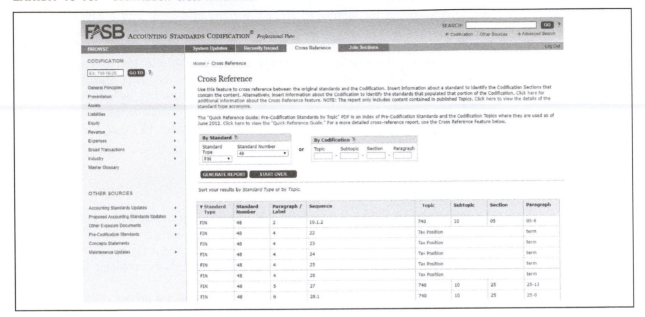

SPOTLIGHT ON TAXATION

ASC 740

As an example of the importance of financial accounting research for tax professionals and the importance of tax research for audit professionals, ASC 740 requires taxpayers to examine each and every tax position taken, and for every uncertain tax position, allows tax benefits to be recognized in financial statements only when it is determined that it is more likely than not (MLTN) that the tax position can be sustained or when the position is ultimately settled via an audit, a negotiation, or a court decision.

A tax position is defined as a position taken in a previously filed return or expected to be taken in a future return. Transactions that create deferred tax assets and liabilities are tax positions, but transactions that create permanent book/tax differences (or no differences at all) are also tax positions. ASC 740 also requires that the taxpayer distinguish between highly certain and uncertain positions.

The application of ASC 740 to an uncertain tax position requires that a tax benefit be recognized when it is MLTN to be sustained based on the technical merits of the position. In determining whether the MLTN threshold is met, taxpayers must assume that the tax position will be examined (audited) by the taxing authorities. Ultimately, the conclusion regarding the financial statement recognition takes into account the tax technical merits, facts, and circumstances of the position.

Prior to the codification, guidance was updated through the issuance of a new standard or statement of position or some other form of standard. Subsequent to codification, changes to guidance are made through accounting standards updates. These updates first take the form of an exposure draft during the public comment period.

EXHIBIT 10-17: Codification Proposed Updates

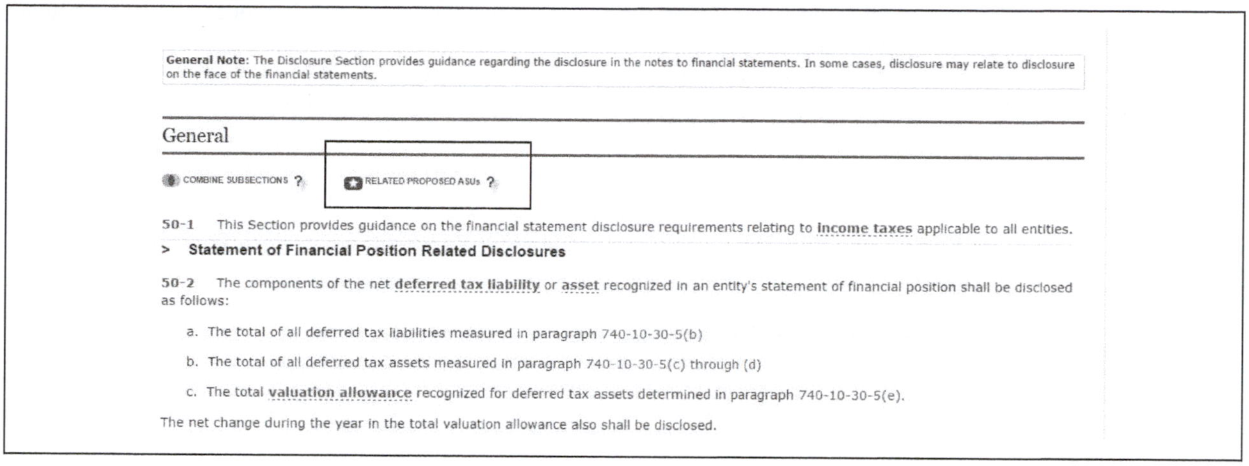

General Note: The Disclosure Section provides guidance regarding the disclosure in the notes to financial statements. In some cases, disclosure may relate to disclosure on the face of the financial statements.

General

⊕ COMBINE SUBSECTIONS ?   ▣ RELATED PROPOSED ASUs ?

50-1   This Section provides guidance on the financial statement disclosure requirements relating to **income taxes** applicable to all entities.
>   **Statement of Financial Position Related Disclosures**

50-2   The components of the net **deferred tax liability** or **asset** recognized in an entity's statement of financial position shall be disclosed as follows:

    a. The total of all deferred tax liabilities measured in paragraph 740-10-30-5(b)

    b. The total of all deferred tax assets measured in paragraph 740-10-30-5(c) through (d)

    c. The total **valuation allowance** recognized for deferred tax assets determined in paragraph 740-10-30-5(e).

The net change during the year in the total valuation allowance also shall be disclosed.

Exposure drafts are proposed updates to the codification and are indexed numerically to show where the update will ultimately be located, should it be approved by the Board.

Once approved, the guidance becomes PENDING CONTENT and is displayed within the paragraphs of the codification in the proper positions until the new guidance becomes effective (an example of pending content was shown in Exhibit 10-11). Once the new guidance is effective, the old guidance is removed and placed in the archived data and is replaced with the new guidance.

For sections for which new guidance may be under exposure draft and awaiting approval, the codification adds a link "Related Proposed ASUs" at the top of the section as shown in Exhibit 10-17. Clicking that link brings the researcher to the FASB page where the exposure draft information is held.

6 Other Sources and Services

The codification is expected to be the primary source of accounting research. However, many companies that provide tax services also offer accounting and audit information within the same platform. Because they operate on the same platform, the research process works in a very similar fashion to that of the tax services, and thus the details of the operations are omitted here. Many offer additional information, however, and a review of the materials available is warranted.

The CCH Accounting Research Manager (ARM) provides an online database (with the same IntelliConnect platform) that provides access to accounting, auditing, governmental, and SEC authoritative literature, plus interpretive guidance and the FASB codification. The ARM also provides access to search Form 10-Ks filed with the SEC. In addition, the ARM offers a series of knowledge-based audit materials to help professionals conduct audits of certain industries, such as financial institutions or employee-benefit plans.

Primary resource information is available for Public Company Oversight Board (PCAOB) rules, releases, and staff materials; IASB accounting standards and IFRS Interpretation Committee (IFRIC) interpretations; Governmental Accounting Standards Board (GASB) statements and related guidance; Governmental Accounting Office (GAO) auditing standards; and others.

Thomson Reuters offers, as part of its Checkpoint series, an accounting based suite with many components, including GAAP compliance, SEC compliance, and FASB and

IASB materials. Similar to CCH, also available are a bevy of analysis and practice aids, such as the Audit and Accounting Disclosure Manual, GAAP Practice Manual, and analysis of international reporting standards.

As discussed earlier, international standards are currently promulgated by the IASB. The standards are currently offered free of charge by the IFRS Foundation (**www.iasb .org**). However, the free subscription does not include implementation guidance or the basis for conclusions. A paid subscription is available and includes electronic versions of all IFRS, older IAS, IFRIC, and Standing Interpretations Committee (SIC) interpretations and IASB-issued supporting documents, including application guidance, illustrative examples, implementation guidance, bases for conclusions, and all appendices. The paid subscription also includes a search function and the capability to have the standards translated into a variety of languages.

Because one goal of the IASB is to adhere to principle-based standards and because the IASB (and its predecessors) has not issued standards for very long, the body of guidance to comb through for information related to income taxes remains reasonably limited. IAS 12 represents the vast majority of guidance on accounting for income taxes (Section 29 for SMEs). As a result, this book will not cover the research process for IFRS. However, as the popularity of IFRS continues to expand and further progress is made toward convergence with U.S. GAAP, the complexity of IFRS may increase. Meanwhile, many of the tax service providers mentioned above include the international standards as part of their offerings, and thus those tools can be used in the same manner as for tax research.

SPOTLIGHT ON TAXATION

IFRS versus U.S. GAAP

The list of differences between IFRS and U.S. GAAP has been, and continues to be, repeatedly analyzed as the two systems of accounting guidance evolve and perhaps converge. Most large accounting firms and numerous other sources have analyzed differences on a standard-by-standard or topic-by-topic basis. One difference that even a financial accounting novice would notice is the size difference between the two sets of guidance. A printed volume (actually four volumes) of the Accounting Standards Codification is about 1,200 pages. The printed version of the international standards is approximately 4,000 pages. Amazingly, the IFRS for SMEs are contained solely within one document approximately 250 pages long. Simplified indeed!

SUMMARY

Tax professionals and CPAs must be able to provide more than just tax advice and compliance services. Tax provision work requires tax professionals to be able to understand not only the tax treatment of a transaction but also the book accounting so that any permanent and temporary differences can be identified and accounted for properly.

Understanding how to navigate the accounting guidance found in the ASC and other sources will enable tax researchers to perform services that are in high demand from accounting firms and businesses of all sizes.

KEY WORDS

By the time you complete this chapter, you should be comfortable discussing each of the following terms. If you need additional review of any of these items, return to the appropriate material in the chapter or consult the glossary to this text.

FASB Accounting Standards
   Codification (ASC),
   p. 355

FASB Accounting Standards
   Codification Research System
   (CRS), p. 357

Financial Accounting Standards
   Board (FASB), p. 355

Generally Accepted Accounting
   Principles (GAAP), p. 354

International Accounting
   Standards Board (IASB), p. 356

International Financial Reporting
   Standards (IFRS), p. 356

Securities and Exchange
   Commission (SEC), p. 355

DISCUSSION QUESTIONS

1. Why should tax professionals know how to conduct financial accounting research?

2. Why are taxes not reflected on financial statements on an as-paid basis?

3. What two bodies have authority to set accounting standards in the United States?

4. What are the responsibilities of the SEC?

5. Who establishes international accounting standards, and what are their principle objectives?

6. Explain whether U.S. and international accounting standards for income taxes are similar.

7. Why did the FASB undertake the codification project?

8. Describe the hierarchy of elements within the codification.

9. How do industry sections differ from other sections?

10. What is an intersection section?

11. How can SEC guidance be distinguished from other guidance?

12. What two methods are available to narrow a search in the codification?

13. Describe how a researcher can find the old standards that became guidance in the codification.

14. What other services provide accounting information as part of their tax services?

EXERCISES

15. Use the codification to answer the following:
    a. Under what general area will you find the Income Taxes topic?
    b. What topics are available under the area Equity?
    c. What nonindustry subtopics are available in Topic 405 Liabilities?

16. Use the codification to answer the following:
    a. Use the Master Glossary and search for the term "deferred tax." How many terms appear in the results?
    b. Which Broad Transaction areas intersect with Topic 740 Income Taxes?
    c. Which industry areas intersect with Topic 740 Income Taxes?

17. Use the codification to answer the following:
    a. What is the citation for the paragraph that provides a description of two basic principles related to accounting for income taxes?
    b. What subtopics of Topic 740 Income Taxes contain sections on implementation guidance?
    c. What is the definition of the term "valuation allowance"?

18. Use the codification to answer the following:
    a. Perform a Join Sections on Topic 740 and Section 25. Which subtopics are on the list?
    b. Using the Search function, search for "push down accounting" and then narrow your search by the Presentation topic. What is the breadcrumb for the resulting paragraph?
    c. Browse to Topic 305, Subtopic 10, Section 05, and then combine all subsections. How many paragraphs are included in the resulting document?

PART IV

Implementing the Research Tools

CHAPTER **11**

Communicating Research Results

LEARNING OBJECTIVES

- Produce a standard format for the construction of a file memorandum to contain the results of one's research efforts and professional judgment.
- Develop skills in using other methods to communicate research results, including client letters, e-mails, text messages, and oral presentations.

CHAPTER OUTLINE

Isabelle Rozenbaum/PhotoAlto Agency RF Collections/Getty Images

Tax FIRMS AND OTHER PROFESSIONALS are looking for new hires who can communicate effectively—both orally and in writing. While solid research skills are critical, the results of your research are only valuable to your supervisor and to your clients if communicated effectively. Accordingly, the purpose of this chapter is to provide students with guidance and practice related to communicating via a variety of forms including research memos, client letters, e-mails, and text messages.

In this chapter, we discuss the means by which the tax professional conveys the results of a tax research project. Directions as to the proper format and content of research memos, of client letters, and of oral presentations are addressed, with the development of professional communication skills as the overriding goal. In addition to discussing the format and content of various communications, we also provide general writing tips and advice for making effective presentations.

1 Communications and the Tax Professional

As we suggested in our initial discussions of the tax research process, illustrated in Exhibit 2-1, a tax research assignment often concludes with some form of communication by the tax professional. The audience for this communication often is the practitioner's supervisor or client, but tax-related communications can take many forms, including the following:

- A telephone call or text message

- An informal discussion in person or via e-mail

- A letter prepared for reading by someone at least as familiar with the tax law as is the writer

- A letter prepared for reading by someone less familiar with the tax law than is the writer

- A letter prepared for reading by someone who is essentially untrained in the tax law

- An article for publication in a newspaper or magazine directed at the general public

- An article for publication in a professional journal read by tax generalists

- An article for publication in a professional journal read by tax specialists

- A directed discussion among tax peers, such as in a tax department meeting

- A speech to a general audience

- A speech at a conference of tax professionals

- A memorandum to be read in the future by the writer or by a peer with similar training

- An appearance on a news broadcast or program with a serious tone

- An appearance on a broadcast with a less serious tone

- A posting on a general, business, or tax-oriented blog

For the most part, the tax professional's preparations for these communications are similar. For the purposes of this chapter, we assume that all the pertinent tax research techniques developed in earlier parts of this text have been planned and conscientiously applied so that the practitioner is qualified and current enough with respect to prevailing tax law to address the audience in terms of the content of the communication. The challenge then becomes how to deliver this information in a manner that will be accepted and understood by the audience.

Communication truly occurs only when the message desired to be sent by the speaker or writer is received by the intended audience. Distractions of all sorts can make this process difficult to accomplish. Thorough research into the nature and expectations of the audience, factors that may interfere with the delivery of the message, and feedback and corrective measures must make up a critical part of the communicator's preparation.

Examples of "noise" that can disrupt the communications process include a mismatching of expectations as to the message, the chosen delivery method, the identity and nature of the sender and receiver of the message, other events competing for the attention of those involved, logistical difficulties, and technological problems. Feedback and corrective devices that can aid in accomplishing the delivery of the desired message include formal and informal evaluation processes, "real-time" opportunities such as question-and-answer periods and written comments received during the drafting of the document, and the sending and receiving of intended and unintended body language or other communicative signals.

Tax professionals generally are almost entirely untrained as to the application of communication methods in conveying tax messages, but this shortcoming can be remedied. The chief ingredients necessary to become an effective tax-content communicator are the desire to learn and improve as a communicator in general and the use of every opportunity possible to obtain and develop skills in the delivery of tax information. Given the nature of today's competitive tax profession, plenty of such opportunities for practice exist, and pressures from others who are competing for clients and promotions provide most professionals with more than enough motivation to make improvements in their communication skills.

SPOTLIGHT ON TAXATION

A Career in Taxation

When I was young, I was taught the story of Jesus and the tax man. The point was that Jesus was good to everyone; so much so that he would even eat with the taxman. The story tells a lot about being good, but it also tells a lot about historical perceptions of the tax collector.

—Christopher Bergin

We begin a more detailed review of the written communication process with some tips and writing advice applicable to all forms of written communication—see Exhibit 11-1. We then review the most common written communications used in a tax practice—the research memo and client letter. We also discuss other forms of written communication, including e-mails and text messages.

EXHIBIT 11-1: General Writing Tips

1	Be organized. Make sure you understand the objective of your communication and organize your thoughts and your message before you start to write.
2	Consider the reader—all audiences are not the same. Writing for another tax professional is very different from writing for a client who is not skilled in tax law.
3	Be professional. Regardless of the form of the writing (even text messages), you should avoid slang, abbreviations, and informal language. Always err on the side of formality in your communications.
4	Use correct grammar and punctuation. While this might seem obvious, invest the appropriate time reviewing and editing your writing to ensure that there are no errors.
5	Be brief and to the point. While your writing must be thorough, do not include extraneous material and references.
6	Write in direct, active voice and use short sentences. Organize your writing in paragraphs and use transition words to help the reader follow your logic and thought process.

2 The Heart of Tax Research Communication: The Research Memo

The tax researcher spends most of his or her time reviewing primary and secondary sources of the federal tax law, redefining pertinent issues, and attempting to discover additional facts concerning the client's situation. On completion of this review, the researcher must integrate the results of the research process into a more usable form.

The **research memo** is designed to:

- Organize the facts, issues, and conclusions of the project.

- Facilitate a review of the research activities by the practitioner's supervisors or colleagues.

- Allow for a subsequent examination of the research issue by the original researcher or by his or her successor, with respect to the same or another client's identical or related fact situation.

Accordingly, the research memo should be constructed in a general, usable format that lends itself to a quick perusal of the pertinent tax facts and issues. It must be able to stand on its own as it is not only being written to answer a specific question today but may also be referred to and relied upon in the future. Many accounting and law firms impose a standardized file memo format.

While specific formats may vary, all include the following:

1. Summary of the facts

2. Summary of the issues

3. Conclusion

4. A list of authorities relied upon. This section may be omitted in situations in which only a few authorities are cited in the analysis section.

5. Analysis and summary

A research memo should start with a brief introductory summary of the relevant facts. While it is important to include only the relevant facts, the writer must at the same time be thorough. It is also helpful to mention where the facts came from—for example, in a letter provided by the client or in a phone conversation with the client.

The next section includes a list of the specific issues researched. Make sure you use technical tax terms in describing the issues. Remember that the audience of a research memo is typically a senior staffer, manager, or partner knowledgeable about the tax law. In all but the most complex instances, these sections should require no more than two paragraphs.

The research memo then includes a short conclusion for each identified issue. This format allows the reader to determine quickly whether each issue is "pro" or "con" for the taxpayer and limits the time required to sort through a number of such memos. If a list of authorities is provided, it should generally be presented next, before the detailed analysis. The rare footnote at this point of the memo should be restricted to current developments, for instance, with respect to an appeal relative to one of the critical cases that is cited in the memo or a statutory amendment. This helps the reader put the issue in context of the relevant authority and allows an experienced reviewer to quickly ascertain if the preparer missed any significant authority. Finally, in the analysis and summary section, a detailed review and evaluation of controlling laws is derived. Unless an authorities section is included in the memo, this section should include full citations presented in the standard format. A more detailed conclusion is typically provided here with enough explanation so that the reader can see how the writer arrived at the conclusion. The "meat" of the memo is presented here, and the strengths and weaknesses of both sides of the tax argument are developed and discussed. Recommendations for subsequent actions with the client may be enumerated, and other strategies as to tax return or audit positions are identified.

Often, the gathering of the pertinent facts is the most challenging of the tax professional's tasks. Tax engagements typically begin with client contact in the form of a phone call or meeting, followed by an exchange of copies of pertinent documents such as letters, spreadsheets, trusts or wills, contracts, life insurance or annuity agreements, employer handbooks, and diaries or logbooks belonging to the client. In reality, though, the initial determination of the facts is likely to be incomplete for reasons that include the following:

- Taxpayers tend to see the issue only from their side so that facts and circumstances may be hidden or "forgotten" if they would cast doubt on the ability to determine or document the pro-taxpayer position.

- Taxpayers are not trained in the details of the technical tax law, so they may be unable to determine which documents or other evidence of the facts are important in determining the controlling tax law.

- For tax research that requires the full professional judgment and experience of the practitioner, there may be no clearly controlling tax statute or precedent, facts may be truly incomplete, or they may unfold as the evaluation of tax law occurs. The researcher may discover that issues of taxpayer motive, knowledge, or other circumstances turn on facts that were not immediately known to be crucial.

Moreover, fact gathering often turns on such intangible factors as the reliability of the memories of the taxpayers and key witnesses, the ability of witnesses to withstand scrutiny in the deposition and testimony phases of the case, the unanticipated death or disappearance of key parties, the destruction of records as a result of natural disasters, and the tendency of some taxpayers to "fix the truth" after the fact.

The tone and nature of the research memo should recognize that its readers will be restricted to fellow tax practitioners who are well versed in federal tax law. Thus, references to primary sources of the tax law should be frequent and complete. One must presume that the ultimate reader of the memo's comments will need no introduction to the hierarchy of the federal tax system nor to statutory citation practices. In addition, it often is helpful to include pertinent references to one or more of the online tax services to which the researcher's firm subscribes, providing a clear electronic trail to facilitate subsequent review and commentary concerning the tax issue.

These practices are illustrated in Exhibit 11-2.

EXHIBIT 11-2: The Research Memo

Sawyers and Gill CPAs

San Francisco, CA

September 30, 20XX

Facts

The Browns live in South Dakota. They own their home and hold investments in the debt of several domestic corporations. The interest that they received on this debt was gross income to them. To diversify their portfolio, the Browns took out a sizable second mortgage on their home and applied a portion of the proceeds to some City of Chandler school bonds. The remainder of the proceeds was used to expand the facilities of Mrs. Brown's dental clinic.

Issue(s)

How much of the mortgage interest paid can be claimed as an itemized deduction by the Browns?

Conclusion

That portion of the mortgage proceeds applied to the dental clinic generates an interest deduction to be claimed against clinic income on Schedule C. No other deduction is allowed.

Authorities

IRC Section 265(a)(2)

Rev. Proc. 72-18, 1972-1 C.B. 740

Wisconsin Cheeseman v. U.S., 388 F. 2d 420

Bradford, 60 T.C. 253

Israelson v. U.S., 367 F. Supp. 1104

Mariorenzi v. Comm., 490 F.2d 92, TC Memo 1973-141

PLR 8631006

Analysis and Summary

The IRC disallows the deduction of interest on indebtedness that is incurred or continued to purchase or carry obligations, the interest on which is exempt from the federal income tax. IRC § 265(a)(2). This provision denies the double benefit that would be enjoyed by the taxpayer who would receive tax-exempt income while simultaneously claiming an investment-interest deduction for the interest expense paid, for example, by incurring a bank loan and using the proceeds to purchase municipal bonds.

The IRS examines evidence to infer the intent of the taxpayer who is incurring the indebtedness. Under Rev. Proc. 72-18, 1972-1 C.B. 740, a taxpayer who purchases exempt bonds can claim an interest deduction if the debt in question has been incurred (1) for personal reasons (e.g., via a mortgage to finance the purchase of residential property), or (2) for valid business reasons, as long as the borrowing does not exceed legitimate business needs.

Several court decisions have emphasized that the existence of such business motives must be documented clearly, as to both presence and amount. *Wisconsin Cheeseman v. U.S.*, 388 F.2d 420 (CA-7, 1968); *Bradford*, 60 T.C. 253 (1973); *Israelson v. U.S.*, 367 F. Supp. 1104 (D. Md. 1973).

Mortgage indebtedness is a classic illustration of an investment that will generate deductible interest expenses for the taxpayer who holds exempt bonds. However, the timing of such a mortgage transaction must be monitored to exhibit the proper motives for the benefit of the IRS. In one case, the taxpayer paid for his home with cash. Only later was an investment program (that included municipal bonds) initiated and a residential mortgage secured. The IRS inferred that the mortgage proceeds were in indirect support of the exempt indebtedness, and the deduction for the mortgage interest was disallowed. *Mariorenzi v. Comm.*, 490 F.2d 92 (CA-8, 1974), T.C. Memo 1973-141. Had the taxpayer secured a mortgage before the home was completed, purchasing the exempt bonds out of savings, it appears that the deduction could have been preserved. The IRS has applied this doctrine outside of the Eighth Circuit, in PLR 8631006.

Because the Browns live in the Eighth Circuit, the *Mariorenzi* doctrine prevails, and no itemized deduction is allowed at all, that is, for that portion of the loan that is applied to the school bonds. Rev. Proc. 72-18 is insensitive to portfolio-diversification motives, and no personal motive appears to exist that supports any other possible deduction. According to the logic of these precedents, the Browns should have sold the exempt bonds and then used the proceeds to finance their portfolio acquisitions.

Actions to Be Taken

Prepare letter, review results with client.

Suggest changes in portfolio holdings to regain the deduction.

Preparer: Mary H. Polzin

Reviewer: Char E. Mano

2-1 Evaluating the Sources of Law

The tax researcher will have made a number of judgments concerning the client's situation before preparing the research memo. For instance, the researcher may select and eliminate competing issues and direct the research process onto one or more pathways to the exclusion of others. Nonetheless, in deriving an analysis of the various elements of the controlling sources of the tax law, the practitioner must attempt to reconcile a number of varied interpretations of the statute and of its (interpretive) regulations and court opinions. If the authority is conflicting, the researcher has to choose the best authority from among these sources to formulate a defensible position for the taxpayer.

Often the researcher will be guided in this regard by the opinions of the most recent of the court cases discovered. Well-written case opinions typically provide a summary of the evolution of the pertinent tax law and a discussion of the competing interpretations by the parties to the lawsuit. In this manner, the researcher can obtain an indication of both the critical facts and issues that the court has identified in the present case and its interpretation as to the distinguishing features of relevant precedents. (In reality, most of these sections of the opinion are written by law clerks or law school students who obtain and retain their positions by preparing thorough and insightful file memos of their own!) Moreover, court opinions often include lengthy dissenting or concurring opinions, from which the researcher can identify additional issues and different angles relating to the opinion and outcome of the case. Logical and legal leads also might be found in a dissenting opinion that could be pertinent in building an appeal to overturn the majority opinion or to argue for a different outcome in a later case with similar facts.

Lacking (or in lieu of) such judicial direction, the researcher's evaluation of the efficacy of a precedent or pronouncement often is guided by no more than a review of the hierarchy of the sources of the federal tax law. (For a review of these sources, see Chapters 3 through 5.) A thorough understanding of the recognized hierarchy of sources of federal tax law is key to properly evaluating the sources of tax law.

In addition, we offer the following points to be considered in the evaluation of a series of apparently conflicting tax laws:

- As discussed in Chapter 4, regulations are seldom held to be invalid by a court. Thus, challenges to the provisions of a regulation should be based on more than a simple challenge to the Treasury's authority or a self-serving competing interpretation of the statute offered by the taxpayer. To successfully challenge a Treasury regulation, the taxpayer generally must convince the court that the regulations are contrary to the intent of Congress, a very high burden.

- Revenue rulings and revenue procedures, however, are frequently modified or otherwise held to be invalid by a court. These pronouncements are nothing more than the IRS's informal opinion as to how the law should be applied to particular situations. Accordingly, the court is more receptive to the taxpayer's attempted recasting of the pertinent law in his or her favor with respect to these administrative pronouncements. As a result, the court's final opinion is likely to be based on the weight of the competing arguments rather than simply on the Treasury's preemptive interpretive rights.

- The decisions of courts that are higher in the judicial hierarchy should receive additional precedential weight. Given an adequate degree of similarity in fact situations, district and circuit court opinions have direct bearing on the taxpayer only if they were issued in the taxpayer's corresponding jurisdiction. On the other hand, opinions of the national courts such as the Court of Federal Claims and Tax Court are binding on the taxpayer, even though they were issued with respect to a taxpayer who works or resides in another jurisdiction, unless the circuit court in the taxpayer's jurisdiction has held differently. Ultimately, the Tax Court must apply the law in each case as that law has been interpreted by the circuit court of the taxpayer's domicile. If the circuit court has not spoken to the issue, the Tax Court's own interpretation controls.

- Thus, a taxpayer who works in Wyoming is not bound by decisions of, say, the Seventh Circuit Court of Appeals or the Alaska district court. Conversely, an Alaska taxpayer's Court of Federal Claims decision is binding on the Wyoming citizen's Court of Federal Claims case. If an earlier Court of Federal Claims decision held in a manner that is detrimental to the Wyoming taxpayer, a different trial court should be pursued.

- Other factors being equal, decisions of the Second, Ninth, and Federal Circuits should be assigned additional precedential value because their opinions are more influential. Among other reasons, this additional weight can be attributed to the inclusion of the cities of New York and Washington, D.C., and the State of California in these circuits.

- Older court decisions should be assigned a geometrically declining degree of importance unless they are Supreme Court cases; they are in the taxpayer's circuit; they are Second, Ninth, or Federal Circuit cases; or they are the only precedents available. Within a taxpayer's circuit, the newer opinions carry more weight. The roster and philosophical makeup of a court change over time and often reflect changing societal culture and philosophies. Thus, recent case opinions are more likely to identify issues that are held to be critical by the sitting judges that the taxpayer will face, and they can be better predictors of the outcome relative to the current taxpayer's issues.

- Tax treatises and journal articles are a useful source by which to identify current, critical tax issues. They also can be used to save research time and jump-start the research process—because they often include both a comprehensive summary of the evolution of the controlling law and a thorough list of citations concerning prior interpretive court decisions.

- IRS agents are bound only by the IRC, administrative pronouncements, and Supreme Court decisions. Some of the most difficult decisions a tax practitioner must face include those in which one must determine whether the time, effort, and expense of litigation will generate a reward that is sufficient to justify, in essence, the construction of new (judicial) tax law; that is, to overcome this narrow scope of the agent's concern. However, sometimes the threat of litigation is the only way to get the IRS to consider unfavorable court precedents issued by the taxpayer's circuit court.

- Court decisions are never completely predictable. Thus, even if absolutely all of the judicial precedent that is available supports the taxpayer's position, the court still may hold against the taxpayer. Negative decisions may be the result of a poor performance by the attorney, other tax adviser, or witnesses who are heard by the court; changes in the makeup or philosophy of the members of the court; changes in societal mores, as reflected by the court; or an incorrect interpretation of the law by the court that hears the present case. The practitioner, however, can do little more than conduct a thorough tax research analysis concerning the case, identify convincing witnesses, exercise good professional judgment in recommending a position, and trust that justice will prevail.

3 Client Letters

Our discussion to this point in the chapter has concentrated on the communication of tax research by the practitioner to other tax professionals in a fairly sophisticated document—a research memorandum. We now shift the focus for the communication to a different audience, namely, the client, and to a different setting, the written or oral presentation.

By far the most common form of substantive communication between the tax professional and his or her client is the telephone call or e-mail. We must stress the danger inherent in most situations in placing too great a dependence on these forms of communication to convey the results of tax research given the intricacies of both the fact situation and the tax adviser's interpretation of controlling law. If the telephone or e-mail must be used to convey tax research results (perhaps because of time pressures or convenience), the practitioner should always send a follow-up **client letter** confirming his or her understanding as to the information that was conveyed and the actions that are to be taken as a result of the call. The final deliverable should be composed using the general writing tips discussed earlier and must communicate the conclusions reached in the research memo using terminology understandable by the client. Of course, this depends on the level of tax sophistication of the client. Writing a letter to the tax director of a client or a tax attorney requires a different approach and language than writing for a CFO with limited tax knowledge or an individual client without a detailed understanding of the tax law.

Except in the most unusual circumstances, client letters should not exceed two pages. This rule should be violated only when the subject of the research is especially complex, perhaps in anticipation of extended litigation or when the tax professional knows other parties will rely on the document. In situations calling for a more in-depth response, the writer should consider the use of a longer, more comprehensive report accompanied by a shorter executive summary.

Responding to client questions is generally easier in a face-to-face meeting. Thus, most practitioners use the client letter to deliver the general conclusions of the research project and to request a follow-up meeting in which questions, comments, and the need for more detail can be addressed.

As with the research memo, the specific format of the client letter may vary by firm. However, all letters should include the following:

- Salutation

- Objective and scope of the research, that is, what you understand the client has asked you to do

- General summary of the research project results

- Statement of the facts as presented by the client

- Summary of critical sources of law

- Implications of the results

- Assumptions and limitations. Here it is important to state that your conclusions are based on the facts as presented by the client and the applicable income tax law as of the date of the letter

- Closing including references to any required follow-up meetings

- Attachments, if any (e.g., engagement letter, file memo, illustrative charts, bibliography), on a separate page

Even if you know the client informally, the tone of the letter should be professional. Follow the general writing tips, use correct grammar and punctuation, and avoid informal language and slang. Exhibits 11-3 and 11-4 illustrate the format and content of typical client letters. The sole difference between these two letters is the degree of sophistication that is possessed by the receiving party.

4 Comprehensive Illustration of Client File

Exhibit 11-5 provides a comprehensive illustration of the two major elements of a client file: a research memo and a client letter. Notice the degree of correspondence between the two documents, in that some portions of the client letter are no more than quotations or paraphrases of the research memo.

The remainder of the internal file for this hypothetical client would include, among other possibilities:

- An engagement letter

- A billing and collection history

- Copies of other correspondence with the client and other parties such as the IRS

Each consulting firm or tax department has its own formatting requirements with respect to client files. Regardless of the format, one must not shortchange the importance

EXHIBIT 11-3: Sample Client Letter—Sophisticated Client

Sawyers and Gill CPAs

San Francisco, CA

November 19, 20XX

M/M Dale Brown 2472

North Mayfair Road

Fillingham, SD 59990

Dear Dale and Rae,

Thanks again for requesting my advice concerning the tax treatment of your mortgage-interest expenses. My research has concentrated on the treatment of mortgage-interest expense that is incurred by taxpayers who purchase tax-exempt bonds with the proceeds. I am sorry to report that only a portion of your expenses can be deducted.

I have uncovered a series of court cases in which the IRS has prevailed over the taxpayer's requests for a deduction that is similar to yours. Unfortunately, the Tax Court's position is that interest such as yours is nondeductible, and additional litigation would be necessary to bring about a more favorable result for you.

My understanding of the facts as you described them to me in your November 10 e-mail is as follows. In order to diversify your portfolio, you took out a sizable second mortgage on your home and used a portion of the proceeds to purchase tax-exempt City of Chandler school bonds. The remainder of the proceeds was used to expand the facilities of Dr. Brown's dental clinic.

Over the past 30 years or so, a number of circuit court decisions have held that a taxpayer effectively must divest himself or herself of investments in such municipal bonds, regardless of portfolio-diversification objectives, before a deduction for the interest payments to the bank is allowed. Fortunately, however, an exception exists relative to business-related loans, so that interest that is related to Dr. Brown's clinic will be allowed as a deduction. Conversely, that portion of the loan that relates to your municipal-bond investment is nondeductible, even though it is secured by your residence.

You may wish to reconsider your use of the mortgage for this purpose, as your tax advantages therefrom are somewhat limited. This appears to be more palatable for you than would be the alternative of expensive (and probably fruitless) litigation of the issue.

My conclusion is based on the facts that you have provided me and on the applicable income tax laws in effect as of the date of this letter.

As you've requested, I've attached a copy of my research memo for you to read and from which you might develop subsequent inquiries. We can discuss any questions that you have on December 15 when we meet to discuss your end-of-year tax planning. I'm sorry that the news from me wasn't more favorable.

Sincerely,

Mary H. Polzin

Sawyers and Gill CPAs

---

of the client file as a road map by which to retrace the researcher's line of thinking that led to the conclusions and recommendations evidenced in the research memo and client letter.

Accordingly, every tax researcher must develop a system by which to cross-reference the steps of the critical thinking and analysis undertaken on the client's behalf. Various software applications will be useful in this regard; not the least of these is the "research trail" feature of many online tax research products that records the detailed sequencing of commands and decisions made during the research project. Regardless of the form this project diary takes, its importance for professional quality control cannot be overstated.

EXHIBIT 11-4:   Sample Client Letter—Less Sophisticated Client

---

Sawyers and Gill CPAs

San Francisco,
CA November 19, 20XX
M/M Dale Brown
2472 North Mayfair Road
Fillingham, SD 59990

Dear Dale and Rae,

Thanks again for requesting my advice concerning the tax treatment of your mortgage-interest expenses. My research has concentrated on the treatment of mortgage-interest expense that is incurred by taxpayers who purchase tax-exempt bonds with the proceeds. I am sorry to report that only a portion of your expenses can be deducted.

My research has uncovered a series of successes by the IRS in several court decisions that have concluded that interest such as yours should not be allowed as a deduction to reduce your taxes.

My understanding of the facts as you described them to me in your November 10 e-mail is as follows. In order to diversify your portfolio, you took out a sizable second mortgage on your home and used a portion of the proceeds to purchase tax-exempt City of Chandler school bonds. The remainder of the proceeds was used to expand the facilities of Dr. Brown's dental clinic.

It seems that the IRS would rather have you purchase the municipal bonds with your own money, rather than with the bank's. The tax law maintains that you get a double benefit from the nontaxability of the school-bond-interest income and the deductibility of the interest expense that is paid to the bank. Thus, that portion of the interest that relates to the bond investment is not allowed. However, the good news is that you can deduct the interest from the loan that relates to Dr. Brown's clinic.

My conclusion is based on the facts that you have provided me and on the applicable income tax laws in effect as of the date of this letter. We can discuss any questions that you have on December 15 when we meet to discuss your end-of-year tax planning. I'm sorry that the news from me wasn't more favorable.

Sincerely,
Mary H. Polzin
Sawyers and Gill CPAs

---

5 E-mail and Text Messages

As previously noted, e-mail should be used with caution and generally not used to convey the results of a research project to a client. However, e-mail and text messages can be a convenient way to communicate other information to clients as well as to staff in your office. When you write an e-mail, you should exercise the same care in crafting your communication as you would in a letter or more formal communication. That means you should follow the writing tips discussed earlier: (1) be organized, (2) consider the reader, (3) be professional and courteous, (4) use correct grammar and punctuation, (5) be brief and to the point, and (6) write in direct, active voice and use short sentences.

As with other forms of writing, err on the side of formality even if you know the recipient in an informal way. E-mail and attachments should be encrypted if they contain any client information. Again, err on the side of caution if anything sensitive or personal is included in the e-mail.

EXHIBIT 11-5: Client File Illustration

RESEARCH MEMO

December 10, 20XX

Sawyers and Gill CPAs

Newport, RI

Facts

On the morning of their wedding, Frieda gave to Harold $400,000 of appreciated stock, pursuant to a prenuptial agreement. Frieda's basis in the stock was $150,000. In exchange for these securities, Harold surrendered all other marital rights and claims to Frieda's assets, under the terms of the agreement.

Issue(s)

1. What are the gift tax consequences of this exchange?

2. What are the income tax consequences of this exchange?

Conclusions

1. Frieda incurs no gift tax liability as the agreement is executed and implemented.

2. Neither Frieda nor Harold recognizes taxable income as a result of the exchange. Asset basis carries over to Harold, the new owner of the securities.

Authorities

Issue 1

IRC § 2501

IRC § 2512(b)

IRC §§ 2503(b) and 2523

Reg. § 25.2511-1(g)(1)

Reg. § 25.2512-8.

Rev. Rul. 69-347, 1969-1 C.B. 227

Merrill v. Fahs, 324 U.S. 308 (1945)

Comm. v. Wemyss, 324 U.S. 303

Issue 2

IRC § 102(a)

IRC §§ 1015(a) and 1041(a)(1)

Reg. § 1.102-1(a)

Rev. Rul. 79-312, 1979-2 C.B. 29

Rev. Rul. 67-221, 1967-2 C.B. 63

Howard v. C.I.R., 447 F.2d 152

Analysis and Summary

Issue One

Donative intent on the part of the donor is not an essential element in the application of the gift tax. Reg. § 25.2511-1(g)(1). The Supreme Court has held that prenuptial transfers in relinquishment of marital rights are not adequate and full consideration in money or money's worth for the transfer of property, within the meaning of IRC § 2512(b) (*Merrill v. Fahs,* 324 U.S. 308 (1945); *Comm. v. Wemyss,* 324 U.S. 303 (1945); Reg. § 25.2512-8. Although the transaction resulted in a gift, no gift tax is imposed due to the application of the annual exclusion and the unlimited gift tax marital deduction (IRC §§ 2503(b) and 2523; Rev. Rul. 69-347, 1969-1 C.B. 227).

IRC § 2501 imposes a tax on the transfer of property by gift; the gift tax is not imposed, though, upon the receipt of property by the donee. Rather, it is the transfer itself that triggers the tax. Since the prenuptial agreement here is enforceable by state law only when consummated by marriage, the transfer has not taken place until after the marriage occurs. Thus, the transfer appears to be eligible for the gift tax marital deduction, regardless of the timing of the transfer relative to the marriage ceremony on the wedding day. Even if the securities had been physically transferred to Harold prior to the completion of the ceremonies, the agreement was only enforceable after the couple was married. The IRS likely would not need or attempt to establish the exact moments of both (1) the transfer of the securities and (2) the consummation of the marriage (*Archbold*, 42 B.T.A. 453 (1940, Acq. in result only)).

Issue Two

Neither Harold nor Frieda recognizes any gross income upon Harold's release of his marital rights. Gross income does not include the value of property that is acquired by gift (IRC § 102(a); Reg. § 1.102-1(a); Rev. Rul. 79-312, 1979-2 C.B. 29; Rev. Rul. 67-221, 1967-2 C.B. 63; *Howard v. C.I.R.*,447 F.2d 152 (CA-5, 1971)). In the typical gift situation, the donee takes the donor's income tax basis in the transferred property. IRC §§ 1015(a) and 1041(a)(1).

Actions to Be Taken

Prepare letter, review results with client.

Place copy of prenuptial agreement in the client file.

Preparer: Karen J. Boucher

Reviewer: Lynne E. Schoenfeldt

Client Letter

Sawyers and Gill CPAs

Newport, RI

December 10, 20XX

Harold and Frieda van Briske

2000 Fox Point Heights

Whitefish Bay, RI 02899

Dear Harold and Frieda,

Thank you again for requesting my advice concerning the tax treatment of a gift of appreciated stock related to your prenuptial agreement. I am happy to report that the transaction will not result in the imposition of any federal gift or income tax for either of you.

My understanding of the facts as you described them to me on the phone are as follows. On the morning of your wedding, Frieda gave to Harold $400,000 of appreciated stock, pursuant to a prenuptial agreement. Frieda's basis in the stock was $150,000. Under the terms of the agreement, in exchange for these securities, Harold surrendered all other marital rights and claims to Frieda's assets.

My research has uncovered a series of court cases concluding that an agreement such as yours is not supported by "full and adequate consideration," and, therefore, that it is to be treated as a gift. Although you did not intend for your property transfer to be a gift, the intent of the parties in such agreements does not control for federal gift tax purposes.

Fortunately, however, the treatment of your transaction as a gift will not result in the imposition of federal gift tax or income tax. Federal income tax is not imposed upon the transfer because gross income is not recognized by either the donor or donee when a gift is made. Although a gift has occurred, no gift tax is due, because the unlimited gift tax marital deduction neutralizes the transfer.

My conclusion is based on the facts that you have provided me and on the applicable income tax laws in effect as of the date of this letter. We can discuss any questions that you have early next year when we meet to begin the process of preparing your tax return for the year.

Sincerely,

Karen J. Boucher, CPA, JD, MST

Sawyers and Gill CPAs

On the other hand, do not use texts for any communication of client information. Text messages should only be used for simple logistical issues and to respond to simple questions—again without including any specific client information. If clients send you a text with sensitive information, the best thing to do is to reply via a more secure method of communication.

6 Oral Presentations of Research Results

Psychologists tell us that most people's greatest fear is speaking before groups of other people. Indeed, the thought of being the only one in the room who is standing, of having your listeners whispering their evaluations of you to each other, of having members of the audience taking notes on (or recording) your comments (certainly so that your errors of omission and commission can be parroted back at a later date), and of fielding extemporaneous questions is enough to bring many people to tears.

Yet public speaking is an important part of the tax practitioner's professional life. As politicians have long known, when one is delivering an oral presentation in an effective and professional manner, the audience becomes convinced that all other professional qualities that they desire from the speaker are also present. Conversely, an ill-prepared or ill-delivered message can do much to erode the audience's confidence in the speaker, not just with respect to the topic of the presentation but in general.

Thus, it behooves the tax professional to develop skill in public speaking. In contexts that range from presenting an award to a colleague or conducting a staff meeting to presenting a keynote address at the annual tax conference of your peers, such skills can mean the difference between enhancing and damaging your reputation.

SPOTLIGHT ON TAXATION

Much speech is one thing, well-timed speech is another.

—Sophocles, Oedipus at Colonus

Whether making a presentation of one's results to a supervisor in one's own firm or elaborating on a research project with the client's board of directors, the communication of tax research results poses special problems that make a review of oral communication procedures all the more valuable. Specifically, we make the following suggestions concerning oral presentations of tax research:

1. General preparation for the talk should include a thorough, frank examination of the following set of questions by the presenter. Nearly all these observations can be characterized as knowledge of the makeup of the audience.

   - *Why me?* Why was I asked to speak? What knowledge do I bring to the event?

   - *What do they want?* What does the audience hope to take away from the presentation? Technical knowledge? General information? Skill development? Should I present an overview or a detailed technical update or analysis?

   - *What is their attitude?* Is the audience coming to the event curious or anxious to hear from me, or must they be persuaded of the relevance or importance of my topics?

- *From what should I stay away?* Are there topics that are taboo for this audience, because of their age, experiences, or existing attitudes? Because tax law is the result of a political process that sometimes strays from sound policy, one must not alienate the audience, wittingly or unwittingly, in any way if the message is to get across.

- *What do they already know?* What is the knowledge base of the audience? It would be ideal to speak to an audience that is homogeneous, especially in the level of knowledge that its members bring into the event, but this seldom is the case. One must decide, then, whether to aim at the median knowledge base, above, or below. The stakes are high in exercising this judgment, though, and either repeating what is common knowledge to the group or presenting information at a high level that is accessible to only a few in the audience can make communication impossible.

- *Who is the audience?* Details as to the audience's demographic characteristics, such as age, education, income level, political leanings, and so forth, can be vital for tailoring one's style, presentation speed and media, references to literature and popular culture, and effective use of humor. Remember to play to as many members of the audience as possible, not just the majority of those in attendance or those who were involved directly in hiring you or retaining your services.

2. Be prepared in the technical aspects of your discussion, particularly the basic research. Spend most of your preparation time on your main points and conclusions rather than on the fine points. If you are caught without a piece of technical information, it is clearly better for you if that information is specific (so that you can refer the questioner to a more detailed reference or to a later, private conversation with you) rather than basic in nature.

3. Direct your remarks to the highlights and general results of the research and leave time for a questions-and-comments period in which more detailed subjects can be addressed. In this manner, you will provide the greatest amount of information to the greatest number of listeners in the audience.

4. Use visual aids effectively. Visualizations should enhance the value and quality of information provided to an audience in a presentation. Handouts, slides, or videos can serve to clarify or emphasize your key points, but you must keep your attention on the audience, not a screen that is behind you. On average, allow at least three minutes of spoken presentation for each slide. Accordingly, limit the number of your slides to the length of your talk in minutes, divided by three. In this way, you will not produce too many slides. In general, visual aids should be used for the following purposes:

- To illustrate ideas that are difficult to convey strictly with words by using a photograph, video, map, or other visualization.

- To simplify comprehension of large amounts of data.

- To save time by consolidating ideas, committing to a time frame or strategy, or listing conflicting viewpoints or tactics.

- To create interest in a subject, perhaps by presenting the concept in a manner with which the audience is unfamiliar (e.g., an extra-large view, a view from "the other side of the issue," or an evolutionary time or growth line).

- To emphasize a point or concept by highlighting a graphic, picture, mnemonic, or list of key words or concepts.

- To organize the introduction, body, or conclusion of the presentation.

- To keep the audience focused on the key discussion points.

- To introduce humor to the event with a tasteful quotation or cartoon.

- To place ideas in the audience's memories through a visual "take away" item.

5. When text is involved in your visual displays, the following general guidelines should be followed:

   - Use the "six and six" rule: no more than six lines of type, and no more than six words on a line. This directive will help to dictate the font chosen and the corresponding size of print.

   - Keep the font style simple. Most designers recommend that no more than two colors of text be used on a slide and that the color scheme of the graphics blend well with that of the text. Be conservative—stick to the primary colors, colors of local sports teams, and multiple shades of gray so as not to frustrate the duplication process for related handout materials.

6. Without exception, find out before the presentation how long your talk is supposed to be, and do not exceed the time limit. You must be fair to the other speakers, if any, who follow your presentation. Moreover, typically the audience also is aware of the schedule for the session, and if the speaker exceeds the allotted time, the audience, at best, will stop paying attention and, at worst, will become restless or angry.

7. Rehearse your presentation, word for word, at least once. The most effective means of preparing yourself in this manner is with a video recorder because your distracting mannerisms (e.g., clearing the throat repeatedly, saying the words "ah" or "you know" too often, or pounding on the lectern) will quickly become apparent. Be kind to yourself in evaluating your video performance, but be observant for "I didn't know I did that" items.

8. In all but the very largest presentation venues, get as physically close to the audience as you can, ideally by removing the lectern, stepping down from the stage or platform, and moving to a series of different spots in the room throughout your speaking time. Use a portable device to control your slideshow, but practice using the device before your presentation begins.

9. Eliminate nervous habits, such as jingling coins, playing with pen and marker tops, and adjusting clothing.

10. Vary the pitch of your voice, avoiding both a dry monotone and a "classic actor" dramatic approach. Many speakers talk too fast or too loud; check yourself throughout the talk on these matters. Test the microphone system before the audience arrives so that you do not need to ask, "Can you hear me in the back?"

11. Do not be afraid of silence. Pauses invariably seem longer to the speaker than they do to the audience, so do not let natural breaks in the talk add to your anxiety. In fact, well-paced pauses can relieve tension (both yours and the audience's), signal changes of pace, and allow you to emphasize the importance of certain ideas.

12. Do not read directly from your outline, except for a selected quotation of three lines or so from the material once or twice in the presentation. If you need notes for very technical or detailed aspects of your presentation, disguise them in the form of comments on hard copies of your slides. Keep your eyes up and on the audience.

13. Be enthusiastic and positive about your comments—do not apologize for a lack of discussion on a tangential point, a logistical snafu, or a misstatement of fact or law. The audience generally wants you to succeed, so do not undermine this trust with self-destructive comments.

14. Rehearse the logistical aspects of the presentation, such as the lighting, projectors, and presentation software, before you begin to speak, ideally both the night before and one hour before your presentation. Have adequate numbers and varieties of markers, pointers, flip chart pads, and remote-control devices. You do not want to encounter any surprises after it is too late to do anything about them! On your script, notecards, or slide masters, make notes to yourself as to when, for instance, to pass out the handout material, turn on or turn off the projector, or refer to a flip chart.

15. Do not take the risk of boring or offending the audience with a joke that they may have heard already or that you might not tell effectively under pressure. This is not to suggest that you avoid humor altogether, however. Audiences, and speakers' reputations, thrive on it. If you are sure of your skill in this area, you might venture a joke, but be careful.

16. Have a "Plan B" ready to go—flexibility is the watchword of the effective speaker. For example, if the time actually allowed for your talk is shorter than you had expected, because of a misunderstanding or unanticipated events, have a list of topics, videos, or slides that can be eliminated without changing the nature of the talk. Practice your question-and-answer-session skills, especially for occasions when more time is available than you had anticipated.

17. Observe audience body language and use signals conveying interest, enthusiasm, boredom, or restlessness to your advantage. Make consistent eye contact with the audience, smile when appropriate, and take a few seconds at the completion of the presentation to accept the audience's show of thanks and savor your job well done.

SUMMARY

The tax professional must become proficient in communicating his or her research results. Recipients of these communications might include oneself or one's peers, via the research memorandum; the client, via a brief letter; or a number of other listeners, via an oral presentation. In each case, the practitioner must be sensitive to the needs, backgrounds, and interests of the recipients of the messages without sacrificing professional demeanor or responsibilities.

KEY WORDS

By the time you complete this chapter, you should be comfortable discussing each of the following terms. If you need additional review of any of these items, return to the appropriate material in the chapter or consult the glossary to this text.

client letter, p. 383   research memo, p. 378

DISCUSSION QUESTIONS

1. What is a research memo designed to do?

2. Briefly list and discuss the general writing tips introduced in the chapter.

3. List and discuss the primary parts of a tax research memo.

4. Discuss some of the key points that the tax researcher must consider with respect to evaluating court cases as part of a research project.

5. Discuss some of the key points that the tax researcher must consider with respect to evaluating administrative sources of law as part of a research project.

6. Identify the major elements of a client letter and briefly discuss the difference between a letter to a sophisticated client and to an unsophisticated client.

7. Give some examples of why gathering pertinent facts can be a challenging task for tax researchers.

8. You are preparing for an audit with an IRS agent for an important client. Your research has uncovered several favorable rulings and court decisions. What are the key points that should guide you in evaluating sources of the law?

9. Briefly summarize the key takeaways regarding the use of visual aids in oral presentations.

EXERCISES

10. Prepare a seven-minute oral presentation on the tax gap. Pay particular attention to the guidelines for the effective use of visual aids as noted in the chapter.

11. Prepare a seven-minute oral presentation on the distribution of income and federal income tax in the United States. Pay particular attention to the guidelines for the effective use of visual aids as noted in the chapter.

12. Prepare a seven-minute oral presentation on the federal estate tax including statistics on who pays it and how much has been collected over the last several years. Pay particular attention to the guidelines for the effective use of visual aids as noted in the chapter.

13. Prepare a seven-minute oral presentation on the primary sources of tax revenue for your state. How has the mix of revenue sources changed over the last five years? Pay particular attention to the guidelines for the effective use of visual aids as noted in the chapter.

14. Prepare a seven-minute oral presentation on the U.S. tax system's treatment of income earned abroad and compare the U.S. system of worldwide taxation to a territorial-type system in place in most countries. Pay particular attention to the guidelines for the effective use of visual aids as noted in the chapter.

CHAPTER **12**

Tax Planning

IN THIS CHAPTER WE return to that element of tax practice consisting of tax planning as it was introduced in Chapter 1. A working knowledge of tax planning concepts is imperative for the researcher because tax planning constitutes both an important part of tax practice and a prime motivation in the open-fact research context.

For most practitioners, tax research and planning represent the glamour end of the business. Properly accomplished tax planning

- Requires the client to identify financial goals and general means by which to achieve them.

- Allows the tax professional to exercise a higher degree of creativity than any other part of the practice.

- Affords the practitioner the greatest possible degree of control over the prescribed transactions and the tax consequences.

The tax planning process finds the tax professional in the roles of technical expert, friend, seer, and confessor priest for the client. It offers an opportunity for the most psychologically and financially rewarding work possible in the context of a tax practice.

1 The Economics of Tax Planning

From both the Treasury and the taxpayer viewpoint, taxes can modify individual decisions. Taxes represent an additional cost of doing business or of accumulating wealth. Assuming that economists are correct in speaking about the ways in which a rational citizen makes day-to-day decisions, taxpayers employ tax planning techniques to accomplish the overall goal of wealth maximization.[1] Because taxes deplete the wealth of the taxpayer, planning behavior is designed to reduce the net present value of the tax liability, which is not the same as a simple reduction of taxes in current, nominal dollar terms—an objective that is often assumed by laypeople, the media, and others, including too many tax advisors.

EXAMPLE 12-1

Sharon can choose between two business plans. One will cost her enterprise $1,000 in taxes today, and the other will cost the business $2,000 in taxes 10 years from now. The plans are identical in all other ways. Prevailing interest rates average 10 percent. Because the present value of the taxes levied with respect to the second alternative is approximately $800, Sharon should choose the latter plan, that is, the one with the higher nominal dollar tax cost but lower present value.

If prevailing interest rates average 5 percent during the 10-year planning period, the present value of the taxes levied under the second alternative would be approximately $1,225, so the first plan, the one that requires an immediate tax payment, should be adopted.

In one important sense, the federal income tax is its own worst enemy. Taxpayers are rewarded more for finding ways to save taxes than for earning an equal amount in the marketplace. This incentive for tax planning is the result of two rules of tax law.

---

[1]We define wealth in its broadest sense here. That is, an individual may choose increased leisure time or other forms of so-called psychic income over traditional forms of wealth. Wealth, the accumulation of which constitutes the overall goal for the specified time period, thus can include measures of happiness, satisfaction, investment, and control over time and other resources.

The first such rule is that the federal income tax itself is not allowed as a deduction in determining taxable income. Consequently, reducing the amount of income taxes that are paid does not decrease one's allowable deductions and, hence, does not trigger any further increase in taxable income. Instead, the full amount of any tax that is saved increases after-tax income; that is, the tax savings themselves do not constitute taxable income. Unlike most profit-seeking activities, tax planning produces benefits that are completely exempt from income taxation.

The second such rule allows a deduction for any business-related expenses that are incurred in connection with the determination of a tax. Most tax planning costs are deductible by business owners and sole proprietors, although only a few employees will qualify for such a deduction. The net cost of a tax planning project, then, is its gross cost minus the amount of the reduction in the tax liability that is generated by the attendant deduction. In concise terms, the after-tax cost of tax planning can be expressed as follows:

$$\mathbf{ATC = BTC \times (1 - MTR), where}$$

$$\mathbf{ATC = after\text{-}tax\ cost}$$

$$\mathbf{BTC = before\text{-}tax\ cost}$$

$$\mathbf{MTR = marginal\ tax\ rate}$$

In relating both rules to tax planning projects, one can see that such endeavors enjoy an economic advantage over most other profit-seeking activities. In evaluating most other investment projects, the decision maker must compare after-tax benefits with after-tax costs. Yet, for tax planning projects, the payoffs are tax-free, while the costs usually remain tax-deductible. Thus, for tax planning activities, one effectively compares pretax benefits with after-tax costs.

EXAMPLE 12-2

Shull Corporation, subject to a marginal state and federal income tax rate of 40 percent, is considering two mutually exclusive alternatives. Alternative 1 is to hire a university accounting major for the summer at a cost of $2,000; his task would be to undertake research on a tax avoidance plan. If it is successful, the plan would save the corporation $1,600 in federal income taxes. The probability of success for the plan is estimated at 80 percent.

Alternative 2 is to hire a university marketing major for the summer at a cost of $1,700; her task would be to undertake research on a marketing plan. If it is successful, this plan would generate new revenues of $2,100. The probability of such success is estimated to be 85 percent. Which, if either, alternative should Shull pursue?

	Alternative 1	**Alternative 2**
Before-tax cost	$2,000	$1,700
Tax reduction (40 percent)	−800	−680
After-tax cost	$1,200	$1,020
Possible pretax payoff	$1,600	$2,100
Probability of success	×0.80	×0.85
Expected pretax payoff	$1,280	$1,785
Tax on expected payoff (40 percent)	−0	−714
Expected after-tax payoff	$1,280	$1,071
Excess of after-tax payoff over after-tax cost	$ 80	$ 51

Decision: Even though Alternative 2 offers a higher pretax payoff, a lower before-tax cost, and a higher probability of success, Alternative 1 should be accepted.

The facts of this example illustrate the apparent built-in economic bias of current tax law for tax planning projects relative to other, seemingly more productive, activities.

The analysis in Example 12-2, as in most of the illustrations in this book, is based on a marginal viewpoint. Its purpose is to determine the effect of the transaction at issue, assuming that all other characteristics of the situation do not change. When it is viewed from this perspective, the after-tax cost of any deductible expenditure decreases if the marginal tax rate is increased. This fact helps explain why lower-income taxpayers, who are subject to lower marginal tax rates, engage in tax planning activities less often than do higher-income taxpayers.

EXAMPLE 12-3

Assume the same situation and opportunities as in Example 12-2, except that Shull's marginal tax rate is 25 percent.

	Alternative 1	Alternative 2
Before-tax cost	$2,000	$1,700
Tax reduction (25 percent)	−500	−425
After-tax cost	$1,500	$1,275
Possible pretax payoff	$1,600	$2,100
Probability of success	×0.80	×0.85
Expected pretax payoff	$1,280	$1,785
Tax on expected payoff (25 percent)	−0	−446
Expected after-tax payoff	$1,280	$1,339
Excess of after-tax payoff over after-tax cost	$(220)	$ 64

Decision: Accept Alternative 2 because it now generates the higher net after-tax payoff. The change in the marginal tax rate alone resulted in a different decision by Shull.

2 Tax Rate Terminology

Regardless of the type of tax involved, the basic formula for computing a taxpayer's liability is

$$\textbf{Tax Liability} = \textbf{Tax Base} \times \textbf{Tax Rate}$$

Accordingly, tax planning at is most basic focuses on reducing or removing something from the tax base or reducing the tax rate applicable to the base.

2-1 Tax Base

The income tax is the most modern of the taxes that are commonly found in contemporary industrialized societies. Most policymakers believe that a tax that is based on ordinary taxable income, allowing deductions for the costs of earning such income and for certain personal expenditures, best reflects the capacity of the taxpayer to support governmental operations.

Previous efforts to base taxation on ability to pay have included taxes on individual consumption and wealth. Consumption taxes are supported by the rationale that the taxpayer receives personal benefit from society in accordance with the amount of goods and services that he or she exhausts during the period; thus, the government should appropriate its share of tax revenue from what people take out of society's "kitty" for personal reasons, not from what they put into it, as is the case under income taxation.

Wealth or property taxes also have been structured to base levies on one's capacity to pay taxes. Most often, wealth taxes take the form of levies against the net holdings of tangible assets that are controlled by the taxpayer at a given time.

2-2 Tax Rates

Most tax scholars identify three distinct tax rate structures: proportional, progressive, and regressive, as illustrated in Exhibit 12-1. The classification of a rate structure depends on the trend of the tax rate as the tax base increases. Under a **proportional tax rate** system, the tax rate is constant. For example, a flat income tax assessed at a rate of 24 percent of income regardless of how much income is earned would be an example of a proportional tax. Most sales and property taxes in the United States employ a proportional rate structure.

EXHIBIT 12-1: Alternative Tax Rate Structures: Graphic Illustrations and Applicable Schedules

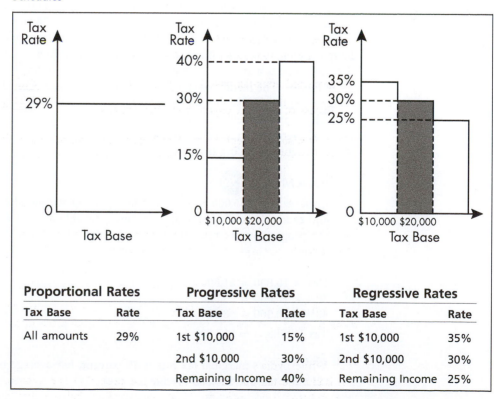

Proportional Rates		Progressive Rates		Regressive Rates	
Tax Base	**Rate**	**Tax Base**	**Rate**	**Tax Base**	**Rate**
All amounts	29%	1st $10,000	15%	1st $10,000	35%
		2nd $10,000	30%	2nd $10,000	30%
		Remaining Income	40%	Remaining Income	25%

Under a **progressive tax rate** system, the applicable tax rate increases as the tax base grows larger. The U.S. individual income tax is a progressive tax rate system in which tax rates increase with income.

Finally, the tax rate decreases as the tax base grows larger under a **regressive tax rate** structure. Most taxpayers and tax professionals consider regressive tax rates to be unfair. No significant U.S. tax to date has employed a system of regressive tax rates.

SPOTLIGHT ON TAXATION

Are Social Security Taxes Regressive?

In 2016, Social Security taxes were imposed on employees at a flat rate of 6.2 percent on all wages up to $118,500. For wages in excess of that amount, there was no additional tax. Technically, the tax is proportional or flat because all covered wages (the tax base) are subject to the same rate of tax. However, many people regard Social Security taxes to be regressive, presumably basing their analysis on the full amount of a taxpayer's income, not just the statutory tax base. Under this view, because the marginal tax rate is zero on wages in excess of $118,500 for the year, the tax is considered regressive.

2-2a Marginal and Average Tax Rates   The marginal tax rate is the present value of the additional tax on one dollar of additional taxable income. Many taxpayers are confused by the appropriate meaning of their **marginal tax rate**. Typically, they assume that if a taxpayer is subject to a 36 percent marginal tax rate (i.e., 36 cents is payable in tax on the next dollar of taxable income), he or she owes 36 percent of the entire taxable income. One often hears people fall victim to this fallacy, when they state, "I wish I hadn't gotten that raise, because it threw me into a higher tax bracket!" The truth is that even under a system of progressive tax rates, one is never left worse off by earning more money. The higher marginal rates that apply to additional income affect only those increments; the tax liability on the original income layers does not change.

Such comments reflect confusion on the part of the taxpayer concerning marginal tax rate and average tax rate. The **average tax rate** is a simple division of the total tax liability by the corresponding tax base.

EXAMPLE 12-4

Lydia earned $55,000 this year. After applying various deductions, exclusions, and exemptions, though, Lydia's statutory taxable income is $40,000. Assuming the progressive tax rate structure of Exhibit 12-1, Lydia's tax is computed as follows.

$$15\% \times 10,000 = \$1,500$$
$$30\% \times 10,000 = 3,000$$
$$40\% \times 20,000 = \underline{8,000}$$
$$\text{Tax liability} = \underline{\$12,500}$$

While Lydia's marginal tax rate is 40 percent, her average rate is 31.25 percent ($12,500 tax due/$40,000 taxable income).

The reader should make sure that he or she understands this distinction between marginal and average tax rates because all tax planning analyses should be based on the marginal tax that the individual will pay or save by adopting a particular course of action. The average tax rate is an interesting statistic, but it is solely the marginal rate that affects the change in tax liability and any corresponding changes in taxpayer behavior.

Of course, our calculation of taxable income allows for certain deductions, exemptions, and exclusions from total receipts in determining the tax base for the year. As a result, we can also distinguish between the nominal average tax rate and the effective average tax rate.

The **nominal average tax rate** can be computed in Exhibit 12-2 by dividing total tax liability by taxable income. Note that before considering Lydia's exclusions, exemptions, and deductions, she had $55,000 of economic income during the year. Thus, Lydia's **effective average tax rate** can be found by dividing the total tax liability by the economic income of $55,000. Exhibit 12-2 summarizes the various tax rate computations that have been introduced in this section.

Calculating marginal tax rates in the presence of net operating losses (NOLs) can be challenging. Although you might expect that the marginal tax rate for a taxpayer who is losing money would be zero, remember that the marginal rate is the tax rate that will be paid on the next dollar of taxable income. An extra dollar of income will reduce the relevant NOL and reduce the tax refund from a carryback of the NOL. Accordingly, if an NOL is carried back, the marginal tax rate in the NOL year will be the marginal tax rate in the year in which the NOL carryback is exhausted.

EXAMPLE 12-5

EDS Corp. has a current year (2017) NOL of $150,000. In each of the last two years (2015 and 2016), the company earned $100,000, and the company expects to make $100,000 in each of the next two years (2018 and 2019). If the appropriate statutory corporate tax rate is 34 percent over the entire five-year period, the company's marginal tax rate in 2017 will be 34 percent. When EDS carries back the NOL to 2015 and 2016, it will receive an immediate refund of $34,000 of taxes paid in 2015 and $17,000 of taxes paid in 2016. If the company earns $1 more of income in 2017, the NOL will be reduced to $149,999, and its refund from 2016 will be reduced to $16,999.66. Accordingly, the extra dollar of taxable income will cost the company an extra $.34 in income tax.

If an NOL is carried forward and used up in a future tax year, the marginal tax rate in the NOL year is the marginal tax rate in the future tax year in which the NOL is exhausted discounted back to the NOL year.

EXHIBIT 12-2: Various Tax Rate Computations Illustrated

Lydia has $55,000 of economic income and $15,000 of exemptions, exclusions, and deductions. Taxable income is $40,000. Tax liability is $12,500 under the prevailing progressive rate system assumed in Exhibit 12-1.

Marginal tax rate	40 percent (from the progressive tax rate schedule, Exhibit 12-1)
Average tax rates	Nominal average rate: $12,500/$40,000 = 31.2 percent
	Effective average rate: $12,500/$55,000 = 22.72 percent

EXAMPLE 12-6

Assume the same facts as in Example 12-5, but now EDS loses $350,000 in 2017. As in Example 12-5, EDS will utilize $200,000 of the NOL by carrying back the NOL to offset taxable income in 2015 and 2016. The remaining $150,000 will be carried over and fully utilized in 2019. If the company earns $1 more of income in 2017, the NOL will be reduced to $349,999, and its refund from 2019 will be reduced by $0.34. However, because this extra tax is not paid until 2019, the present value of the tax payment must be determined. Assuming a discount rate of 6 percent, the present value of the payment is $0.34 × 0.890 discount rate, or 0.3026. Accordingly, the marginal tax rate in 2017 would be 30.26 percent.

3 Tax Planning in Perspective

The entrepreneurial tax professional should not see tax planning as an end in itself. Rather, especially when dealing with individual clients, tax planning must be seen as part of two sets of major services provided by the practitioner, as illustrated in Exhibits 12-3 and 12-4. As we discussed in Chapter 1, tax planning is part of the entire menu of tax services that the tax professional makes available.

Although the compliance and litigation aspects of the profession increasingly are shared with paraprofessionals (who prepare the bulk of tax returns for many professional firms) or attorneys (when a seemingly irresolvable conflict arises, usually between the client and the IRS), tax planning rightly is initiated by the well-educated and experienced tax practitioner.

Similarly, tax planning is but one of the various types of planning services that a tax professional offers to clients. As the U.S. population collectively ages, the importance of portfolio, estate, and retirement planning has increased. As higher education costs have skyrocketed over the last few decades, education planning has grown in importance as well. Planning for cash and risk contingencies is mandatory for business clients, but even the most modestly financially endowed of individual clients can benefit from an introduction to such planning.

Thus, to the extent that the tax professional offers tax planning and counseling services, he or she must be familiar with the rudiments of the planning process and with the dynamic nature of the evolution of the tax law as it affects planning engagements.

EXHIBIT 12-3: Tax Planning in the Typical Tax Practice, by Time and Effort of the Professional Staff

EXHIBIT 12-4: Tax Planning in the Client's Wealth Planning Process

EDUCATION PLANNING
Section 529 Qualified
 Tuition Programs
Coverdell Education
 Savings Accounts
Investment Planning

ESTATE PLANNING
Asset Management
Distributions and Control
Estate and Gift Tax Planning

RETIREMENT PLANNING
Qualified Plans
Nonqualified Plans
Individual Retirement
 Accounts (Traditional and
 Roth)
Planning for Distributions

INCOME TAX PLANNING
Timing
Tax Entity
Exclusions and Deductions
Income Classification
Special Taxes
Withholding
Interest and Penalties

INVESTMENT PLANNING
Risks
Rewards
Control
Purchases/Sales
Asset Allocation
Regulations

CASH PLANNING
Budgeting
Finance

RISK PLANNING
Insurance
Security

4 Fundamentals of Tax Planning

As we noted in Chapter 1, tax planning is a completely legal means for saving taxes. The basic objective of such planning is to arrange one's financial activities in a way that will reduce the present value of tax costs such that maximum wealth accumulation can occur in the time period specified.

Opportunities for effective tax planning almost always are greater when tax effects are given consideration before transactions are finalized rather than after they are completed. Decision makers should constantly be alert for tax-optimizing alternatives in the everyday conduct of their affairs. In other words, the first requirement for effective tax planning is tax awareness on the part of decision makers rather than tax expertise by tax professionals.

EXAMPLE 12-7

Russell and Phyllis Cohen, a married couple subject to a 30 percent marginal tax rate, currently are negotiating the purchase of their first home with the Hacienda Heights Construction Company, a land developer. The company has offered to sell the Cohens a house and lot at a price of $250,000 with a 20 percent down payment and 4 percent interest with annual payments for a five-year period. Under these terms, payments would be as follows:

Year	Beginning Balance	Interest	Principal	Total Payment
0	$ 250,000	$ 0	$ 50,000	$ 50,000
1	$ 200,000	$ 8,000	$ 36,926	$ 44,926
2	$ 163,074	$ 6,523	$ 38,403	$ 44,926
3	$ 124,671	$ 4,987	$ 39,939	$ 44,926
4	$ 84,732	$ 3,389	$ 41,537	$ 44,926
5	$ 43,195	$ 1,728	$ 43,195	$ 44,923
Totals		$ 24,627	$ 250,000	$ 274,627

The Cohens are aware that mortgage-interest payments are tax deductible and that the purchase price of a home is not. Thus, they make a counteroffer to purchase the home at a price of $239,246, with $50,000 down and 6 percent interest on annual payments over a five-year period. Under these new terms, Hacienda Heights receives the same cash payments (and gross income) as it did under the original terms. However, the amount of allowable deductions to the Cohens would be increased, with no change in total cash payments. Note that a complete analysis must consider the other party to the transaction—in this case Hacienda Heights Construction Company. While the company's taxable interest income would increase by $10,758, the gain on the sale would decrease (or the loss increase) by $10,754 (the reduction in the purchase price), effectively making the company indifferent to the terms of the sale.

Year	Beginning Balance	Interest	Principal	Total Payment
0	$ 239,246	$ 0	$ 50,000	$ 50,000
1	$ 189,246	$ 11,355	$ 33,571	$ 44,926
2	$ 155,675	$ 9,340	$ 35,586	$ 44,926
3	$ 120,089	$ 7,205	$ 37,721	$ 44,926
4	$ 82,368	$ 4,942	$ 39,984	$ 44,926
5	$ 42,384	$ 2,543	$ 42,384	$ 44,927
Totals		$ 35,385	$ 239,246	$ 274,631

Often, decision makers can benefit by recognizing how the rearrangement of a planned transaction can produce tax savings, even if the economic substance of the transaction is left unaltered (or altered very little). In Example 12-7, by reclassifying a portion of their housing expenditures as (deductible) interest rather than (nondeductible) principal, the Cohens were able to increase their allowable deductions and save taxes.

SPOTLIGHT ON TAXATION

Radical Tax Planning

A well-timed death is the acme of good tax planning, better even than a well-timed marriage.

—Donald C. Alexander (Former IRS Commissioner)

EXHIBIT 12-5: Goals of Tax Planning Behavior

- Avoiding recognition of taxable income
- Changing the timing of recognition of income, gains, deductions, losses, and credits
- Changing tax jurisdictions
- Changing the character of income
- Tax planning among related taxpayers

Tax planning behavior can be characterized as falling into one or more of the general categories enumerated in Exhibit 12-5. Virtually every tax planning technique employed by the tax professional fits one or more of these overriding planning objectives.

4-1 Avoiding Recognition of Taxable Income

Taxpayers often can reduce their exposure to taxation by avoiding the accumulation of gross income that must be recognized. This is not to suggest that a taxpayer should avoid accumulating real economic income. As long as marginal tax rates remain less than 100 percent, few people would be willing to go to that extreme. Rather, one usually should strive to obtain economic wealth in some manner that does not create recognized income under the tax law.

EXAMPLE 12-8

Julie earned $3,500 when she sold the crop of fruits and vegetables that she grew, and she was subject to income tax on the full amount. Warren also grew a crop of produce of the same size, but he and his family ate the food. Thus, Warren recognized no gross income and paid no income tax relative to his gardening activities, but his family enjoyed $3,500 worth of fruits and vegetables.

EXAMPLE 12-9

Jerry has $50,000 in savings. If the money were invested in securities, the yield on his investment would be taxable, although no deduction would be allowed for his "personal" expense of renting a home. If the $50,000 were invested in a home for his own use, however, the net rental value of the home would escape taxation because such in-kind value is not recognized as gross income under the law.

Another method by which one can avoid recognizing income is through the use of debt. Since neither the borrowing of money nor the receipt of funds that previously were loaned generates gross income, taxpayers sometimes can use loans to avoid the recognition of taxable income on appreciated investments and enjoy the temporary use of the cash.

EXAMPLE 12-10

Doug owns a tract of land that he acquired many years ago for $10,000. Currently, the land is worth $100,000. Doug needs $50,000 in cash to buy a new car. He is considering two alternatives: one is to sell half the land, and the other is to borrow the $50,000 using the land as collateral. If Doug sells half the land, he will recognize a $45,000 ($50,000 minus one-half of $10,000) taxable gain.

However, Doug recognizes no taxable income if he borrows the money, even though the amount that he borrows will be in excess of the basis of the land.

EXAMPLE 12-11

Sarah Carter uses borrowed funds to acquire non-dividend-paying corporate stocks. Appreciation on the stocks is not taxed until it is realized on the sale of the shares. Yet, if Sarah has investment income from other sources, she might be able to claim investment-interest deductions for the interest that she pays on the borrowed funds.

Still another, and perhaps more obvious, way in which one can avoid the recognition of income for tax purposes is to take advantage of the many exclusions that the law permits. For example, an employee might arrange to receive certain nontaxable fringe benefits (such as health insurance) from her employer in lieu of an equivalent value in (taxable) cash salary. This relationship should affect all negotiations as to compensation arrangements: the employer is indifferent between the two choices because both salary and fringe-benefit payments are fully deductible against gross income, but the employee's after-tax wealth increases more when tax-free benefits are received.

EXAMPLE 12-12

Lee Schrader, who is subject to a 40 percent overall marginal tax rate, is better off if she receives a tax-free fringe benefit than if she receives an equivalent increase in her salary.

	If Salary Increases	If Fringe Benefit Is Chosen
Value of compensation received	$2,000	$2,000
Tax on employee's compensation	$ 800	
After-tax increase in employee's wealth	$1,200	$2,000

EXAMPLE 12-13

Albert contributes the maximum amount for the year to a Section 529 qualified tuition plan for his daughter. No immediate deduction is allowed, but the earnings in the account never are taxed. Withdrawals similarly are excluded from gross income when they are used for education-related expenses.

EXAMPLE 12-14

Phil designates a portion of his monthly paycheck for medical and child care expenses through a flexible spending account (FSA) offered by his employer. No payroll taxes are due on these amounts. Phil's employer reimburses him from these funds when it receives documentation from Phil that he incurred medical and child care expenses for the period. By using an FSA such as this, Phil reduces his total tax liability and has more discretionary income for the year.

4-2 Changing the Timing of Recognition of Income, Gains, Deductions, Losses, and Credits

When tax rates are constant, delaying income recognition or accelerating deductions can be beneficial. By delaying the recognition of income, one also delays the payment of the tax and, hence, can continue to enjoy the use of that money. At 4 percent annual interest, the present value of a $1,000 tax that is postponed for 10 years is only $676. For longer periods and/or higher interest rates, the economic significance of the delay would be even greater. A series of tables computing factors to reflect the time value of money is provided on the end pages in the back of the book.

EXAMPLE 12-15

Mike Jones is a self-employed consultant who uses the cash basis of accounting for tax purposes. Mike finished several consulting jobs late in the year. By postponing billing clients (and receiving cash) to next year, Mike can postpone recognition of taxable income and the resulting tax payment.

EXAMPLE 12-16

George itemizes his deductions and generally gives well over 10 percent of his income to charity each year. He is planning a large charitable gift in January when his church begins a major new capital improvement project. By accelerating the contribution to the current year, George can receive tax savings in the current year rather than next year.

Changing tax rates can result in even more interesting and profitable tax planning opportunities, as seen in the following example.

EXAMPLE 12-17

Your employer has had a profitable year and has decided to award you a year-end cash bonus of $25,000. However, you have the option of taking the bonus this year or deferring it and taking the $25,000 at the end of next year. While your tax rate is 39.6 percent this year, you plan to retire in the middle of next year, thus reducing your expected marginal tax rate to 28 percent. If you take the bonus this year, after paying taxes of $9,900 ($25,000 × 0.396) you would have $15,100 to invest for one year. Assuming you can earn 5 percent after tax on your investment, you would have $15,855 after one year. If you forgo taking the bonus until the end of next year, taxes due on the bonus will be reduced to $7,000, leaving you with $18,000 of after-tax wealth.

The general principles of delaying income and accelerating deductions are not always optimal. In unusual circumstances, these principles should be violated purposely to produce a desired effect. Again, however, the tax awareness of the parties is of utmost importance in proper planning activities.

EXAMPLE 12-18

Gretchen's cash-basis business is unincorporated. It has generated an operating loss of $265,000, which Gretchen can deduct on her tax return. Although there may be other tax uses for this loss, Gretchen may want to accelerate the recognition of other gross income into the current year, for example, by selling appreciated investments or simply sending out bills to customers in a more timely fashion. Realization this year will result in no tax liability for Gretchen because of the loss, so income acceleration should be considered.

EXAMPLE 12-19

Brian's gross income is lower than he expected because of an unanticipated decrease in the sale of his homemade sandals. From a tax standpoint, it may be better to delay deductible expenditures of a discretionary or personal nature (e.g., advertising, medical expenses, and charitable contributions) until business picks up again. In this manner, the value of such deductions will increase, as will the marginal income tax rate to which he is subject.

EXAMPLE 12-20

Matt Young is subject to the alternative minimum tax (AMT) for the first time ever this year. State income taxes and property taxes and miscellaneous itemized deductions, among other familiar items, are not allowed as deductions when computing AMT income. Accordingly, Matt should defer the payments of his fourth-quarter state income tax estimates and of the property tax on his home until next year, when the usual definitions of taxable income will apply to him again.

EXAMPLE 12-21

Dolores is subject to the AMT this year, so her marginal tax rate is 24 percent, not the usual 36 percent. She might consider accelerating some gross income into the current year to take advantage of this decrease in her marginal tax rate. However, the tax adviser must be certain to compare the present values of the resulting taxes, not just the nominal dollar amounts.

4-3 Changing Tax Jurisdictions

Tax systems are not universal in breadth, nature, or application. Taxes are adopted by governmental jurisdictions, to be collected from those who live and do business within their boundaries. Often, by moving assets or income out of one tax jurisdiction into another, tax reductions can be achieved. Over time, governments tend to modify their tax systems to prevent the leakage of tax revenues through such cross-border transactions. Yet, in an effort to attract businesses and resulting jobs into their jurisdictions, governments often retain or create border incentives in the form of tax reductions that are limited in time or scope.

EXAMPLE 12-22

While the United States has a worldwide tax system in which earnings from U.S. sources as well as foreign sources are subject to tax, foreign earnings may not be subject to tax in the United States until they are brought back (repatriated) into the United States. Locating subsidiaries in foreign countries with low tax rates can be an effective method of tax planning for multinational companies.

EXAMPLE 12-23

Judy is a well-paid consultant, earning more than $1 million annually. Since she works primarily from her home, choosing to live in Florida (a state without a state income tax) instead of California (a state with a 10.3 percent income tax) could save Judy more than $100,000 in taxes each year.

EXAMPLE 12-24

RGS Inc. has a manufacturing plant, distribution center, and warehouse in State C and a smaller distribution center in State D. Both states utilize an equally weighted three-factor apportionment formula. State C has a 9 percent corporate tax while State D has a 3 percent tax. Moving the distribution and warehouse now located in State C to State D may reduce the company's overall state income taxes.

4-4 Changing the Character of Income

For federal income tax purposes, several distinct categories of income are recognized. The most important of these are as follows:

1. Ordinary income, which is fully taxable at ordinary income tax rates, and ordinary deductions, which decrease the tax base dollar for dollar.

2. Investment or portfolio income, which usually is fully taxable except for tax-exempt state and local bond interest, and related expenses, which typically can be subtracted only against investment income. Some investment income such as dividends may qualify for preferential tax rates.

3. Income from passive activities, such as the ownership of rental property or entities in which the taxpayer does not materially participate, which usually is fully taxable, and passive losses, which can be subtracted only against passive income.

4. Income from long-term capital gains, which historically has often been subject to lower tax rates than ordinary income. This difference in tax rates between ordinary income and capital-gain income produces planning opportunities.

EXAMPLE 12-25

Phil Jankowski is an owner of a family owned business operated as a limited liability company (LLC) that generates $40,000 per year in passive losses. According to the IRC, such losses from passive activities cannot be applied as deductions to offset fully taxable income, such as from Phil's salary or capital-gain transactions. Accordingly, Phil cannot reduce current taxable income by the $40,000 passive loss. However, if Phil materially participates in the activities of the business, the $40,000 loss will no longer be considered passive and can be fully deducted against active and portfolio income.

EXAMPLE 12-26

Amber has $100,000 to invest and is considering a taxable corporate bond that pays 5 percent annual interest or a non-dividend-paying stock that is expected to appreciate by 5 percent each year. Assuming that the investments are of similar risk, the tax liability associated with the expected long-term capital gain on the stock will likely be lower than the tax liability associated with the interest income earned on the corporate bonds, which is taxed as ordinary income.

EXAMPLE 12-27

Amber has $100,000 to invest and is considering a taxable corporate bond that pays 5 percent annual interest or a tax-free municipal bond that pays 3.5 percent annual interest. Assuming that Amber's marginal tax rate is 40 percent, while investing in the corporate bond will earn Amber before-tax interest of $50,000 compared to only $35,000 of before-tax interest income from the municipal bond, investing in the municipal bond will provide a higher after-tax amount. After paying taxes on the interest income from the corporate bond, Amber will be left with only $30,000 of after-tax income. Of course, the municipal bond income is exempt from federal income tax, leaving her with $35,000 of after-tax income. Note that the taxable bond would be preferred by Amber if her marginal tax rate is less than 30 percent.

EXAMPLE 12-28

Ten months ago, Matt invested $10,000 in a stock that has skyrocketed in value and is currently worth $18,000. If he sells the stock today, he will recognize an $8,000 short-term capital gain taxed as ordinary income. If he holds the stock at least two more months, his gain will be characterized as a long-term capital gain and be subject to lower tax rates. However, Matt must consider the risk in that the stock might decrease in value over the next two months.

4-5 Tax Planning among Related Taxpayers

Because different types of legal entities are taxed separately and at different rates, an individual often can produce an overall tax savings by conducting various business and investment activities within separate taxpaying entities. The progressive nature of the various tax rate schedules further tends to increase the advantage of income splitting among related parties. This benefit might result from shifting income, either among different economic entities that are owned by the same individual or among the individual's family members. Accordingly, tax considerations often play an important role both in the selection of organizational forms for a business enterprise and in family financial arrangements.

EXAMPLE 12-29

Bob and Lorraine Whitehead are currently providing for Lorraine's parents' retirement out of after-tax income. Given the Whiteheads' marginal income tax rate of 30 percent, $1,000 of pre-tax income is needed to produce $700 of savings [$1,000 − (0.30 of $1,000) = $700]. Assuming that the parents have a marginal income tax rate of only 18 percent, a transfer to them of $1,000 of pretax income, say, by a gift of cash or income-producing investment assets, would raise the after-tax contribution to the parents' retirement to $820 [$1,000 − (0.18 of $1,000)].

EXAMPLE 12-30

Richie Rich makes certain that he makes gifts of highly appreciated securities every year to each of his adult children, using the entire statutory annual gift tax exclusion. This effectively shifts future appreciation and tax on gains to his children, who face lower tax rates.

SPOTLIGHT ON TAXATION

Fruits of Tax Planning

Tax planning is driven by the fact that under a non-neutral tax law, transactions or arrangements whose economic differences are minor can have significantly different tax consequences.

—James W. Wetzler

Related taxpayers can also exist in the form of corporations and their shareholders. Several types of planning opportunities can be identified and used by the tax planner in these situations. The objective typically is to structure the terms of the transaction so as to decrease taxable income to the taxpayer group as a whole.

EXAMPLE 12-31

Marilyn is the sole owner-employee of a corporation. To the extent that the corporation pays dividends to Marilyn, she will recognize gross income, but the corporation will receive no deduction. To the extent that Marilyn is paid a reasonable salary, she will recognize gross income and the corporation will receive a deduction. To the extent that she receives certain employee fringe benefits, such as medical insurance, Marilyn is not required to recognize taxable income, and the corporation is allowed an ordinary-business-expense deduction. In summary, the payment of dividends increases combined taxable income of a shareholder and the corporation, the payment of salary does not change combined taxable income, and providing qualified fringe benefits reduces combined taxable income.

EXAMPLE 12-32

Don and Ann Smith operate a farm, producing a net taxable income of approximately $30,000 per year. Their nondeductible expenses for housing average $12,000 per year. The Smiths should consider forming a corporation and making a tax-free transfer to the corporation of all the farm property, including their personal living quarters. As shareholders of the corporation, they could hire themselves as employees, with a requirement that they live on the business premises. The value of the lodging would not be taxable to the Smiths as individuals under § 119 of the IRC, but it would be deductible as a business expense of the corporation, thus reducing the corporation's taxable income before salaries to $18,000 ($30,000 minus $12,000).

The Smiths then should have the corporation pay them reasonable salaries totaling $18,000. In this manner, taxable income of $18,000 would be taxed directly to them as individuals, and the corporation's taxable income would be reduced to zero, thus avoiding any double taxation. By using this combination of income splitting and an employee fringe benefit, the Smiths could effectively reduce their taxable income (i.e., from $30,000 to $18,000) by the amount of their lodging costs ($12,000), even though such costs are generally nondeductible by both self-employed persons and employees.

This result is based on the assumptions that $18,000 is a reasonable salary for the work that they perform and that the requirement for living on the farm is for a bona fide business purpose (other than merely for tax avoidance).

EXAMPLE 12-33

Harry Fischer is a 40 percent shareholder and junior executive of Able Corporation. Harry's performance-incentive bonus is set at 30 percent of the corporation's pretax earnings for the year. It is payable on January 31 of the following year. Because the corporation is an accrual-basis taxpayer, the bonus is deductible in the year in which it is earned. As a cash-basis minority shareholder, however, Harry need not recognize the income until the following taxable year (i.e., when he receives it). To the extent of Harry's bonus, the recognition of combined corporate and shareholder income thus is delayed for one year.

EXAMPLE 12-34

Barbara Ward formed a new corporation by investing $100,000 cash. Following the advice of her tax consultant, Barbara designated $60,000 to be used for the purchase of corporate stock and $40,000 as a loan to the corporation. In this way, if Barbara wants to receive large amounts of cash back from the corporation in the future, the entity simply will repay part or all of the loan principal to her, tax free, rather than making a large (taxable and nondeductible) dividend payment. Barbara also can direct the corporation to pay interest on the loan; such payments are deductible by the corporation. Of course, both interest and dividends are taxable to Barbara when she receives them.

5 Avoiding Tax Traps

Ever since the enactment of the first income tax, taxpayers have been trying to find ways to avoid it. Likewise, Congress, the IRS, and the courts have enacted rules and doctrines to prevent, or at least restrict, various avoidance schemes. As a result, current tax law includes a maze of tax traps for the unwary.

5-1 Statutory Tax Traps

Many of the statutory provisions encountered in a tax planning context can best be understood when they are viewed as preventive measures; that is, as rules designed by Congress to prevent certain techniques of tax avoidance. However, remember that any transaction that falls within the scope of a given provision, whether or not it is intended as part of a tax avoidance scheme, is subject to that provision. Thus, a basic knowledge of the tax system is necessary for the tax planner if certain disastrous pitfalls are to be avoided.

As we noted earlier in this chapter, tax planning between related taxpayers often can generate significant tax savings. To be effective for tax purposes, though, the income actually must be earned by the separate entities and not merely assigned by means of artificial transactions. Section 482 gives the IRS the power to reallocate both income and deductions among certain related taxpayers so as to reflect "true taxable income."

In applying § 482, the regulations indicate that the IRS's right to determine true taxable income is not limited to fraudulent or sham transactions but also applies to situations in which income inadvertently has been shifted between controlled parties. The courts have held, however, that there truly must be a "shifting" of income before the IRS's power comes into play. Bona fide business transactions that bring tax advantages in their wake should not subject the related parties to reallocation. In concept, at least, § 482 can be applied by the IRS only where there has been manipulation of income or deductions by the taxpayers.

Thus, while its boundaries are, in practice, both broad and sometimes hazy, § 482 does not prohibit the use of multiple entities for the purpose of earning income. It does, however, give the IRS a potent weapon with which to combat the artificial shifting of income between those entities.

EXAMPLE 12-35

X and Y are two corporations that are fully owned by the same individual. X operates an international airline, and Y owns several hotels that are located in cities served by X. In conjunction with the advertising of its airlines, X often includes pictures of Y's hotels in the airline advertisements. Although the primary benefit of the advertising is to X's airline operations, Y's hotels also obtain patronage by travelers who respond to the ads. X does not charge Y for the advertising. Because an unrelated hotel operator presumably would have been charged for such advertising, the IRS may make an allocation of income from X to Y to reflect the fair market value of the advertising services that were provided.

The kiddie tax was created in 1986 to keep parents from sheltering income by putting accounts in the names of their lower-taxed children. Currently it applies to all children under age 19 and full-time students under age 24. In its original form, a portion of investment earnings held by a child was tax-free. Children can still receive a portion of unearned income tax-free. For 2016, the limit is $1,050, meaning that a child does not have to pay taxes on any interest, dividends, or capital gains up to this amount. The child does have to pay taxes on the next $1,050, but at his or her lower tax rate. Once unearned income exceeds $2,100, however, the preferential treatment ends. The earnings on those excess earnings are taxed at the parent's top marginal tax rate rather than at the child's usually lower tax rate.

Whereas the objective of the kiddie tax may be defensible, the broad provision that was enacted to implement it may create undue hardships in some circumstances because it affects all taxpayers, not only those with the now forbidden income-shifting motivation.

EXAMPLE 12-36

Jimmy, age seven, received an inheritance from his grandmother's estate last year. Grandmother wanted Jimmy to attend college someday, so she invested in securities that produce approximately $10,000 of annual interest income. Jimmy's parents are to see that he accumulates this income for his education. Much of the interest will be taxed at the parents' 40 percent marginal rate, however, and not at Jimmy's lower tax rate, so a smaller after-tax amount of this income will be available for this laudable educational purpose.

5-2 Judicial Tax Traps

In the final analysis, the words of the tax law mean only what the courts say that they mean. Often, judicial decisions must be consulted to determine the allowable limits of various code provisions.

Two pervasive judicial doctrines that often limit the taxpayer's ability to employ effective planning techniques are the concepts of business purpose and substance over form. To be upheld for tax purposes, transactions must possess some nontax, or "business," purpose in addition to that of tax avoidance. Moreover, there is always the possibility that the court may ignore the form of a transaction if it perceives that such structural false colors cloud the actual substance of the arrangement.

Whenever a series of transactions results in significant tax savings, the IRS may attempt to apply the concept of substance over form by collapsing several transactions into one. If it is upheld by a court, this step-transaction doctrine sometimes can negate what had been a good tax plan (where the steps were viewed as separate transactions). To guard against this possibility, the taxpayer should have a bona fide business purpose for each individual step in the transaction. Of course, documenting nontax purposes is usually much easier if the various transactions are separated by reasonable time spans since they are then less likely to be viewed as component parts of an overall plan.

EXAMPLE 12-37

Sandra is the sole shareholder of a real estate development corporation. On January 15, she purchased 10 additional shares of stock from her corporation for $100,000. On the same day, she sold a tract of undeveloped land to the corporation for its fair market value of $100,000. To the corporation, the land will be inventory. For Sandra, it had been a capital asset, having been held for investment purposes since its purchase 10 years previously for $20,000.

If these events are viewed as two separate transactions, Sandra will have increased the basis of her investment in the corporation by $100,000 and realized a fully taxable capital gain of $80,000 ($100,000 minus $20,000). The corporation's basis in the land will be $100,000. Thus, if the corporation were to sell the land for $110,000, for example, its income therefrom would be only $10,000 ($110,000 minus $100,000).

Alternatively, if these events are collapsed into a single transaction, Sandra's payment and receipt of cash would be ignored. Instead, she would be viewed as having given a tract of land in exchange for 10 shares of stock of a corporation that she already controls. Under this single-transaction view, Sandra would recognize no taxable capital gain, and the corporation's basis in the stock would be the same as her prior basis, $20,000.

If the corporation were to sell the land for $110,000, its ordinary income would be $90,000 ($110,000 minus $20,000). Taxpayers are restricted to the actual legal forms of the transactions in which they engage, but the IRS has the option of employing the step-transaction doctrine. Thus, the lack of any time lag between the two transactions effectively gives the IRS its choice as to which interpretation it wishes to follow.

SUMMARY

The study of taxes can be viewed as an examination of various ways to optimize one's tax liability. Tax rules that otherwise might seem as dry as a mouthful of sawdust have a way of becoming interesting, stimulating, and challenging when one realizes their economic significance and the resulting implications for human behavior. Tax optimization, therefore, can be viewed both as the heart of professional tax work and as the most important aspect of taxation for nontax specialists.

KEY WORDS

By the time you complete this chapter, you should be comfortable discussing each of the following terms. If you need additional review of any of these items, return to the appropriate material in the chapter or consult the glossary to this text.

average tax rate, p. 400
effective average tax rate, p. 401
marginal tax rate, p. 400

nominal average tax rate, p. 401
progressive tax rate, p. 400
proportional tax rate, p. 399

regressive tax rate, p. 400

DISCUSSION QUESTIONS

1. How do taxes fit into the general economic goals of most taxpayers?

2. How might a tax adviser ignoring the present-value approach to tax planning arrive at an improper conclusion? Illustrate.

3. Give some examples of U.S. taxes that employ proportional, progressive, and regressive rate structures.

4. Give an example of tax planning between a shareholder/employee and a related corporation.

5. Give one or more examples to show how a taxpayer might take advantage of preferential tax rates on long-term capital gains by structuring transactions to produce capital gains rather than ordinary income.

6. Name two types of tax traps and give an example of each.

7. How does the typical tax practitioner divide his or her time among planning, compliance, research, and litigation?

8. What planning engagements can the tax professional offer? Why is he or she in an ideal position to offer these services?

9. Summarize the most important planning services that a tax professional can offer to a client.

10. Why does tax planning analysis focus on the marginal tax rate?

11. When might a taxpayer undertake transactions seemingly opposite to the usual tax planning principles?

12. Higher-income taxpayers tend to engage in tax planning more than do lower-income taxpayers. Why?

13. Is the objective of tax planning always to minimize taxes? Explain.

EXERCISES

14. Using the following codes, identify the basic approach(es) to tax avoidance that are used in each of the following cases:

    AR Avoiding recognition of taxable income

    CT Changing the timing of recognition of income, gains, deductions, losses, and credits

    CJ Changing tax jurisdictions

    CC Changing the character of income

    RP Tax planning among related taxpayers

   a. Albert invests his savings in tax-exempt state bonds.

   b. Betty invests in non-dividend-paying corporate stocks by using borrowed funds.

   c. Chuck lends $100,000 to his daughter on an interest-free demand note.

   d. Ed invests $100,000 of his savings in a home for his own use.

   e. Frankie invests in a mutual fund that purchases only the indebtedness of the state in which he lives.

15. Using the codes from Exercise 14, identify the basic approach(es) to tax avoidance that are used in each of the following cases:

   a. Retainer Corp. is a U.S.-owned corporation that was incorporated abroad. The U.S. shareholders do not plan to repatriate earnings back to the United States for many years.

   b. Evelyn has her controlled corporation pay her a salary instead of a dividend during the current year.

   c. Georgia grows most of her own food instead of taking a second job.

   d. At retirement, Tom moves from New York (a state with a high income tax) to Florida (a state with no income tax).

16. With respect to the system of coding used in Exercises 14 and 15, create one new illustration in each tax planning category.

PROBLEMS

17. Examples 12-2 and 12-3 in this chapter concern a decision between the same two mutually exclusive alternatives under identical conditions, except for the corporation's marginal tax rate. In Example 12-2, in which the marginal tax rate was 40 percent, the conclusion was to accept Alternative 1. In Example 12-3, in which the marginal tax rate was 25 percent, the conclusion was to accept Alternative 2.

   Determine the marginal tax rate at which the two alternatives would be economic equivalents, that is, they would "break even" and generate the same excess after-tax payoff over after-tax cost. Your answer should be based on all conditions and assumptions stated in Examples 12-2 and 12-3.

18. On creating a new 100 percent-owned corporation, Ben was advised by his tax consultant to treat 50 percent of the total amount that was invested as a loan and 50 percent as a purchase of corporate stock. What tax advantage does this arrangement have over structuring the entire investment as a purchase of stock? Explain.

19. Julia currently is considering the purchase of some land to be held as an investment. She and the seller have agreed on a contract under which Julia would pay $1,000 per month for 60 months, or $60,000 total. The seller, not in the real estate business, acquired the land several years ago by paying $10,000 in cash. Two alternative interpretations of this transaction are (1) a price of $51,726 with 6 percent interest and (2) a price of $39,380 with 18 percent interest. Which interpretation would you expect each party to prefer? Why?

20. George, a high-bracket taxpayer, wishes to shift some of his own taxable income from corporate bonds he owns to his 25-year-old daughter, Debra, so that Debra rather than George is taxed on the interest. One alternative is to make a gift of the interest, and the other is to make a gift of the bonds themselves. Evaluate the pros and cons of each alternative.

21. Assume that a taxpayer can choose when he is to receive $10,000 of fully taxable income. If the taxpayer receives the income at the end of Year 1, he will receive exactly $10,000. If he delays receipt of the income until the end of Year 2, the amount will grow to $11,000. If the taxpayer takes the money at the end of Year 1, he can invest the proceeds and earn a pretax return of 10 percent over the next year.

a. If the taxpayer faces a marginal tax rate of 31 percent in both Year 1 and Year 2, when should he elect to receive the income?

b. At what pretax rate of return will the taxpayer be indifferent to taking the money in Year 1 and Year 2?

c. If the taxpayer's marginal tax rate increases to 35 percent in Year 2, when should he elect to receive the income?

d. What would the tax rate need to be in Year 2 to make the taxpayer indifferent to the alternatives?

22. A taxpayer can invest $10,000 in a taxable 10-year bond that yields an annual pretax return of 6 percent or buy land (a capital asset) for $10,000 that is expected to increase at an annual pretax rate of 4 percent. The taxpayer expects to hold the bond and the land for 10 years and expects to pay capital gains taxes of 20 percent when the land is sold. The taxpayer's marginal tax rate on ordinary income is expected to be 25 percent throughout the 10-year period. Which investment is preferable?

23. Greg Jones lives in Augusta, Georgia, and has the opportunity to rent his condominium during the next Masters golf tournament. He has two offers—one to rent for 10 days at $500 per day and the other to rent for 16 days at $400 per day. Rental expenses will be negligible. What is your advice to Greg?

24. A company has lost money in the past and has a $1.4 million NOL but expects to begin earning money again next year. Assuming future taxable income of $500,000 per year for the next three years, a statutory tax rate of 34 percent, and an after-tax discount rate of 6 percent, what is the company's marginal tax rate during the NOL year if an election is made to carry forward the NOL?

25. In each of the following scenarios should Ferris Corporation elect to forgo the carryback of its $60,000 year 2017 NOL? Ferris is subject to a 16 percent cost of capital. Corporate tax rates are as in IRC § 11.

a.

Tax Year	Actual or Projected Taxable Income
2016	$700,000
2018	$700,000

b.

Tax Year	Actual or Projected Taxable Income
2016	$70,000
2018	$700,000

c.

Tax Year	Actual or Projected Taxable Income
2016	$70,000
2018	($0)
2019	($0)
2020	$700,000

26. In each of the following scenarios should Harris Corporation accelerate $100,000 of gross income into 2017, its first year subject to the AMT? Harris is subject to a 14 percent cost of capital. The corporate AMT rate is a flat 20 percent, and Harris Corporation exceeds the annual AMT exemption phase-out level of income.

a.

Tax Year	Actual or Projected Taxable Income
2018	Regular Tax $700,000
2019	Regular Tax $700,000

b.

Tax Year	Actual or Projected Taxable Income
2018	AMT $700,000
2019	Regular Tax $700,000

c. Tax Year	Actual or Projected Taxable Income
2018	AMT $700,000
2019	AMT $700,000
2020	AMT $700,000
2021	AMT $700,000
2022	Regular Tax $700,000

27. Paris Corporation holds a $100,000 unrealized net capital gain and a capital loss carryforward that will expire in the current year. Paris is subject to a 14 percent cost of capital. Its marginal tax rate is 40 percent. Should Paris accelerate the recognition of this gain from next year to this year, assuming a net capital loss carryforward in each of the following amounts?

    a. $40,000

    b. $10,000

    c. Repeat the computation using the amounts in parts a and b, but this time assume that Paris is subject to a 6 percent cost of capital.

28. Maris Corporation put into service $100,000 of equipment that qualifies for its state's 10 percent research credit. To the extent that the credit is claimed, no cost-recovery deductions are allowed. Maris is subject to a 14 percent cost of capital. If the credit were not claimed, the property would qualify for cost-recovery deductions using a three-year life, straight line with no salvage value, and a half-year convention. The state has a flat income tax rate of 8 percent. What is the net value of the tax credit to Maris Corporation?

29. It is late 2017, and you are a successful executive working in New York for a large company. Tomorrow morning you will have the opportunity to negotiate receiving a $100,000 bonus at the end of the year or an amount of deferred salary in 3 years. Both you and your employer can earn a before-tax rate of return of 10 percent. Your employer's combined federal and state marginal tax rate is 40 percent and is expected to remain constant throughout the 3-year period. Your combined state and federal marginal tax rate is 45 percent. However, you are being transferred to Florida (which does not have an individual income tax) at the beginning of next year. Accordingly, you expect your marginal tax rate to drop to 35 percent in 2018 and remain constant through 2020.

    a. How much deferred salary would your employer be willing to pay you in three years?

    b. How much deferred salary would you be willing to accept from your employer in three years?

    c. What should you do?

30. Rex incurred $8,000 of employment-related meal and entertainment expenses during the year. Rex's employer is trying to determine whether to reimburse Rex directly for the expenses (and claim the $4,000 deduction on its corporate tax return) or to pay him additional salary (in which case Rex would claim the unreimbursed expenses as a miscellaneous itemized deduction on his personal 1040 form). Rex has $5,000 of other miscellaneous itemized deductions and $100,000 of adjusted gross income before any additional salary. Assuming that both Rex and his employer have a 35 percent marginal tax rate, which option is best for the company and for Rex?

CHAPTER 13

Working with the IRS

Isabelle Rozenbaum/PhotoAlto Agency RF Collections/Getty Images

LEARNING OBJECTIVES

- Describe the organizational structure of the IRS and administrative procedures relative to the audit and appeals processes.
- Advise clients as to audit selection factors and probable litigation success.
- Develop decision guidelines as to audit etiquette, working through the appeals system, and constructing taxpayer defenses.
- Explain the application and use of closing agreements and offers in compromise.
- Explain the application of the statutes of limitations as they relate to tax assessments by the IRS and claims for refund by taxpayers.
- Explain rights of taxpayers including client confidentiality privilege accorded to communications between non-attorney accountants and their clients.

CHAPTER OUTLINE

WE HAVE DISCUSSED VARIOUS ASPECTS of tax practice throughout this text, including both the principles of tax research and the structure of the judicial decision-making process. In this chapter we examine in more detail the process of working with the IRS through a better understanding of how tax returns are selected for audit, different types of audits, and the appeals process, with an eye on the opportunities and challenges that face the practitioner in working with the IRS. We also review statutes of limitations and their application to the assessment of taxes by the IRS, requests for refund by taxpayers, as well as requests by the IRS to extend the statute of limitations period. We conclude the chapter with a review of the alternatives and strategies available to taxpayers in making various compromises and agreements with the IRS as a result of the examination process.

1 The Internal Revenue Service

The **Department of the Treasury** is responsible for administering and enforcing the internal revenue laws of the United States. However, most revenue functions and authority have been delegated by the Secretary of the Treasury to the **Commissioner of Internal Revenue**. The commissioner is the chief executive officer of the IRS and is appointed by the President of the United States. The commissioner is responsible for overall planning and for directing, coordinating, and controlling the policies and programs of the IRS.

The IRS is one of approximately a dozen bureaus within the Department of the Treasury. It was established by Congress on July 1, 1862, to meet the government's fiscal needs during the Civil War. At that time, the name of the agency was the Bureau of Internal Revenue. In 1953 the name was changed to the **Internal Revenue Service (IRS)**.

The agency's current mission statement is as follows:

Provide America's taxpayers top quality service by helping them understand and meet their tax responsibilities and by applying the tax law with integrity and fairness to all.

In 2015, the IRS processed almost 240 million returns (most filed electronically) and collected almost $3.3 trillion in tax revenues for the federal government.

1-1 Organization of the IRS

The IRS consists of a national office in Washington, D.C., and a large, decentralized field organization. The IRS organizational chart presented in Exhibit 13-1 illustrates that the IRS is organized to facilitate both the processing of tax returns and the carrying out of its broader goals, using a "shared-services" model like that used by most large businesses.

The IRS's national office is staffed by the office of the Commissioner of Internal Revenue, which includes a deputy commissioner and various chief officers and assistants to

EXHIBIT 13-1: IRS Organizational Chart

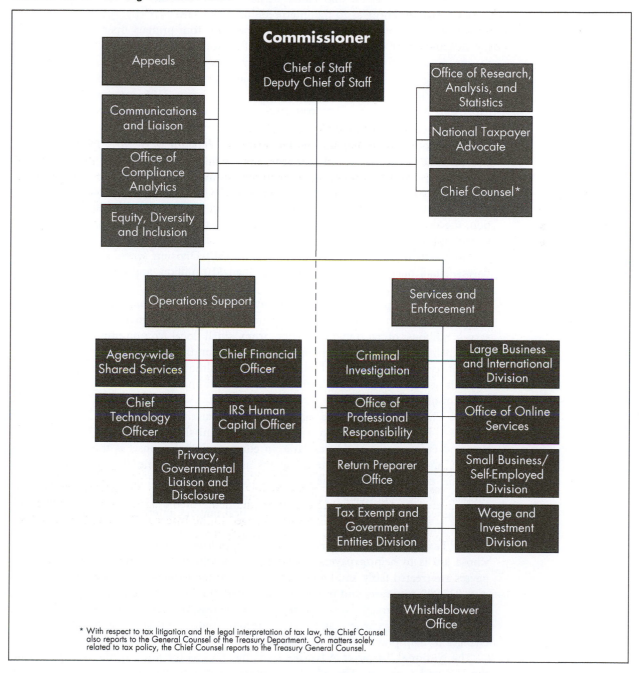

* With respect to tax litigation and the legal interpretation of tax law, the Chief Counsel also reports to the General Counsel of the Treasury Department. On matters solely related to tax policy, the Chief Counsel reports to the Treasury General Counsel.

the commissioner. The IRS commissioner is appointed by the president to a renewable five-year term. He or she is the chief executive officer of the agency and is charged to administer, manage, conduct, direct, and supervise the execution of the federal tax laws.[1] The commissioner's nomination is reviewed by the Senate. He or she advises the

---

[1] IRC § 7803(a).

president as to the person who should be named chief counsel. The commissioner is the agency's final authority as to the interpretation of tax law.

The Deputy Commissioner of the IRS oversees the four primary operating divisions of the IRS and other service and enforcement functions. These operating divisions reflect the major types of tax returns that the agency processes.

The **Wage and Investment (W&I) Division** serves 1040 filers with only wage and investment income (no schedules C, E, or F or Form 2106 for employee business expenses). Most of these filers pay taxes through withholdings, interact with the IRS once a year, and receive refunds.

The **Large Business and International (LB&I) Division** serves C corporations, S corporations, and partnerships with assets of more than $10 million and certain high-wealth individuals. It is organized along six domestic-industry lines: communications, technology and media; financial services; heavy manufacturing and pharmaceutical; natural resources and construction; and retailers, food, transportation, and health care. In addition, the division handles the IRS's international tax compliance efforts, including individual and business compliance issues as well as transfer pricing.

The **Small Business and Self-Employed (SB/SE) Division** serves self-employed taxpayers, small businesses with assets of less than $10 million, and filers of employment, excise, estate, and gift returns.

The **Tax Exempt and Government Entities (TEGE) Division** comprises three business divisions: employee plans, exempt organizations, and governmental entities. It serves millions of customers, ranging from small local community nonprofits and municipalities to major universities, huge pension funds, state governments, and participants in complex tax-exempt bond transactions. Although generally paying no income tax, this sector does pay employment taxes and withholds income and other taxes on behalf of others.

The **Chief Counsel** is the agency's highest ranking legal adviser. He or she is appointed by the president and reports to the commissioner concerning the administration and enforcement of the tax laws. In effect, the chief counsel is the IRS's attorney. Rulings and other written determinations are prepared by the chief counsel's office.[2] The chief counsel represents the agency in Tax Court cases and often assists in preparing proposed legislation, treaties, regulations, and executive orders. Associate chief counsels are assigned duties relating to litigation, technical matters, international transactions, and finance and management.

The **Taxpayer Advocate Service (TAS)** is an independent organization within the IRS whose job is to help taxpayers resolve problems with the IRS and to ensure that taxpayers are treated fairly and know and understand their rights. In 2015 alone, it received over 227,000 new cases and provided at least partial relief in more than 78 percent of the cases it closed. Through its annual report to Congress, the TAS also notes problems and issues affecting taxpayers and makes recommended legislative and administrative changes to help prevent those problems.

The **National Taxpayer Advocate** leads the TAS as the voice of the taxpayer before the IRS and Congress. The advocate reports directly to the commissioner and works through a system of local taxpayer advocates who are independent from IRS examination, collection, and appeals functions. They are responsible only to the National Taxpayer Advocate.

The system is designed to help resolve taxpayer problems or complaints that are not being satisfied through regular agency channels. The primary objective of the advocate

---

[2]IRC § 7803(b).

system is to provide taxpayers with a representative within the IRS who has access to the pertinent regional, district, or service center official. In addition, the program enables the IRS to identify its own organizational, procedural, and systemic problems and to take corrective action as needed.

The system is not intended to circumvent the existing IRS channels of managerial authority, established administrative procedures, and formal avenues of appeal. Rather, it is designed to ensure that taxpayer problems or complaints that have not been resolved adequately through normal procedures are referred and controlled within the program. When a case is referred to a member of the National Taxpayer Advocate team, he or she will ensure that the problem is not lost or overlooked and that it is resolved as promptly and efficiently as possible. Typically, the advocate system is used to resolve billing, procedural, computer-generated, and other problems that taxpayers cannot correct after one or more contacts with the IRS office that is handling the matter.

The National Taxpayer Advocate can issue a **taxpayer assistance order (TAO)** to suspend, delay, or stop actions in which, in the advocate's determination, the taxpayer is suffering or about to suffer a significant hardship as a result of the manner in which the IRS is administering the revenue laws.[3] "Hardships" refer to any circumstance that includes an immediate threat of adverse action for the taxpayer, his or her irreparable injury, a delay of more than 30 days in settling the taxpayer's account, or the incurring of significant costs (such as professional advisory fees) to handle the dispute.[4] The IRS action that is the subject of a TAO must be such that it would offend a person's sense of fairness, given all the related facts.

Typically, a TAO requires remedial actions, such as a release from the IRS's levy of specific property or the cessation of a collection activity, or it gives the IRS a deadline for action. A TAO is binding on the IRS, short of its rescission by the advocate, the commissioner, or a deputy commissioner.

A taxpayer applies for a TAO by filing Form 911, Request for Taxpayer Advocate Service Assistance.

SPOTLIGHT ON TAXATION

Taxpayer Advocate Service—Facts

- In 2015, 236 TAOs were issued by the Taxpayer Advocate Service.
- Identity-theft issues account for almost one fourth of new cases handled by the Taxpayer Advocate Service.

Private-sector input to the IRS is provided through the **IRS Oversight Board**, which functions as part of the Treasury Department. Its major duties include the following[5]:

- Review and approve the IRS's mission, strategic plans, and annual planning documents.

- Review IRS operational functions, including modernization, outsourcing, and training efforts.

- Recommend to the president candidates for commissioner.

---

[3]IRC § 7811.

[4]IRC § 7811(a)(2).

[5]IRC § 7802.

- Review the process of selecting, evaluating, and compensating senior IRS executives.

- Review and approve the IRS annual budget request.

- Ensure the proper treatment of taxpayers.

The board is designed to function like a corporate board of directors. It is made up of six members of the private sector, appointed to five-year terms by the president, and of the Treasury Secretary, the IRS Commissioner, and a representative of IRS employees. The board has no authority to affect tax policy, intervene in IRS personnel or procurement matters, or affect the processing of individual tax cases.

2 The Audit Process

The U.S. federal income tax system is based primarily on an assumption of self-compliance. All persons with taxable incomes that exceed a specific amount are required to prepare an accurate statement of annual income (i.e., an income tax return) and to remit in a timely fashion any amount of tax that is due. The IRS uses the examination of returns as an enforcement device to promote such voluntary compliance with the internal revenue laws. The threat of an IRS audit encourages many taxpayers to accurately report their taxable incomes and to pay any tax liability that remains outstanding.

Because only a small number of tax returns can be audited each year, the IRS attempts to select for examination only those returns that will generate additional revenues for the Treasury. It relies primarily on sophisticated statistical models and computer technology to identify those returns that possess the greatest revenue return for the agency's investment of audit resources. In addition to this scientific selection process, however, many returns are manually selected for examination at an examiner's discretion.

2-1 Preliminary Review of Returns

All business and individual tax returns are reviewed routinely by IRS personnel and computers for simple and obvious errors, such as the omission of required signatures and Social Security numbers. After this initial review, income tax returns are processed through an automatic data-processing system.

One of the most important functions performed by this system is the matching of the information recorded on a return with corresponding data received from third parties, for instance, from an employer on Form W-2. This procedure, which is referred to as the Information Document Matching Program (IDMP), has uncovered millions of discrepancies between the amount of income and deductions that recipients have reported on tax returns and corresponding amounts that have been transmitted by third parties. In addition, the IDMP provides the IRS with a means by which to detect taxpayers who fail to file any return at all.

2-1a Mathematical/Clerical Error Program
The **mathematical/clerical error program** is one of several special programs that are conducted by IRS computers. This program checks every return for mathematical errors, recomputes the tax due after properly applying the numbers that are included in the return, and summarily assesses any additional tax that is due or allows refunds or credits based on (previously) miscomputed deductions or credits. A summary assessment may be made concerning any deficiency that results from a mathematical or clerical error.[6] Consequently, the IRS need not send

---

[6]IRC § 6213(b)(1).

the taxpayer a formal notice of deficiency (i.e., a 90-day letter, as discussed subsequently in this chapter) before the additional tax is assessed.

SPOTLIGHT ON TAXATION

Mathematical Errors on Tax Returns

While the number of routine mathematical errors has declined sharply due to increases in electronic filing, in 2015 the IRS sent out more than 1.6 million notices identifying 2,177,802 math errors on 2014 returns. In addition to computational errors, the program also includes incorrectly transcribed values and omitted entries. The program encompasses more than a dozen types of errors, such as incorrect tax calculations, incorrect numbers of or amounts for exemptions, errors with credits such as the earned-income tax credit, child tax credit, and higher-education credits, errors in claiming itemized deductions or the standard deduction, and errors in calculating the amount of refund due or amount owed to the IRS. In 2015, the most common error was associated with the calculation of various taxes including income tax, the alternative minimum tax, and the self-employment tax.

Source: Internal Revenue Service Data Book, 2015.

When a mathematical or clerical error is identified by the service center, the IRS mails the taxpayer a corrected tax computation and requests that he or she pay the additional tax within 10 days after the date of the notice, or 21 days if the tax underpayment is less than $100,000. If the deficiency is paid within this period, no interest is charged on the underpayment. If the deficiency is not paid in a timely fashion, however, interest is imposed on the unpaid amount for a period that begins on the date of the notice and demand and ends on the date of payment.

A taxpayer may not petition the U.S. Tax Court with respect to a deficiency that results from a mathematical or clerical error. However, other administrative procedures will allow the taxpayer to contest the summary assessment without first paying the tax.

The IRS must give an explanation of the asserted error to the taxpayer. After receiving this explanation, the taxpayer has 60 days within which to request that the additional tax be abated. If a request for abatement is made, the assessment will be canceled automatically. However, the return is then identified for further examination if the taxpayer cannot justify satisfactorily or substantiate the figures that were included on the original return.

When an error results in a taxpayer overpayment of a tax, the IRS usually sends a corrected computation of the tax, together with a brief explanation of the error and a refund of the excess amount that was paid.

The IRS does not consider such a contact that it makes with the taxpayer to be an examination. Therefore, a taxpayer who is contacted under the mathematical/clerical error program is not entitled to the administrative remedies that are available to taxpayers who are involved in a formal examination.

2-1b Unallowable Items Program The IRS conducts another program, similar to the mathematical/clerical error program, called the unallowable items program. Under this program, IRS personnel question items on individual income tax returns that appear to be unallowable by law. These items include such return elements as an overstatement of the standard deduction, a deduction of Social Security taxes paid, the claiming of an incorrect filing status, the deduction of federal income taxes, and the deduction of lost (but not stolen) assets as a casualty loss.

If a return is identified as including an unallowable item, the IRS computes the seemingly necessary adjustment in taxes and notifies the taxpayer by mail. Again, the IRS does not consider the contact that it makes with a taxpayer under the unallowable items program to be an examination.[7] Consequently, it treats an adjustment in this circumstance as a correction of a mathematical or clerical error and does not send the taxpayer a formal notice of deficiency.

If the taxpayer is able to explain the questioned item adequately, the assessment is abated. However, the case will be continued as a correspondence or office audit if the taxpayer's response is deemed unsatisfactory.

2-2 Selection of Returns for Examination

Each year, the IRS determines the approximate number and types of returns that it intends to audit. The national office then prepares an audit plan to allocate its personnel to achieve the desired audit coverage. The IRS's primary goal in selecting a return for examination is to review only those returns that will result in a satisfactory increase in the tax liability.

Computerized and manual methods are used to select returns for examination. Computer programs select certain returns for examination, based on the potential that exists for changes in the tax treatment of certain items on the return. Generally, this is done through the use of mathematical models, including correlations and discriminant functions. IRS personnel also manually select returns that they believe warrant special attention. The IRS describes in nontechnical terms its selection procedures in its annual Publication 1. Selection criteria for audits are not disclosed by the Treasury.[8]

Although most of the initial IRS screening of returns for audit is performed by computers, next a more detailed selection procedure is employed manually in the Examination Division of the local IRS office, where the classification staff ultimately selects specific cases to be examined. The number of returns finally selected by the staff is based on the examination resource (and other) capabilities of the respective offices.

2-2a Discriminant Function System   Once a return has been processed through the IRS automated program, each return is rated by computer for its audit potential by means of a mathematical model, the **discriminant function formula (DIF)**. This formula assigns numeric weights to certain (undisclosed by the IRS) return items, generating a composite score for the return. The higher the DIF score, the greater is the potential for additional tax payments upon audit. Statistics provided by the commissioner show a high correlation between DIF scores and such tax modifications, but the specifics of the formula are not disclosed.[9]

When the computer selects a return that has a high probability for an adjustment, as indicated by a high DIF score, an employee at the service center manually inspects the return to confirm its audit potential. If an acceptable explanation for the DIF score cannot be found after this manual examination of the return and its attachments, including explanatory data that the computer did not consider, the return is forwarded to the examination division at the appropriate local IRS office.

---

[7]Rev. Proc. 94-68, 1994-2 C.B. 803.

[8]IRC § 6103(b)(2); *Long v. U.S.,* 742 F.2d 1173 (CA-9, 1984).

[9]*Feltz v. IRS,* 79 A.F.T.R.2d 97-747 (W.D. Wis. 1997).

2-2b National Research Program The **National Research Program (NRP)** is an initiative designed to furnish the IRS with statistics concerning the type and number of errors that are made on a representative sample of individual income tax returns. These statistics are used to develop and update the DIF formulas. Under the annual NRP procedures, perhaps 15,000 individual income tax returns are selected randomly for an extremely thorough examination. These returns then are examined comprehensively to determine the degree of their accuracy as filed.

Unlike the treatment given to returns that are selected for general audit, the NRP examiner may not exercise any judgment in dealing with an item on the return selected for review. All errors are noted and corrected, regardless of their amount. This procedure is necessary to a determination of the actual error patterns that individual income tax returns exhibit so that the statistics that underlie the DIF procedure are free from any major bias.

NRP audits integrate IRS data files with some of those from the Social Security Administration and the Census Bureau. Some of the NRP audits are transparent to the taxpayer. That is, all the work is done with computer models and by IRS personnel, and the taxpayer does not even know that the audit is being conducted. Most of the rest of the procedures require correspondence by mail with the taxpayer, with no in-person contact required. Taxpayers whose returns are audited and require such in-person contact likely will need professional assistance to meet the IRS data and documentation demands.

2-2c Other Selection Methods In addition to the previously discussed methods for the identification of returns for IRS examination, returns may be selected for a variety of other reasons. For example, returns may be selected for audit when they involve issues or transactions with related taxpayers or other entities, such as business partners or investors, whose returns were selected for examination. For example, a partner's return may be selected as a result of a partnership audit.

An examination may be initiated because of information that is provided by an informant. Moreover, some returns are reviewed automatically by IRS personnel because the reported taxable income, gross receipts, or total assets exceed a predetermined materiality amount. For instance, almost all estate tax returns with gross estates in excess of $10 million are selected for audit. A return may be selected for examination because the taxpayer has filed a claim for refund or otherwise has indicated that an adjustment in the original amount of tax liability is necessary. Finally, area offices may identify returns for audit based on specific local issues or market segments.

"Economic-reality" factors can be considered by the IRS in the selection of returns for audit, but only in situations in which the agency has some other evidence that the taxpayer has underreported taxable income for the year. For instance, manual selection of a return and an economic-reality review might occur when an IRS employee, reviewing data in three consecutive filing periods, finds indications that income might be underreported or deductions might be overstated or misclassified. Some of the factors believed to be perused in an economic-reality audit include the following:

- Significant increases in interest, dividend, and other investment income.

- Significant decreases in mortgage and other reportable interest paid.

- Significant variance in self-employment or farming income during the period relative to industry norms.

- Business and other expenditures not seemingly justified by income levels.

SPOTLIGHT ON TAXATION

Audit Techniques Guides (ATGs)

The Market Segment Specialization Program (MSSP) produces Audit Techniques Guides that assist both examiners and taxpayers. These guides provide the taxpayer insight into issues and accounting methods unique to specific industries. Further, they provide examples of income examination techniques, interview techniques, and approaches used to evaluate evidence. If there are ATGs for your industry, they are must reads prior to any audit.

2-2d Chances of Audit   Taxpayers often want to know their overall probability of selection for an audit for a given year. In general, the IRS selects approximately 1 percent of all returns for examination, outside of the mathematical error program. As can be seen in Exhibit 13-2, the chances of audit vary greatly for different types of tax returns and different size taxpaying entities.

EXHIBIT 13-2:   Various Audit Statistics

Type of Return	Changes of Audit
Individual Income Tax Returns	**0.8%**
Nonbusiness returns with income under $200,000 (without earned-income tax credit and without schedules C, E, or F or Form 2106)	0.3%
Nonbusiness returns with income between $200,000 and $1 million	1.8%
Business returns without earned-income tax credit and gross receipts under $25,000	0.9%
Business returns with income between $200,000 and $1 million	2.9%
All returns (business and nonbusiness) with income of $1 million or more	9.6%
Corporate Income Tax Returns (except Form 1120-S)	**1.3%**
Small corporations with under $250,000 of total assets	0.9%
Large corporations with over $20 million of total assets	64.0%
Estate Tax Returns	**7.8%**
Under $5 million gross estate	2.1%
Between $5 and $10 million gross estate	16.2%
Partnership Returns	**0.5%**
S Corporation Returns	**0.4%**

Source: Internal Revenue Service Data Book, 2015.

3 Examinations

After a return is selected for audit, an IRS agent schedules it for a review in a correspondence, office, or field examination. The type of examination to which the taxpayer is subject generally is determined by the audit potential of the return, the nature of the asserted error, and the type of taxpayer.

3-1 Correspondence Examinations

Many times, IRS personnel question only one or two items on a selected return. In these cases, an examination is typically conducted by mail through a **correspondence examination**. The IRS examiner requests that the taxpayer verify the questioned item of income, deduction, or credit by mailing copies of receipts, canceled checks, or other documentation to the district office or service center. If the taxpayer requests an interview, the issues become too complex, or the taxpayer is unable to communicate effectively in writing, the case is referred to the appropriate district office for resolution as an office or field examination.

Issues that typically are addressed in the correspondence audit setting include itemized deductions for interest, taxes, charitable contributions, medical expenses, and simple miscellaneous deductions such as union dues.

A taxpayer who is subject to a correspondence examination is entitled to the same administrative and judicial appeal rights that are allowed to those who are involved in office or field audits.

3-2 Office Examinations

When a return that has been selected for examination involves one or more issues that will require some analysis and the exercise of the IRS personnel's judgment, rather than a mere verification of record-keeping requirements, the audit usually is conducted at the pertinent IRS office. An **office examination** also will be scheduled if the examiner believes that an office examination is necessary to guarantee that the taxpayer's legal rights are respected.

If the IRS decides to conduct an office examination, the taxpayer is asked to come to the local IRS office for an interview and to bring any records and documents that support the questioned items. Generally, the auditor is given very little time in which to prepare for the session, and the scope of the examination is limited to the items that are listed in the audit notification letter.

Office audits usually are confined to individuals' income tax returns that include no business income. In recent years, however, the IRS has increased the scope of some office audits to include a limited number of small-business returns. Issues that typically are examined in an office-audit setting include dependency exemptions; income from tips, rents, and royalties; income from partnerships, estates, and trusts; deductions for travel and entertainment; deductions for bad debts; and casualty and theft losses.

A field examination may be conducted in lieu of an office audit if it is difficult for the taxpayer to bring the requested records to the district office or if the taxpayer for some other valid reason requests that the audit be conducted on his or her premises or the representative's office.

3-3 Field Examinations

Examinations that present complex issues that require more advanced knowledge of the internal revenue laws and accounting skills usually are conducted at the taxpayer's home, place of business, or accountant's office. A **field examination** is more comprehensive than a correspondence or office audit, and it usually is limited to an examination of corporation and individual business returns. In a field examination, the revenue agent completely reviews the entire financial operations of the taxpayer, including the taxpayer's business history; the nature, amount, and location of taxpayer assets; the nature of the business operations; the extant accounting methods and system of internal control; and other financial attributes of the entity.

While an office audit ordinarily is limited to the items that are specified in the audit notification letter, a field examination may be open-ended. The agent is free to pursue any unusual items that are recorded in the tax return(s) or the records of the taxpayer (i.e., journals, ledgers, and worksheets) and to investigate other areas about which he or she may be suspicious.

The IRS prefers to conduct the field audit on the taxpayer's premises because the taxpayer's books and records may be more accessible and the agent is better able to observe the taxpayer's business facilities and the scope of its operations. However, it is sometimes possible to have the audit conducted at the office of the taxpayer's representative instead. Only one such inspection of taxpayer books and records may be made for a tax year.[10] The IRC includes a broad set of restrictions regarding access to the taxpayer's physical office by the IRS.[11] Taxpayers refusing to admit IRS personnel are subject to a $500 fine.[12]

SPOTLIGHT ON TAXATION

Virtual Audits

The IRS is testing technology that would allow taxpayers to bring documentation to a local IRS office and see their correspondence exam auditor virtually using a webcam and video-conferencing software. This would allow a taxpayer to provide documentation to the IRS, which could then determine in real time if it is sufficient.

3-4 Dealing with an Auditor

Most practitioners develop over time a list of "dos and don'ts" for negotiating with a government auditor. In the very best case, one will have dealt with the same auditor many times and will have become familiar with the nuances of that particular auditor's mode of operation. Whether or not this is the case, the following guidelines, dictated as much by common courtesy and decorum as by ethics and hardcore negotiating techniques, are likely to be useful:[13]

- Do conduct yourself courteously and professionally, showing that you have prepared yourself for the audit.

- Do review the strengths and weaknesses of your position before the agent arrives.

- Do cooperate with the auditor and promptly respond to all requests.

- Do establish internal timetables and responsibilities for completing the audit.

---

[10]IRC § 7605(b).

[11]IRC § 7606.

[12]IRC § 7342.

[13]Some of the material is adapted from a talk entitled "The Audit Process," by Robert E. Dallman, Milwaukee, Wisconsin.

- Do provide the auditor with adequate work accommodations.

- Do not impede the audit process.

- Do not allow the auditor free access to and through the taxpayer's building.

- Do not let the agent browse through taxpayer information.

- Do not volunteer comments or information not requested by the agent.

- Do not attempt to bully or intimidate the auditor.

- Do assign one person to be the primary on-premises contact with the auditor—he or she cannot interview taxpayer employees on a random basis.

- Do verify the auditor's credentials before providing any information.

- Do request that all communications be in writing.

- Do keep track of time spent (by taxpayer, practitioner, and auditor) on the audit.

- Do meet at least daily with the auditor to review issues.

- Do agree to disagree on major irreconcilable issues.

- Do conduct a concluding conference to discuss audit recommendations.

- Do obtain copies of all governmental work papers affecting the potential assessment.

- Do request clarification on the rest of the appeals process.

3-5 Conclusion of Examination

Upon conclusion of the examination, the IRS auditor or agent must explain to the taxpayer any proposed adjustments to the tax liability. A written **revenue agent's report (RAR)** is prepared by the agent and is given to the taxpayer. The RAR is important to the taxpayer and the preparer because it explains with code sections, and/or case law, the rationale for the position of the IRS. This report allows the taxpayer and preparer to understand why the IRS has taken its position. The RAR contains a brief explanation of the proposed adjustments and lists the balance due or the overpayment. A deficiency action results when a tax return is audited and the IRS determines that there is a deficiency in tax paid. As noted in Exhibit 13-3, at any stage in the process, the taxpayer can pay the deficiency and file a claim for refund. If the taxpayer disagrees with the RAR, they are given a 30-day letter (discussed later in the chapter) and must then file a protest. In Exhibit 13-3, note that the case goes to the Appeals Office after a protest is filed. As discussed later, the Appeals Office has complete authority to settle the case.

The RAR also includes a waiver of the restrictions on assessment (Form 870), which the taxpayer is asked to sign if he or she agrees with the proposed modifications. This waiver permits the IRS to assess any deficiency in tax immediately without sending the taxpayer a formal notice of deficiency. This means that the taxpayer cannot go to the U.S. Tax Court to dispute the tax.

Even though the taxpayer may agree with the proposed adjustments to his or her return and sign the form, thereby indicating acceptance of the proposal, the case technically is not closed until the agent's report is reviewed and accepted by the district office review staff. Therefore, it is possible that an agreement that is worked out with the agent might not be accepted by the IRS.

EXHIBIT 13-3: Income Tax Appeal Procedure

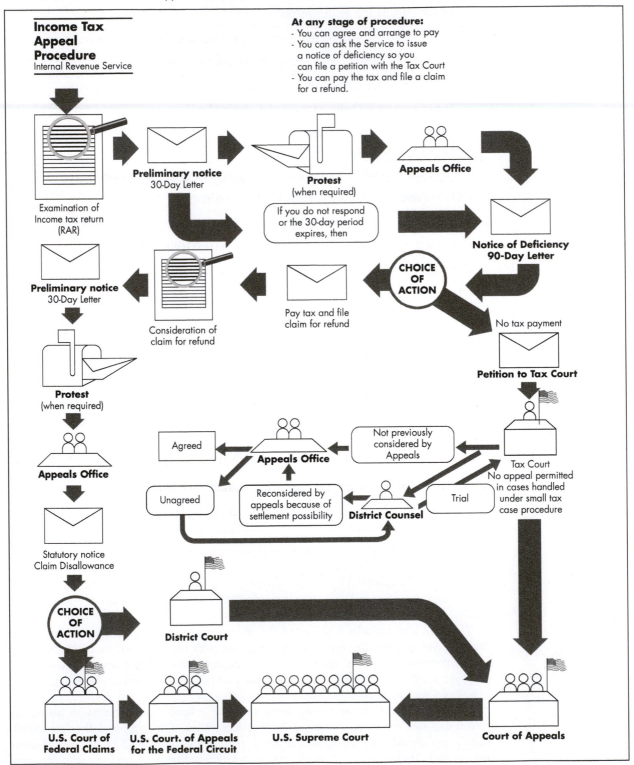

After the taxpayer agrees to any increase in tax, he or she may either make an advance payment of the deficiency and accrued interest (to eliminate additional interest charges) or wait for a formal request for payment from the service center.

If the taxpayer disagrees with the agent's proposals, the IRS makes an immediate attempt to resolve the disagreement. The taxpayer normally is given an opportunity to discuss the proposed adjustments with the agent's group supervisor or with an appeals officer. If an immediate interview is not possible or if the issues remain unresolved after such an interview, the taxpayer receives a preliminary notice of deficiency, which is also referred to as a 30-day letter.

3-6 30-Day Letter

In situations in which the taxpayer does not agree with the agent's proposed adjustments, a **30-day letter** is issued. This correspondence formally notifies the taxpayer of the examiner's findings, requests that the taxpayer agree to the proposed adjustments, and informs the taxpayer of his or her appeal rights. If the taxpayer does not respond to the notice within 30 days, he or she receives a **statutory notice of deficiency**, also known as a **90-day letter**, discussed later in this chapter.

The taxpayer has 30 days from the date of the 30-day letter to request a conference with an appeals officer. This request may be made orally with respect to an office examination or if the total proposed additional tax and penalties total $2,500 or less. The taxpayer's appeal must be in writing if the total proposed additional tax and penalties exceed $2,500,[14] and a formal protest, setting forth the specific facts and applicable law or other authority in support of the taxpayer's position, is required if the proposed tax and penalties exceed $10,000.[15]

3-7 File a Protest or Go Straight to Court?

In deciding whether to file a protest and request a hearing in the Appeals Office or to allow a 90-day letter to be issued and skip directly to the courts for satisfaction, the taxpayer and his or her adviser must consider a number of factors.[16]

3-7a Factors in Favor of the Protest/Appeals Process

- An appeals officer can consider the hazards of litigation. This allows for the possibility of a settlement without the costs of litigation.

- The litigation path remains a possibility even if an appeal is pursued.

- The appeals process allows a further delay in the payment of the disputed tax. This criterion can be important if funds are not available with which to pay the tax or if the taxpayer can earn more on the funds during the administrative period than will be assessed in the form of interest.

- During the appeals process, the taxpayer will discover more of the elements of the government's position. In addition, the taxpayer gains additional time in which to formulate or polish his or her own position.

---

[14]Reg. §§ 601.105(c)(2)(iii), 601.105(d)(2)(iv).

[15]Reg. §§ 601.105(d)(2), 601.106(a)(1)(ii).

[16]Saltzman, *IRS Practice and Procedure,* Warren, Gorham & Lamont; ¶ 9.05(1).

- Recovery of some court costs and attorney fees is available if the court finds that the government's case was largely unjustified and all administrative remedies were attempted. Thus, working through the appeals process is required if any costs are to be recovered.

3-7b Factors in Favor of Bypassing Appeals

- The likelihood of the government finding and raising new issues during the appeal is eliminated.

- The government receives a psychological message that the taxpayer is firmly convinced of his or her position, and negotiating advantages for the taxpayer may result.

- The conclusion of the dispute, whether for or against the taxpayer, is expedited.

4 The Appeals Process

To minimize the costs of litigation in both time and money, the IRS encourages the resolution of tax disputes through an administrative appeals process. If a case cannot be resolved at the examination level, the taxpayer is allowed to appeal to a separate division of the IRS, known as the **Appeals Office**.

The Appeals Office has the exclusive and final authority to settle cases that originate in a district that is located within its jurisdiction. This division is under the supervision of the commissioner of the IRS, with input from the chief counsel. The appeals function provides the taxpayer with a final opportunity to resolve tax disputes with the IRS without incurring litigation costs. Its objective is to resolve tax controversies without litigation on a basis that is fair and impartial to both the government and the taxpayer. This broad authority allows the appeals officer to settle a case based on an evaluation of the "hazards of litigation," that is, the chance that if the case goes to court, the government will prevail. This expanded authority permits the appeals officer to look at evidentiary issues, witness availability, the credibility of witnesses, and various arguments of law.

4-1 Appeals Conference

The conference with the appeals officer is an informal proceeding. Although the appeals office may require allegations to be submitted in the form of affidavits or declarations under penalty of perjury, testimony typically is not taken under oath.[17] The taxpayer, or his or her representative, meets with the appeals officer and discusses the dispute informally. According to the IRS's conference and practice rules, the appeals officer is to maintain a standard of strict impartiality toward the taxpayer and the government.

The appeals officer has the authority to settle all factual and legal questions that are raised in the examiner's report. He or she also can settle a tax dispute on the basis of the hazards of litigation. However, no settlement can be made that is based on the nuisance value of the case to the government.

The appeals officer may use a considerable amount of personal judgment in deciding how to handle the disputed issues of a case. He or she can split or trade issues when substantial uncertainties exist as to the law or the facts. On the other hand, the appeals officer may defer action on, or refuse to settle, a case or an issue to achieve greater uniformity concerning the application of the revenue laws and to improve the overall

---

[17]Reg. § 601.106(c).

voluntary compliance with the tax laws. If a settlement is reached, Form 870-AD is typically signed by both parties reflecting the terms of the agreement. While not technically a closing agreement (see page 446), once signed by the commissioner of the IRS or his or her designee, it is considered binding on both parties. Absent fraud, malfeasance, concealment, or misrepresentation of a material fact, the IRS will not reopen the case. At the same time, the taxpayer is precluded from suing for an additional refund.

4-2 90-Day Letter

If the taxpayer and the IRS cannot agree on the proposed adjustments after an appeals conference, the regional director of appeals will issue a statutory notice of deficiency.[18] The statutory notice also is issued if the taxpayer does not request an appeals conference.

A statutory notice of deficiency, commonly referred to as a 90-day letter, must be sent to the taxpayer's last known address by certified or registered mail before the IRS can assess the additional taxes that it believes are due.[19] Once a formal assessment has been made, the IRS is entitled to collect and retain the tax. However, a statutory notice is not required relative to deficiencies that result from mathematical errors or from the overstatement of taxes that were withheld or paid as estimated taxes.

After the statutory notice of deficiency is mailed, the taxpayer has 90 days (150 days if the letter is addressed to a taxpayer who is outside the United States) to file a petition with the U.S. Tax Court for a redetermination of the deficiency. If such a petition is not filed in a timely fashion, the deficiency is assessed and the taxpayer receives a notice and demand for payment of the tax.[20] Once this 90-day period expires, the taxpayer cannot contest the assessment without first paying the tax, filing a claim for refund, and, if the IRS denies the claim, instituting a refund suit in a district court or the U.S. Court of Federal Claims within two years of the payment date. Generally, no assessment or collection effort may be made during the 90-day period, or, if a Tax Court petition is filed, until after the decision becomes final.

A mailing of the statutory notice to the taxpayer's last known address is sufficient to commence the running of the 90-day period, unless the commissioner has been notified formally of a change of address.[21] The statute does not require that the taxpayer receive actual notice; therefore, a notice that is sent by certified or registered mail to the proper address is effective even though it is never actually received by the taxpayer.[22]

After a case has been scheduled (docketed) for review in the Tax Court, the taxpayer is invited to attend a pretrial settlement conference with an appeals officer and an IRS attorney. However, this conference typically is offered only if the case was not considered previously by the appeals office and if no related criminal prosecution is pending.

If the taxpayer and the IRS agree to settle the dispute at this stage, they will enter into a written agreement stipulating the amount of any deficiency or overpayment. This stipulation is filed with the Tax Court, which will enter a decision in accordance with the agreement. The Tax Court can levy a penalty of up to $25,000 if it determines that the taxpayer unreasonably did not pursue the available administrative remedies prior to approaching the court.[23]

---

[18]IRC § 7522.

[19]IRC § 6212(a), § 6212(b)(1).

[20]IRC § 6213(c).

[21]IRC § 6212(b); *McIntosh v. U.S.,* 85 A.F.T.R.2d 98-6501 (S.D. Ohio).

[22]IRC § 6212(a); *Lifter,* 59 T.C. 818 (1973); *U.S. v. Ahrens,* 530 F.2d 781 (CA-8, 1976).

[23]IRC § 6673(a)(1)(c).

Exhibits 13-4 and 13-5 offer sample 30-day and 90-day letters for the reader's perusal.

EXHIBIT 13-4: Sample 30-Day Letter

Notice of Adjustment—30-Day Letter

IRS Department of the Treasury

Date:

Social Security or Employee Identification Number:

Tax Year Ended:

Person to Contact:

Contact Telephone Number:

Contact Address:

Dear: _____.

Enclosed are two copies of our report explaining why we believe adjustments should be made in the amount of your tax. Please look over this report and let us know whether you agree with our findings.

If you accept our findings, please sign the consent to assessment and collection portion at the bottom of the report and mail one copy to this office within 30 days from the date of this letter. If additional tax is due, you might want to pay it now and limit the interest charge; otherwise, we will bill you. (See the enclosed Publication 5 for payment details.)

If you do not accept our findings, you have 30 days from the date of this letter to do one of the following:

- Mail us any additional evidence or information you would like us to consider.

- Request a discussion of our findings with the examiner who conducted the examination. At that time you may submit any additional evidence or information you would like us to consider. If you plan to come in for a discussion, please phone or write us in advance so that we can arrange a convenient time and place.

- Discuss your position with the group manager or a senior examiner (designated by the group manager), if an examination has been held and you have been unable to reach an agreement with the examiner.

If you do not accept our findings and do not want to take any of the above actions, you may write us at the address shown above or call us at the telephone number shown above within 30 days from the date of this letter to request a conference with an Appeals Officer. You must provide to the examiner all pertinent documentation and facts concerning disputed issues before your case is forwarded to the Appeals Office. If your examination was conducted entirely by mail, we would appreciate your first discussing our findings with one of our examiners.

The Appeals Office is independent of the District Director. The Appeals Officer, who had not examined your return previously, will take a fresh look at your case. Most disputes considered by Appeals are resolved informally and promptly. By going to Appeals, you may avoid court costs (such as the U.S. Tax Court filing fee), clear up this matter sooner, and prevent interest from mounting. An Appeals Officer will promptly telephone you and, if necessary, arrange an appointment. If you decide to bypass Appeals and petition the Tax Court, your case will normally be assigned for settlement to an Appeals Office before the Tax Court hears the case.

Under Internal Revenue Code section 6673, the Tax Court is authorized to award damages of up to $25,000 to the United States when a taxpayer unreasonably fails to pursue available administrative remedies. Damages could be awarded under this provision, for example, if the court concludes that it was unreasonable for a taxpayer to bypass Appeals and then file a petition in the Tax Court. The Tax Court will make that determination based upon the facts and circumstances of each case. Generally, the Service will not ask the court to award damages under this provision if you make a good faith effort to meet with Appeals and to settle your case before petitioning the Tax Court.

The enclosed Publication 5 explains your appeal rights.

If we do not hear from you within 30 days, we will have to process your case on the basis of the adjustments shown in the examination report. If you write us about your case, please write to the person whose name and address are shown in the heading of this letter and refer to the symbols in the upper right corner of the enclosed report. An envelope is enclosed for your convenience. Please include your telephone number, area code, and the most convenient time for us to call, in case we find it necessary to contact you for further information.

If you prefer, you may call the person at the telephone number shown in the heading of this letter. This person will be able to answer any questions you may have.

Thank you for your cooperation.

Sincerely yours,
IRS Examinations

Enclosures:
Examination Report (2)
Publication 5
Envelope

EXHIBIT 13-5: Sample 90-Day Letter

Notice of Deficiency—90-Day Letter

IRS Department of the Treasury

Date:

Social Security or Employer Identification Number:

Tax Year Ended and Deficiency:

Person to Contact:

Contact Telephone Number:

Dear: ___.

We have determined that there is a deficiency (increase) in your income tax as shown above. This letter is a NOTICE OF DEFICIENCY sent to you as required by law. The enclosed statement shows how we figured the deficiency.

If you want to contest this deficiency in court before making any payment, you have 90 days from the above mailing date of this letter (150 days if addressed to you outside of the United States) to file a petition with the U.S. Tax Court for a redetermination of the deficiency. To secure the petition form, write to U.S. Tax Court, 400 Second Street, NW, Washington, D.C. 20217. The completed petition form, together with a copy of this letter, must be returned to the same address and received within 90 days from the above mailing date (150 days if addressed to you outside of the United States).

The time in which you must file a petition with the court (90 days or 150 days, as the case may be) is fixed by law and the court cannot consider your case if your petition is filed late. If this letter is addressed to both a husband and a wife, and both want to petition the Tax Court, both must sign the petition or each must file a separate, signed petition.

If you dispute not more than $50,000 for any one tax year, a simplified procedure is provided by the Tax Court for small tax cases. You can get information about this procedure, as well as a petition form you can use, by writing to the Clerk of the Tax Court at 400 Second Street, NW, Washington, D.C. 20217. You should do this promptly if you intend to file a petition with the Tax Court.

You may represent yourself before the Tax Court, or you may be represented by anyone admitted to practice before the court. If you decide not to file a petition with the Tax Court, we would appreciate it if you would sign and return the enclosed waiver form. This will permit us to assess the deficiency quickly and will limit the accumulation of interest. The enclosed envelope is for your convenience. If you decide not to sign and return the statement and you do not timely petition the Tax Court, the law requires us to assess and bill you for the deficiency after 90 days from the above mailing date of this letter (150 days if this letter is addressed to you outside the United States).

If you have questions about this letter, please write to the person whose name and address are shown on this letter. If you write, please attach this letter to help identify your account. Keep the copy for your records. Also, please include your telephone number and the most convenient time for us to call, so we can contact you if we need additional information.

If you prefer, you may call the IRS contact person at the telephone number shown above. If this number is outside your local calling area, there will be a long-distance charge to you.

You may call the IRS telephone number listed in your local directory. An IRS employee there may be able to help you, but the contact person at the address shown on this letter is most familiar with your case.

Thank you for your cooperation.

Sincerely yours,
Commissioner

By
Enclosures:
Copy of this letter
Statement
Envelope

5 Entering the Judicial System

If a taxpayer cannot resolve his or her dispute with the IRS administratively, he or she may seek judicial relief. As we have discussed earlier in the text, the taxpayer can choose from among the U.S. Tax Court, the pertinent district court, and the U.S. Court of Federal Claims to initiate the lawsuit against the government (see Exhibit 13-3).

The Tax Court will review the taxpayer's case provided that he or she files a petition with the court within 90 days after the date of his or her statutory notice of deficiency. The district courts and the Court of Federal Claims cannot hear the taxpayer's case unless he or she is suing for a refund. Consequently, the taxpayer first must pay the disputed tax and then file an (unsuccessful) claim for refund to obtain a judicial review in either of these latter two forums.

6 Statutes of Limitations

The IRC establishes a specific period of time, commonly referred to as a **statute of limitations**, within which all taxes must be assessed and collected and all refund claims must be made. After the pertinent statute of limitations expires, certain actions may not be taken because the expiration establishes an absolute defense for the party against whom legal action is brought. In other words, a taxpayer cannot be required to pay taxes that he or she rightfully owes if these taxes are not assessed and collected within the time periods that the code has established.

Although the statute of limitations appears to be a legal loophole that rewards delinquent taxpayers who avoid detection, Congress believes that, at some point, the right to be free of stale claims must prevail over the government's right to pursue them. If the statutes permitted an extended period of time between the initiation of a claim and its pursuit, the defense could be jeopardized because witnesses might have died or disappeared, memories might have faded, and records or other evidence might have been lost.

Moreover, some statutes of limitations are designed solely to protect the government (e.g., the statute of limitations on credits or refunds). A number of such statutes limit the

SPOTLIGHT ON TAXATION

Deciding to Litigate

One should not consider tax litigation lightly. The additional costs to the taxpayer for attorney and accountant fees, in addition to filing and processing fees and the cost and time involved in gathering supporting documentation for the taxpayer's position, finding and coaching expert and other witnesses, and providing for one's own travel to the site of the hearing, make litigation a costly prospect. Given the right combination of facts and law, though, a suit might be the taxpayer's only chance to achieve an equitable solution.

Remember, nonetheless, that the IRS tends to litigate only cases that it expects to win and that it expects will make good precedent to discourage other taxpayers. Moreover, because many taxpayers represent themselves before the Tax Court, procedural errors occur, usually to the detriment of the taxpayer. Thus, it is not surprising that the deck appears to be stacked against the taxpayer once he or she enters the judicial system.

National Taxpayer Advocate Nina Olson, in her *2015 Annual Report to Congress,* listed the 10 tax issues most litigated in the federal courts. Of the 640 cases involving those issues, taxpayers prevailed in whole or in part in 143, or roughly 22 percent. Taxpayers who were represented by counsel did somewhat better when the numbers were broken down—they won 28 percent, or 69 of 244 cases; pro se taxpayers prevailed in 19 percent, or 74 of 396 cases.

time period within which assessment, collection, and claim for refund or credit activities must be conducted.[24]

6-1 Assessment

Assessment of a federal income tax generally must be made within three years of the later of the date that the return was actually filed or the unextended due date of the return. A return that is filed prior to its due date, for this purpose, is deemed to be filed on its due date. The assessment period for a return that is filed after the due date starts on the day that follows the actual filing date (the date the return is received by the IRS), regardless of whether the return is delinquent or the due date was extended properly.

The period in which a tax may be assessed is extended to six years if the taxpayer omits from his or her reported gross income an amount that is greater than 25 percent of the reported gross income.[25] For this purpose, IRC § 61 gross income is used in the 25 percent computation, with two exceptions. First, the gross income of a business is not reduced by cost of sales. Second, income that is omitted from the return is ignored for purposes of constructing the base for the 25 percent test, if the omission is disclosed in the return or in an attached document.[26]

Although the limitations period is extended for a substantial omission of income, it (surprisingly) is not extended where the taxpayer has overstated the amount of his or her deductions, regardless of the amount of the overstatement. However, as explained

---

[24]IRC § 6501.

[25]IRC § 6501(e)(1)(A).

[26]IRC § 6501(e)(1)(A)(i), (ii).

SPOTLIGHT ON TAXATION

Original Due Dates and Extended Due Dates

Exhibit 1: Noncorporate filings

Tax filing	Original due date	Extended due date
Form 1065, *U.S. Return of Partnership Income* (calendar year end)	March 15	Sept. 15
Form 1041, *U.S. Income Tax Return for Estates and Trusts* (calendar year end)	April 15	Sept. 30
Form 990, *Return of Organization Exempt From Income Tax* (calendar year end)	May 15	Nov. 15

Exhibit 2: Corporate filings

Tax filing	Original due date	Extended due date
Form 1120, *U.S. Corporation Income Tax Return* (calendar year end)	April 15	Tax years beginning before Jan. 1, 2026: Sept. 15 Tax years beginning after Dec. 31, 2025: Oct. 15
Form 1120 (June 30 year end)	Tax years beginning before Jan. 1, 2026: Sept. 15 Tax years beginning after Dec. 31, 2025: Oct. 15	Tax years beginning before Jan. 1, 2026: April 15 Tax years beginning after Dec. 31, 2025: April 15
Form 1120S, *U.S. Income Tax Return for an S Corporation* (calendar year end)	March 15 (unchanged)	Sept. 15 (unchanged)

Source: "A Look at the Impact of New Federal Filing Deadlines," *The Tax Adviser*, May 2016, AICPA.

in the following Spotlight on Taxation feature, for returns filed after July 31, 2015, any overstatement of basis that results in a substantial omission (in excess of 25 percent) of gross income also results in a six-year statute of limitations period.

An exception to the normal three-year assessment period also applies in situations in which required information related to certain international transactions and foreign transfers is not disclosed with a return. The statute of limitations is suspended and will not begin until the missing information is supplied to the IRS.[27] All items on the return are subject to adjustment during this time period unless the failure to provide information is a result of reasonable cause. If the failure to furnish information is a result of reasonable cause, the suspension will apply only to the item or items not furnished, not the entire return.[28]

---

[27]IRC § 6501(c)(8)(A).

[28]IRC § 6501(c)(8)(B).

SPOTLIGHT ON TAXATION

Six-Year Statute and Overstated Basis

A 2012 Supreme Court decision (*Home Concrete & Supply LLC v. United States* (132 S. Ct. 1836)) resolved a dispute as to whether an overstatement of basis in property resulting in an understatement of gain could extend the normal three-year statute of limitations to the six-year window applicable when a taxpayer substantially understates income through an omission. In ruling that the three-year statute applied, the Court relied on its earlier ruling in *Colony Inc. v. Commissioner*, 357 U.S. 28 (1958), holding that the plain meaning of *omit* is to leave out and that the taxpayer in *Colony* as well as *Home Concrete* had reported the transaction on the tax return. However, in 2015 Congress overruled the Supreme Court decision by amending IRC § 6501(e)(1) and specifically noting that "an understatement of gross income by reason of an overstatement of unrecovered cost or other basis is an omission from gross income" (§ 6501(e)(1)(B)(ii)).

A tax may be assessed at any time when a taxpayer files a false or fraudulent return with the intent to evade tax liability.[29] Once the fraudulent return is filed, the limitations period remains open indefinitely. A later filing of a nonfraudulent amended return will not start the running of the three-year (or six-year) limitation period.[30] When a taxpayer fails to file a return, the tax may be assessed at any time. For this purpose, one's failure to file need not be willful. A taxpayer who innocently or negligently fails to file still is subject to an unlimited period of assessment for the tax.[31]

Generally, the filing of an amended return does not affect the length of the limitations period. However, the limitations period is extended by 60 days if the IRS receives, within 60 days of the expiration of the applicable statute of limitations, an amended return that shows the taxpayer owes an additional tax.[32] This provision was enacted to discourage taxpayers from waiting until the limitations period on an assessment was about to expire before submitting an erroneous amended return. For § 6501(c)(7) to apply, the IRS must actually receive the amended return before the normal assessment limitation period expires. In CCA 201052003, the IRS now takes the position that the "mailbox rule," "timely mailed equals timely filed" does not apply.

Prior to the enactment of this provision, it was beneficial for the taxpayer to wait to file an amended return this way because the IRS would not have enough time to assess more tax if an examination of the original return uncovered additional unreported errors or omissions.

The usual three-year assessment period can be reduced to 18 months if a request for a prompt assessment is filed with the IRS.[33] This request usually is made for an income tax return of a decedent or an estate, or for a corporation that is in the midst of a dissolution. Generally, a prompt assessment is requested when all the involved parties wish to accelerate the final determination of the tax liability.

---

[29]IRC § 6501(c)(1).

[30]*Badaracco v. Comm.*, 464 U.S. 386 (1984).

[31]IRC § 6501(c)(3).

[32]IRC § 6501(c)(7).

[33]IRC § 6501(d).

A deficiency for a tax year in which a net operating loss, capital loss, or unused research or general business credit is carried back can be assessed at any time before the expiration of the limitations period for the year in which the loss occurred or the credit originated. This extension in the period of assessment for the carryback year is necessary to ensure that there is adequate time to process the refund claim and to allow the IRS to examine the return that gave rise to the carryback item.[34] The period for assessment is not extended when a net operating loss, capital loss, or unused credit is carried forward. However, in *Springfield St. Railway Co.*, 312 F.2d 754 (Ct. Cl. 1963), the court allowed a taxpayer to adjust its NOL carryback amount in a closed year to claim a refund in an open one. The IRS has consistently followed this interpretation in Rev. Rul. 81-88 explaining in the Internal Revenue Manual that "errors in a closed year are corrected for purposes of determining the taxable income of an open year" (Internal Revenue Manual Section 4.11.11.6(10)).

An extension of the period of limitations typically may be requested by the IRS when an audit or an appellate review cannot be completed until after the statute of limitations expires. When requesting to extend the statute of limitations, the IRS will ask the taxpayer to sign Form 872 (Consent to Extend the Time to Assess Tax), which is for a specific period of time but cannot be shortened by the taxpayer. An alternative which can be used by the IRS is Form 872-A, which is an open-ended consent for up to 10 years. However, its use gives the taxpayer the option to request termination of the extension by filing a Form 872-T. Upon filing the 872-T the IRS will have 90 days from receipt to prepare and send a Statutory Notice of Deficiency.

In general, while a fixed statute date may be preferred to an open-ended one, the ability to terminate an 872-A extension by filing a Form 872-T is important. Agreeing to an 872-A extension will also show the taxpayer's willingness to administratively resolve the issues if that becomes a question when requesting court costs and attorney fees. Taxpayers may also request that a consent be restricted to specific issues.

The taxpayer is not bound to agree with such a request, but such a refusal may prompt the IRS to stop negotiations prematurely and assess a deficiency against the taxpayer. Although the issuance of a statutory notice of deficiency does not preclude the taxpayer from obtaining a negotiated settlement with the IRS, he or she will be required to undertake a more costly procedure and file a petition with the U.S. Tax Court or pay the assessment and file a claim for refund.

Consequently, a taxpayer normally should not refuse to sign a waiver of the statute of limitations, as requested by the IRS, unless the agent has completed the examination and there exist one or more unagreed-upon issues that the taxpayer is ready to litigate.

6-2 Collection

All taxes must be collected within 10 years after a timely assessment has been made.[35] **Collection** can be made either by IRS levy or by the agency's commencement of an action in court. If the tax is not collected administratively by levy within the 10-year period, the IRS must commence an action in court to reduce the assessment to a judgment before the statute of limitations expires.

Once a judgment for the assessed tax is awarded, the tax may be collected at any time after the normal period of collections has expired. Thus, collection is not barred after the 10-year period expires, provided that the IRS has obtained a timely judgment against the taxpayer.

---

[34]IRC § 6501(h)–(k).

[35]IRC § 6502(a)(1).

The taxpayer and the IRS may agree to an extension of the normal collection period. The IRS will request such an extension whenever the taxpayer has agreed to extend the period of limitations for assessment of the tax. In addition, the taxpayer may request an extension to allow additional time in which to raise and submit any delinquent taxes. If the taxpayer agrees to extend the period of limitations on collections, the IRS may agree not to seize and sell the taxpayer's property to satisfy the tax liability.

The 10-year period of limitations begins only after an assessment is made. If an assessment can be made at any time, for instance, because the taxpayer failed to file a return or filed a fraudulent return, then the tax may be collected within 10 years of the date of assessment, regardless of when it eventually is made.

6-3 Claim for Refund or Credit

A taxpayer must file a timely and valid claim at the service center for the district in which the tax was paid to receive a refund or credit of an overpayment of tax. The claim should be made by individuals on Form 1040X, Amended U.S. Individual Income Tax Return, and by corporations on Form 1120X, Amended U.S. Corporation Income Tax Return.

Generally, an overpayment can be refunded or credited only to the person who was subject to the original tax. However, the IRS can apply overpayments to delinquent support obligations and certain certified nontax debts that are owed to the federal government. Refunds in excess of $2 million may not be made until they have been reviewed by the Joint Committee on Taxation.[36]

A taxpayer who reports a net operating loss, capital loss, or credit carryback can accelerate the processing of the refund by filing an Application for Tentative Refund on Form 1045 (for individuals) or Form 1139 (for corporations). The IRS has 90 days from the later of the date on which the application was filed, or the last day of the month in which the return for the loss is due, to examine the application and accept or deny the claim.[37]

If the application is denied, however, the taxpayer cannot bring a suit for recovery of the overpayment because the IRS's determination is only tentative. Instead, the taxpayer must file a refund claim on the appropriate form and wait for six months from the date on which the claim was filed, or until the IRS denies the refund claim, before legal action can be started.

Before a refund or credit can be issued, the IRS must review the taxpayer's claim. Even if the commissioner agrees that the taxpayer has overpaid a tax, he or she has no authority to refund or credit the overpayment unless the taxpayer files the claim within the allowable period. Any refund of an overpayment that is made after the period for filing a timely claim expires is considered erroneous, and a credit is considered void.

A taxpayer who has filed a return must file a claim for credit or refund within three years of the date on which the return was filed or two years of the date on which the tax was paid, whichever is later. Returns filed early are deemed to be filed on the due date. If the taxpayer did not file a return (e.g., because taxes were withheld from the taxpayer's wages, but the taxpayer did not file a return because his or her taxable income did not exceed the applicable exemptions and standard deduction), the claim for credit or refund must be made within two years of the date on which the tax was paid.[38]

---

[36]IRC § 6405(a).

[37]IRC § 6411(b); Reg. §1.6411-1(b).

[38]IRC § 6511(a).

The period within which a claim for credit or refund may be filed is extended when the taxpayer and the IRS agree to extend the statute of limitations on assessments. A claim can be filed within six months after the expiration of the extended assessment period.[39] The limitations period is also extended in situations in which an overpayment results from a business bad debt or from a discovery of worthless securities.[40] A claim for refund or credit that is attributable to losses sustained from worthless securities or business bad debts may be filed within seven years from the date that the return was due without regard to any extension for filing the return. This period is extended further if the debt or loss increases a net-operating-loss carryback because the taxpayer is entitled to three additional years for the filing of a claim that is based on the carryback.[41]

This provision was enacted because the determination of the date on which a debt or share of stock becomes worthless is a question of fact that may not be determined until after the year in which the loss actually occurred. If taxpayers were not allowed additional time in which to file refund claims for these items, they could incur substantial losses without the receipt of any tax benefits because the deductions must be taken in the taxable year of the loss, not in a later year.

The period for filing a claim for refund is extended when the claimed overpayment results from the carryback of a net operating loss, capital loss, or certain credits. If a claim for credit or refund is attributable to the carryback of a net operating loss, net capital loss, or business credit, it can be filed within three years of the extended due date of the return for the year in which the losses occurred or the credits originated, rather than within three years of the due date of the return for the carryback year. Again, this provision was enacted because the existence and amount of these items might not be known until after the expiration of the usual three-year period for filing the claim.

If a claim for refund or credit is filed in a timely fashion, the amount of the taxpayer's refund or credit is limited to the portion of the tax that was paid during the three immediately preceding years, plus the period of any extension for filing the return.[42] The amount of tax that is subject to the claim may include amounts that were withheld and estimated payments that were made more than three years before the date on which the claim was filed, because these amounts are all deemed to have been paid on the due date of the return.

If a claim is filed after the three-year period, the amount of any refund or credit is limited to the portion of the tax that was paid during the two years that immediately preceded the filing of the claim. This two-year period also is effective if a claim is filed for a year in which a return was not filed. Because this claim relates only to a two-year period, it may not protect payments that were made with the original return.

6-4 Suspension of Period of Assessment and Collection

Usually, a tax must be assessed within three years after the filing of a tax return, and it must be collected within six years of the assessment. Under certain circumstances, however, the running of the statutes of limitations on assessment or collection is suspended.

When the IRS mails a statutory notice of deficiency (i.e., a 90-day letter) to the taxpayer, the assessment and collection period is suspended for 150 days (210 days if the letter is addressed to a person who is outside the United States).[43] The statutes of

---

[39]IRC § 6511(c)(2).

[40]IRC § 6511(d).

[41]IRC § 6511(d)(2)(A).

[42]IRC § 6511(b)(2)(A).

[43]IRC § 6503(a)(1).

limitations on assessment and collection also are suspended when a case is pending before the U.S. Tax Court. This suspension period begins when the taxpayer files a petition in the Tax Court contesting the deficiency, and it continues until 60 days after the decision of the Tax Court becomes final.

When a taxpayer submits an offer in compromise for consideration by the IRS, the statute of limitations on assessment is suspended. This suspension period begins when the offer is submitted, and it continues until one year after the offer is terminated, withdrawn, or formally rejected.[44]

In addition to the circumstances just discussed, the statute of limitations also can be suspended in the following instances:[45]

- The taxpayer's assets are in the custody of the court.

- The taxpayer is outside the United States for six or more consecutive months.

- The taxpayer's assets are wrongfully seized.

- A fiduciary or receiver is appointed in a bankruptcy case.

- The IRS is prohibited under bankruptcy law from any assessment or collection of a tax.

- The collection of excise or termination taxes on certain retirement plans or private foundations is suspended.

The filing of an amended return does not extend the statute of limitations and is accepted at the discretion of the IRS.[46] Because the statute of limitations is not extended by the amended return, it encourages the IRS to ignore the amended return and force the taxpayer into a refund action. The IRS would be severely disadvantaged to refund any alleged overpayment only to find out that they had no additional time to audit the return. That is why it is important to look at the self-assessed amount on a filed return. The preparer must always inform the taxpayer that the IRS cannot be forced to audit a return and the taxpayer may have to pay the tax along with any penalties and interest in order to initiate an IRS or court review. If the taxpayer can pay the tax, then a Claim for Refund is filed. The taxpayer will then be offered the appeals process (as outlined in Exhibit 13-3).

If a claim for refund is denied, the IRS issues a Statutory Notice of Claim Disallowance to the taxpayer. The taxpayer then has two years to initiate a refund action in district court or the Court of Federal Claims. It is important to remember that the appeals process is different in district court from that of the Court of Federal Claims. On the flow chart (Exhibit 13-3), note that appeals from a district court decision are to the Court of Appeals which controls their particular circuit. In contrast, an appeal from the Court of Federal Claims is to the Court of Appeals for the Federal Circuit. The appellate court in the circuit where the taxpayer lives may have a different opinion of the transaction than that of the Federal Circuit. Since the taxpayer has the ability to select the court in which to file the case, a careful analysis is required. Assuming that the U.S. Supreme Court has not spoken on the issue, the different appellate courts are controlling.

---

[44]Reg. § 301.7122-1(f).

[45]IRC § 6503(b)–(f). This section also contains other, less frequently encountered suspension possibilities.

[46]*Goldstone v. Commissioner*, 65 T.C. 113 (1975), *Badarocco v. Commissioner*, 464 U.S. 386, (1984), Rev. Rul. 83-36, 1983-1CB 358.

6-5 Mitigation of Statute of Limitations

Generally, the IRS cannot make an assessment and a taxpayer cannot obtain a refund after the statute of limitations has expired. However, IRC §§ 1311–1314 include a complex set of rules designed to prevent the taxpayer or the IRS from taking advantage of an oncoming expiration of the period of limitations on assessment, collection, or refunds.

When an error has been made in the inclusion of an item of income, allowance, or disallowance of a deduction or other tax treatment of a transaction that affects the basis of property, the mitigation provisions will allow a submission of the error to be corrected, even though the normal period of limitations has expired for that year.

7 Statutory Agreements

The IRC provides for two types of agreements that may be used to resolve tax disputes: closing agreements and offers in compromise.

7-1 Closing Agreements

A **closing agreement** is a formal, written agreement that is made between a taxpayer and the IRS. It is the only agreement that the IRC recognizes as being binding. Once it is approved by the Treasury, a closing agreement is final and conclusive as to both the government and the taxpayer unless there is a showing that either party has committed fraud or malfeasance or made a misrepresentation of a material fact.[47]

The purpose of a closing agreement is either to enable the taxpayer and the IRS to resolve, finally and completely, a tax controversy for any period prior to the date of the agreement and to protect the taxpayer against the reopening of the matter at a later date; or to determine a matter in a tax year that arises after the date of the agreement.

The IRS is authorized by the Treasury to enter into a closing agreement in any case in which there appears to be a benefit to the government in closing the case permanently and conclusively, or in which the taxpayer demonstrates a need to close the case and the government's interests are not harmed. Typically, a closing agreement is used in cases in which the IRS and the taxpayer have made mutual concessions relative to the case, and it is necessary or desirable to bar further actions by either party. Such an agreement also may be used when a corporation is winding up its business affairs or when a taxpayer needs some authentic evidence of his or her tax liability, for instance, to satisfy creditors.

As a matter of practice, the IRS discourages the use of closing agreements because of their finality. Moreover, the IRS would have a difficult time processing a large number of requests for these agreements since they must be signed by the Treasury. Consequently, it prefers to use informal agreements that might not resolve conclusively the tax dispute that is under examination or might not provide for the same degree of finality as would a closing agreement.

7-2 Offers in Compromise

The commissioner can accept an **offer in compromise** for any civil or criminal case (as long as it does not involve sales of illegal drugs) prior to the time that the case is referred to the Justice Department for prosecution or defense. Once the case is referred to the Justice Department, however, the U.S. Attorney General has the final authority to

---

[47]IRC § 7121(b).

compromise the case.[48] Compromise proposals entailing more than $50,000 in tax also must be supported by an opinion of the chief counsel.

In this context, the government will compromise a case only if there is doubt as to the liability or collectability of the assessed tax. The IRS will not enter into a compromise with the taxpayer if the liability has been established by a valid judgment and there is no doubt as to the ability of the IRS to collect the amounts due.

A compromise agreement may cover the principal amount of tax, plus any corresponding interest or penalties. Ordinarily, the IRS will not compromise a criminal tax case unless it involves a violation of a regulatory provision of the IRC or of a related statute that was not deliberately violated with intent to defraud.

A compromise agreement relates to the entire liability of the taxpayer, and it conclusively settles all the issues for which an agreement is to be made. It is a legally enforceable promise that cannot be rescinded unless there has been a misrepresentation of the assets of the taxpayer by falsification or concealment or a mutual mistake relative to a material fact.

Consequently, a taxpayer cannot decide later to bring a suit for refund with respect to any item that is so compromised. Moreover, if a taxpayer defaults on a compromise agreement, the IRS may collect the original tax liability, minus any payments that were actually made, or sue to enforce the agreement.

An offer in compromise typically is made via Form 656, Offer in Compromise or Form 656-L, Doubt as to Liability, and must be accompanied by a comprehensive set of the taxpayer's financial statements. The offer may be revoked or withdrawn at any time prior to its acceptance. An offer in compromise is perhaps most appropriate in the following circumstances:

- There is doubt as to the taxpayer's liability for the tax (i.e., disputed issues still exist).

- There is doubt as to the collectability of the tax (i.e., the taxpayer's net worth and earnings capacity are low).

- Payment of the disputed amount would constitute an economic hardship for the taxpayer. For instance, the taxpayer is incapable of earning a living because of a long-term illness or disability, or liquidation of the taxpayer's assets to pay the amount due would leave the taxpayer unable to meet basic living expenses.

The IRS investigates the offer by evaluating the taxpayer's financial ability to pay the tax. In some instances, the compromise settlement includes an agreement for final settlement of the tax through payments of a specified percentage of the taxpayer's future earnings. This settlement procedure usually entails lengthy negotiations with the IRS, but the presumption is that the agency will find terms upon which to enter into a compromise with the taxpayer. The IRS is charged to use a "liberal acceptance policy" in compromising with taxpayers and to increase educational efforts so that taxpayer rights and obligations are better known.

The IRS has statutory authority to enter into a written agreement allowing taxes to be paid on an installment basis if that arrangement facilitates the tax collection.[49] The agency encourages its employees to use installment plans, and an individual is guaranteed the right to use an installment agreement when the amount in dispute does not exceed $10,000. The taxpayer uses Form 9465 to initiate the installment plan.

The IRS provides an annual statement accounting for the status of the agreement. The agreement may be modified or terminated later because of inadequate information, a

---

[48]IRC § 7122(a).
[49]IRC § 6159.

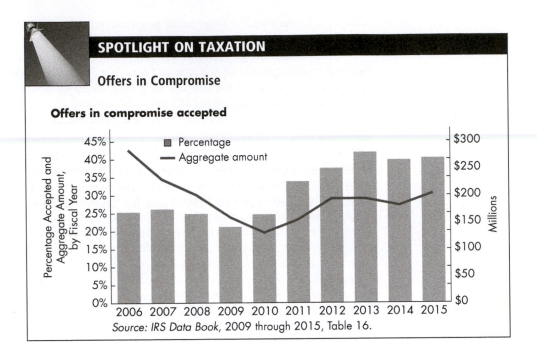

SPOTLIGHT ON TAXATION

Offers in Compromise

Offers in compromise accepted

Source: IRS Data Book, 2009 through 2015, Table 16.

subsequent change in financial condition, or a failure to pay an installment when due or to provide requested information.

8 Taxpayer Rights

Under various provisions of the Internal Revenue Code, taxpayers are guaranteed various rights to representation before the IRS, a recording of any proceedings, and an IRS explanation of its position relative to the pertinent disagreement. Specifically, the taxpayer has a right to know why the IRS is requesting information, exactly how the IRS will use the information it receives, and what might happen if the taxpayer does not submit the requested information. Accordingly, prior to an initial audit or collection interview, an IRS employee or officer must explain, orally or in writing, the pertinent aspects of the procedures to come.[50]

A taxpayer may be represented by an attorney, certified public accountant (CPA), or other person who is permitted to represent a taxpayer before the IRS and who has obtained a properly executed power of attorney. Absent an administrative summons, a taxpayer cannot be required to accompany the representative to an interview.[51]

If the taxpayer complies with a 10-day notice requirement, the taxpayer is allowed to make a recording of the IRS interview using the taxpayer's own equipment. Similarly, if the IRS intends to record an interview with a taxpayer or his or her representative, it must give 10 days' notice to the taxpayer. In addition, upon receiving a request from the taxpayer and a reimbursement for duplication costs, the IRS must make available to the taxpayer a transcript of the interview or a copy of its recording.[52]

---

[50]IRC § 7521(b)(1).

[51]IRC § 7521(c).

[52]IRC § 7521(a); Notice 89-51, 1989-1 C.B. 691.

To protect the rights of so-called innocent spouses on joint returns, the IRS must inform spouses of their joint and several liabilities for tax deficiencies, and both spouses must receive separately mailed notices as to audit, appeals, and Tax Court proceedings.[53] This may be especially important in situations in which the spouses have divorced or separated subsequent to filing the original joint return.

The IRS must inform taxpayers of their rights to representation in disputes with the agency. The taxpayer can suspend at any time an interview with IRS personnel so as to include a representative.[54]

An interesting provision in the code allows the taxpayer to recover court costs and attorney fees from the Treasury when the taxpayer defeats the government in the Tax Court (§§ 7430(a) and (c)). Recovery of costs such as those paid to a taxpayer's expert witness is allowed under §§ 7430(a) and (c). The costs are recoverable when all of the following conditions are met.

- The taxpayer pursued the case through IRS administrative appeals (§ 7430(b)(1)).

- The taxpayer "substantially prevailed" in the Tax Court (§ 7430(c)(4)(A)(i)(I)).

- The taxpayer's net worth does not exceed $2 million (§ 7430(c)(4)(A)(ii)).

- The taxpayer did not unduly prolong the litigation (§ 7430(b)(3)).

If these conditions are met, then the taxpayer can recover from the United States reasonable costs of the litigation. The statutory rate of $125 per hour for attorney fees and other costs is increased for inflation and for 2016 was $200 per hour.[55] A higher amount may be charged when "special factors" are present. Concerning an expert witness, special factors may be present when a particular expertise is brought to the trial, say by a neurosurgeon, or when the needed expertise is not available locally.

Section 7430(g) also allows taxpayers to make **qualified offers** to the IRS to settle the amount of the taxpayer's liability. Qualified offers may be made at any time after a 30-day letter is received or after the statutory claim of disallowance is received following a claim for refund action. If the IRS pursues a case to court and the amount awarded is equal to or less than the qualified offer, the taxpayer is entitled to receive litigation costs including accounting and attorney fees incurred after the date of the offer.

Qualified offers must be in writing and labeled as such—there are no set forms that must be completed to submit an offer. It must be submitted to the IRS office that has jurisdiction over the case or, in the case of a refund action, to the Justice Department's Tax Division that is responsible for the case. An individual applicant must have a net worth of less than $2 million or $4 million if a joint return is filed. If the applicant is a business, the net worth must be less than $7 million. Offers remain open until the earliest of the date the offer is rejected by the IRS, the date the trial begins, or for 90 days. The taxpayer may make multiple offers, but only one at a time. The offer may be in a dollar amount or expressed as a percentage of the proposed adjustment.

The availability of qualified offers provides an important strategic tool for taxpayers in that although the IRS may win on an issue they could potentially end up paying some administrative costs of the taxpayer. From the government's point of view, this additional "hazard of litigation" must be considered. Due to the potential costs that the government could incur, offers are evaluated by the IRS field counsel. The field counsel

---

[53]IRC § 6103(e)(1)(B).

[54]IRC § 7521(b)(2).

[55]Rev. Proc. 2015-53.

must prepare a formal written acceptance or rejection of the offer. The sheer amount of work required to respond to a qualified offer may encourage settlement of the case.

SPOTLIGHT ON TAXATION

Taxpayer Rights

In 2014, the IRS adopted an updated **Taxpayer Bill of Rights** to better inform taxpayers of their rights regarding interactions with the IRS. The *Taxpayer Bill of Rights* categorizes the rights embedded and scattered throughout the tax code and groups them into 10 broad categories:

1. The right to be informed
2. The right to quality service
3. The right to pay no more than the correct amount of tax
4. The right to challenge the IRS's position and be heard
5. The right to appeal an IRS decision in an independent forum
6. The right to finality
7. The right to privacy
8. The right to confidentiality
9. The right to retain representation
10. The right to a fair and just tax system

These rights are also included as part of Publication 1 sent to all taxpayers when they receive IRS notices on issues such as audits and collections.

8-1 Tax Confidentiality Privilege

Section 7525(a) provides authorized practitioners such as CPAs and enrolled agents a limited **client confidentiality privilege**. While the code provides that, with respect to tax advice, the same common law protections of confidentiality which apply to communications between a taxpayer and an attorney apply to communications between a taxpayer and an accountant, there are several exceptions. First, this nonattorney–client privilege may not be asserted in a criminal tax proceeding before the IRS or a federal court.[56] In addition, this confidentiality privilege usually does not apply to the preparation of tax returns or the giving of accounting or business advice. It also does not extend to written communications regarding tax shelters[57] or to the client's work papers used to determine tax expense for financial statements. This federally authorized privilege does not apply to state tax matters, although a number of states have their own accountant–client privilege statutes.

In contrast, attorney–client privilege provides a wider range of protection for communications (both verbal and written) between a taxpayer and an attorney. Accountants who are hired by attorneys in connection with a tax engagement may fall under this wider attorney–client privilege when the accountant is necessary or highly useful to the attorney in order to provide the client with legal advice.[58] It should be noted that

---

[56]IRC § 7525(a)(1).

[57]IRC § 7525(b).

[58]*Kovel*, 296 F.2d 918.

communications between a nonattorney tax professional and a client before the tax professional is hired by an attorney are not generally protected. Particularly in situations in which criminal action is possible, it is important for nonattorney tax practitioners to work directly with attorneys in providing assistance on a client's case.

SUMMARY

In counseling clients, the tax professional must be aware of the organization and inner workings of the IRS. Strategic and tactical decisions as to how and when to appeal within the administrative system of the IRS, if and when to agree to requests by the IRS to extend the statute of limitations period, assessing the strengths and weaknesses of the client's case, and determining available remedies can be made only with a thorough understanding of the agency and its operating style. Some of the most valuable advice that a client receives can be in the context of an audit selection letter or the handling of settlement alternatives thereafter.

KEY WORDS

By the time you complete this chapter, you should be comfortable discussing each of the following terms. If you need additional review of any of these items, return to the appropriate material in the chapter or consult the glossary to this text.

30-day letter, p. 433
90-day letter, p. 433
Appeals Office, p. 434
assessment, p. 439
chief counsel, p. 422
client confidentiality privilege, p. 450
closing agreement, p. 446
collection, p. 442
Commissioner of Internal Revenue, p. 420
correspondence examination, p. 429
Department of the Treasury, p. 420
discriminant function formula (DIF), p. 426

field examination, p. 429
Internal Revenue Service (IRS), p. 420
IRS Oversight Board, p. 423
Large Business and International (LB&I) Division, p. 422
mathematical/clerical error program, p. 424
National Research Program (NRP), p. 427
National Taxpayer Advocate, p. 422
offer in compromise, p. 446
office examination, p. 429
qualified offers, p. 449

revenue agent's report (RAR), p. 431
Small Business and Self-Employed (SB/SE) Division, p. 422
statute of limitations, p. 438
statutory notice of deficiency, p. 433
Tax Exempt and Government Entities (TEGE) Division, p. 422
Taxpayer Advocate Service (TAS), p. 422
taxpayer assistance order (TAO), p. 423
Taxpayer Bill of Rights, p. 450
Wage and Investment (W&I) Division, p. 422

DISCUSSION QUESTIONS

1. Why must the tax professional be cognizant of how tax law administration works?

2. What are the major functions of the national office of the IRS?

3. What are the chief responsibilities of the following?
   a. The IRS commissioner
   b. The IRS chief counsel
   c. The National Taxpayer Advocate
   d. Local taxpayer advocates

4. List three of the items included in one of the Taxpayer Bills of Rights.

5. Distinguish between the mathematical/clerical error program and the unallowable items program.

6. What are the chances of having a tax return audited this year?

7. What techniques other than the random selection of returns for audit does the IRS use in its enforcement function?

8. Why might it be desirable to settle with an agent rather than continue by appealing to a higher level within the IRS?

9. Relate some of the "audit etiquette" tactics that you have heard taxpayers or tax professionals discuss.

10. Distinguish among the various means by which the IRS selects a tax return for examination. For this purpose, examine the criteria of:
    a. Scope of review
    b. Probability of selection
    c. Preservation of taxpayer constitutional rights

11. Add two items to the "dos and don'ts" list included in the discussion of audit etiquette.

12. Suggest other information documents that the IRS computers could add to the IDMP.

13. Identify several items that you believe are included in the prevailing DIF model.

14. Carol takes some very aggressive positions on her tax return. She maintains, "With the downsizing of the government, my chances of getting caught are virtually zero." Is Carol's approach correct?

15. Should the IRS audit more or fewer returns every year? What issues would you consider in this regard if you were a politician? A wealthy individual?

16. The IRS's budget has been severely cut in recent years, dropping 17 percent since 2010 since adjusting for inflation. The budget cuts have led to reductions in the number of enforcement staff and the delay of upgrades to information technology systems. Write a memo to the current chairs of the House and Senate Appropriations Subcommittees on Financial Services and General Government either supporting or opposing the budget cuts.

17. What is the role of the statute of limitations in the federal income tax system?

18. What are the statutes of limitations for the IRS and taxpayers? Why did Congress create them? When can they be shortened, extended, or suspended?

19. Examine some tax journal articles and treatises to put together a checklist, "How to Prepare for a Tax Audit."

20. Examine some tax journal articles and treatises to put together a checklist, "How to Prepare for an Appeals Conference."

21. Update Exhibit 13-2 for the most recent year and comment on any changes you see in audit activity over the past few years.

EXERCISES

22. Which of the following methods is used to select tax returns for audit? More than one answer may be correct.
    a. DIF procedures
    b. Random samples
    c. Amount of gross income
    d. Type of income, such as business or wages

23. Which type of audit is used most often to substantiate the reported items of income or deduction for individuals who have only wages?
    a. Field
    b. Office
    c. Correspondence

24. A revenue agent may do which of the following in an attempt to negotiate a settlement after the completion of an audit? More than one answer may be correct.
    a. Attempt to settle an unresolved issue based on the hazards of litigation
    b. Settle a question of fact
    c. Reach an agreement that will be accepted unconditionally by the IRS
    d. Turn the case over to the Appeals Office

25. When an agreement cannot be reached with a revenue agent, a letter is transmitted stating that the taxpayer has 30 days to do which of the following?
    a. File a suit in the U.S. Tax Court
    b. Request an administrative appeal
    c. Pay the tax
    d. Find additional facts to support his or her position

26. A statutory notice of deficiency gives the taxpayer 90 days to do which of the following?
    a. Pay the tax
    b. Request an administrative appeal
    c. File a suit in the U.S. Tax Court
    d. File a protest

27. Make a chart that distinguishes among the various types of examinations that the IRS conducts relative to individual income tax returns, namely, office, correspondence, field, and NRP audits. For this purpose, examine the following criteria:
    a. Scope of review
    b. Type of documentation that typically is required of the taxpayer
    c. Use of IRS personnel time and other resources
    d. Opportunity for agent to use professional judgment in resolving issues

28. Respond to the following client comment: "We have a better than even chance of winning in the Tax Court, according to an article I read. Let's sue the government!"

29. How should the tax professional advise a client whose charitable contributions are double that of the U.S. norm for his or her income level?

30. In early 2017, the IRS selected Amber's 2014 return for audit with respect to Schedule C expenses and employee business expenses claimed on the return. Amber met with an IRS agent, who disallowed many of the expenses and who claims that Amber owes $2,500 of additional taxes. Discuss Amber's alternatives.

31. Distinguish between the receipt of a 30-day letter and a 90-day letter.

32. Indicate whether, after both parties sign a closing agreement, the following result(s) occur. More than one answer may be correct.
    a. The taxpayer still may appeal to a higher level of the IRS.
    b. The agreement is binding on both the taxpayer and the IRS.
    c. The tax must be paid, but a suit for refund can be filed in the district court or U.S. Court of Federal Claims.

33. Construct a scenario in which the tax adviser should recommend that the client terminate an IRS challenge with the following:

    a. Lawsuit

    b. Offer in compromise

    c. Closing agreement

    d. Appeals conference

    e. Office audit

    f. Correspondence audit

34. Indicate whether the following statements are true or false:

    a. The statute of limitations for assessment of taxes never extends beyond three years from the filing of a return.

    b. There is no statute of limitations relative to a taxpayer's claim for a refund.

35. What is the applicable filing period under the statute of limitations in each of the following independent situations?

    a. No return was filed by the taxpayer.

    b. The taxpayer incurred a bad-debt loss that she failed to claim.

    c. A taxpayer inadvertently omitted a large amount of gross income.

    d. Same as item c, except that the omission was deliberate.

    e. A taxpayer inadvertently overstated her deductions by a large amount.

36. Ace filed her 2016 income tax return on January 25, 2017. There was no material understatement of income on her return, and the return was properly signed and filed. The statute of limitations for Ace's 2016 return expires on:

    a. January 25, 2020

    b. April 15, 2020

    c. January 25, 2023

    d. April 15, 2023

37. Blanche filed her 2016 income tax return on April 4, 2017. On December 14, 2017, she learned that 100 shares of stock that she owned had become worthless in 2016. Because she did not deduct this loss on the 2016 return, Blanche intends to file a claim for refund. This claim must be filed by no later than April 15 of what year?

    a. 2018

    b. 2021

    c. 2023

    d. 2024

    e. There is no expiration date for the statute of limitations in this context.

38. Carl purposely omitted from his 2017 tax return $40,000 of the gross receipts that he collected as the owner of a restaurant. His 2017 return indicated collective gross receipts of $25,000. The IRS no longer can pursue Carl with the threat of collection of the related tax, interest, and penalties, as of April 15 of what year?

    a. 2019

    b. 2022

    c. 2024

    d. 2025

    e. There is no expiration date for the statute of limitations in this context.

39. David accidentally omitted from his 2016 tax return $40,000 of the gross receipts that he collected as the owner of a restaurant. His 2016 return indicated collective gross receipts of $25,000. The IRS no longer can pursue David with the threat of collection of the related tax, interest, and penalties, as of April 15 of what year?

    a. 2018

    b. 2021

    c. 2023

    d. 2024

    e. There is no expiration date for the statute of limitations in this context.

40. Michal accidentally omitted from her 2016 tax return $4,000 of gross receipts she collected as the owner of a restaurant. Her 2016 return indicated collective gross receipts of $35,000. The IRS no longer can pursue Michal with the threat of collection of the related tax, interest, and penalties as of April 15 of what year?

    a. 2018

    b. 2020

    c. 2023

    d. 2024

    e. There is no expiration date for the statute of limitations in this context.

41. Jenna and Sam sold a piece of property for $300,000, claiming that their basis was $150,000 and report a taxable gain of $150,000. Their 2016 return filed in February 2017 reported gross income of $250,000. Jenna and Sam later determine that the property's basis was actually $50,000, not $150,000, resulting in a $100,000 understatement of income on the 2016 return. The statute of limitations period in which the IRS may assess additional tax in this situation expires on April 15 of what year:

    a. 2019

    b. 2020

    c. 2023

    d. There is no expiration date for the statute of limitations in this context.

Tax Practice and Administration

- Identify various penalties that may be applied to taxpayers whose returns reflect improper amounts and related computations of interest charges.
- Identify various penalties that may be applied to tax practitioners who fail to perform as directed by the IRS.
- Understand the various provisions providing relief from joint and several liability available to spouses.

CHAPTER OUTLINE

THE ADVERSARIAL NATURE OF the federal tax system is apparent in discussions throughout this text, especially in Chapter 13. The revenue system is based on the notion of self-assessment, but a taxpayer's failure to comply in detail with the requirements of the tax law can lead to painful negotiations with the Internal Revenue Service (IRS) and prolonged litigation.

Yet the U.S. Treasury need not wait for a resolution of the disputed tax issues alone to collect revenues. Penalties and interest play an ever-increasing role in the makeup of the federal tax system—in many cases, the accumulated penalties and interest assessed by the IRS equal 50 percent or more of the disputed tax.

The Treasury assesses interest in such a way that the taxpayer gains no advantage or disadvantage with respect to the time value of money in deciding how to handle a tax dispute—to the extent that interest rates are developed to parallel those of the rest of the financial market, both parties are indifferent as to cash-flow issues, and the negotiations can center on the tax issues alone. Taxpayer penalties have become more prominent in the federal tax system for several reasons, as follows:

- In an environment in which nominal tax increases are politically unpopular, penalty increases can supplement revenues in a manner that is acceptable to the public.

- Politics aside, penalties increase the tax cost of negotiating with the Treasury and may discourage challenges to tax precedents when the challenges are not founded in sound tax law.

- Penalties can bolster the self-assessment process by discouraging taxpayers from behaviors that the Treasury wants to repress, such as participating in tax shelters and ignoring filing deadlines and requirements.

As professional tax preparers and advisers play a more important role in the filing of tax returns and the development of tax return positions, the behavior of such third parties has increasingly become more and more regulated as well, resulting in a number of penalties aimed at tax preparers. As a result, the tax professional must incorporate into her decision-making model the penalty-based costs of being too aggressive in taking a tax return or litigation position.

1 Taxpayer Penalties

To promote and enforce taxpayer compliance with the voluntary self-assessment system of taxation in the United States, Congress has enacted a comprehensive array of penalties. Tax penalties may involve both criminal and civil offenses. Criminal tax penalties are imposed only after the usual criminal process of law is carried out, during which the taxpayer is entitled to the same constitutional guarantees that are given to nontax criminal defendants.

Normally, a criminal penalty provides for imprisonment. Civil tax penalties are collected in the same manner as other taxes, and they usually provide only for monetary fines. Criminal and civil penalties are not mutually exclusive; therefore, a taxpayer may be liable under both types of sanctions.

1-1 Civil Penalties

The IRC imposes two types of **civil penalties**. **Ad valorem penalties** are additions to taxes that are based on a percentage of the delinquent tax. Unlike assessable penalties, ad valorem penalties are subject to the same deficiency procedures that apply to the underlying taxes. **Assessable penalties** typically are expressed as a flat dollar amount and are usually imposed on third parties (e.g., tax return preparers, tax shelter promoters, and information providers). Because of the absence of Tax Court jurisdiction or a specific statutory exemption, assessable penalties are not subject to review by the Tax Court. The IRC characterizes tax penalties as additions to tax; thus, they cannot subsequently be deducted by the taxpayer.[1]

Civil penalties are imposed when the tax statutes are violated without **reasonable cause**, as the result of **negligence** or unwillful disregard of pertinent rules, or through a willful disobedience or outright **fraud**. The most important civil penalties include the following:

- Failure to file a tax return

- Failure to pay tax

- Accuracy-related penalties

- Civil fraud

- Failure to make estimated payments

- Failure to make deposits of taxes

- Giving false information with respect to withholding

- Filing a frivolous return

1-1a Failure to File a Tax Return　When a taxpayer fails to file a required tax return, a penalty is imposed unless it is shown that the failure is the result of some reasonable cause and not the taxpayer's willful neglect. The **failure-to-file penalty** is 5 percent of the amount of the tax, less any prior payments and credits, for each month (or fraction thereof) that the return is not filed. The maximum penalty that may be imposed is 25 percent (or five months' cumulative penalty). A fraudulent failure to file is subject to a 15 percent monthly penalty, to a 75 percent maximum.[2]

If the taxpayer's failure to file is because of **willful neglect**, there is a minimum penalty for a failure to file an income tax return within 60 days of the due date, including extensions. Effective for returns filed for calendar years after 2015, this minimum penalty is the lesser of $205, or the full amount of taxes that are required to be shown on the return. The penalty does not apply if the failure is the result of reasonable cause.[3] This penalty is applied in lieu of, rather than in addition to, some other penalty.

No statutory or administrative definition exists for the term "reasonable cause." However, some courts define it to include such action as would prompt an ordinary, intelligent person to act in the same manner as did the taxpayer under similar circumstances. One of the most commonly encountered examples of reasonable cause is the reliance on the advice of competent tax counsel.[4] However, a recent Tax Court decision held that a

---

[1] IRC § 6665(a)(1).

[2] IRC § 6651(a)(1), (f).

[3] IRC § 6651(a)(3).

[4] See, for example, *Chamberlin*, T.C. Memo 2000-50. However, in this case, the taxpayer offered no evidence to show that his paid preparer was the cause of his failure to file federal income taxes in a timely manner. According to the appeals court for the second circuit, the Tax Court appropriately relied on the fact that the taxpayer was sufficiently educated to know (or should have known) that he was obliged to file taxes each year (88 A.F.T.R. 2d 2001-5151).

corporation was liable for employment tax penalties for failure to file its employment taxes on time even though the company had relied on a CPA to file the returns.[5]

Other examples of reasonable cause that the Internal Revenue Manual describes include the following:

- A timely mailed return that is returned for insufficient postage.

- Death or serious illness of the taxpayer or his or her immediate family.

- Destruction of the taxpayer's residence, place of business, or records by fire or other casualty.

- Proper forms were not furnished by the IRS.

- Erroneous information obtained from IRS personnel.

- A timely mailed return sent to the wrong IRS address.

- An unavoidable absence by the taxpayer.

- An unavoidable inability to obtain records necessary to compute the tax.

- Some other inability to obtain assistance from IRS personnel.

However, the penalty will not be excused for any of the following reasons:

- The taxpayer lacks the necessary funds with which to pay the tax.[6]

- The taxpayer was hospitalized and suffered from an illness that was not incapacitating.[7]

- The taxpayer was incarcerated.[8]

- The taxpayer allegedly was ignorant of the law.[9]

To avoid the penalty, the taxpayer must meet the burden of proof that the failure to file was the result of reasonable cause. In these situations, the IRS's determination of the penalty is presumed to be correct.

Civil penalties also apply for failure to file partnership or S corporation returns. The penalty is a statutory dollar amount of $195 per partner or shareholder for each month (or fraction of a month) that the return is not filed, up to a maximum of 12 months.[10] Assuming a 50-person partnership and a 12-month maximum penalty period, the maximum penalty that may be imposed for the failure to file the partnership return is $117,000 (12 months × 50 partners × $195).

1-1b Failure to Pay Tax   If a taxpayer fails to pay either a tax that is shown on his or her return or an assessed deficiency within 10 days of an IRS notice and demand, a **failure-to-pay penalty** is imposed. The 10-day period becomes 21 days when the tax due is less than $100,000.[11] The penalty is 0.5 percent of the required liability, after adjusting for any prior payments and credits, for each month (or fraction thereof) that the tax is not paid—but it increases to 1 percent of the underpaid tax per month after

---

[5]*McNair Eye Center, Inc.*, T.C. Memo 2010-81.

[6]*Langston*, 36 T.C.M. 1703 (1977).

[7]*Hernandez*, 72 T.C. 1234 (1979).

[8]*Jones*, 55 T.C.M. 1556 (1988).

[9]*Lammerts Estate v. Comm.*, 456 F.2d 681 (CA-2, 1972).

[10]IRC §§ 6698(b)(1), 6699(b)(1).

[11]IRC § 6651(a)(3).

SPOTLIGHT ON TAXATION

When Is a Return Filed?

To avoid the IRC § 6651 penalty, a return must be "filed." Some taxpayers think that sending in a blank form, or neglecting to sign the return, is enough to avoid this penalty, but the tax law says otherwise. The taxpayer information must be included in a readable format, almost always on the correct IRS form, mailed by the due date, and signed by the appropriate parties. There must be enough information on the return so as to compute the correct amount of tax; thus, leaving lines or checkboxes empty will void the filing, and the penalty will be assessed.

When electronic filing requirements are imposed on various taxpayers, both to speed up the system and to eliminate the possibility of errors, IRS software will not accept an incomplete or frivolous return. This is also a way to verify tax identification numbers to immediately identify taxpayers with other delinquent accounts or with inadequate filing credentials.

---

notice and demand is issued by the IRS.[12] The maximum penalty that may be imposed is 25 percent of the outstanding tax. This penalty does not apply if the failure to pay is attributable to a reasonable cause or to the failure to pay an estimated tax for which there is a different penalty.

For this purpose, reasonable cause is defined in a manner that is identical to that discussed in conjunction with the failure-to-file penalty except that, if an individual is granted an automatic filing extension, reasonable cause is presumed to exist provided that the balance due does not exceed 10 percent of the total tax.[13]

The failure-to-file penalty is reduced by the 0.5 percent failure-to-pay penalty for any month in which both apply. Thus, no more than a 5 percent total (nonfraud) penalty typically can be assessed against a taxpayer for any month. Nonetheless, after rendering sufficient notice to the taxpayer, the IRS can assess both the failure-to-pay and the failure-to-file penalties.

A taxpayer can avoid the failure-to-file penalty if an extension of the return's due date is granted by the IRS. With the two exceptions just discussed, however, the failure-to-pay penalty is imposed when the total amount of the tax is not paid by the unextended due date of the return.

EXAMPLE 14-1

John Gray, a calendar-year taxpayer, filed his 2016 income tax return on October 20, 2017, paying an amount due of $1,000. On April 1, 2017, John had obtained a six-month extension of time in which to file his return. However, he could not assert a reasonable cause for failing to file the return by October 15, 2017 (the extended due date), nor did he show any reasonable cause for failing to pay the tax that was due on April 15, 2017. Gray's failure to file was not fraudulent. As a result, Gray is subject to a $35 failure-to-pay penalty and a $45 failure-to-file penalty, determined as follows:

---

[12]IRC § 6651(a)(2), (d)(1). The monthly penalty rate is cut in half for taxpayers paying delinquent taxes under an installment agreement. IRC § 6651(h).

[13]IRC § 6654(d)(1)(B)(i).

Failure to pay

Underpayment	$1,000
Penalty percentage	× 0.005
Penalty per month outstanding	$ 5
Months (or fractions thereof) for which required payment was not made	×7
Failure-to-pay penalty	$ 35

Failure to file

Underpayment	$1,000
Penalty percentage	× 0.05
Penalty per month outstanding (before reduction)	$ 50
Months (or fractions thereof) for which return was not filed	×1
Unreduced penalty	$ 50
Less: concomitant failure-to-pay penalty (portion of October) [1 month × (0.005 × $1,000)]	−5
Failure-to-file penalty	$ 45

1-1c Accuracy-Related Penalties   Major penalties relating to the accuracy of the return data, including the negligence penalty and the penalty for substantial understatement of income tax liability, are combined in a single code section. This consolidation of related penalties into a single levy eliminates the possibility of the stacking of multiple penalties when more than one type of penalty applies to a single understatement of tax.

The **accuracy-related penalty** amounts to 20 percent of the portion of the tax underpayment that is attributable to one or more of the following:

- Negligence or disregard of applicable federal tax rules and regulations.

- Substantial understatement of income tax.

- Substantial valuation overstatement.

- Substantial overstatement of pension liabilities.

- Substantial understatement of estate and gift tax valuation.

- Disallowance of claimed tax benefits by reason of a transaction lacking economic substance (within the meaning of IRC § 7701(o)) or failing to meet the requirements of any similar rule of law.

- Any undisclosed foreign-financial-asset understatement.

Underpayment is defined in § 6664 as the correct amount of tax, less the sum of the amount of tax reported by the taxpayer on the return, plus any amount previously assessed or collected, less the amount of rebates made. Congress amended § 6694 in 2015 to provide that the amount of tax reported on the return is reduced by the amount of refundable credits and that the resulting amount can be below zero. The practical result is that an underpayment penalty may be assessed when a taxpayer claims in error refundable credits in excess of tax.

When the accuracy-related penalty applies, interest on the penalty accrues from the due date of the return rather than merely from the date on which the penalty was imposed.

The practitioner is likely to most frequently encounter two of the elements of this penalty: negligence or disregard of rules and substantial understatement of tax. In the first penalty, "negligence" includes any failure to make a reasonable attempt to comply with the provisions of the code.[14] This might occur when the taxpayer fails to report gross income, overstates deductions, or fails to keep adequate records with which to comply with the law. "Disregard" includes any careless, reckless, or intentional disregard of the elements of the tax law.

The negligence component of the penalty is waived when the taxpayer has made a good-faith attempt to comply with the law, as indicated by a full disclosure of the non-frivolous position that may be contrary to that of the IRS. Such disclosure is made by completing Form 8275, the first page of which is reproduced as Exhibit 14-1, and attaching it to the return. If the return position is contrary to the language of a regulation, Form 8275-R is used.

The second commonly encountered penalty, substantial understatement of income tax, occurs if the determined understatement exceeds the greater of 10 percent of the proper tax liability or $5,000. The understatement must exceed the lesser of the following for a corporation other than an S corporation or a personal holding company:[15]

- 10 percent of the proper tax liability, or

- $10,000, if greater

or

- $10 million

Occasionally, a valuation-overstatement penalty is encountered. This 20 percent penalty applies when an asset value has been overstated on a return, for example, to substantiate a charitable-contribution deduction. It is assessed when the valuation used is 150 percent or more of the actual value, resulting in an underpayment of more than $5,000 ($10,000 for C corporations).

Similarly, a 20 percent transfer-tax valuation-understatement penalty is assessed in situations in which the claimed value is 65 percent or less than the asset's actual value, resulting in an underpayment of more than $5,000.

The rate of both penalties is 40 percent if a gross valuation misstatement is made; that is, the income tax valuation was at least 200 percent of actual value or the transfer tax value was 40 percent or less of actual value.[16] In the case of any portion of an underpayment that is attributable to one or more undisclosed noneconomic substance transactions or undisclosed foreign-financial-asset understatements, a 40 percent penalty also applies.

The amount that is subject to this penalty is reduced if the taxpayer has **substantial authority** for the position that was taken on the return[17] or makes a full disclosure of the position (where there is a reasonable basis for the position) on Form 8275 or 8275-R.[18] While not quantified in the Code or regulations, many practitioners consider reasonable basis for a position to be having at least a 20% probability of a tax return position succeeding on its merits if challenged by the IRS. Substantial authority is often defined as having at least a 40% probability of a position succeeding on it merits.

For this purpose, "substantial authority" includes the IRC, regulations (proposed and temporary), court decisions, administrative pronouncements, tax treaties, IRS information and press releases, IRS notices and announcements, letter rulings, technical advice

---

[14]IRC § 6662(c).

[15]IRC § 6662(d)(1).

[16]IRC § 6662(e)–(h).

[17]IRC § 6662(d)(2)(B). Tax shelters cannot use this provision.

[18]IRC § 6662(d)(2)(B).

EXHIBIT 14-1:   Disclosure Statement

Form **8275** (Rev. August 2013) Department of the Treasury Internal Revenue Service	**Disclosure Statement** Do not use this form to disclose items or positions that are contrary to Treasury regulations. Instead, use Form 8275-R, Regulation Disclosure Statement. ▶ Information about Form 8275 and its separate instructions is at *www.irs.gov/form8275*. ▶ Attach to your tax return.	OMB No. 1545-0889 Attachment Sequence No. **92**

Name(s) shown on return	Identifying number shown on return

If Form 8275 relates to an information return for a foreign entity (for example, Form 5471), enter:
Name of foreign entity ▶ _____
Employer identification number, if any ▶ _____
Reference ID number (see instructions) ▶ _____

Part I   **General Information** (see instructions)

	(a) Rev. Rul., Rev. Proc., etc.	(b) Item or Group of Items	(c) Detailed Description of Items	(d) Form or Schedule	(e) Line No.	(f) Amount
1						
2						
3						
4						
5						
6						

Part II   **Detailed Explanation** (see instructions)

1 _____

2 _____

3 _____

4 _____

5 _____

6 _____

Part III   **Information About Pass-Through Entity.** To be completed by partners, shareholders, beneficiaries, or residual interest holders.

Complete this part only if you are making adequate disclosure for a pass-through item.

Note: *A pass-through entity is a partnership, S corporation, estate, trust, regulated investment company (RIC), real estate investment trust (REIT), or real estate mortgage investment conduit (REMIC).*

1 Name, address, and ZIP code of pass-through entity	**2** Identifying number of pass-through entity
	3 Tax year of pass-through entity / / to / /
	4 Internal Revenue Service Center where the pass-through entity filed its return

For Paperwork Reduction Act Notice, see separate instructions.	Cat. No. 61935M	Form **8275** (Rev. 8-2013)

memoranda, general counsel memoranda, committee reports, and "Blue Book" explanations of tax legislation.[19] Substantial authority does not include conclusions reached in tax treatises, legal periodicals, and opinions rendered by tax professionals.[20]

Clearly, greater weight is placed on the IRC and regulations than will be assigned to letter rulings and IRS notices, but a weighted average derived from all competing positions with respect to a given tax question is not likely to be obtained easily.

SPOTLIGHT ON TAXATION

Tax Court Rejects TurboTax Defense

In his Senate confirmation hearing, former Treasury Secretary Timothy Geithner appeared to blame TurboTax for the errors on his tax returns in which he failed to pay self-employment taxes on the payments he received from the International Monetary Fund. However, in *Parker v. Commissioner,* T.C. Summary Opinion 2010-78 (June 21, 2010), the Tax Court rejected the "TurboTax defense" used by Geithner and refused to waive the accuracy-related penalty for reasonable cause as provided for by IRC § 6664(c).

In so doing, the court noted that "regardless of the facts and circumstances relating to the case to which petitioner refers involving U.S. Secretary of the Treasury Timothy Geithner, petitioner is required to establish on the basis of the facts and circumstances that are established by the record in his own case that there was reasonable cause for, and that he acted in good faith with respect to the underpayment...."

1-1d Civil Fraud   If any part of an underpayment of tax is attributable to fraud, a substantial civil penalty is imposed. In addition, the taxpayer may be liable for a criminal penalty, which will be discussed later in this chapter. The civil fraud penalty is 75 percent of the underpayment that is attributable to the fraud.[21]

The burden of proof in a fraud case is on the IRS; it must show by clear and convincing evidence a fraudulent intent for the underpayment. This intent usually entails more than mere negligence; instead, a plan to defraud the government, often including a series of actions over time to evade the tax, must be shown.

Under an all-or-nothing rule, if the IRS establishes that any portion of an underpayment is attributable to fraud, the entire underpayment is treated as attributable to fraud, and the penalty applies to the entire amount due. If the taxpayer shows that any part of an underpayment is not attributable to fraud, however, then the fraud penalty is not imposed with respect to that amount.[22] Neither the failure-to-file, the failure-to-pay, nor the civil accuracy-related penalty is assessed in these circumstances. However, the penalty for underpayment of estimated tax (discussed later) may still be assessed, and interest is assessed from the (extended) due date of the return.

Fraud is not defined in either the IRC or the regulations. One longstanding judicial definition of fraud describes it as "... actual, intentional wrongdoing ... the intent

---

[19]Reg. § 1.6662-4(d)(iii).

[20]Notice 90-20, 1990-1 C.B. 328.

[21]IRC § 6663(a), (b).

[22]IRC § 6663(b).

required is the specific purpose to evade a tax believed to be owing."[23] This definition has been expanded to include acts that are done without a "bad or evil purpose." In *U.S. v. Pomponio,* the Supreme Court held that "willfulness," which is a crucial element of fraud, is present when the taxpayer's actions constitute "... a voluntary, intentional violation of a known legal duty."[24] Consequently, what distinguishes fraud from negligence or from other actions taken to avoid taxation is the taxpayer's deceptive or misleading conduct, not the presence of some (inherent or documented) evil purpose.

SPOTLIGHT ON TAXATION

Proving Fraud

The courts factor in the education and experience of the taxpayer when determining whether fraud has occurred. Is the taxpayer "smart" enough in terms of business and accounting training to construct a plan to defraud and then to carry it out? In cases of a complicated tax law or tax-reduction device, the taxpayer might successfully plead ignorance and avoid the fraud charge.

Ordinarily, the evidence that indicates that a taxpayer's conduct was fraudulent is circumstantial. Thus, the court must infer the taxpayer's state of mind from the evidence. Examples of fraud include the following:

- Keeping two sets of books, one in English and one in Japanese.[25]
- Making false accounting entries.[26]
- Destroying books or records.[27]
- Concealing assets or sources of income.[28]
- Consistently understating income or overstating deductions.[29]
- Purposely avoiding the making of business records and receipts.[30]

1-1e Failure to Make Estimated Payments A penalty is imposed on both individuals and corporations that fail to pay quarterly estimated income taxes. This penalty is based on the amount and duration of the underpayment and the rate of interest that currently is established by the IRC. This rate, for instance, was 4 percent in the third quarter of 2016.[31] Unlike the similar interest computation, however, this penalty is computed without any daily compounding and is not deductible.

The penalty is calculated separately for each quarterly installment. Each penalty period begins on the date on which the installment was due, and it runs through the

---

[23]*Mitchell v. Comm.,* 118 F.2d 308, 310 (CA-5, 1941).

[24]429 U.S. 10 (1976).

[25]*Noro v. U.S.,* 148 F.2d 696 (CA-5, 1945).

[26]*U.S. v. Lange,* 161 F.2d 699 (CA-7, 1947).

[27]*U.S. v. Ragen,* 314 U.S. 513 (1942).

[28]*Gendelman v. U.S.,* 191 F.2d 993 (CA-9, 1952).

[29]*Holland v. U.S.,* 348 U.S. 121 (1954) and *Ragen, op.cit.*

[30]*Garispy v. U.S.,* 220 F.2d 252 (CA-6, 1955).

[31]Rev. Rul. 2016-12.

earlier of either the date that the amount is paid or the due date for filing the return. Any overpayment is first applied to prior underpayments, and the excess is credited to later installments.[32] In this regard, the taxpayer must balance cash-flow concerns with the payment requirements of the code.

EXAMPLE 14-2

The taxpayer is required to have $100 paid in as estimates for the year. Payment schedule A would likely incur an underpayment penalty, while schedule B would not.

Quarter	Schedule A	Schedule B
1	$10	$40
2	40	10
3	10	40
4	40	10
Total	$100	$100

An individual's underpayment of estimated tax is computed as the difference between the amounts that were paid by the quarterly due dates and the least of the following:

- 90 percent of the tax that is shown on the current year's return.

- 100 percent of the prior year's tax, if a return was filed for that tax year of 12 months. The threshold increases to 110 percent if the adjusted gross income reported on that return is more than $150,000.

- 90 percent of the tax that would be figured by annualizing the income that was earned during the year, up to the month in which the quarterly payment is due.[33]

For this purpose, unless the taxpayer can prove otherwise, taxes that are withheld are considered to have been remitted to the IRS in equal quarterly installments.[34]

The underpayment penalty will not apply if less than $1,000 in underwithheld tax is due. Thus, an individual can avoid the estimated-tax-underpayment penalty if the preceding taxable year included 12 months, the individual did not have any tax liability for the preceding year, and he or she was a citizen or resident of the United States throughout the preceding taxable year.[35]

The IRS can waive the estimated-tax-underpayment penalty (but not the penalty that is based on the outstanding interest attributable thereto) if the failure to make the payment was the result of a casualty, disaster, or other unusual circumstance such that it would be inequitable to impose the penalty. The IRS can also waive the penalty if the failure was the result of reasonable cause rather than willful neglect during the first two years after the taxpayer retires after reaching age 62, or becomes disabled.[36] The fourth installment penalty is waived if the corresponding tax return is filed with full tax payment by the end of the first month after the tax year-end (January 31 for calendar-year taxpayers).

---

[32]IRC §§ 6654(b), 6655(b).

[33]IRC § 6654(d). The rule is 110 percent of the prior-year tax if that year's AGI was more than $150,000.

[34]IRC § 6654(g).

[35]IRC § 6654(e)(1), (2).

[36]IRC § 6654(e)(3).

An underpayment on the part of a corporation is defined as the difference between the amount of the installment that would be required to be paid if the estimated tax was equal to 100 percent of the tax that is shown on the return (or, if no return was filed, 100 percent of the actual tax that is due), and the amount that was actually paid on or before the prescribed payment date.[37] The underpayment penalty will not apply if less than $500 in tax is due or if the total payments that are made by the applicable installment date are equal to the least of the following:

1. 100 percent of the nonzero amount of tax that is shown on the corporation's tax return for the preceding year, provided that the preceding year contained 12 months.

2. 100 percent of the current-year tax liability.

3. 100 percent of the tax that is due using a seasonal installment method, or annualizing the current year's income received for (1) the first two or three months, relative to the installment that is due in the fourth month of the tax year; (2) the first three, four, or five months, for the installment that is due in the sixth month; (3) the first six, seven, or eight months, for the installment that is due in the ninth month; or (4) the first nine, ten, or eleven months, for the installment that is due in the twelfth month as elected.[38]

Exception 1 does not apply to a "large corporation," that is, one that had a taxable income of $1 million or more in any of its three immediately preceding taxable years. To avoid an underpayment penalty, a large corporation can use the prior year safe harbor for the first-quarter estimate but must remit quarterly estimated tax payments for the rest of the year that are equal to its current year's tax liability, or it must meet Exception 3, as discussed.[39]

1-1f Failure to Make Deposits of Taxes   The IRC requires employers to collect and withhold income and Social Security taxes from their employees. Amounts that are withheld are considered to be held in a special trust fund for the United States, and they must be deposited in a government depository on or before certain dates prescribed by the statutes and regulations. An employer that does not have either the inclination or sufficient funds to meet its deposit obligations may be tempted to postpone the making of these deposits, that is, to "borrow" from the government the cash provided by employees.

Consequently, the IRC imposes heavy civil and criminal penalties on those who are responsible for the failure to make a timely deposit of the withheld funds.[40] A responsible party may be an officer or board member of a corporation rather than the corporation itself, even for charities and other exempt entities. Although officers of a corporation are routinely asserted to be "responsible persons" for the trust fund penalty, under IRC § 6672, persons who are neither corporate officers nor employees can also be responsible for collecting and paying over trust fund taxes. A responsible person could be a creditor/lender,[41] a trustee/fiduciary,[42] or even an attorney.[43]

---

[37]IRC § 6655(b)(1).

[38]IRC § 6655(d), (e), (f).

[39]IRC § 6654(d)(2), (g)(2). The prior-year exception can be used in making the first-quarter installment, however. IRC § 6654(d)(2)(B).

[40]IRC § 6656.

[41]*Commonwealth National Bank v. U.S.*, 665 F.2d 743 (5th Cir. 1982). Lender and its president were responsible parties if lender barred debtor from using funds to pay taxes.

[42]*Keller v. U.S.*, 46 F.3rd 851 (8th Cir 1995), personal representative of estate ultimately responsible for the estate; *U.S. v. Cole*, 733 F.2d 651 (9th Cir. 1984), escrow holder of the proceeds from sale of assets was required to pay United States before other creditors.

[43]*Brown v. U.S.*, 464 F.2d 590 (5th Cir. 1972), Cert. denied, 410 U.S.908 (1973), attorney became nominal president of client's corporation.

If an employer fails to deposit on a timely basis taxes that were withheld from employees, a penalty equal to a percentage of the underpayment is imposed. This rate varies from 2 to 15 percent, depending on when the failure is corrected.[44] The penalty may be avoided in situations in which the taxpayer can show that his or her actions were the result of reasonable cause and not willful neglect.

If any person who is required to collect, truthfully account for, and remit employment taxes willfully fails to do so, a penalty equal to 100 percent of the tax is imposed.[45] Therefore, when a corporate employer willfully does not pay to the government employment taxes that it withheld from an employee, the IRS effectively may collect the tax from those who are responsible for the corporate actions, such as the corporate directors, president, or treasurer.[46]

In addition to the civil penalties that have been discussed, criminal penalties may be imposed in an aggravated case of nonpayment.

1-1g Giving False Information with Respect to Withholding   All employees are required to give their employer a completed Form W-4, Employee Withholding Allowance Certificate. This form notifies the employer of the number of withholding exemptions that the employee is entitled to claim. The employer then calculates the amount of tax that must be withheld from each employee. A civil penalty of $500 is imposed on any person who gives to his or her employer false information with respect to withholding status or the number of exemptions to which he or she is entitled. This penalty is not imposed in situations in which there was a reasonable basis for the taxpayer's statement. Moreover, the IRS may waive all or part of the penalty if the actual income taxes that are imposed are not greater than the sum of the allowable credits and estimated tax payments.[47]

Employers who receive a Form W-4 from an employee on which he or she claims more than 10 exemptions must submit a copy of the form to the IRS.[48]

1-1h Filing a Frivolous Return   A separate $5,000 civil penalty is assessed when the taxpayer is found to have filed a **frivolous return**.[49] Returns of this sort have been used to assert that the taxpayer's Fifth Amendment rights are violated by tax return disclosures,[50] that the taxpayer objects to the use of his or her tax receipts for defense or other uses,[51] that the government can collect taxes only in gold-based coins and certificates (which no longer circulate freely in the United States), or some other argument. Specifically, the penalty applies in the following situations:

- When the return does not contain information by which to judge the completeness of the taxpayer's self-assessment (e.g., if the return is blank).

- When the return contains information or statements that on their face indicate that the self-assessment requirement has not been met (e.g., a "tax protester" statement is attached).

---

[44]IRC § 6656(b)(1).

[45]IRC § 6672(a).

[46]IRC §§ 6671(b), 7809(a).

[47]IRC § 6682.

[48]Reg. § 31.3402(f)(2)-1(g).

[49]IRC § 6702.

[50]*Welch v. U.S.*, 750 F.2d 1101 (CA-1, 1985).

[51]*Fuller v. U.S.*, 786 F.2d 1437 (CA-9, 1986).

- When the return otherwise takes positions that are frivolous or are meant to impede the administration of the tax law, such as when it takes a return position contrary to a decision of the U.S. Supreme Court, or it is not presented in a readable format.

1-1i Other Civil Penalties   A variety of other civil penalties may be imposed on taxpayers who fail to comply with the IRC. Most of these penalties involve specialized areas of the tax law and ordinarily are not encountered by taxpayers. Consequently, one should be aware of the existence of such sanctions and refer to the code and regulations when working in such a specialized field to identify the events that might trigger such penalties.

SPOTLIGHT ON TAXATION

Frivolous Returns

The $5,000 penalty will not be assessed in the course of a typical dispute over the amount of tax due, for instance, in an audit where both sides have defensible positions concerning the law. The penalty also is not applied in the case of a mathematical or clerical error. However, the penalty relates to the original return as filed; that is, the penalty is not waived if the taxpayer "fixes" the problem by filing an amended return.

The frivolous-return penalty applies even if the taxpayer legitimately owes zero tax, and if the taxpayer was not required to file a return (e.g., because of low taxable income) but did so anyway.

1-1j Reliance on Written Advice of the IRS   The Secretary of the Treasury must abate any civil penalty or addition to tax that is attributable to the taxpayer's reliance on erroneous written advice furnished by an IRS officer or employee. This abatement is available only with respect to advice given in response to a specific request by the taxpayer, and it is negated if the IRS error was made as a result of a lack of information provided by the taxpayer.[52]

There is no abatement of a penalty on the taxpayer for the reliance on general information published by the Internal Revenue Service. In *Bobrow v. Commissioner*, T.C. Memo 2014-21 (2014), the court upheld the imposition of an accuracy-related substantial understatement penalty against a taxpayer even when the taxpayer relied on information published by the Internal Revenue Service. In this case, the Internal Revenue Service incorrectly stated the facts of a code section in Publication 590. The taxpayer relied on the IRS publication and was subsequently penalized. The court stated in its opinion that the IRS "published guidance is not binding precedent" and that taxpayers "rely on IRS guidance at their own peril."

1-2 Criminal Penalties

In addition to the civil penalties that we have discussed so far, the IRC prescribes a number of **criminal penalties** for certain acts of taxpayer noncompliance. The criminal

---

[52]IRC § 6404(f).

penalties are intended "to prohibit and punish fraud occurring in the assessment and collection of taxes."[53] They are imposed only after the implementation of the constitutional criminal process, under which the taxpayer is entitled to the same rights and privileges as other criminal defendants.

1-2a Nature of Criminal Penalties   Ordinarily, criminal prosecutions are limited to flagrant offenses for which the IRS believes it is virtually certain to obtain a conviction. As a result, the IRS usually limits its charges to the civil penalty provisions. In the typical context, criminal prosecutions are limited to cases in which the additional tax that will be generated from a successful prosecution is substantial, the crime appears to have been committed in three consecutive years, or the taxpayer's flagrant or repetitive conduct was so egregious that the IRS believes that it is virtually certain to obtain a conviction. As a result, the IRS usually will not engage in a criminal prosecution when the taxpayer's noncompliance can be corrected by imposing civil penalties.

However, criminal and civil penalties are not mutually exclusive. If a taxpayer is convicted of criminal fraud under § 7201, he or she cannot contest a civil fraud determination. Since the wording of § 7201 is identical to that of § 6663 (the civil fraud statute), the taxpayer is "collaterally estopped" from arguing that the civil fraud penalty should not also apply. However, if the taxpayer is convicted of criminal fraud under § 7206, he or she may then contest the civil fraud penalty.[54] As the language in § 7206 is not identical to that of § 6663, a separate action is needed to prove civil fraud.

In addition, a charge that the taxpayer is guilty of criminal fraud may be contested when a civil fraud determination has been upheld. In a criminal fraud case, the IRS must prove "beyond a shadow of any reasonable doubt" that the taxpayer's actions were fraudulent. In a civil fraud case, there must be "clear and convincing evidence" that the taxpayer committed fraud.

1-2b Criminal Tax Offenses   The principal criminal offenses that are addressed by the IRC include the following:

- Willful attempt to evade or defeat a tax (i.e., tax evasion)—a felony offense that is punishable by a fine not to exceed $100,000 ($500,000 for corporations), reimbursement of the government's cost of prosecution, and/or imprisonment for a period not to exceed five years.[55]

- Willful failure to collect, account for, and remit any tax by any person who is required to do so—a felony offense that is punishable by a fine not to exceed $10,000, reimbursement of the government's cost of prosecution, and/or imprisonment for a period not to exceed five years.[56]

- Willful failure to file a return, supply information, or pay tax or estimated tax—a misdemeanor offense that is punishable by a fine not to exceed $25,000 ($100,000 for corporations), reimbursement of the government's cost of prosecution, and/or imprisonment for a period not to exceed one year (five years and felony status for

---

[53]*U.S. v. White*, 417 F.2d 89, 93 (CA-2, 1969).

[54]*Wright v. Commissioner*, 84 T.C. 636,643 (1985).

[55]IRC § 7201.

[56]IRC § 7202.

returns relative to money laundering rules, that is, large amounts of cash received by a business).[57]

- Willful making, subscribing, or aiding or assisting in the making of a return or other document that is verified by a declaration under the penalties of perjury, and that the person does not believe to be true and correct as to every material matter—a felony offense that is punishable by a fine not to exceed $100,000 ($500,000 for corporations), reimbursement of the government's cost of prosecution, and/or imprisonment for a period not to exceed three years.[58]

- Willful filing of any known-to-be-false or fraudulent document—a misdemeanor offense that is punishable by a fine not to exceed $10,000 ($50,000 for corporations) and/or imprisonment for a period not to exceed one year.[59]

- Disclosure or use of any information that is furnished to a person who is engaged in the business of preparing tax returns, or providing services in connection with the preparation of tax returns, for purposes other than the preparation of the return—a misdemeanor offense that is punishable by a fine not to exceed $1,000 and/or imprisonment for a period not to exceed one year.[60]

SPOTLIGHT ON TAXATION

Tax Criminals

As you have seen throughout the book, prosecutions for tax crimes have brought down some highly visible individuals, including political and entertainment figures, but the penalties can be used against any taxpayer, as the following IRS information on criminal investigations demonstrates:

IRS Criminal Investigation Statistics

	FY 2015	FY 2014	FY 2013
Investigations Initiated	3853	4297	5314
Prosecution Recommendations	3289	3478	4364
Informations/Indictments	3208	3272	3865
Convictions	2879	3110	3311
Sentenced*	3092	3268	2812
Percent to Prison	80.8%	79.6%	80.1%

*Sentenced includes confinement to federal prison, halfway house, home detention, or a combination of all three.

Data Source: Criminal Investigation Management Information System, **www.irs.gov/uac/Current-Fiscal-Year-Statistics**

---

[57]IRC §§ 7203, 6050I.

[58]IRC § 7206.

[59]IRC § 7207.

[60]IRC § 7216.

In addition to the penalties just described, the IRC prescribes a number of other criminal penalties that ordinarily are not encountered on a regular basis. Most of these penalties involve specialized areas of the tax law. Consequently, one should be aware of the existence of such sanctions and refer to the code and regulations when working in such a specialized field to identify them.

1-2c Defenses to Criminal Penalties The standard for conviction in a criminal case is the establishment of guilt beyond a reasonable doubt. With respect to criminal tax cases, taxpayers have had some success—that is, to establish some doubt in the mind of the court or the jury—in presenting one or more of the following defenses:

- Unreported income was offset fully by unreported deductions.[61]

- Unreported income was in reality a gift or some other excludible receipt.[62]

- The taxpayer was confused or ignorant as to the applicable law, and one cannot intend to violate the tax law if he or she does not know what that law is.[63]

- The taxpayer relied on the erroneous advice of a competent tax adviser.[64]

- The taxpayer has a mental disease or defect and so could not have acted willfully to violate the tax law.[65]

- The statute of limitations (discussed in Chapter 13) has expired.

- The taxpayer enters a plea bargain and accepts conviction on a lesser offense.

2 Relief from Joint and Several Liability

Married taxpayers often choose to file a joint income tax return because of benefits that the filing status provides. However, when joint returns are filed, both taxpayers are jointly and individually responsible for the tax as well as any interest and penalties due on the joint return—even if they later divorce and even if the income is only attributable to one of the taxpayers.

Relief from joint and several liability can be requested by a spouse under the provisions of IRC § 6015. Under § 6015, there are three ways that a requesting spouse can obtain relief:

1. Request "**innocent spouse**" relief under the provisions of § 6015(b),

2. Request an allocation of liability between the spouses under § 6015(c) or § 6015(d), and

3. Request equitable relief under § 6015(f).

---

[61]*Koontz v. U.S.*, 277 F.2d 53 (CA-5, 1960).

[62]*DiZenzo v. Comm.*, 348 F.2d 122 (CA-2, 1965).

[63]*U.S. v. Critzer*, 498 F.2d 1160 (CA-4, 1974). This is not a mere disagreement with the law, which is not an acceptable defense. *U.S. v. Schiff*, 801 F.2d 108 (CA-2, 1986), cert. den.

[64]*U.S. v. Phillips*, 217 F.2d 435 (CA-7, 1954).

[65]*U.S. v. Erickson*, 676 F.2d 408 (CA-10, 1982).

2-1 Innocent Spouse Relief from Joint and Several Liability under § 6015(b)

To obtain relief from **joint and several liability** on a joint return under § 6015(b), the requesting spouse must show that:

1. A joint return has been made for a taxable year;[66]

2. There is an understatement of tax attributable to erroneous items of one individual filing the joint return;[67]

3. The other individual filing the joint return establishes that in signing the return, he or she did not know, and had no reason to know, that there was such understatement;[68]

4. Taking into account all the facts and circumstances, it is inequitable to hold the other individual liable for the deficiency in tax for such taxable year attributable to such understatement;[69] and

5. The innocent spouse seeks the benefits of this subsection not later than the date which is two years after the date the secretary has begun collection activities with respect to the individual making the election.[70]

Looking at the components of relief under § 6015(b), there must be an understatement (in contrast to an underpayment) of tax. An understatement is the difference between the full amount of tax that should have been reported on the return and the amount of tax actually shown. The regulations define an erroneous item as "any item resulting in an understatement or deficiency in tax to the extent that such item is omitted from, or improperly reported in an individual income tax return."[71] There also must not be a knowledge or a reason to know that an understatement in the tax occurred.[72] The requesting spouse must prove this by a preponderance of evidence. Factors that would be taken into consideration to prove lack of knowledge are as follows:

1. Type of tax item,

2. The financial position of the taxpayers,

3. The educational background and business experience of the requesting spouse,

4. The requesting spouse's participation in the business or activity that would cause a reasonable person to inquire about the action,

5. Whether the requesting spouse asked about the items on the return when the return was signed, and

6. Whether the position/items on the return were different than on prior years' returns.[73]

---

[66]IRC § 6015(b)(1)(A).

[67]IRC § 6015(b)(1)(B).

[68]IRC § 6015(b)(1)(E).

[69]IRC § 6015(b)(1)(C).

[70]IRC § 6015(b)(1)(D).

[71]IRC § 1.6015-1(b)(4).

[72]IRC § 6015(b)(1)(C).

[73]Reg. § 1.6015-2(c).

2-2 Allocation of Liability under § 6015(c) and § 6015(d)

A spouse can also ask for relief from joint and several liability under § 6015(c). This relief is for separate liability because the parties are no longer married, the nonrequesting spouse is dead, the parties are legally separated, or the parties have been living apart from one another for a period of 12 months from the date that the return was filed.[74] The requesting spouse has the burden of showing the amount of any deficiency that should be allocated to him or her. Relief is not available for amounts attributable to fraud or certain transfers of disqualified assets.[75]

For separate liability relief, the knowledge standard is increased. The knowledge standard under § 6015(b) is a "reason to know," but under § 6015(c) it is heightened to "actual knowledge."[76] Actual knowledge is defined by the Tax Court as "actual and clear awareness (as opposed to reason to know) of the existence of an item which gives rise to the deficiency (or portion thereof)."[77] With the heightened knowledge requirement, relief under § 6015(c) becomes somewhat easier than under § 6015(b). Facts and circumstances will always control the level of knowledge required. Regulations suggest that a requesting spouse's knowledge of how the erroneous item was treated on the tax return does not show actual knowledge.[78]

While § 6015(c) provides for limiting the tax liability for taxpayers that are no longer married, are separated, or are not living together, § 6015(d) allows for the apportionment of taxes as if no joint return was filed. Under this apportionment election, each taxpayer will be responsible for his or her respective taxes.

2-3 Equitable Relief under § 6015(f)

If relief is unavailable under § 6015(b) or (c), a taxpayer may be eligible for relief under § 6015(f) if it would be otherwise inequitable to hold the taxpayer liable for the underpayment or deficiency considering the facts and circumstances.

Unlike § 6015(b) and § 6015(c), which only provide relief from a proposed or assessed deficiency (i.e., an understatement of tax as previously defined), § 6015(f) also provides relief from under payments of tax. For example, your 2016 return shows that you and your spouse owed $12,000. You paid $10,000 with the return. You have an underpayment of $2,000. In addition, the two-year deadline for filing for equitable relief found in § 6015 (b) and § 6015(c) does not apply to § 6015(f).[79] Instead, requests for equitable relief may be filed within the 10-year statute of limitations period for collections under § 6502 or for any credit or refund of tax within the two- or three-year period under § 6511.

The innocent spouse can be relieved of all the year's liability or a pro rata percentage. In granting this relief, the IRS has wide latitude when looking at the facts and circumstances. Rev. Proc. 2013-34 lists some of the factors that the IRS will look for when deciding whether granting relief is appropriate. These factors include:

1. Marital status,

2. Economic hardship,

3. Knowledge or reason to know of the understatement or that the tax would not be paid,

---

[74]IRC § 6015(c).

[75]IRC § 6015(c)(4) and (d)(3)(C).

[76]IRS § 6015(c)(3)(C).

[77]*Cheshire v. Commissioner,* 115 TC 183 (2000).

[78]Reg. § 1.6015-3(c)(2)(ii).

[79]Notice 2011-70, 2011-32 IRB 135.

4. Legal obligations of the nonrequesting spouse,

5. Significant benefits to the requesting spouse, and

6. Compliance with income tax laws.[80]

Under previous guidance, spousal abuse was considered as a separate factor.[81] The new guidance under Rev. Proc. 2013-34 removes abuse as a factor but clarifies the effect abuse has on the other factors, specifically as to whether the spouse had knowledge of the understatement of tax and whether he or she received any benefits.

3 Penalties on Return Preparers

Individuals who prepare income tax returns or refund claims for compensation are subject to a number of disclosure requirements and penalties for improper conduct in the preparation of those documents. These provisions were added to the IRC as more and more taxpayers utilized some form of professional assistance in preparing their income tax returns. Moreover, a significant percentage of returns that were prepared by return preparers indicated some fraud potential.

The return-preparer penalties apply to all federal tax returns. Most of them are mild, ranging from $50 for the failure to furnish an identification number to $1,000 for the aiding and abetting of an understatement of a tax liability. Because these sanctions may be applied cumulatively, however, their magnitude can become more substantial. In addition, the criminal penalties that may be imposed on the return preparer provide for substantial monetary fines and jail terms.

For both taxpayer and tax preparer, the penalty system encourages a lawful application of the tax rules by all participants by raising the cost of the tax when specific requirements are violated.

3-1 Definition of Return Preparer

A **tax return preparer (TRP)** is any person who prepares for compensation, or employs one or more persons to prepare for compensation, all or a substantial portion of a tax return or a claim for income tax refund.[82] Returns include not only income tax returns but also estate and gift tax returns, employment tax returns, excise tax returns, returns for tax exempt organizations, and information returns that report information that may be reported on another taxpayer's return.[83] The regulations distinguish between the signing preparer who has primary responsibility for the overall accuracy of the return and nonsigning preparers who prepare substantial portions of a return or claim for refund.[84]

A person must prepare a tax return for compensation if he or she is to be subject to the return-preparer sanctions. If a return is prepared gratuitously, the preparer is not a TRP. The preparer also must prepare all or a substantial portion of a return if the TRP sanctions are to apply.

In determining whether the work that has been performed by the party is substantial, a comparison must be made between the size and complexity of the item relative to the

---

[80]Rev. Proc. 2013-43, I.R.B. 397.

[81]Rev. Proc. 2003-61, 2003-2 C.B. 296.

[82]IRC § 7701(a)(36)(A).

[83]Reg. § 301.7701-15(b)(4)(i).

[84]Reg. § 301.7701-15(b)(1) and (2).

taxpayer's gross income and the size of the understatement attributable to the item compared to the taxpayer's reported tax liability.[85]

The regulations provide two safe harbors for nonsigning preparers in determining whether they have prepared a substantial portion of a return. Time spent on advice that is given after events have occurred that represents less than 5 percent of the time spent by the individual with regard to the position giving rise to an understatement can be disregarded.[86] In addition, a schedule or other portion of a return is not considered substantial if it involves amounts less than $10,000 or less than $400,000 and also less than 20 percent of the gross income (or adjusted gross income) shown on the return.[87]

SPOTLIGHT ON TAXATION

The Package Deal

Under Rev. Rul. 86-55, a car dealership was deemed a preparer although its employees only reviewed the return as part of a "package deal" where the refund was applied to the purchase of an automobile. The car dealership did not charge for the review nor bill the taxpayer.

A person is not a TRP merely because he or she[88]

- Furnishes typing, reproducing, or other clerical assistance.

- Prepares a return or refund claim of his or her regular employer or of an officer or employee of the employer.

- Prepares as a fiduciary a return or claim for refund.

- Prepares a claim for refund during the course of an audit or appeal.

- Provides general tax advice to a taxpayer.

- Is an employee or official of the IRS, while performing job-related duties.

- Prepares the return for no compensation.

- Works for IRS-sponsored programs such as Volunteer Income Tax Assistance, Tax Counseling for the Elderly, or a low-income tax clinic.

Being classified as a TRP is not directly based on the attainment of a certificate or degree or the completion of continuing education requirements, but on the substantial completion of a tax return for compensation.[89]

---

[85]Reg. § 301.7701-15(b)(3)(i).

[86]Reg. § 301.7701-15(b)(2)(i).

[87]Reg. § 301.7701-15(b)(3)(ii)(A).

[88]IRC § 7701(a)(36)(B); Reg. §§ 301.7701-15(f).

[89]Reg. § 301.7701-15(d).

3-2 Preparer Disclosure Penalties

Five key **preparer penalties** may be imposed on those who do not comply with certain disclosure requirements, as follows:[90]

- A penalty of $50 for each return may be imposed on a TRP if the taxpayer is not given a complete copy of the return when it is presented to him or her for signature.

- A penalty of $50 for each return may be imposed on a TRP if he or she fails to sign the return.

- A penalty of $50 for each return is imposed on a TRP if the preparer's identification number or that of his or her employer, or both, is not listed on each completed return.

- A penalty of $50 for each failure is imposed on a TRP if he or she does not retain a copy of all returns he or she prepared. Alternatively, he or she may retain a list of all the taxpayers, including their identification numbers, for whom returns were prepared for the previous three years.

- A penalty of $50 for each failure to retain, and $50 for each item that is omitted, is imposed on a TRP who does not retain records that indicate the name, identification number, and place of work of each preparer who is employed during the 12-month period that begins on July 1 of each year.

In each instance, the maximum penalty for any calendar year is $25,000.

3-3 Preparer Conduct Penalties

The IRC contains a number of civil and criminal penalties that may be imposed on return preparers as a result of misconduct. The civil penalties were added to the code because Congress found that a significant number of return preparers were engaging in improper practices, such as guaranteeing refunds or having taxpayers sign blank returns. Except for the criminal penalty of aiding and assisting in the preparation of a false return, however, there were no lesser sanctions that could be applied to return preparers who were guilty of misconduct.

Civil penalties that may be imposed on preparers relate to the following:

- Endorsing or negotiating a refund check.

- Understatements due to unreasonable positions.

- Willful understatement of tax liability.

- Organizing, assisting in organizing, or promoting and making or furnishing statements with respect to an abusive tax shelter.

- Aiding and abetting the understatement of a tax liability.

Return preparers always have been subject to criminal prosecution for willful misconduct. The two principal criminal preparer penalties involve:

- Aiding or assisting in the preparation or presentation of a false return, affidavit, claim, or other document[91]

- Disclosure or use of information for other than return preparation purposes.[92]

---

[90]IRC § 6695.
[91]IRC § 7206(2).
[92]IRC § 7213(a)(3).

3-3a Endorsing or Negotiating a Refund Check   A TRP may not endorse or otherwise negotiate an income tax refund check that is issued to another person. A preparer who violates this rule is subject to a $500 penalty.[93]

3-3b Understatements Due to Unreasonable Positions   A tax preparer incurs a penalty for each occurrence of an understatement of tax that results from the taking of an unreasonable position in the return. A position is "unreasonable" unless there is substantial authority for it.[94]

The substantial-authority standard under IRC § 6694 should be similar to the substantial-authority standard under IRC § 6662. In general, substantial authority exists if the weight of authorities supporting the taxpayer's treatment is substantial in relation to the weight of those that take a contrary position. For tax shelters and reportable transactions, the law requires a more stringent "more likely than not" standard [IRC § 6694(a)(2)(C)]. In contrast to the generally accepted 40 percent substantial authority requirement, the "more likely than not" standard requires a greater than 50 percent likelihood of success.

IRC § 6662(d)(2)(C)(ii) defines a tax shelter as a partnership or other entity, any investment plan or arrangement, or any other plan or arrangement that has as a significant purpose the avoidance or evasion of federal income tax. A reportable transaction is any transaction for which information must be included with a return or statement because, as determined under regulations issued under IRC § 6011, the transaction has a potential for tax avoidance or evasion.

The penalty applies to a tax return position that is taken on a federal tax return or a claim for refund. The amount of the penalty does not relate to the amount of understated tax, which is the manner of computing most tax penalties. Rather, the unreasonable-position penalty is computed as the greater of $1,000 or one-half the return preparer's fees derived from the engagement.[95]

The penalty is not applied when the position is properly disclosed under IRC § 6662(d)(2)(B)(ii)(I) and the preparer shows both that there is a reasonable basis for the understatement and that the preparer acted in good faith [IRC § 6694(a)(3)].

EXAMPLE 14-3

Josie prepares a tax return that includes the claiming of a deduction that is contrary to a revenue ruling. Because of a new court decision in another circuit that is favorable to the deduction, Josie believes that there is a 70 percent chance that the position would be sustained in a suit relative to the deduction. No unreasonable-position penalty applies to Josie, whether the client wins or loses in court, and she need not disclose in any way her variance on the return from the government's position.

EXAMPLE 14-4

Return to the facts of Example 14-3, except that Josie believes that the position has a 30 percent probability of success in a court hearing. To avoid any unreasonable-position penalty, Josie must disclose the position, revealing where and how she has deviated from the government's position relative to the deduction. As long as there is a reasonable basis for the disclosed position and Josie acted in good faith, the penalty can be avoided.

---

[93]IRC § 6695(f).

[94]IRC § 6694(a)(2)(A).

[95]IRC § 6694(a)(1).

EXAMPLE 14-5

Return to the facts of Example 14-3, except that Josie believes that the deduction has a 5 percent probability of prevailing in court. Josie cannot take this filing position on any tax return. This is a frivolous position and would trigger an unreasonable-position penalty.

3-3c Willful Understatement   A preparer is subject to a penalty if any part of an understatement of a taxpayer's liability is attributable either to the preparer's willful attempt in any manner to understate the liability or to the reckless or intentional disregard of IRS rules or regulations.[96] A preparer is considered to have willfully attempted to understate the tax in this manner if he or she disregards information that has been supplied by the taxpayer, or by any other person, in an attempt wrongfully to reduce the taxpayer's levy. The penalty is computed as the greater of $5,000 or one-half the return preparer's related fees.

3-3d Organizing Abusive Tax Shelters   A civil penalty may be imposed on any person who organizes, assists in organizing, or (even indirectly) participates in the sale of any interest in a tax shelter, and who makes or furnishes a statement regarding an expected tax benefit that the person knows or has reason to know is either false or fraudulent or contains a gross valuation understatement on a material matter.[97]

For this purpose, a gross valuation understatement is a statement of the value of any property or service that exceeds 200 percent of the amount that is determined to be its correct value, if the value of the property or service is directly related to the amount of any allowable deduction or credit.[98] Accordingly, there does not need to be an understatement of tax before this penalty can be applied. The penalty, equal to one-half of the party's related fees from the engagement, can be triggered without an IRS audit, and it can be based only on the shelter's offering materials.

The amount of a valuation-overstatement penalty is the lesser of $1,000 or 100 percent of the gross income that is derived, or is to be derived, from the activity by the taxpayer. The IRS may waive all or a portion of the penalty that is attributable to a gross valuation understatement if there was a reasonable basis for the valuation and it was made in good faith.[99]

Although the penalty is not aimed specifically at tax preparers but rather at the tax shelter industry itself, professional tax advisers may be subject to the penalty because they often assist in organizing tax shelter projects.

3-3e Aiding and Abetting Understatement   The IRC imposes a civil penalty on any person who aids, assists, procures, or advises in the preparation or presentation of any portion of a return or other tax-related document, if he or she knows or has reason to believe that the return or other document will be used in connection with any material tax matter, and that this use will result in the understatement of another person's tax liability.[100] This penalty may also be imposed on a person who acts in violation of the statute through a subordinate (e.g., an employee or agent) by either ordering or causing

---

[96]IRC § 6694(b).

[97]IRC § 6700.

[98]IRC § 6700(b)(1).

[99]IRC § 6700(a)(2), (b)(2).

[100]IRC § 6701(a).

the subordinate to act, or knowing of and not attempting to prevent the subordinate from acting, wrongfully.[101]

The amount of the penalty is $1,000 ($10,000 for corporations) for each understating taxpayer. This penalty may be imposed only once per year for each understating taxpayer who is serviced by the TRP. However, it may be imposed in addition to other penalties. Thus, the preparer may also be prosecuted under the criminal statutes.[102]

3-3f Aiding or Assisting in the Preparation of a False Return

A criminal penalty may be imposed on any person who willfully aids or assists in the preparation of a return or other document that is false as to any material matter. This penalty is the criminal equivalent to the civil penalty for aiding and abetting the understatement of any tax liability.

A person who is convicted of violating this statute is guilty of a felony and is subject to imprisonment for up to three years and a fine not exceeding $100,000 ($500,000 for corporations). This is one of the most severe tax-preparer penalties under the IRC.[103]

The persons who are prosecuted under this statute usually are accountants or other return preparers. However, a person who supplies false information that is used in the preparation of a return may also be subject to this penalty. The penalty can be assessed when it is merely a false tax-related document (like a Form 1099 or W-4), and not a tax return, that is prepared.

SPOTLIGHT ON TAXATION

Abusive Return Preparers

Criminal Investigation Statistical Information on Abusive Return Preparers

	FY 2015	FY 2014	FY 2013
Investigations Initiated	266	305	309
Prosecution Recommendations	238	261	281
Indictments/Informations	224	230	233
Sentenced	204	183	186
Incarceration Rate*	80.4%	86.3%	78.0%
Average Months to Serve	27	28	27

*Incarceration may include confinement to a federal prison or a halfway house, home detention, or a combination of all three.

Data Source: Criminal Investigation Management Information System, **www.irs.gov/uac/Statistical-Data-Abusive-Return-Preparers**

---

[101]IRC § 6701(c).

[102]IRC § 6701(b).

[103]IRC § 7206(2).

3-3g Disclosure or Use of Information for Other than Return Preparation Purposes

The IRC imposes a civil penalty on any return preparer who discloses or uses any tax return information for other than the purpose of preparing a tax return. This penalty amounts to $250 per improper use; a preparer's maximum penalty for any calendar year is $10,000. The IRC also imposes a criminal penalty on any return preparer who knowingly or recklessly discloses or uses any tax return information for other than the specific purpose of preparing a tax return. One who is convicted of violating this statute is guilty of a misdemeanor and is subject to imprisonment for not more than one year and a fine not to exceed $1,000.[104]

The definition of a TRP for purposes of this criminal penalty is broader than that under the civil preparer statutes. For instance, a clerical assistant who types or otherwise works on returns that are completed by the preparer is a TRP for purposes of this provision. However, he or she would not be considered a TRP for purposes of the civil-preparer penalty statutes.

The preparer, as here defined, may disclose information that is obtained from the taxpayer without being subject to the civil or criminal penalty if such disclosure is pursuant to any other provisions of the code or to a court order.

See Exhibit 14-2 for a summary of the most important of the civil and criminal penalties that may apply to taxpayers, preparers, and shelter distributors.

EXHIBIT 14-2:   Summary of Tax-Related Penalties

Criminal and civil penalties are not mutually exclusive, so a taxpayer or a preparer may be liable for both. Unlike civil penalties, which are collected in the same manner as would be true for the regular tax, criminal penalties are imposed only after the completion of the normal criminal process, in which the defendant is entitled to a number of constitutional guarantees and other rights, that is, he or she is deemed to be innocent until proven guilty.

IRC §	Type of Infraction	Penalty
Civil Penalties		
6694(a)	Understatement as a result of unreasonable position	$1,000 or one-half of income derived, per return
6694(b)	Willful understatement of liability	$5,000 or one-half of income derived, per return
6695(a)	Failure to furnish copy to taxpayer	$50 per failure
6695(b)	Failure to inform taxpayer of certain record-keeping requirements or to sign return	$50 per failure
6695(c)	Failure to furnish identifying number	$50 per failure*
6695(d)	Failure to retain copy or list	$50 per failure
6695(e)	Failure to file correct information return	$50 per failure to file; $50 per omitted item
6695(f)	Negotiation or endorsement of refund checks	$500 per check
6695(g)	Failure to be diligent in applying eligibility rules for earned-income tax credit	$100 per failure
6700	Organizing (or assisting in doing so) or promoting and making or furnishing statements with respect to abusive tax shelters	Greater of $1,000 or 100 percent of gross income derived by preparer from the project
6701	Aiding and abetting an understatement of tax liability	$1,000 per return; $10,000 per return if taxpayer is a corporation
6713	Improper disclosure or use of return data	$250 per improper use; annual maximum $10,000

---

[104]IRC §§ 6713, 7216(a).

IRC §	Type of Infraction	Penalty
Criminal Penalties		
7201	Attempt to evade or defeat tax	Felony; fine of not more than $100,000 ($500,000 if a corporation) and/or imprisonment for not more than five years
7202	Willful failure to collect or pay over a tax	Felony; fine of not more than $10,000 and/or imprisonment for not more than five years, plus costs of prosecution
7203	Willful failure to file return, supply information, or pay tax	Misdemeanor; fine of not more than $25,000 ($100,000 if a corporation) and/or imprisonment for not more than one year (five years and felony relative to willful violation of cash-receipts rules)
7204	Fraudulent statement or failure to make statement to employees	Fine of not more than $1,000 and/or imprisonment for not more than one year
7205	Fraudulent withholding exemption certificate or failure to supply information	Fine of not more than $1,000 and/or imprisonment for not more than one year
7206	Fraud and false statements; concealing or removing property	Felony; fine of not more than $100,000 ($500,000 if a corporation) and/or imprisonment for not more than three years
7207	Fraudulent returns, statements, or other documents	Fine of not more than $10,000 ($50,000 if a corporation) and/or imprisonment for not more than one year
7210	Failure to obey summons in tax matter	Fine of not more than $1,000 and/or imprisonment for not more than one year
7212	Attempts to interfere with administration of internal revenue laws, corruption, threats of force	Fine of not more than $5,000 and/or imprisonment for not more than three years
7216	Disclosure or use of information by preparer of return	Misdemeanor; fine of not more than $1,000 and/or imprisonment for not more than one year

*Annual maximum penalty = $25,000.

4 Injunctions

The IRS is empowered to seek **injunctions** against two classes of persons of interest to our discussion: TRPs and promoters of abusive tax shelters. An injunction is a judicial order that prohibits the named person from engaging in certain specified activities. The courts have broad authority to structure any injunctive relief that is granted to fit the circumstances of the case as appropriate.

4-1 Action to Enjoin TRPs

The IRS may seek an injunction against a TRP who is guilty of certain misconduct to prohibit him or her from engaging in such misconduct or from practicing as a return preparer. Before such an injunction can be issued, however, the preparer must have:

- Violated a preparer penalty or a criminal provision of the IRC.

- Misrepresented his or her eligibility to practice before the IRS.

- Guaranteed the payment of any tax refund or the allowance of a credit.
- Engaged in other fraudulent or deceptive conduct that substantially interferes with the administration of the tax laws.

In addition, it must be shown that the injunctive relief is appropriate to prevent the conduct from recurring. An injunction to prohibit the person from acting as a TRP may be obtained if the court finds that the preparer continually or repeatedly has engaged in misconduct and that an injunction prohibiting such specific misconduct would be effective.[105]

4-2 Action to Enjoin Promoters of Abusive Tax Shelters

The IRS may obtain an injunction against a person who is guilty of promoting abusive tax shelters, or of aiding and abetting an understatement of the tax liability, to prohibit him or her from engaging in such conduct or activities. Before such an injunction is issued, a court must find that injunctive relief is appropriate to prevent this conduct from recurring.[106]

5 Interest

The IRC provides for the payment of interest on underpayments and overpayments of tax, at an adjustable rate, compounded daily. The objective of these provisions is to compensate offended parties for the use of their funds. Moreover, the interest charge eliminates the benefits that taxpayers (or the government) could obtain by adopting aggressive positions in the creation or processing of tax returns in order to postpone or avoid the payment of their taxes.

5-1 Interest-Computation Conventions

Interest on underpayments is payable at a federally specified rate from the last date that is prescribed for the payment of the tax to the date on which the tax is actually paid. The last date that is prescribed for payment of the tax is usually the unextended due date of the return that reports the amount of tax that is due.[107]

Interest is compounded on a daily basis.[108] The IRS has published interest-factor tables that automatically calculate the daily compounding for various rates of interest.[109] The rate of interest that is used for underpayments and overpayments is adjusted quarterly to reflect the federal short-term interest rate for the first day of the quarter.[110] The new prevailing rate is published in a timely fashion, typically in a revenue ruling.

For taxpayers *other* than corporations, the overpayment and underpayment rate is the federal short-term rate plus 3 percentage points. Generally, in the case of a corporation, the underpayment rate is the federal short-term rate plus 3 percentage points and the overpayment rate is the federal short-term rate plus 2 percentage

---

[105]IRC § 7407.

[106]IRC § 7408.

[107]IRC § 6601(a), (b).

[108]IRC § 6622(a).

[109]Rev. Proc. 95-17, 1995-1 C.B. 556.

[110]IRC § 6621.

points. The rate for large corporate underpayments is the federal short-term rate plus 5 percentage points. The rate on the portion of a corporate overpayment of tax exceeding $10,000 for a taxable period is the federal short-term rate plus one-half (0.5) of a percentage point.

SPOTLIGHT ON TAXATION

Interest Rates

For purposes of calculating the interest rate on overpayments and underpayments, the federal short-term interest rate is rounded to the nearest full percent. As of November 2016, the federal short-term rate was 0.68 percent, resulting in a 1 percent interest rate for purposes of determining the following:

- The rate for overpayments for noncorporate taxpayers (4 percent),
- The rate for overpayments for corporations (3 percent),
- The rate for underpayments (4 percent),
- The rate for large corporate underpayments (6 percent), and
- The rate for the portion of a corporate overpayment exceeding $10,000 (1.5 percent)

In situations in which the taxpayer is subject to both underpayment and overpayment computations for the same time period, whether the prior disputes involve income, transfer, or employment taxes, the amounts due from and payable to the government are netted, and a zero interest rate applies to those amounts.

EXAMPLE 14-6

Mary Brown, a calendar-year taxpayer, filed her 2016 tax return and showed a balance due of $1,000. The return was filed on June 30, 2017, pursuant to a properly executed extension of time to file, and the tax was paid in full with the return. The prevailing IRS interest rate that applies to Brown's underpayment was 4 percent. She must pay $8.36 of interest with her return, determined as follows:

Total tax outstanding	$ 1,000
Factor from Rev. Proc. 95-17, for 4 percent	
Interest and 76 days' late payment	× 0.008363088
Interest assessed	$ 8.36

If Brown does not remit the interest that she owes when she files the return, interest will continue to accrue, on both the tax and the $8.36 of interest itself, until the obligation is paid in full. If this amount is paid within 10 days of the receipt of an IRS notice and demand for payment, however, no further interest accrues.

Interest accrues on the full amount of the tax liability that is appropriate under the IRC, regardless of the amount of tax that is entered on the return. Moreover, interest is imposed on an assessable penalty, additional amount, or addition to the tax if these amounts are not paid within 21 calendar days of the date on which the IRS requests its payment. Interest on penalties generally is imposed only from the date of this IRS notice and demand and not from the due date of the return. However, the fraud, accuracy-related, and failure-to-file penalties run from the (extended) due date of the return.[111]

No interest is charged on criminal penalties or delinquent estimated-tax payments. However, recall that a nondeductible penalty is imposed in lieu of interest with respect to delinquent estimated-tax payments. This penalty is computed in the same manner as would be the required interest, except that daily compounding of the penalty is not required.

In general, the IRS has no authority to forgive the payment of interest. Consequently, a taxpayer is required to pay the total amount of interest assessed on any underpayment even though the delinquency was attributable to a reasonable cause, including an IRS loss of records or the illness, transfer, or leave of a pertinent IRS employee. However, the IRS can abate such interest when it is attributable to an unreasonable error or delay caused by an employee or officer of the IRS in response to the taxpayer's filing a claim on Form 843. Such a delay cannot be one that is traceable to an interpretation of the tax law but must relate to nondiscretionary, administrative, or managerial duties of procedure or return processing, including an IRS loss of records or the illness, transfer, or leave of a pertinent IRS employee.[112]

The government is required to pay interest at the applicable federal rate to any taxpayer who has made an overpayment of tax. Interest on an overpayment runs from the date of the overpayment to the date on which the overpayment is credited against another tax liability, or, in the case of a refund, to a date that is not more than 30 days before the date of the refund check.

However, the IRS is allowed a specific period in which it may refund an overpayment without incurring interest. This interest-free period runs for 45 days after the unextended due date of the return or, if the return is filed after its due date, for 45 days after it is actually filed. If the refund is not made within this 45-day period, interest begins to accrue from the later of the due date of the return or the date on which the return was actually filed.[113]

EXAMPLE 14-7

Joan Jeffries, a calendar-year taxpayer, filed her 2014 federal income tax return on October 1, 2017. Her return showed an overpayment of $2,500, for which Jeffries requested a full refund. If the IRS refunds the $2,500 overpayment on or before November 14, 2017, no interest is due from the government. If the refund is paid after November 14, 2017, however, interest accrues from October 1, 2017, through a date that is not more than 30 days before the date of the refund check.

The date that is stated on the government's refund check determines whether the overpayment is refunded within the 45-day interest-free period. The date on which the refund is actually received does not control for this purpose. Thus, an interest-free refund may be paid even though it is not received by the taxpayer until the 45-day period has expired.

---

[111]IRC § 6601(e)(2). Interest begins to run after 10 business days for amounts exceeding $100,000.

[112]IRC § 6404(e); *Dormer*, T.C. Memo 2004-167; TD 8789 (1998).

[113]IRC § 6611(e).

SUMMARY

In dealing with tax underpayments, the stakes include more than just the disputed tax. Interest charges accrue, and both the taxpayer and tax adviser can be subjected to significant amounts of civil and criminal penalties. The tax professional must include these sanctions in the research process, communicating their effects to the client as needed. The tax professional must also understand the relief provisions available for innocent spouses.

In today's tax practice, the professional must have a full working knowledge of the details of the tax administration process, so as best to serve clients.

KEY WORDS

By the time you complete this chapter, you should be comfortable discussing each of the following terms. If you need additional review of any of these items, return to the appropriate material in the chapter or consult the glossary to this text.

accuracy-related penalty, p. 462
ad valorem penalties, p. 458
assessable penalties, p. 459
civil penalties, p. 458
criminal penalties, p. 470
failure-to-file penalty, p. 459

failure-to-pay penalty, p. 460
fraud, p. 459
frivolous return, p. 469
injunctions, p. 483
innocent spouse, p. 473
joint and several liability, p. 474

negligence, p. 459
preparer penalties, p. 478
reasonable cause, p. 459
substantial authority, p. 463
tax return preparer (TRP), p. 476
willful neglect, p. 459

DISCUSSION QUESTIONS

1. Should prevailing interest rates bear on tax decision making in either or both of the following situations?
   a. The taxpayer is contemplating litigation in either the Tax Court or the Court of Federal Claims.
   b. An understatement of estimated tax payments is discovered late in the tax year.

2. Describe the civil fraud penalties, the definition of fraud, and the all-or-nothing rule for civil fraud. What are the differences in individual and corporate penalties for failure to make adequate estimated payments? What is a frivolous return?

3. Explain the imposition of criminal penalties. What is the relationship between criminal and civil penalties? What are the defenses against criminal penalties?

4. Discuss the penalties imposed on TRPs. Who is a preparer, what is defined as a tax return preparation, and what is not considered preparation?

5. What is an injunction, and when may the IRS seek an injunction?

6. How has Congress used tax penalties to discourage the development of certain tax shelters?

7. Define and illustrate the following terms or concepts:
   a. Fraud
   b. Negligence
   c. Reasonable cause
   d. Lack of reasonable cause
   e. Civil penalty conviction
   f. Criminal penalty conviction

8. Indicate whether the following statements are true or false:

   a. The government never pays a taxpayer interest on an overpayment of tax.

   b. Penalties may be included as an itemized deduction on an individual's tax return.

   c. An extension of time for filing a return results in an automatic extension of the time in which the tax may be paid.

9. The client's return is found by the U.S. Tax Court to have included improper business deductions. The court agreed that the taxpayer's position had some statutory and judicial merit, but it held for the government nonetheless. Which of the following could the IRS charge with a preparer penalty?

   a. Taxpayer

   b. Partner of the accounting firm that prepared the return

   c. Employee of the client, who provided the accounting firm with the deduction data

   d. Staff member of the accounting firm, who used the deduction data to prepare the return

   e. Secretary of the accounting firm, who made copies of the return

10. Discuss which penalties, if any, the tax adviser might be charged with in each of the following independent circumstances. In this regard, assume that the tax adviser:

    a. Provided information about the taxpayer's federal income tax returns to the pertinent state income tax agency.

    b. Provided information about the taxpayer's federal income tax returns to the pertinent county's property tax agency.

    c. Provided information about the taxpayer's federal income tax returns to the FBI, which was interested in gathering evidence concerning the client's alleged drug-dealing activities.

    d. Suggested to the client various means by which to acquire excludible income.

    e. Suggested to the client various means by which to conceal cash receipts from gross income.

    f. Suggested to the client means by which to improve her cash flow by delaying for six months or more the deposit of the employees' share of federal employment taxes.

    g. Suggested to the client means by which to improve her cash flow by delaying for six months or more the deposit of the employer's share of federal employment taxes.

    h. Kept in his safe deposit box the cash receipts referred to in item e.

11. Discuss which penalties, if any, the tax adviser might be charged with in each of the following independent circumstances. In this regard, assume that the tax adviser:

    a. Suggested that the client invest in a real estate tax shelter.

    b. Provided a statement of assurance as to the accuracy of the financial data that are included in the prospectus of a real estate tax shelter.

    c. Suggested to the promoters of a real estate tax shelter that a specific accounting technique, not recognized by generally accepted accounting principles, should be used to construct the prospectus.

    d. Failed, because of pressing time conflicts, to conduct the usual review of the client's tax return. The IRS discovered that the return included fraudulent data.

    e. Failed, because of pressing time conflicts, to conduct the usual review of the client's tax return. The IRS discovered a mathematical error in the computation of the taxpayer's standard deduction.

12. When Maggie accepted employment with Martin Corporation, she completed a Form W-4, listing 14 exemptions. Given that Maggie was single and had no exemptions, she misrepresented her tax situation in an attempt to increase her cash flow. To what penalties is Maggie exposed?

13. What is joint and several liability?

14. Briefly discuss the three ways that a spouse can request relief from joint and several liability.

15. What are the rules for innocent spouse relief under the provisions of IRC Section 6015(b)?

16. What are the rules for equitable relief?

17. Define erroneous items for purposes of innocent spouse relief under the provisions of IRC Section 6015(b).

18. Jack and Jill filed a joint return in 2014 showing Jill's wages of $50,000 and Jack's self-employment income of $30,000. Jack and Jill divorced in 2015. In 2016, the IRS audited their return and found that Jack did not report $20,000 of self-employment income. Jill had knowledge of the omitted income. The additional income resulted in $6,000 of understated tax plus interest and penalties. Can Jill file for separate liability relief? Why or why not?

EXERCISES

19. Julie filed a valid extension for her 2017 tax return, giving her until October 15, 2018, to file her return. She filed her return on November 1 and paid $2,000 of tax due. For what period of time will Julie be subject to interest? For what period of time will Julie be subject to the failure-to-file and failure-to-pay penalties?

20. Jim received a six-month extension (to October 15, 2018) to file his 2017 tax return. Jim actually filed the return on October 20, 2018, paying the $20,000 amount due at that time. He has no reasonable cause for failing to file the return by October 15 or for failing to pay the tax that was due on April 15, 2018. Compute the failure-to-pay and failure-to-file penalties.

21. Joan filed her unextended 2017 tax return on November 15, 2018, paying the $5,000 amount due at that time. Joan has no reasonable cause for failing to file the return by October 15 or for failing to pay the tax that was due on April 15, 2018. Compute the failure-to-pay and failure-to-file penalties.

22. John, a calendar-year taxpayer subject to a 34 percent marginal tax rate, claimed a charitable-contribution deduction of $15,000 for a sculpture that the IRS later valued at $10,000. Compute the applicable overvaluation penalty.

23. Samantha, a calendar-year taxpayer subject to a 34 percent marginal tax rate, claimed a charitable-contribution deduction of $170,000 for a sculpture that the IRS later valued at $100,000. Compute the applicable overvaluation penalty.

24. Susan, a calendar-year taxpayer subject to a 34 percent marginal tax rate, claimed a charitable-contribution deduction of $400,000 for a sculpture that the IRS later valued at $150,000. Compute the applicable overvaluation penalty.

25. Beth, a calendar-year taxpayer subject to a 34 percent marginal tax rate, claimed a charitable-contribution deduction of $600,000 for a sculpture that the IRS later valued at $100,000. Compute the applicable overvaluation penalty.

26. Todd, who is subject to a 35 percent marginal gift tax rate, made a gift of a sculpture to Becky, valuing the property at $7,000. The IRS later valued the gift at $15,000. Compute the applicable undervaluation penalty.

27. Greg, who is subject to a 35 percent marginal gift tax rate, made a gift of a sculpture to Karen, valuing the property at $80,000. The IRS later valued the gift at $150,000. Compute the applicable undervaluation penalty.

28. Brian, who is subject to a 40 percent marginal gift tax rate, made a gift of a sculpture to Adam, valuing the property at $100,000. The IRS later valued the gift at $250,000. Compute the applicable undervaluation penalty.

29. Krista, who is subject to a 40 percent marginal gift tax rate, made a gift of a sculpture to Ann, valuing the property at $100,000. The IRS later valued the gift at $500,000. Compute the applicable undervaluation penalty.

30. Compute the overvaluation penalty for each of the following independent cases involving the taxpayer's reporting of the fair market value of charitable-contribution property. In each case, assume a marginal income tax rate of 35 percent.

Taxpayer	Corrected IRS Value	Reported Valuation
a. Individual	$30,000	$40,000
b. C Corporation	30,000	50,000
c. S Corporation	40,000	50,000
d. Individual	150,000	210,000
e. Individual	150,000	250,000
f. C Corporation	150,000	900,000

31. Compute the undervaluation penalty for each of the following independent cases involving the executor's reporting of the value of a closely held business in the decedent's gross estate. In each case, assume a marginal estate tax rate of 50 percent.

Reported Value	Corrected IRS Valuation
a. $20,000	$25,000
b. 100,000	150,000
c. 150,000	250,000
d. 150,000	500,000

32. Kim underpaid her taxes by $15,000. Of this amount, $7,500 was the result of negligence on her part because her record-keeping system is highly inadequate. Determine the amount of any negligence penalty.

33. Compute Dana's total penalties. She underpaid her tax by $50,000 as a result of negligence and by $150,000 as a result of civil fraud.

34. Trudy's AGI last year was $200,000. Her federal income tax came to $40,000, which she paid through a combination of withholding and estimated payments. This year, her AGI will be $300,000, with a projected tax liability of $60,000, all to be paid through estimates. Ignore the annualized-income method. Compute Trudy's quarterly estimated-payment schedule for the year, assuming that she wants to make the minimum necessary payments to avoid any underpayment penalties.

35. Kold Corporation estimates that its 2018 taxable income will be $900,000. Thus, it is subject to a flat 34 percent income tax rate and incurs a $306,000 tax liability. For each of the following independent cases, compute the minimum quarterly estimated-tax payments that will be required from Kold to avoid an underpayment penalty.
    a. Taxable income for 2017 was ($100,000). Kold carried back all its loss to prior years and exhausted the entire net operating loss in creating a zero liability for 2017.
    b. For 2017, taxable income was $200,000, and tax liability was $68,000.
    c. For 2016, taxable income was $2 million, and tax liability was $680,000. For 2017, taxable income was $200,000, and tax liability was $68,000.

36. White Corporation estimates that its 2018 taxable income will be $800,000 and its tax liability will be $272,000. For each of the following independent cases, compute the minimum quarterly estimated-tax payments that will be required to avoid an underpayment penalty.

a. White Corporation's 2017 tax return showed taxable income of $700,000 and a tax liability of $238,000.

b. White Corporation's 2017 tax return showed a net loss and $0 tax liability for the year.

37. Mimi had $40,000 in federal income taxes withheld in 2016. Because of a sizable amount of itemized deductions, she figured that she had no further tax to pay for the year. For this reason and because of personal problems, and without securing an extension, she did not file her 2016 return until July 1, 2017. Actually, the return showed a refund of $2,400, which Mimi ultimately received. On May 10, 2020, Mimi filed a $16,000 claim for refund of her 2016 taxes.

a. How much of the $16,000 will Mimi rightfully recover?

b. How would your analysis differ if Mimi had secured from the IRS an automatic six-month extension of time for filing her 2016 return?

38. Examples of erroneous items for purposes of innocent spouse relief include:

a. a deduction by your spouse of $10,000 of advertising expenses on her Schedule C even though nothing was ever paid for advertising.

b. a deduction of $5,000 for the payment of fines which are not deductible.

c. Deducting $4,000 for security costs related to a home office which were actually veterinary and food costs for your family's two dogs.

d. All of the above are examples of erroneous items.

Chapter 1

Note: Unless otherwise noted, assume all CPAs in the following cases are in public practice.

1-1 Ahi Corporation is one of your clients in Hawaii. The company owes the IRS $100 million, due on March 15. There are no penalties or interest assessed by the IRS. One of Ahi's employees approaches you with the following plan to benefit from the so-called float on the large payment to the government. First, Ahi Corp. will courier its tax return and payment to the U.S. Virgin Islands. There, the tax return will be mailed to the IRS Service Center in Fresno by certified mail on the return's due date, March 15. By doing this, the employee thinks it will take at least six days for the tax return to reach the IRS and for them to cash the $100 million check. Ahi can earn 3 percent after tax on its money, so the interest earned during these six days because of the float is $8,219 per day [($100,000,000 × .03/365 days]. Thus, the total interest earned on the float for six days would be $49,314 ($8,219 × 6 days).

  a. Would you recommend Ahi complete this transaction?

  b. What potential ethics issues do you see in this situation?

1-2 John Haddock owns 75 percent of Haddock Corporation. The other 25 percent of the stock is held by John's wife, Marsha. You are a tax manager assigned to prepare the corporate tax return for Haddock. While working on the return, you note that Haddock Corp. pays rent to John for a building he owns with his son, John, Jr. The rent being paid is at least three times the normal rate for rentals of similar property in that area of town. You report this observation to the partner on the engagement. She tells you that it is all right to deduct the payments because Haddock Corp. has been doing it for several years, and the IRS never has objected. Under your firm's policy, managers sign the tax return for clients.

  a. Would you sign this tax return?

  b. What potential ethics issues do you see in this situation?

1-3 You are negotiating a transaction for your client, Shark Corporation. Parties on the other side of the deal ask you for information about the structural stability of a building, which is a significant part of the transaction. Coleman, Shark's tax director, tells you to say that everything is all right when, in reality, the building has substantial hidden damage. Coleman tells you to say this because it would be more favorable to Shark's position in the transaction.

  a. How would you respond to Coleman's request?

  b. What if you have already told the other side that the building is fine when you learn about the problems?

1-4 Big CPA Firm has many partners in one of its local offices. Two of these partners are Tom, a tax partner, and Alice, an audit partner. Because of the size of the office, Tom and Alice do not know each other very well.

  Tom has a tax client, Anchovy Corporation, that is in severe financial trouble and may have to file for bankruptcy. Anchovy is a customer of Sardine Corporation, one of Alice's audit clients. Accounts receivable on Sardine's books from Anchovy are significant. If Anchovy goes bankrupt, it could cause serious problems for Sardine. Alice is unaware of the bad financial condition of Anchovy.

  a. Can Tom disclose to Alice the problems at Anchovy?

  b. What if Anchovy goes under and takes Sardine with it?

  c. What potential ethics issues do you see in this situation?

1-5 You are the tax manager in a CPA office. One of your clients, Snapper Corporation, is also an audit client of the firm. The CFO of Snapper invites you and the audit manager for a one-week deep-sea fishing trip to Mexico, all expenses to be paid by Snapper. The audit manager says that you both should go and just not tell your supervisor at the CPA firm any details (like who paid the expenses) about the trip.

    a. Would you go on the trip?

    b. Would you tell your supervisors at the CPA firm if the audit manager went on the trip without you?

    c. What other potential ethics issues do you see in this situation?

1-6 Clara comes to an attorney's office in need of assistance with her husband's estate. Her husband, Phil, a factory worker, had been a saver all his life and owned approximately $1.5 million in stocks and bonds. Clara is relatively unsophisticated in financial matters, so the attorney agrees to handle the estate for 17 percent of the value of the estate. The normal charge for such work is 3 to 5 percent of the estate. The widow agrees to the 17 percent arrangement. The attorney then hires CPA Charles for $10,000 to compute Phil's estate tax on Form 706 and to prepare other appropriate documents.

    a. Under Circular 230, does Charles have any responsibility to inform the widow that she is being significantly overcharged by the attorney?

    b. What potential ethics issues do you see in this situation?

1-7 Darlene works for Big CPA Firm. When she was being interviewed, Darlene was told by a partner in the firm that she was not to underreport her time spent on various engagements. However, after working for a few months, she discovers that everyone in her office "eats time." Because she is not eating time like everyone else, Darlene is always over budget. She is beginning to get a reputation as a "budget buster." As a result, none of the senior tax staff wants her on their engagements. She is getting the worst clients and bad reviews from the people for whom she works. It appears that unless she starts eating time, Darlene's future with the firm is limited.

    a. What would you recommend Darlene do?

    b. What potential ethics issues do you see in this situation?

1-8 Freya is an accountant working on the tax return of a high-tech client. After reviewing the work papers, she discovers that there is a pattern of double billing the U.S. Navy for various projects done by the tax client. She brings this to the attention of her manager on the job, and he tells her that it is not the CPA firm's business what the client does since this is not an audit engagement.

    a. What would you recommend Freya do at this point?

    b. What potential ethics issues do you see in this situation?

1-9 Jenny is an accountant for an international energy corporation (not in public practice). She oversees the accounting for certain associated offshore entities. The amount of funds involved in the entities is substantial. At the end of the year, she notices that the accounting information from the offshore entities is not included in the consolidated financial statements of the corporation but is reported on the consolidated tax return. She inquires about this and is told that the corporation does not report the financial information from the offshore entities since it would lower the earnings of the main corporation. Jenny is sure that this is not the proper accounting and tax treatment for the entities.

    a. What would you recommend Jenny do at this point?

    b. What potential ethics issues do you see in this situation?

1-10 Eric is a tax manager for a national CPA firm that audits Penny-Pinching Bank (PPB), a public company. Eric and his staff prepare and review the tax return for PPB. One day, at an alumni football tailgate party, he meets another alumnus who Eric discovers is on the Audit Committee of PPB. The Audit Committee member/alumnus was unaware that Eric's CPA firm is doing PPB's tax return.

a. What would you recommend Eric do at this point?

b. What potential ethical and practice issues do you see in this situation?

1-11 For the last 10 years, Ricky, 40, and Lucy, 35, were married, and you prepared their joint tax returns for those years. Last year they divorced, and both remained as your tax client. Under the dissolution decree, Ricky has to pay Lucy $4,000 per month alimony, which he does for the current year. You as an EA have completed Ricky's tax return for the current year, and you deducted the required alimony payments to Lucy on his Form 1040. Lucy comes to you to prepare her tax return and refuses to report her alimony received as income. She states, "I am not going to pay tax on the $48,000 from Ricky." She views the payments as "a gift for putting up with him for all those years of marriage." Lucy will not budge on reporting this alimony as income.

a. Under Circular 230, could you sign the paid preparer's declaration on this return? Cite a specific Circular 230 section to support your answer.

1-12 Dewin Auer Best (DAB) CPAs has an audit and tax client named Meyers, Inc. Meyers is a closely held C corporation whose majority shareholder, Alicia Meyers, is also its CEO. Alicia also is a tax client of DAB. During the latest year, Meyers, Inc. allowed Alicia to use a company credit card to make numerous personal purchases, but she did not reimburse the company for any of these expenditures. She also has a company car that she uses for all her transportation needs, business and personal. You are a first-year professional and have been asked by your partner, Sarah Best, to prepare Form 1120 for Meyers, Inc. and Form 1040 for Alicia Meyers. When you start to prepare the Form 1120, you notice that Meyers, Inc. has reported these charges and the total amount of operating costs for the automobile as deductible items. When reviewing Alicia's personal tax information, you note that on her W-2, box 1, the amount listed as salary is exactly the contracted amount reported in the board of directors minutes and does not include any additional amounts for the unreimbursed expenses or automobile usage. In addition, box 14 is blank and does not contain any reported fringe benefits. Consult Circular 230, the SSTSs, and the AICPA Code of Professional Conduct. What issues must be resolved before you can recommend that Sarah Best should sign this tax return? Ignore the standards that a return preparer must satisfy under the Internal Revenue Code.

1-13 Robert has been a CPA for over 20 years, primarily doing tax compliance engagements for individuals. One of his long-time clients indicates that she is considering a transaction that would involve creating an employee stock ownership plan (ESOP) so she can transfer control of her closely held business to her employees. She asked Robert to assist with this transaction because she has always relied on his integrity and she trusts him. Robert knows what an ESOP is from general knowledge but has never worked professionally with ESOPs, nor has he ever helped implement one for a client. What ethical issues does Robert face? How do you advise him to proceed?

1-14 Lorraine Newman, CPA, has developed considerable tax expertise in business acquisitions and is widely recognized in her geographic practice area as the go-to person for such transactions. She is currently representing DanAck, Inc. in the acquisition of a potential subsidiary, BillMur, Inc. BillMur is represented by Ida No, who just graduated from college and has not yet taken the CPA exam and is not an EA. It is obvious to Lorraine that Ida is totally unfit to represent BillMur and does not understand the tax issues or consequences that would apply under the proposed terms for the transaction. Lorraine is convinced that if BillMur follows Ida No's advice it will suffer significant adverse tax consequences. Does Lorraine have any ethical issues to consider as she represents DanAck in these circumstances?

1-15 Paul Monroe, CPA, has been in public practice and a member of the AICPA for 25 years. He signs over 300 individual tax returns each year, most of which have been initially prepared by his staff and reviewed by other staff and himself. In reviewing tax returns for the current filing season, Paul notices that several transactions were improperly handled for the prior year return. Upon further review, Paul realizes that this error exists not only on prior year returns for his current clients but also on prior returns for individuals who are no longer his clients. Consider Circular 230, the SSTSs, and the AICPA Code of Professional Conduct in analyzing Paul's situation.

1-16 Sarah Smart, CPA, is a member of the AICPA and has been in practice for over 10 years. She recently acquired a new tax compliance client, NewCo, Inc. NewCo's in-house accountant (not a CPA) had previously prepared its returns. In reviewing NewCo's prior returns, Sarah discovers some significant error, resulting in underpayment of tax, that will impact the current year return. Sarah meets with the client representative and informs him of the errors and possible corrective action. Initially the client indicates that it will not correct the prior returns but instead allow the IRS to find the mistakes on audit. In the course of the conversation, the client also suggests that it could make a counterbalancing entry to the current return that would result in an increase in tax sufficient to offset the prior underpayments of tax. Based on Circular 230, the SSTSs, and the AICPA Code of Professional Conduct, how should Sarah proceed?

Chapter 2

2-1 Your client, Barney Green, and his wife, Edith, attended a three-day program in Maui entitled "Financial, Tax, and Investment Planning for Investors." The Greens went to Hawaii several days early so that they could adjust to the jet lag and be ready for the seminar. The $8,000 cost of the trip included the following expenses:

First-class airfare	$2,500
Hotel (seven days)	2,000
Program fee	2,000
Meals and other expenses	1,500

The Greens have records to substantiate all the above expenditures in a manner that is acceptable under IRC § 274.

a. List as many possible tax research issues as you can to determine whether the Greens can deduct any or all of the $3,000 of expenditures on their current-year tax return.

b. After completing your list of tax research issues, list the keywords you might use to construct an online tax research query.

c. Execute an online search using your query. For simplicity, select the IRS Publications database from whichever online tax service you use. Summarize your findings.

2-2 Ban Vallew has a son, Katt, by a previous marriage. Ban's ex-wife has custody of Katt. Katt Vallew has a history of emotional problems, for which he has seen a psychiatrist for several years. This year he has become so disturbed, manifesting violence at home and school, that he was enrolled in a special school in Arizona for problem children. Ban pays Katt's school expenses, $3,000 per month. Ban would like to determine whether he is entitled to the medical-expenses deduction (over 10 percent of adjusted gross income) for the cost of sending his son to this school.

a. List as many possible tax research issues as you can to determine tax treatment(s) available to Ban on the payments to the school.

b. After completing your list of tax research issues, list the keywords you might use to construct an online tax research query.

c. Execute an online search using your query. For simplicity, select the IRS Publications database from whichever online tax service you use. Summarize your findings.

2-3 Linda Larue has arthritis. Her chiropractor advised her that she needed to swim daily to alleviate her pain and other symptoms. Consequently, Linda and her husband, Philo, purchased for $400,000 a new home that had a swimming pool, after selling their old home for $325,000. If the Larues had constructed a pool at their former residence, it would have cost $75,000 to build, and it would have increased the value of their home by $50,000.

a. List as many possible tax research issues as you can to determine whether the Larues can deduct any of their current-year expenditures for Linda's arthritis.

b. After completing your list of tax research issues, list the keywords you might use to construct an online tax research query.

c. Execute an online search using your query. For simplicity, select the IRS Revenue Rulings database from whichever online tax service you use. Summarize your findings.

2-4 Gwen Gullible was married to Darrell Devious. They were divorced two years ago. Three years ago (the year before their divorce), Darrell received a $500,000 retirement plan distribution, of which $100,000 was rolled over into an IRA. At the time, Gwen was aware of the retirement funds and the rollover. The distribution was used to pay off the couple's mortgage, purchase a car, and cover living expenses. Darrell prepared the couple's joint return, and Gwen asked him about the tax ramifications of the retirement distributions. He told her he had consulted a CPA and was advised that the retirement plan proceeds used to pay off a mortgage were not taxable income. Gwen accepted that explanation and signed the return. In fact, Darrell had not consulted a CPA.

One year ago (after the divorce), Gwen received a letter from the IRS saying it had not received the tax return for the last full year of marriage. On advice from a CPA, Gwen immediately filed the return (she had a copy of the unfiled return). The IRS notified Gwen that no estimated payments on the retirement distribution had been paid by Darrell, and that she owed $140,000 in tax, plus penalties and interest.

a. List as many possible tax research issues as you can to determine whether Gwen is liable for the tax, interest, and penalties.

b. After completing your list of tax research issues, list the keywords you might use to construct an online tax research query.

c. Execute an online search using your query. For simplicity, select the IRS Revenue Rulings database from the online tax service you use. Summarize your findings.

2-5 Trevor recently purchased a beautiful house on a hillside in sunny California at a cost of $1 million. One evening while enjoying a barbeque on his patio and after a particularly heavy rain, Trevor is surprised to see his neighbor's house disappear in a mudslide. Visibly shaken, Trevor makes immediate efforts to sell his home. Although the view from his lot has improved considerably, he meets severe buyer resistance when forced to explain why he lacks one set of neighbors. Trevor's best offer, made by a family just arrived in town, is $500,000. Trevor reevaluates his life insurance portfolio, places his personal affairs in order, and decides not to sell. Presuming the landslide caused no physical damage to his property, does Trevor have a casualty loss?

a. List as many possible tax research issues as you can to determine Trevor's potential casualty-loss deduction from the decrease in value of his house.

b. After completing your list of tax research issues, list the keywords you might use to construct an online tax research query.

c. Execute an online search using your query. For simplicity, select the IRS Publications database from whichever online tax service you use. Summarize your findings.

Chapter 3

3-1 Staff sergeant G. I. Jane was a soldier in the Iraq War. Her salary was $2,600 per month, and she was in the war zone for eight months. How much of her salary is taxable for the eight months? In answering this case, use only the Internal Revenue Code for your research.

3-2 Carol received a gift of stock from her favorite uncle. The stock had a fair market value of $30,000 and a basis to the uncle of $10,000 at the date of the gift. How much is taxable to Carol from this gift? In answering this case, use only the Internal Revenue Code for your research.

3-3 Maria is an independent long-haul trucker. She receives a speeding ticket for $500, which she pays. Can Maria deduct the cost of the ticket on her Schedule C? In answering this case, use only the Internal Revenue Code for your research.

3-4 Julie loaned her friend Nathan $2,500. Nathan did not repay the debt and skipped town. Can Julie claim any deduction for this bad debt? In answering this case, use only the Internal Revenue Code for your research.

3-5 In December of the previous tax year, Ann's 12-year-old cousin, Susan, came to live with her after Susan's parents met a sudden death in a car accident. In the current tax year, Ann provided all normal support (e.g., food, clothing, education) for Susan. Ann did not formally adopt Susan. If Susan lived in the household for the entire year, can Ann claim a dependency exemption for her cousin for the current tax year? In answering this case, use only the Internal Revenue Code for your research.

3-6 John and Maria support their 21-year-old son, Bill. The son earned $12,200 last year working in a part-time job. Bill went to college part time in the spring semester of the current year. To complete his degree, Bill started school full time in the fall. The fall semester at Bill's college runs from August 20 to December 20. Can John and Maria claim Bill as a dependent on the current year's tax return, even if Bill earns this level of gross income? Assume any dependency test not mentioned has been met. In answering this case, use an online tax service with only the Internal Revenue Code database selected. State your keywords and which online tax service you used to arrive at your answer.

3-7 George and Linda are divorced and own a house from the marriage. Under the divorce decree, Linda pays George $5,000 per month alimony. Because the real estate market has collapsed in the area where they live, George and Linda cannot sell the house. Since they are still friends, they decide to live in separate wings of the house until the real estate market recovers. If George and Linda live together for the entire current year, can Linda claim a deduction for the alimony paid to George? In answering this case, use an online tax service with only the Internal Revenue Code database selected. State your keywords and which online tax service you used to arrive at your answer.

3-8 Juan sold IBM stock to Richard for a $10,000 loss. Richard is the husband of Juan's sister, Carla. How much of the loss can Juan deduct in the current year if Juan's taxable income is $55,000 and he has no other capital transactions? In answering this case, use an online tax service with only the Internal Revenue Code database selected. State your keywords and which online tax service you used to arrive at your answer.

3-9 Tex is a rancher. This year her herd of cattle was infested with hoof-and-mouth disease and had to be destroyed. Tex's insurance policy reimburses her for an amount in excess of the tax basis in the cattle, thereby creating an "insurance gain." After receiving the insurance proceeds, Tex buys a new herd of cattle. Can Tex defer the recognition of this insurance gain on the destroyed herd? In answering this case, use an online tax service with only the Internal Revenue Code database selected. State your keywords and which online tax service you used to arrive at your answer.

3-10 Betty owed Martha $5,000. In payment of this debt, Betty transferred to Martha a life insurance policy on Betty, with a cash surrender value of $5,000. The face value of the policy is $100,000. Martha names herself as beneficiary of the policy and continues to make the premium payments. After Martha has paid $15,000 in premiums, Betty dies and Martha collects $100,000. Is any of the $100,000 Martha received taxable? In answering this case, use an online tax service with only the Internal Revenue Code database selected. State your keywords and which online tax service you used to arrive at your answer.

3-11 On May 1, Rick formed a new corporation, Red, Inc. He spent $3,000 in legal fees and paid the state $600 in incorporation fees. Red, Inc. started operating its business on May 10. How much, if any, Rick or Red, Inc. deduct either of these organizational fees? In answering this case, use an online tax service with only the Internal Revenue Code database selected. State your keywords and which online tax service you used to arrive at your answer.

3-12 Maria Gonzalez lives in San Diego, CA. Over a decade ago, Maria's family emigrated from the Jalisco region of Mexico (a small town known as Etzatlan) to the U.S. and obtained U.S. citizenship shortly thereafter. During the current tax year, brush fires ravaged large parts of Jalisco. Although Maria had no close relatives left in the region, her family history stimulated her generosity and she made a $3,000 cash contribution to the Associacion Comunitaria De Autosuficiencia A.c., a registered Mexican charity that helps farmers engage in more sustainable techniques (the fires were attributed in part to farmers burning their fields). She found the charity after reading an internet news item on the fires. The funds were used to provide immediate food, shelter and clothing to fire victims and to develop communications to discourage field burning as a farming technique. Maria generated adjusted gross income of $60,000 in the current year. Is Maria's charitable contribution deductible for income tax purposes? In answering this case, use an online tax service with only the Internal Revenue Code database selected. State your keywords and which online tax service you used to arrive at your answer.

3-13 Curtis is 50 years old and has an individual retirement account (IRA) that contains substantial funds. His son, Curtis Jr., was accepted to Yale University upon graduating from high school. Curtis had not planned for this and needs to draw $25,000 per year out of his IRA to help pay the tuition and fees at Yale. What are the tax consequences of the withdrawals from the IRA? In answering this case, use an online tax service with only the Internal Revenue Code database selected. State your key words and which online tax service you used to arrive at your answer.

3-14 Cathy Coed is a full-time senior student at Big Research University (BRU). Cathy is considered by most as a brilliant student and has been given a $35,000-per-year scholarship. In the current year, Cathy pays the following amounts to attend BRU:

Tuition	$26,000
Required lab fees	$300
Required books and supplies	$1,000
Room and board	$7,500

What are the tax consequences (i.e., how much is income) of the $35,000 current year's scholarship to Cathy? In answering this case, use an online tax service with only the Internal Revenue Code database selected. State your key words and which online tax service you used to arrive at your answer.

3-15 Dennis is an executive of Gold Corporation. He receives a one-for-one distribution of stock rights for each share of common stock he owns. On the date of distribution, the stock rights have a fair market value of $2 per right, and the stock has a fair market value of $20 per share. Dennis owns 10,000 shares of the stock with a basis of $5 per share. If Dennis does not make any special elections with regard to the stock rights, what is his basis in the rights?

a. Locate the code section(s) that deals with this situation. State the section number(s).

b. Review the code section(s). Does it raise a need for new information to solve this question?

c. Are you able to reach a conclusion about the research question from this code section? If so, what is your conclusion(s)?

3-16 Monica purchased two acres of land with an old building on it for $1 million. The purchase was made to acquire the land for a new store she wanted to open on the property. Shortly after completing the purchase, Monica pays $80,000 to have the old building demolished. How does Monica treat the $80,000 demolition payment for tax purposes?

   a. Locate the code section(s) that deals with this situation. State the section number(s).

   b. Review the code section(s). Does it raise a need for new information to solve this question?

   c. Are you able to reach a conclusion about the research question from this code section? If so, what is your conclusion(s)?

3-17 Lihue Inc. sells timeshares in Hawaii. Gene buys a timeshare from Lihue Inc. Gene agrees to pay $10,000 down, and Lihue Inc. will finance a seven-year note for the balance of the purchase price at the current market rate of interest. Can Lihue Inc. use the installment method to report its gain on the sale of the Hawaiian timeshare to Gene?

   a. Locate the code section(s) that deals with this situation. State the section number(s).

   b. Review the code section(s). Does it raise a need for new information to solve this question?

   c. Are you able to reach a conclusion about the research question from this code section? If so, what is your conclusion(s)?

3-18 Sara Student is a full-time first-year student at Small State University (SSU). Her tuition for the year is $42,000, which is paid by Sara's mother, Susan. Sara also has a job as a model, earning substantial money; therefore, Sara does not qualify as Susan's dependent. Assuming no phase-out of the credit due to income, can Sara's mother claim the American Opportunity Credit for the tuition she paid? Can Sara claim the American Opportunity Credit on any unused portion of the tuition?

   a. Locate the code section(s) that deals with this situation. State the section number(s).

   b. Review the code section(s). Does it raise a need for new information to solve this question?

   c. Are you able to reach a conclusion about the research question from this code section? If so, what is your conclusion(s)?

3-19 Homer and Marge Owner are married and file jointly. Seven years ago, Homer and Marge bought a new home that they have lived in since. The home cost $640,000 for which they paid $120,000 as a down payment and financed the balance through a mortgage. This year, interest rates reached new lows and Homer and Marge decided to refinance the mortgage. At the time of the refinancing, the mortgage balance was only $535,000. Because rates were so much lower, the Owners decided to refinance for a new mortgage of $545,000 and paid off their existing car loan. Can the Owners deduct the interest expense on their new mortgage?

   a. Locate the code section(s) that deals with this situation. State the section number(s).

   b. Review the code section(s). Does it raise a need for new information to solve this question?

   c. Are you able to reach a conclusion about the research question from this code section? If so, what is your conclusion(s)?

   d. Could the Owners have structured the debt in a different manner that might have affected its deductibility?

3-20 Dr. Stephen Kolbert is a professor of television and movie production at Hollywood University (and thus an employee of the university). He often meets with his doctoral students, who call him Dr. K, in his home. In his home, Dr. K has a room that he uses solely to conduct business related to the classes he teaches at Hollywood University. In the room, he and his students review the movies and shows the students have made to satisfy requirements in their doctoral program. Dr. K has an office on campus, but he has found that his movie and show reviews are more efficient when he and his students can watch the programs on his 72-inch LED flat-screen television and sit on the comfortable couch in his home office rather than the 19-inch television and chairs in his office.

a. Locate the code section(s) that deals with this situation. State the section number(s).

b. Review the code section(s). Does it raise a need for new information to solve this question?

c. Are you able to reach a conclusion about the research question from this code section? If so, what is your conclusion(s)?

3-21 Odiferous Chemical Company (OCC) manufactured pesticides that were toxic. Over the course of several years, the toxic waste contaminated the air and water around the company's plant. Several employees and people living near the plant suffered toxic poisoning, and the Environmental Protection Agency (EPA) cited the company for violations. A federal district court judge found OCC guilty and imposed a fine of $15 million, which OCC paid to the EPA. You have been asked to assess the deductibility of the payment of the fine.

a. Locate the code section(s) that deals with this situation. State the section number(s).

b. Review the code section(s). Does it raise a need for new information to solve this question?

c. Are you able to reach a conclusion about the research question from this code section? If so, what is your conclusion(s)?

3-22 The Reverend Shaman Oracle is an ordained minister in the Church of Prophetic Prophecy in Palm Desert, California. In the current year, Shaman receives payments of $150,000 from the church for his services. Of this amount, the church designates $60,000 for compensation and $90,000 as a housing allowance. Shaman and his wife own a home and have actual expenditures during the year for the home of $72,000. The house is located in a well-established rental market, and the fair market rental value of the home for the current year is $55,000. Shaman wants to know how he and his wife should report these amounts on their current year's tax return.

After appropriate research, write a letter to Shaman explaining your findings. His address is P.O. Box 1234, Palm Desert, California 92211.

Chapter 4

4-1 Lance asks you to explain why his employer, the Good Food Truck Stop, an establishment that employs more than 30 waiters and waitresses on any given day, included $2,400 in tip income in Box 8 on his Form W-2 for the year. Although he has not informed the truck stop, Lance always has kept track of the tips he actually received, and he has reported them in full on his tax return.

4-2 Joe incurred $38,000 of investment interest expense in the current year. He also generated $35,000 in dividend income and had a $65,000 passive loss for the year. What is the amount of Joe's interest deduction?

4-3 Georgia won the Massachusetts lottery, which means that she will receive $28,000 per year for the next 30 years. Georgia purchased the lucky ticket in March, and she was selected the winner in June. Georgia regularly spent $100 per month on lottery tickets, one-third for Massachusetts tickets and two-thirds for Vermont tickets, but is not considered to be in the gambling business.

a. What is Georgia's gross income from this prize?

b. Is there any corresponding deduction?

4-4 Dieter won the lottery this year, which means that he will receive $400,000 per year for the next 30 years. The present value of Dieter's prize is about $3.75 million. Conscious of the tax benefits of income shifting, Dieter irrevocably assigned one-fifth of every annuity payment to his daughter Heidi. What are the effects of these events on Dieter's taxable income?

4-5 Ace High and Lady Luck live together and have pooled their funds for several months to purchase food and other household necessities and to buy an occasional state lottery ticket. Ace used part of these pooled funds to buy a lottery ticket that won $3 million. When they discovered that the lottery proceeds could be paid only to one recipient under state law, Ace and Lady executed a "separate ownership agreement." The agreement created an equal interest in the ticket for both Ace and Lady. Must Ace pay gift tax on the transfer of a one-half interest in the ticket to Lady? What is the value of the gift?

4-6 Shaky Savings and Loan has a depositor named Olive who opened an account last year. At that time, Olive gave Shaky her Social Security number (SSN) as a taxpayer identification number (TIN). The IRS notified Shaky that Olive's SSN was invalid. This year, Shaky asked Olive for a corrected number, which she provided. Later this year, the IRS notified Shaky that the new SSN also was invalid. What should Shaky do at this point about backup withholding on Olive's account? Prepare (in good form) a research memorandum to the file.

4-7 Alpine Corporation is a qualified small business corporation eligible to elect S corporation status. Albert is a shareholder in Alpine. On February 1 of the current year, Albert dies before signing the proper S corporation election form. The stock passes to Albert's estate. Ellen is appointed executor of Albert's estate on May 1 of the current year. On March 10 of the current year, Alpine filed Form 2553, the election form to be an S corporation, properly signed by all March 10 shareholders, and Ellen (the executrix) on behalf of Albert. Is this a valid S corporation election? Prepare (in good form) a research memorandum to the file.

4-8 Joe Bacillus owns Bacillus's Italian Restaurant. A friend of Joe's who owns a sports bar comes to Joe and wants to form a partnership with Joe to buy an old building, renovate it, and then move both the restaurant and the sports bar into it along with other tenants. Joe would like to make this investment. He needs approximately $200,000 for his share of the buy-in of the partnership that will purchase, renovate, and manage the building. Because of other recent large expenses, however, Joe finds himself short of cash at the present time. His only large liquid asset is his self-directed IRA, which currently owns $225,000 in stock and bonds. Joe proposes that he direct the IRA to sell the securities and to use the proceeds to invest in the building renovation partnership. Conduct appropriate research (including an online search) to determine if Joe's plan is workable. Prepare (in good form) a research memorandum to the file.

4-9 The Pima and Southern Railroad (PSRR) is a small railroad operating in rural Arizona. It exists by carrying freight to remote areas of the southwest. This year the PSRR needs to replace a 30-mile section of its track. The PSRR has bids from a contractor to replace the track for the following amounts:

Cost of new track	$5,000,000
Installing new track	3,000,000
Road bed grading and improvements	2,500,000
Removing old track (net of salvage)	1,500,000
Total	$12,000,000

The old track is fully depreciated, and the cost shown is net of $200,000 salvage value received for the scrap metal. The new track is an improved type, and it is expected to last 35 to 40 years. The controller of PSRR, Casey Jones, comes to you and wants to know the tax treatment of the above expenditures. He specifically wants to know if any costs can be deducted or if all must be capitalized and written off over a period of years. He is also concerned about any potential problems with the uniform capitalization rules under § 263A. Prepare (in good form) a research memorandum to the file.

4-10 Your client, Ned Bovine, purchased a $2 million life insurance policy from the Nickel Life Insurance Co. (NLIC) of Dime Box, Texas. Ned's wife is the beneficiary of the policy. The policy was purchased 10 years ago when Nickel Life Insurance was a mutual insurance company. In the current year, Nickel Life Insurance converted from a mutual company to a stock company in a tax-free reorganization. As part of the conversion, Ned received 800 shares of the new publicly traded (NASDAQ) Nickel Life Insurance Co. Three weeks after receiving the shares, Ned sold all his shares at $15 each. The total premiums paid by Ned on the policy before the conversion was $20,000.

a. Locate the IRS pronouncement(s) that deals with this situation. State the pronouncement number(s).

b. Review the IRS pronouncement(s). Does it raise a need for new information to solve this question?

c. Are you able to reach a conclusion about the research question from this IRS pronouncement(s)? If so, what is your conclusion(s)?

4-11 At age 65, Carlota's financial position was better than her health. She had a large balance in an IRA that she wanted to move to a different IRA. Carlota withdrew $100,000 from the IRA and planned to roll over the funds into another IRA. Unfortunately, she died before completing the rollover. Carlota's son, Andres, discovered what his mother had done a week after her death. Andres was both executor of Carlota's estate and beneficiary of her IRA.

Can Andres, in his role as executor, complete the rollover for his deceased mother by depositing the $100,000 in another IRA within the 60-day rollover period?

a. Locate the IRS pronouncement(s) that deals with this situation. State the pronouncement number(s).

b. Review the IRS pronouncement(s). Does it raise a need for new information to solve this question?

c. Are you able to reach a conclusion about the research question from this IRS pronouncement(s)? If so, what is your conclusion(s)?

4-12 The Venganza Tribe is a federally recognized Indian tribal government described in IRC § 7701(a)(40)(A). The Venganza Tribe would like to invest some of its cash resulting from its newly opened casino in a real estate development, Vista de Basura Inc., an S corporation. Is the Indian tribal government an eligible shareholder for S corporation purposes?

a. Locate the IRS pronouncement(s) that deals with this situation. State the pronouncement number(s).

b. Review the IRS pronouncement(s). Does it raise a need for new information to solve this question?

c. Are you able to reach a conclusion about the research question from this IRS pronouncement(s)? If so, what is your conclusion(s)?

4-13 Fred Forgetful parks his personal car on a hill in sunny California and fails to properly set the brake or curb the wheels. As a result of Fred's negligence, the car rolls down the hill, damages Lucky's front porch, injures Lucky (who was sitting on the porch), and damages Fred's car. Because of the accident, Fred is forced to pay the following unreimbursed amounts:

Medical expenses for Lucky's injuries	$5,500
Repairs to Fred's car	7,000
Repairs to Lucky's porch	8,500
Fine for traffic violation	275

Using only the regulations and code, determine which of these payments, if any, would qualify for casualty loss treatment (before any percentage limitations) as to Fred.

4-14 Your client, Mustang Racing Parts Inc. (MRP), is engaged in the production, transmission, distribution, and sale of racing headers for Ford Mustangs (inventory property). The client is also involved in the distribution of other racing parts manufactured by other suppliers (inventory property). During the tax year, MRP produces numerous identical dies and molds using standardized designs and assembly line techniques (noninventory property). The dies and molds are mass-produced. MRP uses the dies and molds to produce particular automobile racing components and does not hold them for sale. The dies and molds have a three-year recovery period for purposes of IRC § 168(c). The client wants to know if it can elect to use the "simplified service cost method" to calculate the amount capitalized under § 263A on the dies and molds.

a. Locate the IRS pronouncement that deals with this situation. State the pronouncement number.

b. Review the pronouncement. Does it raise a need for new information to solve this question?

c. Are you able to reach a conclusion about the research question from this pronouncement? If so, what is your conclusion(s)?

4-15 Your client, Manny Mendacious, invested $70,000 in the stock of a new start-up company that opened a chain of fried pickle fast-food restaurants called The Cooked Cucumber. As might be expected, this venture has not been very successful, and Manny's stock has lost its value. Manny knows that worthless securities are normally treated as a capital loss, which means the $3,000 annual maximum deduction and other limits apply. While talking to one of his co-investors, he discovers that her tax adviser (Shamus Sham, the taxman) contends that if a taxpayer "abandons" a security it is not subject to the capital loss limitation. Manny is very excited about this and is anxious to assert he "abandoned" the Cooked Cucumber stock and deduct the entire $70,000 loss in the current year.

   a. Locate the regulation that deals with this situation. Give the regulation's citation and when the regulation was finalized.

   b. Review the regulation. Does it raise a need for new information to solve this question?

   c. Are you able to reach a conclusion about the research question from this regulation? If so, what is your conclusion(s)?

   d. Does the code allow for Manny to treat his loss as ordinary if The Cooked Cucumber stock meets certain requirements?

4-16 David Dental, DDS, and his unmarried partner Sally Surgeon, MD, have lived together for the past five years. Both are at the peak of their careers and decide to buy a new "showcase" home in La Jolla, California. After looking at several homes in the area, they buy one for $2 million. They put a 20 percent down payment ($400,000) on the house and finance the balance ($1.6 million). Each takes out a separate mortgage for $800,000, for a total of $1.6 million. There is no additional debt (e.g., a home equity loan) on the residence.

   a. Locate the chief counsel advice (CCA) that deals with this situation. Give the CCA citation.

   b. Review the CCA. Does it raise a need for new information or authority to solve this question?

   c. Are you able to reach a conclusion about the research question from this CCA? If so, what is your conclusion(s)?

4-17 During a properly declared U.S. war with Outer Altoona, Harriet, a single taxpayer, was killed in action. Current year federal taxable income to the date of Harriet's death totaled $19,000, and federal income tax withholding came to $2,300.

   a. What is Harriet's tax liability for the year of her death?

   b. What documentation must accompany her final Form 1040?

Chapter 5

5-1 Snidely Limited spent $1 million this year to upgrade its manufacturing plant, which had received several warnings from the state environmental agency about releasing pollution into the local river. Late in the year, Snidely received an assessment of $700,000 for violating the state's Clean Water Act. After he negotiated with the state, which cost $135,000 in legal fees, Snidely promised to spend another $200,000 next year for more pollution control devices, and the fine was reduced to $450,000. How much of these expenditures can Snidely Limited deduct for tax purposes?

5-2 Last year, only 4 of 32 professional sports teams in a new league turned a nominal accounting profit. Betty purchased such a team this year. Betty operates the franchise in a business-like manner, but has no expertise in the area of sports franchises (Betty's primary source of income is from her cardboard packaging business). She attends all the games (as she loves the sport) and spends some time managing the business, but has hired a general manager to run the day-to-day operations. As a "turnaround expert," Betty is comfortable she can make this franchise profitable; however, she may have overstepped her ability since the league is struggling overall. Her loss for the year was determined to be $950,000. Can she deduct this loss?

5-3 Herbert, a collector of rare coins, bought a 1916 Spanish Bowlero for $2,000 in 2004. He sold the coin for $4,500 in January of the current tax year. Herbert was surprised at how easy it was to turn a profit selling rare coins and since he was at the appropriate age, he retired from his loading dock job in June and began actively buying and selling rare coins. By December of the current tax year, Herbert's realized gain from such activities was $21,500. What type of taxable income was January's $2,500 gain?

5-4 Steve is an usher at his local church. Can he deduct commuting expenses for the Sundays that he is assigned to usher for church services?

5-5 Sam Shiatsu is a self-employed massage therapist and is the brother-in-law of a partner in the CPA firm where you work. During the current tax year, Sam worked as an assistant supervisor and clinician for the Western College of Oriental Massage in Gila Bend, Arizona, an institution owned by Massage Center, Inc. (MCI). Sam was paid $20,500 with checks issued by MCI for services he provided to MCI pursuant to a contract, which stated that MCI would file a Form 1099-MISC, Miscellaneous Income, with the IRS and that Sam would be responsible for paying any tax liability that resulted from the payments. Sam has a B.S. degree in accounting, a master's degree in industrial relations, and a B.S. degree in nutrition. Sam, although not an attorney, also has four years of experience as a justice of the peace in Blanco, Texas.

Sam did not file a tax return for the current tax year, and he did not pay any federal income tax or make any payments of estimated tax for that year. He did not file a return because he claims he is a citizen of the "Republic of Arizona" and therefore not subject to the U.S. federal income tax. On February 25th, two years after the current tax year, the IRS mailed Sam a notice of deficiency setting forth respondent's determination of a deficiency in petitioner's income tax for the current tax year and additions to tax. Tracy (your boss) asks you to research this issue and determine Sam's exposure for not filing his tax return. Summarize in a short internal memo the key points you find.

5-6 Professor Stevens obtained tenure and promotion to full-professor status many years ago. Yet he continues to publish research papers in scholarly journals to satisfy his own curiosity and to maintain his professional prestige and status within the academic community. Publications are also necessary in order for Professor Stevens to receive pay raises at his university. This year, Dr. Stevens spent $750 of his own funds to travel to southern Utah to collect some critical pieces of data for his work. What is the tax treatment of this expenditure?

5-7 The local electric company requires a $200 refundable deposit from new customers in lieu of a credit check. Landlord Pete, a cash basis taxpayer, pays this amount for all his new-to-town tenants. When the tenant has paid the electric bill without delay, the electric company credits the deposit from the subsequent bill(s) until the entire amount is refunded. Pete allows the tenants to keep the credits on their utility account. The rent charged remains more or less at market value for the apartments; thus Pete is using the deposit as a way of attracting tenants. Can he deduct the $200 payments on his tax return?

5-8 High-Top Financing charges its personal loan holders a 2 percent fee if the full loan principal is paid prior to the due date. What is the tax effect of this year's $50,000 of prepayment penalties collected by High-Top?

5-9 Cecilia died this year, owning mutual funds in her IRA worth $120,000. Under the terms of the IRA, Cecilia's surviving husband, Frank, was the beneficiary of the account, and he took a lump-sum distribution from the fund. Both Cecilia and Frank were age 57 at the beginning of the year.

a. How does Frank account for the inheritance assuming that he rolls it over into his own IRA in a timely manner?

b. Would your answer change if Frank were Cecilia's brother?

5-10 Jerry Baker and his wife, Hammi, started a church known as the Church of Tropical Worship (CTW) about two years ago. The CTW was organized under state law as a separate legal entity, and has a set of charter rules that other CTW churches (of which there are currently) none must follow. The rules, largely prescribed by Jerry, require any new minister in the church to undergo an education training process that consists of a trip to a tropical location such as the South Pacific or Caribbean where the minister must devote his or her time to tropical activities such as tanning, luaus, tropical drinks, snorkeling, etc. The trips are often taken during the winter because the church meets regularly only during the summer months. There are currently over 125 registered members in the church but only 20-30 show for any particular church service, held at the only existing church location, an elementary school rented out on Sundays during the summer. To practice their beliefs, the Bakers took a two-week trip to Tahiti this year to worship the tropical lifestyle. The cost (e.g., airfare, hotels) of this religious "pilgrimage" was $5,250. Jerry wants to know if he can deduct the cost of this trip as a charitable deduction on his Form 1040, Schedule A.

5-11 Willie Waylon is a famous country-and-western singer. As an investment, Willie started a chain of barbecue restaurants called Willie's Wonderful Ribs. Willie's friends and associates invested $500,000 in this venture. The restaurant chain failed, and the investors lost all their money. Because of his visibility and status in the entertainment community, Willie felt that he personally had to make good on the losses suffered by the investors to protect his singing and business reputation. Consequently, he personally paid $500,000 to reimburse the investors for their losses. What are Willie's tax consequences (if any) from the reimbursement?

5-12 Paul Preppie is an accountant for the Very Big (VB) Corporation of America, located in Los Angeles. When Paul went to work for VB, he did not have a college degree. VB required that Paul earn a B.S. degree in accounting, so he enrolled in a local private university's night school and obtained the degree. VB Corporation does not reimburse employees for attending night school, and because Paul attended a private university, the tuition and other costs were relatively expensive. Under California law, once Paul has his degree, he is eligible to sit for the CPA exam and can become a CPA in California. Can Paul deduct any of the $10,500 he paid in tuition and other costs during the current tax year?

    Prepare (in good form) a research memorandum to the file. (See Chapter 2 for an illustration of the structure of a tax memo.)

5-13 Several years ago, Carol Mutter, a cash-basis taxpayer, obtained a mortgage from Weak National Bank to purchase a personal residence. In December 2016, $8,500 of interest was due on the mortgage, but Carol had only $75 in her checking account. On December 31, 2016, she borrowed $8,500 from her sister, Pearl, evidenced by a note, and the proceeds were deposited in her checking account. On the same day, Carol issued a check in the identical amount of $8,500 to Weak Bank for the interest due. Is the interest expense deductible for the 2016 tax year?

    Prepare (in good form) a research memorandum to the file. (See Chapter 2 for an illustration of the structure of a tax memo.)

5-14 Phyllis maintained an IRA account at the brokerage firm ABC. On February 11 of the current year, she requested a check for the balance of her account. She received the check made out in her name and deposited it the same day in a new IRA account at the brokerage firm XYZ. Phyllis then requested a check on May 8 from XYZ, which was deposited in another new IRA account 35 days later. Is the May 8 distribution taxable to Phyllis?

    Prepare in good form a research memorandum to the file. (See Chapter 2 for an illustration of the structure of a tax memo.)

5-15 Crystal Eros is a devout Pyramidist and a member of the Religious Society of Yanni, a Pyramidist organization. She adheres to the fundamental tenets of Pyramidist theology, including the belief that the Spirit of God is in every person and that it is wrong to kill or otherwise harm another person. Crystal's faith dictates that she not voluntarily participate, directly or indirectly, in military activities. Because federal income taxes fund military activities, Crystal believes that her faith prohibits her from paying such taxes. Is there any legal substantiation for Crystal's position?

    Prepare (in good form) a research memorandum to the file. (See Chapter 2 for an illustration of the structure of a tax memo.)

5-16 Last year, your client, Roberto Dinero, mailed an automatic extension for his tax return on April 15. He enclosed a check for $10,000 with the extension request. The IRS cashed the check on April 28. Later, the

IRS assessed Roberto late filing penalties of $2,900 because they claim he did not mail the extension request on time. On the same date, Roberto mailed an income tax extension request and check to the state of California. The California check was cashed on April 23. You requested that the IRS send you a copy of the extension request envelope showing the postmark; however, the IRS has lost it. The IRS recently attached Roberto's bank account for the $2,900, thereby seizing the funds directly. You have known Roberto for years, and he could be described as a good, law-abiding, taxpaying citizen. He always pays his taxes on time, has never been in trouble with the IRS, and is not a tax protester. Roberto asks you to recommend whether he should engage a tax attorney and sue for a refund, knowing that the legal fees for such an action will probably exceed $10,000.

After appropriate research, write a letter to Roberto explaining your findings. His address is 432 Lucre Street, Tecate, CA 91980.

5-17 Your client, Luther Lifo, is a professor who runs a CPA review course. He comes to you with the following tax questions:

Question One. Luther teaches CPA review courses on either a guaranteed or a nonguaranteed basis. Under the contractual guaranteed program, students pay higher tuition and, if they fail the CPA examination, are entitled to a full refund within two weeks of the release of the results. The CPA review course contracts require him to place the tuition in a set-aside escrow account until the students pass the exam; he established an escrow account as a qualified trust account for this purpose. The registration fee and tuition must be paid in full before the classes begin. Thus, students enrolled in the class that started in January 20x1 paid their tuition in December 20x0. In 20x0, Luther deposited registration fees and tuition, including $30,000 in guaranteed tuition payments for the winter 20x1 courses, into a qualified trust escrow account. Also during 20x1, he paid refunds to guaranteed students who failed the 20x1 exams from that account. Does Luther report the $30,000 as income in 20x0 or 20x1? How are the refunds paid in 20x1 treated for tax purposes? State the authority for your conclusion.

Question Two. Luther is a majority shareholder in a corporation that owns an office building. He leases space in the building for use in his CPA review course. Luther pays approximately $20 per square foot in annual rent. The corporation leases the remaining space in the building to a LSAT, GMAT, SAT, and GRE review course run by other taxpayers for approximately $10 per square foot. Luther's main intent in negotiating the discounted lease was to secure the additional traffic generated by the other review courses in order to enhance the potential revenue for the CPA review course. What is the amount of rent that Luther can deduct in connection with the CPA review course? State the authority for your conclusion.

After appropriate research, write a letter to Luther explaining your findings. His address is 321 Fifo Street, Temecula, CA 91980.

5-18 Austin Towers is a convicted former spy for the former Soviet Union. Austin received a communication from a current Russian agent that $2 million had been set aside for him in an account upon which he would be able to draw. Austin was told that the money was being held by Russia, rather than in an independent or third-party bank or institution, on the petitioner's behalf. Over the next few years, Austin drew approximately $1 million from the account. During that period, Austin filed annual tax returns with his wife showing taxable income of approximately $65,000 per year. When Austin's espionage was discovered by the U.S. government, they confiscated the remaining $760,000 of cash found stuffed in various cookie jars, mattresses, and other hiding places. Conduct appropriate research to determine Austin's tax liability for the $1 million in spy fees.

After appropriate research, write a letter to Austin explaining your findings. His address is Lompoc Federal Prison, Cell #123, Lompoc, CA 93401.

5-19 Your client, Teddy Chow, and his wife Abby filed a lawsuit to recover damages for personal injuries Teddy sustained in an auto accident in 2008. In 2012, a jury awarded Teddy $1.62 million in damages. In addition, delay damages in the amount of $1.08 million were then added to that award, resulting in a total judgment of $2.7 million. The defendants appealed the award, and while the appeal was pending, the parties reached a settlement, which provided for payment to Teddy of $2.55 million. In 2017, after attorney fees of $850,000 were subtracted, Teddy received $1.7 million. Teddy wants to know how these amounts are treated for tax purposes.

After appropriate research, write a letter to Teddy and Abby explaining your findings. Their address is 654 Hops Street, Golden, CO 78501.

5-20   Cabrito Ranch Inc. is a family ranch owned and operated by two brothers, Billie and Bubba Cabrito. The corporation made in-kind bonus payments, in the form of goats, to its two officers (Billie and Bubba) in exchange for their performance of agricultural labor. The two brothers are the only employees to receive goat bonuses. The transfers of the goats to the officers occurred within days after the date Cabrito Ranch would have sold the goats within the ordinary course of its business. The two officers/brothers did not market their bonus goats separately from other Cabrito Ranch goats; rather, the bonus goats were loaded onto the same trucks and sold to the same goat buyer on the same terms as other Cabrito Ranch goats. The officer/brothers' goats were sold for $70,000 ($35,000 to each brother). Cabrito Ranch wants to know how to treat the cash from the goat bonuses for FICA purposes.

After appropriate research, write a letter to Billie and Bubba explaining your findings. Their address is 247 Angora Road, Mohair, TX 77501.

5-21   Gwen Gullible was married to Darrell Devious. They were divorced two years ago. Three years ago (the year before their divorce), Darrell received a $250,000 retirement plan distribution, of which $50,000 was rolled over into an IRA. At the time, Gwen was aware of the retirement funds and the rollover. The distribution was used to pay off the couple's mortgage, to purchase a car, and for living expenses. Darrell prepared the couple's joint return, and Gwen asked him about the tax ramifications of the retirement distributions. He told her he had consulted a CPA and was advised that the retirement plan proceeds used to pay off a mortgage were not taxable income. Gwen accepted that explanation and signed the return. In fact, Darrell had not consulted a CPA.

One year ago (after the divorce), Gwen received a letter from the IRS saying it had not received the tax return for the last full year of marriage. On advice from a CPA, Gwen immediately filed the return. (She had a copy of the unfiled return.) The IRS notified Gwen that no estimated payments on the retirement distribution had been paid by Darrell, and that she owed $60,000 in tax, plus penalties and interest. The deficiency notice provided that the retirement distribution, minus the amount rolled over, was income to the couple.

After appropriate research, prepare (in good form) a research memorandum to the file. (See Chapter 2 for an illustration of the structure of a tax memo.) Then write a letter to Gwen explaining your findings. Her address is 678 Surprise Street, Houston, TX 77019.

5-22   Ned Naive operated several franchised stores, and at the home office's suggestion he consolidated the stores' payroll and accounting functions with Andy the Accountant. Andy is not a CPA. Last year, Andy began embezzling taxpayer's escrowed tax withholdings and failed to remit required amounts for the four quarters. The IRS assessed Ned $10,000 in penalties for failing to make the proper withholding deposits during the year.

After appropriate research, prepare (in good form) a research memorandum to the file. (See Chapter 2 for an illustration of the structure of a tax memo.) Then write a letter to Ned explaining your findings. His address is 4567 Brainless Street, Phoenix, AZ 91234.

5-23   Phred Phortunate won his state lotto two years ago. His lotto ticket was worth $10 million, which was payable in 20 annual installments of $500,000 each. Phred paid $1 for the winning ticket. The lotto in Phred's state does not allow winners to receive their payout in a lump sum. Phred wanted all his money now, so he assigned his future lotto winnings to Happy Finance Company for a discounted price of $4.5 million. Assignment of lotto winnings is permitted by Phred's state lotto. Phred filed his tax return and reported the assignment of the lotto winnings as a capital gain ($4.5 million, $1 basis) taxable at a 15 percent rate.

After appropriate research to determine if Phred correctly reported his lotto winnings assignment, prepare (in good form) a research memorandum to the file. (See Chapter 2 for an illustration of the structure of a tax memo.) Then write a letter to Phred explaining your findings. His address is 2345 Ecstatic Street, White River Junction, VT 05001.

5-24 Your client, Gary Gearbox, wholly owned and worked full time for a C corporation in the business of repairing autos. His wife, Tammy, wholly owned and worked full time for another C corporation that provided mobile auto-windshield repairs. Both corporations' offices were located in the Gearboxes' home. The corporations paid the Gearboxes rent for the use of this office space. In addition to renting this portion of their home, the Gearboxes also owned five rental properties. On their last three tax returns, the Gearboxes reported net income from leasing office space to their C corporations of $40,000, $24,000, and $22,000, respectively. During these years, the combined losses from the five other rental properties exceeded the income derived from their office leases. On their last three tax returns, the Gearboxes offset the losses from the rental properties against the income from the office leases and, as a result, paid no tax on the rental income paid to them by their corporation.

After appropriate research to determine if Gary and Tammy correctly reported their rental income, prepare (in good form) a research memorandum to the file. Then write a letter to the Gearboxes explaining your findings. Their address is 7895 NASCAR Way, Talladega, AL 35160.

5-25 Your client, Jack Benny, and his wife were divorced last year. Jack had been employed by the city of Rancho Cucamonga for 30 years. Jack was a participant in a defined-benefit pension plan. He had been eligible to start receiving pension benefits five years ago, but he kept working and did not collect his pension. The divorce decree gave Jack's wife one-half of the community interest in the pension plan. If Jack had retired on the date of the divorce, she would have been entitled to receive $2,200 per month. Because Jack did not retire, however, the divorce court ordered him to pay his former spouse $2,200 per month until he retired. The divorce court also ordered the pension plan to make the same monthly payments to Jack's ex-wife after his retirement. Jack paid his former spouse $26,400 in the current year as ordered in the divorce decree. Jack is still working and has not yet retired.

After appropriate research to determine if Jack can deduct the payments to his ex-wife as alimony on his current tax return and prepare (in good form) a research memorandum to the file. Write a client letter to Jack with your findings. His address is 543 Camino Disolución, Rancho Cucamonga, CA 91730.

5-26 Many years ago your client Lucy Hapless (currently single and age 48) started working with Sham Credit Swap (SCS) Inc., where she participated in the company's 401(k) plan. Five years ago, she took out a home loan from her 401(k) plan. The loan was repayable with interest through semimonthly payroll deductions over a 10-year term. Lucy made the scheduled payments until she was laid off this early this year. The outstanding balance of the loan became due and payable at the time of Lucy's termination, but she did not have the money to pay off the loan, nor was she able to refinance it. No payments were made on the loan after her layoff, and the loan went into default. The 401(k) plan sent Lucy a letter, notifying her that she had a deemed distribution from the plan equal to the then unpaid loan balance of $72,000. The 401(k) plan sent Lucy a check for $98,000, which represented the balance of her plan account minus federal tax withholding of $24,500. Six months ago, after Lucy received the check, she deposited the entire $98,000 into her checking account and has been using the money for living expenses, because she has been unable find another job.

After appropriate research to determine if determine Lucy's tax consequences from this 401(k) plan loan payoff and prepare (in good form) a research memorandum to the file. Write a client letter to Lucy with your findings. Her address is 789 Hard Luck St., Carefree, AZ 85377.

5-27 Mary and Manny Muffler were involved in an auto accident several years ago with an uninsured motorist. The uninsured motorist was at fault and caused significant injuries to Mary. Because of her injuries, Mary was unable to work for more than a year. At the time of the accident, Mary and her husband had two vehicles insured under separate automobile liability insurance policies through Farm State Automobile Insurance Co. (Farm State). Both insurance policies were purchased by Mary and her husband and had endorsements for uninsured and underinsured motorist (UM/UIM) coverage with policy limits of $50,000.

Although Mary filed a lawsuit against the motorist who was at fault in her accident, her counsel ascertained that the defendant had neither significant assets nor any insurance. Mary submitted a claim under her UM/UIM coverage to Farm State for compensation for her injuries in the automobile accident. Farm State took the position that Mary was entitled to recover under the UM/UIM coverage of only one of the two policies she and her husband held, resulting in an effective limit on recovery of $50,000. In taking this position, Farm State relied on antistacking provisions in its insurance contracts with Mary and her husband, under which the insured was precluded from aggregating or "stacking" his or her UM/UIM coverage under multiple Farm State policies. Mary agreed to settle her claim with Farm State for $32,000 plus $18,000 in attorney fees ($50,000 total).

After receiving the $32,000 payment several years ago, Mary became a member of a class action against Farm State that alleged that the antistacking rules constituted a breach of contract and a breach of a covenant of good faith and fair dealing in their insurance contracts, and that she was entitled to collect on the second policy. Farm State settled the claim. As a result, Mary received an additional $53,000 ($50,000 plus interest) payment pursuant to the settlement agreement as her pro rata portion of the settlement funds. During that year Mary was issued a Form 1099-MISC, Miscellaneous Income, reflecting the payment.

After appropriate research, determine how Mary (who has since divorced Manny) should report the $53,000 payment on her current year's tax return and prepare (in good form) a research memorandum to the file. Write a client letter to Mary with your findings. Her address is 789 Mustang St., Shelby, CA 92111.

5-28 David Dental, DDS, and his unmarried partner, Sally Surgeon, MD, have lived together for the past five years. Both are at the peak of their careers and decide to buy a new "showcase" home in La Jolla, California. After looking at several homes in the area, they buy one for $2 million. They put a 20 percent down payment ($400,000) on the house and finance the balance ($1.6 million). Each takes out a separate mortgage for $800,000 for a total $1.6 million. There is no other debt (e.g., a home equity loan) on the residence.

   a. Locate any courts cases that might provide insight in how to treat this tax situation. Give the citation(s) of any cases you find.

   b. Review any case(s) you found. Does it raise a need for new information to solve this question? Do any case(s) you found help the conclusion you reached in Chapter 4 on this fact pattern?

5-29 Several years ago, Maurice and Maureen (both Mo, for short) Morris, a married couple from Ohio, purchased a used piano at an auction sale for $500, and their daughter used the piano for piano lessons. In the current year, while cleaning the piano, Mo and Mo discovered $14,467 in cash tucked inside the piano. Being unable to ascertain who put the money there, and after consulting with local authorities, the Morrises kept the $14,467 (which, in accordance with Ohio law, is legal).

   a. List as many possible tax research issues as you can to determine whether the Morrises are liable for any tax on the money they found.

   b. After completing your list of tax research issues, list the keywords you might use to construct an online tax research query.

   c. Execute an online search using your query.

Chapter 10

10-1 Which paragraphs in the ASC discuss the effects of tax holidays on accounting for income taxes?

10-2 What is the basic recognition threshold for the financial statement effects of a tax position? (Include your citation.)

10-3 In a prior year, Bradley Corp. took a very aggressive tax position on its tax return that the predominance of the evidence indicated Bradley would be unable to benefit from if detected under review by the taxing jurisdiction. In the current year, the taxing authorities discovered the tax position and reversed the deduction that Bradley had taken. Bradley was required to pay the tax liability associated with the reversal of the tax item. Rather than pursue a settlement with the revenue agent, Bradley has elected to appeal the issue to the Tax Court. Is the issue "effectively settled" under Topic 740?

10-4 For $1 million, Dempsey Inc. purchased stock in a corporation that held only one asset, an FCC license, and thus is unable to treat the purchase as a business combination. The tax basis in the asset was $0. What method should Dempsey use to assign the value to the asset and the deferred tax liability?

10-5 Donovan Corp., a calendar-year-end company, operates a profitable division in Jurisdiction A. In January 2017, Jurisdiction A enacted a tax law that changed the tax rate structure from 30 percent to 35 percent. Donovan wants to know whether it needs to adjust its December 31, 2016, tax provision to reflect the rate change. Also, if not in 2016, when does it need to recognize the effect of that change?

10-6 Altidore Inc. operates a calendar-year-end business that suffers from dramatic seasonal variation in taxable income. For example, it often operates at a net loss for the first two quarters of the year and then operates profitably for the last two quarters and, for as long as anyone can remember, finishes the year with taxable income. The new tax director has been asked to help calculate the deferred tax assets at the end of the first quarter. After looking at the quarterly loss, he claims that since there is no net income, there are no deferred tax assets because the effective tax rate is zero. (Carrybacks and carryforwards are not allowed in this jurisdiction.) Is the tax director correct in his assessment of the effective tax rate for calculating the deferred tax assets?

10-7 ASC 740 provides a two-step process in accounting for uncertain tax positions. What are these two steps?

10-8 How are interest and penalties treated on uncertain tax positions? What is the classification of the unrecognized tax benefits?

10-9 What are the necessary disclosures for uncertain tax liabilities for public companies, and do they differ for nonpublic companies?

10-10 According to ASC 740, in what order should tax effects be allocated? (Hint: This has to do with intraperiod allocation.)

10-11 What are the six exceptions to the basic requirements of ASC 740? Briefly describe each of the exceptions.

10-12 Yankee Corporation has suffered a large net operating loss. Which sources of income should be considered when estimating the future realization of a tax benefit from this loss? Briefly describe each. Provide examples when possible.

10-13 How and what type of evidence is analyzed to determine the need for a valuation allowance? Describe the process for this analysis.

10-14 What is the tax basis of an asset under ASC 740? What is the book basis?

10-15 ASC 740 has been described as a balance sheet (or asset and liability) approach. Explain why that is an apt description.

10-16 Charger Corp. has $500,000 of income from continuing operations and $300,000 of income from discontinued operations. In the prior year, Charger finished the year with a $1.2 million net operating loss that was attributable to losses generated from what is now the discontinued operations and determined that a full valuation allowance was required. In the current year, Charger has determined that no valuation allowance is required based on current-year income and future income projections in excess of $700,000. Assuming a 40 percent tax rate, how should the total tax expense going be allocated between continuing operations and discontinued operations in the current year?

Chapter 13

13-1 The IRS has issued a summons for the tax file held by CPA Ann Whitman for her clients, the Harberts. The file consists of paper and electronic spreadsheets in which Whitman detailed some tax computations using assumptions that the IRS would find to be "too aggressive." In addition, the file includes notes from meetings with the Harberts, income and balance sheet data as to their personal assets, and other technical correspondence, including email messages. In a memo to the tax research file, summarize the current status of the law as to whether the privilege of confidentiality protects these documents from the government.

13-2 Your supervisor says that the U.S. Constitution forces the IRS to reveal the make-up of the DIF formula that it uses to select tax returns for audit. Prepare a research memo assessing the supervisor's assertion.

13-3 Max and Annie are roommates sharing an apartment. Although they know each other well, they have respect for each other's privacy. Thus, when Max's Form 1040 was audited by the IRS, he made no mention of the audit to Annie. When Annie was clearing the answering machine that they shared, she heard the following message: "Max, this is Richard, the IRS auditor. My figures show that you owe the government $10,000 in taxes and another $4,500 in penalties and interest."

When Annie brought up the message during dinner conversation that night, Max was furious. How could the IRS be so careless as to broadcast this news to a stranger? Did he not have any privacy and confidentiality rights? Max calls you to determine whether he might have a case against the IRS or Richard, the agent. Prepare a research memo assessing Max's position.

13-4 You have just rendered service for a taxpayer as an expert witness in a case heard by the U.S. Tax Court. The taxpayer is requesting reimbursement for your fees and for those amounts paid to her attorney in presenting the case. Your billing rate for this type of engagement is $500 per hour, the market rate for such services in your city, plus out-of-pocket expenses (e.g., auto mileage, duplication charges). How much of your fee will the taxpayer recover?

13-5 Duane paid his 2011 federal income taxes in January 2014 in the amount of $10,000 and then paid $4,000 interest and penalties on this amount in May 2015. In April 2017, Duane filed a claim for refund of the $1,000 as a result of a sizable operating loss from his business in tax year 2016. Can he recover the 2011-related amounts?

13-6 Tobey was late in filing his federal income tax refund claim, but he requested an extension of the statute of limitations, citing the financial-disability exceptions of IRC § 6511(h). Tobey's mother is chronically ill, and he must make four-day-a-week trips to another city to care for her. Will the IRS grant Tobey's request?

Chapter 14

14-1 The Bird Estate committed tax fraud when it purposely understated the value of the business created and operated by the decedent, Beverly Bird. Executor Wilma Holmes admitted to the Tax Court that she had withheld several contracts and formulas that, had they been disclosed to the valuation experts used by the government and the estate, would have added $1 million in value to the business and over half that amount in federal estate tax liabilities. Summary data include the following:

	Reported on Form 706	Other Amounts
Gross estate	$12 million	$1 million understatement
Deductions on original return Interest on estate tax deficiency, professional fees incurred during administration period	$2 million	$400,000

Holmes asks you for advice in computing the fraud penalty. Ignore interest amounts. She wonders whether to take the 75 percent civil penalty against the full $1 million understatement or against the $600,000 net amount that the taxable estate would have increased had the administrative expenses been incurred prior to the filing date of the Form 706. Write to Holmes, an experienced certified public accountant with an extensive tax practice, a letter stating your opinion.

14-2   Blanche Creek has engaged your firm because she has been charged with failure to file her 2016 federal Form 1040. Blanche maintains that the "reasonable cause" exception should apply. During the entire tax-filing season in 2017, she was under a great deal of stress at work and in her personal life. As a result, Blanche developed a sleep disorder, which was treated through a combination of pills and counseling.

Your firm ultimately prepared the 2016 tax return for Blanche, but it was filed far beyond the due date. Blanche is willing to pay the delinquent tax and related interest. However, she feels that the failure-to-pay penalty is unfair, as she was ill. Consequently, she could not be expected to keep to the usual deadlines for filing.

Write a letter to Blanche concerning these matters.

14-3   The Church of Freedom encourages its members to file "tax protestor" returns with the IRS, objecting to both the government's failure to use a gold standard in payment of tax liabilities and its sizable expenditures for social welfare programs. These returns routinely are overturned by the Tax Court as frivolous, with delinquent taxes, penalties, and interest due, and the church has engaged in a long-standing, sometimes ugly, battle with the IRS over various constitutional rights. Meanwhile, church members continue to file returns in this manner.

Ellen overheard church members talking about "roughing up" the IRS agents who were scheduled to conduct an audit of various members' returns. She went to the IRS and informed them of the danger they might encounter. At the IRS's direction, Ellen then took a key clerical job at church headquarters. In this context, she had access to useful documentation and over a period of a few months gave to the IRS copies of church mailing lists and other data. She also helped record key conversations among church leaders and search the church's trash for other documents. In other words, Ellen helped the IRS build a case of civil and criminal tax fraud against the church and various members.

All these materials were given voluntarily to Ellen by church leaders in her context as an employee. Church members never suspected that she was working with the IRS. After delivering the various materials to the IRS, Ellen quit her job with the church and severed all communications with the IRS.

After the parties were charged with fraud, the government's case was found to be insufficiently supported by the evidence, and no penalties were assessed. Afterward, church leaders sued Ellen in her role as IRS informant, charging that she had violated their First Amendment rights of free association and their Fourth Amendment rights against illegal search and seizure. Governmental employees are immune from such charges, but Ellen was only an informant to the IRS and not its employee. Can the church collect damages from Ellen for informing on them?

14-4   Butcher attended meetings of tax protestors for many years in which the constitutionality of the federal income tax and its means of collection were routinely challenged. Members of various protest groups were provided with materials to assist them in preparing returns such that little or no tax would be due, for example, on the basis that only gold-backed or silver-backed currency need be submitted to pay the tax or that a tax bill had originated in the Senate rather than the House of Representatives. Some of the groups maintained that no returns need be filed by individuals at all on the grounds that the current law supporting a federal income tax violates various elements of the U.S. Constitution.

The U.S. Tax Court routinely has overturned such means of avoiding the tax, charging that such returns were frivolously filed and charging the protestors with delinquent taxes, interest, and a variety of negligence and other accuracy-related penalties, especially where taxpayers failed to file altogether. The results of these cases never were discussed in the meetings that Butcher attended, though. Thus, although he never joined any of the groups, Butcher felt comfortable with the arguments of the protestor groups and never filed a federal income tax return for himself or his profitable sole-proprietorship carpentry business.

When the IRS discovered his failure to file and charged him with tax, interest, and penalties, Butcher went to the tax library and found that judicial precedent and administrative authority were stacked against him. He asked the court for relief from the civil fraud penalties related to his failure to file and failure to pay tax on the basis of his good-faith belief that the tax protestor information he had received was an acceptable interpretation of the law. Under this argument, a taxpayer cannot be found to willfully have failed to file and pay if he or she had a good-faith belief that no such requirement was supported by the Constitution. Should Butcher be required to pay civil fraud penalties?

14-5 Chang wants to claim a cost-recovery deduction for the acquisition of original artwork to be hung in the reception area of her dental office. The paintings were specially chosen because of their tendency to relax the patients who would be viewing them, thereby facilitating the conduct of Chang's business. Chang lives and works in the Fifth Circuit. A recent Eleventh Circuit case seems to support such a deduction, in limited circumstances. Complete the following chart, indicating for each independent assumption the actions that Chang can take without incurring the civil penalty for substantial understatement of taxes, but still maximizing her legitimate deductions for the year:

Probability of Success in Court	Claim the Deduction?	File a Form 8275 Disclosure?
80%		
40%		
20%		
2%		

14-6 Your client, Lee Ann Harkness, has been accused of criminal tax fraud. A high-school dropout, she received hundreds of thousands of dollars over the years from Bentley, an elderly gentleman, in exchange for love and companionship. When Bentley died and Harkness was left out of the will, she sued the estate for compensatory payments earned throughout her years of tending to Bentley. The government now accuses Harkness of fraud for failing to file income and self-employment tax returns for the open tax years. Construct a defense on Harkness's behalf.

14-7 The Scooter Company, owned equally by Julie (chair of the board of directors) and Jeff (company president), is in very difficult financial straits. Last month, Jeff used the $100,000 withheld from employee paychecks for federal payroll and income taxes to pay off a creditor who threatened to cut off all supplies. To keep the company afloat, Jeff used these government funds willfully for the operations of the business, but even that effort was not enough. The company missed the next two payrolls, and today other creditors took action to shut down Scooter altogether. From whom and for how much will the IRS assess taxes and penalties in the matter?

14-8 For the completion and filing of his 2017 federal income tax return, Ron retains the services of a tax preparer. Because of a particularly hectic tax preparation season, the preparer does not complete and file the return until June 2018. Is Ron excused from the failure-to-file and failure-to-pay penalties under the reasonable-cause exception?

14-9 Joan, a traveling sales representative, kept no formal books and records to summarize her gross receipts for the year, but she retained copies of all customer invoices and reported her gross income for the year from these totals. Is she liable for a negligence penalty under IRC § 6662 for failing to keep any books and records?

14-10 Pealii Loligo owned and operated three House of Calamari restaurants from 2009 through 2011. His wife, Cleopatra Decacera, assisted with the management of the restaurants.

In May 2010, Ms. Decacera and Mr. Loligo purchased a $900,000 home. In relation to this home purchase, in 2008 and 2009 they signed mortgage loan applications indicating joint annual incomes of $235,000 and $321,000, respectively. On their 2008 joint federal income tax return, however, Ms. Decacera and Mr. Loligo reported that they earned no salaries and had net losses of $55,000; and on their 2009 joint tax return, they reported that Mr. Loligo earned a salary of $23,000, and that they had net losses of $77,000.

During 2010–2012, Ms. Decacera and Mr. Loligo paid approximately $70,000 for home furnishings, $30,000 for a swimming pool, and $40,000 for Ms. Decacera's jewelry. In addition, they leased two Mercedes-Benz automobiles and took Ms. Decacera's parents on vacations to Florida and Nevada.

In 2014, Ms. Decacera and Mr. Loligo were indicted and charged with filing false tax returns in 2008 and 2009. Mr. Loligo pled guilty, while Ms. Decacera signed a deferred prosecution agreement and admitted filing false returns. The couple divorced in 2015, and in 2016 the IRS issued a deficiency notice for the 2008 and 2009 taxes. In September 2016, Ms. Decacera filed a petition in which she requested relief from joint and several liability for the income taxes. During January 2017, Mr. Loligo filed his "notice of intervention." In July, an IRS appeals officer determined that Ms. Decacera did not qualify for innocent spouse relief under § 6015(f).

After appropriate research, prepare (in good form) a research memorandum to the file. Then write a letter to Ms. Decacera explaining your findings. Her address is 4567 Whome Lane, Escondido, CA 92069.

14-11 Mark and Leslee Jones were married in 2000. Mark has an MBA from Harvard and worked in the financial markets in New York City. Leslee has a degree in hotel administration and worked for the Hilton Hotel until two years ago, when Mark and Leslee moved to California. They moved because Mark lost his job. He had been accused of embezzlement, and formal charges had been filed against him. However, the charges were dropped because the firm for which Mark worked did not want to be involved in a public scandal. Mark admitted the embezzlement to Leslee and promised that if they stayed married and moved, he would never embezzle again. In California, Mark obtained a job as the chief financial officer of a mid-sized company. His salary, while approximately 60 percent of his former salary, was still more than $200,000.

Mark likes to gamble. He does so by betting on horse races, going to Las Vegas, playing in the stock market, and making speculative real estate investments. The reason he had embezzled the money at his former job was to cover his gambling and stock market losses. While in California, he continued to bet on horse races and visit Las Vegas to gamble. Leslee accompanied him to the race tracks and to Las Vegas. Because Mark was known as a big gambler, their rooms were always provided for free, as were any costs associated with their stays in Las Vegas. Leslee would watch Mark gamble for a while, get bored, and then go to see shows or go shopping. Leslee liked to shop and spent thousands of dollars at a time.

As to the investments, Leslee did not help in the decisions to purchase stock or real estate. However, she did sign all purchase-and-sale agreements for real estate, because California is a community property state. Any proceeds from the sales were paid to both Mark and Leslee. She endorsed all checks, which were deposited in their joint checking account. Leslee and Mark both wrote checks out of this account. What Leslee did not know is that Mark had a separate bank account into which he deposited much of his gambling winnings and stock gains.

In the current year, the Jones's prior two tax returns are audited and material omissions are found. The embezzled money never had been reported, gambling gains were substantially understated, and gains on the sale of stock and real estate were omitted from the returns. Shortly after the Jones received notice from the IRS as to their findings regarding the audits, Leslee filed for divorce, for obvious reasons.

What tax-related advice do you have for Mark and Leslee? Will Leslee qualify for innocent-spouse protection from the tax liabilities? She claims that she had no knowledge of any of the underreporting on their tax returns. Mark and Leslee always used a CPA to prepare their returns.

General Research Cases

Note: Develop solutions and appropriate documentation for the cases assigned by your instructor. Follow the writing and presentation tips as discussed in Chapter 11 in preparing your solutions using one or more of the following means of communicating your research results:

- Research memorandum

- Letter to tax-sophisticated client

- Letter to unsophisticated client

- Outline for a tax department meeting

- Article for local business newsweekly

- Speech to local chamber of commerce

- Article for *Practical Tax Strategies*

- Presentation to a group of CPAs

- Presentation to client's board of directors

- Presentation to client's senior counsel

- Posting to the Internet Tax Blog for Practitioners

- Posting to the Internet Tax Help group for taxpayers

G-1   Frances moved in with her mother, Beatrice, when Beatrice's health started to fail. Frances cared for her mother as a devoted child would and never expected anything in return. When Beatrice needed to move to a nursing home, she legally transferred the home to Frances for $1,000 and "other valuable consideration." The house had cost Beatrice $50,000 many years ago, and on the date of the transfer it was valued at $150,000. At the time of the transfer, Beatrice was insolvent, as she owed the IRS $250,000 in back taxes and interest for several years. A few months after the transfer of the house, the IRS filed a notice of federal tax lien for Beatrice's unpaid taxes. The IRS has filed against Frances for $150,000 of her mother's taxes, as Frances is in possession of the only valuable asset Beatrice has owned. Can the IRS collect from Frances?

G-2   The IRS audited the Loser Corporation's return filed two years ago. The IRS found substantial underreporting of income and is proposing to review Loser's returns for the six prior years. Loser knows it underreported its taxable income on its timely filed tax return five years ago. It reported $80,000 of gross sales, $10,000 product returns, and $60,000 costs of goods sold. Its actual amounts were $100,000 gross sales, $2,000 returns, and $40,000 cost of goods sold. Does the IRS have the right to audit this return from five years ago?

G-3   Magnus has been divorced from his wife, Irina, for three years. In the divorce, Magnus lost custody of the two children he fathered and one adopted child. Irina has moved to Russia to be close to her parents. Magnus misses having children, so he pays for in vitro fertilization of his sperm with two anonymous donors' eggs and has the resulting embryos carried by women, unrelated to him, who give birth to the two children. Can Magnus take the costs for these procedures as a medical expense?

G-4   Ozzie and Sherrie Johnson lived in Bishop, California. The Johnson's 15-year-old son, Jack, was addicted to illegal drugs and experienced both physical and behavioral problems. In 2015, without the consultation of a psychiatrist or psychologist, the Johnsons sent Jack to a therapeutic boarding school, the Lonely Bridge School, in Idaho. Lonely Bridge was well known as a school in which celebrities and wealthy persons could enroll their "troubled" teens for 365 days a year for therapy and a high school education, and the school had a strong reputation nationally. The Johnsons paid tuition of $48,000 in 2015 and incurred $12,000 in travel costs (airfare, rental cars, and lodging) to attend required parent-therapy sessions at the school. They also deposited $3,000 into a "personal account" that was used to cover expenses associated with therapy and was required to maintain matriculation at Lonely Bridge; the money was spent during the year. Jack stayed most of 2015 and 2016 at Lonely Bridge before running away in late 2016. Although he no longer is physically addicted, his behavioral issues remain. In 2017, it was discovered that some of the staff at Lonely Bridge, although therapists, were not credentialed as had been previously thought and that the school was not accredited as parents had been led to believe. In addition, a number of high-profile "incidents" involving alleged unusual therapy methods and abuse resulted in Lonely Bridge closing in 2017. Prepare a tax research memo for your files regarding whether the Johnsons can deduct the tuition, travel costs, and personal account expenses for tax purposes as a medical deduction (in excess of the floor).

G-5   Paul and Patty Nelson own a home in Nelsonville, Ohio, and maintain apartments in Lexington, Kentucky, New York City (part year), and Philadelphia (part year). Their cars are registered in Kentucky, and they have driver's licenses from Kentucky. However, the Nelsons consider Nelsonville their "home" because their house was inherited from Paul's parents and has been in the family for more than 150 years. During the year, Paul traveled between Kentucky and Nelsonville numerous times. Patty did not usually accompany Paul, as she works for a consulting firm on engagements in New York City and Philadelphia. The home office of her employer is in Chicago, but she never works in Illinois. Paul's sales region for his job is Kentucky and Indiana. For purposes of taking expenses while away from home, Paul and Patty use their Nelsonville home. Is this correct? Where is the Nelsons' tax home?

G-6   Jason Deruler was diagnosed with depression three years ago. Since stress increases the symptoms, he left his public accounting job to become an accountant at a manufacturing firm. His symptoms subsided substantially after this move. Then last year, the firm hired a new accounting manager, Sheila, who is very high strung and demanding. Worst yet, Jason uncovers that Shelia is double billing customers that she believes will not notice the overcharges. All of this causes Jason to suffer a recurrence of his depression and he copes with his issues by overeating. Because of his eating habits and resulting obesity, Jason suffers insomnia, nausea, and migraines such that his doctor recommends he take a leave of absence, which he does. Shelia fires Jason and Jason sues. When the settlement payment is made for wrongful discharge, Jason receives back wages, attorney fees of $100,000; and $50,000 identified ambiguously in the lawsuit as "nonemployee compensation." Can Jason exclude the $50,000 as a payment for sickness or injury?

G-7   Candidate Feldman ran for Congress in 2016, raising $4.7 million for the campaign, including $800,000 in federal matching amounts. Five months after his opponent was sworn into office, auditors discovered that Feldman used $500,000 of campaign donations for a personal vacation, taken immediately after the unsuccessful campaign. What are the tax consequences of this use of election funds?

G-8   Ann is required under a divorce decree to pay alimony of $2,000 per month and child support of $3,000 per month. Ann has only been paying $4,000 per month because she thinks the child-support obligation is too high. On Ann's tax return, which portion of the payments does she treat as alimony and which part is considered child support?

G-9   Tom and Katie divorced in 2014. Under the divorce decree, Tom is required to pay alimony of $3,000 per month and child support for their daughter, Suri, of $2,000 per month. In 2016, at age 17, Suri married the multibillionaire inventor of freeandclear.com, a website that allows individuals to cleanse their social media pages of any and all unacceptable content with a few simple clicks. As a result, Suri has substantial individual wealth of her own and no longer needs the child support. Suri and Tom discussed Suri's new wealth and agreed that Tom would cease child support payments immediately. Tom has a copy of the e-mail exchange with Suri, and a reasonable reading of those e-mails would indicate that Suri agreed to the reduction. Katie did not pursue the matter with Tom because she also benefitted from Suri's wealth and did not see the need for any more child support payments, but she did continue to receive her alimony and include the monthly $3,000 as income. Tom does not have any contemporaneous documentation of Katie's acquiescence to the decision to reduce child support other than Suri informing him of her mother's agreement through a telephone conversation. The divorce decree did *not* contain any stipulation that if Suri married or attained substantial wealth, child support could stop. Prepare a tax memo to the files that communicates your findings concerning the effect of Tom ceasing child support payment on his ability to deduct alimony before and after Suri's marriage.

G-10   Which of the following items qualifies for the child-care credit claimed by the Rodriguez family?

- Salary for nanny.

- Employer's share of FICA tax for nanny, paid by Rodriguez.

- Employee's share of FICA tax for nanny, paid by Rodriguez.

- Nanny's health insurance premiums, paid by Rodriguez.

- One-half of nanny's hotel bill while on her own during a European vacation, paid by Rodriguez.

- Dry cleaning bills for nanny's clothes soiled by youngsters and paid by Rodriguez.

G-11   Colbert has been a waiter at the Burger Report in Starkville, Mississippi for four years. The Burger Report treats its employees well, allowing them a 60 percent discount for any food that they buy and consume on the premises (for example, a $10 meal will cost only $4). In 2016, the value of the discount for Colbert amounted to $2,500 for days on which he was working and $1,500 for days when he was not assigned to work but still stopped by during mealtimes. The average profit the Report earns on a meal is 25% (i.e, the cost of a $10 meal is about $8.00). There is no requirement that Colbert eat at the Report during his breaks and some days he does and others he does not. Fortunately, there are a number of other eating establishments near the Report that Colbert can walk to and still get back to his fryolator with plenty of time before his shift starts again. The Report is adequately staffed so it's not as if Colbert needs to stay at the restaurant to be "on call," after all, there is no such thing as a "burger emergency!" Prepare a tax research memorandum in good form that provides your conclusion on Colbert's treatment of the meals provided by his employer at a discount in 2016 for federal tax purposes. Do NOT consider any reporting by the Report on Colbert's W-2 – focus on only Colbert's responsibility.

G-12   Ollie died this year in September, after a long illness. His wages prior to death totaled $15,000, and his state taxes thereon came to $600.
    a.   Who must file Ollie's last tax return?
    b.   How is the return signed?
    c.   Who collects Ollie's $440 federal refund?

G-13   When Fifi, a sheriff's deputy, was injured on the job, she was allowed under her contract with the state to choose between a $1,000 weekly sick-pay distribution and an $850 weekly workers' compensation payment. Which one should Fifi select?

G-14   Willie was tired of cleaning up the messes that his wife, Barbara, made in their house. One morning, he found a crumpled facial tissue on the bathroom vanity, so he disgustedly flushed it down the toilet. Unfortunately, the tissue was wrapped around Barbara's engagement ring, which she had removed the previous evening after cutting her finger while shoveling snow. Is the couple allowed a deductible casualty loss for federal income tax purposes under IRC § 165?

G-15 Louella was born into a low-income family and lives in a poverty-stricken neighborhood. She recently landed a job as wardrobe consultant at High Fashions Ltd., a retailer of expensive women's clothing at an Elm Grove shopping mall. Can Louella claim a § 162 business expense deduction on her federal income tax return for the cost and upkeep of the expensive Yves St. Laurent outfits that she is required to wear on the job?

G-16 Steve is a member of a local church. May he deduct as a charitable contribution the commuting expenses for the Sundays that he is assigned to usher?

G-17 Phil is a used-car dealership manager. To obtain advanced skills in management and marketing, he enrolls in the weekend MBA program at State University, located 20 miles from his home. Does Phil qualify for an educational credit? Which items associated with Phil's education are deductible as an employee business expense, assuming that he receives no reimbursements for any of them?

G-18 Frank and Sharon have been married for five years. Without Frank's knowledge, Sharon has been operating an escort service from the local pub. This year's operations were very profitable. In fact, if Sharon had reported the net escort income, their joint federal income tax liability would have increased by $50,000. When Sharon finally is nabbed by the police, she is taken to jail. Frank is unable to locate any of Sharon's earnings in their personal bank or brokerage accounts. Can Frank fend off the IRS's charge that he should pay the $50,000 in tax, plus interest and penalties, from his salary as an engineer?

G-19 Maria has an unusually strong constitution, which produces the highest quality blood and plasma available for transfusions. She manages to stay healthy while donating blood at the hospital two or three times per week. For each blood donation, the hospital pays Maria $175. Maria drives 40 miles round trip to the hospital to make her donation. Moreover, she spends approximately $135 every month for vitamins and other pills prescribed by her physician to ensure that her general health and blood quality do not degenerate in light of her frequent donations. Last year, Maria quit all of her part-time jobs and now survives financially solely by these blood donations. Specify the tax consequences of this regular activity.

G-20 Chang, a brain surgeon, subscribes to the *Journal of Brain Research*. With a special subscription offer, Chang pays $3,000 this year for the full three-year subscription for this weekly scientific journal. Normally, the journal charges $1,500 for an annual renewal. In what year(s) can Chang deduct this $3,000?

G-21 Jamie is an elementary school teacher, and her adjusted gross income is $31,000. For this year, she spent $450 of her own funds on special school supplies for those children who could not afford to purchase the necessary supplies. She bought these supplies at a specialty educational store that is a 70-mile round trip from her home. Can she deduct any portion of these amounts?

G-22 Ted's sister, April, was injured while performing her duties as a police officer. She was in the hospital for three weeks before she died from her wounds. The city paid directly to Ted the worker's compensation benefits due to April before she died, as he is April's only surviving relative. How much gross income does Ted recognize upon receiving the benefits?

G-23 Peggy had been a heavy tobacco user until she joined the Norwood Tobacco-Free Program. She had spent a substantial amount of money on nicotine patches and other nonprescription treatments without much success. Her father recently died from lung cancer, and his death made her realize that to kick the habit she would need to get professional help before her smoking created serious medical problems. While she is very pleased at being tobacco free for the first time in 10 years, she is wondering whether any of the vast amounts spent on the cure are deductible.

G-24 Sally sells her home to Bob and pays $9,000 in points for Bob's mortgage, by receiving $9,000 less in sale proceeds. Determine the tax effects on both parties.

G-25 Ethel and Rick spent $4,500 in allocable interest and taxes and $1,100 in advertising and maintenance for their "bed and breakfast" inn. This year's rental income from the inn came to $4,900. Determine the tax effects of conducting the B&B using one-third of Ethel and Rick's residence.

G-26   Carline's son, Leon, 10, is a musical prodigy. Carline, also a musical person, has spent a significant amount of time teaching Leon music and promoting his possible career. When Leon finally receives a recording contract, Carline is designated in the contract to receive one-half of Leon's total earnings. Discuss the proper recognition of gross income and related deductions concerning this arrangement.

G-27   Barbara owns an incorporated consulting business and has spent many years building its respectable reputation. However, business recently has dropped dramatically because of the unprofessional behavior of Cliff, Barbara's husband. Barbara feels that the only way to protect her business is to divorce Cliff. Cliff demands 50 percent of the stock in Barbara's business. The divorce will be costly because Cliff and Barbara cannot reach an agreement about the business's stock. Are the costs of the divorce deductible to Barbara or to Cliff?

G-28   Newark Marine Food Service (NMFS) sells hot lunches and snacks to the crews of ships that dock at the Port of Newark. According to custom, the officers of the visiting ships receive a 5 percent "commission" from all sales, so that NMFS can retain its "exclusive rights" to the seamen's business. Are the commissions deductible by NMFS?

G-29   Clara, a community college graduate, works at the Pamper U Hotel in Lake Tahoe. Clara's job is to provide relaxation demonstrations, teach yoga, provide massage therapy, and give lectures on stress management. Since Clara possessed no formal training in any of these subjects, she decided to attend seminars all over the United States on the topics related to her job. She also attended the local university and took physiology classes to learn more about the body and how it functions. Can Clara receive any tax benefits from these educational expenses?

G-30   Mary Madeline is a college student with a very active social life. Over the last year she purchased a variety of birth control devices. She tried birth control pills as prescribed by her physician but did not like the side-effects. She also tried the contraceptive sponge, a diaphragm, and condoms, all of which are available without a prescription but were recommended by her doctor as possible substitutes for birth control pills with fewer side effects. Mary is interested in understanding to what extent, and under what circumstances, such items qualify for a medical expense deduction. She understands the 10% AGI floor and the itemized deduction requirement so there is no need to address those issues.

G-31   Phyllis sued Martin's estate and won a $65,000 settlement. She showed the probate court that she carried out her end of a compensatory arrangement with her companion, under which she provided "traditional wifely services" without benefit of matrimony during Martin's life in exchange for all of his estate. Martin left his entire estate to his faithful dog Sparky via a trust. How much gross income is recognized by Phyllis?

G-32   How much gross income is recognized by Carol, who received $10,000 damages (two months' salary) for pain and suffering because of the school administration's critical reaction to her negative comments about ineffective recruiting of athletes who graduate with legitimate academic majors?

G-33   Carol and Jerry, LLP, pays the Good Eats Cafe each month for the lunches the two accountants eat there each work day. While at lunch, Carol and Jerry always discuss some business. Often Carol and Jerry invite friends who work at other CPA firms to join them, so they can keep up with what is happening in the accounting community. Are these meals deductible?

G-34   Lila personally bought three insurance policies on her life. She borrowed $28,500 and prepaid the first five years' worth of annual payments on a whole life policy. In addition, she borrowed $4,200 and paid one of the two required premiums on a group term policy through her professional organization. Finally, she borrowed $3,000 and bought utilities mutual fund shares. The principal and interest of the fund's assets are to be appropriated in a timely fashion by Lila to make payments on a five-premium endowment contract. Interest charges for the three loans were $2,500, $420, and $310, respectively. How much of this interest can Lila deduct?

G-35   CPA Joe reimburses a client for a $75,000 tax liability that is traceable to Joe's ineffective tax advice. For fear of increasing his already steep malpractice-insurance premiums, Joe does not file a claim with the insurer. Can Joe deduct the $75,000 loss?

G-36   Tony, a gardener, loaned Harry, his friend, his new $500 lawn mower. Harry ruined the lawn mower but replaced it with a $425 model. Later in the same year, Tony loaned Harry $5,000 for bail, $3,000 to start a fencing operation, and $15 for a meal. According to Harry's parole officer, none of these items will ever be paid back. Can Tony deduct any of these losses?

G-37   Three years ago, Geraldine bought a Kandinsky painting for her art collection from a mail-order advertisement for $310,000. This year, Geraldine's art dealer told her that the painting was actually painted by Kansky and is not worth more than $310. What is her deductible loss upon discovery of the forgery?

G-38   Chickfer Cooperative is a horticultural cooperative located in Arkansas that markets fertilizers created by its members especially for use by commercial greenhouses. It grossed $25 million in sales for the current year. Is Chickfer able to qualify for the domestic-production-activities deduction?

G-39   Bob Carburetor is the new owner of Carburetor Cars, an accrual-based corporate taxpayer. At Carburetor Cars, when a vehicle is sold, the dealership tries to sell an auto service contract. The amounts received for these contracts are placed into an escrow account. The agreements grant the buyers the right to have parts or components covered by the contract repaired or replaced whenever the covered parts experience a mechanical difficulty. The dealer will either provide the services or reimburse the car buyer for the reasonable cost of repair or replacement. Normally, the buyer returns the vehicle to the dealer for repair, but this is not required. In either case, the repairs or replacements must be authorized in advance by an administrator hired by Carburetor Cars. Fees to the administrator of the contracts are paid out of the escrow account. What is the proper tax treatment for the income from the service contracts? When are the payments to the administrator deductible?

G-40   Betty Jo Harris lives in Maine with her son, Rick, and husband, Walter Reed. Rick has Lou Gehrig's disease. Rick's physician encourages Betty Jo to go to a conference at the Mayo Clinic in Rochester, Minnesota, for caregivers of persons with Lou Gehrig's disease so she can learn how to better take care of Rick. Betty takes the advice and flies to Rochester. Besides the cost of the plane ticket, Betty Jo incurs the following types of expenses: meals, lodging, phone calls home, dry cleaning (she dumped her taco salad on her lap at lunch), and conference registration fees. The leading speaker at the conference suggested that caregivers take their patients to destinations in warm climates to improve their state of mind and general condition. When Betty returns home, she arranges a two-month trip (January and February) to the Bahamas for Rick and herself. One week after they arrived in the Bahamas, Rick's father, Walter, arrives and stays for a couple of weeks. Advise Betty Jo as to whether any of these expenses are deductible as medical expenses.

G-41   Several years ago, Agnes and Wyman Booth bought a home for $200,000. They lived in the home for 10 years and then moved into an apartment. Unable to immediately sell the home, starting in 2014 they rented it for two years, earning $24,000 in rents and taking $14,000 in depreciation. After the two rental years, the Booths exchanged the house for $30,000 cash and a duplex worth $300,000. The Booths will hold the duplex as rental property. How much taxable income do the Booths have from the exchange?

G-42   King and Knight is a personal service corporation that has been in existence for five years. In the current year, it makes a § 444 election to have its year end become October 31. King and Knight incurs a net operating loss (NOL) for the current year amounting to $100,000. How should King and Knight treat this NOL for tax purposes?

G-43   Clarence is a packrat. He has clothes from when he was in high school some 20 years ago that he never wears. He also has household items that have accumulated over the past 15 years. Some of these household items have not been used by Clarence in years, and he is not sure if they even work. Clarence is buying a new home and wants to clean out his closets before he moves into his new house. He would like to give all his old clothes and household items to local charities. What restrictions apply to charitable deductions of old clothes and household items?

G-44   Ramon, Clarita, and Juan are shareholders in the computer consulting firm 3Geeks. Because the business has had several years of success, Juan is ready to leave the business and requests to be bought out. After negotiations among the owners, it is agreed that Juan will receive $300,000 for his stock and $500,000 for agreeing not to provide any computer consulting services for one year starting October 1 of the current year. This $500,000 is the same amount Juan was guaranteed to receive each year as salary. How should 3Geeks treat the $500,000 payment to Juan?

G-45   Handy Corporation assists its relocated executives by buying their homes if an acceptable sale cannot be completed before their move. Purchase is made at the appraised value. What is the nature of Handy's gain or loss on the subsequent sales?

G-46   John accompanied his wife, Ling, on a business trip to San Diego because Ling is paralyzed from the waist down and confined to a wheelchair. John was not associated with Ling's business directly, but he performed services such as helping Ling overcome architectural barriers, carrying Ling's luggage, facilitating security inspections of Ling at airports, and helped Ling board the airplanes. What is the tax treatment of the incremental expenses for John accompanying Ling on the trip?

G-47   After his divorce, Brown paid the expenses of maintaining the family home, which continued to be the principal residence of his ex-wife and their three children. Thus, he owns the house, but he no longer lives there. Instead, Brown maintains another home as his principal residence. Can Brown claim head-of-household status, assuming that the divorce decree grants him the dependency exemptions for his children?

G-48   Alice, the chair of the School of Accountancy, entertains the faculty at her home each semester and has a holiday party at the end of December for the faculty and their families. When a faculty member is promoted or has a paper published in an exceptionally prestigious journal, Alice hosts a "social hour" at her house. She also sponsors a picnic for the faculty and graduate students at the start of the fall semester to let them get acquainted with each other. To what extent are these expenses deductible?

G-49   Cambro Construction Company hires union carpenters for home building. Cambro requires, as a condition of employment, that the carpenters provide and maintain various tools of their trade. Cambro pays each carpenter a set amount per hour as a "tool allowance" to cover the costs of the tools. This amount is determined quarterly based on national compiled data on the costs of carpenters' tools. How should this employee reimbursement be treated for tax purposes?

G-50   Matt injured Buddy in an automobile accident. The court awarded Buddy $30,000 in damages, but Matt was only able to pay Buddy $12,000. They both then considered the matter closed. Under these terms, compute the amount of gross income to Buddy and Matt from this event.

G-51   Con man Floyd sold Larry the Library of Congress for $150,000. Since Larry did not have that kind of money, he embezzled the $150,000 from his employer to make the purchase.
   a.   How much gross income should Larry and Floyd report as a result of this event?
   b.   For tax purposes, how will Larry treat any repayment of the embezzlement to his (former) employer?

G-52   Reverend Ruth receives a yearly salary of $50,000 and a parsonage allowance of $12,000. She paid $9,000 in rent for the house in which she lives, and she spent $1,500 on housing-related purchases. What is her gross income from these items?

G-53   Jill received a research grant from the University of Minnesota for $10,000 for her time and $3,000 for related supplies and expenses. She purchased a $28,000 Audi the day after depositing the university's check. Jill is a candidate for a master's degree in philosophy and ethics. What is her gross income from the grant?

G-54   Earl is a golf course superintendent. He recently was hired by the Jack Nicks Corporation to construct an 18-hole course in Wyoming. There will be substantial earth-moving costs in creating the landscape desired for the course. The fairways will have planted grass, but the greens will be "modern greens" containing sophisticated drainage systems. The greens must be replaced when the underlying drainage systems are replaced. Earl would like to know what costs are expensed and what costs are capitalized, either as part of the land or as depreciable assets.

G-55   Barry's wife, Terra, died in an accident, leaving him with four young children to raise on his own. Shortly after Terra's funeral, Barry and the children move from the house that Barry and Terra owned for eight years, mainly because they need a change. Barry buys a new house with the help of Lisa, a realtor. Lisa and Barry start dating, and within one year Barry and Lisa are married. Lisa has four children of her own. Given that neither Lisa's nor Barry's home is large enough for the combined family of eight children, Lisa and Barry both sell their homes and buy a new six-bedroom house. Lisa owned her home for six years, but Barry has owned his most recent house for only one year. All of the houses show realized gains on the sales. How are these sales of personal residences treated for tax purposes?

G-56   Professor Dodd receives examination copies of textbooks without charge from book publishers. To what extent should the professor include these books in gross income if he donates them to a local library and takes a charitable-contribution deduction?

G-57   Tony, a single parent, spent $3,600 on after-school care for his six-year-old son. Tony received $1,200 as aid to families with dependent children from the state Department of Social Services (DSS) for child care as part of the welfare assistance program in which he is enrolled. In determining his child-care credit, how much of the DSS payments are included in gross income, and what is the amount of Tony's child-care costs for computing the child-care credit?

G-58   Carmella really wants to be an actor, but she is having trouble getting that "big break" she so desperately needs. To keep food on the table, Carmella has a small tax-preparation business and nets approximately $30,000 per year. She has received small parts in several movies and on television, earning approximately $10,000. However, she incurs substantial expenses associated with her acting career that amount to $15,000. Can Carmella deduct her acting expenses, and/or can Carmella qualify for the qualified-performing-artist deduction?

G-59   Yukio was seriously injured when he fell through an open manhole. Yukio was awarded compensatory damages of $500,000 for his injuries, loss of current wages, reduced future earning ability, and the suffering he incurred and may incur in the future. Is any of the settlement taxable to Yukio? Specifically, is the amount for lost wages taxable?

G-60   Walt was convicted of murder and sent to prison for life. Walt continued to profess his innocence and his sister, Wanda, believed him. After spending three years in law school and two years gathering facts, she proved that he was innocent. Walt and Wanda assigned the book, movie, and photo rights concerning their story to Sundance Films for $500,000. As of yet, no book, movie or photos have been written or created but Sundance anticipates getting started soon by interviewing Walt and Wanda. How is this payment treated by Walt and Wanda?

G-61   Hugo was planting a tree when he unearthed 100,000 certificates of ITT bearer bonds, with a current value of $4 million. He speculated that they had been placed there by the home's former owner (now deceased), at a time when they were worth nearly $400,000. Hugo did not sell the bonds by the end of the year. Must Hugo recognize any gross income with respect to the bonds?

G-62   Karla is a single parent with two children, aged 7 and 11. She is a full-time student and earns $12,000. Both children receive dividends and capital gains from mutual funds acquired for them by their grandparents. Karla has elected to include her children's income on her return for the kiddie-tax computation. Since it is on her tax return, does her children's income affect the computation of Karla's earned-income credit?

G-63   At gunpoint, Roger lent $2,000 from the cash register at his hardware store to four large youths who told Roger that they wanted a loan to set up their own business. Not having the phone number of any of the sprightly entrepreneurs, Roger could not recover any of the invested funds. Can Roger claim any deduction with respect to this loan? In what tax year?

G-64   Phyllis, a Virginia resident, owns some property in Florida. Every year, she travels to Florida (coincidentally, during baseball's spring-training season) to inspect the property, initiate repairs, interview new tenants, and search for new properties in which to invest. She also attends approximately 20 ball games. Determine Phyllis's deductible travel expenses.

G-65   Bruce wanted to be an Olympic skater. His family paid $12,000 in 2016 and $14,000 in 2017 for travel and training expenses related to skating practices and competitions. Bruce made the 2018 U.S. Olympic team. While the U.S. Olympic Committee is a tax-exempt organization, Bruce did not make any payments directly to the organization. How much of Bruce's expenses are deductible and when?

G-66   Harold installed a safe and an alarm system and bought a German shepherd dog to protect his vintage paperback and comic book collection. What are his deductible items?

G-67   Donna's and Albert's children attend a parochial grade school. The school charges $1,500 annual tuition and $200 for uniforms for Donna's children, but only $500 tuition and $100 for uniforms for Albert's children because he is a member of the congregation. Albert contributed $800 to the church this year. Can Donna and Albert withdraw amounts out of their children's Coverdell Educational Savings Accounts to pay for this private primary-school education? What is the amount of Albert's charitable contribution for the year?

G-68   Julie is a professional singer who also performs in the nonprofit City Symphony Chorus (CSS). CSS requires that all members wear traditional formal wear (i.e., $800 tuxedos for the men and $1,300 long black gowns for the women) during performances. In addition, because of her annual $15,000 contribution to the CSS patron drive, Julie is a member of CSS's board of directors. The board chooses the works to be performed, sites for the concerts, and the resident conductor. How much of Julie's expenditures this year can she deduct?

G-69   The farmers in Whitman County are concerned about the prices they are receiving for their crops. They decide to create the Whitman County Farm Commission, whose purpose is to encourage farmers to band together when selling their crops, educate legislators on farming issues, and instruct farmers on methods to control pests and weeds in the most environmentally safe manner. Does this organization qualify for tax-exempt status?

G-70   Three friends form a film-production partnership. Will the operations of this partnership qualify for the domestic-production-activity deduction in the current year?

G-71   Can a business traveler to your city use the high-cost-city meal allowance for travel away from home overnight? What would the meal allowance be for a business trip to Washington, D.C.?

G-72   Nancy and Curtis had not spoken to each other since their mother's funeral in 2001. Nancy broke the family discord this year by selling Curtis a family heirloom, basis to her $14,000, for $1,700. What are the tax consequences of this transaction?

G-73   Zarco, a very profitable corporation, was owned by Julio, Tilly, and Martinez. Julio and Martinez purchased all of Tilly's Zarco Corporation stock for $50,000 and a $100,000 promissory demand note guaranteed by Zarco. Tilly demanded payment on the note, and Zarco, rather than Julio and Martinez, paid the note. What are the tax consequences of this transaction?

G-74   Dolores is a limited partner in the Houston Hopes partnership. This year, she was forced under the terms of the agreement to make a $50,000 contribution to capital because the general partners were unable to meet the entity's operating expenses. Dolores's basis in the partnership prior to the contribution was $40,000, but her at-risk amount was zero because of her limited-partner status and her prior-year pass-through losses. What is her at-risk amount after the $50,000 cash call?

G-75   The IRS acquires vast amounts of sensitive information about individual taxpayers. The government is required to keep this information confidential. May a state child-support agency obtain access to an individual's Form 1040 information when determining the person's ability to pay child support?

G-76   John is a shady real estate broker. In 1980, he sells Roy homestead rights to 500 acres in Nevada. In the current year, the land has become moderately valuable, and Roy sells his rights to Velma. When Velma tries to exercise the rights, she discovers that Roy never had the rights. She sues Roy for return of the money and legal fees. Roy would like to sue John, but he has long since skipped town, never to be found. Roy wants to know if he can claim a theft-loss deduction for the damages paid to Velma and all his court costs as result of this breach of title warranty. Roy thinks that he was the victim of a swindle when he bought the nonexistent rights from John.

G-77   Emily's department is required to attend a business meeting in Orlando, Florida. To reduce the costs, the employer charters a 16-passenger plane. Because only 10 employees are attending the meeting, Emily is permitted to bring her husband and daughter along on the flight. How much income will Emily recognize for this fringe benefit?

G-78   Cary Bean is a product manager for a high tech firm, Apps R Us, that develops apps for smart phones. The Global Conference on Technology is being held in Sint Maarten in 2017 and her employer agrees that she may attend in spite of the conference program being only tangentially related to her business. This conference is largely considered a boondoggle by most in the tech industry but it is tech-related. The cost of the conference is $800 and travel and lodging are $1,400. How much of the conference costs can Apps R Us deduct?

G-79   Ike and Tina were married in 2010 and shortly thereafter purchased a home by taking out a $300,000 mortgage. In 2017, Ike and Tina divorced. The divorce decree gave sole possession and ownership of the house to Ike. However, Tina was to continue making the mortgage payments as part of her spousal maintenance obligation. Are these payments deductible in full or in part by Tina as home-interest expense or alimony, or are they payments on a debt obligation and not deductible?

G-80   Todd bought a used speedboat by writing a check for $23,000. When the seller presented the check to Todd's bank, it was rejected, with the bank indicating that Todd no longer had an account at the bank. The seller then requested Todd come back for an item he left behind, but the police were waiting and Todd was arrested for theft. He was handcuffed in front of his family, taken to jail, and put in a holding area with drunks until bail could be arranged. Once it was determined that the bank had made a terrible mistake, Todd sued the bank for false imprisonment and defamation. He received $200,000. Although Todd suffered no physical injury from the arrest and detention, he did have nightmares and sought psychological help for several months, and the bank paid the bills. Because Todd was physically held against his will, he thinks the $200,000 is not taxable. Is Todd correct?

G-81   Rose is a state legislator for a small district located 300 miles from the state capital. Thus, while the legislature is in session (generally 60 days of the year), Rose lives in the capital. If there is a special session, she may have to stay another 30 days. She is rarely gone for more than 100 days. The remainder of the year, Rose is a farmer. Can Rose deduct her costs of attending the legislature as travel expenses because she is away from her home?

G-82 Chris and Sue are 50 percent shareholders in the BackBone personal service corporation. BackBone provides chiropractic services in four small towns: Troy, Union, Vista, and Willow. Chris is the main chiropractor in the Troy office, and Sue heads the Vista office. The two other offices have chiropractor employees running the practices, but that is where BackBone's trouble lies. Charlie, the main chiropractor in the Willow office, does not see eye-to-eye with Chris and Sue on management styles. Charlie does not take well to any interference in how he runs the office, the hours he keeps, or the therapy techniques he employs.

Firing Charlie is not an option for two reasons. First, it is difficult to find chiropractors who want to work and live in small towns. Second, and most important, if Charlie were to leave BackBone, he would start his own practice in Willow. He is very good with patients and easily would be able to take at least 80 percent of the clients in Willow. Sue and Chris have noticed that some of the patients in Union drive to Willow because they prefer Charlie to Joe, the chiropractor in their Union office. Chris and Sue do not want to compete with Charlie and would prefer that the parties come up with an arrangement that would make everyone happy. They already pay Charlie handsomely, so more salary is not the solution. For Charlie, it seems to be a matter of control. Chris and Sue may be willing to give up control of the Willow office, but they do not want to completely lose the profits this office adds to BackBone. Chris and Sue have come to you for some suggestions on how to solve this problem with the lowest tax cost. Provide BackBone with several options and the tax consequences of each. Support your conclusions with primary citations.

G-83 Joe Roberts, 22 years old, is the star of the State University basketball team. He will likely be selected in the first round of the NBA draft. Needless to say, Joe is being wined and dined by several sports agents, and each has been providing Joe with "incentives" to be selected as his agent. These incentives range from trips to Las Vegas to Rolex watches. This is all overwhelming for Joe, as he grew up on a farm in Kansas. His parents are also being wined and dined in hopes that they can influence him in his choice of agents.

After finally selecting an agent, the time has come to negotiate with the basketball team that selected him. Joe relies completely on the agent in these dealings. Joe is just interested in playing ball, and he does not really care much about the financial details. Joe's agent is in the final negotiating stages with the San Antonio Spurs. The potential offer is $3.5 million for the first year, a signing bonus, and incentive bonuses based on his and the team's performance plus fringe benefits. These benefits will include health and dental insurance, life insurance, a team car, a clothing allowance, a travel allowance for him and his family, free tickets to each game, and all the training and fitness coaching he needs. A retirement plan is a separate benefit to be negotiated. Joe has come to your firm for tax guidance with regard to the package offered by the Spurs. Provide Joe with a tax analysis of the compensation package. Suggest any tax planning that could help Joe maximize his lifetime wealth.

G-84 Ella works at an accounting firm and, like many accountants, tends to spend more than 40 hours a week at the office preparing and reviewing tax returns and providing tax advice to her clients. Recently, Ella decided to move out of her one-bedroom condominium and into a larger single-family home. Rather than sell the condominium, however, Ella elected to start renting it and was able to secure a reliable tenant. Shortly after Ella began renting out the condominium, one of the kitchen appliances needed replacement at a cost of approximately $1,400. Ella wishes to immediately expense the cost of this appliance under IRC § 179. Prepare a memo that describes the qualifications for immediate expensing under § 179 and whether Ella's cost will qualify as deductible.

G-85 Phil recently received a permit to open a medical-waste incineration center in Newark, New Jersey. He has been working on the project for some time with his colleague Karen. Now that they have received a permit, they are going to establish an S corporation to handle operating the new business, with Phil as the CEO and Karen as the COO. They feel comfortable that the new business venture is going to make large profits, because other similar businesses have done well (the key, as it turns out, is working with federal, state, and local agencies to obtain the permit). Phil wants to limit the amount of employment taxes he pays on his compensation from the S corporation and is thus considering paying himself a very low salary and taking the bulk of his profits from the business as a distribution from the S corporation. Prepare a memo that explains how reasonable compensation can be established for Phil; include techniques from both the circuit in which he resides and any other circuit for addressing the issue of reasonable compensation.

G-86   Ernie and Julie Paltrow purchased a 57-acre property in Temecula, California, in 2014. They began developing approximately 40 acres of the property for vineyards and incurred substantial costs to prepare the land for the vines, purchase the rootstock for the wine grapes they wish to grow, and, of course, plant numerous vines around the acreage in hopes of eventually producing a fine wine. This took approximately two years, and during that time, the Paltrows capitalized the costs until 2016, when the vines started to grow. At that point, the Paltrows put the vineyard into service, and now they wish to deduct the $800,000 vineyard-related costs as quickly as possible. They placed in service only nominal amounts of other assets in 2016 and are expecting a healthy profit (more than $2 million) from the sale of the wine. Based on the law in effect in 2016, what is the Paltrows' best alternative for recovering these business-related costs as quickly as possible?

G-87   Swoosh, Inc. is a shoe manufacturer. Consider each of the following activities and explain in a memo whether these activities will qualify for the research and experimentation credit.

   a.   Swoosh researches how well different running shoe designs, shapes, and forms perform. By determining the ideal shape, form, and design, Swoosh will be able to improve the performance of its shoes.

   b.   Swoosh performs an experiment using many different shoes that all perform very well, but Swoosh is uncertain which model of shoe is ideal. Using computer models and simulations and by paying athletes to run in the different types of shoes, Swoosh is able to determine the best alternative for the new brand of shoe.

   c.   Swoosh performs research to determine the ideal placement of the logo on its shoes. Swoosh's study determines that customers are more likely to buy the shoes if its logo is placed approximately in the middle.

   d.   Swoosh undertakes to engineer a basketball shoe that prevents ankle injuries in basketball players. It designs several shoes with different sizes and materials for the laces and ankle support and tests each to determine which combination puts the least amount of stress on the ankle. The equipment used to test the shoes measures the physical forces being put on the ankle area of the shoe during normal movement.

   e.   Swoosh tests different designs and asks focus group participants to wear the shoes and report, on a scale of 1 to 10, which shoe felt the best around their ankles.

G-88   Sarah came home one day to find significant water damage in her home. Apparently one of the hoses to her washing machine had worn out and split, spilling water all over the place. Over the next month, mildew appeared as well. Is there any casualty-loss deduction for Sarah? Ignore any computational floors and assume that she did not have any homeowner's insurance.

G-89   Richie is a wealthy rancher in Texas. He operates his ranch through a grantor trust set up by his grandparents. Richie does not like to get his hands dirty, so he hires a professional management company to run the ranch. The property generated a $500,000 loss this year. Can Richie deduct this loss on his Schedule E given the material-participation rules of IRC § 469?

G-90 Maggie could not conceive a child using natural means, so she sought out a woman who would donate an egg to be surgically implanted in Maggie. Which of the following items are deductible by Maggie in her process to find an egg donor?

    a. Payment to a search firm to find donor candidates.

    b. Payment to Maggie's attorney.

    c. Payment of a fee to the egg donor.

    d. Payment to medical staff to run physiological and psychological tests on the prospective donor.

G-91 Larry and Mary obtained a divorce, and the decree as negotiated allowed alimony payments to Mary of $3,000 on the 15th of each month. The divorce was final on July 5, but Mary was short of cash, so Larry made the payments to her starting in March. What is Larry's alimony deduction for the year?

G-92 Sally incurred a 90-mile round-trip commute every day, mainly because she could not get along with her supervisor at the sales office located four miles from her home. Sally works under a one-year contract, and her assignment to the nearer office is affirmed in the current year's contract, but management has allowed her to travel to the more distant location. How many deductible commuting miles does Sally accumulate on a work day?

G-93 Professor White operates a popular CPA exam review course as a sole proprietor. He charges $2,000 tuition to each student, and he guarantees a full refund of the tuition if the student passes an in-course exam but does not pass the actual CPA exam on the first try. White is bold enough to do this because the first-time-pass rate for his students is more than 80 percent. He collected $150,000 tuition for his fall 2017 review section, but he reported the gross receipts on his 2018 Form 1040 because the grades for those taking the fall review are not released until February 2018. Thus, White asserted that he had no constructive receipt of the tuition until February 2018. Is this treatment correct?

G-94 Lisa, usually a stay-at-home mother, went to the hospital one day for some outpatient surgery. She hired a babysitter for $35 to watch her four-year-old son while she was gone. What tax benefits are available to Lisa for this cash payment?

G-95 Same as G-94, except that Lisa paid the sitter while she worked as a scout leader for the Girl Scouts.

G-96 Tex's credit union has provided him with financing to acquire his $200,000 home. The loan is set up as a three-year note with a balloon payment, but the credit union always renews the loan for another three years at the current interest rate. This year, the credit union renewed Tex's loan for the third time, charging $3,000 in points. In what year(s) can Tex deduct this $3,000?

G-97 Amelia and Dave are married and have one child. Detail the tax effects to the couple of making the IRC § 1(g)(7)(A)(iv) election to include their seven-year-old daughter's $10,000 unearned income on their current-year joint return.

G-98 Eighty percent of the Willigs's AGI comes from their submarine sandwich shop operated as a sole proprietorship. In 2017, the Willigs lost an IRS audit and owed $12,000 in 2015 federal income taxes, all attributable to inventory computations in their business. Interest on this amount totaled $3,200. All amounts due were paid by the end of 2017. How much of the interest can the Willigs deduct on their 2017 Schedule C?

G-99 Al and Amy are divorced. In which of the following circumstances can legal fees be deducted?

    a. Al pays an attorney $5,000 for help with getting the court to reduce his alimony obligation.

    b. Amy pays an attorney $5,000 for help with getting the court to increase her alimony receipts.

    c. Al pays Amy's attorney fees in part b, as required by the original divorce decree.

G-100 Katie is a one-third owner of an S corporation. After a falling out with the other shareholders, Katie signed an agreement early in January 2017. Under the terms of the agreement, Katie took $200,000 of her capital from the corporation and had eight months to negotiate a purchase of the stock of the other shareholders. She did not complete this task by the end of August 2017. On March 1, 2018, Katie sells all her shares to the remaining shareholders for a $2.5 million gain. For how many of these months does Katie report flow-through income from the S corporation?

G-101 Can an individual make a contribution to an IRA based on the receipt of unemployment compensation?

G-102 SlimeCo spent $250,000 to build underground storage tanks for its waste byproducts. This is a recurring expenditure for SlimeCo because once the tanks are filled, new ones must be built. When can SlimeCo deduct the $250,000?

G-103 Prudence was named a shareholder in her law firm, which operates as an S corporation. Her payments into the firm's capital were to start in approximately nine months, when an audit would determine the full value of the firm and a new corporate year would commence. Paperwork with the pertinent state offices was completed, naming Prudence as a shareholder and director and adding her name to that of the firm. However, Prudence left the firm eight months after the announcement, that is, before she paid any money for shares. Is Prudence liable for tax on her share of the entity's earnings for the eight months?

G-104 Cal's son has been labeled a "can't miss" NBA prospect since middle school. This year, while the son is a college freshman and classified as an amateur under NCAA rules, Cal spent $14,000 for special clothing, equipment, camps, and personal trainers to keep improving his son's skills. Can Cal deduct these items?

G-105 CPA Myrna forgot to tell her client, Freddie, to accelerate the payment of state income and property taxes in a year when Freddie was in an unusually high tax bracket. Upon discovering the error, the parties negotiated a $15,000 payment from Myrna (and her insurance company) to Freddie to compensate Freddie for Myrna's inadequate professional advice. Is this payment gross income to Freddie?

G-106 How much of the $100,000 interest that is paid on a loan from Everett National Bank can Ben deduct if he invests the loan proceeds in the following? Consider each item independently.

    a. South Chicago School District bonds

    b. AT&T bonds, paying $125,000 interest income this year

    c. Computer Futures Inc. shares, a growth stock that pays no dividend this year

    d. A life insurance policy on Betty, Ben's wife

G-107 Lilly leases a car that she uses solely for business purposes. The car would be worth $40,050 on the market, and Lilly paid $7,400 in lease payments this year. How are these items treated on her tax return?

G-108 Pete is an engineering professor at State University. Under his contract, Pete's inventions while employed at the university are the property of the Board of Regents, but Pete receives an addition to his salary equal to one-third of the royalties received by the university on his patents. This year, Pete received $75,000 on top of his salary, as royalties allocated to him. Does Pete recognize this amount as ordinary income or capital gain?

G-109 Dean and Robin owned a family business, each holding the shares as community property. When they were divorced in 2014, the court did not force them to split the shares, citing damage to the business that could occur if the public learned that ownership of the enterprise was changing. Now it is 2017, and Robin wants to remarry. She and her new husband want to have the business retitle one-half of the shares in Robin's name only. The original divorce court agrees in 2017. Is this transfer subject to income tax? Is it subject to gift tax?

G-110 Dave made a $100,000 cash withdrawal from his IRA. He bought $100,000 of Microcraft stock, and within the rollover period he transferred the stock to another IRA. Does Dave report any gross income?

G-111 Gold Partners wanted to complete a like-kind exchange just before it liquidated. Accordingly, it sold the real estate it meant to transfer to the other party, and a qualified intermediary held the resulting cash. When the intermediary found acceptable replacement realty, the intermediary transferred cash and the like-kind property directly to the partners, thereby liquidating Gold. Does IRC § 1031 apply?

G-112 HelpCo pays Hank two $100,000 salaries per year, one through its WestCo subsidiary and one through its EastCo subsidiary. How do Hank and HelpCo treat his Social Security tax obligations?

G-113 Zhang lived in Atlanta from 2011 through 2013 to carry out her duties as an employee of YourTV.com, receiving an annual salary of $150,000. She was transferred to the San Jose office for 2014 through 2016, and then in 2017 she took an executive position with the Web2.2 LLC in Austin. Zhang owned a home in Atlanta, but she rented an apartment in San Jose. When she withdraws money from her IRA to submit a down payment on her Austin condominium, is a 10 percent penalty due?

G-114 Give three examples of situations in which the IRS would waive the two-year rule for applying the IRC § 121 exclusion of gain from the sale of a principal residence as a result of "unforeseen circumstances."

G-115 LaFollette lives in a condominium with Tourneau. The two are not married, but they each hold a one-half interest in the deed for their unit. In the current year, the condominium association installed a solar water heater. The association paid for the water heating system, but it assessed LaFollette and Tourneau $7,500 for this expenditure, as it did for other unit owners. Tourneau was short of funds, so LaFollette paid the entire assessment before the end of the year. Compute LaFollette's IRC § 25D credit against her Form 1040 liability for the year.

G-116 On December 6, Ed Grimely appeared on the game show, "The Wheel of Fate." As a result of his appearance, Grimely won the following prizes:

	Manufacturer's Suggested List Price	Fair Market Value	Actual Cost to the Show
All-expenses-paid trip to Hawaii	$8,432	$6,000	$5,200
One case of Twinkies	16	12	0
Seven music lessons for the calliope	105	35	0
One year of free haircuts	120	60	15

a. Assuming that Grimely received all these prizes by the end of the year, compute his gross income for the year as a result of his winnings.

b. Will this amount change if Grimely refuses to accept the calliope lessons immediately after the program's taping session is completed?

G-117 Sing-Yi receives a $100 debit card every month from her employer, the Porter Group. The debit card is limited so that it can be used only to purchase fare cards and passes on the Metro Transit line that operates trains and subways in town. Sing-Yi throws away the card when it expires at the end of the month, and she is not required to provide any records to Porter about how the card was used. The card logo says "American Airlines Visa," and Sing-Yi picks her own password for the card. Does the card represent $100 monthly gross income to Sing-Yi? Explain.

G-118 HardCo spent $4 million this year on a new graphic design for its product, a yo-yo. Under the prior design, HardCo's name and logo only appeared on the box and wrapping paper, which were discarded by most customers once they started using the product. The new design displayed HardCo's name and newer, flashier logo on both sides of the yo-yo, with a paint that also made it glow in the dark. When can HardCo deduct the $4 million?

G-119 Fred was the owner of a three-bedroom cabin in California. During 2016, he contracted with a property-management company to rent the cabin to third parties. In exchange for its services, Fred paid the company a 35 percent commission on all rental income received. The property-management company was responsible for maintaining the property, cleaning the cabin, paying all utilities, providing linens, and so on. The cabin was rented three times during the year for a total of 12 days and nine nights, with the average rental period being three days. Fred visited the cabin eight times during the year and stayed 19 nights and 27 days. Fred claimed $15,000 of Schedule E expenses relating to the rental of the cabin on his return under the active-rental-real-estate exception. Was Fred entitled to the deduction?

G-120 Gina was falsely imprisoned as the result of an auto dealer's criminal complaint against her. Although the charges were later dropped, she was arrested and detained for approximately eight hours. She was not hurt or abused during the arrest and detention, but she did see a psychologist for several sessions. She sued the auto dealership for malicious prosecution and received a $25,000 settlement payment from the company. Can Gina exclude the settlement payment from income?

G-121 Four individuals formed Triangle Properties as a C corporation in 2011. The corporation is domiciled in North Carolina. The corporation invested in commercial rental properties that generated passive-activity losses. The shareholders made a Subchapter S election for Triangle Properties effective on January 1, 2017. On the date of conversion, Triangle Properties had $118,000 of suspended passive-activity losses from its commercial rental properties. In 2017, the properties generated $44,000 of net rental income. Can Triangle Properties carry forward and deduct the suspended passive losses incurred when it was a C corporation against the passive rental income earned while it was an S corporation?

G-122 Sal was born male but diagnosed with gender identity disorder. As a result, he suffered persistent psychological discomfort with his gender and decided to have a sex-change operation. As part of the treatment regimen, Sal had to undergo various hormonal treatments for several years, followed by a period in which he changed his name to Sally and lived for two years as a female before finally having gender-reassignment surgery in 2017. Is Sally entitled to a medical deduction for the costs of the hormone treatment, surgeries, and related expenses?

G-123 Jim Jones owns 50 percent of the stock of an S corporation. In 2017, Jim obtains a health insurance plan providing coverage for himself, his wife, and their two children. Jim makes all premium payments to the plan during 2017 and furnishes proof of the payments to the S corporation, which then reimburses him for the payments and reports the premium payments as wages on Jim's W-2 for the year. Jim reports the amounts as gross income on his 2017 personal tax return. Jim's income from the S corporation exceeds the amount of premiums for the health coverage, and he does not participate in any subsidized health plans maintained by another employer or an employer of his spouse. Is Jim allowed to take a deduction on his personal tax return for the health insurance premiums paid during the year?

G-124 Chico is a corporation operating in several states on the accrual basis. Chico received a state income tax refund this year (Year 4) based on the following sequence of events. In which tax year does Chico recognize the refund as gross income?

Year 1: Generated the operating loss.

Year 2: Filed the loss carryback form with the state.

Year 3: Received notice that the refund was approved.

Year 4: Received the refund check.

G-125 After her employer transferred her to another town, Rosemary put her house up for sale. After two years of Internet listings, open houses, repairs, and price cuts, a buyer finally came along. By this time, the house had sat empty for 25 months before the closing occurred, and Rosemary rented it out just to help with the mortgage payments. Rosemary claimed a $40,000 business loss with respect to the house. Do you agree with this filing position?

G-126 Edna is a well-paid executive with ADley, a firm that uses stock options and deferred compensation as well as high salaries to compensate its most successful employees. When Edna and Ron were divorced, Ron received the rights to a bundle of these deferred-compensation rights. Complete the following table, indicating the required tax results:

Tax Year	Market Price for Edna's Option Transferred to Ron	Event	Tax Consequences to Edna	Tax Consequences to Ron
2009	$9	Divorce is settled.		
2012	$14	Ron exercises stock options with $10 cash payment, then holds stock received.		
2015	$20	Edna terminates employment with ADley; $100 lump sum of deferred compensation is distributed to Ron.		
2017	$22	Ron sells shares received via option contracts.		

G-127 Wes and Donna were the only members of an LLC, and they fended off unwanted takeover suitors with a clause in the charter that shares could change hands only with unanimous approval from all the other owners. Wes is now 70 years old, so he wants to start phasing out of the business. He makes a gift of 10 percent of the LLC shares to his son Jeffrey, as agreed to by Donna. The shares are worth $20,000. What is Wes's taxable gift to Jeffrey in the year of the transfer?

G-128 Peg worked with a local IRS-approved charity whose mission was to capture and neuter feral cats and take care of them until they could be released back into the wild. Peg incurred more than $6,000 of expenses for food and medical care for more than 50 cats under her care. Is Peg able to claim any of the $6,000 as a charitable deduction on her tax return?

G-129 As a result of financial difficulties, Acme Company, located in Raleigh, North Carolina, closed all its retail stores and terminated all its employees. The company adopted a plan to compensate terminated employees based on job grade and management level, and each terminated employee received a severance payment as a lump-sum payment. The payments were treated as taxable income to the employees for federal income tax purposes, and Acme reported the payments as wages on W-2 forms. Do the company and the laid-off workers owe Social Security and Medicare taxes on the payments?

G-130 A local law firm recently remodeled its offices. In addition to new office furniture and computers, the company purchased six large paintings from a local art gallery. These paintings are more than 100 years old and cost more than $100,000. The paintings are on display in the offices alongside more recent paintings by lesser-known artists. Are the paintings depreciable for tax purposes?

G-131 Chris Mac, a local CPA, is a self-employed tax return preparer. Chris works from home in a room that is exclusively used on a regular basis as the principal place of business. Last year, Chris built a new bathroom across the hall for his clients' use. Although the vast majority of use of the bathroom is from clients, occasionally a family member or guest uses the bathroom. Can Chris deduct the additional bathroom space as a home office?

G-132 The Downtown Wellness Clinic, a tax-exempt organization, sells memberships to corporations so that their employees can work out before and after office hours. Three blocks away, the Power Up Fitness Center has similar facilities and also wants to sell memberships to corporate neighbors. Is the clinic subject to federal income tax on its membership sales?

State Research Cases

S-1 Tom and Verna are going to combine their fishing businesses to become more profitable. Tom currently lives in Mississippi, and Verna lives in Louisiana. They would prefer to set up the business as an S corporation, but only if it will not be subject to state taxation. Since Verna and Tom live within 20 miles of each other, they do not have a preference as to the state of incorporation. Does it make a tax difference which state they choose?

S-2 New City, California, charged Rick a real estate transfer tax when his property was relinquished to the Federal Housing Administration (FHA) in its capacity as his loan guarantor. The amount charged was the same as the amount Rick was required to pay the county. Can Rick be required to pay this tax, or should the FHA pay it?

S-3 TimberCut Corporation transferred all the rights to timber growing on its land located in Spokane County, Washington, to its wholly owned subsidiary, PineCo. The Department of Revenue has imposed a real estate excise tax on TimberCut because PineCo. transferred $1 million cash to TimberCut. Is TimberCut's transfer a sale of timber land subject to the taxes imposed?

S-4 WaterWorks Corporation has decided to sell off one of its amusement parks located in Texas. Several businesses have been identified as possible buyers. It is unlikely that one of these businesses by itself will purchase all the assets of the amusement park, but WaterWorks is confident that it can sell all the assets to various parties within a six-month period. Is this sale subject to Texas sales tax?

S-5 A tribal nation in Kansas is considering building a gas station to accommodate people traveling through their reservation. Before undergoing the considerable expense for construction, the tribe members want to know whether the fuel sold will be subject to state fuel taxes. This will make a difference in the profitability of the project. Is gasoline sold on a federally recognized reservation subject to the fuel tax imposed by Kansas?

S-6 A town in Vermont wants to charge property tax on a lot and building used by a not-for-profit organization as its administrative office. To be exempt from property taxes, the property must have the following characteristics:

- Be dedicated to public use.

- Have its primary use directly benefit a class of persons who are part of the public.

- Be owned and operated on a not-for-profit basis.

Does administrative use of the building meet the definition for the exemption?

S-7 Iowa imposes a tax on the operation of slot machines. The rate is graduated based on slot machine revenues. Can Iowa charge a higher maximum rate to racetrack owners than it does to riverboat owners without violating the equal protection clause of the U.S. Constitution?

S-8 The Pluto Corporation has been mining ore in Oklahoma for many years. A new mine just developed is producing ore that contains uranium. Pluto would like to know the rate of the severance tax on mined uranium and upon what base the tax is assessed.

S-9 The Peppermint Partnership operates a successful candy business. It is considering taking the partnership public and becoming a master limited partnership. If it does so, will it be subject to the corporate franchise tax in New York, where its headquarters and operating plant are located?

S-10 Rodney has been in the South Carolina National Guard for the past 20 years. This is his last year as an active member. When Rodney turns 65 in August of this year, he will begin collecting Social Security benefits and Guard retirement pay. His employer laid him off in January, and Rodney qualified for unemployment compensation. Rodney received severance pay of $50,000 when terminated by his employer. Which of these amounts are taxable to Rodney in South Carolina?

S-11 Poplar Inc.'s corporate headquarters, plants, and warehouses are located in Vermont. Until this year, all of Poplar's sales have been made in Vermont. Poplar's first out-of-state sale of $1 million (cost of sales, $300,000) is shipped by a common-carrier trucking firm from its warehouse to the purchaser's dock in Indiana. The truck stops for gasoline in New York and Ohio, and its driver spends a night in Ohio. To which states must Poplar apportion income from the sale? How much income is taxed in each such state?

S-12 A religious organization is considering spreading its message into Illinois by opening several churches in the state. As part of its ceremonies, wine is consumed by its members. The church would like to know the consequences for the alcoholic beverage tax if it ferments its own wine. What if, instead of making the wine, the church purchases it from an importing distributor?

S-13 Crazy Freddie's is a mail order and internet based electronic retailer incorporated and based in Grand Rapids, MI. Crazy Freddie's takes significant measures to avoid triggering income tax nexus with any state except Michigan. The state of Ohio recently passed a new Commercial Activity Tax (CAT). The CAT is an annual tax imposed on gross receipts for the privilege of doing business in Ohio. It is not limited to those with substantial nexus (and thus, is not intended to be limited by P.L. 86-272). Crazy Freddie's does about $1.5 million in sales to Ohio customers each year but has no physical presence in Ohio. Is Crazy Freddie's subject to Ohio's CAT.

S-14 Travis Smith and Carmela Jones operate a successful law firm in Portland, Oregon. They are considering opening another office across the Columbia River, in Vancouver, Washington. Travis and Carmela would like to know if they then would be subject to any business or personal taxes in Washington. If they are subject to any taxes, can they use those taxes as a credit or a deduction on their Oregon income tax returns as taxes paid to another state?

S-15 Jie Wang wants to open a new funeral parlor in Colorado. She would like to know the sales and use tax implications for this business. Are morticians considered to be rendering services, selling tangible personal property, or a combination of both? Specifically, Jie needs to know whether she should contract funeral services as one lump sum, or whether it would be more beneficial to itemize the charges for caskets, urns, and so on separately from the services offered.

S-16 Brock and David are equal shareholders of an S corporation that manufactures electric razors. They are interested in opening a plant in the south. They want to know whether Florida or Alabama would be the best state to move to, considering only tax consequences. The main concerns are income taxes (corporate and personal), franchise taxes, and intangible asset property taxes. Brock and David expect the S corporation to generate $400,000 in annual taxable income.

S-17 Melkry, an Ohio corporation, provides tugboat services on the Great Lakes to vessels weighing at least 800 tons. Each of Melkry's tugboats weighs approximately 100 tons. Michigan has assessed use tax on repair materials, fuel, and capital assets purchased by Melkry for its operations. Is Melkry subject to the use tax?

S-18   EmiLu Corporation is a private delivery company that hires independent contractors with their own trucks to deliver car parts to various auto repair shops in Pennsylvania. EmiLu contracts with the manufacturers of the car parts to make the deliveries, and then it hires the drivers in Pennsylvania to deliver the parts. EmiLu has no property, employees, or customers in Pennsylvania. EmiLu is incorporated in Delaware, where all the car-part-manufacturing customers are located. Is EmiLu subject to the corporate franchise tax in Pennsylvania?

S-19   Earl and Kathy live on the "Big Island" of Hawaii in the town of Captain Cook. Because the altitude is high, they grow coffee plants on their property. Most of their neighbors grow coffee as well. Earl and Kathy collect the coffee from their property and that of their neighbors, and then they dry the coffee in a special building they have constructed on their land. Does this activity affect their qualification for the home exemption for Hawaii property taxes?

S-20   Chuck Taylor owns a fish-processing plant in Alaska. Some of the processing chemicals and fish remains could be considered hazardous wastes. What possible state and local taxes does Chuck need to be concerned about when disposing of these materials?

S-21   Jefferson W. Clinton is a resident of Arkansas but has not filed an income tax return nor paid any tax liabilities for the last few years. Does Arkansas currently have a tax amnesty program that would relieve Jefferson of some of the penalties and interest on his unpaid liabilities?

S-22   Chicago Tool and Die Corporation (CTDC) recently purchased an aircraft for the top executives to use for customer visits, transporting employees from one location to another, and matters relating to acquisitions and lawsuits. Upon purchase, no Illinois sales tax was charged, as the seller did not have Illinois sales-tax nexus. The aircraft was hangared in Ohio but made numerous trips (more than 200) in and out of Illinois airports. In the year of purchase, was CTDC liable for Illinois use tax?

S-23   James Bulger works at a sandwich shop in Ames, Iowa. During his coffee break each afternoon, he enjoys a candy bar that his employer sells to him at an employee discount. Candy bars are not exempt (as food) from sales tax in Iowa, and his employer charges him sales tax on the purchase. Recently, James noticed that his employer was charging him sales tax on the retail sales price ($1), not the employee discount price ($.80) that James actually pays. What is the proper amount to calculate the sales tax on, the actual (reduced) price or the retail price?

S-24   Sal Bermuda recently invested in a new flavored water that he is bottling and selling at street vendor carts throughout the city of Chicago. Sal's water is flavored with natural ingredients and just a touch of sweetener. Some of Sal's customers have been explaining how happy they are that Sal has not been charging them a $0.05 bottled-water tax. Sal has never heard of such a tax and is wondering if there are any other taxes aimed specifically at his bottled water product.

S-25   Apache and Alice Swearingen moved to Minnesota in 2012. Apache retired in early 2015, and the Swearingens purchased a motor home, started traveling extensively, and put their Minnesota home up for sale. Due to lack of interest, however, they took their home off the market late in the year. In 2016, they spent approximately 15 days in South Dakota. While there, they registered a mailbox address with a private company and, using that address, obtained South Dakota driver's licenses, opened a bank account, registered to vote, and registered their vehicles in South Dakota. In March 2016, they relisted their Minnesota home for sale. In April 2016, they returned to Minnesota from their road trip to South Dakota (and other states as well), and in June 2016 they finally sold the Minnesota home. They spent the rest of 2016 traveling the country in their motor home. Are the Swearingens required to file a Minnesota resident income tax return for 2016?

S-26   Evgenia is a resident of California. She recently purchased two computers from an online retailer that did not charge California sales tax. The retailer happened to be offering a steep discount if two computers were purchased in a single transaction. She gave one of the computers to her sister (also a California resident) for her birthday a few days after the computers arrived. Because Evgenia already had a fully functional computer, she stored the other computer for the next 18 months before finally upgrading to a new one. Is Evgenia responsible for California use tax for one, both, or neither computer, and when is the use tax due?

S-27   Coldbear Inc., a California corporation, recently entered into two new contracts with clients in Georgia and Utah. In order to service those clients, Coldbear will hire a couple of additional employees (based in California) who will make five or six trips to the client's offices in Utah and Georgia to provide the services required under the contract. Coldbear employees will work at the client's offices in each location and stay in hotels during the trips. (Coldbear does not see any need to open new offices in either state.) Please describe, in detail, how Coldbear will calculate the numerator of the sales apportionment factor for state income tax purposes in all three states (California, Georgia, and Utah).

S-28   Professional athletes are required by many states to consider "duty days" when determining taxable income. What are duty days? Does the state in which your university is located have duty days? Compare and contrast the definition of duty days between California and Michigan, specifically with reference to different treatment of different sports.

S-29   Compare and contrast additions to unadjusted federal income in Utah, Delaware, and New Mexico.

S-30   Compare and contrast subtractions to unadjusted federal taxable income for Maine, Montana, and Kansas.

S-31   Many states use the Internal Revenue Code as the backbone of their tax code. Determine the level of conformity with the Internal Revenue Code for Nebraska, Kansas, Oklahoma, and Missouri. Compare that approach to the one taken by Arkansas.

S-32   Compare and contrast the rules for allocating nonbusiness gains and losses in Mississippi, Maryland, and Hawaii. Based on the corporate tax rate structure, which state would be most desirable for allocating a nonbusiness gain? How about a nonbusiness loss?

International Research Cases

I-1   VanDelay, a citizen of the United States but a resident of Dulcinea, is an important sculptor. This year, he came to the United States to appear at an exhibition of his work in San Francisco. The United States has no tax treaty with Dulcinea. Does the $250,000 that VanDelay netted from the show qualify for the IRC § 911 earned-income exclusion?

I-2   State University invites Dr. Byko, a Russian citizen, to become a member of the faculty for a three-year period to work on a large grant the university obtained from the National Aeronautics and Space Administration (NASA). Dr. Byko accepts the invitation and enters the United States on a J-1 visa. His university pay is entirely funded by the NASA grant. Based on the Russian treaty, Dr. Byko thinks his income is exempt because it is from a grant. Determine whether Dr. Byko is correct.

I-3   Haruo, a resident alien, obtained a divorce in the United States from his wife, Wakana, two years ago. Last July, Wakana returned to Japan, but Haruo remained in the United States. For all of the current year, Haruo paid alimony to Wakana in the amount of $10,000 per month. Does Wakana have income subject to U.S. taxation or withholding?

I-4   Rainbow Corporation has a contract with the National Science Foundation to conduct research in Antarctica. Harriet, a U.S. employee of Rainbow, spent all of last year and part of this year working at McMurdo Station on Ross Island, Antarctica. When filing her return for last year, Harriet excluded her income from the contract, based on the fact that she worked outside of the United States. Her income was not in excess of the excludible ceiling. Is Harriet correct in her treatment of last year's income?

I-5   Moonsoo, a Republic of Korea citizen, went to San Diego, California, on a vacation. Because he liked San Diego, Moonsoo purchased five acres of land, on which he wants to build luxury condominiums. He also bought the majority interest in a construction corporation that specializes in condominium construction. Moonsoo could not get the zoning clearance to build the condominiums, so he sold both the land and his stock in the construction corporation. Is Moonsoo taxed in the United States on his gains from these sales?

I-6   Ireland imposes a tax on the net market value (less certain deductions) of the taxable assets of those individuals residing in Ireland. Although she is a U.S. citizen, Katherine has been residing in Ireland for the past five years. She owns property located in Ireland and property located in the United States. Much of her property consists of stocks and bonds, but she also has large holdings of land in both countries. Does this Irish tax qualify for the foreign tax credit and/or as a deduction for U.S. tax purposes?

I-7   Paul Thomas and Karen Jackson are both in the U.S. Armed Forces, and each receives combat zone pay. Karen is a commissioned officer, whereas Paul is enlisted personnel. How is each taxed on the combat zone pay? How does Paul treat his combat zone pay when computing his earned income tax credit?

I-8   Three international students are paid $1,000 per month to be teaching assistants in their university's Department of Accounting. The students from India and China have been in the United States for six years, and the student from Spain arrived one year ago. How is each of the students taxed in the United States for the current year?

I-9   A group of Russian tourists spent a week in Las Vegas. Kolzak, one of the tourists, was very lucky at the roulette table and won $50,000. Is Kolzak subject to U.S. income tax, and is the casino required to withhold taxes on her winnings?

I-10   Which of the following payments by International Partners Inc., a Montana corporation, qualifies for the foreign-tax credit?

     a.   Income tax paid to Germany, covered by an existing treaty.

     b.   Income tax paid to Adagio, with which the United States has no income tax treaty.

     c.   Value-added tax paid to Largetto, with which the United States has no income tax treaty.

     d.   Oil-extraction tax paid to Tedesco, with which the United States has no income tax treaty.

     e.   Transportation tax paid to Santa Lucia, with which the United States has no income tax treaty. The tax is reduced dollar for dollar when International provides consulting services in designing Santa Lucia's new bullet train system. This year, International incurred $1 million in taxes, but it earned a $600,000 reduction for its services.

I-11   Chris Renaldo, a U.S. tax resident who resides in the United States, heard that the Bank of Spain is paying above-market returns for savings accounts. Determine whether interest payments from the bank to Chris will be subject to withholding at the source.

I-12   Hardy Kicker plays on the U.S. men's soccer team. He recently played in a soccer tournament in South Africa. The South African tournament organizers will pay Hardy $20,000 to play. Determine whether payments to Hardy by the organizers will be subject to tax withholding under South African statute, and separately whether they be subject to withholding considering the U.S.–South Africa tax treaty.

I-13   Sally James is the CFO of a domestic corporation with a small subsidiary in Mexico. The subsidiary earned taxable profits of $1 million for the year just ended. What amount should be accrued for profit sharing for the Mexican employees?

I-14   Boxian Wu is a real estate developer in China. She recently sold an office building for 4 million yuan. She paid 2 million yuan for the land use rights and 1 million yuan for the cost of developing the building. What is Boxian's Chinese land-appreciation tax on the transfer of this real estate?

I-15   Taylor Joseph has held stock in Foreign Corporation, classified as a passive-foreign-investment corporation (PFIC), for the last three years. Starting with the current year, Foreign will no longer meet the definition of a PFIC. Determine whether Taylor must continue to treat his investment in Foreign as a PFIC.

I-16   Jamaica Corp. (established under the laws of Jamaica) seeks to borrow funds from a Jamaican financial institution. In order to process the loan, the local Jamaican bank requires that U.S. Corp., the sole shareholder of Jamaica Corp., provide a guarantee on the loan. Jamaica Corp. pays its loan off in accordance with the terms of the loan, and no call is made on U.S. Corp.'s guarantee. Does the mere presence of a guarantee require U.S. Corp. and Jamaica Corp. to reflect transfer pricing costs under IRC § 482?

Advanced Research Cases

AC-1   Helen Hanks, who lives in San Francisco, California, has just been promoted to manager of a divisional office. However, the divisional office is located in Portland, Oregon. Helen's significant other, Tom Hunt, will be moving with her to Portland. Helen's children from a previous marriage will also be joining her in Portland. The children have been living with their father in Spain for the past year.

Helen easily sells the San Francisco house in which she and Tom live. Helen is the sole owner of the house. However, she has a harder time finding the right home in Portland. Helen has to make several trips to Portland before buying a house under construction. It will not be available for occupancy for at least 20 days after she arrives in Portland. Tom accompanied Helen on the house-hunting trips to give his opinion on the houses and to look for a new job.

The actual move takes place as follows. The movers arrive on Wednesday to pack up Helen's and Tom's household items. Thursday, the movers pack up Helen's items from a storage unit located outside the city, along with her sailboat.

The movers then leave for Portland. Helen hires a college student to drive her car to Portland; the driver leaves on Friday. On Saturday, after dropping Helen at the airport for her flight to Portland, Tom leaves to drive his car to Portland via Salt Lake City, Utah, where he also visits his brother. Helen and Tom stay in a hotel from Wednesday to Friday while still in San Francisco and upon arriving in Portland until the house is ready for occupancy. The moving company stores their household items at its warehouse until Helen and Tom are ready to move into their new house. Helen's children arrive two weeks later.

In November of the current year, Helen pays for all the costs involved in selling the San Francisco home and moving Tom, the children, and herself to Portland. Helen's employer eventually reimburses her (in March of the next year) for 75 percent of all costs of moving the household items (Helen's and Tom's), Helen's car, and two house-hunting trips. The employer also reimburses Helen for 50 percent of the total hotel and meal costs while she and Tom were in Portland and waiting for the completion of their home. Advise Helen on the tax consequences of the above events.

AC-2   Charles Nobel works as a television talk show host for Broadcast Inc. In the current year, Charles generated substantial income from his employment. His wages from Broadcast were approximately $250,000. The show is taped four days per week, and taping lasts only a few hours each day. The crew of writers and Charles's ability to effortlessly read the teleprompter provide Charles with an extremely well-paid job for approximately 20 hours' work per week. This leaves Charles with time away from work that most U.S. employees would find enviable. Charles found a way to use that extra time by becoming, in his words, a "professional slot machine gambler." On approximately 50 days during the current year, Charles played the slots in casinos in and around southern California, winning payouts of $102,000. However, during those same 50 days, Charles lost $116,000. Because of the level of play and money spent at the casinos, Charles was probably one of the top 1 percent or 2 percent of gamblers in all of southern California. In fact, he was frequently invited to slot machine tournaments based on his gambling and celebrity status.

Charles also kept meticulous records of his gambling endeavors. He had detailed books and records that tracked the amounts played each day, the amounts won and lost, and various other expenses incurred. It seemed clear that Charles took his gambling very seriously. In previous years, Charles had played the slots less frequently but had managed to generate net gambling winnings (his wins exceeded his losses) and truly believed he could make money playing slots "professionally." On his current year tax return (Schedule C of Form 1040—Profit or Loss from Business), Charles reported the following:

Gross income	$102,000
Car and truck expenses	(2,323)
Supplies	(212)
Travel	(400)
Other expenses:	
Gambling losses	(116,000)
Telephone expenses	(65)
Net loss	$(17,000)

Prepare a tax research memorandum to the files that provides your opinion on the proper treatment of Charles's gambling activities as it relates to calculating his taxable income (i.e., what is the taxable income or loss from Charles's gambling?). For the purposes of this memo, you may assume that his gambling activities rise to the level of a trade or business. You may also assume that all Charles's expenses are ordinary and necessary business expenses that are fully supported and directly related to his gambling business.

AC-3 Dr. Gerald W. Colbert, DFA, is a professor of television and movie production at Hollywood University (and thus an employee of the university). He often meets with his doctoral students, who call him Dr. C, in his home. In his home, Dr. C has a room that he uses solely to conduct business related to classes he teaches at Hollywood University. In the room, he and his students review the movies and shows the students have made to satisfy requirements in their doctoral programs. Dr. C has an office on campus, but he has found that his movie and show reviews are more efficient when he and his students can watch the programs on his 52″ flat screen TV and sit on the comfortable couch in his home office rather than use the 19″ television and chairs in his office. Prepare a tax research memorandum to the files that explains whether Dr. C can deduct expenses related to his home office. As part of this memo you *must* include a discussion of § 280A as it relates to this issue.

AC-4 The Griffins were driving in a blizzard when a truck hit them as it was sliding off the road. The truck driver received minor injuries, but Wanda and Frank died at the scene of the accident. Amy, their eight-year-old daughter, was in the back seat and was seriously injured. Amy will eventually recover, but it will take a long time, and there will be some lasting physical damage. Frank and Wanda have a will that leaves all their assets to Amy. These assets include their house and its contents, investments, traditional IRAs, 401(k) retirement funds, and a life insurance policy with Amy as the beneficiary. The Griffins indicated that in case of their deaths, Wanda's only sister, May, should be Amy's guardian. Frank and Wanda requested that a trust be set up to control the money Amy will receive.

May filed a lawsuit against the driver of the truck, the company for which he works, and Frank and Wanda's car insurance company. The accident was determined to be 90 percent the fault of the truck driver and 10 percent the fault of Frank, who was driving. The jury awarded Amy a large sum for the death of her parents and to cover Amy's current and future medical costs. The jury also awarded amounts to cover the medical and funeral costs for Wanda and Frank. Amy received compensation for any mental anguish and for the partial loss of use of her right hand and arm. May was awarded a sum for the loss of her sister, Wanda.

May contacted your supervisor regarding the car accident, the deaths of Frank and Wanda, and the lawsuit. Please advise May on the current tax treatment of the inheritance that Amy is receiving as well as the compensation that Amy and May received from the lawsuit.

AC-5   Thomas and Nicole Eirgo have been married for 20 years and have three children, Candice, age 18, and twin boys, Trevor and Julian, age 12. Nicole has an undergraduate degree in accounting and worked in public accounting while Thomas was obtaining his law degree. Five years ago, they quit their jobs and started TechKnow, a C corporation that develops legal and tax software specifically for accountants and lawyers with high-tech clients. Thomas and Nicole work more than full time at TechKnow and have received only modest salaries. No dividends have been paid. The business has finally started to make substantial profits, but success, unfortunately, has brought problems. Thomas and Nicole have very different opinions regarding TechKnow's future. Thomas would like to continue to reinvest most of the profits for the development of software for other specialties, whereas Nicole would like to focus on the lines they have and enjoy their success by distributing some of the profits. Since they cannot come to an agreement, the earnings are being retained, and no new software is being developed.

These business disagreements are having a disastrous effect on their marriage. The only solution Thomas and Nicole see is to divorce. As might be expected, Thomas and Nicole cannot decide on how to separate their ownership interests in TechKnow. Some options they are considering include redeeming Nicole's stock, having Thomas and/or the children buy the stock, or dividing the business in some manner between Nicole and Thomas.

One thing Nicole has decided is to fulfill a lifelong dream of obtaining a doctoral degree in accounting. She will be entering a Ph.D. program in the fall, by which time the divorce should be final. Since Candice also will be attending college, she will live in an apartment with her mother. Thomas will keep the house, and the boys will live with him. Thomas will pay Nicole alimony and child support while she and Candice are in school. The terms and amounts of these payments will be determined at the time the divorce is final.

Advise the Eirgos on the tax consequences of the above events. Support your conclusions with primary citations.

Cumulative Research Cases

C-1   Anh Nguyen, a single 24-year-old, recently completed her undergraduate degree in accounting at Vietnamese National University in Hanoi. She applied to and was accepted into Southern California University, located in Burbank, California, to pursue a master's degree in taxation. She received her F-1 student visa and arrived at Los Angeles International Airport in the summer of 2013 and started her courses almost immediately. She was extremely excited because this was her first trip to the United States. Although Anh was an exceptionally bright student, she was thoroughly enjoying the southern California lifestyle and took only enough courses to maintain her full-time-student classification. As a result, it was going to take Anh a little longer to complete her master's degree in tax. Although Anh missed her family and friends back in Vietnam, international travel was very expensive, and so she returned home only on limited occasions. Her international travel schedule was as follows:

Arrival in the United States	Departure from the United States
8/12/2013	12/25/2013
1/6/2014	5/12/2014
6/10/2014	12/26/2014
1/4/2015	–

Anh remained in the United States from January 4, 2015 through the end of 2016. During 2016, Anh managed to get an on-campus job that paid her $6,000 as compensation for working as a graduate assistant assisting SCU Professor Ira Ess with his research and grading.

Anh noticed that she had income tax and FICA taxes withheld from her paycheck. When she received her Form W-2 statement in early 2017, she realized that she needed to file a U.S. tax return to get back her withholding.

Prepare a memo that addresses three issues: (1) How is Anh going to be treated for U.S. tax residency purposes? (2) Is Anh's income from her student job taxable in the United States? (3) Is Anh subject to FICA taxes? Be sure and support your memo with primary sources.

Cumulative Research Case—State Implications

C-2   As mentioned previously, Anh really enjoyed the lifestyle in southern California. After living in student housing her first year, she immediately moved off campus into a nearby apartment. Over time, Anh started to grow quite comfortable in the United States. Her English improved a great deal, she managed to get a California driver's license, and she even bought a used car that she registered in California so she could drive back and forth to school (and perhaps occasionally to the beach). She became very good friends with a number of her classmates and from time to time even dated one or two. At the end of 2016, she had been dating one student for approximately four months; the relationship was showing signs of becoming serious but it was still too early to tell. Although Anh missed her friends and family back in Vietnam terribly, she was beginning to think maybe she could stay in the United States after she finished her degree, but only if she could find a firm to sponsor her work visa. Prepare an addendum to the previous memo that discusses the California residency treatment of Anh in 2016 and determine whether her income is taxable in California.

Cumulative Research Case—International Implications

C-3   As a result of the income she generated from her on-campus job, Anh found herself with a small amount of disposable income. In early 2016, she took $1,000 of her disposable income and purchased shares in Jefferson Realty Trust, a real estate investment trust (REIT) for which shares are traded on a major U.S. stock exchange. In late 2016, she realized she needed to purchase some holiday presents for her friends, including her previously mentioned significant other, and sold all her shares in the REIT for a gain of almost $800. She sold the REIT prior to the trust paying any dividends. What is the U.S. treatment of Anh's gain on the sale of the REIT shares?

The following definitions pertain specifically to the manner in which the identified terms are used in a tax research context. Other uses for such terms are not examined.

30-day letter A notice from the Internal Revenue Service (IRS) formally notifying the taxpayer of the results of an examination of the return and requesting that the taxpayer agree to the proposed modifications to the tax liability. A taxpayer's failure to respond to the letter triggers the statutory notice of a tax deficiency, that is, the 90-day letter demanding the payment of the tax or a petition to the Tax Court.

90-day letter A statutory notice from the IRS that the taxpayer has failed to pay an assessed tax. An issuance of such a letter usually indicates that the taxpayer has exhausted all of his or her appeal rights within the IRS and that the next forum for review will be a trial-level court. The taxpayer has 90 days to petition the Tax Court to be relieved of the deficiency assessment. If no such petition is filed, the IRS is empowered to collect the assessed tax.

Accuracy-related penalty A civil tax penalty assessed in situations in which the taxpayer has been negligent in completing the return or is found to have acted with a disregard of IRS rules and regulations or in which a substantial understatement of the income tax, a substantial valuation or pension-liability overstatement, or a substantial transfer-tax-valuation understatement exists. A 20 percent penalty usually applies to the pertinent understatement, and related interest accrues from the due date of the return, rather than the date on which the penalty was assessed.

Acquiescence A pronouncement by the IRS that it will follow the decision of a court case to the extent the court held in favor of the taxpayer. Announced in the Internal Revenue Bulletin. Modifies the citation for the identified case.

Action on decision (AOD) A memorandum prepared when the IRS loses a court case and that recommends the action, if any, that the IRS should take in response to the adverse decision. See also Acquiescence; Nonacquiescence.

Administrative sources Federal tax law that is created by the appropriate use of power that is granted to the U.S. Treasury Department by Congress. These sources of the law have a presumption of the authority of the statute, but they are subject to taxpayer challenge. Such sources include regulations, rulings, revenue procedures, and other opinions that are used by the Treasury Department or the IRS.

Ad valorem penalties Additions to tax based on a percentage of the delinquent tax.

Advance Citator In Checkpoint's RIA Citator, the source of the most recent cases and rulings.

AFTR (American Federal Tax Reports) The citation abbreviation for the tax case reporter, American Federal Tax Reports. The first series of the reporter includes cases concerning pre-1954 Internal Revenue Code litigation, and the second and third series include cases that address issues relative to the 1954 and 1986 codes, respectively. Includes most tax case opinions issued by federal courts other than the Tax Court.

American Bar Association (ABA) The professional organization for practicing attorneys in the United States.

American Institution of Certified Public Accountants (AICPA) The professional organization of practicing certified public accountants (CPAs) in the United States.

The AICPA Code of Professional Conduct Originally adopted in 1988, it provides a comprehensive code of ethical and professional conduct applicable to members of the AICPA.

Annotated tax service A commercial tax research reference collection, that is, a secondary source of federal tax law. Includes the Internal Revenue Code, regulations, ruling analyses, judicial case notes, and other indexes and finding lists, organized by code section number. The two most important annotated services are published by Commerce Clearing House and Research Institute of America.

Annotation An entry in an annotated tax service indicating a summary of a primary source of the federal tax law that is pertinent to one's research, for example, a court case opinion digest or a reference to a controlling regulation.

Announcements and notices The IRS issues announcements and notices concerning items of general importance to taxpayers.

Annual Filing Season Program A voluntary program administered by the IRS in which noncredentialed tax return preparers complete continuing education training and receive a certificate from the IRS.

Appeals Office   The internal group of the IRS that has the greatest authority to come to a compromise solution with a taxpayer concerning a disputed tax liability. Can consider the "hazards of litigation" in its deliberations. Failure to reach an agreement at this level of the IRS means that the only subsequent appeal by either party to the dispute must be before a court of law.

Assessable penalties   Penalties expressed as a flat dollar amount rather than a percentage of the delinquent tax.

Assessment   The process in which the IRS fixes the amount of a taxpayer's tax liability. Although the U.S. tax system exhibits some degree of self-assessment, the IRS has the ultimate authority to assess the liability of every taxpayer.

Average tax rate   The percentage of a taxpayer's income that is paid in taxes (i.e., computed by dividing the current-year tax liability by the taxpayer's income). The average tax rate is computed as a percentage of total taxable income (this generates the taxpayer's average nominal tax rate) or as a percentage of the taxpayer's total economic income (this generates the taxpayer's effective average tax rate).

BNA Bloomberg Tax and Accounting Center (BNA)
Offers numerous products covering all areas of tax and accounting, including the BNA Daily Tax Report and BNA Tax Management Portfolios (see respective entries).

BNA Daily Tax Report   A daily collection of the latest regulations, rulings, case opinions, and other tax law revisions, as well as news reports, press releases, congressional studies and schedules, interviews, and other items of interest to the tax practitioner. Available through the mail and on various electronic tax services. One of the most important tax newsletters published because of its breadth of topics and its quality of analysis. In addition, the newsletter provides interviews with governmental officials, articles reviewing the day's events, and the full text of key documents discussed in the newsletter.

BNA Tax Management Portfolios   A topical tax service published by BNA in a collection of more than 400 magazine-size portfolios, dedicated to U.S. income, foreign income, and estate and gift taxation. Each portfolio is prepared by an identified expert in the field and includes a detailed analysis of the topic, working papers with which to implement planning suggestions, and a bibliography of related literature. Supplemented by a biweekly newsletter, the portfolio series includes a topical index and case name and code section finding lists.

Board of Tax Appeals   An earlier name for the U.S. Tax Court, which did not have full judicial status. Opinions are recorded in the Board of Tax Appeals reporter, the citation abbreviation for which is BTA.

Boolean connectors   A deductive logic search that allows for the intersection of terms by using connectors such as "or" and "and" as well as searching for a word or phrase within a certain proximity of other words.

Case brief   A concise summary of the facts, issues, holdings, and analyses of a court case. Used in a tax research context to allow subsequent review of the case by its author or another party. Includes complete citations of the briefed case and other items addressed in the brief to facilitate additional review when necessary.

CCH Citator   A citator published by Commerce Clearing House that is part of the IntelliConnect platform.

CCH Federal Tax Weekly   A weekly newsletter published by CCH that covers IRS tax guidance, tax litigation, congressional developments, and practitioner reaction to tax planning news and trends.

CCH IntelliConnect   The online platform for Commerce Clearing House (CCH) tax research services. It is designed to be intuitive, and the entire CCH library can be searched from one screen. It is one of the most prominent tax services used by accountants.

CCH Tax Briefings   Short newsletter-style documents published by CCH that cover major tax legislation recently passed. Tax Briefings typically provide highlights of the new tax law and explanations of expected effects on taxpayers or groups of taxpayers.

Certified public accountant (CPA)   An individual who has passed the CPA exam and has been licensed by his or her state board of accountancy. In addition to specific educational requirements, licensing often requires specific work experience under the supervision of a CPA. Maintaining a CPA license typically requires 40 hours annually of continuing education.

Checkpoint   A commercial tax and accounting research service offered by Thomson Reuters. Checkpoint offers integrated source materials and analysis for tax, accounting, auditing, and corporate finance.

Checkpoint Catalyst   A research tool intended to make tax research more intuitive.

Chief Counsel   The chief legal officer of the IRS. Responsible for making litigation and acquiesce/nonacquiesce decisions and for developing the agency's interpretive materials, including rulings and memoranda.

Circular 230   A tax regulation detailing the requirements and responsibilities of those who prepare federal tax returns for compensation. Includes educational, ethical, and procedural guidelines.

Citations   A means of conveying the location of a document. Appendix B of this text offers a standard format for citations used by tax researchers.

Citation search   A method of finding documents in Checkpoint by citation—the code section, regulation, ruling, paragraph, case number, and so forth.

Citator   A research resource that presents the judicial history of a court case and traces subsequent references to the case. When these references include the citing case's evaluations of the cited case's precedents, the researcher can obtain some measure of the efficacy and reliability of the original holding.

Cited case   With respect to a citator, the original case that is cited, whose facts or holding are referred to in the opinion of the citing case.

Cited favorably   In a citator, a notation that indicates that the court cited a case and used the holding in the cited case to support the current case.

Cited without comment   In a citator, a notation that indicates that the case was cited but might not have been an important determining factor in the subsequent case.

Citing case   With respect to a citator, the subsequent case, which includes a reference to the original (cited) case.

Civil penalty   In a tax practice context, a fine or other judgment that is brought against a taxpayer or preparer for a failure to comply with one or more of the elements of the federal tax law. Examples include penalties for failure to file a return or pay a tax in a timely fashion.

Client confidentiality privilege   I.R.C. Section 7525(a) provides authorized practitioners such as CPAs and enrolled agents a limited client confidentiality privilege. While the code provides that, with respect to tax advice, the same common law protections of confidentiality which apply to communications between a taxpayer and an attorney apply to communications between a taxpayer and an accountant, there are several exceptions.

Client letter   A primary means by which to communicate one's research results to the client. Includes, among other features, a summary of the controlling fact situation and attendant assumptions, a summary of the critical sources of the tax law that led to the researcher's conclusions, specific

implications of the project's results, and recommendations for client action.

Closed transactions   A tax research situation is closed when all pertinent transactions have been completed by the taxpayer and other parties, such that the research issues may be limited to the proper nature and amount of disclosure to the government on the tax return or other document, and to preparation activities relative to subsequent government review.

Closing agreement   A form with which the taxpayer and the IRS finalize their computations of a disputed tax liability.

***Cohan* rule**   The doctrine that allows taxpayers to use estimates to claim a tax deduction when they can show there is some factual foundation on which to base a reasonable approximation of the expense.

Collateral estoppel   The legal principle that limits one's judicial exposure relative to a disputed item to one series of court hearings. In a tax environment, the principle can present hardships for the taxpayer who wishes to raise additional issues during the course of a judicial proceeding.

Collection   The process by which the IRS extracts an assessed tax liability from a taxpayer. Usually takes the form of the receipt of a check or other draft from the taxpayer but can include liens or other garnishments of taxpayer assets.

Commerce Clause   The clause of the U.S. Constitution indicating that Congress has the power to regulate commerce with foreign nations, among states, and with Native American tribes. It grants powers to Congress and places constraints on the states' ability to tax interstate trade.

Commercial tax service   A resource that organizes primary sources of law into a single database system and provides editorial explanations and expert analysis of primary tax law.

Commissioner of Internal Revenue   The chief operating and chief executive officer of the IRS. Holds the ultimate responsibility for overall planning and for directing, coordinating, and controlling IRS policies and programs.

Committee report   A summary of the issues that were considered by the House Ways and Means Committee, Senate Finance Committee, or Joint Conference Committee, here relative to proposed or adopted changes in the language of the Internal Revenue Code. Useful in tax research as an aid to understanding unclear statutory language and legislative history or intent. Published in the Internal Revenue Bulletin.

Conference committee   A committee formed to reconcile differences in versions of a tax bill passed by the U.S. House of Representatives and U.S. Senate.

Contents search   A search that treats electronic tax services as if they were printed published services. Accordingly, researchers can drill down through the table of contents of a service just as they would thumb through the pages if they had books in front of them.

Contingent fee   The practice under which a professional bases his or her fee for services on the results obtained. The American Institute of Certified Public Accountants has held that the performance of services for a contingent fee may be unethical; one exception is available, though, in situations (as in tax practice) in which the results are subject to third-party actions (here the government, in an audit setting). Several states are relaxing this restriction, allowing certified public accountants to mix the form of their compensation between fixed and contingent fees.

Convention   Another name for a tax treaty. There are two influential model tax conventions — the United Nations and OECD Model Conventions.

Correspondence examination   An audit of one's tax return that is conducted largely by telephone or mail. Usually involves a request for substantiation or explanation of one or more items on a tax return, such as filing status, exemptions, and itemized deductions for medical expenses, interest, taxes paid, charitable contributions, or miscellaneous deductions.

Court of Federal Claims   A trial-level court in which the taxpayer typically sues the government for a refund of overpaid tax liability. Hears nontax matters as well in Washington, D.C., or in other major cities.

Courts of appeals   A federal appellate court that hears appeals from the Tax Court, Court of Federal Claims, and district courts within its geographical boundaries. Organized into geographical circuits, although there are additional circuits for Washington, D.C., and for cases appealed from the Court of Federal Claims.

Criminal penalty   The punishment for a severe infraction of the elements of the federal tax law by a taxpayer or tax preparer. Felony or misdemeanor status for tax crimes can be accompanied by substantial fines or jail terms. Examples of tax crimes include tax evasion and other willful failures to comply with the Internal Revenue Code.

Cumulative Bulletin (C.B.)   An official IRS publication, consolidating the material that first was published in the Internal Revenue Bulletin in a (usually semiannual) hardbound volume. Cumulative bulletins were discontinued after 2008, but older rulings will use the C.B. citation format instead of the more recent I.R.B. format.

Department of the Treasury   Federal agency that is responsible for administering and enforcing the internal

revenue laws of the United States. The IRS is a bureau of the Department of the Treasury.

Determination letter   An IRS pronouncement issued by the local IRS office relative to the agency's position concerning a straightforward issue of tax law in the context of a completed transaction.

Discriminant function formula (DIF)   A means by which, on the basis of probable return to the IRS in terms of collected delinquent tax liabilities, the IRS selects tax returns for examination.

District court   A trial-level court that hears tax and nontax cases. Organized according to geographical regions. Jury trials are available.

Due diligence   The care a reasonable person should take in preparing or assisting in the preparation, approval, and filing of tax returns, documents, and other papers relating to IRS matters. See Circular 230, subpart B, § 10.22.

Due Process Clause   Found in the 14th Amendment to the U.S. Constitution, the clause (among other things) limits the territorial scope of a state's taxing authority, particularly in regard to interstate commerce.

Effective average tax rate   The proportion of a taxpayer's economic income that was paid to the government as a tax liability (i.e., it is computed by dividing the tax liability by the taxpayer's economic income for the year). Economic income includes nontaxable sources of income, such as gifts, inheritances, and tax-exempt interest.

Enrolled agent (EA)   A person who is qualified to practice before the IRS by means other than becoming an attorney or certified public accountant. Typically, a person must pass a qualifying examination and meet other requirements to become an enrolled agent.

Equal Protection Clause   The Equal Protection Clause of the 14th Amendment of the Constitution provides that "no state shall … deny to any person within its jurisdiction the equal protection of the laws." In a tax setting, it prevents states from implementing discriminatory tax classifications.

Ethical standards   Boundaries of social or professional behavior derived by the culture or its institutions. Tax ethics are described in various documents of governmental agencies or professional organizations.

Fact issue   A tax research issue in which the practitioner must determine whether a pertinent question of fact was satisfied by the taxpayer; for example, determining whether an election was filed with the government in a timely manner, or determining what the taxpayer's motivation was for the redemption of some corporate stock.

Failure-to-file penalty   A penalty imposed on taxpayers who fail to file a required tax return. The penalty can be waived for reasonable cause and is coordinated with the failure-to-pay penalty.

Failure-to-pay penalty   A penalty imposed on taxpayers who fail to pay a tax that is shown on their return. The penalty is generally .5 percent of the required liability for each month that the tax is not paid, up to a maximum penalty of 25 percent.

FASB Accounting Standards Codification (ASC)   The source of authoritative generally accepted accounting principles (GAAP) recognized by the Financial Accounting Standards Board (FASB) to be applied to nongovernmental entities.

FASB Accounting Standards Codification Research System (CRS)   Online system to document and research the FASB Accounting Standards Codification.

Federal Tax Coordinator (FTC)   Checkpoint's most comprehensive editorial source, analyzing in a topical arrangement the IRC and all important federal tax legislation, regulations, cases, and rulings.

Federal Tax Handbook   Checkpoint's less-detailed reference for day-to-day tax questions on the most current tax years.

Field examination   An audit of the taxpayer's tax return that is conducted on the taxpayer's premises. These audits are usually more involved and comprehensive than correspondence or office audits.

Finance Committee   The committee of the U.S. Senate that deals with matters of taxation.

Financial Accounting Standards Board (FASB)   The designated organization in the private sector for establishing standards of financial accounting that govern the preparation of financial reports by nongovernmental entities in the United States.

Flush language   Language in the Internal Revenue Code that does not appear to be associated with any particular subsection, paragraph, or other element of the section.

Foreign tax credit   A reduction of U.S. tax liability for taxes paid or accrued to a foreign country on foreign source income and also subject to U.S. tax.

Fraud   In a tax practice context, a taxpayer action to evade the assessment of a tax. Criminal fraud requires a willful intent by the taxpayer. The IRS bears the burden of proof relative to fraud allegations.

Frivolous matter   With respect to tax law, a matter in which the intent is to delay the revenue collection process and the proceedings are found to be groundless or in which the taxpayer unreasonably failed to pursue available administrative remedies.

Frivolous return   A return that does not include enough information to figure the correct tax, contains information or statements that on their face indicate that the self-assessment requirement has not been met, or takes positions that are meant to impede the administration of the tax law.

Generally Accepted Accounting Principles (GAAP)   The body of accounting guidance governing the financial reporting by nongovernmental entities contained within the FASB Accounting Standards Codification (ASC).

***Golsen* rule**   Tax Court decisions are appealed to the federal court of appeals for the taxpayer's place of work or residence. The decisions of the courts of appeal are not always consistent. Under the *Golson* rule, when a taxpayer whose circuit has ruled on a given issue brings a case that includes that issue before the Tax Court, the Tax Court follows the holding of the pertinent circuit, even if the Tax Court disagrees with the holding, or if another circuit has issued a contrary holding. This can lead to contradictory Tax Court rulings based solely on the state of the taxpayer's residence.

Good-faith belief   A good-faith belief (such as that required to meet the realistic possibility standard of SSTS No. 1) is a belief that is based on reasonable interpretations of the tax law.

Headnote   Numbered paragraphs in which the editors of the court reporter summarize the court's holdings on each issue. These paragraphs appear in the court reporters before the text of the actual court case.

Independence   The American Institute of Certified Public Accountants requires the certified public accountant (CPA) who renders an opinion relative to a client's financial statements to be (and to appear to be) independent from the client. This principle entails restrictions as to the CPA's direct and indirect financial dealings with the client and the CPA's simultaneous role as financial auditor.

Index search   A search method using indexes created for Checkpoint. Index searches can help identify effective terms for keyword searches. With indexes, the *tax meanings of the* *words* are considered as well as the context in which the words are found.

Injunction   The action by which the IRS or a court prevents (enjoins) a taxpayer, preparer, or tax shelter distributor from undertaking a specified action (e.g., preparing tax returns for compensation or offering a tax shelter for sale).

Innocent spouse   Innocent spouses may request relief from joint and several liability if the nonrequesting spouse or former spouse failed to report income, reported income improperly, or claimed improper deductions or credits.

Internal Revenue Bulletin   An official weekly publication of the IRS that includes announcements, Treasury decisions, revenue rulings, revenue procedures, and other information of interest to the tax researcher.

Internal Revenue Code   The primary statutory source of the federal tax law, a collection of laws that have been passed by Congress and incorporated in Title 26 of the U.S. Code. The code was last reorganized in 1954. It is presently known as the Internal Revenue Code of 1986. The chief subdivision of the code is the section.

Internal Revenue Service (IRS)   A division of the Department of the Treasury, the federal agency that is charged with the collection of federal taxes and the implementation of other responsibilities that are conveyed by the Internal Revenue Code.

Internal Revenue Service (IRS) Oversight Board
A group of at least nine individuals that acts as the board of directors of the IRS. They are responsible for overseeing the agency's operational and internal control functions, approving mission plans and strategies, reviewing the agency's budget, and ensuring the proper treatment of taxpayers.

Internal Revenue Service (IRS) Publications   Documents published by the IRS which are arranged by topic and include an easy-to-read description of how the tax law works on that topic. IRS Publication 17, Your Federal Income Tax, is a large publication that covers almost all facets of completing the individual income tax return and contains many examples and worksheets to assist taxpayers with individual tax compliance.

International Accounting Standards Board (IASB)   The independent standard-setting body responsible for the development and publication of the International Financial Reporting Standards (IFRS).

International Financial Reporting Standards (IFRS)
A single set of high-quality financial reporting standards developed by the International Accounting Standards Board (IASB) for use globally.

Interpretive Regulation   A regulation issued under the general authority granted to the IRS to interpret the language of the Internal Revenue Code, usually under a specific code directive of Congress and with specific congressional authority.

Intuitive search   A search method from Thomson Reuters Checkpoint that analyzes the natural language of the key words and provides the most relevant results based on historical usage.

Joint and several liability   Joint and several liability means that each taxpayer is legally responsible for the entire tax, including any interest and penalties assessed on a jointly filed return.

Judicial sources   Certain federal court decisions that have the force of the statute in constructing the federal tax law. The magnitude of this authority depends upon the level and location of the courts that issued the opinions.

Keyword search   A search method in Checkpoint, CCH IntelliConnect, and other tax research databases in which key words are used to search primary and editorial source materials.

Large Business and International (LB&I) Division   An operating division of the IRS serving large C corporations, S corporations, partnerships, and certain high-wealth individuals and handling international tax compliance efforts.

Law issues   A tax research question in which one must determine which provision of the federal tax law applies to the client's fact situation. This entails the evaluation of various statutory, administrative, and judicial provisions with respect to the client's circumstances; for example, whether the client's charitable contribution is subject to the 30-percent-of-adjusted-gross-income limitation.

Legislative regulation   A regulation by which the IRS is directed by Congress to fulfill a lawmaking function and to specify the substantive requirements of a tax provision.

LexisNexis Academic   A version of the LEXIS and NEXIS database services designed for use at public libraries, universities, and law schools.

Lexis Advance Tax   A LexisNexis online research service exclusively for tax practitioners.

Marginal tax rate The proportion of the next dollar of gross income (or other increase in the tax base) that the taxpayer must pay to the government as a tax. Thus, the marginal tax rate conveys the proportionate value of an additional deduction or the cost of an increase to the tax base. Tax-effective decisions must take into account the marginal (and not the average or nominal) tax rate.

Mathematical/clerical error program A program that checks every return for mathematical errors, recomputes the tax due after properly applying the numbers that are included in the return, and assesses any additional tax that is due. The IRS need not send the taxpayer a formal notice of deficiency (i.e., a 90-day letter) before the additional tax is assessed.

Memorandum decision A decision of the Tax Court that, in the opinion of the chief judge, does not address a new or unusual issue of tax law. While generally not considered as important as regular Tax Court decisions, memo decisions should nonetheless not be ignored by researchers.

Model Rules of Professional Conduct Adopted by the American Bar Association in 1983, the rules are intended as a guide for attorneys' professional conduct. The Model Rules deal with issues such as confidentiality and conflicts of interest in the client–lawyer relationship, responsibilities to nonclients, and so on.

Multistate Tax Commission (MTC) Created in 1967 by the Multistate Tax Compact. the MTC adopted the Uniform Division of Income for Tax Purposes Act (UDITPA) as part of its articles, issued regulations interpreting the UDITPA, and continues to urge states to develop and adopt uniform laws and regulations.

National Research Program (NRP) A means by which the IRS develops its discriminant function formulae. The taxpayer's return is selected randomly for an extensive review, during which the government challenges every item of income, credit, deduction, and exclusion. The results of such reviews are used (other than to adjust the examined taxpayer's liability) to delineate criteria by which other taxpayers' returns are selected for examination.

National Taxpayer Advocate Leads the Taxpayer Advocate Service (TAS) as the voice of the taxpayer before the IRS and Congress. The advocate reports directly to the commissioner and works through a system of approximately 2,000 local taxpayer advocates.

Negligence In a federal tax context, a (nonwillful) failure to exercise one's duty with respect to the Internal Revenue Code or to use a reasonable degree of expected or professional care. Examples include the unacceptable failure to attempt to follow the IRS's rules and regulations in the preparation of a tax return for compensation.

Nexus A sufficient business connection with a locality such as to give the locality taxing authority over the business.

Nominal average tax rate Determined by an inspection of the applicable rate schedule. The average nominal rate at which the taxpayer's total taxable income is taxed is computed by dividing the taxpayer's total tax liability by his or her taxable income. Tax-exempt income is not included in the denominator of this fraction.

Nonacquiescence An announcement by the IRS that it will not follow the decision of a court in a tax decision that was adverse to the agency. Notation is included in the proper citation of the disputed case. Announced in the Internal Revenue Bulletin.

Notice of Proposed Rulemaking (NPRM) Once a regulation is drafted, an NPRM is issued announcing the proposed regulation. The NPRM includes a preamble explaining the purpose of the regulations, asks for public input, announces a public hearing (if one is to be held), and contains the text of the proposed regulations themselves. Before and during the hearings process, the NPRMs are referred to as proposed regulations and, unlike final regulations, do not have the effect of law.

Offer in compromise The means by which the government offers to reduce the amount of an assessed tax, usually because of some doubt as to the collectability of the tax. A legally enforceable promise that cannot be rescinded, an offer in compromise relates to the entire liability of the taxpayer, and it conclusively settles all issues for which an agreement can be made.

Office examination An audit of one's tax return that is conducted at a local IRS office. These audits are typically more involved than correspondence audits and often deal with multiple issues that will require some analysis and exercise of judgment by the auditor.

Open transaction A tax research issue is open when not all pertinent transactions have been completed by the taxpayer or other parties, such that the researcher can suggest to the client several alternative courses of action that generate differing tax consequences.

Permanent citation A Tax Court citation assigned to a Tax Court decision; contains the case name, volume number, reporter page number, and year of the decision.

Practice before the IRS   The privilege to sign tax returns as preparer for compensation and to represent others before the IRS or in court in an audit or appeal proceeding. This privilege is granted by the IRS and controlled under Circular 230.

Precedential value   A document has precedential value if it can be used as authority, support, or a basis for a subsequent decision in a similar situation.

Preparer penalties   A series of fines and other levies by which the IRS encourages taxpayers and preparers to fulfill their responsibilities under the Internal Revenue Code. Examples include penalties for failure to sign returns, keep or furnish copies of returns, and provide required information to federal agencies.

Primary authority   An element of the federal tax law that was issued by Congress, the Department of the Treasury, the IRS, or a federal court.

Private letter ruling   A written determination published by the IRS relative to its position concerning the tax treatment of a prospective transaction. It cannot be applied to any taxpayer other than the one who requested the ruling. Text or summaries thereof are included in various commercial tax services.

Progressive tax rate   The term for a tax rate schedule in which the marginal rates increase as the magnitude of the tax base increases.

Proportional tax rate   The term for a tax rate schedule in which the marginal rates remain constant as the magnitude of the tax base increases.

Proposed regulation   An interpretation or clarification of the provisions of a portion of the Internal Revenue Code, issued by the Department of the Treasury and available for comment (and possible revision) in a public hearing.

Protocol   In reference to tax treaties, a protocol is an agreement that diplomatic negotiators formulate and sign as the basis for a final convention or treaty.

Proximity connector   Used in keyword searches to find terms within a certain proximity (number of words, sentence, paragraph) of another term.

Public Law 86-272   U.S. federal law that prohibits a state from imposing a net income tax if a company's only activities pertaining to the state are solicitation of orders for sales of tangible personal property that are sent outside the state for approval or rejection and are filled from outside the state.

Qualified offers   I.R.C. Section 7430(g) allows taxpayers to make qualified offers to the IRS to settle the amount of the

taxpayer's liability If the IRS pursues a case to court and the amount awarded is equal to or less than the qualified offer, the taxpayer is entitled to receive litigation costs including accounting and attorney fees incurred after the date of the offer.

Realistic possibility   Under the AICPA's SSTS No. 1, a member should have a good-faith belief that a tax return position has at least a realistic possibility of being sustained administratively or judicially on its merits if challenged. Realistic possibility is considered to be a one-in-three chance of success. This standard applies if the applicable taxing authority has no written standards with respect to recommending a tax return position or preparing or signing a tax return, or if its standards are lower than the standards set forth in the SSTS.

Reasonable cause   A means by which a taxpayer or preparer can be excused from an applicable penalty or other sanction. For instance, if the taxpayer failed to file a tax return on a timely basis because of illness or if the underlying records were destroyed by natural cause, the taxpayer likely would be excused from the penalty (but not from the tax or any related interest) because of this reasonable cause.

Regressive tax rate   The term for a tax rate schedule in which the marginal rates decrease as the magnitude of the tax base increases.

Regular decision   A decision issued by the Tax Court that generally involves a new or unusual point of law, as determined by the chief judge of the court.

Regulation   An interpretation or clarification of the provisions of a portion of the Internal Revenue Code, issued by the Department of the Treasury under authority granted by Congress. Legislative regulations directly create the details of a tax law. Both general and legislative regulations carry the force of the statute unless they are held to be invalid in a judicial hearing.

Research Memorandum   A primary means by which to communicate the results of a research project to the tax researcher, his or her supervisor, and/or the researcher's successor. Includes, among other features, a statement of the pertinent facts and assumptions, a detailed outline (and citations of) controlling tax law, a summary of the researcher's conclusions, and a listing of action recommendations for the client to consider.

Revenue agent's report (RAR)   A report prepared upon the completion of the examination of a tax return to explain to the taxpayer the sources of any adjustments to the reported tax liability. If the taxpayer agrees to this recomputation, the associated tax, penalty, and interest become due. Lacking such agreement, other aspects of the appeals process are undertaken.

Revenue procedure   A pronouncement of the IRS concerning the implementation details of a specific code provision. Published in the Internal Revenue Bulletin.

Revenue ruling   A pronouncement of the IRS concerning its interpretation of the application of the Internal Revenue Code (typically) to a specific taxpayer-submitted fact situation. Published in the Internal Revenue Bulletin. Can be relied on as precedent by other taxpayers who encounter similar fact patterns.

RIA Citator   The online citator included in the Checkpoint tax research service. Citators are used to determine the history and reliability of court cases and IRS administrative rulings.

Rule 155   When the Tax Court reaches a decision without calculating the tax, the decision is said to be entered under Rule 155.

Secondary authority   An element of the federal tax law that was issued by a scholarly or professional writer, for example, in a textbook, journal article, or treatise, and thus carries less precedential weight than elements of the tax law issued by primary sources.

Securities and Exchange Commission (SEC)   A federal agency in the United States with responsibilities that include enforcing federal securities laws and regulating the securities industry. The SEC also has statutory authority to establish financial accounting and reporting standards for publicly held companies in the United States.

Senate Executive Report   In reference to tax treaties, a document prepared by the Senate Foreign Relations Committee.

Shepardizing   Term used in the legal profession to describe the process of using Shepard's citator.

Shepard's Citator   The original citator service, responsible for coining the term "shepardizing" a case. Shepard's Citator uses a unique signal marker system to indicate the validity and status of a case in the citing references.

Small Business and Self-Employed (SB/SE) Division   An operating division of the IRS serving self-employed taxpayers and small businesses.

Small tax case procedures   A division of the Tax Court that can try cases of taxpayers whose disputed tax liability does not exceed $50,000. Procedural rules of the division are somewhat relaxed, and taxpayers often represent themselves.

Small tax case decisions are not published, nor can either party appeal the division's holdings.

Standard Federal Tax Reporter   The Commerce Clearing House (CCH) flagship annotated tax service offered through CCH IntelliConnect.

Statute   A law written and passed by a legislative body.

Statute of limitations   The maximum amount of time within which one or both parties in the taxing process must perform an act, such as file a return, pay a tax, or examine a return. Various time limits apply relative to the Internal Revenue Code, although both parties can, by mutual agreement, extend one or more of these time limitations.

Statutory notice of deficiency   See 90-day letter.

Statutory sources   The Constitution, tax treaties, and the Internal Revenue Code are the statutory sources of the federal tax law. They have the presumption of correctness unless a court modifies or overturns a provision in response to a taxpayer challenge. In this regard, legislative intent and history can be important in supporting the taxpayer's case.

Substantial authority   A taxpayer penalty may be incurred if a tax return position is taken and not disclosed to the IRS and no substantial authority (generally, statute, regulation, court decision, or written determination) supports the position.

Summary opinion   Tax Court small tax case decisions, called summary opinions, are not officially published by the government but are available from commercial publishers. Small tax case decisions cannot be used as precedent when dealing with the IRS. However, they do provide insight into how the Tax Court has treated similar tax situations.

Supremacy Clause   The clause in the U.S. Constitution that confers superiority to federal laws over state laws. That is, federal laws are "the supreme law of the land" and trump state laws. If a state law or constitutional provision is in conflict with a federal law, the state provision is invalid.

Supreme Court   The highest federal appellate court, which hears very few tax cases. The court approves a writ of certiorari for the cases that it hears.

Tax Analysts   A tax research service provider traditionally known for their *Tax Notes* and *Tax Notes Today* products.

Tax avoidance   The legal structuring of one's financial affairs so as to optimize the related tax liability. Synonym for tax planning.

Tax compliance   An element of modern tax practice in which a practitioner works with a client to file appropriate tax returns in a timely manner and represents the client in administrative proceedings.

Tax confidentiality privilege   The Internal Revenue Code provides authorized practitioners with a limited client confidentiality privilege with respect to tax advice.

Tax Court   A trial-level court that hears only cases involving tax issues. Issues regular and memorandum decisions. Meets in Washington, D.C., and in other major cities. Formerly called the Board of Tax Appeals.

Tax evasion   The reduction of one's tax liability by illegal means.

Tax Exempt and Government Entities (TEGE) Division   An operating division of the IRS serving employee pension plans, exempt organizations, and governmental entities.

Tax journal   A periodic publication that addresses legal, factual, and procedural issues encountered in a modern tax practice. As a secondary source of federal tax law, analyses in tax journals can be used in support of a taxpayer's case before a government agency or, especially, before a court.

Tax litigation   An element of modern tax practice in which a practitioner represents the client against the government in a judicial hearing.

Tax periodical   Journals and other publications containing articles and news briefs that are designed to keep readers up to date in specific or general areas of the tax law.

Tax planning   See Tax avoidance.

Tax research   An examination of pertinent sources of the state, local, and federal tax law in light of all relevant circumstances relative to a client's tax problem. Entails the use of professional judgment to draw appropriate conclusions and the communication of such conclusions or alternatives at a proper level to the client.

Tax Research Consultant (TRC)   The Commerce Clearing House (CCH) topical tax service offered through CCH IntelliConnect. It is a hybrid between a CCH in-house service and a BNA outside-authored topical service.

Tax return preparer (TRP)   Any person who prepares for compensation, or employs one or more persons to prepare for compensation, all or a substantial portion of a tax return or claim for income tax refund.

Tax treaties   An act of Congress that addresses the application of certain Internal Revenue Code provisions to a taxpayer whose tax base falls under the taxing statutes of more than one country. Published in the Internal Revenue Bulletin, among other resources. Generally, treaties are negotiated to prevent double taxation by providing reduced tax rates or exempting certain types of income from taxation. The income receiving reduced rates, tax holidays, and exemptions vary among countries.

Tax treatises   Editorial analyses that provide in-depth coverage of a particular tax area. Written by prominent experts in the specific field, a treatise offers numerous examples and insights on a single tax area.

Taxpayer Advocate Service (TAS)   An independent organization within the IRS whose job is to help taxpayers resolve problems with the IRS and to ensure that taxpayers are treated fairly and know and understand their rights.

Taxpayer assistance order (TAO)   A method for a taxpayer to request to engage an IRS taxpayer advocate to delay the implementation of an IRS action, such as a collection or seizure activity, if it appears the taxpayer has received less than fair treatment through the agency's administrative procedures.

Taxpayer Bill of Rights   Signed into law in 1996, it guarantees various rights to representation before the IRS, a recording of any proceedings, and an IRS explanation of its position relative to the pertinent disagreement. Specifically, the taxpayer has a right to know why the IRS is requesting information, exactly how the IRS will use the information it receives, and what might happen if the taxpayer does not submit the requested information.

Technical advice memorandum (TAM)   A pronouncement of the national office of the IRS stating the agency's position relative to the tax treatment of a taxpayer whose return is under audit. Text or discussion thereof may be included in the body of a commercial tax service.

Technical Explanation   In reference to tax treaties, a guide to help understand the treaty and the policies behind treaty provisions, as well as agreements reached during the negotiations with respect to the application and interpretation of the treaty.

Temporary citation   A Tax Court citation assigned to a Tax Court decision; contains the case name, volume number, reporter, case number, and year of the decision. The page number is not included because the opinion has not yet been published.

Temporary regulation   An administrative pronouncement of the IRS, typically concerning the application of a recently enacted or detailed provision of the tax law, especially in situations in which there is insufficient time to carry out the public-hearings process that usually accompanies the enactment of regulations. Temporary regulations carry the force of law, although citations differ from those for permanent regulations with regard to the prefix.

Terms and connectors   The LexisNexis form of a Boolean search.

Territorial model   A structure of international taxation under which a country only taxes profits that are earned within its own borders.

Topical tax service   A professional tax research reference collection, that is, a secondary source of federal tax law. Includes code, regulation, and ruling analyses; judicial case notes; and other indexes and finding lists organized by general topic. The most important topical tax services are published by the Research Institute of America and the Bureau of National Affairs.

Transfer pricing   The price-setting process between related parties.

Treasury decision (TD)   A regulation that has not yet been formally integrated into the published tax regulation collection. Often issued in the Internal Revenue Bulletin. Typically provides digest-style summaries of current court decisions, administrative pronouncements, and pending or approved tax legislation cross-referenced to the organization system of the tax service. Helps the practitioner to keep current relative to breaking tax developments.

Unauthorized practice of law   Activities of modern tax practice that nonattorneys are forbidden from engaging in, entailing, for example, the issuance of a legal opinion or the drafting of a legal document for the client. Legal or professional penalties may be imposed for the unauthorized practice of law.

Unconscionable fee   A fee for tax work that is not in accordance with what is just or reasonable; the charging of unconscionable fees is prohibited. See Circular 230, subpart B, § 10.27(a).

Uniform Division of Income for Tax Purposes Act (UDITPA)   Drafted in 1957 by the National Conference of Commissioners on Uniform State Laws to create a greater uniformity and consistency in the measurement of business income.

U.S. Master Tax Guide   Published by CCH and organized by topic, the U.S. Master Tax Guide is a quick way to find general information about a tax topic of interest.

U.S. Tax Cases (USTC)   The citation abbreviation for the Commerce Clearing House reporter, U.S. Tax Cases. Includes most of the tax decisions of federal courts other than the Tax Court.

U.S. Tax Reporter (USTR)   The annotated tax service offered through Thomson Reuters Checkpoint.

Wage and Investment (W&I) Division   An operating division of the IRS serving Form 1040 filers with only wage and investment income.

Ways and Means Committee   The committee of the U.S. House of Representatives that deals with matters of taxation.

Westlaw   Online database, provided by the West Group, that consists of the text of court decisions, administrative rulings, and selected law review articles. Researchers can search these files for tax (and other) law sources that may be relevant to the research problem. This database is meant primarily for legal research and thus contains a broader array of court cases and other authority than Checkpoint or IntelliConnect.

Westlaw Campus Research   A less comprehensive version of Westlaw available to many colleges and universities.

Willful neglect   A conscious, intentional failure or reckless indifference. Many IRS penalties may be abated if the underlying act resulted from reasonable cause rather than willful neglect.

Worldwide model   A tax system in which a country imposes taxes on residents based on their worldwide income, regardless of its source.

Writ of certiorari   Document issued by the U.S. Supreme Court indicating the Court will hear the petitioned case. If the case will not be heard, certiorari is said to be denied.

J

Time Value of Money Tables

FUTURE VALUE OF $1

Periods	4%	6%	8%	10%	12%	14%	20%
1	1.040	1.060	1.080	1.100	1.120	1.140	1.200
2	1.082	1.124	1.166	1.210	1.254	1.300	1.440
3	1.125	1.191	1.260	1.331	1.405	1.482	1.728
4	1.170	1.262	1.360	1.464	1.574	1.689	2.074
5	1.217	1.338	1.469	1.611	1.762	1.925	2.488
6	1.265	1.419	1.587	1.772	1.974	2.195	2.986
7	1.316	1.504	1.714	1.949	2.211	2.502	3.583
8	1.369	1.594	1.851	2.144	2.476	2.853	4.300
9	1.423	1.689	1.999	2.358	2.773	3.252	5.160
10	1.480	1.791	2.159	2.594	3.106	3.707	6.192
11	1.539	1.898	2.332	2.853	3.479	4.226	7.430
12	1.601	2.012	2.518	3.138	3.896	4.818	8.916
13	1.665	2.133	2.720	3.452	4.363	5.492	10.699
14	1.732	2.261	2.937	3.797	4.887	6.261	12.839
15	1.801	2.397	3.172	4.177	5.474	7.138	15.407
20	2.191	3.207	4.661	6.727	9.646	13.743	38.338
30	3.243	5.744	10.063	17.449	29.960	50.950	237.376
40	4.801	10.286	21.725	45.260	93.051	188.884	1469.772

FUTURE VALUE OF AN ANNUITY OF $1 IN ARREARS

Periods	4%	6%	8%	10%	12%	14%	20%
1	1.000	1.000	1.000	1.000	1.000	1.000	1.000
2	2.040	2.060	2.080	2.100	2.120	2.140	2.200
3	3.122	3.184	3.246	3.310	3.374	3.440	3.640
4	4.246	4.375	4.506	4.641	4.779	4.921	5.368
5	5.416	5.637	5.867	6.105	6.353	6.610	7.442
6	6.633	6.975	7.336	7.716	8.115	8.536	9.930
7	7.898	8.394	8.923	9.487	10.089	10.730	12.916
8	9.214	9.897	10.637	11.436	12.300	13.233	16.499
9	10.583	11.491	12.488	13.579	14.776	16.085	20.799
10	12.006	13.181	14.487	15.937	17.549	19.337	25.959
11	13.486	14.972	16.645	18.531	20.655	23.045	32.150
12	15.026	16.870	18.977	21.384	24.133	27.271	39.581
13	16.627	18.882	21.495	24.523	28.029	32.089	48.497
14	18.292	21.015	24.215	27.975	32.393	37.581	59.196
15	20.024	23.276	27.152	31.772	37.280	43.842	72.035
20	29.778	36.786	45.762	57.275	72.052	91.025	186.688
30	56.085	79.058	113.283	164.494	241.333	356.787	1181.882
40	95.026	154.762	259.057	442.593	767.091	1342.025	7343.858